DATE DUE

GAYLORD			PRINTED IN U.S.A.

Handbook of

Instrumentation

HANDBOOK OF INSTRUMENTATION

Andrew Stiller

ILLUSTRATIONS BY JAMES STAMOS

UNIVERSITY OF CALIFORNIA PRESS

BERKELEY   LOS ANGELES   LONDON

University of California Press
Berkeley and Los Angeles, California

University of California Press, Ltd.
London, England

LIBRARY OF CONGRESS
CATALOGING IN PUBLICATION DATA

Stiller, Andrew.
Handbook of instrumentation.

Bibliography: p.
Includes index.
1. Instrumentation and orchestration.
2. Musical instruments.   I. Title.
MT 70.S78   1985   781.6′4   82–20184
ISBN 0–520–04423–1

Printed in the United States of America

1 2 3 4 5 6 7 8 9

In memory of

MICHAEL PRAETORIUS

who got it right the first time

Contents

Figures

FIGURES **xi**

Preface and Acknowledgments

As no book of this sort has previously appeared in English, it will perhaps forestall misunderstandings if its scope and intent are outlined at the start.

Handbook of Instrumentation is a guide to the potentials and limitations of every instrument currently in use for the performance of classical and popular music in North America. Non-Western, folk, and educational instruments are not covered; and while over ninety percent of what is included here applies equally well to Europe, Central and South America, and Australia, no special attempt has been made to delineate the differences between the musical practices of those regions and of North America. Further, the book is strictly limited to current practice and is in no sense a history either of instruments or of instrumentation. It is for this reason that, at least in Part One, very few of the works cited as examples pre-date the twentieth century.

Within these limits I have endeavored to be as comprehensive as possible, and to anticipate every question, naïve or sophisticated, that could conceivably arise from any quarter. I am well aware that such an attempt can never be entirely successful, and I would like to beg of my readers not only their indulgence for any sins of omission or commission perpetrated in these pages, but their aid in pointing out to me any areas where expansion or correction might be desirable.

In order that the book be as useful as possible to students as well as professionals, I have not cast it in dictionary or encyclopedia form, but in that of a text, which may profitably be read straight through. Instruments are covered in standard orchestral order, and those who wish to look up a specific point will find that most instruments can be easily located simply by flipping through and looking at the illustrations and chapter subheads. The index is designed for quick reference and glossary use. The main or defining entry for each term is given in boldface.

A compendium of this sort cannot be put together without the aid of many people. I must of course bear the final responsibility for the information contained between these covers, but that does not make any less real my debt to all those who have patiently borne my constant badgering for information, or who have submitted their instruments to strange experiments in order to determine under what conditions such-and-such an effect is possible or impossible. I am particularly grateful to Dr. Charlotte Roederer for convincing me to begin the project; to my uncle, Richard Stiller, for guiding me through the ins and outs of book publishing; and to Carol Bradley and the rest of the staff of the Music Library at the State University of New York at Buffalo for their unfailing and unflappable help in locating and even acquiring for the library "many a quaint and curious volume of forgotten lore." Donald Miller, Ernestine Steiner, and Robin Willoughby provided valuable advice in the rendering of the musical examples.

The following people assisted me with all or part of the chapters under which their names are listed.

Chapter II: Lejaren Hiller, Paul Schlossman, Edward Yadzinsky. Chapter III: Frank Cipolla, Don Harry, Roger Larsson, Lee Lovallo, Ronald Mendola, Donald Montalto. Chapter IV: Sylvia Dimiziani, Eve Harwood, Judith Kerman, Elaine Moise, Roger Parris, Robert and Robin Willoughby. Chapters V–VII: John Boudler, Albert Furness, Donald Knaack, Elaine Moise, Jan Williams. Chapter VIII: Steven Bradley, David Cohen, Mark Freeland, Christos Hatzis, Guy Klucevsek, Jean Laurendeau, Kathleen Law, Ernestine Steiner. Chapter IX: Jackson Braider, Emmett Chapman, Mario Falcao, Mark Freeland, John Green, Marsha Hassett, Elias Kaufman, Steve Marvin, Norbert Osterreich, Greg Piontek, Jennifer Stiller, Geoffrey Stokes, Robin Willoughby. Chapter X: Steven Bradley, Robert Coggeshall, Lejaren Hiller, Norbert Osterreich. Chapter XII: Floyd Green, Philip Levin, John Lindberg, Elaine Moise. Chapter XIII: Marsha Hassett, John Hsu, John Lindberg, Ernestine Steiner, Barbara Wise. Appendix III: Timothy Fox, William Ortiz Alvarado.

Handbook of

Instrumentation

I

INTRODUCTION

PRELIMINARY

Instrumentation is both an art and a craft. As an art it is a matter of choosing, ordering, and blending timbres—one facet of the greater art of composition, which also involves choosing, ordering, and blending pitches, dynamics, and durations. As with all arts, it cannot be reduced to rules or formulas but must be learned through intuition, imitation, and painstaking trial and error.

The *craft* of instrumentation, with which this book is concerned, is a purely factual discipline, consisting of the knowledge and understanding of the capabilities, limitations, and idiosyncracies of the numerous devices that are used to transform music from dots on a page into sound. The musical devices involved include not only everything that can be called a musical instrument but also the human voice and a wide variety of electronic equipment; these are included in the term "instrument" wherever it occurs in this book.

Musical instruments have traditionally been classified into a number of broad categories, based on the manner in which the sound is produced: **winds** (subdivided into **woodwinds** and **brasses**), **voices**, **percussion**, **keyboards**,* **strings**, and **electronic equipment**. In scores of all sorts it is the usual practice to order the instrumental lines according to these categories; the order of the categories is standardized, and the position of instruments within each category is also standardized.

* Many writers do not recognize the keyboards as a distinct group, but instead divide them among the various other categories.

CLASSIFICATION OF INSTRUMENTS

Woodwinds	*Brasses*	*Voices*	*Strings*
flutes	horns	children	harp
oboes	trumpets	women	guitars
clarinets	trombones	men	violins
saxophones	tubas	*Percussion*	*Electronics*
bassoons		*Keyboards*	

The position of voices, keyboards, and electronics within this scheme is not fully standardized, and alternative page-positioning of these instruments is discussed at the beginning of the appropriate chapters. The instruments in Part One of this book are discussed in score order.

Most instruments are made in a variety of different sizes, comprising a **family** of instruments all basically the same in timbre and technique but differing in pitch range. When several sizes of the same instrument are used together in a score, the highest (smallest) variety appears first, followed by the others in descending order. Thus, for instance, the piccolo will be found at the top of any system in which it appears, since the flutes come first in the basic order and the piccolo is the highest of the flutes. It should be understood, however, that each line of music in score corresponds to a single *player*, not necessarily to a single instrument: if a player is required to **double**, that is, to play two or more different instruments, the position of the player's line in the score does not change relative to the others even though this may put an instrument out of sequence. This is particularly important in the percussion, since percussionists are expected to play all the instruments in that category, and a part may require a dozen or more different instruments. This aspect of percussion writing is discussed at length in Chapter V.

The instruments covered in Part Two of this book have discontinuous histories—they were all extinct for greater or lesser periods of time before being revived in the twentieth century for the performance of early music. The vast majority of them were extinct throughout the period when the traditional score-order discussed above was being developed, and hence there is no standard place for them in that order. Suggestions as to appropriate placements for them are advanced in Chapter XI. The "early" instruments are of course technologically simpler than the modern instruments discussed in Part One, and are less flexible, more idiosyncratic. Because of this, and because they are rather infrequently required in new compositions, they have been relegated to a separate section and should probably be studied only after the material in Part One has been absorbed.

In both parts of the book, the discussion of each family of instruments is headed by two or more diagrams. The first of these is a line drawing of all the members of the family drawn to the same scale, with a drawing of a meter-stick for comparison. The second diagram gives the "vital statistics" of each instrument in the family: its full name, the most commonly used abbreviations for that name, its written range, its transposition* (if any), and its availability. The range of most instruments varies depending on the abilities of the player and small differences in construction between individual instruments; in the vital-statistics charts the limits of the normal range are given with open ("white") notes, and any **extension range** is

* *Transposition* is explained in Chapter II.

shown with filled ("black") notes. The normal range given in each case is that expected as a matter of course from all professionals and first-rate amateurs; student players, however, may not be able to cover even this normal range completely (see Appendix II). When extension tones are available only on specially constructed instruments, the approximate percentage of such instruments presently in the hands of professionals and competent amateurs is usually indicated. Extension tones other than these can be produced on ordinary instruments but require the abilities of a virtuoso player.

The "extra" open and filled notes in the ranges of most instruments are provided as guideposts for the **dynamic range**, given just beneath; the loudest and softest dynamic levels an instrument can attain in the various parts of its pitch range are given there. It must be understood that, despite the appearance of these charts, changes in the dynamic range from note to note are usually gradual, not abrupt.

Traditionally, the notation of dynamics has been a compromise between two distinct concepts: the amount of effort exerted by the player to play loudly or softly, and the actual loudness of the sound. The exact balance between these concepts varies from composer to composer. If one strictly follows the first concept, a single invariant dynamic range will apply to all instruments at all points in their ranges, and different instruments may have to be assigned different dynamic levels to produce the same loudness. An example of this can be seen at rehearsal number sixteen in the *Sinfonia de Antigona* of Chavez, where in a duet for alto flute and heckelphone the two parts are marked, respectively, *ff* and *ppp*, the obvious intent being that both should produce a moderately soft sound. In this book, dynamic indications refer to the loudness of the sound, not to the effort put out by the player. Nine evenly spaced degrees of loudness are distinguished, from *ppp* (barely audible) to *ffff* (threshold of pain).*

The **availability** of each instrument is indicated by one of five terms (**ubiquitous, common, usually available, rare, very rare**). All the information in this book is based on U.S. and Canadian practice, and although in most respects European practice (or Australian or whatever) is not significantly different from that described here, the availability of many instruments abroad is not the same as in North America. It is, unfortunately, impossible to generalize about this.

Following the discussion of each family of instruments is a list of musical examples for each instrument in the family. These are pieces that prominently feature the instrument, displaying a wide range of effective and idiomatic writing for it. With a few exceptions, all these pieces are available both on record and in published score. At the end of each chapter is an additional list of pieces featuring large mixed groups of the instruments covered in that chapter.† Finally, at the end of Chapter IX is a list of works displaying the full resources of the orchestra. All these lists are divided approximately equally between works written before and after 1950, and *at least* one piece of each period should be studied in detail for each instrument, so that a balanced perception of their sound and general "feel" will be acquired. In studying the older scores, one should remember that the *instrumentarium* even of the early twentieth century was somewhat different from that of today. Instruments will be encountered that are now extinct (usually with good reason), and techniques now taken for granted may appear cautiously employed and elaborately footnoted. It is because of this constant evolutionary change in instrumentation that very few pre-twentieth-century pieces are

* Calculated for a moderate-sized hall of average acoustics.
† All percussion examples are listed at the end of Chapter V.

FIGURE I. *Pitch names.*

♯ = ¼ *tone sharp*   ǀ = ¼ *tone flat*

♯♯ = ¾ *tone sharp*   ǀ♭ = ¾ *tone flat*

FIGURE 2. *Quarter-tones.*

cited here: the vast majority of instruments now in use differ quite radically in construction and technique from those used in the nineteenth century.

Students lacking access to a large music library should at least be able to borrow—or, better yet, acquire—the following works, which display most of the instruments in the book.

Stravinsky: *Le Sacre du printemps*
    Agon
Schoenberg: *Theme and Variations*, Op. 43a
Varèse: *Ecuatorial*
    Déserts

Messiaen: *Chronochromie*
Cage and Harrison: *Double Music*
Xenakis: *Oresteia Suite**
Crumb: *Ancient Voices of Children*

For Part Two, see any demonstration album of medieval and Renaissance instruments. Also, Mauricio Kagel's *Musik für Renaissanceinstrumente* is a veritable compendium of contemporary techniques for these instruments.

In the body of this text, capital letters without subscript numerals are used to refer to general pitch-classes. Individual pitches are identified by a now universal system of capital and lower-case letters and sub- and superscript numerals; this notation, summarized in Figure 1, should be memorized. Although the use of quarter-tones is by now quite common, their notation is not yet completely standardized. In this book the system given in Figure 2 is used. In addition, this book uses upward- and downward-pointing arrows to indicate "very slightly sharp" or "very slightly flat."

THE PHYSICS OF INSTRUMENTAL SOUNDS

Sound is created by any object vibrating in a fluid medium such as air. As the object moves through the medium, it strikes the molecules in its path, propelling them in its own direction at a speed that varies with the density of the medium. Since air is approximately the same density everywhere, this speed ("the speed of sound") is essentially constant. The air mole-

* At this writing (1981) the score to the *Oresteia Suite* is available only on rental. Until a study score of this important work becomes available, *Akrata* may be substituted.

cules so propelled "run into" the stationary air adjacent to them, creating a zone of high pressure and transferring most of their motion to the adjacent molecules, which in turn transfer their motion to still other molecules further down the line. The net result is a burst of high pressure that is propagated through the air at the speed of sound until its energy has been dissipated—much like a wavelet spreading outward from the spot at which a pebble is thrown into a pool of water. Note that individual molecules move only a short distance: it is the *wave* that does the traveling. With each oscillation of the vibrating object a new burst of pressure is sent out in the same way; and since the bursts all travel at the same speed, when they reach the ear they have the same frequency with which they left the vibrating object.

In the ear the bursts of pressure are transferred through the eardrum and the three auditory ossicles to the fluid in the cochlea. Within the cochlea different frequencies resonate in different places; the vibrations are registered by the auditory nerve and transmitted to the brain, which interprets the *location* of each stimulus within the cochlea as a pitch.

The human ear can register frequencies between approximately 16 and 16,000 Hertz (= complete back-and-forth vibrations per second),* that is, from about C_2 to c^7; however, the ability to discriminate differences in pitch is largely absent above about 8,000 Hz (c^6). Frequencies below 16 Hz, though they cannot be heard, can be felt by the whole body.

The relationship between frequency and pitch is exponential: two notes an octave apart have frequencies in the ratio of 2:1. Thus, since a^1 has a frequency of 440 Hz, a^2 lies at 880 Hz, a^0 lies at 220 Hz, and so on.

The vibration of a real object is not as simple and straightforward as one might think; there are wiggles and bends in its shape, slight hesitations in its motion. These complexities are reflected in the sound waves it produces in the air, and are heard by the ear as its **timbre**. In reality, any waveform, no matter how complex, can be analyzed as a combination of a number of pure tones called **partials**. Of these, the lowest (which is usually also the loudest and thus heard as "the" pitch of the note) is called the **fundamental**; the others (usually much softer) are called **overtones**. The exact relationship among the frequencies of the various partials depends on the nature of the vibrating object.

As an example, let us consider a plucked string. Theoretically, there are an infinite number of ways that a string can vibrate, but all of them involve division of the string into equal segments (Fig. 3). Each of these **modes of vibration** produces a different pitch, and since the actual vibration of a string contains some component of every mode, all the pitches are represented: these are the partials of string tone. The simplest mode of vibration, in which the whole string vibrates back and forth as a unit, produces the fundamental. The second vibratory mode, which divides the string into two equal parts, produces a frequency twice that of the fundamental; the third mode, dividing the string into three parts, produces a frequency three times that of the fundamental, and so forth, so the frequencies of all the partials are simple integer multiples of the fundamental frequency: 1/1, 2/1, 3/1, 4/1, etc.

Since the relationship between frequency and pitch is exponential, this linear series of frequencies produces a logarithmic series of pitches (shown in Fig. 4). This **harmonic series** is characteristic of the timbres not only of stringed instruments (both bowed and plucked) but also of all wind instruments (as explained in detail in Chapter II), the human voice (Chapter IV), and electronically produced triangle, square, and sawtooth waves

---

* Below the age of forty or so, most people can hear as high as 20,000 or 30,000 Hz. Young children can hear frequencies as low as 10 Hz.

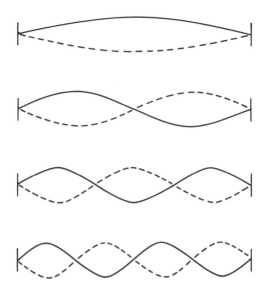

FIGURE 3. *Modes of vibration of a plucked string.*

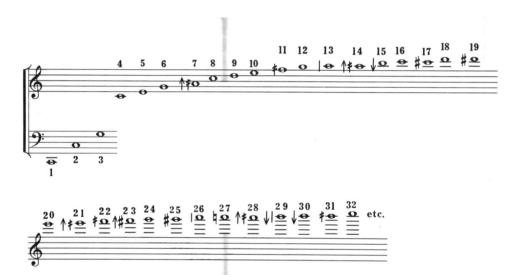

FIGURE 4. *The harmonic series of the note C₀.*

(Chapter X). The vibratory modes of drumheads and solid objects (Chapter V) are much more complex, and their frequencies, which can only be calculated by the use of some rather fearsome mathematics, are heard simply as irrational collections of sounds. These **inharmonic partials** give the sound of drums and bells a characteristic clangor that is also typical of such phenomena as multiphonics (Chapter II) and ring-modulation (Chapter X).

The harmonic spectrum of a sound is not the only determinant of its timbre. Equally important is the **envelope**—the contour of the sound as it develops over time, its pattern of attack and decay. The most important timbre-forming part of the envelope is the attack pattern; the recorded sounds of instruments as diverse as the piano, cello, and baritone horn become virtually indistinguishable if the attacks are removed. A typical attack pattern involves several features. First of all, the sound must start from zero and build up to its steady-state volume, and this may happen with great suddenness, gradually, or at some intermediate

FIGURE 5. Trompe-l'oreille *effect from voice-crossing in identical timbres: (a) as written; (b) as heard.*

speed. Frequently the attack volume builds to a point *above* the steady-state volume and then comes back down. During the attack the harmonic spectrum changes, both in the relative volume of the various partials (the fundamental often enters rather late) and in their pitches, which often start out inharmonically. Finally, the **attack noise**—the sound of the woodwind player's tongue pulling back from the reed, of the brass player's lips parting, of a finger releasing a string—is an independent sound unrelated to the pitch produced. Attack noise can be heard very clearly, for example, when the highest notes of the piano are played *fortissimo*; indeed, in this case the attack noise is the loudest component of the sound. The attack noise has its own envelope, independent of that of the tone itself, and this has usually died away completely by the time the steady tone is set up. As far as decay is concerned, the most important point for the composer is the distinction between **sustaining instruments**, such as the violin or clarinet, in which the tone can be maintained at a constant or even increasing volume throughout its duration, and **nonsustaining instruments**, such as the piano, guitar, or vibraphone, in which the sound dies away automatically following the attack.

COMBINING INSTRUMENTS

Three factors must be considered when writing for instruments in groups: these are **balance**, **timbre matching**, and **timbre mixing**. The factor of balance is best learned through familiarity with the dynamic ranges of the instruments as given in the "vital statistics" charts. Its importance may be gauged from the fact that a differential of as little as one dynamic level is sufficient to make a single instrument stand out clearly from a mass of as many as fifty. An *ffff* roll on the tam-tam will completely drown out a hundred-piece orchestra, most of whose members can play no louder than *fortissimo*.

Timbre matching is the trickiest single aspect of instrumentation and is the area in which errors are most frequently made by the student. For purposes of timbre matching, pairs of instruments may be considered to have **identical**, **similar**, or **unlike** timbres. Identical timbres are possessed only by identical instruments; even closely related instruments from the same family have similar rather than identical tone qualities. Identical timbres are ideal for homophonic writing in which a single full sonority is wanted and in which the vertical aspect of the music is more important than the horizontal. Counterpoint in identical timbres does not readily admit of voice-crossing, for the ear will misinterpret the voice-leading (Fig. 5). This *trompe-l'oreille* effect can be avoided by assigning different dynamic levels or articulations to the two parts or by placing the players far apart.

No clear line can be drawn between similar and unlike timbres, but the distinction is an important one since the less similar two timbres are, the less well they will blend. Extremely dissimilar timbres produce an effect of superposition: the two parts appear to occupy entirely different harmonic worlds, without harmony or counterpoint between them.*

The degree of blend is strongly affected by the horizontal and vertical density of the parts to be instrumented and by the overall height or depth of pitch. Parts that lie close together blend more easily than those that are widely separated in pitch, rhythmically similar parts blend more easily than those that are rhythmically diverse, and a little experimentation at the piano will show that low notes blend with each other much more easily than high ones. In addition, there are two general principles which should be remembered:

1. Sustaining and non-sustaining instruments blend with each other poorly at best, though each blends well with others of its own type.

2. Woodwinds, brasses, voices, and string instruments with fingerboards sound most distinctive (i.e., stand out most clearly, blend least well) at the bottom of their ranges; all other instruments sound most distinctive in the middle of their ranges.

The way all this works in practice can only be learned through frequent and intense analytical listening, score in hand—particularly to chamber music, in which the interactions between pairs of instrumental lines can be observed clearly. In the musical examples listed in the following chapters, one should study not only the specific instrument cited but also the ways in which that instrument reacts with the other instruments in the ensemble. In a wind quintet (flute, oboe, clarinet, horn, bassoon), for instance, the instruments blend well only at high pitches and the composer must constantly fight the tendency of this diverse ensemble to fly apart into its component parts in an unmediated five-voice wrangle. Contrast this with the string quartet (two violins, viola, cello), in which, because of the homogeneity of the ensemble, the blend is virtually perfect at all pitches. Or take the example of a sustaining instrument accompanied by piano—a song, for instance, or a sonata. Here almost the whole harmonic world of the piece is created by the piano, which in most musical circumstances quite literally "accompanies" the solo line rather than interacting with it, except by opposition and dialogue, both of which stress the relative immiscibility of the two sounds.

Timbre mixing requires less caution and more imagination than timbre matching. Just as a painter mixes the colors on the palette to produce new colors, so in instrumentation the tone colors of the various instruments can be mixed to form timbres unobtainable from any single instrument. Most timbre mixing is simple unison doubling, and the simplest form of unison doubling is **massing**, in which two or more identical instruments play the same material. The most familiar examples of massing are the five standard sections of massed bowed strings in the orchestra and the three sections of massed clarinets in the concert band. The sound of massed instruments has somewhat less character than the equivalent solo timbre; in particular, the attack patterns of the individual instruments are largely lost in the mass sound. In partial recompense, the sound of massed instruments has a unique turbulent quality, due to slight differences in pitch. The greater the number of players involved in producing a massed timbre, the more pronounced these characteristics become. The differences between

* This is just as true of music composed of noises or "sound events" as it is of more traditionally conceived material. References in this book to "harmony," "counterpoint," and so on should be interpreted in this light.

solo and massed timbre can be heard clearly in violin concertos, in which the solo violinist is regularly contrasted with the two orchestral sections of massed violins.

The violin concerto is also a good illustration of another feature of massed sound, viz., that massing produces very little augmentation of the volume of sound. As mentioned above, it takes a massed body of roughly fifty players to produce a sound one dynamic level higher than the sound of the individual players within the mass. The reason for this lies in the acoustical phenomenon of **interference**: the high-pressure crests of the sound waves from one instrument may correspond with the low-pressure troughs of sound waves from another, in which case the two cancel each other, producing a reduced volume or, if the correspondence is perfect, complete silence. In reality, the suppression of sound by interference within a mass of instruments almost exactly cancels the increase in volume one would expect from having multiple instruments.*

Mixed unison doubling is a very simple matter. The sound produced by a unison of nonidentical instruments is exactly intermediate between the instruments involved, in a very obvious way. One soon becomes able to imagine the sound of such combinations even when one has not heard them before. The only detail worth mentioning on this subject is that when a sustaining instrument is mixed with a non-sustaining instrument, the tone of the latter will have its effect for the most part only at the beginning of the combined sound and will be heard as a special attack pattern appended to the beginning of the sustaining instrument's tone. The most striking mixed unisons are those that involve unlike timbres, for when the two parent timbres are very distinct from each other their combined sound will also be distinctive.

A more complex and subtle form of timbre mixing involves the building up of a new timbre "from scratch" by assigning instruments to play not only the note itself but also upper partials of the note being doubled. A simple example of such an **artificial timbre** is the cliché octave doubling of the nineteenth century. Doubling of non-octave partials has been little explored (it occurs most frequently in the works of French composers from Debussy on), and it is admittedly tricky to fool the ear with such sounds. For such a combination to be successful the following conditions should generally be observed: first, that lower partials should be louder than higher ones, with the fundamental and/or second partial being loudest of all; second, that the fundamental should have a strong, bright timbre of its own, while the upper partials should be comparatively smooth and pure. A good example of a complex artificial timbre of this type can be found after rehearsal number 5 in Ravel's *Bolero*, where five partials of the melody are doubled. It is possible to construct artificial timbres with inharmonic partials, but these are more difficult to bring off than are those built on harmonic ratios. In order for the ear to be convinced that the sounds produced really are a single sound, either the partials must be many and dense (as in the sound-blocks of Ligeti and other Eastern European composers), or the fundamental must be at least two dynamic levels louder than any of the other partials. An example of an inharmonic artificial timbre is found at number 40 (and again at number 87) in Messiaen's *Couleurs de la cité céleste*.

* Interference takes its toll even when the instruments are playing different pitches. The totally *divisi* string sections of Ligeti and Penderecki are only marginally louder than ordinary massed unisons.

PART ONE

Modern

Instruments

II

THE

WOODWINDS

GENERAL CONSIDERATIONS

The term "woodwind" is misleading, for although all the instruments covered by the designation are winds, barely half of them are made of wood. Nor, as we shall see, does the material of which a woodwind is made have much effect on its tone or technique.

ACOUSTICS

Basically, a woodwind instrument consists of a tube, open broadly at one end and narrowly at the other, that contains and controls a vibrating column of air. The vibrations are produced at the narrow end of the tube by either of two rather different means.

In the flutes (and recorders—see Part Two) a narrow stream of air is directed across a small hole in the instrument. A well-known principle of physics requires that the moving air is lower in pressure than the still air around it, and some of this still air thus gets drawn into the stream. The still air directly beneath the stream lies inside the instrument, and as this air is drawn into the stream the pressure in the enclosed space will drop until, theoretically, it approaches that of the stream. The air pressure outside the instrument remains constant, however, and because of this differential the stream itself is pushed down into the instrument. This of course sends blown air into the instrument, and the pressure there builds rapidly until it is higher than that of the outside air, whereupon the stream is deflected back out of

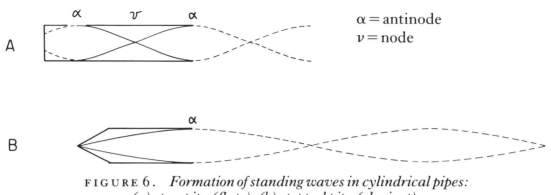

α = antinode
ν = node

FIGURE 6. *Formation of standing waves in cylindrical pipes:*
(a) open pipe (flute); (b) stopped pipe (clarinet).

the instrument. This process repeats itself over and over as long as the airstream is maintained, and by this means the air inside the instrument is set into oscillation.

It oscillates most strongly, and in opposite directions, at the ends of the tube, where the air is most free to move. There it forms the two antinodes of a **standing wave** (Fig. 6a). At the fundamental pitch of the tube there is a single node (place where the air is still) between these antinodes, but in higher modes of vibration (which produce the upper partials of the tube) two, three, four, or more nodes spaced evenly with antinodes between them lie between the two terminal antinodes. Thus, the wavelength of the standing wave produced in the tube (as well as the wavelengths of all its partials) is a function of the length of the tube; in fact, the wavelength of the fundamental frequency is exactly twice the length of the tube in which it is produced. Since the speed at which the molecules move back and forth within the tube is for all practical purposes constant, the frequency of the standing wave is a simple inverse function of its wavelength: the longer the tube, the lower the pitch. The frequency determined by the tube imposes itself on the oscillating air stream that generates the sound, much as a bouncing basketball imposes its natural rate of bouncing on the hand of the person dribbling it, and the stream thus oscillates at this same frequency, forming a **coupled system** with the tube.

All woodwinds other than the flutes are provided with a thin, flexible **reed** made of cane. In clarinets and saxophones a single flat piece of cane is attached to a hollow **mouthpiece** that is open down one side (Fig. 7). The reed almost closes this off, leaving between the tip of the reed and the tip of the mouthpiece a narrow slit that allows for the inflow of air. All other reed instruments have a **double reed**—two pieces of cane tied tightly together with wire and/or string to form a tube flattened at one end (Fig. 8). Air enters the instrument between the two blades of the reed.

Unlike the flutes, reed instruments are played by actually blowing air through the instrument. After the initial burst of high pressure as the note is started, the pressure of the moving air inside the reed (or between the reed and the mouthpiece) is much lower than that of the air outside the reed, which is being compressed by the player's lungs and mouth cavity; the tip of the double reed is forced almost closed, while that of the single reed is pressed against the mouthpiece. With the flow of air thus cut off, the pressure inside the instrument returns to normal, and the reed reopens. The rate at which this process recurs is controlled, just as with flutes, by the length of the tube. Because the end of the tube is effectively blocked by the reed, reed instruments behave acoustically as **stopped pipes** with a node at the reed end of the tube and an antinode at the far end. In the clarinet, which has a cylindrical **bore**

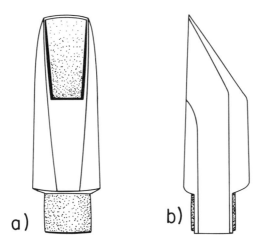

FIGURE 7.　*Clarinet mouthpiece: (a) rear view; (b) longitudinal section.*

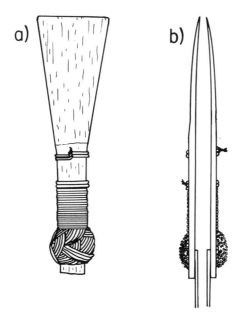

FIGURE 8.　*The double reed: (a) bassoon reed; (b) longitudinal section of reed in place.*

(internal contour of the instrument), the standing wave forms normally, and because there is only the one node and the one antinode, the fundamental wavelength is four times, rather than twice, the length of the tube and the pitch is thus an octave lower than would otherwise be expected (Fig. 6b). Additionally, since in all modes of vibration there must always be an antinode at one end and a node at the other, the even-numbered partials (which would demand antinodes at both ends of the tube) ought to be missing from the instrument's tonal spectrum. In fact, however, the clarinet is not a perfect stopped pipe: a little air does get past the reed. Furthermore, the reed must transmit its vibration energy to the air in the tube, which it could not do if the node at that end of the instrument were perfect. Thus, even-numbered partials *are* present in the clarinet's tonal spectrum, but they are very weak, especially in the low register, and their suppression gives the clarinet its characteristic tone-color.

	Cylindrical Bore	*Conical Bore*
SINGLE REED	clarinet	saxophone
DOUBLE REED	——	oboe, bassoon

FIGURE 9. *Modern reed instruments classified by bore shape and reed type.*

All modern reed instruments other than the clarinet have conical bores,* which are acoustically much more complicated than cylindrical ones. In a conical bore, first of all, although the antinodes occur where they should, all the nodes are shifted in position by varying degrees from where they theoretically ought to be. This, combined with the fact that the speed of sound in a conical pipe varies according to the diameter of the pipe, produces a standing wave half the wavelength (and twice the frequency) that might be expected. All the partials are similarly altered in their frequencies, so that in fact a conical stopped pipe acts exactly like an **open pipe** such as the flute, which is truly open at both ends.

Aside from the shape of the bore, the major factor affecting the timbre of reed instruments is the type of reed. Double-reed instruments tend to sound more coarse and "reedy" than single-reed ones, and generally have narrower dynamic ranges. Modern instruments exist with three of the four possible combinations of reed type and bore contour, as is shown in Figure 9. For a double-reed, cylindrical-bore instrument we must look to Renaissance forms such as the crumhorn. The oboe and bassoon are similar enough in sound that they have always been treated as a single family of instruments, the high and medium-pitched members built as oboes, the low-pitched ones as bassoons; experimental bass oboes and tenoroons have never really caught on. Although other characteristics besides reed and bore affect the tone of a woodwind, they are of distinctly subsidiary importance, and one of the least important is the material of which the instrument is made. Many people believe that the difference in sound between a clarinet and a saxophone is due to the one being made of wood, the other of metal: however, as we have seen, the difference in sound is caused by their differing bore contours. A metal (or plastic or glass) clarinet sounds almost exactly like any other clarinet of similar workmanship, and a wooden sax, were such a thing to be built, would sound almost exactly like its metal brethren.

FINGERING

The full length of a woodwind instrument is needed only for its lowest note. The other notes are produced by means of holes bored into the instrument at various places along its length. These can be closed by the player's fingers either directly or by means of pads at the ends of keys. The sounding length of the instrument is the distance between the player's mouth and the first open hole, since the length of instrument beyond this hole usually has little effect on the pitch produced. By opening or closing the various holes all the pitches in the instrument's range can be produced. The keys themselves are mostly simple first-class levers. When the

---

* It should be mentioned that the acoustical properties of a tube are affected very little by its being bent or thrown into a curve. The curved or twisted shapes of many low-pitched wind instruments were developed simply to make them easier to handle.

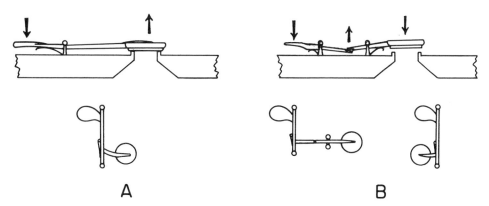

FIGURE 10. *Key mechanisms: (a) standing closed; (b) standing open.*

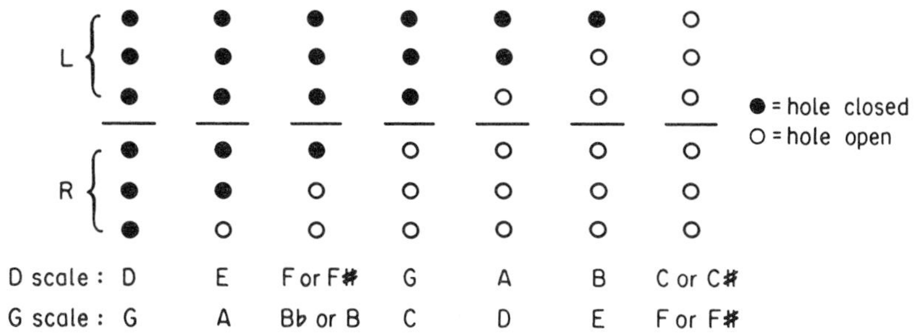

FIGURE 11. *Fundamental scales of woodwinds.*

key is depressed, the pad on the other side of the fulcrum is raised; when the key is released the pad is returned to its place by the force of a needle spring that the finger counteracts in depressing the key (Fig. 10). Many keys are designed to "stand open," that is, the spring acts to open the tone hole rather than close it. Such keys are designed either as second-class levers (pad on the same side of the fulcrum as the key) or as two interlocking first-class levers (Fig. 10b). Additionally, all modern woodwinds have one or more "automatic" mechanisms to simplify the fingering of certain notes or passages. These mechanisms consist of complex interlocking sets of keys designed so that the depressing of one key will, under certain conditions, raise or lower another.

The fingering systems used by the various instruments are by no means as complex, inconsistent, or irrational as might be expected. The instruments are all descended from much simpler ancestors with no keys and only six to nine tone-holes covered directly by the fingers, and this simple pattern continues to be reflected in the modern instruments. Basically, each instrument has a **fundamental scale** produced by depressing, one after the other, the second, third, and fourth fingers of the left hand followed by the second, third, and fourth fingers of the right hand.* There may be a hole or key for the left thumb which must be closed first of all; for most woodwinds, the right thumb is used only to support the instrument. There are really only two different fundamental scales, and all modern woodwinds use one or the other of them. A number of other keys are almost as highly standardized. For instance, all woodwinds are provided with three keys for the right fifth finger which produce

* The left hand lies above the right in the fingering of all modern woodwinds.

low C–C♯–D♯ (D-scale) or F–F♯–G♯ (G-scale) when added to the fingering for D or G, respectively, and almost all have a key for the left fifth finger which produces G♯ (D-scale) or C♯ (G-scale) when added to G or C.

It will be noted that the difference between all-fingers-down and all-fingers-up is only about an octave. Notes above this **lower register** are produced by the process of **overblowing**, in which, by means of a tighter **embouchure** (manner of holding the instrument in the mouth) the instrument is forced to speak at the second partial, thus raising all the notes one octave. This process is usually aided by one or more **speaker** or **octave keys** operated by the left thumb. These keys open a tiny hole in the air column at approximately the location of an antinode of the second partial. The formation of this antinode suppresses the fundamental but has no effect on the second partial, which has an antinode at that position anyway. The second octave is called the **upper register**, but even higher notes (the **altissimo register**) can be produced by forcing the instrument to speak a few notes each at the third, fourth, fifth, and sixth partials. These notes have rather chaotic fingerings because openings must be left at various points along the air column in order to generate the proper antinodes, and because compensations have to be made to bring the notes into tune. The clarinet, which has no even-numbered partials to speak of, creates its upper register on the third partial and thus overblows at the twelfth rather than the octave. This means that more than the usual number of keys are needed in the lower (chalumeau) register (in order to fill a twelfth), and that the notes of the upper (clarion) register belong to pitch classes different from those of the equivalently fingered lower-register notes. In fact, the G-scale is used for the lower register, the D-scale for the upper. The clarinet's altissimo register is provided by notes from the fifth, seventh, and ninth partials.

Readers with no previous woodwind experience would do well at this point to examine in detail one of the fingering charts included in this chapter, to see how all this works in practice. In these charts the tone holes of the fundamental scale (or the keys that cover them) are indicated on the instrument by the Roman numerals I to VI, and the closing of these holes (or depressing of the keys) is noted in the body of the chart by filled circles, as in Figure 11. Keys not involved in the fundamental scale of the instrument are named after the note they normally determine when they are depressed; a few have other specialized functions, and one or two have been given picturesque names by the instrumentalists. Every effort has been made to ensure that the names used for keys in these fingering charts correspond to those used or at least understood by the players themselves. When two different keys are used to determine two notes exactly an octave apart, they are differentiated here by using a capital letter for the lower of the two. (This should not be confused with the use elsewhere in this book of upper- and lower-case letters together with sub- or superscript numerals to indicate the exact octave in which a given note lies.)

The separate charts of trill fingerings show secondary fingerings for use in very rapid passages for which the normal fingering would be too clumsy. For several reasons, these fingerings are not part of the normal fingering patterns of the instruments. The trill fingerings are themselves rather clumsy for all uses save the one for which they were invented; many of them have odd timbres that would be obtrusive in a slow passage (needless to say, these timbres can be exploited for their special effect, but since not all trill fingerings have special timbres, nothing can be deduced from the trill charts in this regard—one must simply become acquainted with the sounds of these fingerings); finally, some of them are slightly out of tune. Nor does a special fingering exist for every possible contingency. On all woodwinds certain trills and other combinations of notes are flatly impossible to play at high speed. Whenever the writing of an extremely rapid passage is contemplated, the fingering charts should be consulted to make sure that the passage is playable.

In addition to all the notes listed in the fingering charts, all woodwinds are capable of producing quarter-tones throughout most of their range, by means of special fingerings or by "lipping up" or "lipping down" an ordinary note. Fingerings for these are by no means standardized, so no charts have been provided for them; however, one should bear in mind that most quarter-tones require awkward combinations of keys or an unusual embouchure and thus cannot be executed very swiftly.

The desire to have all woodwinds conform to one or the other of the two fundamental scales has led many of them to be treated as **transposing instruments**, whereby the player's music is not notated at actual pitch but is transposed up or down by a specific interval. The transposition is usually given as part of the instrument's name, for instance "E♭ alto saxophone"—meaning, in this case, that when the note written as C is played, the actual pitch produced is the E♭ below the C, for the instrument sounds a major sixth lower than written pitch. This means that parts must be written a major sixth *higher* than they are intended to sound. If a key signature is used, this must be altered as well—in this case, the key of E♭ having three more flats than the key of C, the player's part must have three flats *subtracted* from (or three sharps added to) the key signature. All this is a headache for the composer but a great convenience for the player, since it enables him or her to play all the members of the saxophone family, irrespective of their transpositions, without having to deal with changes in the relationship between fingerings and pitches—the one saxophone fingering chart given in this chapter is valid in almost every detail for every saxophone, from soprano to bass. Similar situations exist within each of the other families of woodwinds.

In addition to this sort of transposition, the much simpler octave transposition is also used. The parts for a number of low-pitched instruments (and a few high-pitched ones) are notated an octave or two higher (or lower) than they sound, in order to avoid an excess of ledger lines. The two kinds of transposition can exist together. Thus, the clarinet, bass clarinet, and contrabass clarinet are all pitched in B♭, but while the regular clarinet sounds only a major second lower than written, the bass clarinet sounds a major ninth (= one octave plus a major second) lower than written, and the contrabass clarinet sounds two octaves plus a major second lower. One result of this procedure is that such extremely low-pitched instruments as the contrabass clarinet and bass saxophone are notated in the treble clef.

Although the performance material for transposing instruments must be transposed, contemporary practice allows the *score* to be notated at actual pitch. One cannot be inconsistent in this, however: all the transposing instruments in a given score must be transposed or they must all be untransposed, with the possible exception of instruments, such as the piccolo and contrabassoon, which are pitched in C and use octave transpositions.

As mentioned above, the institution of transposing instruments makes it very easy for one player to "double" on all the members of a given family of woodwinds. It is much less widely realized, however, that the same institution makes doubling *between* families of woodwinds much easier than might be expected. In fact, until the nineteenth century, woodwind players were expected as a matter of course to be able to play *all* woodwinds. Popular musicians have of course never stopped doubling, but among classical musicians a mystique has grown up that holds that it is impossible to play more than one kind of woodwind adequately. Nonetheless, a fairly large number of woodwind players do double, and composers wishing to save time, space, and/or money by availing themselves of this fact will find that the following combinations are not at all rare: clarinet and sax; flute and sax; oboe and sax; bassoon and clarinet; bassoon, clarinet, and sax; oboe, clarinet, and sax.

Whenever doubling is required, whether within a single family of woodwinds or between two families, one must allow time for the player to switch from instrument to instrument. If both instruments are of the short, straight type that can be held in the lap, the change from one to the other can be negotiated in as little as five seconds. If, however, one or both of the instruments are large and/or curved or bent, the change will take longer, since such instruments must be carefully placed on the floor or on a special stand when not in use and be picked up equally carefully: a safe minimum time in such circumstances would be about ten seconds. Whenever possible, players should be allowed more than the minimum time to switch, so that the new instrument can be properly warmed up and adjusted before it is required. For woodwinds of all sorts this process can be completed in about thirty seconds.

SPECIAL TIMBRES

The nineteenth century valued uniformity in the sound of its instruments, and the basic philosophy of woodwind manufacture and performance remains to this day the production of the most uniform tone possible at all pitches and dynamic levels. Nonetheless, woodwinds are by nature heterogeneous in tone, and the differences in timbre between the various registers of an instrument are sometimes quite marked. In addition, players can alter the timbre of individual notes by using unusual embouchures and/or special fingerings. Such timbre variation, though easily produced, is not a normal performance technique, and composers must specify whenever such a departure from the usual sound is desired. The timbre can be altered either in the direction of a harsh, cutting sound (**hard** or **glassy tone**) or in that of a thick, stifled one (**muffled** or **muddy tone**). Hard tone is most effective and easily produced at high dynamic levels, muffled tone at low ones. A third possibility is a **breathy tone**, also best at low dynamic levels.

A special type of tone production developed since World War II is manifested in **multiphonics**, often incorrectly called "multiple stops" in the mistaken belief that these complex and irrational sounds are actually chords. Multiphonics are created by using fingering and embouchure to set up an unstable acoustic situation wherein the instrument is equally prone to play either of two notes from different partials. Both notes are produced simultaneously, together with a wide variety of **combination tones** (or "heterodyne frequencies") generated by the interference of these two frequencies with each other. Although the ear can readily pick out individual pitches from a multiphonic (which can then be heard as a chord), the sound produced is really unitary and is heard as such by the casual listener. The sound produced by bells and chimes is very similar to that of multiphonics, and it is equally easy to aurally pick out individual pitches from their tonal spectra; but no one would claim that the sound of a chime or bell was in reality a chord.

Multiphonics vary tremendously in their harmonic structure, and hence in the way they sound. Some produce major or minor triads, and these sound like particularly live or bright versions of the normal timbre of the instrument. Others are highly dissonant and harsh. Some contain widely separated pitches; others have components so close in pitch that a combination tone of only one or two Hz is produced, heard in the form of audible beats. Some are extremely pungent and cutting in timbre, while others have a fuzzy or muffled sound.

There have been many attempts to codify and name the multiphonics. Unfortunately, these attempts have all come to grief because an individual multiphonic varies both in sound and ease of production from instrument to instrument, reed to reed, and player to player. One clarinetist, for example, may with a given fingering easily produce a sweet-sounding, triadic multiphonic, while another using a different instrument and a different reed may only be able to produce from that fingering a harshly dissonant multiphonic, and a third player may not be able to produce any sound at all. There are in fact a small number of multiphonics that are so stable that they do come out the same under all conditions, but the players and composers involved with multiphonics research have not, so far, been interested in finding out which these are. One should be wary of the extensive lists of multiphonics that have been published—particularly those for reed instruments. These lists are almost always based on experiments with only one or two players and one or two instruments, the results of which are not nearly so universally applicable as their authors seem to think. If one is oneself a woodwind player, or knows players willing to experiment, it is possible to discover one or another of the few truly generalizable multiphonics.

Multiphonics are quick of speech only on double-reed instruments. On other woodwinds they can—with rare exceptions—be produced only gradually: the first sound that emerges will be an ordinary note, usually of highly muffled timbre, that is one of the multiphonic's main components; the remaining components are then added by adjusting the embouchure. Once a multiphonic has been produced, however, one can easily slur to any related multiphonic, or even produce a multiphonic trill.

The notation of multiphonics remains an unsolved problem. The only systems so far in use for notating multiphonics consist of either giving a complete fingering diagram for each multiphonic as it is used, or writing out the harmonic spectrum of the multiphonic as if it were a chord. Since both notations are extremely cumbersome to write and hard to read (the "chord" system of is no use to the player at all), I have developed a tablature-like system of notation that players can read very easily once it is explained to them. This system is, however, not widely known and will require explanation whenever it is used unless and until it becomes common practice; furthermore, it perhaps requires a greater familiarity with woodwind fingerings than composers usually possess. Those who do not wish to use this or some other precise system of multiphonic notation should specify merely whether they wish a multiphonic to be high or low, sweet or sour, etc., and let the player find one that is appropriate.

In my tablature system each multiphonic is notated as a variant of one or two ordinary notes, following these two principles:

1. The left and right hand can be given separately; thus, this very generalizable bassoon multiphonic

   (whose harmonic spectrum comprises a D♭ major triad) is to be played by fingering d^0 with the left hand and adding the right-hand fingers used to play B♭$_0$.

2. If necessary, a multiphonic may be notated (either as above or with a single note) with instructions to add or subtract one or two specific keys, thus: In this example

for English horn the player must finger e¹, adding the low c¹ key and sliding the finger partly off the a¹ plate to produce a **half-hole** fingering. On the flute, clarinet, and saxophone, in which multiphonics cannot usually be produced directly unless they are slurred, the notation should be given at the point at which the multiphonic fingering is first used, with the later commencement of the multiphonic itself either left to the player or indicated with an arrow or other notation.

ARTICULATION AND BREATHING

On woodwinds, articulation is effected by means of the tongue and the diaphragm. Notes are attacked with the syllable "da" or "ta"—of course, without using the vocal cords. Where a distinct release is needed, as in staccato delivery or when a note is followed by a rest, the note is ended by simply stopping the breath. Slurs are performed by continuing to blow while changing the fingering.

It is difficult to rapidly slur large leaps (an octave or more) downward on reed instruments, because the instrument tends to stay on a higher partial once it has been forced there, and it is difficult to get the instrument vibrating at the lower partial without bending the pitch or giving a clear attack to the new note. Upward slurs are no problem; however, even detached notes are difficult to produce securely if high and low notes are interspersed in rapid

passages such as which would be extremely difficult to play on any woodwind.

Detached notes can be played on reed instruments only as fast as the tongue can say "ta" repeatedly; thus, frequent recourse is made to a "fake" called "slur two, tongue two"

whereby is rendered The difference is seldom noticed. A notorious example is the bassoon solo in the last movement of Beethoven's fourth symphony, which cannot be played any other way. On flutes only, the syllable "ka" can also be used to attack a note, and very fast detached notes are easily performed by alternating, "takatakataka"—a process known as **double-tonguing**.

If the normal attack and release process is reversed, so that the tone is started with the diaphragm and stopped with the tongue, the note will sound as if it were played backward on tape. The "ha" attack from the diaphragm has been ignored largely because of the relatively long time it takes for the tone to build up and because it is difficult to control the pitch at high volume levels. If either this effect or the abrupt choking-off of the tone by the tongue is desired, some instruction to the player will have to be written out, as there is no standard notation for it (though the letter "h" placed above a note is beginning to become established as a designation for the former).

Another specialized articulation is the **fluttertongue**, executed by performing a rolled, Spanish-type "r." This is not a true form of articulation, since the speed of the roll cannot really be controlled, nor can individual notes be articulated rapidly by fluttertonguing. Though one can play rapid notes while fluttertonguing, the result will *not* be a series of separately attacked notes. Fluttertongue is actually a special sound-texture rather than a method

of articulation. It is notated thus: ♪. Formerly the abbreviation "flzg." (standing for the German "flatterzunge") was added as a precautionary measure, but this is no longer necessary. One should take care to distinguish notationally between

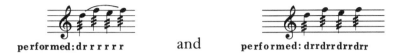

performed: dr r r r r r   and   performed: drrdrr drrdrr

On reed instruments, fluttertongue is somewhat problematic and cannot usually be executed at the softest dynamic levels. Particularly on double-reeds, it tends to be out of tune, but a good player can compensate for this.

On single-reed instruments a special kind of attack called **slap-tongue** is occasionally required. In this technique, which was invented by jazz musicians, the tongue creates a vacuum between the tip of the reed and the top of the mouth; when the tongue is pulled back, air enters the mouthpiece with an explosive snap. This is equivalent to the alveolar click [ɕ] (see Chapter IV), and will produce both a snapping sound and the appropriate pitch. In the low register it will produce pitches even without blowing: this effect is very similar musically to the snapped Bartók pizzicato of stringed instruments. It has no standard notation.

Another technique pioneered by jazz musicians is that of humming into the instrument while playing it. The resultant sound is not simply a duet, for the voice and instrument share the same resonating chambers, and prominent **difference tones** (equal to the difference between the two frequencies being produced by the voice and the instrument) can be heard. This effect is extremely easy to perform on the flute but is much more difficult on reed instruments, in which the humming tends to interfere with the player's control of the airflow through the instrument. Because of the difference tones, humming into a woodwind while playing often sounds surprisingly like a multiphonic.

One factor that must be kept in mind in writing for woodwinds is the necessity for the player to stop playing every so often in order to breathe. This can be accomplished in a small fraction of a second, so that passages in detached notes are not usually a problem unless they proceed for a long time in very small note values; Baroque music frequently poses great problems of where to breathe precisely because of this. For slurs and long-held notes a good rule of thumb is that a woodwind can hold a note (or slurred passage) for about as long as a singer could at the same loudness; it should be noted, however, that low-pitched instruments demand proportionally more air in this respect, the extreme cases being the bass flute and the contrabassoon. The woodwinds are on the average slightly more efficient acoustically than the voice, and can hold notes slightly longer. The single-reed instruments are particularly good in this regard, and on the clarinet the only limit on a *ppp* note is the length of time the player can hold his or her breath—theoretically a matter of a minute or more; but in performance players are usually too wrought up to go more than 45 seconds without a breath. A comma placed through or above the top line of the staff is the standard symbol to indicate the place in the music at which a breath should be taken. It is written to aid phrasing or to help the player through a passage where places to breathe are few.

The recently introduced technique of **cyclic breathing** offers wind players a way to play indefinitely without interrupting the sound. The technique makes use of air stored in the mouth to play the instrument while simultaneously the lungs are replenished by inhaling through the nose. Cyclic breathing is a very difficult technique to acquire, and so far only a few players have bothered to learn it, but it is potentially so useful that it will doubtless eventually become a part of every player's training. If a passage requiring cyclic breathing is written, a cautionary note to the player should accompany it, since players are quite used to seeing in traditional music notes too long to play, which they break with a breath in the least obtrusive spot.

FLUTES

THE INSTRUMENTS

Except for the piccolo, which is usually made of wood, members of the flute family are generally made of metal, although a few flutes are wooden. Flutes are built in three pieces called, respectively, the head joint, body, and foot joint. The head joint contains the blow-hole, across which the breath is directed to create the tone, and it is closed at the left end. The blow-hole is set in an **embouchure plate** on which the player rests the lower lip. In the bass flute the head joint makes a complete 180° turn in order to bring the blow-hole closer to the tone holes in the body of the instrument. Flutes are tuned by inserting the head joint more or less deeply into the body of the instrument.

The body of the instrument contains all the keywork except the keys for the right fifth finger, which are on the foot joint. A few flutes are made with extra-long foot joints provided with one or two extra keys for that finger, extending the range down to b^0 or bb^0. The 25 percent and ½ percent figures cited in Figure 13 apply to all flutes in the hands of competent players; the figure would be much higher if only professionals were considered, higher still if one considered only those professionals in orchestras. The vast majority of piccolos have no foot joint at all, and thus descend only to the written d^1; the key for $d\sharp^1$ is placed on the body of the instrument.

In the best flutes (called **French-model** flutes) the pads that lie beneath the three middle fingers of each hand are (except for that for the left index finger) pierced by holes so that the fingers themselves cover part of each tone hole. This enables the player to make subtle gradations of pitch by sliding a finger partly off the hole while still depressing the ring around it (**half-hole** technique). Many players, however, use the less flexible (and often less expensive) **plateau-model** flute, in which there are no such holes, and therefore cannot employ the half-hole technique. All piccolos, alto flutes, and bass flutes are plateau-system instruments. Bass flutes and most alto flutes lack the B♭ trill key (see fingering chart), and many bass flutes lack the D and D♯ trill keys as well; these instruments are otherwise fingered identically to the regular flute.

The octave gap between the flute and the piccolo is very imperfectly occupied by the rare eb^1 **flute**, which, sounding only a minor third above the ordinary flute, is too close to it in range and timbre to be of any real use. A flute in f^1 or (more symmetrically) g^1 would be a much more worthwhile instrument.

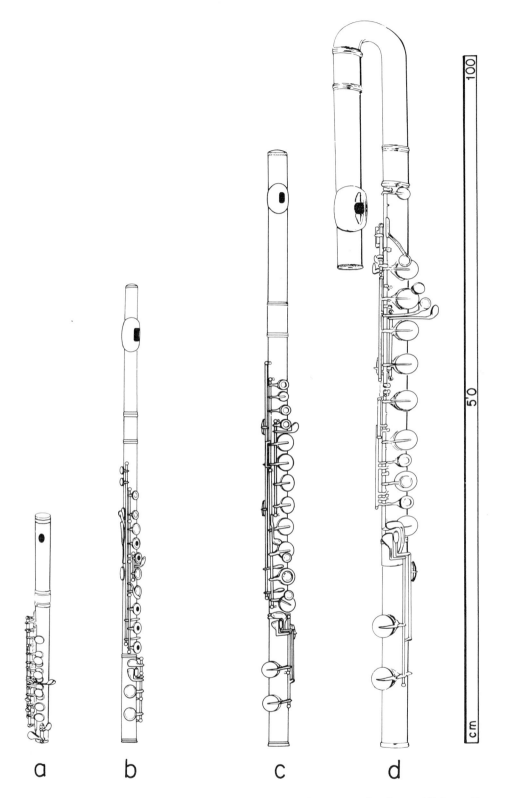

a   b   c   d

FIGURE 12.   *The flute family: (a) piccolo; (b) flute; (c) alto flute; (d) bass flute.*

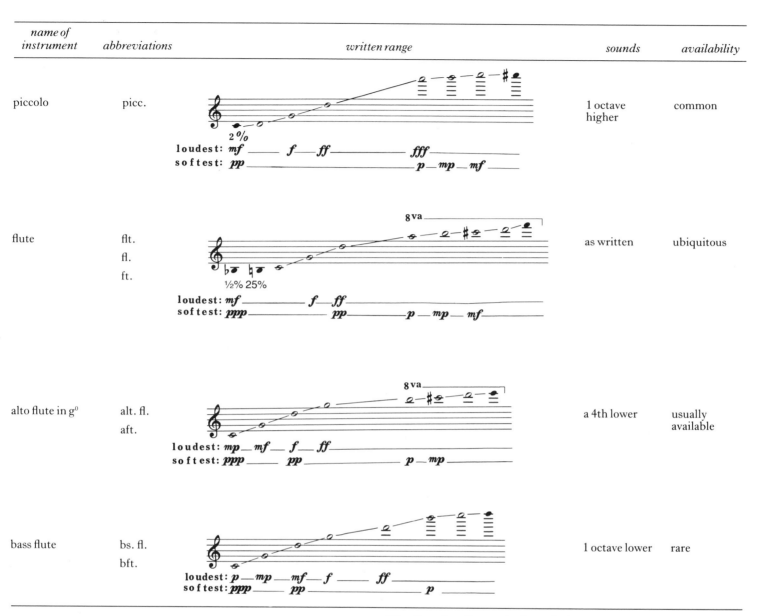

name of instrument	abbreviations	written range	sounds	availability
piccolo	picc.	loudest: *mf* ___ *f* — *ff* ___ *fff* ___ softest: *pp* ___ *p* — *mp* — *mf* ___ 2%	1 octave higher	common
flute	flt. fl. ft.	loudest: *mf* ___ *f*—*ff* ___ softest: *ppp* ___ *pp* ___ *p* — *mp* — *mf* ½% 25%	as written	ubiquitous
alto flute in g⁰	alt. fl. aft.	loudest: *mp*—*mf*— *f* — *ff* ___ softest: *ppp* ___ *pp* ___ *p* — *mp* ___	a 4th lower	usually available
bass flute	bs. fl. bft.	loudest: *p* —*mp* — *mf*— *f* ___ *ff* ___ softest: *ppp* ___ *pp* ___ *p* ___	1 octave lower	rare

FIGURE 13. *The flute family—vital statistics.*

PERFORMANCE CHARACTERISTICS

Flutes of all sizes are normally played with an attractive vibrato generated by the diaphragm. If it is desired to have the instrument play without vibrato, the instruction "senza vibr." must be used. The speed and intensity of the vibrato may also be varied, within limits.

Members of the flute family vary considerably in timbre from one end of their compass to the other. The lowest notes, from about written g¹ down, have on the regular, alto, and bass flutes a particularly warm, velvety quality and a great deal of **presence** so that, although soft, they sound "big" and full. On the piccolo these same notes are strangely thin and wispy—the sound has been compared to "a ghost whistling in a rain barrel." The remaining low-register tones (up to written c♯²) have some of the same quality as the lowest tones, but

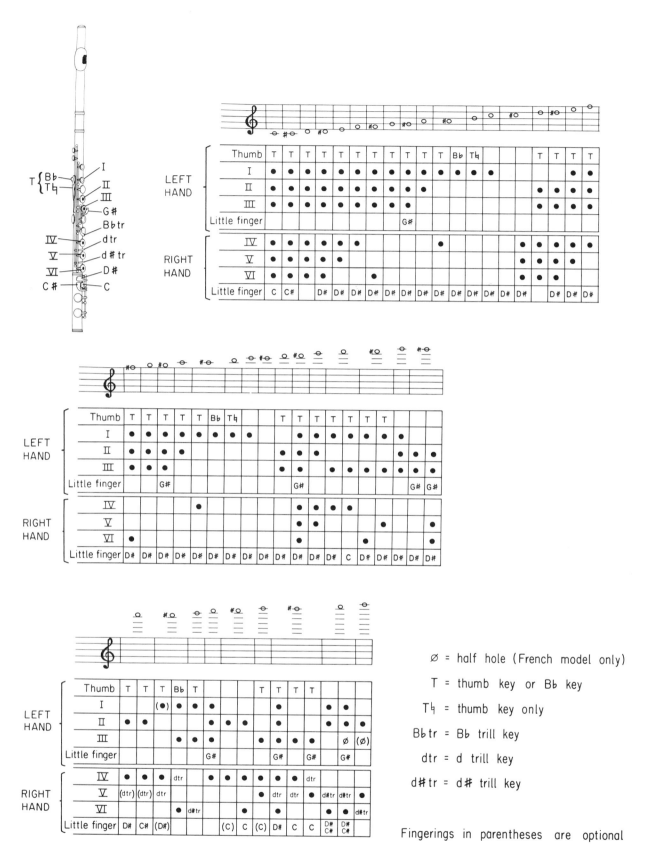

FIGURE 14. *Fingering chart for the flute.*

∅ = half hole (French model only)

T = thumb key or B♭ key

T♮ = thumb key only

B♭tr = B♭ trill key

dtr = d trill key

d♯tr = d♯ trill key

Fingerings in parentheses are optional

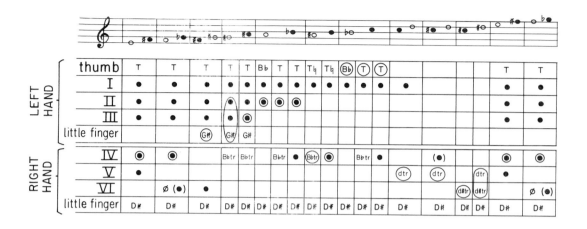

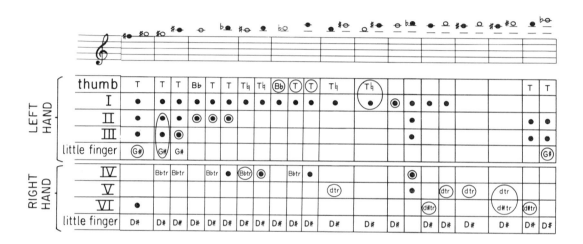

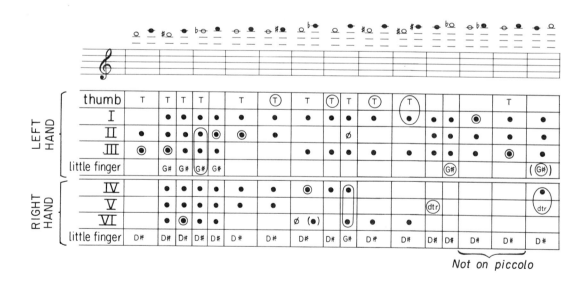

Not on piccolo

FIGURE 15. *Special trill fingerings for the flute. The complete fingering shown produces the open note. When the circled keys are raised, the filled note is produced.*

| | | thumb | I | II | III | little finger | IV | V | VI | little finger |

Special trill fingerings for the flute — fingering chart:

	1	2	3	4	5	6	7	8	9	10
thumb		T	T		T	B♭	T	T♮	(B♭)	(T♮)
I							•	•	•	•
II	•	•	(•)	•	•	⊙	⊙			
III	•	⊙	(•)	•			ø	•	•	•
little finger	G♯	G♯	G♯	G♯						
IV		•			•		⊙	⊙	⊙	
V	(dtr)	•	(dtr)					d♯tr		
VI			(d♯tr)	(d♯tr)		•		d♯tr	d♯tr	
little finger	D♯	D♯	D♯	D♯	D♯	D♯				(D♯)

Not on piccolo

Special trill fingerings for the flute, continued.

for the most part they partake of the instrument's most characteristic timbre, a very pure and liquid sound with few overtones, found in the range from about g¹ to a³ written. In this range the tone of the piccolo is so poor in overtones that it is an almost characterless piping, although the use of vibrato does help to make the tone seem more alive. The alto and bass flutes, on the other hand, sound somewhat warmer in this range than the ordinary flute does. They also sound distinctly breathy, largely because of the rather long time it takes the tone to build after each attack. In fact, rhythms on these two instruments tend to sound mushy, and a loud, sharp staccato is flatly impossible on the bass flute, in the lower register of the alto flute, or in the lowest fifth of the ordinary flute. The topmost notes of the flute and piccolo are harsh and piercing—the piccolo can easily cut through a loud orchestral tutti with these notes. On the alto and bass flutes these notes are also somewhat harsh, but rather than being piercing they sound very breathy, almost out-of-breath, and they take a great deal of air for the volume of sound produced.

A special additional timbre is available to the flutes because only one note (written d³) normally makes use of the instruments' third partial. A perfectly good series of notes on the third partial exists on the flute, but these are not needed in the course of normal playing; instead, they are used as a special tone-color effect, and are called **harmonics**. They are

notated with a small circle above the note head, just like the harmonics of stringed instruments. The notes in question lie in the range from g² to g♯³ inclusive, and are produced by overblowing from the fingerings used for c¹ to c♯²; the note a³ can also be produced as a harmonic by overblowing the d² trill fingering. The harmonics above g³ are unfortunately almost incurably flat. In tone, all the harmonics are of an oddly denatured and whistling quality. Although there is no reason why this effect should not be used by all members of the flute family, it has in practice mostly been written for the flute itself. On the piccolo a harmonic-like timbre can be obtained for the note a¹ (written) by fingering low d¹ and covering the end of the instrument with the little finger of the right hand.

Another series of flute harmonics (producing written c³ to b³) makes use of the fourth partial. These have no particularly individual timbre; rather, they are used by the player to "fake" rapid scalewise passages at the top of the instrument's range.

Similar to harmonics are the **whistle tones**, tiny, whistle-like sounds produced on the fingerings for the notes a² to b³ (written) by blowing with very low pressure. The pitches produced are slightly sharper than the normal tones produced from these fingerings, and since they can be raised as much as a half-step by moving the tongue but cannot be brought all the way down to pitch by any means, they should be thought of as lying in the range from a ♮² to c³—though they are produced by the lower fingerings. These sounds can only be produced *ppp*, and not all players can learn to produce them. They must be produced with a "ha" attack, and their speech is slow and uncertain, so it is unrealistic to expect one of them to be produced immediately on cue or simultaneously with another musical event. There is no standard notation for whistle tones.

It may be observed that flutes of all sizes are hampered by having a narrow dynamic compass: somewhat so at the top of the range, where notes cannot be played very softly, and extensively so at the bottom, where the notes cannot be played loudly at all. The bass flute in particular is so handicapped in this respect that the instrument was never more than an experimental curiosity until the development of electronic amplification made practical its use alongside more robust instruments. Its main use continues to be in film and television scores, where the amplifier can solve all balance problems. To compensate, at least partially, for this dynamic inflexibility, the flutes are the most agile of all the woodwinds. In particular, slurs involving a drop from a higher to a lower partial without any great fingering change are not much of a problem, and passages such as

which would be virtually impossible to play on a reed instrument with a similar fingering pattern present no great difficulty for a flutist.

The flutes can produce quarter-tones and other microtonal shadings throughout their range (including the low c♮¹) by varying the embouchure and using special fingerings. Unfortunately, many bass flutes have ribbed embouchure plates (to help direct the large airstream) which so stabilize the pitch that bent tones are for the most part out of the question, and quarter-tones can only be produced by special fingerings—they can be produced only in the range from written b♮¹ up—and even then the written d♮² is impossible. A true glissando can only be approximated by sliding the fingers very slowly onto or off the keys. By this means, and by playing tricks with the embouchure, a rather "lumpy" glissando can be produced—some parts of the slide will be louder than others, there will be changes in tone color, and the speed of the glissando will vary from moment to moment; there will probably even be a few outright leaps from one tone to another, but it will be a glissando of sorts. Naturally, this can all be done much more easily and effectively on a French-model instrument, but by means of rather athletic embouchure adjustments it can be done in the lowest fifth (only) of plateau-model instruments, including piccolos, alto flutes, and those bass flutes without ribbed embouchure plates.

FIGURE 16. *Notation of the true glissando.*

FIGURE 17. *Notation of the key rip.*

A true glissando on all instruments should be notated as a thick straight line attached to the head of the note whose pitch begins the glissando and whose rhythmic value is that of the entire glissando. If the glissando does not connect directly to the next steady tone, its last pitch should be given as a small, stemless note-head attached to the far end of the line. If the contour of the glissando is to change while it is being performed, this may be indicated either by using curved lines or, more precisely, by combining short line-segments, giving the correct rhythmic value for each (Fig. 16).

A very short glissando (of grace-note proportions) is notated as a thin line that does not touch the notes that begin and end it: This effect is called **portamento**.

The **key rip**, a very rapid, unsystematically negotiated scale with glissando effect, may either be notated note-for-note or as in Figure 17.

Flute multiphonics are very beautiful and bell-like; unfortunately, most of them are difficult to produce and sustain. In partial recompense for this, the flute—because of the absence of any finicky reed—has an unusually large number of multiphonics that work on all flutes. It must be remembered that even if a given multiphonic is found to work on all flutes, there is no guarantee that it will also work on piccolo, alto flute, or bass flute.

SPECIAL EFFECTS

The best-known and longest-established of the various special effects called for in contemporary flute music is the so-called *key slap*. This is produced by closing one or more keys with such force that a percussive noise is produced by the closing pad. This noise resonates briefly inside the instrument, and the pitch governed by the fingering in question is heard clearly. In practice this can only be done with the pads underlying the middle three fingers of both hands, with the low c^1 key, and with the two left-thumb keys. The effect produces only low-register tones, and cannot be performed any louder than *piano*. It can be used alone or to provide a percussive attack with notes which are also blown. The commonest notation for it is a + over the note, but an explanation to the player is probably still necessary—definitely so if the simultaneous blowing and "percussing" of a note is wanted.

If the blow-hole is completely blocked with the tongue, the instrument becomes a stopped pipe, and key slaps will produce notes about a major seventh lower than usual. These tones, mostly below the flute's normal range, can also be produced by first fingering the note and then jamming the tongue into the blow-hole. Naturally, these notes cannot be blown.

A similar effect to the key slap is the *pop attack*, performed by folding in the lips and then blowing them out to make a popping sound. This is analogous to the slap-tonguing of clarinets and saxophones, and like that technique can be used alone to produce a brief low-register tone, or in combination with the breath to color the attack of any note. This effect is perhaps more commonly performed by making the retroflex "t" ([t] in the International Phonetic Alphabet—see Chapter IV), but this sound must be used to begin a normally blown note. In fact, almost any consonant in the I.P.A. (Chapter IV) can be used to start a note on the flute. This combined with humming into the instrument (on any rounded vowel) enables one to approximate actual speech or song while playing.

Some other effects that have been written for flute include:

1. Removing the head joint and playing on it alone. The pitch produced depends on the exact length of the head joint, which varies from instrument to instrument. If the end of the joint is covered tightly with the right hand, it becomes a stopped pipe, producing a hooty sound about an octave lower than the unaltered pitch. The hand need not cover the end of the tube completely, however, and by varying the extent to which the end of the head joint is covered all the pitches between the completely stopped and completely open ones can be obtained—unfortunately, without much accuracy. A beautiful glissando of about an octave can, however, be obtained in this fashion.

   The head joint can be made into a slide whistle by using a pencil wrapped with electric tape as a slide. Notes between approximately e^1 and d^2 can be produced in this way.

2. Extending the instrument with a cylindrical tube of the appropriate diameter. The pitch produced by fingering the lowest note on the instrument can in this way be dropped as much as a third. The next higher note will be completely unusable, and several pitches above that will be severely out of tune. The "extension" note will be very soft.

3. Blowing directly into the blow-hole through the lips, as for a brass instrument. The whole lower register can be played in this manner, sounding *approximately* a major seventh lower because of the cylindrical bore, and more or less badly out of tune. The notes produced can be quite powerful. Notes up to fingered g^1 played in this manner can be *overblown* a twelfth, producing notes up to (written) d^2. This effect is easier and more effective on alto flute than on the regular instrument; it cannot be played on bass flutes with ribbed embouchure plates, and it is useless on piccolos since the tube of that instrument is too short to control the vibration of the lips.

4. **Colored noise**. The instrument can be played with any degree of pitch quality, from a hiss that is merely colored by fingering the notes of the lower register, through a hiss dominated by a distinct pitch, to the normal sound of the instrument.

MUSICAL EXAMPLES

FLUTE:

    Varèse, *Density 21.5*
    Stravinsky, *Dumbarton Oaks Concerto*,
        Agon
    Maxwell Davies, *Missa super l'homme armé*

PICCOLO:

> Varèse, *Octandre* (2nd mvt.)
> Messiaen, *Oiseaux exotiques*
> Maxwell Davies, *Missa super l'homme armé*

ALTO FLUTE:

> Boulez, *Le Marteau sans maître*
> Crumb, *Night of the Four Moons*

BASS FLUTE:

> Chihara, *Willow, Willow*
> Crumb, *Lux Aeterna*

OBOES

THE INSTRUMENTS

The members of the family of modern double-reeds form a singularly motley crew. Not only is the design of the oboes completely different from that of the bassoons, but the three sizes of oboe are the sole surviving members of three different, though closely related, families of instruments. Later we shall see that similar differences exist between the bassoon and contrabassoon.

The oboe itself has for all practical purposes existed in only one size since its alto variety, the *taille des hautbois*, was replaced in the eighteenth century by the English horn. The English horn is a member of the **oboe d'amore** family, differing from a true oboe chiefly in having a bulbously expanded bell (the **Liebesfuss**) designed to make the tone, particularly of the lowest few notes, more gentle. The type instrument of this family, the oboe d'amore in a^0, retains a precarious hold on life only because of the numerous important parts written for it by J. S. Bach. As the trend toward using instruments of Baroque pattern for the performance of Baroque music continues, it is likely that the modern, fully keyed oboe d'amore will become even rarer. In the meantime, the instrument is so close in pitch to the English horn as to be virtually indistinguishable from it in sound, and is thus, from a contemporary standpoint, superfluous. The heckelphone is the last surviving member of a complete family of heckelphones, from sopranino to contrabass, invented by the renowned bassoon maker Heckel of Biberich. It has a *Liebesfuss*, like the English horn, but has a considerably larger **scale** (angle of bore expansion) than other oboes. Fortunately, the English horn and heckelphone are almost exactly identical to the oboe in fingering.

Although the heckelphone has been around since 1905, its position as the tenor of the oboe family is not yet standardized, and heckelphone parts are occasionally performed on any of a variety of other tenor oboes, all of even more shadowy reality than the heckelphone. Since tenor oboes of all sorts, including the heckelphone, are very rare, one cannot afford to be picky in this respect; and since no tenor oboe other than the heckelphone descends below written low b^0, it may not be wise to write the low bb^0 or a^0.

FIGURE 18. *The oboe family: (a) oboe; (b) English horn; (c) heckelphone.*

name of instrument	*abbreviations*	*written range*	*sounds*	*availability*
oboe	ob.	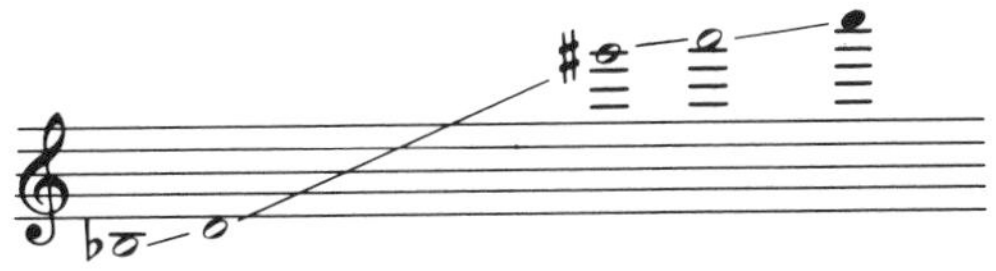 **loudest:** ***ff*** — **softest:** ***p***–***pp*** — ***p***	as written	common
English horn in f^0	E.h. Engl. hn.	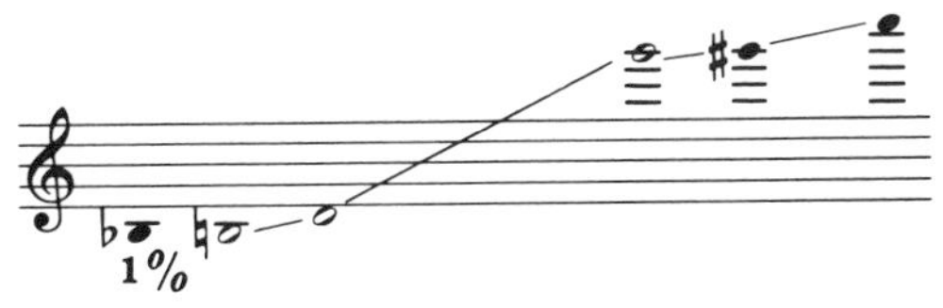 **loudest:** ***ff*** — **softest:** ***p*** — ***pp*** — ***p***	a 5th lower	usually available
heckelphone	heck.	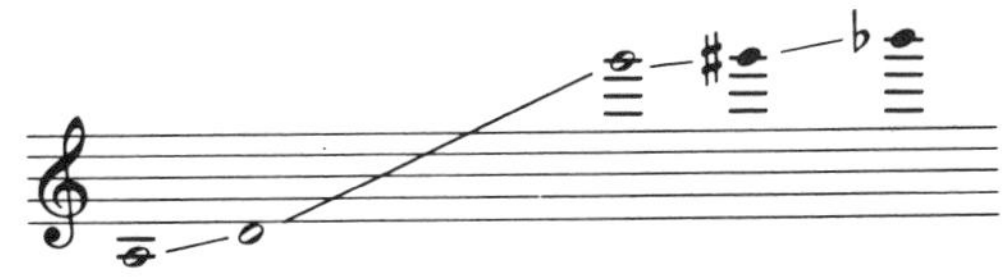 **loudest:** ***ff*** — **softest:** ***p***–***pp*** — ***p***	1 octave lower	very rare

FIGURE 19. *The oboe family—vital statistics.*

Oboes of all sizes are made of wood (student instruments may be plastic) in three pieces—the upper joint, lower joint, and bell. To these the English horn and heckelphone add a **bocal**: a thin, curved, conical metal tube over one end of which the reed is placed and which is inserted into the top of the upper joint. In the oboe there is an equivalent metal tube called the **staple**, which is, however, permanently attached to the reed (with thread) and is considered a part of it; the oboe reed thus inserts directly into the the top of the upper joint. The division between the upper and lower joints is made between the tone holes for the left ring finger and the right index finger; there are keys for fingers of both hands on both joints, and two keys interlock between the joints. The bell contains the lowest tone hole and the pad that closes it to produce the low b♭^{0}. This interlocks with the remainder of the b♭^{0} key mechanism, which is on the lower joint. Because of the difficulty of placing such a tone hole in a *Liebesfuss*, the English horn descends only to the written b♮^{0}. A very few English horns do have the low b♭^{0}, mounted on a lower joint made longer than usual. The key is put there mostly to accommodate the distressingly large number of composers who have apparently been unaware that this note was not supposed to be available! On the heckelphone the division between the bell and the body lies well above the *Liebesfuss*, and the pads for written low b♭^{0} and a^0 are located on the conical portion of the bell. The keys for these notes are operated by the left thumb.

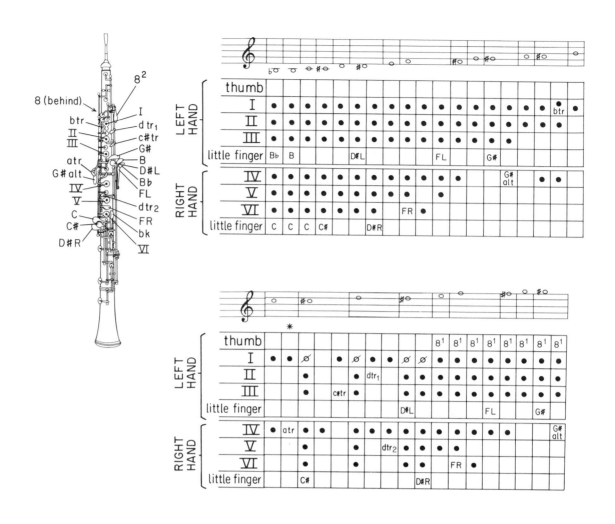

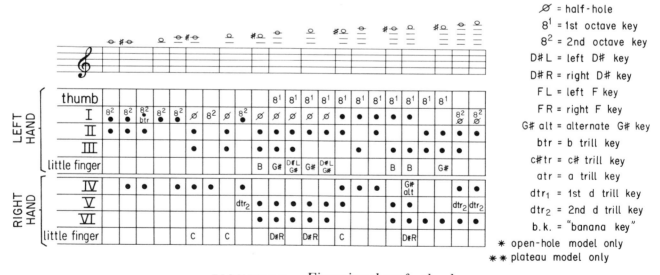

∅ = half-hole
8¹ = 1st octave key
8² = 2nd octave key
D#L = left D# key
D#R = right D# key
FL = left F key
FR = right F key
G# alt = alternate G# key
btr = b trill key
c#tr = c# trill key
atr = a trill key
dtr₁ = 1st d trill key
dtr₂ = 2nd d trill key
b.k. = "banana key"
* open-hole model only
** plateau model only

FIGURE 20. *Fingering chart for the oboe.*

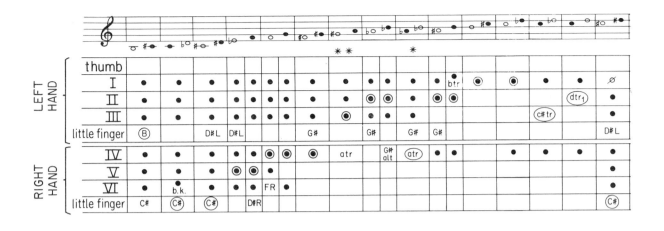

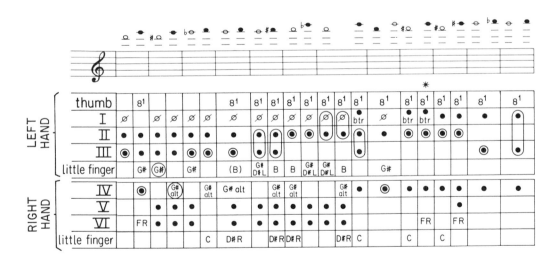

FIGURE 21. *Special trill fingerings for the oboe. The complete fingering shown produces the open note. When the circled keys are raised, the filled note is produced.*

Oboes are normally played with a vibrato generated by the diaphragm (rarely, by the lips), and the instruction "senza vibr." must be used if the vibrato, which may also be varied in speed and amplitude, is not desired. The tone of all three instruments is nasal, reedy, and somewhat coarse. These characteristics are strongest in the pitches below written d¹, notes that also cannot be played very softly; and it was to soften the almost honking character of these notes that the *Liebesfuss* was developed. The notes of the altissimo register are brilliant and piercing even when they are not very loud. To play the notes above a³, many oboists must "bite" the reed, i.e., hold it directly between the teeth rather than between the lips. Throughout its range the English horn sounds somewhat smoother and more velvety than the oboe, and the heckelphone sounds much the same; but the heckelphone's broadly expanding bore renders it so powerful that it has acquired a somewhat unfair reputation as a honking monster.

Like the flute, the oboe has a number of good third-partial notes that are not normally used. They have a slightly more "aloof" timbre than the equivalent second-partial tones, and are called "harmonics" by oboists. This timbre is available for the notes f² to c³ written (produced by overblowing written b♭⁰ to f¹—octave key added) and is notated, as for the flute,

with a small circle above the note, thus: ⁰♩ .

The oboe can only be tuned within very narrow limits, by inserting the reed more or less deeply into the upper joint; the English horn and heckelphone cannot be easily tuned at all. It was because of this inflexibility that the oboe was originally assigned to give the pitch in an orchestra, since most of the other instruments are more capable of adjustment.* In practice, oboists keep in tune by adjusting the reed—a time-consuming process usually done outside rehearsal time.

The oboes are only barely capable of a normal six-value scale of dynamics through most of their range. Relatively extreme measures must be taken to produce the *fortissimo* and *pianissimo*, and many players—even first-rate professionals—squeeze everything they play into the range between *piano* and *forte*, since the tone qualities associated with the more extreme dynamics are equated with the genuine faults of "blasting" (*ff*) or "pinching" (*pp*) the notes. A player who takes care to clearly differentiate six dynamic levels may even be accused of playing unmusically.

The oboes can produce quarter-tones from written e|¹ up to the top of their range; a problematic, "lumpy" glissando like that described for the flute is also possible from written e¹ up. Double-reeds excel in the production of multiphonics, and the oboe possesses dozens, perhaps hundreds, of stable ones, high and low, raucous and ethereal, that are easily produced and controlled. The multiphonics produced by the English horn and heckelphone are mostly *not* the same as those of the oboe, and it is not safe to assume that if a given one can be produced on the oboe the same fingering will generate the same multiphonic on the lower instruments.

The oboe can be **muted** very effectively, by inserting into the bell a soft-plastic trumpet mouthpiece case, a handkerchief, or even a crumpled-up dollar bill. As with the more "offi-

* As the only woodwind universally present in the Baroque orchestra, at the time the choice was obvious.

cial" mutes of brass and stringed instruments, the mute affects, not the dynamic range of the instrument, but the timbre, which is rendered more gentle and oddly distant, as if the instrument were being played in another room. With the mute in place the notes b^0 and bb^0 are not usable. The English horn and heckelphone can be similarly muted by balling up a handkerchief inside the *Liebesfuss*.

SPECIAL EFFECTS

The oboe key-slap is very weak. The lower-register pitches can be produced in this way, as on the flute, but certainly no louder than *pianissimo*. A more useful form of key percussion is the rattling of the keys. This produces an indefinite percussive rattling, *piano* or *pianissimo*. It cannot be done while blowing, unless it is not important what sounds the blowing produces.

Other miscellaneous effects include:

1. Playing the reed alone. This produces a high tone rather like a party noisemaker, and can be modulated over a range of about a fourth.

2. Blowing directly into the upper joint through pursed lips. This sounds amazingly like a cornett (Part Two) and can produce all the notes between written g^1 and a^2, though mostly out of tune. Many oboists have difficulty with this technique. It is not really feasible on the lower instruments.

3. Lowering the pitch of the lowest note as much as a whole step by means of a tubular extension. Notes so produced can only be played loudly, and the other notes below written d^1 will be out of tune or unplayable. On the low oboes one can also make use of extensions with the bell removed, which will slightly alter the timbre of the instrument.

4. Blowing air through the instrument without making the reed vibrate. The resulting hiss can be colored by any of the low-register fingerings.

MUSICAL EXAMPLES

OBOE:

Berio, *Sequenza VII*
Varèse, *Octandre*
Maderna, Concerto for oboe, chamber ens., tape *ad lib* (1962)
Xenakis, *Dmaathen*

ENGLISH HORN:

Hindemith, *Sonata for English horn and piano*
Stockhausen, *Zeitmäße*
Maderna, Concerto for oboe, chamber ens., tape *ad lib* (1962)

HECKELPHONE:

Chavez, *Sinfonia de Antigona*
Hindemith, Sonata for heckelphone, viola, and piano

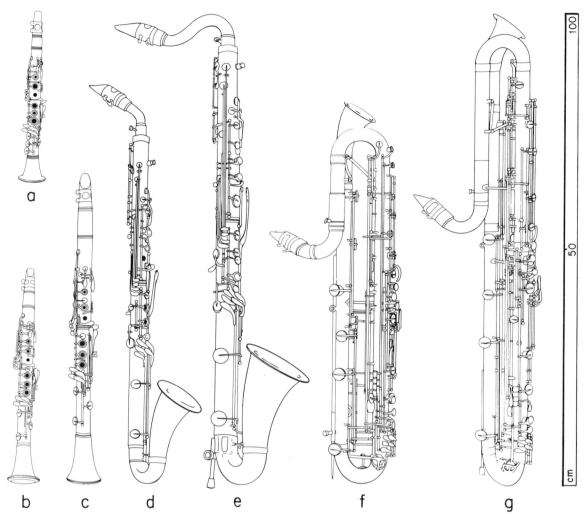

FIGURE 22. *The clarinet family: (a) A♭ clarinet; (b) E♭ clarinet; (c) B♭ clarinet; (d) alto clarinet; (e) bass clarinet; (f) contra-alto clarinet; (g) contrabass clarinet.*

CLARINETS

The clarinet can be considered the most successful of all woodwinds, since it outstrips all others both in sheer numbers of instruments made and in the number of different sizes in which the instrument is available. As Figure 23 shows, clarinets are made in seven clearly distinct sizes, of which only the uppermost can be considered rare.

THE INSTRUMENTS

The piccolo clarinet in a♭¹ (usually called simply "A♭ clarinet") is built at that odd pitch because the more logical b♭¹ instrument would be too small to hold. As it is, the player's fingers jostle each other, and it takes some practice to avoid missing a key or tone hole once in a while. The sopranino instrument (usually called "E♭ clarinet") is considerably easier to use, and like the A♭ clarinet is simply a miniature replica of the standard clarinet in b♭⁰, called "B♭ clarinet" or simply "clarinet."

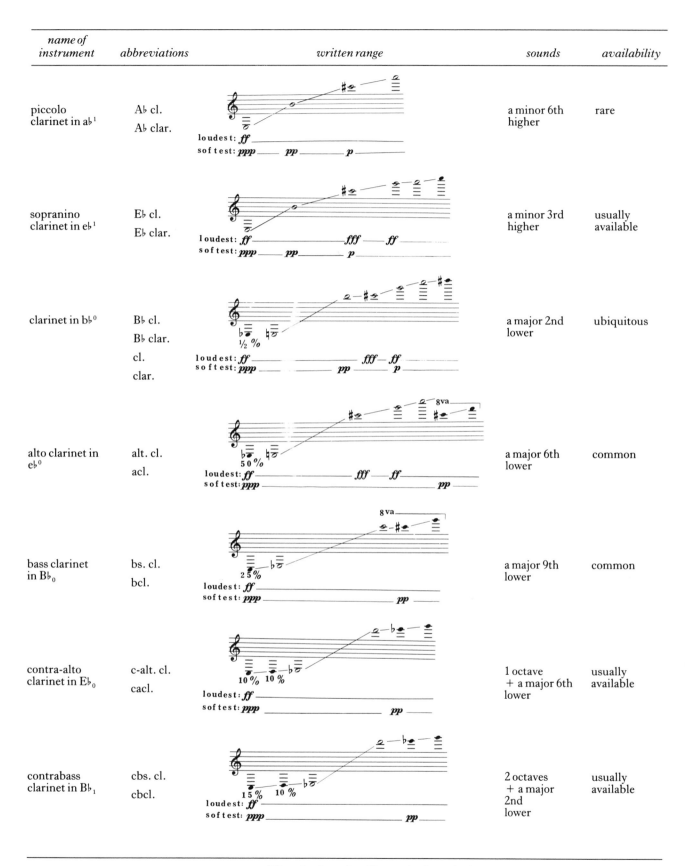

name of instrument	abbreviations	written range	sounds	availability
piccolo clarinet in ab¹	Ab cl. / Ab clar.		a minor 6th higher	rare
sopranino clarinet in eb¹	Eb cl. / Eb clar.		a minor 3rd higher	usually available
clarinet in bb⁰	Bb cl. / Bb clar. / cl. / clar.		a major 2nd lower	ubiquitous
alto clarinet in eb⁰	alt. cl. / acl.		a major 6th lower	common
bass clarinet in Bb₀	bs. cl. / bcl.		a major 9th lower	common
contra-alto clarinet in Eb₀	c-alt. cl. / cacl.		1 octave + a major 6th lower	usually available
contrabass clarinet in Bb₁	cbs. cl. / cbcl.		2 octaves + a major 2nd lower	usually available

FIGURE 23. *The clarinet family—vital statistics.*

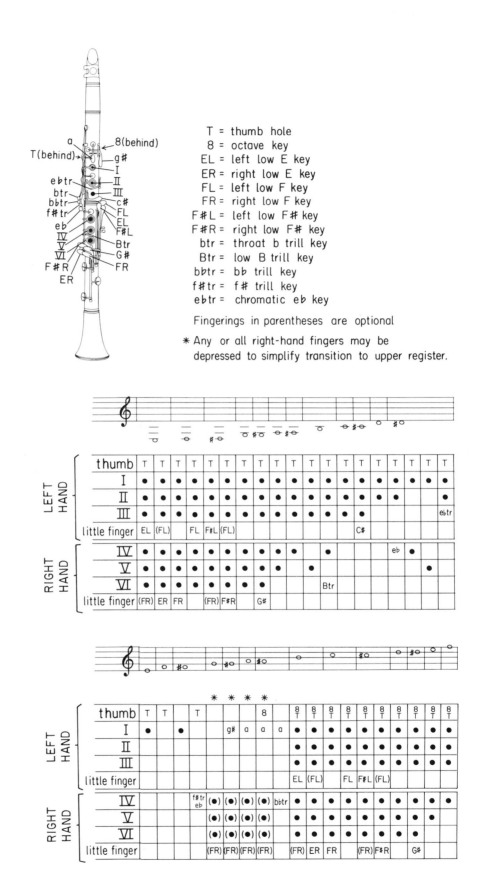

T = thumb hole
8 = octave key
EL = left low E key
ER = right low E key
FL = left low F key
FR = right low F key
F#L = left low F# key
F#R = right low F# key
btr = throat b trill key
Btr = low B trill key
bbtr = bb trill key
f#tr = f# trill key
ebtr = chromatic eb key

Fingerings in parentheses are optional

* Any or all right-hand fingers may be depressed to simplify transition to upper register.

FIGURE 24. *Fingering chart for the clarinet.*

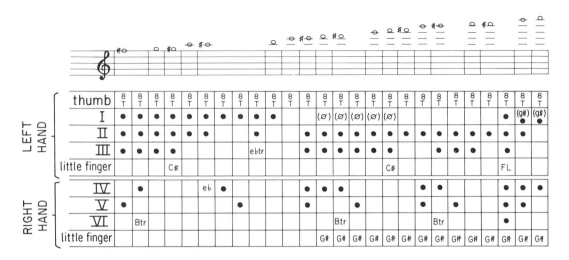

Fingering chart for the clarinet, continued.

Between the B♭ clarinet and the alto clarinet are two quite common instruments which are nonetheless of little use. The **clarinet in a⁰** ("A clarinet") was originally developed to play music in sharp keys, because the clarinet of the eighteenth and early nineteenth centuries was not tonally very flexible, so that such music would have been awkward to play on the B♭ instrument. Modern clarinets are of course perfectly capable of being played with ease in any key, and with the demise of functional tonality the whole issue has become moot. However, despite the fact that the two are indistinguishable in tone unless one is a clarinetist or has perfect pitch, virtually every professional clarinetist owns both instruments. Less and less has been written for the A clarinet as the twentieth century has progressed, and although the instrument is quite common it may well be on the way to extinction.

As the oboe d'amore owes its continued survival to Bach, so the **bassett horn** in f⁰ owes its life to Mozart, who wrote a great deal of beautiful music for the instrument. And just as there is no need for the modern oboe d'amore when an English horn is available, so there is no need for the modern bassett horn beside the true alto clarinet. The bassett horn is a peculiar instrument when considered in the context of the rest of the clarinet family. Its bore is of a much narrower scale (here, ratio to width to length) than usual, enabling the player to use the same mouthpiece for the B♭ (and A) clarinet as for the bassett horn. Normally, the bassett horn also has four **bassett keys** for the little fingers and right thumb, extending the range down to written c⁰. Strangely enough, nearly half the bassett horns made lack those keys; it is difficult to imagine to what use these instruments are put, since Mozart (as well as the few other composers who have written for the bassett horn) regularly demands the extra notes. Note that at least some bass, contra-alto, and contrabass clarinets are also equipped with bassett keys. A very few B♭ and A clarinets have recently been built with the low c⁰ extension, since Mozart required such **bassett clarinets** in *La Clemenza di Tito* and the original version of his clarinet concerto.

With the alto clarinet in e♭⁰ we return to normalcy. This instrument has so far been confined almost entirely to the concert and marching band, where it is held in totally undeserved bad esteem. In a vicious cycle, poor players are given the instrument to play, so com-

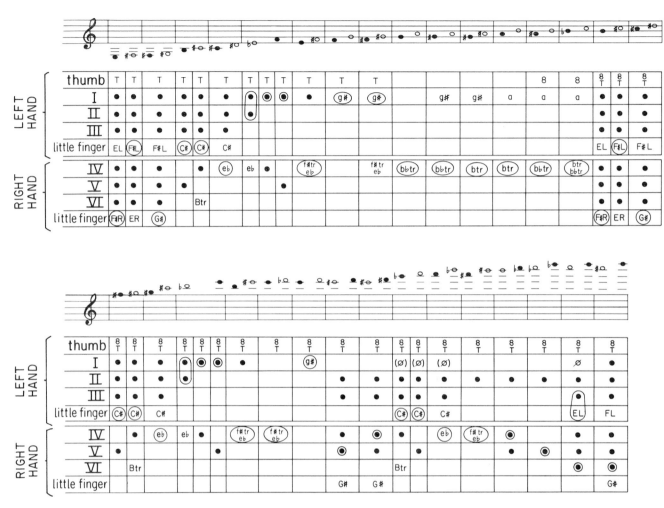

FIGURE 25. *Special trill fingerings for the clarinet. The complete fingering shown produces the open note. When the circled keys are raised, the filled note is produced.*

posers give it unimportant parts, all carefully doubled in the third clarinets and alto saxes, so that the instrument is never heard, which is why it is given to poor players. In the hands of a good player, however, the alto clarinet is one of the most versatile and beautiful-sounding of all the clarinets.

The clarinets from alto down are known collectively as "the low clarinets": these sizes are all bent in various ways to keep them physically manageable. In the alto clarinet the mouthpiece end is bent back toward the player and the bell is recurved out and up. In the bass clarinet (which logically ought to be called "tenor") the bell is similar, but the mouthpiece end is bent out and down in an S-curve. Some contra-alto and contrabass clarinets are built in a "stretched" version of this shape, but most are in the so-called "paper-clip" format patented by the Leblanc company (see Fig. 22). Despite the complexities of a key system that must be seen to be believed, these Leblanc instruments are popular due to their comparative cheapness, ruggedness, and reliability. The clumsy term "contra-alto" is applied to the second-lowest member of the clarinet family because the term "bass" was preempted. Considerable confusion continues to be generated by the incorrect use of the name "E♭ contrabass" for this instrument—a reflection of the fact that many band directors consider the contra-alto and contrabass clarinets to be slightly different versions of the same instrument. Worse, the illiteracy "*contralto* clarinet" is still encountered from time to time.

The true contrabass clarinet in $B\flat_1$, long an experimental curiosity, is by now firmly established and readily available. It is used in bands as an underpinning to the clarinet choir, and occasionally in the orchestra as a foil to the contrabassoon, the only other contrabass woodwind.

Clarinets of all sizes except the $A\flat$ are usually made in five pieces: mouthpiece, barrel, upper joint, lower joint, and bell; in the $A\flat$ clarinet the upper and lower joints are unified. All the keywork is on the upper and lower joints,* which divide, as with the oboe, between the tone holes for the fourth finger of the left hand and the second finger of the right. There are one or more points at which the keywork of the two joints interlocks. The instrument is tuned by adjusting the depths to which the mouthpiece and upper joint are inserted into the barrel. Since the tenons involved are about the same length for all sizes of clarinet, the higher instruments are more flexible in this regard than the lower ones; fortunately, the low clarinets are less affected by changes in temperature and humidity than are the high ones. The curved barrel and bell of the low clarinets are made of metal. Mouthpieces of all sizes are almost always made of plastic. The body of the instrument may be of wood, plastic, or metal, wood being the material of choice.

"Contra" clarinets in paper-clip format are made only of metal. When these instruments are provided with an extension to written low d^0 or c^0, the pads and tone holes for the extra notes are sometimes incorporated into a short extra joint called the low D joint or low C joint. Other extended-range clarinets simply have a longer lower joint.

All low clarinets normally descend at least to written $e\flat^0$. The key for this note is operated by the right fifth finger. While the alto clarinet has not yet been standardized in this respect, a few $B\flat$ clarinets are provided with this key to enable them to cover the lowest note of parts written for clarinet in A. Most clarinets with low $e\flat^0$ keys are provided with an alternate fingering for written $g\sharp^0/d\sharp^2$, usually in the form of a duplicate G♯ key for the left fifth finger, but sometimes in the form of an automatic mechanism whereby $g\sharp^0/d\sharp^2$ can be produced by fingering

(8)

For notes lower than written $e\flat^0$, the distribution of keys has not yet been standardized. The most common setup gives d^0 with the left fifth finger and $c\sharp^0$ and c^0 with the right thumb, which normally only supports the instrument. Some instruments, however, also give the d^0 key to the right thumb, and a few extended bass clarinets even have the $e\flat^0$ key in that position.

* The lowest tone-hole and its pad are on the bell in straight-format low clarinets.

On some alto, bass, and "contra" clarinets the octave key (so-called, though it actually speaks the twelfth) is double, one key for notes from written b♭¹ to g² and the other for notes above that.

On all high clarinets (and some alto clarinets as well) the six tone holes for the middle three fingers of each hand are closed directly by the fingers, five of the six holes (sometimes all six) being surrounded by metal rings that are depressed whenever the finger covers the hole and which connect to various keys and pads. Except for the best alto clarinets all low clarinets are plateau-model instruments, with the exception that the plate for the left index finger is usually pierced by a small hole to enable the altissimo register to be produced by the normal half-hole technique (see Fig. 24).

PERFORMANCE CHARACTERISTICS

Alone among woodwinds, the clarinet has normally been played without any vibrato, only Eastern Europe dissenting from the prevailing feeling that adding this feature to the instrument's already sweet tone would be gilding the lily. Since about 1960, however, the vibrato has been gaining in favor worldwide, and practice now varies from player to player. If a vibrato is either particularly desired or particularly undesired, the instruction "vibr." or "senza vibr." should be given. The vibrato is produced by the diaphragm (rarely, by the lips), and can be varied in speed and intensity.

Because its partials are so widely separated, the three registers of the clarinet have very distinctive timbres. The lower register (called the **chalumeau** register, after the non-over-blowing instrument from which the clarinet is descended) is dark, sweet, and liquid—it has been described as sounding "chocolatey." This tone-color is even stronger on the alto than on the B♭ clarinet, and it is stronger still on the bass clarinet. On the "contra" clarinets, some very high upper partials of these notes become audible, and as a result the lowest tones of these instruments have an almost rattling quality, like the lowest strings of a large grand piano. On the high E♭ clarinet, the lower register, while still sweet and liquid, is much less dark than on the B♭ instrument and tends to sound somewhat characterless and detached. This is even more true of the A♭ clarinet, whose sweet, soul-less lower register can seem almost psychotic.

The highest tones of the chalumeau register, written f♯¹ to b♭¹, are called the **throat tones**. These notes tend to sound thin, stuffy, and unconvincing, and the ability to unify these notes timbrally with the others is the mark of a fine instrument and a fine player. On the high E♭ and A♭ instruments this is considerably less of a problem than on the other members of the family.

The upper register of the B♭ clarinet is smooth, brilliant, and powerful. Its almost trumpet-like timbre has led it to be called the **clarion register** and has given the instrument its name. On the E♭ clarinet the upper register tends to be rather shrill, but as with the upper register of almost any woodwind it will sound impassioned and intense when given lyrical material to play. The A♭ clarinet is irredeemably shrill in this register, but not necessarily unpleasant—as with the piccolo, the small number of audible partials renders the tone rather characterless. On the alto clarinet the clarion register is somewhat smoother, more liquid, and gentler-sounding than on the B♭ clarinet. It also tends to be slightly stuffy. The upper register of the bass clarinet is quite weak and thin—it is usually described as sounding "watery." The two "contras," on the other hand, produce an almost saxophone-like honk, albeit rather muffled, in this range.

The altissimo register of all the high clarinets is brilliant, squeaky, shrill, and piercing. That of the alto clarinet is also brilliant, but powerful and intense; the bass clarinet's altissimo sounds oddly disembodied and thin. The "contra" clarinets yield this register only in the hands of a dedicated high-note specialist (the high c#³ and d³ written are produced with clarion-register trill fingerings). This is particularly frustrating to clarinetists, because the harmonic spectrum of these instruments is so rich that the addition of just one special speaker key would be sufficient to give them all ranges even greater than that of the bass clarinet—which, it should be noted, has when played by a virtuoso a greater range than any other woodwind.

The clarinets also have a broader and more flexible dynamic range than any other woodwind. The extremes given in Figure 23 are, in contrast to the situation found among double-reed instruments, achievable without great effort or distortion of the sound.

Quarter-tones are available on the clarinet from written a|⁰ up, with the exception that written c ♮², c #², and d ♮² are not possible. Low clarinets with plateau-system keywork cannot produce written a|⁰, a ♮⁰, e|², or e ♮². The clarinet comes closer than other woodwinds to producing a truly convincing glissando, but some sort of "fudge" must nonetheless be used to get past the register breaks. The glissando is most effective in the upper register, and it is not possible below written g⁰. Because the ability to bend pitches with the embouchure is very restricted in clarinets, glissandos are out of the question for plateau-model instruments. Pitches can be bent (downward only) by the embouchure more in the altissimo than in the other registers, more in the lower clarinets than in the high ones, and more when few tone holes are closed than when many are. With some exceptions (the open g¹ written, for instance) they can be bent more than a quarter-tone only in the altissimo register.

Clarinets of all sizes can produce a great variety of multiphonics, but every one is, as mentioned earlier, slow and/or uncertain of speech. Once a given multiphonic has been generated, however, it is easy enough to slur to others. Because of the large gaps between partials, the components of a clarinet multiphonic tend to cover a wide range of pitch.

Special effects on the clarinets include:

1. Key percussion, possible only for notes from written f#¹ down. It can be performed as loudly as *piano* on plateau-model instruments, on open-hole clarinets no louder than *pianissimo*. The effect can be taken up exactly an octave and made slightly louder by the simple expedient of removing the reed, thus turning the instrument into an open pipe.

2. Playing on the mouthpiece alone, a siren-like sound. The pitch can be varied over a range of about a fourth. The difference in pitch between an A♭ clarinet mouthpiece and a contrabass clarinet mouthpiece is only about an octave.

3. Removing the mouthpiece and blowing into the barrel through pursed lips, in the lower register only. This is most effective on the lowest notes but the notes are out of tune throughout. A better sound but one even more out of tune is produced when the barrel is removed as well. This technique is not really feasible on low clarinets.

4. Removing the mouthpiece of a B♭ clarinet and replacing it with that of a contra-alto or contrabass clarinet, which fits *over* the barrel. An unearthly, hollow, whooping sound is produced, about a third lower than the usual lower-register notes. It is thoroughly out

of tune, and the embouchure can vary the pitch downward by as much as a third for each note. The instrument will not overblow under these conditions, but the lowest notes of the instrument can be *underblown* so that their pitch drops about a fourth. This effect has not been investigated acoustically, but it is probably allied to the "privileged frequency" pedals of brass instruments (q.v.).

5. Blowing through the instrument without causing the reed to vibrate. The fingerings of the lower register will color the resulting *piano* or softer hiss without giving any real impression of pitch change.

6. Removing the reed altogether, turning the mouthpiece around, holding the instrument like a flute, and blowing across the opening (**lay**) of the mouthpiece. The tones of the lower register will emerge, one octave higher (and in tune!) with a very breathy, vaguely flute-like sound. This can be done no louder than *mezzo-forte*, and, obviously, only on straight members of the family.

7. Lowering the pitch of the lowest note by removing the bell and replacing it with a tubular extension. By this means notes as much as an octave and a half below the normal range can be produced. The longer the extension, the more restricted the dynamic range of the note becomes; and in the extreme case, the note can only be blown *piano* or softer. In any event, the note immediately above the affected one will be out of tune.

MUSICAL EXAMPLES

Bb CLARINET:
> Messiaen, *Quatuor pour la fin du temps*
> Maxwell Davies, *Hymnos*
> > *Missa super l'homme armé*
> Xenakis, *Anaktoria*

Eb CLARINET:
> Chavez, *Sinfonia India*
> Janáček, Concertino for piano and chamber orchestra (2nd mvt.)

Ab CLARINET:
> There does not appear to be any independent literature for this instrument. Whole sections of Ab clarinets are used in Italian carabinieri bands, where they play opera transcriptions, etc.

ALTO CLARINET:
> Stravinsky, *Elegy for J.F.K.*
> Henze, *The Raft of the Medusa*

BASS CLARINET:
> Schoenberg, *Pierrot lunaire*
> Nono, *Polifonica-Monodia-Ritmica*

CONTRA-ALTO CLARINET:
> Martirano, *Octet*
> Penderecki, *Pittsburgh Overture*

CONTRABASS CLARINET:
Xenakis, *Akrata*
Penderecki, *Capriccio* for violin and orchestra

SAXOPHONES

The saxophone family is the newest of the modern woodwind groups, and all the sizes (plus eight others now extinct)* were developed simultaneously. There is thus a remarkable unity of timbre and unanimity of fingering among the various members of the family, and the fingering system is admirably flexible, rational, and simple. In addition, each instrument is almost invariant in timbre from one end of its range to the other. The upshot of all this is that saxophones are the easiest of all woodwinds to play well, a fact that as much as anything else accounts for their continuing popularity.

The rather subtle differences in timbre between the different sizes of saxophone seem to be a function more of the keys in which they are built than of the sizes of the instruments. Thus, the soprano, tenor, and bass saxes, all pitched in B♭, sound relatively coarse and throaty compared to the alto and baritone, both in E♭, which sound smooth and velvety. All saxes, regardless of size, show a considerable similarity to the human voice in tone quality— an attribute that led to their early and permanent adoption in jazz and other forms of popular music. The vast majority of professional saxophonists also play clarinet.

Except for the soprano, saxes are made in three pieces: mouthpiece, neck, and body. Part of the octave key mechanism lies on the neck, but all the rest of the keywork is on the body. The soprano sax has no separate neck. The mouthpiece of a saxophone may be of either metal or plastic, but the rest of the instrument is always made of metal. Saxophones are by necessity all plateau-model instruments, for even on the soprano sax the tone holes are very large and could not possibly be covered by the fingers alone. Rather like the clarinets, saxes are tuned by adjusting the extent to which the neck is inserted into the mouthpiece and body.

PERFORMANCE CHARACTERISTICS

Saxes are played with or without vibrato, depending on the player and the musical context; if either the vibrato or its absence is particularly desired, the player must be so instructed. As usual, vibrato speed and amplitude can be varied. There is a remarkable evenness of timbre throughout the range of the saxophone, the only notes with any distinctive quality being those below written d^1, which honk rather vulgarly no matter how gently they are treated, and which, as on the oboe, cannot be played very softly. Until fairly recently the altissimo register of the saxophone (called by saxophonists the "top tones") was a mystery revealed only to a handful of virtuosi. Now, however, it is being taught on a fairly regular basis as an advanced technique. There is no doubt that the altissimo register is more difficult to produce

---

* In addition to the instruments listed, an e♭^{1} sopranino saxophone is still occasionally manufactured as a publicity gimmick ("look how complete our line is!"). It is almost impossible to play in tune and well deserves complete extinction.

FIGURE 26. *The saxophone family: (a) soprano saxophone;*
(b) alto saxophone; (c) tenor saxophone; (d) baritone saxophone; (e) bass saxophone.

on the saxophone than on other woodwinds; it appears likely, however, that these notes will eventually come to be considered a normal part of the instrument's compass. The fingering chart reflects the currently unsettled state of affairs; it should be borne in mind that only one or two of the numerous fingerings given for each of these notes will be feasible on any given instrument.

The saxophone has a broad dynamic range, but must be counted the loudest of the woodwinds because it is most comfortably played *forte*. The *fortissimo* throughout the range is so powerful as to approach the *fff* of brass instruments, and the sax is the only woodwind that can be played on a nearly equal footing with a group of brass instruments.

Quarter-tones are possible on the saxophone from written e♭¹ up. Because the opening in the mouthpiece (the **lay**) covered by the reed is proportionally much longer in the saxophone than in the clarinet, the pitch of individual notes can be inflected by the embouchure much more strongly in the former than in the latter—up to half a step downward for all notes from written g¹ up, much less than that upward. Below written g¹, intonation is less flexible,

name of instrument	abbreviations	written range	sounds	availability
soprano saxophone in b♭⁰	sop. sax s.s.	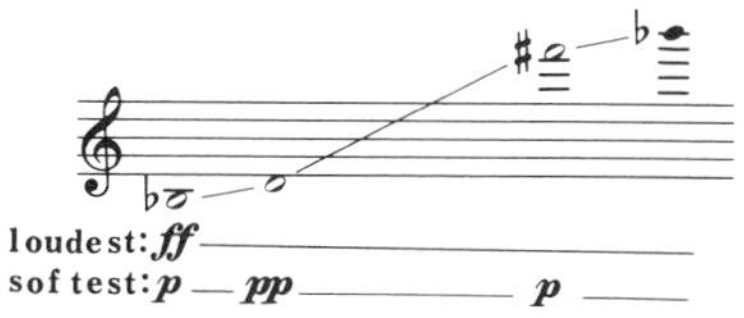 loudest: *ff* softest: *p* — *pp* — *p*	a major 2nd lower	common
alto saxophone in e♭⁰	alt. sax a.s.	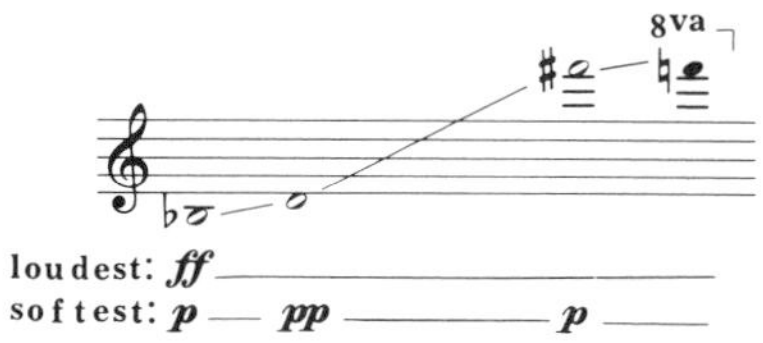 loudest: *ff* softest: *p* — *pp* — *p*	a major 6th lower	ubiquitous
tenor saxophone in B♭₀	ten. sax t.s.	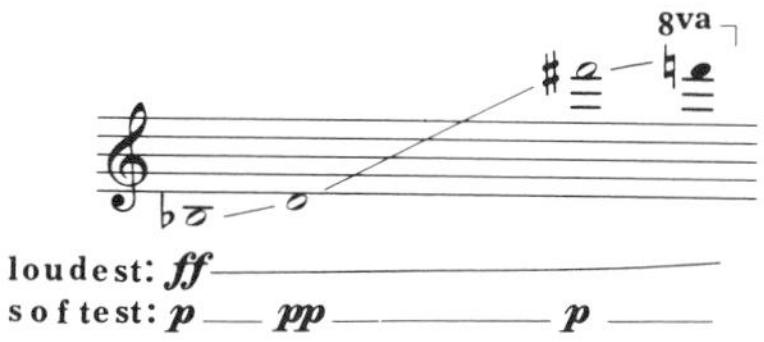 loudest: *ff* softest: *p* — *pp* — *p*	a major 9th lower	ubiquitous
baritone saxophone in E♭₀	bar. sax bt.s.	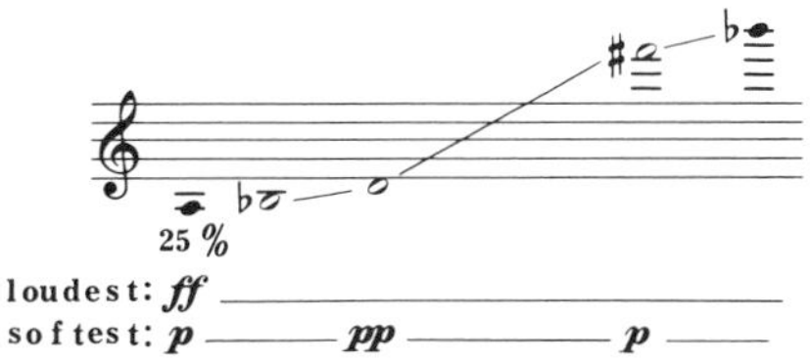 25 % loudest: *ff* softest: *p* — *pp* — *p*	1 octave + a major 6th lower	common
bass saxophone in B♭₁	bs. sax bs.s.	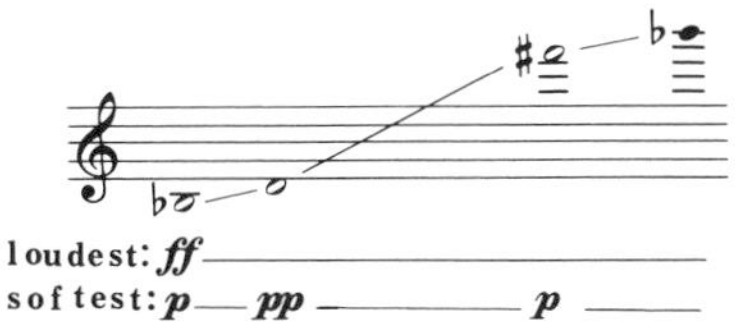 loudest: *ff* softest: *p* — *pp* — *p*	2 octaves + a major 2nd lower	rare

FIGURE 27. *The saxophone family—vital statistics.*

and notes below written d^1 can scarcely be adjusted at all. Even a "lumpy" glissando is out of the question on the saxophone except in the range from written c^3 to f^3.

As do the flute and clarinet, the saxophone produces and sustains multiphonics only slowly and with difficulty. There are fewer of these sounds on the sax than on any other woodwind, and those that do exist have not been widely exploited.

Mutes resembling those used by brass players are or have been manufactured for the saxophone, but they are very rare. A sufficiently large piece of cloth wadded up and stuffed

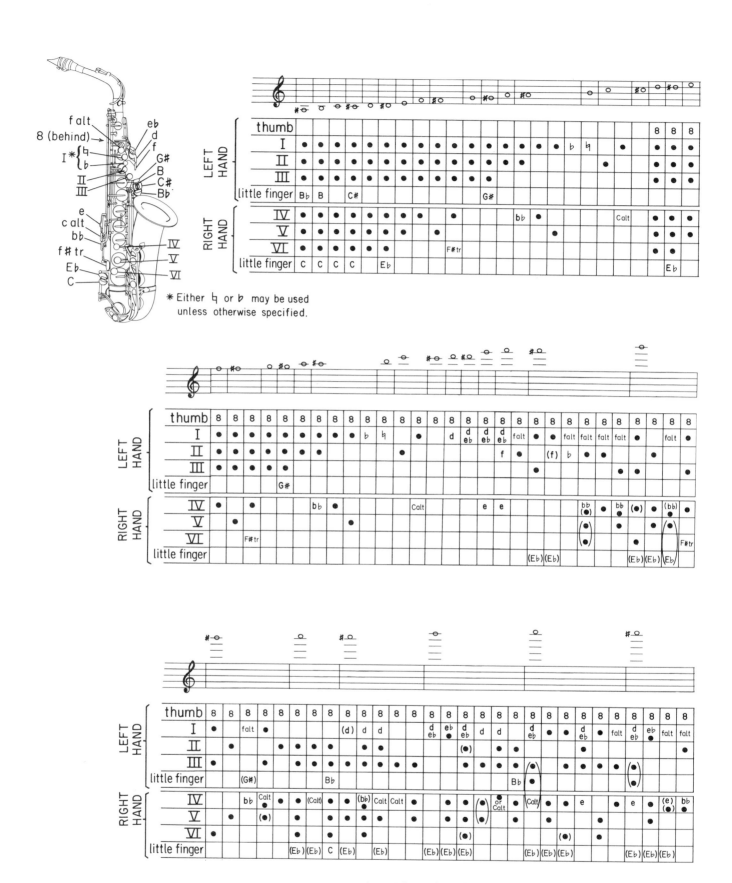

FIGURE 28. *Fingering chart for the saxophone.*

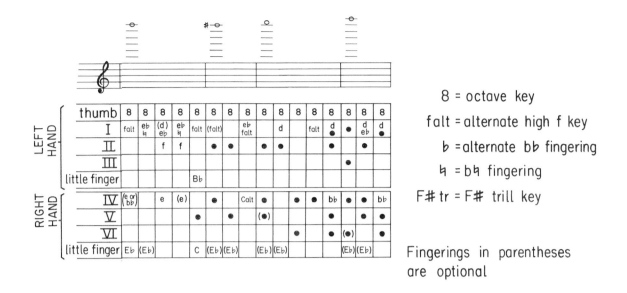

8 = octave key

falt = alternate high f key

♭ = alternate b♭ fingering

♮ = b♮ fingering

F# tr = F# trill key

Fingerings in parentheses
are optional

Fingering chart for the saxophone, continued.

into the bell makes a satisfactory substitute. As with the oboe, the sound is rendered not so much soft as gentle and distant. The low written b♭^{0} and b♮^{0} will be unusable and the written c^1 may be out of tune.

The key slap of the saxophone can be even stronger than that of the flute, but nonetheless cannot be produced louder than *piano*. A *mezzo-piano* can be attained by combining this effect with slap-tonguing. The key slap is subject to the same restrictions as on the flute, oboe, and clarinet, and can be performed only from written c^2 down.

Played by itself, a sax mouthpiece sounds much like a clarinet's, but the pitch can be varied a bit more—about a fifth. Hissing air through the instrument without vibrating the reed produces **colored noise** from the low register-fingerings, as for the clarinet. The illusion of a continuously sounding pitch can be produced by combining this effect with the key slap.

A written low a^0 or a♭^{0} can be obtained by inserting a rolled-up newspaper or other tubular extension of appropriate length into the bell and fingering b♭^{0}. As usual, the b^0 will be muffled and out of tune.

Finally, the mouthpiece can be removed and the instrument played by blowing air between the pursed lips directly into the barrel. The soprano sax sounds and behaves much like the oboe in this respect; the effect is more restricted on lower instruments, e.g., on the baritone sax only written g^1 to c#^{2} can be obtained. As usual, this effect is out of tune.

MUSICAL EXAMPLES

SOPRANO SAXOPHONE:

Koechlin, *Les Bandar-Log*
Copland, Piano Concerto (2nd mvt.)
Ravel, *Bolero* (a sopranino sax part almost invariably played on soprano)

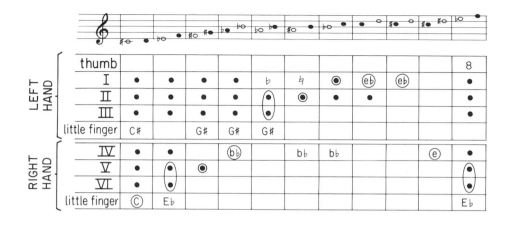

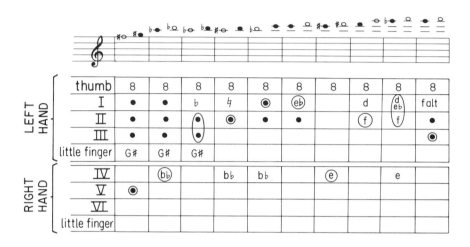

FIGURE 29. *Special trill fingerings for the saxophone. The complete fingering shown produces the open note. When the circled keys are raised, the filled note is produced.*

ALTO SAXOPHONE:

    Hindemith, Symphony in B♭ for concert band (2nd mvt.)
    Stravinsky, *Ebony Concerto*
    Nono, *Polifonica-Monodia-Ritmica*
    Curtis-Smith, *Unisonics*

TENOR SAXOPHONE:

    Ravel, *Bolero*
    Stravinsky, *Ebony Concerto*
    Webern, Quartet, Op. 22

BARITONE SAXOPHONE:

    Stravinsky, *Ebony Concerto*
    Weill, *Die Dreigroschenoper* ("Ballade von der sexuellen Hörigkeit")
    Penderecki, *Capriccio* for violin and orchestra

BASS SAXOPHONE:
Schoenberg, *Von Heute auf Morgen*
Schmitt, *Dionysiaques*

BASSOONS

The bassoon and contrabassoon provide the bass and contrabass of the oboe family but are so markedly different from the oboe in construction and fingering system that they are rightly considered to comprise a separate family of their own. On top of that, the bassoon and contrabassoon are so different from each other that their constructions must be discussed separately, and they require separate fingering charts.

THE INSTRUMENTS

The bassoon is simultaneously the most peculiar and the most archaic of all modern woodwinds. For example: the bore makes a sharp 180° turn at the bottom of the instrument, the ascending and descending portions of the U being housed in the same piece of wood; the mechanism of two keys actually runs *through* the body of the instrument, traversing the partition between the branches of the U-bend; the instrument descends to a depth of nine semitones below the lowest note (G_0) of its fundamental scale; both thumbs are used in play; and there are nine keys operated by the left thumb alone; notwithstanding which, the key system is so primitive that the tone holes for three fingers are not even provided with a ring; in consequence, complicated *fork-fingerings* are needed for sixteen notes. Finally, in order to have the tone holes of the fundamental scale lie under the fingers, these holes are made unusually deep (through wood left thick for that purpose) and communicate with the bore at sharp angles. All these irrational and primitive features have been retained in the instrument because all attempts to "modernize" the bassoon result in the destruction of the instrument's characteristically gentle, veiled tone quality, which is dependent on precisely these long, slanted tone holes, the sharply angled bore, and the extra length provided for the lowest tones.

Bassoons are made of wood (student instruments may be made of plastic) in five pieces. The reed (Fig. 8) fits snugly over the end of the curved metal **bocal** (or **crook**), which in turn fits into the top of the **wing joint**, so called from its rather flattened shape. This corresponds to the upper joint of the oboe or clarinet, and holds the keys and tone holes for the left index, middle, and ring fingers, and five keys for the left thumb. The tone holes for the middle three fingers of the left hand are all covered directly by the fingers, and only the hole for the ring finger is provided with a ring. The wood through which these tone holes pass is unusually thick in order that the holes may be properly elongated and slanted, and this extra thickness of wood gives the joint its "wing" shape.

The U-shaped portion of the bore lies within the **butt joint** (or "boot joint") and the wing joint inserts into the descending branch of the U. Actually, only straight portions of the bore lie in the wood of this joint; the very sharp turnaround is negotiated by a semicircular

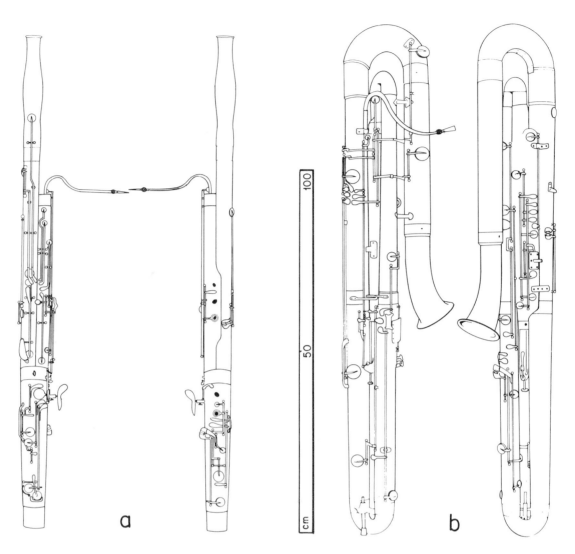

FIGURE 30. *The bassoon family: (a) bassoon; (b) contrabassoon.*

metal tube, exactly like a sink trap, which is tightly sealed to the bottom of the boot joint with a gasket, and protected/disguised by a removable metal cover. The boot joint contains all the keywork for the right hand. The tone holes for the right index and middle fingers are covered directly by those fingers, the latter being provided with a ring. The tone hole for the right ring finger is covered by a pad at the end of a long and complicated key.

Into the ascending portion of the boot joint is fitted the **bass joint**, which is provided with the keywork for the left little finger and four keys for the left thumb. The pad and tone hole for the low B♭$_1$ are located on the **bell**, which, however, is not even remotely bell-shaped.

Contrabassoons, invariably built of wood, are made in only two or three pieces, but the bore of a contrabassoon is folded back on itself three or four times. The various ascending and descending sections are all permanently attached to each other, and only the bocal and sometimes the bell are detachable. The bocal is inserted into the the top of the first descending section, a thin metal tube with only one tiny tone-hole. This tube curves 180° and reascends a short distance to the point at which it is attached to the first ascending section. This section, which is wooden, corresponds to the wing joint of the bassoon. The keys of this

name of instrument	abbreviations	written range	sounds	availability
bassoon	bsn. bn.	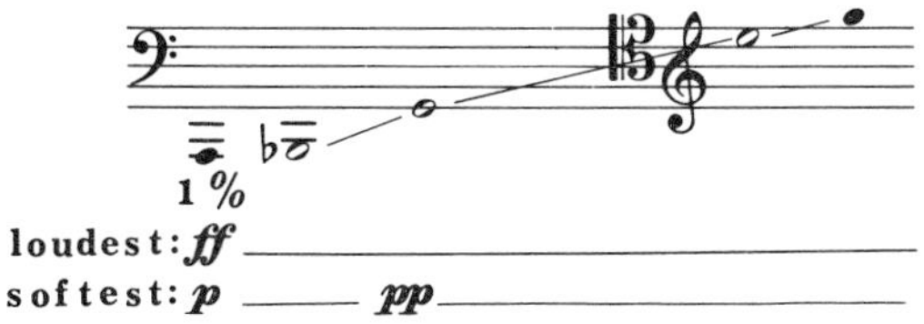 1 % loudest: *ff* softest: *p* — *pp*	as written	common
contrabassoon	cbsn. cbn.	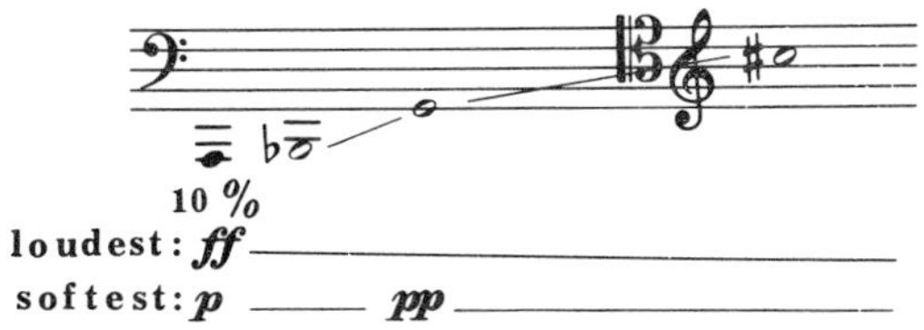 10 % loudest: *ff* softest: *p* — *pp*	1 octave lower	rare

FIGURE 31. *The bassoon family—vital statistics.*

section are so arranged that, although they control the tone holes of an ascending length of pipe, they are depressed by the fingers in *descending* order, as on the bassoon. At the top of this section the tube makes another 180° bend, through a metal loop like that in the butt joint of the bassoon.

The second descending section, which corresponds to the butt joint of the bassoon, is really two separate lengths of wooden tubing, joined end to end. At the bottom of this section (the bottom of the instrument) is another metal turnaround leading to the second ascending section. This section, too, is in two connected pieces and is roughly equivalent to the bass joint of the bassoon. It is surmounted by a bell, which is usually detachable and may take either of two forms. Most commonly, the bell curves broadly over the top of the instrument and flops down, forming what is essentially a third descending section of the instrument. Such bells are made in three interconnected pieces, viz., the (wooden!) curve over the top of the instrument, which holds the low B_2 pad and tone hole; a straight descending section on which the low $B\flat_2$ (and A_2, if present) tone hole and pad are placed; and the bell proper, which is made of metal and curves down and out. On contrabassoons descending to A_2, the key for that note is operated by the left little finger. The other form of contrabassoon bell continues straight up from the second ascending segment of the body, and contrabassoons with such bells tower over everything else in the orchestra. This kind of bell is in only two sections, a lower wooden section bearing the low $B\flat_2$ tone hole and pad (the $B\natural_2$ is on the second ascending section), and an upper metal section that curves so as to project the sound upward and outward.

The contrabassoon is such a sturdy and expensive instrument that it is said that none of those built since the key system was "perfected" in the 1870s has been retired from service. Whatever the truth of this statement, it is certain that there are some very old "contras" still in use, including, unfortunately, some instruments descending only to low C_1.

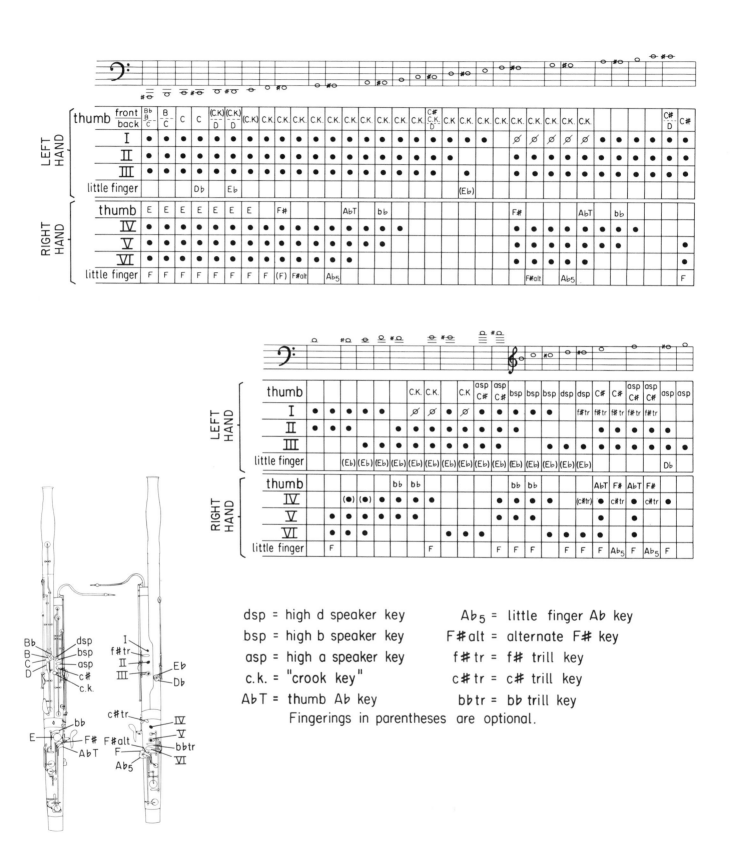

dsp = high d speaker key   Ab₅ = little finger Ab key

bsp = high b speaker key   F#alt = alternate F# key

asp = high a speaker key   f#tr = f# trill key

c.k. = "crook key"   c#tr = c# trill key

AbT = thumb Ab key   bbtr = bb trill key

Fingerings in parentheses are optional.

FIGURE 32. *Fingering chart for the bassoon.*

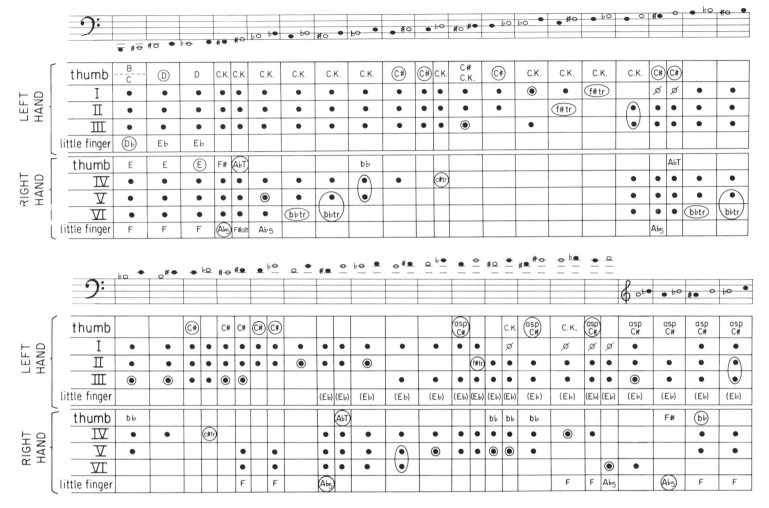

FIGURE 33. *Special trill fingerings for the bassoon. The complete fingering shown produces the open note. When the circled keys are raised, the filled note is produced.*

PERFORMANCE CHARACTERISTICS

Parts for bassoon and contrabassoon are normally written in the bass clef except for high-lying passages, which have traditionally been put in the tenor clef. As the range of both instruments has been gradually expanded upward during the twentieth century, the use of treble clef in bassoon parts has become more frequent, and all bassoonists now read high notes easily in that clef. Accordingly, the use of tenor clef has been decreasing, and it seems likely that composers will discontinue its use altogether in the near future—there is certainly no need for it. In the meantime, bassoonists are used to reading parts in the bass clef up to about b^1, in the tenor clef from d^0 to d^2, and in the treble clef from e^1 up. The appearance of notes much outside these ranges will cause confusion, incredulity, and resentment.

The bassoon and contrabassoon, like the oboes, are normally played with a diaphragm (sometimes lip) vibrato which must be specifically countermanded if it is not desired, and whose speed and intensity can be varied by the player. The timbre of the bassoon is nasal, but somewhat veiled, velvety, and melancholy. Because of the instrument's manifold peculiari-

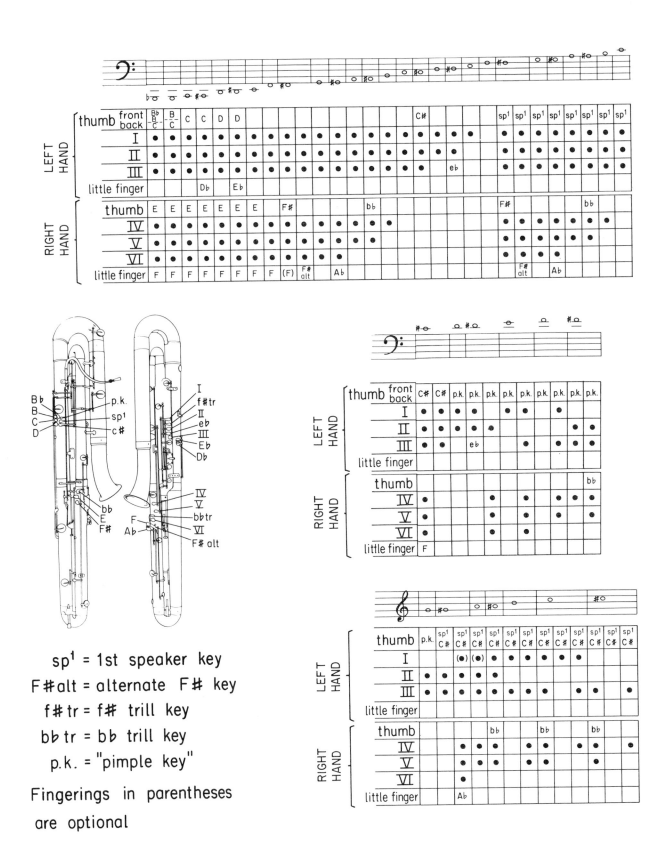

sp¹ = 1st speaker key

F#alt = alternate F# key

f#tr = f# trill key

b♭tr = b♭ trill key

p.k. = "pimple key"

Fingerings in parentheses
are optional

FIGURE 34. *Fingering chart for the contrabassoon.*

ties, the tone varies considerably in different parts of the range—not necessarily corresponding to the different registers. The most characteristic sound is that of the lower-register notes from Bb_1 to $c\#^0$; those below G_0 cannot be played very softly, but on the bassoon, unlike the oboe or saxophone, the lowest notes do not sound particularly coarser than the rest of the low register. The notes from d^0 to $f\#^0$ are the most nasal on the instrument, and it is in this range that the bassoon sounds most like an oboe—these pitches have almost exactly the same sound when played on the heckelphone. The notes g^0 to d^1 match the lower register in tone; but eb^1 to $c\#^2$ have a particularly smooth and dark timbre which can also be extended to d^1 and $c\#^1$ by the use of alternate **fork fingerings** (see Fig. 32). The remaining high notes sound increasingly unearthly the higher they get.

The contrabassoon is a different matter; here the veiling of the tone produces an effect more of hourseness or coveredness, and the instrument sounds somewhat coarse throughout its range. Written d^0 to f^0 are rather nasal and thin, d^1 to $f\#^1$ almost unpleasantly nasal, thin, and very coarse. Because of its great length (the contrabassoon behaves like an open pipe, remember, and is thus twice as long as the equally low contrabass clarinet) it takes a relatively long time for the standing wave to be set up when a note is attacked, and a similarly long time for the air column to adjust to the opening or closing of a tone hole. While this does not affect the instrument's agility (the extremely rapid passagework in Beethoven's *Ninth Symphony* or Strauss's two late wind sonatinas is not at all unidiomatic), it strongly affects the timbre, and this slowness of speech is heard by the ear as awkwardness or sloppiness—one can clearly hear the air column "shift gears" whenever there is a slur across a register break, for instance. It is thus almost impossible for the contrabassoon to sound "dignified" in any kind of moving passage; and it is not by accident that the two extended contrabassoon solos cited below as musical examples were intended to represent, respectively, physical ugliness and vain stupidity. Indeed, if one is looking for an all-purpose contrabass woodwind, the contrabass clarinet is superior to the contrabassoon in almost every respect. Nonetheless, the contrabassoon is a valuable timbre, and if its idiosyncrasies are taken into account it can be used with very telling effect; witness the striking way in which two contrabassoons are played off against tuba, trombone, and contrabass clarinet in Xenakis's *Akrata*.

The dynamic potential of the bassoon is restricted exactly as the oboe's is—extreme measures must be taken to achieve a genuine *pianissimo* or *fortissimo*. Many players do not trouble to take these measures, squeezing everything into the space between *piano* and *forte*. The situation for the contrabassoon is exactly the same.

The bassoon can be muted by stuffing a handkerchief or other object into the bell. The low Bb_1 will be unavailable and the $B\natural_1$ out of tune. The resulting change of timbre is a much more subtle affair than it is on the oboe.

Quarter-tones are feasible on the bassoon from $G\natural_0$ up, with the exception of $f\#^0$, which is impossible. The notes $E\natural_0$, $D\natural_0$, and $C\natural_0$ are also possible; these three low quarter-tones are not possible on the contrabassoon. The usual sort of "lumpy" glissando can be produced from G_0 up, but the contrabassoon is not really suited to glissandos, though individual pitches in this range can be bent with the lips, sometimes as much as a half-step downward.

Both the bassoon and contrabassoon rival the oboe family in the number and variety of multiphonics they can produce. The lower-pitched among the contrabassoon multiphonics are mostly unearthly rattling, gargling, or coughing sounds one would not think a woodwind capable of producing.

Special effects on the bassoon are much like those of the oboe. The reed, played alone, sounds like a party noisemaker, about a fifth lower than an oboe reed; the contrabassoon reed sounds a fifth lower still. The key slap is not worthwhile on either instrument, but a very similar effect can be produced on both bassoon and contrabassoon by fingering any lower-register note and ramming the tongue against the reed (without blowing through the instrument). This cannot be performed louder than *pianissimo.* Additionally, the keys can be rattled, as with the oboe, producing a clatter as loud as *mezzo-piano* when the left-thumb keys are struck simultaneously by the palm of the left hand.

Blowing through the instriment without letting the reed vibrate produces a hiss that can be colored by any low-register fingering. The contrabassoon, however, is so low-pitched and cavernous that different fingerings do not have much audible effect.

Bassoonists are quite used to placing a cardboard or metal tube in the bell to obtain the low A_1 that is occasionally written; theoretically one could also get an Ab_1 by using a longer tube. In any event, the B_1 will be stuffy and perhaps out of tune whenever an extension is used. Similar extension of the contrabassoon, while theoretically possible, is hardly practical in view of the inordinate length and width of extra tubing that would be required. The contrabass clarinet is a much better candidate for such experiments.

Musical Examples

BASSOON:

Hindemith, *Kleine Kammermusik*
Stravinsky, Octet for winds
Chihara, *Branches*
Xenakis, *Anaktoria*

CONTRABASSOON:

Ravel, *Ma Mère l'oye* ("Entretiens de la belle et la bête")
Koechlin, *Les Bandar-Log*
Xenakis, *Akrata*

Additional Examples

WOODWINDS IN LARGE GROUPS

Stravinsky, *Symphonies of Wind Instruments*
Schoenberg, Theme and Variations, Op. 43a
Hindemith, Symphony in Bb for concert band
Grainger, *A Lincolnshire Posy*
Messiaen, *Oiseaux exotiques*
          Et exspecto resurrectionem mortuorum
Xenakis, *Akrata*

III

THE

BRASSES

GENERAL CONSIDERATIONS

Organologically, brass instruments belong to the category of *lip-vibrated aerophones*, a term that correctly emphasizes the way in which the air column is set in motion rather than the material of which the instrument is made. Although most "brasses" are in fact made of brass, they may be constructed of some other soft-metal alloy, and some cheap instruments are even made of fiberglass. The sound of all these instruments is produced by the vibration of the player's lips when air is forced between them, and it is this that gives them their "brassy" tone quality.

ACOUSTICS AND MECHANISM

Acoustically the brass are very similar to woodwinds. All behave as stopped, conical pipes, and thus share many tonal properties with the saxophone, oboe, and bassoon. They are all, however, built to a much narrower scale than any woodwind; this property enables the player to overblow (by tightening the lips to a greater or lesser extent) a great many more partials than are available on a woodwind, while simultaneously making the fundamental (called "pedal" by brass players) difficult to produce. Figure 35 shows the various partials that may theoretically be used by an alto or tenor brass instrument pitched in C. For instruments built in other pitches, this pattern should be transposed up or down by the appropriate interval.

FIGURE 35. *Notes produced on a brass instrument by overblowing C_0.*

In reality, only the horn makes regular use of all of these partials,* but even on the relatively inflexible trumpet all partials from the second to the ninth are used in the normal course of play.

Note that *all* these notes are produced by the lips alone. If one ignores the fundamental, the largest gap between any two adjacent partials is only a fifth, and all that is necessary to give a brass instrument a completely chromatic range from the second partial up is some means of producing the six tones between the second and third partials; these six tones can themselves then be overblown to fill in the other gaps. The trombone's movable slide fills the gap with elegant simplicity: by pushing out the sliding portion of tube, the instrument as a whole is lengthened by the extent necessary to lower the pitch any amount up to six semitones. Thus, with the slide drawn all the way in, the notes $B\flat_1$, $B\flat_0$, f^0, $b\flat^0$, etc., can be produced with the lips alone; while with the slide slightly extended the pitches A_1, A_0, e^0, a^0, etc., can be produced, and so forth.

Brasses other than the trombone effect a similar lengthening of the tube by means of a system of **valves**. These valves operate so that when a lever is depressed, the windway, rather than running straight through the valve, is shunted through an extra length of tubing. This is accomplished by one of two rather different mechanisms. The **rotary valves** usually found on horns (Fig. 36) are internally simpler than the **piston valves** (Fig. 37) usual in trumpets, but rotary valves require a complicated and delicate mechanism for converting the linear motion of the valve spatula into the rotary motion of the valve itself. Both types of valve are returned to their "off" position by a spring when the spatula (rotary valve) or button (piston valve) is released. The **valve tubing** added to the windway when the valve is depressed is fitted with a movable section (like the slide of a trombone) by means of which the pitch of the valve can be adjusted. A similar **tuning slide** in the main part of the instrument enables the player to tune the instrument as a whole.

Typically there are three valves, arranged in a row and placed so as to be operated by the middle three fingers of the right hand (the horn is played left-handed). Of these three valves, the first (operated by the index finger) lowers the pitch of the instrument by a major second, the second valve lowers the pitch by a minor second, and the third lowers the pitch by a minor third. The valves can be used either alone or in combination; when all three are depressed together, the pitch is lowered a minor third plus a minor second plus a major second, i.e., a tritone. However, since the length of tubing needed to lower the pitch by a given amount is a function of the length of tubing already in use, a valve that is perfectly in tune when used by itself will be slightly sharp when added to a tube already slightly lengthened by the depressing

* Even on the horn the quarter-tone seventh, eleventh, thirteenth, and fourteenth partials are usually avoided.

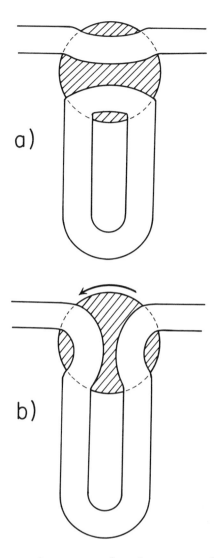

FIGURE 36. *Diagrammatic cross-section of a rotary valve: (a) closed; (b) open.*

of another valve. This discrepancy is not important when only two valves are considered, but when all three are depressed the combined sharpness is severe. To solve this problem, the third valve is tuned so as to be perfectly in tune when combined with the first valve. This results in acceptable intonation for the combinations 2 + 3 and 1 + 2 + 3, but leaves the third valve badly flat when used alone. Thus the fingering system shown in Figure 38 is produced. Where absolutely necessary the third valve *can* be used by itself to replace the combination 1 + 2—for instance, if in the example in Figure 38 one were to trill from g^0 to a^0. In trumpets a ring or (less commonly) a lever attached to the third-valve slide and operated by a finger of the left hand allows for instantaneous adjustment of the third valve in all combinations. Sometimes this mechanism is attached to the first valve as well or instead. Partials above the third are separated from each other by smaller and smaller intervals, so that as the scale is ascended, more and more notes have alternative fingerings. The third valve is not used at all when it can be avoided. Notes produced without depressing any valves are called **open** notes, and by analogy notes produced on the trombone with the slide pulled all the way

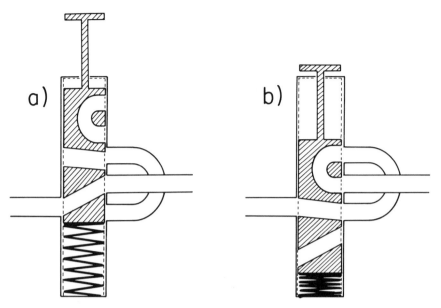

FIGURE 37. *Diagrammatic cross-section of a piston valve: (a) up; (b) down.*

FIGURE 38. *Normal fingering system of three-valve brass instruments.*

in are also called open. Exceptions to this basic three-valve fingering system (and they are numerous) will be covered as they arise in the discussion of the various instruments.

A brass instrument that normally reads in the treble clef will be written for as a transposing instrument if its open fundamental is any note other than C. Those whose parts are usually written in the bass clef are invariably non-transposing.

TIMBRE AND ARTICULATION

The brasses are timbrally a much more homogeneous group than the woodwinds, differing no more among themselves than do the various conical reed instruments. The tone is affected mostly by the bore, which may be narrowly conical (horn), mostly cylindrical (trumpets and trombones), or broadly conical (tubas). Trumpet and trombone differ only in that the one has valves, the other a slide. Another factor affecting the timbre is the internal contour of the mouthpiece (Fig. 39). Funnel-shaped mouthpieces give a smooth, mellow tone, while cup-shaped mouthpieces produce a more brilliant and cutting sound. In practice, all modern brass mouthpieces are compromises between these extremes, with horn mouthpieces tending to be funnel-shaped, trumpet mouthpieces cup-shaped, and tuba mouthpieces somewhere in between. Most players own several different mouthpieces with slightly differing contours for use in different musical circumstances.

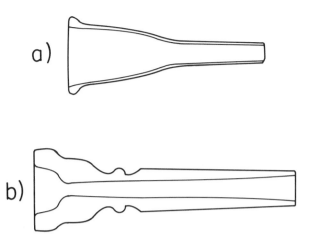

FIGURE 39. *Extremes of brass-instrument mouthpiece shape: (a) funnel-shaped; (b) cup-shaped.*

	PLAYER CAN USUALLY DOUBLE						
player's main instrument	piccolo trumpet	flügel-horn	tenor trumpet	alto horn	bass trumpet	baritone horn	contrabass trombone
trumpet	●	●	●	●	●		
horn				●		●	
trombone					●	●	●
tuba						●	●

FIGURE 40. *Common brass doublings.*

The more unusual brass instruments are usually handled by players of an instrument of similar size (depth of pitch), regardless of whether the instrument is of the trumpet, horn, or tuba type. The most common doublings are given in Figure 40. One should allow at least ten seconds for a player to switch instruments, and preferably thirty seconds or more to allow him or her to warm up the new instrument before playing it.

Articulation in brass instruments is very similar to that of the flute: notes are tongued by forming the consonant "d" or "t"; double-tonguing ("tktktk") is used for rapid detached notes, and fluttertonguing is available as a special texture. As with woodwinds, care should be taken to differentiate notationally between slurred fluttertongue notes (♪ ♪) and detached ones (♪ ♪). In addition to these articulations, brasses can start a tone with the sound "p." Tones are cut off as with woodwinds, by simply stopping the breath; in addition, they can be cut off with the tongue as a special effect.

A brass instrument requires slightly more air to produce the tone at a given dynamic level than does a woodwind of similar pitch, so the player must breathe somewhat more frequently. The horn is the most acoustically efficient in this regard, comparing favorably to the various tenor woodwinds; the contrabass tuba, on the other hand, requires more air than any other wind instrument, but a single soft, mid-range note can be held for twenty seconds or more. Cyclic breathing is as much of a possibility on brass instruments as on woodwinds. Remember that few players have mastered this difficult technique. It is also possible to play a brass instrument on the inhale, but the tone will be a bit coarse, and the highest and lowest notes of the range cannot be played thus.

Although brass instruments have broad dynamic ranges, they are most comfortably played *forte* and must be carefully scored when combined with strings or woodwinds. If the absolute maximum loudness is desired, one may instruct the player to direct the sound upward and outward with the instruction "bell in the air" or "campana in aria." At the highest dynamic levels (*ff*, *fff*) a special blaring quality can be obtained from the brass. The instruction for this is the word "brassy" or "cuivré." This technique is discussed in more detail in the section on the horn.

Brass players normally use a vibrato only when playing solo passages of a lyric character. If the presence or absence of vibrato is particularly desired, an indication to that effect should be written into the part. As with woodwinds, the speed and amplitude of the vibrato are variable.

The pitch ranges of brass instruments are not sharply delineated at either end. It is probably not much of an exaggeration to say that on any one of the brass instruments it is *possible* to play any pitch from the highest note of the piccolo trumpet to the lowest note of the contrabass tuba. One does, however, reach a point of diminishing returns: at the high end of an instrument's range, the partials begin to lie so close together that the player cannot be certain of pinpointing the correct one with the lips, and at the other end of the scale the tube exercises so little control over the player's lips that "any note can be played from any fingering," and intonation becomes extremely problematic. Even in the middle of the range the lips exercise tremendous control over the pitch, both through lipping notes up and down (particularly low ones) and through selecting the precise partial to overblow. Because of this, brass players must, like singers, have a good idea of what the note is *before* an attempt is made to play it; and because this is most crucial at the ends of the range, sudden leaps from one extreme to the other are likely to result in cracked or burbled notes. A passage such as:

is impossible to play on any brass instrument.

Because of the great control exerted by the lips over the pitch, a brass instrument can easily produce quarter-tones throughout its range.

A trill executed on a brass instrument is one of the fiercest sounds imaginable. Trills can be produced with the regular valve fingerings, with the special third-valve fingerings mentioned above, or, in a few cases, with the lips. These **lip trills** can only be executed between partials, such as the eighth and ninth, that lie a second apart.

additional notes available on 4-valve instruments

FIGURE 41. *Fingering chart of half-valve octaves,*
calculated for an instrument whose open fundamental is C_0.
A slash through a number indicates that the valve in question is to be half-valved.

SPECIAL EFFECTS

By depressing one or more valves only halfway, a peculiar strangled sound can be produced. This **half-valve technique** is most useful in the production of glissandos and microtones but can of course be used simply as a special timbral effect. Curiously, the greater the amount of valve tubing involved, the more normal the instrument will sound; thus, if the second valve alone is used to create the effect the sound will be extremely weak, thin, and pinched, while if all three valves are used together the tone will be only slightly muffled. Half-valving depresses the maximum dynamic level that can be attained, and in the most extreme case (when only the second valve is half-valved) the player cannot exceed *mezzo-piano*.

Under certain conditions, the depressing of a valve *exactly* halfway will cause the pitch of the instrument to leap exactly an octave. This occurs wherever a note can be produced either with a valve up or (on a neighboring partial) with the same valve down. When the valve is depressed only halfway the higher octave is produced, because the acoustically ambiguous state into which the windway has been thrown suppresses all the odd-numbered partials of the specific pitch being produced; in effect, a second-partial "harmonic" of that pitch is generated. Those who are by now utterly confused may avail themselves of the fingering chart in Figure 41, which is based on a hypothetical instrument whose open fundamental is C_0 but which is of course transposable up and down the scale. Despite their extreme altitude, these half-valve notes can be played on any given instrument with *exactly as much effort* as the normal note an octave lower. In fact, since the removal of the odd partials occurs *after* the tone has been created by the lips, the player may not even be aware that the octave has been leapt. These *half-valve octaves* are tricky to produce on cue and are best avoided altogether on instruments whose open fundamental is higher than C_0. The best way to ensure that the octave will be produced is to start with the lower note, then have the player adjust the valve while playing to bring out the upper octave, thus:

If the player starts with the valve up, half-valving will cause the pitch of the note to drop slightly before leaping the octave. If, however, she or he starts with the valve down and raises it in order to half-valve, the pitch will *rise* slightly before the leap, thus giving the effect of a quick glissando or portamento between the notes.

There is no standard notation yet for half-valve octaves, but the "harmonic" symbol (a small circle over the note) used here seems logical. Because the portion of the instrument between the valve system and the player's lips continues to vibrate at the lower pitch, both notes will be heard (at about equal volume), and the notation

may therefore be preferred. Whatever notation is used must be explained to the player, and it would be wise also to provide fingerings.

Multiphonics can be produced on brass instruments in two ways. One way involves setting the lips exactly halfway between two adjacent partials, both of which will then sound, producing a smooth and mellifluous multiphonic. Unfortunately, this is a very narrow fence to sit on, and such multiphonics are difficult to produce reliably. The player should be given plenty of time to produce the sound, which can best be arrived at by playing one of the two notes and then bringing in the other. These multiphonics are best notated by the two pitches being written together as a chord.

The other type of brass multiphonic, easier to produce but less predictable in effect, involves setting one side of the mouth to produce one note while the other side is set to produce a different one. The result is an aggressive but not particularly harsh growling or whining sound. This type of multiphonic is also best produced by slur from one of the notes it contains; but if the exact sound produced is not critical, a brass player can come up with such a multiphonic on cue without slurring. These multiphonics are probably best notated simply by writing the instruction "multiphonic" and indicating the general pitch-level desired.

Multiphonics of both types can only be produced between the second and eighth partials, except on the horn, where the limits are the third and tenth partials.

As a special effect a brass instrument can be played with a double reed or with a single-reed mouthpiece. The double reed (bassoon reed for trombone, bass trumpet, tuba, and baritone horn; oboe reed for all others) can be inserted into the brass mouthpiece or replace it at the end of the instrument, the former procedure being preferable because the player can store the reed in the cheek until it is needed, then insert it with the tongue in less than a second. When the reed is used, the instrument will sound harsh and nasal and will have the dynamic range of a woodwind. The reed can be used to produce high-pitched squeals at and just above the top of the instrument's normal range, and, lower down, to produce some harsh, woodwind-type multiphonics. The instrument *cannot* be played normally with the reed.

The single-reed mouthpiece is a somewhat different proposition. Here, the brass instrument's mouthpiece must be replaced by a saxophone or clarinet mouthpiece of appropriate dimensions (the saxophone mouthpiece being tonally the more flexible). Two sounds can be produced with such a mouthpiece. One is a low rattle in the instrument's pedal range; the exact pitch produced depends on the mouthpiece, reed, and embouchure, but it can be varied across approximately a tritone by using various valve combinations or slide positions. The other sound is a high-pitched squeal on approximately the pitch the mouthpiece would produce if it were unattached to the instrument. This squeal can be modulated across a number of the instrument's high partials (all sounding out of tune) so that a number of higher pitches can (not very securely) be produced; this must be done with the lips, since the valves have little effect on the sound. The squeal and the rattle can be combined as a multiphonic.

A number of other special effects common to all brass instruments should be mentioned here. **Popping the mouthpiece** involves striking the opening of the mouthpiece with the palm of the hand. The resulting pop has a clearly audible pitch, and when the various valve combinations are fingered the seven pitches of the instrument's fundamental can be produced by this means. This effect can be performed as loudly as *mezzo-piano*. The **valve flutter** is produced by very rapidly and unsystematically alternating the valves while controlling the pitch with the lips. The sound produced is an odd, fluttery burble, only vaguely pitched but quite strong in timbre. **Playing on the mouthpiece alone** produces a thin buzz with only slightly more character than the sound of the lips by themselves. The range of pitches that can be produced is the same as that producible by the lips without the mouthpiece. **Singing into the instrument while playing** is particularly effective on brass instruments, since the sound of the voice coming through the instrument is very similar to that of the instrument itself. Combination tones generated by the conflict of the two vibrating mechanisms may create the illusion that three- or four-part chords are being played. Simultaneous singing and playing is somewhat easier to do on low-pitched instruments, and is easiest to control when the sung and played notes have frequencies in simple harmonic ratio.

THE HORN

THE INSTRUMENT

The horn (now called "French horn" only when some ambiguity might arise from simply calling the instrument "horn") is the most smooth and mellow-sounding of the brasses. Its role has traditionally been to mediate timbrally between the woodwinds and the other brass, and to add unobtrusive body to the sound of the full orchestra. The mellow tone arises from the instrument's very narrow bore and funnel-shaped mouthpiece, and in the normal course of play is enhanced even more by the player's right hand being held in the bell of the instrument, where it muffles and dampens the sound. The position of the bell also assures that the sound is directed backward and to the right, i.e., away from the audience, and this too helps to "gentle" the sound. The instrument is designed to be played with the hand in the bell, and when the hand is removed the sound is not only coarse and trombone-like but very sharp in pitch.

The horn's extremely narrow bore emphasizes the production of very high partials, and the horn is easiest to play and sounds most characteristic in the upper two-thirds of its range. Parts for the instrument are therefore normally written in the treble clef, the bass clef being used only when the instrument dips into the lowest part of its range. Horn players are used to seeing notes as low as c^0 written in the treble clef, but are accustomed to reading in the bass clef up to written c^1 if necessary.

The horn is a transposing instrument, sounding a fifth lower than written in both treble and bass clefs. Prior to the beginning of the twentieth century it was, for no very good reason,

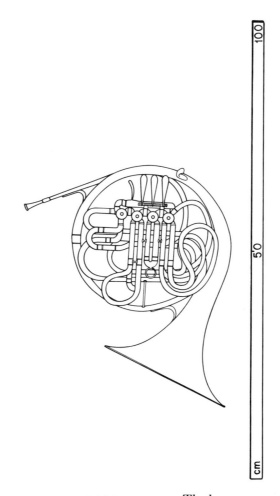

FIGURE 42. *The horn.*

name of instrument	abbreviations	written range	sounds	open fundamental (actual pitch)	availability
horn in f⁰	hrn. hr. hn.	 loudest: *mf* — *f* — *ff* — *fff* — softest: *pp* — *p* —	a perfect 5th lower	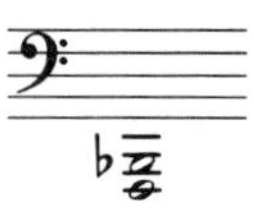	common

FIGURE 43. *The horn—vital statistics.*

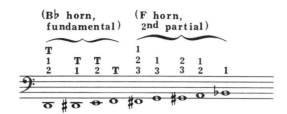

FIGURE 44. *Valve combinations for the lowest notes of the horn.*
T = thumb valve. Pitches are given as notated for the horn.

universal practice when writing for the horn in the bass clef to notate the part an octave too low, i.e., a fourth down rather than a fifth up. Since the more logical modern practice did not become universal until quite recently, many twentieth-century horn parts are notated in the old system, and horn players are occasionally uncertain as to which system is intended even in brand-new works.

Except for some student instruments, all modern horns are **duplex instruments**: two horns, pitched a fourth apart, are placed side by side and share only mouthpiece, bell, and valves—even the valve tubing is duplicated. The switch from one of the two halves of the **double horn** to the other is negotiated by a valve operated by the left thumb: when this valve is depressed the shorter, B♭-horn side of the instrument is engaged and the pitch of the instrument is raised a fourth; when the valve is released the longer, F-horn side of the instrument takes over. It should be understood that parts for the horn are notated in f^0 for both sides of the horn; the additional transposition for B♭ horn is handled by the player.

The double horn was originally invented to help the intonation of certain notes and to make the highest notes more secure. Paradoxically, the addition of the B♭ horn to the simplex instrument in F also extends the effective range downward, since a number of pedal tones (= fundamental pitches) that can only be "faked" on the F horn can be produced clearly on the B♭ horn. The fingerings used for the lowest notes of the double horn are shown in Figure 44. All notes above the written B♭$_0$ can be played on either the F or B♭ side of the instrument. It should be emphasized that the use of the B♭ horn does not extend the range of the instrument upward: the highest notes can be played on both the F and B♭ sides of the horn—they are simply somewhat more secure on the B♭ horn.

PERFORMANCE CHARACTERISTICS

The lowest notes of the horn (up to written B♭$_0$) sound weak and flabby if they are forced, if they are played rapidly, or if they are dropped upon suddenly from above. But if well-prepared and played softly and slowly they can sound peaceful and serene, secure and in tune. Because of the very weak control exerted by the valves in this range, rapid runs or trills sound like so much mud—the player simply executing a valve flutter would achieve the same effect. By the same token, a sharp staccato is impossible in this range.

Between approximately written B_0 and c^1 the player has much more control, although rapid runs and trills still sound rather blurred. The sound of notes in this range is warm and vocal when they are played softly, but when they are played loudly their quality becomes covered, dark, and menacing.

The most characteristic timbre of the horn is that produced in the two octaves between written c^1 and c^3. This is one of the most physically beautiful of all timbres, beloved of many otherwise totally unmusical people, and is the subject of much Romantic hyperbole. Such blatant and easy gorgeousness has lately been out of fashion, and the mid-twentieth-century horn literature is accordingly rather small. One consequence of the horn's smooth, rounded timbre is that rapid legato leaps in either direction tend to sound like portamentos. This can be heard very clearly, for instance, in the "Market-place at Limoges" movement of Ravel's orchestration of *Pictures at an Exhibition*.

When the instrument is played *triple-forte*, the metal of the instrument begins to vibrate in sympathy with the air column and the sound becomes ringing, fierce, and clangorous. This effect, called by the French term **cuivré**, can also be forced by the player at a slightly lower (*ff*) dynamic level. The not infrequent demand for this effect at *all* dynamic levels by various (mostly French) composers does not reflect acoustic reality.

The notes above written c^3 (which not all players can produce) sound forced, strained, and thin at any dynamic level. The British firm of Paxman offers horns in F/high F and even a **triple horn** in F/B♭/high F to make these notes more accessible.

A special timbre, available only on the horn,* is that of **stopped** notes. By placing the right hand so that it almost completely blocks the windway, the acoustic characteristics of the instrument are altered so that (1) the pitches of all notes on the F horn are raised one half-step; and (2) the timbre becomes thin, buzzy, nasal, stuffy, and distant—in short, totally un-hornlike. This effect sounds most distinctive when played *cuivré*. Stopping is notated with a plus-sign above each note affected, or by the word "stopped" (or its Italian equivalent, "chiuso") at the beginning of a stopped passage. It is canceled by a large "O" above the note (not the small "o" used to indicate harmonics) or by the word "open" or "aperto." Stopped tones should be written in f^0, like ordinary notes; the extra half-step transposition will be made automatically by the player. On the B♭ horn, stopped notes are raised by three-quarters of a step rather than a half-step, so quarter-tone stopped notes are easily produced. The pedal tones of the B♭ horn (which are not duplicated on the F horn) can be lipped the quarter-step into tune. Stopping lowers the maximum loudness of the horn by one dynamic level throughout its range; the minimum loudness also drops one dynamic level. Below about written $b♭^0$, stopped tones become increasingly uncertain in speech and intonation, particularly at the highest and lowest dynamic levels, and the stopped pedal tones are only barely negotiable. Low stopped notes can be produced more securely when a **stopping mute** is used instead of the hand. This mute seals off the windway and raises the pitch just as hand-stopping does, but has the disadvantage of requiring at least half a second of rest for its insertion or removal.

The ordinary horn mute (equivalent to the **straight mute** of trumpets and trombones) does not entirely block the windway. It is held in place by cork wedges on its sides, allowing the passage of some air between the sides of the bell and the sides of the mute. This mute changes the timbre of the instrument but has no effect on the pitch or dynamic range. The

* But see the discussion of Renaissance mutes in Part Two, and that of the plunger mute in the section on the trumpet.

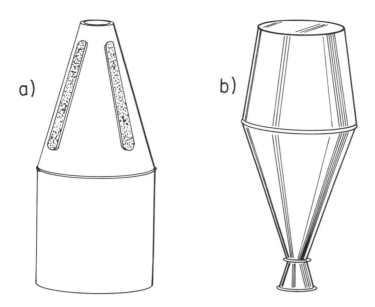

FIGURE 45. *Horn mutes: (a) regular mute; (b) stopping mute.*

sound of the muted horn is nasal and distant, without the thin stuffiness of the stopped horn sound (the right hand is of course not held in the bell while the mute is in place). Normally a couple of seconds of rest must be allowed to give the player time to pick up the mute with the right hand and insert it, and another couple of seconds, later, to remove it and put it down. If necessary, the mute can be held on a strap around the wrist, in which case it can be inserted or removed in as little as half a second. The instruction for muting is the indication "with mute" or the Italian abbreviation "con sord."; removal of the mute may be indicated by the instruction "via sord." at the spot where this occurs, but the indication "senza sord." immediately before the first unmuted note is more usual.

Subtle inflections of pitch can be performed on the horn not only with the lips but with the right hand as well. By the technique of **half-stopping**, in which the windway is closed off more than usual, but not completely as in full stopping, the pitch can be dropped any amount up to a half-step without affecting the timbre. This technique can be used to produce quarter-tones and half-step glissandos. Note that half-stopping *lowers* the pitch, while full stopping raises it. If the right hand is moved so as to gradually block the windway while a note is held, the pitch will slowly drop a half-step, then suddenly leap up a whole step, simultaneously acquiring the "stopped" timbre. True glissandos larger than a half-step can only be negotiated by the use of half-valve technique (the **valve smear**), in which one or more valves are partially depressed: the glissando is executed while the instrument is in this acoustically ambiguous condition. The resultant glissando will sound somewhat weaker in both volume and timbre than the notes that begin and end it.

For large upward glissandos, at least, a much more satisfactory sound can be obtained by means of the **lip gliss**, or **rip**. This is an upward slur across a number of partials, executed by the lips with or without any shift of valve configuration. It should be notated as a slurred group of notes, optionally with the added indication "gliss." to tell the player that the passage is meant to sound like a glissando. There are many such lip glisses notated very clearly in Stravinsky's *Sacre du printemps*. The lip gliss, valve smear, and half-stop may be combined.

HORN:
Mahler, Symphony No. 4
Stravinsky, *Le Sacre du printemps*
Hindemith, Sonata for 4 horns
Varèse, *Octandre*
Nono, *Polifonica-Monodia-Ritmica*
Xenakis, *Anaktoria*

TRUMPETS

THE INSTRUMENTS

The trumpet family is not the tidy affair that Figure 47 would make it seem. Rather than five discrete sizes of trumpet, it would perhaps be more accurate to speak of an uninterrupted continuum of trumpets, built in a wide variety of pitches, ranging between the extremes represented by the piccolo trumpet and the bass trumpet. For any given trumpet part, the player may use an instrument in c^2, bb^1, g^1, f^1, eb^1, d^1, c^1, bb^0, f^0, eb^0, d^0, c^0, or Bb_0, and his or her choice will be governed not so much by the composer's wishes in the matter as by how high or low the part lies, what instruments happen to be available, and any prejudices the player may have against one or another of them. This state of affairs is due to the indecision, confusion, and apathy of composers, the opportunism of instrument manufacturers, and, above all, to the fact that transposition on brass instruments is so easy that a part written for an instrument in, say, F can be played with little difficulty on an instrument in, say, Eb, if that's what happens to be available. The following discussion attempts to untangle this mess in terms of the existing reality, the choices realistically available to composers, and a hypothetical ideal.

Let us start with the ideal, for it is the easiest to describe. The main point of having a family of like instruments in different sizes is to extend to its limits the range of pitches in which the basic timbre of the instrument will be available; this condition can be satisfied by the piccolo and bass trumpets alone, for between the two of them the entire range of the trumpet family is covered without a gap. There is, however, another reason for instruments to be built in families. Instruments of sufficiently different size will have significantly different timbres even if they are constructed identically, and each of these timbres is valuable in its own right. For there to be such a consistently perceptible difference in their timbre, two like instruments must be pitched a fourth or more apart. Thus, it makes no sense to write, as many composers do, for trumpets in c^1 and d^1 in the same piece, for the sounds of these two instruments can only be distinguished by trumpet players. Two trumpets in bb^0 and d^1 *can* be told apart, barely, but if the higher instrument is pitched in eb^1 instead of d^1, the difference between it and the bb^0 instrument will be clearly and consistently audible.

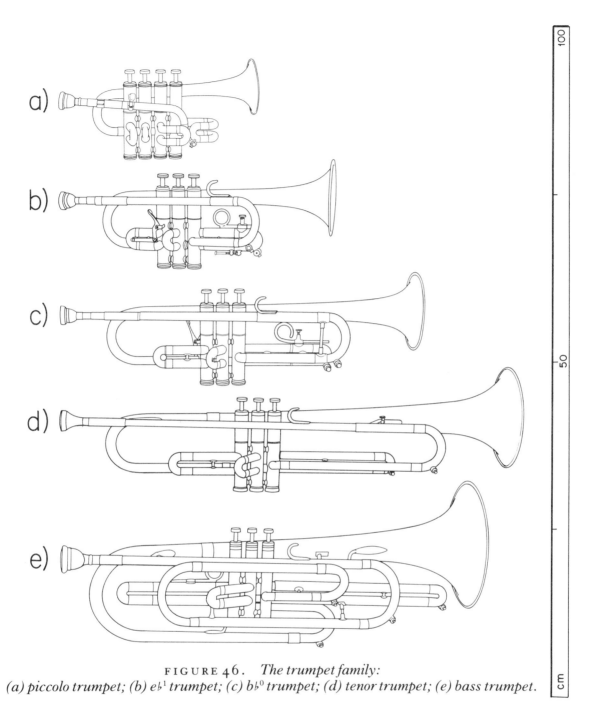

FIGURE 46. *The trumpet family:*
(a) piccolo trumpet; (b) $e\flat^1$ trumpet; (c) $b\flat^0$ trumpet; (d) tenor trumpet; (e) bass trumpet.

If, then, we were to choose from among the existing trumpets an ideal family of trumpets with the maximum pitch range and the maximum number of clearly distinguishable timbres, we would come up with something like the following:

> piccolo trumpet in $b\flat^1$ or c^2
> "soprano" trumpet in $e\flat^1$ or f^1
> "alto" trumpet in $b\flat^0$ or c^1
> tenor trumpet in $e\flat^0$ or f^0
> bass trumpet in $B\flat_0$ or c^0.

name of instrument	abbreviations	written range	sounds	open fundamental (actual pitch)	availability
piccolo trumpet in b♭¹	picc. tr. / picc. trp. / picc. trpt.	 loudest: mp — ff — fff softest: pp — p	a minor 7th higher		rare
trumpet in e♭¹, d¹, e♭¹/d¹	E♭ tr. (trp., trpt.) / D tr. (trp., trpt.)	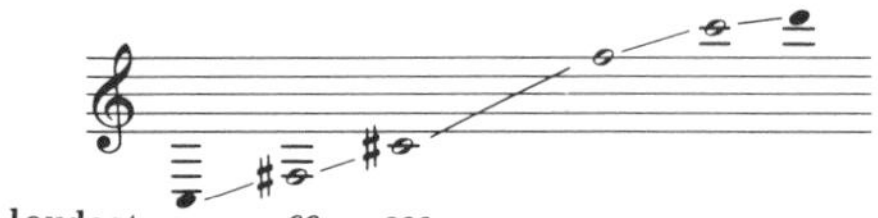 loudest: mp — ff — fff softest: pp — p	a minor 3rd higher, or / a major 2nd higher, or / either one	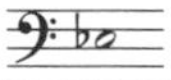  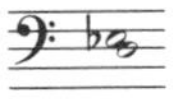	usually available / common / usually available
trumpet in c¹, b♭⁰	(B♭) tr. / (B♭) trp. / (B♭) trpt.	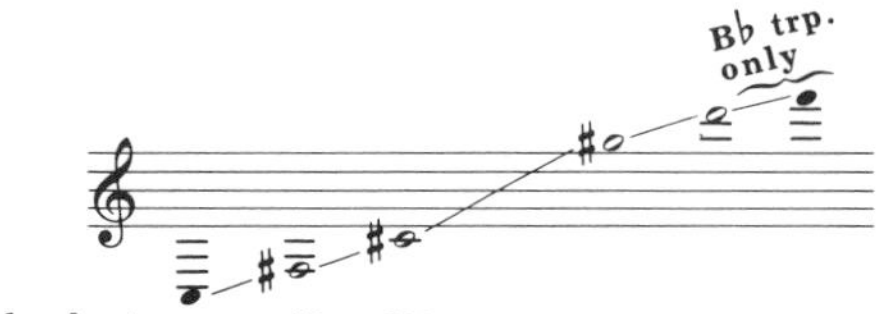 B♭ trp. only loudest: mp — ff — fff softest: pp — p	as written, or / a major 2nd lower	 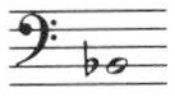	common / ubiquitous
tenor trumpet in e♭⁰	ttr. / ttrp. / ten. trp. / ten. trpt.	 loudest: mp — ff — fff softest: pp — p	a major 6th lower	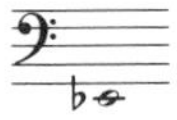	very rare
bass trumpet in B♭₀	btr. / bs. trp. / bs. trpt.	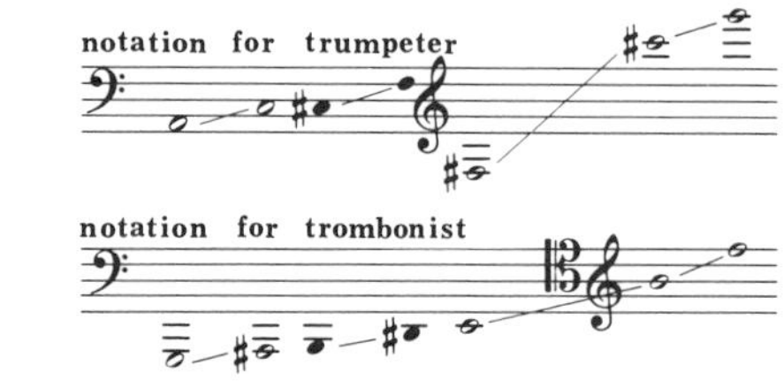 notation for trumpeter / notation for trombonist / loudest: fff — mf — fff softest: p — pp — p	a major 9th lower / as written	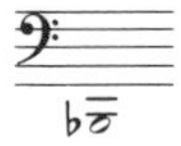	rare

FIGURE 47. *The trumpet family—vital statistics.*

In this family we have a piccolo trumpet which sounds thin and piercing, a brilliant and piercing "soprano," an "alto," also brilliant but somewhat more mellow, a tenor that is somber and somewhat dark, and a rich and powerful bass. If one is interested in the differentiation of a variety of trumpet timbres, one should write for these five alone and ignore the others. Even accepting this restriction, however, we still have ten trumpets to choose from where only five are needed. In this regard it should be pointed out that the various F and C trumpets are all less readily available than the equivalent B♭ and E♭ instruments, as Figure 48 shows, so the best bet would be to write only for the B♭/E♭ series.

	In F or C	In B♭ or E♭
Piccolo	very rare	rare
"Soprano"	very rare	usually available
"Alto"	common	ubiquitous
Tenor	very rare	very rare
Bass	very rare	rare

FIGURE 48. *Relative availability of trumpet in C, B♭, F, and E♭.*

In the real world, as we have seen, thirteen or more sizes of trumpet are jostling for attention by composers. Let us start at the top and work our way down through the heap. The **piccolo trumpet in b♭^{1}** was invented to play the trumpet part in Bach's second Brandenburg Concerto—which was originally conceived for a narrow-bore, valveless instrument three times as long as this trumpet—and it is to this piece and a handful of other extremely high Baroque trumpet parts that the instrument owes its continued existence. Since 1960 composers have written a number of important parts for the piccolo trumpet. Recently, increasing numbers of piccolo trumpets have been built with a fourth valve (to extend the range downward, thus making the instrument more generally useful). This fourth valve lowers the pitch of the instrument a perfect fourth, and is combined with the other three valves just as the fourth valve of the tuba is. The severe pitch discrepancies arising from the use of the fourth valve in combination are corrected with the third-valve slide. Other trumpets invented to play the second Brandenburg are the **piccolo trumpets in c^2, f^1 and g^1**. The f^1 instrument is extremely rare, as is the one in c^2; the g^1 trumpet is slightly more common, but nowhere near as frequently available as the b♭^{1} trumpet—which is also a more useful instrument. For all four instruments g^3 (actual pitch) is the highest reliably obtainable note.

The **trumpets in e♭^{1} and d^1** were invented for the performance of Baroque and early Classical trumpet parts written for valveless instruments twice their length, but the d^1 trumpet has since acquired a secure place in the modern repertoire. The best instruments of this type can be switched between e♭^{1} and d^1 by means of a special lever or by adjusting the tuning slides. The trumpet in d^1 has been much more frequently called for by modern composers than the one in e♭^{1}, but the higher instrument is much commoner than one would suspect from this fact. As mentioned above, if an instrument genuinely different in sound from the standard trumpet in c^1 or b♭^{0} is desired, the e♭^{1} trumpet is superior to the one in d^1.

The term "trumpet," unmodified, refers to the instrument in c^1 or b♭^{0}. Of these, the **b♭^{0} trumpet** is both more common and more useful, since it is timbrally more flexible and has a potentially greater range. Nonetheless, composers have increasingly preferred the **trumpet in c^1**—probably because it doesn't transpose—and this instrument is gaining in popularity. Most players own both.

The **tenor trumpet in e♭^{0}** is one of the most underexploited of all instruments. It has a huge range and a unique and beautiful timbre, but has seldom been written for, and is unfortunately quite rare. Rarer still is the virtually identical **tenor trumpet in f^0**. A very few e♭^{0} tenor trumpets have a special valve that drops the pitch of the instrument to d^0. Tenor trumpets are often erroneously called bass trumpets, and the two are frequently confused.

The **bass trumpet in B♭$_0$** is identical to the trombone in every respect save that it has valves instead of a slide. Since it is a much rarer instrument than the trombone, one should write for it only when its unique capabilities—trills and rapid legato runs not possible on the trombone—are needed. There is also a much rarer **bass trumpet in c⁰**. B♭₀ bass trumpets shaped like a trombone are called **valve trombones**; those shaped like tubas are called **tromboniums**. Since the bass trumpet is usually played by a trombonist rather than a trumpet player, it may be notated as written rather than as a transposing instrument a ninth higher.

PERFORMANCE CHARACTERISTICS

The characteristic brilliant, blaring sound of the trumpet is that of the notes from about written c♯¹ upward. The notes between written f♯⁰ and c¹ are weaker and sound somewhat flabby and growling except in the bass trumpet, which retains full power in this range. The extension tones below f♯⁰ are the so-called pedal tones—extremely weak, flabby, covered-sounding notes which many trumpet players do not bother to master and which are seldom called for by composers. These notes are uniformly slow of speech and uncertain of intonation, and if written they must be well prepared, moving slowly if at all.

The reader may have noticed that only notes from written c⁰ down are "true" pedal tones using the instrument's first partial; the production of the notes between c♯⁰ and f⁰ appears to be an acoustic impossibility. That these notes *are* producible is due to a phenomenon not previously discussed in this book, that of **privileged frequencies**. On a wind instrument such as the trumpet (or any other brass instrument) where the column of air is dominated by the massiveness of the vibrating mechanism (the lips), the air column can be forced to vibrate not only at whole-number multiples of its fundamental frequency (the various partials), but also at such fractional multiples as 4/3, 3/2, or 5/3, and thus notes between the first partial (1/1) and the second partial (2/1) can be produced, with difficulty. These fractional "partials" are, together with the true partials, called "privileged frequencies."* The intonation of all trumpet "pedal tones" of whatever provenance is so highly influenced by the lips that the valve combination used makes little difference in the production of the note. The "true" pedal tones of the bass trumpet are much more secure than those of other trumpets, with the same powerful, blatty sound as the equivalent notes of the trombone. The notes between written c♯⁰ and f⁰ are just as weak and insecure as they are on the smaller trumpets.

If desired, the note f⁰ written can be obtained in the second partial of any size trumpet by putting the instrument into **German cavalry fingering**. This alternative (and generally inferior) system of valve tuning involves pulling out the third valve slide far enough to lower the pitch an additional semitone. The fingerings shown in Figure 49 are then used. Note that the starred fingerings will be out of tune and must be lipped to pitch. On most trumpets the third-valve slide is (by means of an attached ring) directly under the control of a finger of the left hand, and such instruments can be put into German cavalry fingering in a fraction of a second. Where this is not the case, at least five seconds must be allowed for the operation. If an f⁰ is written with no further explanation of the composer's intent, the player will almost certainly use German cavalry fingering rather than attempt the clumsy and uncertain pedal-

* The situation is actually even more complicated. The construction of brass instruments is such that the fundamental is displaced acoustically to a much lower pitch than the one it should theoretically hold. The "fundamental" actually used by brasses is in fact one of these fractional privileged frequencies, itself displaced to lie where the real fundamental belongs.

FIGURE 49. *German cavalry fingering. The intonation of the valve combinations marked by asterisks must be corrected with the lips.*

tone. Those piccolo trumpets with four valves can play in the second partial down to written c♯⁰, and the notes thus obtained can be played as loudly (*ff*) and clearly as the "ordinary" second-partial notes.

By means of a rather awkward contortion of the left hand, half-stopping similar to that of the horn can be managed on the trumpet, lowering the pitch any amount up to a half-step. This technique (which must be explained to the player, since it is by no means traditional) is most useful in the production of microtones and slow glissandos of a half-step or less. Larger glissandos can be produced by means of valve smears (half-valving) and lip glisses, subject to the same limitations as on the horn. Of these two techniques, the valve smear is somewhat more effective on the trumpet than the horn, the lip gliss somewhat less so.

MUTES

A wide variety of mutes are available for the trumpet. Longitudinal sections of the most common types are shown in Figure 50; mutes other than these are rare or very rare and are either synonyms or minor variants of these eight basic types. The standard trumpet mute is the **straight mute**. If the general instruction "with mute" or "con sord." is used without any further specification, the straight mute will be used. This is the oldest of the modern trumpet mutes and is entirely analogous to the mutes of the horn and tuba and to the straight mute of the trombone. It is a hollow cone, made of metal, plastic, or pasteboard, with an opening at the top. On the outside near the top of the cone are three or four longitudinal strips or wedges of cork that enable the mute to be wedged into the bell without blocking it off entirely. The sound of the instrument resonates inside the cone but must exit via the narrow channel between the mute and the bell of the instrument. The resulting sound is thin, nasal, and somewhat distant. The material of which a straight mute is made has a slight effect on its sound, metal mutes being generally somewhat harsher and more cutting in timbre than cardboard ones; plastic mutes fall somewhere between these. Some composers specify the exact type of straight mute they desire, but the differences in effect are actually quite small and may safely be ignored. Straight mutes of whatever type have no effect upon the dynamic range or response of the trumpet, but except for the very best they do affect the intonation slightly, requiring correction of some notes by the lips and/or third-valve slide, or an adjustment of the main tuning slide.

The other mutes fall into two general categories: mutes that make the tone harsh and thin and those that make it muffled and sweet. In the first category are the harmon, solotone, and practice mutes. All these mutes differ from the straight mute in having a complete ring of cork around the top of the mute, which prevents any air from escaping past the sides of the mute and forces all the sound to travel into the mute itself, escaping finally by some sort of

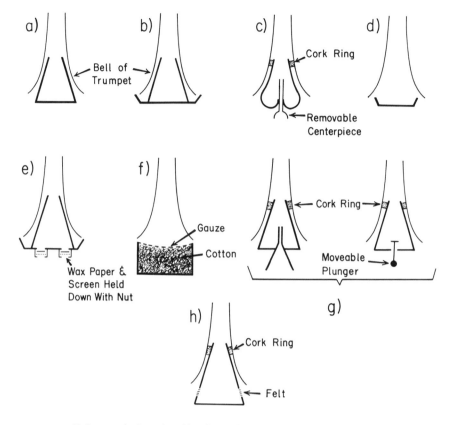

FIGURE 50. *Schematic longitudinal sections of various trumpet mutes in place:*
(a) straight mute (ubiquitous); (b) cup mute (common); (c) harmon mute (common);
(d) plunger mute (usually available); (e) buzz mute (rare); (f) bucket mute (rare);
(g) two types of solotone mute (rare); (h) practice mute (usually available).

restricted opening in the base of the mute. With all these mutes the second-partial notes are weak and uncertain, and pedal tones are impossible.

In the **harmon mute** the opening at the end takes the form of a single hole about a centimeter in diameter, into which is normally inserted a snugly fitting but movable tube only a bit shorter than the mute itself. Thus, although the body of the mute acts as a resonating chamber, the sound must exit through the long, narrow tube. The tube (called the **stem**) ends in a tiny "bell" that helps to project the severely pinched sound once it has left the mute. The stem, as has already been mentioned, is movable, and variations of the basic harmon timbre can be obtained by either pulling out the stem to a greater or lesser extent without actually removing it or by removing it altogether. The normal sound of the harmon mute (with the stem inserted all the way up to its bell) is very thin, pinched, and distant. When played loudly a *cuivré* effect begins and the tone becomes extremely harsh and cutting. As the stem is extended the tone becomes increasingly more distant and pinched but somewhat less thin and nasal, the *cuivré* effect becoming less unpleasant. With the stem removed, the sound becomes gentler, covered and even cavernous, and the *cuivré* effect disappears. All three of these timbres can be varied by loosely covering the bell of the stem (or the hole into which it inserts, if it has been removed) with the palm of the left hand; this gives the tone a covered quality and makes it less metallic. Though one might guess otherwise, the vowel sounds obtainable with the plunger mute (see below) cannot be duplicated with the harmon—only the sounds [wɑ] and [ɑu] will have any vocal quality. This effect has led to the harmon sometimes being called the *wawa mute*, a familiar term unfortunately also used for

the plunger mute. Muffling with the hand is indicated by ♩⁺ and canceled by ♩⁰ or the word "aperto" or "open."

The **solotone mute** is a modification of the harmon mute designed to project the tone forward while retaining the basic harmon timbre. The sound produced is somehow unsettling—one would almost say "distressing" or "irritating"—and can quickly get on one's nerves. This mute exists in two rather different forms (Fig. 50g). In one the sound, after emerging from a small hole at the end of an immovable tube within the mute, is projected forward with a megaphone-like extension of the mute. In the other, the sound emerges from an extremely tiny hole in the bottom of the mute, and there is no internal tube; because of this, the thin bottom wall of the mute acts as a diaphragm and vibrates sympathetically with the air column, producing a sort of "cardboard *cuivré*" very similar in sound to the megaphone-type mute. This second type of solotone mute has a further refinement in the form of a movable metal rod with a brass disk at one end and a knob at the other that fits loosely through the hole from which the sound emerges. By pulling the rod (called the *plunger*) out so that the brass disk inside the mute covers the hole, a sound is produced analogous to that made by muffling the harmon mute with the hand; pushing the rod in restores the normal sound. On the megaphone type of solotone mute, harmon-like "wawa" effects can be produced more naturally by covering the end of the megaphone with the left hand. The notation for this effect on either type of mute is the same as for the harmon mute.

The **practice mute**, as its name implies, was devised to enable players to practice without disturbing the neighbors. Here the sound is forced into the mute, from which it must exit via a number of small "windows" in the outer rim of the mute, each of which is stuffed with felt. The sound of this mute is very similar to that of the straight mute, but very tiny and distant, and it reduces the instrument's dynamic level to the range between *ppp* and *p*. This mute, sometimes referred to by the brand name "**Whispa mute**," must be used if a true *ppp* is desired from the trumpet.

The remaining varieties of trumpet mute are designed to make the tone sweet and gentle. All have in common a dish- or bowl-shaped component that lies flat across the very end of the bell of the trumpet, forcing the air (and the sound) to exit around the rim of the bell.

The simplest and most versatile of these mutes is the **plunger mute**, so called because in its oldest form it consists of nothing more than the business end of a plumber's helper—nowadays a pie-plate-like affair with a strap on the back for the player's hand is more common. This mute is also called "wawa mute" because of the vocal effects of which it is capable (unfortunately this name is also used for the harmon mute). The beauty of the plunger mute is that it remains in the player's left hand at all times and can be quickly and easily manipulated so as to mute the instrument to a greater or lesser extent. By this manipulation the sounds of the vowels [ɑ], [ɔ], [o], and [u] can be very closely approximated (for the meaning of these phonetic symbols see Chapter IV). The consonants [m], [w], and [β] can also be produced, and such word-like combinations as [βɑ͡umɔwo] can easily be done. Remember in this regard that the additional consonants [t], [p], [k], and [ʔ] can be made by the player with the mouth

while playing. Traditionally, the notation for plunger mute has been ♩⁺ = bell closed by mute, and $\overset{0}{\vphantom{|}\raisebox{0pt}{$\mathord{|}$}}$ = bell open (by analogy with the notation for stopped notes on the horn); but composers are now beginning to use the phonetic symbols instead, since these indicate more precisely than the older notation the exact degree to which the bell is to be blocked. If the phonetic symbols are used, they should be bracketed, as here. [ɑ] represents the open position, [u] the usual closed position, and [m̩] the most closed normal position. Note that before either form of notation is used, the player must be instructed that the mute is going to be needed. By using the mute to block the bell altogether, a stopped sound like that of the horn can be obtained. The pitch of open notes so produced is raised a half-step, while notes requiring all three valves will be raised only a quarter-step, the other valve combinations showing intermediate raising. If phonetic symbols are used to represent the usual plunger-mute sounds, a + over the note can be used to indicate stopping.

A variant of the plunger mute, called simply "the hat" (because early jazz players used their hats for this purpose), differs from the plunger in that the bell of the instrument fits into the rim of the mute rather than vice versa. It sounds exactly like the plunger but cannot make as many different sounds. It should be mentioned at this point that the hand can be used without a mute to muffle the sound of the instrument. The effect, though quite clear, is much less strong than it is when one of the "wawa" mutes is used. The notation for this effect is the usual $\overset{+}{\vphantom{|}\raisebox{0pt}{$\mathord{|}$}}$ and $\overset{0}{\vphantom{|}\raisebox{0pt}{$\mathord{|}$}}$, together with the indication "muffle with hand."

Closely related to the plunger mute is the **cup mute**. This resembles a pie plate with a straight mute welded to its center, and sounds almost exactly the same as a plunger mute in closed ([u]) position. Some players prefer an [m̩] sound from the cup mute; they file down the cork wedges to make the mute fit more tightly. Some mutes are adjustable with a set screw, but the adjustment is time-consuming and requires removal of the mute. The advantage of the cup mute is that when this typical timbre is desired for an extended period of time, without any fancy vocalisms or rapid alternation between closed and open sounds, the mute will stay in place, freeing the player's left hand for supporting the instrument and turning pages. The sound of the cup mute is very gentle and sweet—almost woodwind-like—and does not become less so when the instrument is played loudly. With the cup mute in place the trumpet can be played no louder than *fortissimo*.

The **buzz mute** is a specialized variant of the cup mute: the bottom of the mute is pierced by three small, round "windows," each of which is covered by wax paper and a piece of brass screening. The wax paper and screen are held loosely in place by an adjustable hex-nut; whenever the instrument is played the paper vibrates sympathetically against the screen, producing a rattling buzz that sounds exactly as if the instrument were being played into a kazoo—which in fact it is. By obscuring the "windows" with the left hand, simple "wawa" effects can be produced like those of the harmon mute.

Finally, there is the **bucket mute**, a cylindrical metal pail filled almost to the brim with cotton and covered with gauze. This is attached to the trumpet with three prongs that grab the outer rim of the bell—in place, the mute bears an unfortunate resemblance to a horse's feedbag. In sound this mute corresponds almost exactly to the lay conception of what a mute does: the sound is muffled and deadened without its fundamental character being significantly altered.

As mentioned above, the basic instruction "with mute," "mute," or "con sord." is understood to call specifically for the straight mute. The best way to ask for some other mute is simply to put the name of the mute immediately before the passage to be muted. For the removal of any mute the instruction "mute off" or "senza sord." is sufficient. To change from one mute to another without any intervening unmuted passage, the instruction "change to x mute" or "muta in x mute" should be used. Any mute can be inserted in a fraction of a second, but two or more seconds must be allotted somewhere for the player to *pick up* the mute. If the place in the music at which the mute is to be picked up is not immediately before the muted passage, the instruction "pick up x mute" should be written at the appropriate spot, followed by "mettere sord." or "mute on" when the mute is to be inserted.

Except for the straight mute, which is available for all sizes of trumpet, all these mutes are manufactured only for the ordinary trumpet in $b\flat^0$ or c^1. All the mutes can be used, albeit rather clumsily and imperfectly, on the d^1 and $e\flat^1$ trumpets, but the piccolo trumpet is restricted to the straight mute.* An identical series of mutes is available for the trombone, and the bass trumpet makes use of these; the tenor trumpet, by using some $b\flat^1$ trumpet mutes and some trombone mutes, can also employ the whole series.

MUSICAL EXAMPLES

PICCOLO TRUMPET:
> Xenakis, *Oresteia Suite*
> Berio, *Allelujah II*

TRUMPET IN D/E♭:
> Stravinsky, *Le Sacre du printemps*
> Messiaen, *Et exspecto resurrectionem mortuorum*

TRUMPETS IN B♭, C:
> Stravinsky, *Ebony Concerto*
>   *Agon*
> Chavez, *Sinfonia de Antigona*
> Varèse, *Octandre*
> Xenakis, *Eonta*

TENOR TRUMPET:
> Stravinsky, *Le Sacre du printemps* ("Action rituelle des ancêtres")
> Schoenberg, *Gurrelieder*
> Feldman, *Eleven Instruments*

BASS TRUMPET:
> Janáček, *Sinfonietta* (1st mvt.)
> Ruggles, *Men and Angels* (1922)

TROMBONES

THE INSTRUMENTS

As mentioned above, the trombone and trumpet families are virtually identical acoustically, differing only in that trombones have a slide mechanism rather than valves. The usual

---

* It should be fairly simple to jury-rig a plunger mute for this instrument.

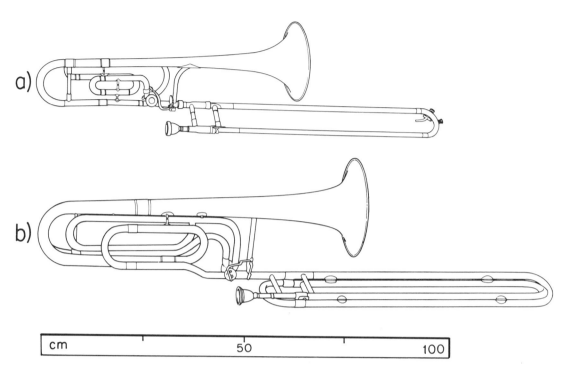

FIGURE 51. *The trombone family: (a) trombone; (b) contrabass trombone.*

name of instrument	abbreviations	written range	sounds	open fundamental (actual pitch)	availability
trombone	trb. trbn.	 loudest: *f—ff—fff* softest: *pp* ————— *p*	as written	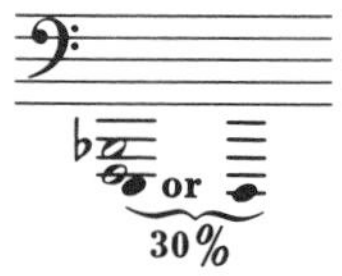	common
contrabass trombone	cb. trb. cbs. trbn.	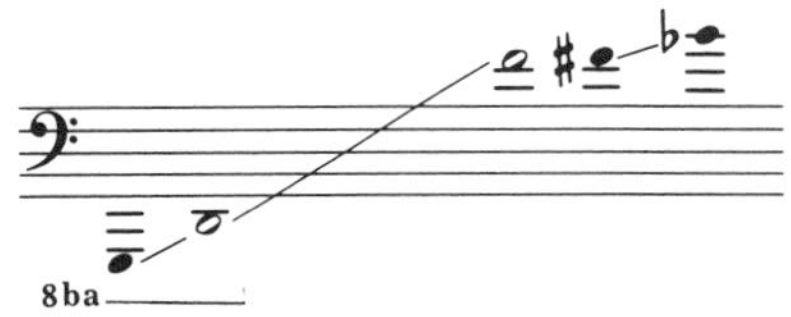 loudest: *ff—fff* softest: *pp* ————— *p*	as written		very rare

FIGURE 52. *The trombone family—vital statistics.*

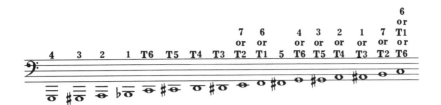

FIGURE 53. *Slide positions for the low register of the trombone (T = trigger depressed).*

modern trombone, however, is a duplex instrument like the horn, and thus possesses, in addition to the slide, a single valve designed to lower the pitch of the instrument a perfect fourth. This valve, called the "trigger" or "rotor," is operated by the left thumb; when depressed, it lowers the open fundamental from Bb to F_1. The trombone is thus said to be "in Bb/F" even though it is not a transposing instrument. The original simplex intrument was in Bb, and the trombone is designed and played as a Bb instrument with an F-attachment—the trigger is used only where necessary or particularly convenient.

Trombonists speak of seven numbered "positions" of the slide, corresponding to the seven equal-tempered semitones on each partial. When drawn all the way in, the slide is in first position; when completely extended it is in seventh. When the trigger is depressed the instrument becomes longer, and the slide must be moved slightly further to achieve each semitone gradation in pitch. In this case there are only six slide positions, and the sixth position requires a greater extension of the slide than seventh position does on the unaltered instrument. The F-attachment is most often used in the lower register, where it fills a gap between the first and second partials and simplifies passages such as ♩ that would be uncomfortably athletic to perform without it. Figure 53 should make this clear. Note that the pitch $B\natural_1$ is not usually available on the trombone; it can be faked by lipping down the C above it or with a privileged frequency, but it will be weak, flabby, and uncertain of speech and intonation.* Note also that passages such as ♩ that require rapid and extreme changes of slide position are impossible to play. Even ♩ would be extremely difficult. Such awkward shifts of the slide are never required above G_0.

The usual sort of trombone, which we have been discussing so far, is more specifically called the **tenor-bass trombone**. Instruments of slightly different design are used by players for parts that lie unusually high or low. The old, simplex **tenor trombone** is used for the performance of music that lies consistently high in the range, such as nineteenth-century alto trombone parts. These instruments not only lack an F-attachment but generally have narrower bores, smaller bells, and shallower mouthpieces than tenor-bass trombones. No player is likely to use such an instrument for any part that descends below E_0; on the other hand,

---

* The tuning slide for the F-valve is marked so that it can be quickly and accurately lowered to E, thus making the low B_1 possible, but this is an emergency measure, requiring at least five seconds for the player to adjust the instrument both before and after the note is played.

attempts may be made to use a tenor trombone for a high-lying part that really demands the flexibility provided by an F-attachment, and in such cases composers should provide a cautionary instruction.*

Parts that mostly exploit the lower end of the trombone's range are often played on the **bass trombone**. Bass trombones have broad bores, large bells, and wide, deep mouthpieces, and usually have two triggers for the left thumb. The second trigger depressed simultaneously with the first lowers the instrument an additional half-step to E or minor third to D, enabling the player to produce a secure $B\natural_1$. The D trigger is superior to the E trigger in that it gives this low B in fourth position rather than sixth, making passages such as

much easier to play.† Because of this advantage, the D trigger is now commoner on new instruments and seems likely to oust the E trigger entirely. In the meantime, some bass trombones have F, E, *and* D triggers. At any rate, all parts requiring frequent use of B_1 or $B\flat_1$ should be specifically labeled "bass trombone" rather than simply "trombone." Because bass trombones are designed to play low notes more easily than high ones, it is probably unwise to write for them above c^2.

While the tenor, bass, and tenor-bass trombones are only slightly different varieties of what is essentially the same instrument, the **contrabass trombone** is distinctive in tone, range, and appearance. Its distinguishing characteristic is its double-barreled slide, two equal and parallel U-shaped tubes that are attached to each other and move in and out together. Because of this doubling the slide has the same seven positions as that of the tenor-bass trombone. The instrument is usually built in B♭, an octave below the tenor-bass trombone, and most have an F-attachment as well, sounding an additional fourth down. With the trigger depressed the slide has six positions, again as for the tenor-bass trombone. Because a great deal can be done with the lips at such low pitches, the notes B_2–$E\flat_1$ can be produced even on a simplex instrument but, needless to say, they are (except for the B_2 itself) much more secure and better in tune when there is an F-attachment. Some contrabass trombones are provided with valves rather than a slide—presumably to enable a tuba player to double on the contra trombone. While this may be fine for Wagner's *Ring* operas, more recent parts not infrequently call for glissandos impossible to play adequately on these "contrabass trumpets." Unfortunately, the contra trombone in any form is so rare that one is unlikely to have any choice in the matter. Valved contras have four rotary valves, the fourth replacing the F-attachment. Strangely enough, no octave transposition is used in notating for contrabass trombone.

PERFORMANCE CHARACTERISTICS

Both trombone and contrabass trombone normally read in the bass clef. Traditionally the tenor clef has been used for high notes, but the treble clef has gradually been replacing it.

* In early-twentieth-century scores the term "tenor trombone" refers indifferently to both the tenor-bass and true tenor trombones.

† There is also the quarter-tone $B\downarrow_1$, which must be lipped from $B\natural_1$ on an instrument with an E trigger but is easily played in 4½ position with a D trigger.

Trombonists are used to reading in the bass clef up to about bb^1, in the tenor clef from about Bb_0 to d^2, in the alto clef (for old alto trombone parts) from c^0 to f^2, and in the treble clef from e^1 up.

The tone of the trombone is powerful, resonant, and somewhat vocal, blaring at high dynamic levels, rich and velvety at low ones. Notes below E_0 tend to sound somewhat blatty, even flatulent, especially when played loudly. The extension pitches at the bottom of the range sound increasingly weak, flabby, and uncertain. The bass trombone has a somewhat smoother, fuller tone in the low register than does the tenor-bass instrument. The timbre of the contrabass trombone is considerably darker, fuller, and less blaring than that of the ordinary trombone; it is intermediate in quality between that instrument and the tuba.

Mutes are available for the trombone in all the types described above for the trumpet. These mutes are identical to the equivalent trumpet mutes in design, timbre, technique, and availability. With the plunger mute the trombone can imitate human speech to an uncanny degree: its timbre is more voice-like than that of the trumpet, and it can reproduce with its slide the variable, fluctuating pitches of actual speech. Only a straight mute is available for the contrabass trombone; however, the instrument can use the baritone-horn bucket mute, and a plunger mute can be jury-rigged.

Normally, legato passages are executed on the trombone by performing the smoothest possible tenuto and moving the slide during the almost imperceptible break in the tone. In many cases the legato so produced rivals that of other brasses. Even fairly large shifts of the slide can be covered in this way, provided they are accompanied (as they usually are) by a shift of partial. Only the following slurs may be called impossible, and even they can be faked:

FIGURE 54. *Awkward trombone slurs.*

Note that a bass trombone equipped with a D trigger would have no trouble with any of these. Because of the large arm motions required in moving the slide, passages such as

while technically possible, are not idiomatic for the trombone and will sound much better (and be much more easily played) on the bass trumpet.

Trills are possible on the trombone provided that the two notes of the trill are from adjacent partials and that the slide is not required to move more than one position back and forth. Trills that involve the trigger and/or the slide are of necessity somewhat slower and more awkward than those executed with the lips alone.

The trombone glissando is so famous that many composers assume that a smooth glissando can be executed between any two notes. In reality, the trombone cannot produce a true glissando in excess of a tritone in width, and the tritone can only be reached where the end tones of the glissando lie in first and seventh positions on the slide. A little thought will make it clear that any trombone glissando must lie on a single partial, entirely between the two extreme positions of the slide, with the trigger(s) either engaged or disengaged for the entire duration of the glissando.

   Glissandos that do not meet these rules are usually executed as combined slide and lip glissandos. Such combination glissandos can be quite effective if performed rapidly, but they will have perceptible breaks or rough spots. Composers should be aware of the distinction and notate the "true" and "false" glissandos differently. For example, the huge glissandos in the last bar of Varèse's *Intégrales*, which are written thus:

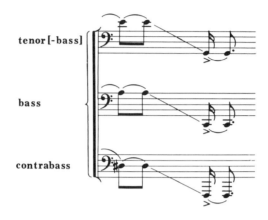

must be performed:

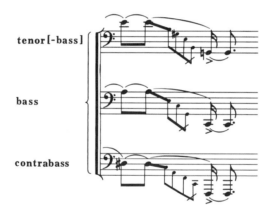

and should have been so notated. The various half-valve effects are possible from the trigger but have not been widely exploited.

MUSICAL EXAMPLES

TROMBONE:
   Hovhaness, Symphony No. 4 (3rd mvt.)
   Stravinsky, *L'Histoire du soldat*
   Bartók, *The Miraculous Mandarin*
   Berio, *Sequenza V*
   Xanakis, *Eonta*

CONTRABASS TROMBONE:
   Varèse, *Intégrales*
   Ligeti, *Requiem*

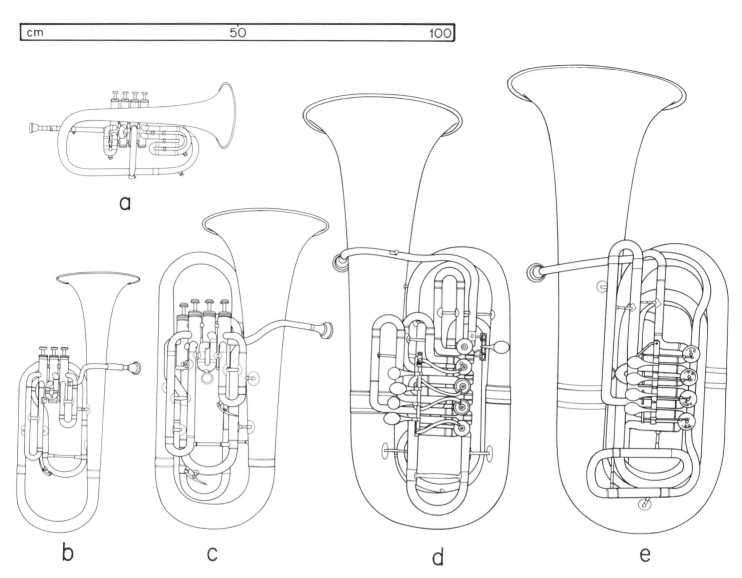

cm   50   100

FIGURE 55. *The tuba family: (a) flügelhorn;*
(b) alto horn; (c) baritone horn; (d) bass tuba; (e) contrabass tuba.

TUBAS

The tuba family arose from the addition of valves to the valveless military bugle. This basic idea was hit upon and/or pirated so many times in the course of the nineteenth century that half a dozen or more "different" families of tubas are still in competition with each other, and most musicians (including composers) remain unaware of the essential similarity of them all. All instruments of the valved-bugle type, whether called "tuba," "saxhorn," "flügelhorn," or what-have-you, are characterized by a broadly expanding conical bore, which gives them a coarse, full, somewhat mellow tone with a tremendous amount of **presence**—the quality of filling a room with sound even at low dynamic levels.

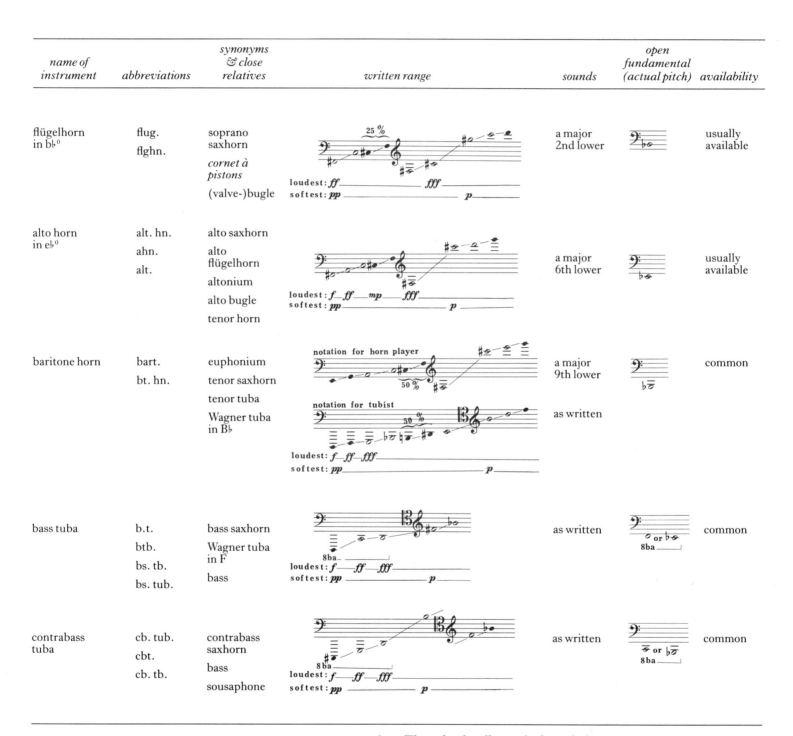

name of instrument	abbreviations	synonyms & close relatives	written range	sounds	open fundamental (actual pitch)	availability
flügelhorn in b♭⁰	flug. flghn.	soprano saxhorn *cornet à pistons* (valve-)bugle		a major 2nd lower		usually available
alto horn in e♭⁰	alt. hn. ahn. alt.	alto saxhorn alto flügelhorn altonium alto bugle tenor horn		a major 6th lower		usually available
baritone horn	bart. bt. hn.	euphonium tenor saxhorn tenor tuba Wagner tuba in B♭		a major 9th lower / as written		common
bass tuba	b.t. btb. bs. tb. bs. tub.	bass saxhorn Wagner tuba in F bass		as written		common
contrabass tuba	cb. tub. cbt. cb. tb.	contrabass saxhorn bass sousaphone		as written		common

FIGURE 56. *The tuba family—vital statistics.*

FIGURE 57. *Valve combinations for the lower register of the contrabass tuba in B♭.*

THE INSTRUMENTS

The "different kinds" of tubas are for the most part different in name only, being identical to each other in sound and virtually identical in construction. The only variants with some claim to an independent existence are the Wagner tubas and the old *cornet à pistons*. Wagner tubas (nowadays increasingly called simply **tubens**) are designed to be played by horn players (they have deep, funnel-shaped mouthpieces and are built left-handed) and are usually erroneously described as bass members of the horn family. The funnel-shaped mouthpiece gives these instruments a *very* slightly mellower and gentler tone than the ordinary tenor and bass tubas; it is doubtful that even the most confirmed Wagnerite would notice if the ordinary instruments were substituted for Wagner's invention, especially if appropriate mouthpieces were used. The *cornet à pistons* of the nineteenth century was essentially a soprano Wagner tuba, for it too had a basically funnel-shaped mouthpiece. The modern cornet, its direct descendant, is utterly indistinguishable from the trumpet. A handful of modern cornets are still built with bores wide enough to qualify them as tubas, and these, not surprisingly, sound much like flügelhorns; the cornet, in short, no longer has any truly independent existence.

The names used here for the five different sizes of modern tuba are those most commonly in use in North America. Ideally, of course, one ought simply to speak of soprano, alto, tenor, bass, and contrabass tubas and have done with the mess forever; unfortunately, at least as of this writing, no one would understand a reference to "soprano tuba" as indicating the flügelhorn.

The term "tuba" used alone refers to either the bass or contrabass instrument. Most tuba players play all their music on one or the other, regardless of which is specified by the composer, but the two instruments are somewhat different in both range and timbre. In *Et exspecto resurrectionem mortuorum*, for example, Messiaen makes good use of both bass and contrabass tubas in parts of differing character. Bass tubas may be built in F or E♭, contrabasses in C or B♭; since neither is a transposing instrument, this is no problem for the composer. All good contrabass tubas have *at least* four valves, the fourth extending the range downward and compensating for the intonation problems of the third valve. The severe intonation problems of the fourth valve (more than a half-step sharp when combined with the other three) are corrected by the addition of a fifth valve and/or by means of tuning slides that adjust either manually (with the player's free left hand) or automatically. The way the fourth valve is combined with the other three is shown in Figure 57. Professional-quality bass tubas are now made with a minimum of *five* valves; the fifth valve lowers the pitch either a major third or a major second, depending on the instrument.

The baritone horn ("baritone," for short) appears only occasionally in orchestral scores, but it is a standard member of the concert band. There it is traditionally considered both as a transposing instrument in $B\flat_0$ and as a non-transposing instrument, and duplicate parts are provided by publishers. This reflects the fact that most players of the instrument have come to it from the trumpet, and beginners who have not yet mastered the bass clef use the (treble-clef) transposing parts. In orchestral scores the baritone is frequently written for doubling by a horn player rather than a tuba player or trombonist, and here too the transposing notation is used;* in all other cases the instrument should be notated at pitch.

Of those baritones used by professionals and first-rank amateurs, about half have four valves rather than three. Without the fourth valve the notes B_1 to $E\flat_0$ can be played only weakly and uncertainly as privileged-frequency pedals, and should thus be avoided; with four valves these notes are readily available. In band use the three-valve instruments are sometimes called "baritones" and the four-valve ones "euphoniums," but this is by no means standard.

The alto horn in $e\flat_0$ is almost exclusively a band instrument, used on the marching field to replace the "French" horn. Like the alto clarinet, the alto horn has a bad reputation which is largely undeserved: Hindemith's sonata for the instrument barely scratches the surface of its capabilities. All alto horns have three valves. The "false" pedal tones (from written f^0 to $c\sharp^0$) are as weak and uncertain as the corresponding tones of the tenor trumpet, but the "true" pedals (from written c^0 down) are quite strong.

The flügelhorn in $b\flat_0$ is shaped like a trumpet and played by trumpeters, but it is a true tuba. In North America it appears only occasionally in the concert band. Its primary use is by jazz musicians, who appreciate its muffled, vocal tone. Traditionally the instrument has been built with three valves; it is now occasionally (and increasingly) seen with four. Four-valve flügelhorns can descend to written $c\sharp^0$ on the second partial—three-valve instruments have only weak and uncertain "false" pedal tones from f^0 to $c\sharp^0$—but both four- and three-valve instruments have a surprisingly good set of "true" pedals below this.

All the trumpet mutes exist in variants usable on the flügelhorn. The harmon and solo-tone mutes destroy the instrument's presence, however; when these mutes are used the flügelhorn sounds essentially the same as a trumpet similarly muted.

For tubas other than the flügelhorn only straight and bucket mutes are available, and the bucket mutes are very rare. The straight mute for the bass or contrabass tuba comes in a wide variety of sizes and shapes, only about half of which perform their proper function of rendering the timbre thin, nasal, and distant. With either the straight or bucket mute the quality of presence that distinguishes all members of the tuba family is unaffected. A good straight mute will make a tuba of any size sound simultaneously very close and very distant. The mutes of the deeper tubas (from baritone horn down) are large, ponderous affairs that cannot be inserted or removed unobtrusively. While one need not go as far as the composer who said, "The only excuse for a tuba mute is theater," the theatrical aspects of its use should be taken into account.

PERFORMANCE CHARACTERISTICS

Even compared to other brass instruments, tubas are remarkably even in timbre from one end of the range to the other. As mentioned above, the most distinctive quality of all these

* In *Le Sacre du printemps* Stravinsky writes the tenor-tuba parts an octave too low.

instruments is the room-filling character of their tone. Aside from this presence, the tone of the various tubas is best described by reference to other brass instruments: the flügelhorn sounds like a particularly coarse, dark, mellow trumpet; the alto horn has a tone halfway between trumpet and "French" horn; and the baritone sound is halfway between horn and trombone. The bass and contrabass tubas sound almost as if they could be low-pitched members of the horn family, with the bass tuba being more obviously coarse and powerful in a typically tuba-like fashion; the contrabass sounds thick and muffled even in its high register.

Although tubas *sound* ponderous, they are in fact as agile as trumpets, and one need not fear to write rapid runs, trills, valve-smears, and lip glisses as readily as one would for trumpets of equivalent size. Only below D_1 is any caution required, and even there, a passage such as

while it might raise some eyebrows, is possible (if difficult) to play. A truly sharp staccato is, however, impossible below D_1.

Musical Examples

FLÜGELHORN:
> Stravinsky, *Threni*
> Schoenberg, Theme and Variations, Op. 43a

ALTO HORN:
> Hindemith, Sonata for alto horn and piano
> Berlioz, *Les Troyens* ("Royal Hunt and Storm")*

BARITONE HORN:
> Janáček, *Capriccio* for piano (left hand) and winds
> Schoenberg, Theme and Variations, Op. 43a
> Stravinsky, *Le Sacre du printemps* (Part I)

BASS TUBA:
> Revueltas, *Sensemayá*
> Stravinsky, *Le Sacre du printemps*
> Varèse, *Déserts*
> Messiaen, *Et exspecto resurrectionem mortuorum*

CONTRABASS TUBA:
> Varèse, *Déserts*
> Messiaen, *Et exspecto resurrectionem mortuorum*

* Most instruments—including the alto horn—have changed quite a bit since Berlioz's time. One must bear in mind when studying this score that it documents an historical practice—even if modern instruments are used to play the piece. Compare this book with Berlioz's orchestration treatise.

TUBA (BASS OR CONTRABASS):
L. Hiller, *Malta*

ADDITIONAL EXAMPLES

BRASS IN LARGE GROUPS:
Stravinsky, *Ebony Concerto*
Schoenberg, Theme and Variations, Op. 43a
Hindemith, Symphony in B♭ for concert band
Grainger, *A Lincolnshire Posy*
Varèse, *Ecuatorial*
Messiaen, *Et exspecto resurrectionem mortuorum*
Xenakis, *Akrata*

IV

THE

VOICE

GENERAL CONSIDERATIONS

More ink has been spilled on the subject of the voice, vocal training, and the art of singing than on any other aspect of music. Unfortunately for singers and composers, much of what has been taught and written is narrow-minded, culture-bound, or just plain nonsensical. Opinions on the subject are often held with the force of dogma, and an inordinately high proportion of trained singers are likely to reject any new or unconventional vocal technique either as physiologically impossible or as literally damaging to their vocal organs; nor will such opinions be readily discarded even after the technique has been demonstrated to them.

The reader should accordingly be aware that some of what follows in this chapter is controversial. Caution is particularly necessary in acting upon the discussions of registers, vibrato, and styles of singing. It should be emphasized, however, that the vocal phenomena treated below are not in any way freakish or dangerous; they are all a normal part of the potential repertoire of almost any trained voice.

CLASSIFICATION OF SOUNDS

The most striking characteristic of the human voice is the incredible variety of sounds it can produce. Equally remarkable is the fact that 80 or 90 percent of these sounds are used to form words in one or another of the world's languages and dialects. The study and classification of vocal sounds has thus fallen largely to linguists and semanticists, who have dealt with them according to their function as fundamental units of speech, or "phonemes."

These are divided into sounds that are essentially static and self-contained (vowels) and those that are transitory (consonants). Vowels are described on the basis of the configuration of the lips and position of the tongue. Those formed with rounded lips, such as the vowel sounds in "b*oa*t" and 'b*oo*t," are called **rounded** vowels; all others, such as those in "b*ee*t" and 'b*u*t," are **unrounded**. By the position of the tongue a vowel is classed as high or low, front, back, or central. The italicized vowel sounds in the following words are, respectively, high front, low front, low back, high back, and central:

p*ea*t   p*a*t   f*a*ther   f*oo*d   ad*a*m*a*nt

Consonants are divided into those such as "p," "d," and "k," in which the stream of air is completely stopped for an instant (**plosives**, or **stops**), those such as "v," "s," and "h," in which the stream is merely constricted so as to produce a hissing sound (**fricatives**), and those such as "m," "r," and "l," in which an otherwise vowel-like sound is used in a transitory fashion (**frictionless open consonants**). A further broad division is made between **voiced** consonants such as "b," "z," and "l," which involve the use of the vocal cords, and **unvoiced** ones such as "p," "s," and "h," which do not. In addition, consonants are classified by the manner in which the blockage or constriction of the airstream is formed, as follows:

Constriction or Blockage Formed by	*Type of Consonant*	*Examples*
both lips	bilabial	"m," "p," "w"
upper teeth against lower lip	labiodental	"f"
tip of tongue against upper teeth	dental	"th"
tip of tongue against bump (*alveolus*) behind upper teeth	alveolar	"l," "n," "r," "s," "t"
underside of tongue tip against alveolus	retroflex	(no English examples)
top of tongue just behind tip against hard palate	palatal	"y"
sides of tongue against back teeth	lateral	"l"
middle of tongue against soft palate	velar	"k," "ng"

Constriction or Blockage Formed by	Type of Consonant	Examples
back of tongue against hanging flap (*uvula*) at back of soft palate	uvular	(no English examples)
constricted throat	pharyngeal	"h"

It should be obvious that the Roman alphabet is totally inadequate to distinguish all the possible vowels and consonants. The International Phonetic Association has devised an alphabet that is internationally recognized and uniform. Though this **International Phonetic Alphabet** is no longer used much by linguists (real languages are not as tidy as use of the I.P.A. suggests), it is a godsend to the composer, since it provides a universally accepted notation for all the minimally distinguishable sounds used in human speech. Listed and described below are the letters of the I.P.A., with its diacritical marks, by means of which still more sounds may be notated. Figures 58 and 59 show the configuration of lips and tongue for each of the alphabet's twenty-four vowels plus the sounds [u+] and [ɯ+]. (In composition, phonetic letters and phonetically spelled words should be enclosed in brackets, as here, in order to differentiate them clearly from ordinary letters and words.)

Despite the comprehensiveness of the I.P.A., the reader will easily be able to find sounds not included in it and not describable with its diacritical marks—the voiced and unvoiced labiodental plosives, for example, and a wide variety of clicks and "Donald Duck" noises. If such sounds are worked into a piece, they should be notated by symbols not readily confusable with the letters of the I.P.A.

THE INTERNATIONAL PHONETIC ALPHABET

Vowels

i   as in English "f*ee*t"

ɪ   as in English "f*i*t"

e   as in French "th*é*" or German "b*e*ten" (English "long A" is usually pronounced [eɪ])

ɛ   as in English "p*e*t"

æ   as in English "c*a*t"

a   as in French "p*a*tte." Halfway between [ɑ] and [æ]

ɑ   as in English "f*a*ther"

ʌ   as in English "c*u*t"

ɣ   like [o], but unrounded. Halfway between [ʌ] and [ɯ]

ɯ   like [u], but unrounded. High, back, unrounded vowel

ɨ   Russian letter ы ("yery"). Centralized [ɪ]

ə   as in French "l*e*," German "bitt*e*," English "app*e*tite"

ɐ   as in English "tub*a*"

ɒ   as in British "h*o*t"

y   as in French "l*u*ne" or German "H*ü*te"

ʏ   as in German "Gl*ü*ck." Like [ɪ], but rounded

ø   as in French "bl*eu*" or German "sch*ö*n"

œ   as in French "b*œu*f" or German "Götter"

ɔ   as in English "s*aw*"

o   as in French "d*o*s" or German "S*oh*n" (English "long O" is usually pronounced [o͡u])

ω or ʊ   as in English "b*oo*k"

u   as in English "sp*oo*k"

ʉ   halfway between [ω] and [y]

ɵ   halfway between [o] and [ø]

Diacritical Marks for Vowels

ˌ   Placed beneath fricative or frictionless open consonant; indicates consonant sustained and treated as a vowel

—   Placed after a vowel; indicates that it is fronted

˷   Placed under a vowel; indicates that it is rounded (labialized)

°   Placed above or below a vowel; indicates that it is whispered

˜   Placed above a vowel; indicates nasalization

⌢h   [h]-colored vowels ligature [h]

ˌ   Attached to lower right corner of a vowel; indicates [ɹ]-colored

Diphthongs are ligatured: "pie" = [pa͡ɪ]; "cow" = [ka͡u]; "boy" = [bo͡ɪ]; "theater" = [θɪ͡ətɹ]

Small superscript letters give fine shades of pronunciation.

Consonants

p   as in English "*p*et"

b   as in English "*b*et"

⊙   bilabial pop

t   roughly as in English "*t*op." More precisely, English (alveolar) "t" is [t̠]; French (dental) "t" is [t̪]

d   roughly as in English "*d*og." More precisely, [d̠] (alveolar); contrast French [d̪] (dental)

ʇ   dental click (unvoiced). English "*t*isk"

ʗ   alveolar click (unvoiced)

ʈ   like [t], but retroflex

ɖ   like [d], but retroflex

c   unvoiced palatal plosive; halfway between [k] and [t]

ɟ   voiced palatal plosive; halfway between [g] and [d]

ʖ   lateral click (unvoiced)

k   as in English "*c*at"

g   as in English "*g*et"

ʞ   velar click (unvoiced)

q   unvoiced uvular plosive

ɢ   voiced uvular plosive

ʔ   glottal stop (for many speakers of English, used in words like "bu*tt*on")

ˌ   glottal stop superimposed upon the consonant it precedes or follows

m   as in English "ti*m*ing"

ɱ   like [m], but labiodental rather than bilabial

n   as in English "o*n*us"

ɳ   like [n], but retroflex

ɲ   as in English/French "cog*n*ac"

ŋ   as in English "si*n*k"

N   like [ŋ], but uvular rather than velar

ɸ   unvoiced bilabial fricative. Like [f], but bilabial

β   voiced bilabial fricative. Like [v], but bilabial

ʙ   rolled bilabial fricative (English "*brrr*")

w   as in English "a*w*ay"

ɥ   as in French "n*u*it." Formed like [y]

ʋ   like [w], but labiodental

ʍ   like [w], but unvoiced (for many speakers of English, used in words like "*wh*ite")

f   as in English "o*ff*er"

v   as in English "a*v*oid"

θ   as in English "*th*ick"

ð   as in English "*th*en"

σ   simultaneous [s] and [f]

ʑ   simultaneous [z] and [v]

ʮ   simultaneous [ʃ] and [f]

ʒ̧   simultaneous [ʒ] and [v]

s   as in English "a*s*ide"

z   as in English "*z*oo"

ʃ   as in English "*sh*ip"

ʒ   as in English "vi*s*ion"

ç   intermediate between [s] and [ʃ]

ʑ   intermediate between [z] and [ʒ]

ʂ   like [ʃ], but retroflex

ʐ   like [ʒ], but retroflex

ɼ   like [ʒ], but r-colored, as in Czech "Dvo*ř*ák"

r   rolled "r" of Spanish, Italian, Russian

ɾ   like [r], but with just one tap rather than a full roll

ɽ   like [r], but retroflex

ɹ   intermediate between [d] and [l]

ɻ   as in English "*r*abbit"

ç   unvoiced palatal fricative, as in (high) German "i*ch*"

j   voiced palatal fricative, as in English "we *y*ield" (English "y" in most positions is pronounced [ɪ̯])

ɫ   unvoiced lateral fricative

ɮ   voiced lateral fricative

l   as in French "a*ll*er" or German "a*ll*e" (English "l" is usually pronounced [ɫ])

ɭ   like [l], but retroflex

ʎ   like [l], but palatal

x   unvoiced velar fricative, as in German "a*ch*" or Spanish "*J*uan"

ɣ   voiced velar fricative, as in German "bewe*g*t"

χ   unvoiced uvular fricative

ʀ   rolled uvular "r," as in French "a*rr*acher"

ʁ   unrolled uvular "r," as in French "peu*r*"

ʄ   simultaneous [x] and [ʃ]

h   as in English "*h*at"

ɦ   like [h], but voiced; roughly as in English "uh-*h*uh"

ɧ   like [ɦ], but nasal

ħ   like [h], but with throat constricted (pharyngealized) (the sound of a polite cough is roughly [ʔħ])

ʕ   like [ħ], but voiced

Diacritical Marks for Consonants

˅ Placed beneath voiceless consonant; indicates voiced form

˚ Placed above or below a voiced consonant; indicates voiceless (whispered) form

˘ Placed above a vowel; indicates vowel shortened and treated as a consonant

˜ or ˉ Placed above a consonant; indicates pharyngealization or velarization (constriction of throat)

ˬ Placed beneath a consonant; indicates labialization (rounded lips)

ʒ Attached to lower right corner of consonant; indicates palatalization (middle of tongue raised, as for [ç] or [j])

η̑ Nasalized consonants ligature [η]

Small superscript letters give fine shades of pronunciation.

TEXT UNDERLAY

The text of any voice part, whether consisting of real words or meaningless sounds phonetically notated, should be written out syllable by syllable below the staff. Traditionally there must be at least one note for each syllable, but occasionally the pronunciation of a word is telescoped into fewer than the usual number of syllables. In such cases a ligature should be used to indicate the elision, as in the following examples:

"trying," when pronounced [tɹɑɪn], should be written "tryi͡ng"
"every," when pronounced [ɛvɹi], should be written "ev͡ery"

Each syllable should be placed directly under the first note on which it is sung, and if this results in a word being broken on the page, hyphens should be used to bridge the gaps, thus: "di---a-mond." If the last syllable of a word is to be sung on several notes, a solid line should be drawn from the end of the word up to the last note involved, thus: "im--pact__." Note that terminal consonants are given as part of the syllable to which they belong, not separately at the end of the line like this: "im--pa____ct." Punctuation, if any, can be placed either before or after such a line, but one should maintain consistency.

Vocal music is now notated just like instrumental music. Until fairly recently, however, the system in Figure 60 was used. The old system is still occasionally seen in new music.

The position of vocal parts in a score is not entirely standardized. The commonest and perhaps most logical solution is to place them between brass and percussion, but often scores show the voices at the top, at the bottom, between percussion and keyboards, or between keyboards and strings.

VOWEL FORMANTS

When writing for voice, the effect of pitch on the perceptibility of vowels must be taken into account. The distinctive timbre of each vowel is determined by a number of frequency bands called **formants** (the lowest pair of which is the most important) that are not dependent

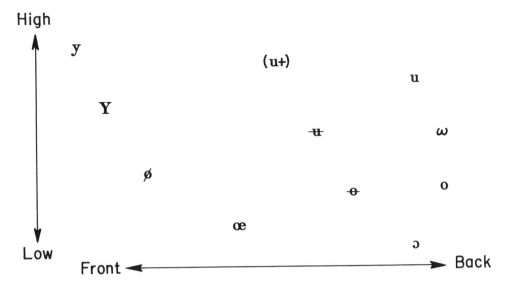

FIGURE 58. *Placement of the tongue for rounded vowels.*

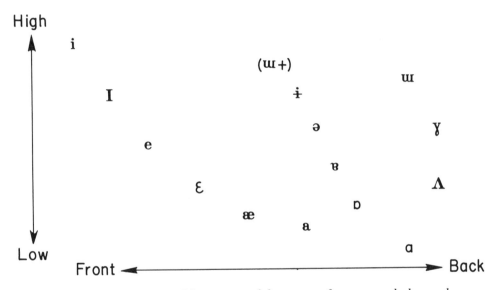

FIGURE 59. *Placement of the tongue for unrounded vowels.*

upon the pitch at which the vowel is sung. If the sung pitch is so high that only one or two partials lie within the lower two formant bands, the vowel is difficult to distinguish from others; and if the fundamental pitch lies above both bands the vowel disappears altogether, becoming a colorless, neutral sound. Figure 61 gives the *approximate* pitches at and above which different pairs of vowels become indistinguishable from each other. It will be noted that most of the vowels of the standard European languages are mutually indistinguishable above c^3, and that therefore words sung at or above this pitch are largely unintelligible. It is probably this more than anything else that has established c^3 as the traditional top of the vocal range, for, as we shall see, many women and almost all children can sing well above "high C." Singers are used to altering high-pitched vowels, partly to aid intelligibility and partly to

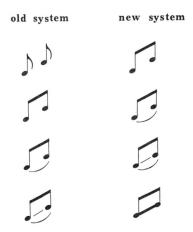

old system   new system

FIGURE 60. *Comparison of old and new systems of vocal notation.*

make them easier to sing. As a general rule, high and front vowels will be increasingly lowered and backed as the scale is ascended above about f^2. If this is not desired, some special instruction to the singer is probably necessary.

Nasal vowels have a very high harmonic development, and as a result of this they are distinguishable, as a group, from non-nasal vowels at even the highest singable frequencies. A pair of nasal vowels become indistinguishable from *each other*, however, at approximately the same pitch as the equivalent pair of non-nasal vowels. Because nasal vowels have such strong partials, those within the lowest formant band can easily be picked out by the ear. If one holds any pitch from about c^1 down and, starting with the sound [m̩], gradually opens the lips to [ã], then gradually fronts and raises the tongue to [ĩ], the lower formant will "scan" the audio range, picking out one after another the various upper partials of the note sung, starting with the second or third and ending somewhere between the sixth and the twelfth, depending on how low the sung pitch is. In his *Stimmung*, Stockhausen successfully bases an entire one-hour piece on this effect. The I.P.A. is insufficient in and of itself to specify this effect: if it is desired, one should notate the vowel as precisely as possible, appending a note to the singer such as "bring out fifth partial."

VOCAL TYPES AND REGISTERS

Acoustically, the voice resembles both strings and winds. The motion of air past the vocal cords causes them to vibrate against each other, like the lips of a brass player or the blades of a double reed; unlike these wind instruments, however, the frequency of the vibration is almost entirely determined by the length, mass, and tension of the cords themselves—exactly like a taut string. The cavities of the throat and mouth, while they strongly affect the timbre of the note produced, are too short and irregularly shaped to govern the vibrating frequency of the vocal cords. Rather, the frequency of a sung note is determined by the tension put on the vocal cords by the muscles of the larynx.

These muscles can cause the cords to vibrate in four distinct ways. These "modes of vibration" are somewhat analogous to the registers of woodwinds. The analogy is imperfect, however: although different partials are emphasized in each of these vocal *registers* (as they

104   MODERN INSTRUMENTS

	ɒ	ɵ	ʁ	ə	ʉ	ɨ	u+	ɯ+	u	ɯ	ω	ɤ	o	ʌ	ɔ	ɑ	a	œ	æ	ø	ɛ	e	ʏ	ɪ	y
i	$a^3{+}$	$g\sharp^3$	$g\sharp^3$	$b\flat^2$	$b\flat^2$	c^3	$a^3{+}$	$a^3{+}$	e^3	c^3	c^3	d^3	$a^3{+}$	e^3	$a^3{+}$	d^3	d^3	c^3	c^3	$a^3{+}$	$a\sharp^2$	e^2	$a\sharp^2$	c^3	e^3
y	$a^3{+}$	$b\flat^2$	d^3	c^3	$f\sharp^2$	$a\sharp^2$	c^3	c^3	$a\sharp^2$	$a\sharp^2$	$a\sharp^2$	c^3	d^3	c^3	d^3	$a^3{+}$	$g\sharp^3$	$g\sharp^2$	$a^3{+}$	c^3	c^3	c^3	e^2	c^3	
I	c^3	c^3	d^3	$b\flat^2$	$f\sharp^2$	e^2	$g\sharp^3$	$a\sharp^2$	$b\flat^2$	c^3	c^3	$a\sharp^2$	d^3	d^3	$b\flat^2$	d^3	d^3	c^3	$a\sharp^2$	$g\sharp^2$	e^2	c^2	$f\sharp^2$		
Y	$f\sharp^3$	$f\sharp^3$	c^3	d^2	$g\sharp^2$	d^2	c^3	$f\sharp^2$	c^3	c^3	e^2	$a\sharp^2$	$a\sharp^2$	$g\sharp^3$	d^3	c^3	c^3	$f\sharp^2$	$a\sharp^2$	$f\sharp^2$	$f\sharp^2$	$g\sharp^2$			
e	$f\sharp^3$	$a\sharp^2$	d^3	$g\sharp^2$	$g\sharp^2$	$b\flat^2$	$a^3{+}$	c^3	$f\sharp^3$	$g\sharp^2$	$a\sharp^2$	$g\sharp^2$	$b\flat^2$	$g\sharp^2$	$g\sharp^2$	d^3	c^3	$b\flat^2$	$a\sharp^2$	$g\sharp^2$	e^2				
ɛ	$a^3{+}$	$g\sharp^2$	c^3	$a\sharp^2$	d^3	$g\sharp^2$	e^3	$f\sharp^2$	c^3	$a\sharp^2$	$a\sharp^2$	$a\sharp^2$	$b\flat^2$	$g\sharp^2$	$g\sharp^2$	d^3	$a\sharp^2$	$d\sharp^2$	$a\sharp^2$	$f\sharp^2$					
ø	$g\sharp^2$	$f\sharp^2$	$f\sharp^2$	d^2	$g\sharp^2$	e^2	$a^3{+}$	e^3	$f\sharp^2$	e^3	$f\sharp^2$	e^2	e^2	$g\sharp^2$	$g\sharp^2$	$g\sharp^2$	c^3	$f\sharp^2$	$a\sharp^2$						
æ	$b\flat^2$	$g\sharp^2$	$g\sharp^2$	$g\sharp^2$	$g\sharp^3$	$a^3{+}$	$a^3{+}$	$a^3{+}$	$f\sharp^3$	$f\sharp^3$	d^3	$b\flat^2$	$b\flat^2$	$g\sharp^2$	$b\flat^2$	d^3	$a\sharp^2$	e^3							
œ	$b\flat^2$	$f\sharp^2$	$f\sharp^2$	$b\flat^2$	d^3	e^2	$a^3{+}$	$b\flat^2$	$f\sharp^2$	$f\sharp^2$	$f\sharp^2$	$f\sharp^2$	$f\sharp^2$	$g\sharp^2$	$g\sharp^2$	e^2									
a	e^2	$f\sharp^2$	$f\sharp^2$	$b\flat^2$	$a^3{+}$	$g\sharp^2$	$a^3{+}$	$b\flat^2$	$f\sharp^2$	$f\sharp^2$	c^3	$f\sharp^2$	$b\flat^2$	$f\sharp^2$	$b\flat^2$	$g\sharp^2$									
ɒ	$f\sharp^2$	$g\sharp^2$	$f\sharp^2$	$g\sharp^2$	$b\flat^2$	$b\flat^2$	$a^3{+}$	$a^3{+}$	d^3	$f\sharp^2$	e^3	$f\sharp^2$	d^3	e^2	e^3										
ɔ	$f\sharp^2$	$f\sharp^2$	$b\flat^2$	$b\flat^2$	$g\sharp^2$	$g\sharp^2$	$a^3{+}$	$a^3{+}$	d^3	$g\sharp^2$	$b\flat^2$	e^2	d^2	d^2											
ʌ	$b\flat^2$	$g\sharp^2$	d^2	$f\sharp^2$	$g\sharp^2$	$b\flat^2$	$a^3{+}$	$a^3{+}$	e^3	$f\sharp^2$	$f\sharp^2$	c^2	c^2												
o	$b\flat^2$	$f\sharp^3$	e^3	c^3	e^2	$g\sharp^2$	$a^3{+}$	c^3	d^2	e^2	e^2	e^2													
ɤ	e^2	$f\sharp^2$	$f\sharp^2$	$g\sharp^2$	$f\sharp^2$	d^2	d^3	$f\sharp^3$	c^3	c^2	e^2														
ω	$f\sharp^2$	$g\sharp^2$	c^3	$g\sharp^2$	$g\sharp^2$	$b\flat^2$	$b\flat^2$	$f\sharp^2$	$b\flat^2$	$g\sharp^2$															
ɯ	$f\sharp^2$	e^2	e^2	e^2	e^2	$f\sharp^3$	e^2	d^2	$f\sharp^3$																
u	$f\sharp^2$	$g\sharp^2$	e^2	$g\sharp^2$	$f\sharp^2$	$g\sharp^2$	$g\sharp^2$	e^2																	
ɯ+	$g\sharp^2$	e^2	c^3	c^3	$b\flat^2$	$g\sharp^2$	$b\flat^2$																		
u+	$g\sharp^3$	$g\sharp^2$	e^2	e^2	$b\flat^2$	$g\sharp^2$																			
ɨ	c^3	$g\sharp^2$	c^3	c^3	$f\sharp^2$																				
ʉ	$b\flat^2$	$f\sharp^2$	d^2	e^2																					
ə	$g\sharp^2$	e^2	c^2																						
ʁ	e^2	c^2																							
ɵ	$g\sharp^2$																								

FIGURE 61. *Approximate pitches at (and above) which pairs of vowels are indistinguishable from each other. Those marked "$a^3{+}$" are still distinguishable at a^3.*

are in fact called), there is no true overblowing. An equally valid analogy could be made to the muscles of the legs, which behave differently in the three modes of ambling, walking, and running. From top to bottom, the four vocal registers are the whistle register, falsetto or head register, chest register, and growl register. Of these, only the chest and falsetto registers have been widely exploited.

The characteristic sound of each register is partially a function of the pitch range in which it is used. Thus, the average woman's chest register sounds very similar to that of a high-pitched man; on the other hand, the chest register of children, because it lies in essentially the same range as their falsetto register, is virtually indistinguishable from it in timbre.

The **chest register** is the one normally used in speaking. A few women speak with the falsetto register instead, as do many children. A very few men speak with their growl register—soft, gravelly, and very deep.

The chest register of both men and women is warm, rich, and sonorous. It is the most

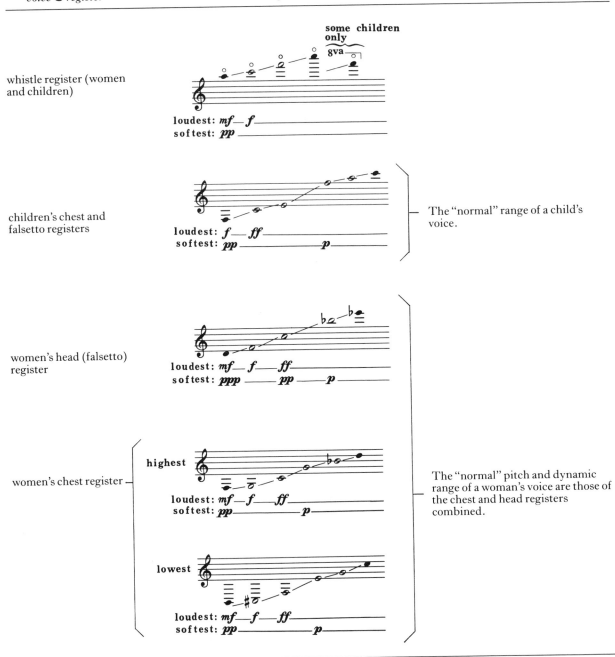

FIGURE 62. *The voice—vital statistics.*

clearly "vocal" in quality of the four registers, and most clearly conveys to the listener the immense load of emotional and psychological associations the voice always bears in speech however deadpan, in song however abstract. The chest register is the only one of the four that varies much in pitch from person to person, and because it is so important, the voice as a whole is regarded as high, medium, or low almost entirely on the basis of whether the chest

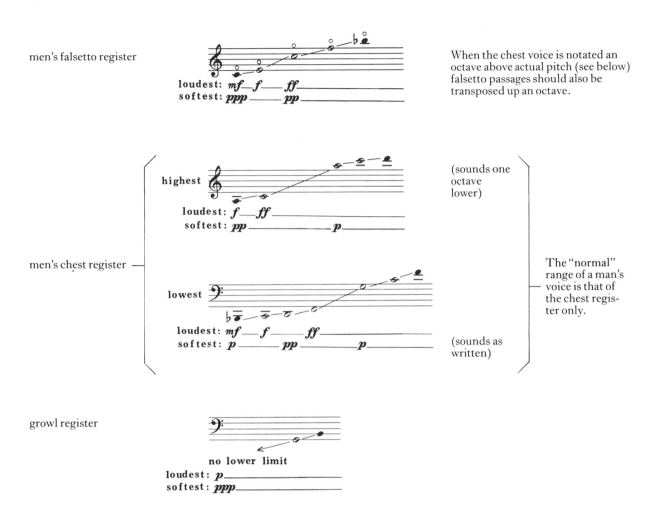

The voice—vital statistics, continued.

register is high, medium, or low. In this regard it should be mentioned that the extreme ranges given in Figure 62 are the highest and lowest that are common enough not to be considered freakish or physiologically abnormal. The extension tones given for all four registers are not a matter of training but of biology, and while voices do exist with both the bottom and top extension tones as indicated, such voices are *extremely* rare, and one will be the more likely to find a singer the less extreme the range demanded. Similarly, intermediate-range voices are much more common than the high and low extremes given in Figure 62. In writing for massed voices (chorus), the range of each part should not generally exceed two octaves for women, or a major thirteenth for men or children.

The chest register is considerably less agile than the falsetto register, and rapid runs and ornaments tend to sound blurred and muddy. As mentioned above, the chest register of children is almost completely overlapped by the falsetto register, and is very similar to it in tone. Boys' parts are occasionally written down to f^0, the additional notes being available in the chest register of some boys when their voices are just about to break.* A few girls also have these low notes, and their speaking voices have a startlingly grown-up quality.

Compared to the chest register, the **falsetto register** is relatively thin and colorless—though it has a great deal more character than the tone of, say, the flute. When trained, it can be quite brilliant and powerful in the range above about c^2, but it will always be somewhat weak and thin below that pitch. In ordinary adult speech it is used only in shrieks. It also appears (inadvertently) when the chest voice has been exhausted by prolonged loud talking or when one is in the grip of a strong emotion.

In traditional Western classical music the falsetto register of men has been used only by specialists called **countertenors** (about whom more later), who are not expected to use the chest register; otherwise it occurs only rarely, as a parody of a woman's voice or to signify (through its emotional flatness) madness or idiocy. In a traditionally trained woman's voice, however, the falsetto register takes over the main job of singing, and the chest register is completely subordinated to it. It is for this reason that women's voices are supposed to sound different from men's, although in ordinary speech and certain kinds of popular singing (as well as in most non-Western vocal styles) the difference is actually very small.

The falsetto register of both men and women is very agile and flexible, capable of executing with precision the most rapid runs and trills. A child's falsetto register is just as flexible, but it is extremely rare to find a child with the intelligence, musicianship, and dedication necessary for the acquisition of a coloratura technique. When composing for children's voices it is necessary to take into account these technical limitations; the maximum credible demands upon a child soprano are made in the soprano solos of Bach's cantatas, which can be adequately sung by only a handful of boys in each generation. The falsetto register of children of both sexes (as well as the virtually interchangeable chest register) is strong and liquid in tone; the difference between this sound and that of a woman's falsetto register is mostly due to the very small size of the resonating cavities in the child's mouth, nose, and chest. Despite great similarities, boys' and girls' voices do differ slightly in timbre, and as the boys' sound is the more distinctive there has been much more written for boys' voices than for girls'. †

The **whistle register** is most frequently heard in the incredibly high-pitched shrieks of children at play. It is a normal component of every child's voice, but has never been used in music, probably because of the indistinguishability of vowels at such high frequencies. Most adult women retain a usable whistle register, but it is rather difficult to control, and the vast majority of singers are, for no particular reason, not trained to use it. It is a colorless, thin, piping sound whose musical potential has been so far almost completely ignored. The few places this register has been required (invariably mixed with some falsetto component) are for the most part intended to portray a spectacular kind of insanity—Mozart's psychotic

* When a boy's voice breaks, the chest register parts company from the falsetto register and, in the space of one or two years, descends to its adult pitch. During this time the chest register is absolutely useless for singing, and to attempt to train the voice then may damage it. The adolescent's suddenly lengthened vocal cords are as clumsy as his suddenly lengthened limbs, and will "trip" into the falsetto register at unpredictable moments. Girls' voices also change at puberty, but much less dramatically than boys'—there is no sudden break, and no loss of control.

† It should be remembered, however, that the initial impetus for the use of boys' voices was the liturgical prohibition of female singing in church. A girl's voice is, with the rare exceptions mentioned earlier, clearly identifiable as a child's voice, and the distinction between boys' and girls' voices has almost certainly been overstressed by our culture.

Queen of the Night is perhaps the best and best-known example. There is no reason why this should always be the case, although it must be admitted that this sound, which forms no part of normal human speech, can be decidedly eerie. Very few men possess a whistle register, and those who do have merely a few harsh and painful squeaks widely separated from the rest of their range.

If the chest, falsetto, and whistle registers are roughly analogous to the lower, upper, and altissimo registers of woodwinds, then perhaps the **growl register** is best compared to the privileged-frequency pedals of brass instruments. It is a weak, flabby, low-pitched noise of rather indefinite pitch. Because they are so poorly resonated by the body, these tones are more an undefined rattle or buzz than a specific pitch, and it is very difficult for the singer to pinpoint a pitch when producing this register. Accordingly, it should be composed only as a non-pitched sound, or at least as *sprechstimme* (q.v.). Incredible as it may seem, there is no lower limit to the growl register, and with a little practice anyone can produce isolated clicks at frequencies of 1 Hz or less. These are, needless to say, almost inaudible, and are certainly not heard as pitches. For some reason the growl register, in contrast to the other registers, is most easily performed on the inhale.

Everything that has been said so far in this chapter about registers applies to the voice as an unmodified bio-acoustical entity, as reflected in the speech and song of ordinary people all over the world. When we examine voices that have received a traditional Western classical training the situation becomes more complex.

Classically trained singers are taught to suppress as much as possible all distinctions between registers; for the most part, this is accomplished by mixing the registers. Since the registers of the voice are created by the use of specific combinations of throat muscles, it is possible to mix registers by using intermediate or combined muscular configurations, and by this means the timbre of the voice can be made smoothly continuous across a large portion of its range. Women singers borrow from the chest voice to shore up the power of their falsetto register below c^2 or d^2, and modify the upper part of the chest register to make it sound as much like falsetto as possible. Because the lowest fourth or fifth of the chest register cannot be convincingly modified in this way, it is usually sacrificed. At the other end of the scale, high-note specialists (**coloratura sopranos**) borrow from their whistle register to make the notes above c^3 more secure and less of a strain. Many singers consider the range between approximately d^1 and c^2, where the chest and falsetto (head) registers are strongly blended, to have a distinct register of its own, the "throat" or "middle" register. This "register" is, however, an artifact of training; it is simply a mixture of chest and falsetto tone.

The chest and falsetto registers of men are so distinct from each other in range that the subtle blending accomplished by women is out of the question. Accordingly, since uniformity of timbre is a major goal of classical voice training, the falsetto register is sacrificed altogether, and singing is restricted to the pure chest register. Classically trained male voices of all ranges do, however, borrow from their falsetto register to make their highest chest tones smoother and more secure, calling the resultant mixed timbre the "head register" by faulty analogy with the female voice. The rare **basso profundo**, with chest tones below D_0, reinforces these low notes by borrowing from the growl register. For the performance of early music, some men are trained as **countertenors**, singing for the most part only in the falsetto register, with the lowest tones shored up by some chest quality, and perhaps a few modified chest tones at the bottom to take the compass down to f^0. Countertenors usually have trained

		Light	*Dark*
Women:	high	lyric soprano	dramatic soprano
	medium	lyric mezzo	dramatic mezzo
	low	×	alto
Men:	high	lyric tenor	dramatic tenor
	medium	baritone	bass-baritone
	low	basso cantante	basso profundo

Women with a tone quality of intermediate darkness are often called **spintos**. Light-voiced and spinto women with great range and agility are called **coloratura** sopranos or mezzos.

FIGURE 63. *Classical vocal types classified by basic vocal range and timbre.*

chest registers, too, and can sing a perfectly good tenor, baritone, or bass, but the use of *both* registers equally in the same piece is not found prior to about 1960.*

In addition to being uniform in timbre, a classically trained voice must be able to project clearly to the back of a large hall, and compete unamplified with an orchestral tutti. To this end singers are taught to acquire a timbre that is somewhat darker and fuller than that of the untrained voice. Persons with naturally dark, rich voices are rare, but many singers are able to acquire this sound through training. The extent to which one is born with or can acquire the dark quality determines the kind of voice into which one is trained (see Fig. 63).

Note that the pitch ranges associated with these various vocal types do not exactly jibe with the actual range of the voice concerned. A woman with a light, low voice (an extremely common type) will *not* be trained to sing alto, but will more likely be taught to sacrifice her "unsuitable" chest register and end up as a lyric soprano! Bass-baritones are expected to be strongest at the bottom of their range, despite the fact that that range may be no different from that of an ordinary light baritone, and bassi profundi are expected to sing as much as a fourth lower than bassi cantanti. A trained voice often becomes darker with age, and because naturally dark voices are so rare, most singers whose voices fall into one of the dark categories tend to be at least in their late thirties: that is why so few Siegfrieds and Brünnhildes come up to Wagner's expectations of youth and beauty. In writing for dark voices, one must be aware that their power is gained at the expense of both agility and pitch range—dramatic sopranos who attempt a light coloratura role usually fare disastrously. Women who have trained their voices to darkness are likely to have suppressed their whistle register altogether.

In writing for the voice, one must expect to hear the part sung in one or another of the traditional vocal styles described above. If one desires a "natural," popular, non-Western, or otherwise non-traditional vocal quality it should be specified. The easiest way to make such a specification is either to name the style involved or to refer to a famous singer who uses that style. Whistle-register notes should be notated as if they were harmonics, as should individual male falsetto tones. If unmixed chest or falsetto tone is desired in the throat-register range of a woman's voice, the term "pure chest" or "pure head" should be used (many women singers use the term "falsetto" to refer to the whistle voice, so "head voice" is less ambiguous).

* Prior to about 1830, it was customary for tenors to take high notes in falsetto, rather than straining after b^1s and c^2s in the chest register as they do now.

PERFORMANCE CHARACTERISTICS
OF THE VOICE

Let it be stated at the outset, at the risk of belaboring the obvious, that singers must be allowed to breathe! Though professional singers sing somewhat more efficiently than other people, their breath control is nonetheless limited, and one will never go wrong in restricting vocal writing to passages that one can oneself take in a single breath. In fact, a good general rule for vocal writing is: "If *you* can sing it, *they* can sing it." Cyclic breathing is *not* possible for the voice, but it is possible to sing on the inhale. Unless the singer has practiced this unorthodox technique long and hard, the sound will invariably be somewhat gasping. In writing for inhaled singing, extremes of pitch or dynamics should be avoided. The alternation of inhaled and exhaled song does not enable the production of an indefinitely continuable tone as cyclic breathing does—because each time the direction of the breath changes the sound must stop for an instant—but it does enable the production of nonstop sixteenth-note chatter. Whenever inhaled singing is desired it must be specified, and the composer should bear in mind that inhaled plosives (**implosives**) sound different from exhaled ones.

VIBRATO

It is not generally realized, even by singers, that four distinct types of vibrato are available in singing. **Diaphragm vibrato**, the type used by wind players, is employed by singers in exactly the same way. It causes a fluctuation in the loudness of the tone without affecting either pitch or timbre, and can be varied in both speed and amplitude. The **throat vibrato** is made with the muscles of the pharynx, is also variable in both speed and amplitude, and affects only the loudness of the tone. It is most easily produced at a somewhat higher speed than the diaphragm vibrato. At high amplitude it becomes the *trillo* ("goat's trill") of Monteverdi and his contemporaries; at even higher amplitude it becomes a series of glottal stops.

The **laryngeal vibrato**, often confused with the throat vibrato, is an entirely different entity. This is the so-called "natural" vibrato that does indeed come naturally to most untrained singers and forms an invariable part of the tone of all classically trained singers except children and countertenors. This kind of vibrato is formed in the larynx, probably as an interaction between two adjacent registers. Into the actual register in which the note is sung is admixed a small but fluctuating component of the other register, which creates a vibrato affecting both pitch and timbre. The fluctuation is the result of a natural give-and-take of the muscle groups involved, responding to the physiological/acoustical instability inherent in the mixing of registers, and the frequency of a laryngeal vibrato is usually a fixed and invariable quality for any given singer. The amplitude of this vibrato can, however, be adjusted; it can be suppressed entirely if desired, or augmented to help form a trill—in fact, the usual classical trill is performed in just this way.* Men do not seem to be able to produce a laryngeal vibrato when singing falsetto, nor does this kind of vibrato come very easily to children; since the laryngeal vibrato is the only kind usually recognized in classical voice training, children

* Trills can, however, be produced by other means, and are not limited to the range and registers in which the laryngeal vibrato can be produced.

and countertenors are usually taught to sing without any vibrato at all. In practice, the laryngeal vibrato is occasionally supported by a superimposed throat or diaphragm vibrato.*

Unlike the other three kinds of vibrato, the **mouth vibrato** forms no part of classical voice technique. It is produced by moving the jaw and/or tongue, and is thus a fluctuation of timbre rather than of pitch or loudness. Mouth vibrato is normally used in the West only in certain kinds of popular singing. It is variable in both speed and amplitude, and can be performed simultaneously with any of the other forms of vibrato—at a different speed if so desired.

To sum up: all trained singers (except countertenors and children) and most untrained singers will normally sing with a mild to moderate laryngeal vibrato, possibly supported by the throat or diaphragm. If it is desired to have a passage sung without vibrato, the instruction "senza vibr." should be used. If any modulation of vibrato speed or amplitude is desired, instructions to that effect must of course be given, and if mouth vibrato is desired it must be specified. Modulation of the vibrato speed will automatically be performed with the requisite diaphragm or throat vibrato without any special instruction to that effect—nonetheless, one occasionally finds singers so tied to the laryngeal vibrato that they must be taught, or at least reminded, that other possibilities exist.

PITCH LOCATION

Within a given register the voice can produce infinitely subtle gradations of pitch, the only limit being the acuteness of the singer's ear. In order to reproduce a pitch accurately, the singer must be able to feel, at least subconsciously, the precise adjustment of the laryngeal muscles necessary to produce that pitch, and accordingly must be able to hear the note clearly in his or her head *before* attempting to sing it. This, combined with the fact that the singer's "feel" for the laryngeal muscles is disoriented when their configuration must be greatly changed, means that large leaps cannot be executed at the fastest speeds. This is particularly true when awkward intervals are involved, so that while

may be possible for some singers (and I do not claim that it is),

certainly is not. Again, the limits on vocal acrobatics are much stricter for children than adults.

* It is physiologically impossible to perform combinations of these three types of vibrato at different speeds simultaneously.

Singing	Speaking
voice moves from one discrete pitch to the next	pitch constantly fluctuates
usually with vibrato	without vibrato
tone supported by the diaphragm and rib cage and focused by the throat muscles*	tone unsupported and unfocused except in stage speech
all registers used	usually only chest register used
rhythm usually moves in discrete, proportional units	rhythm free, flexible
dynamic range usually broad	dynamic range usually narrow
pitch, rhythm, and dynamics have *musical* meaning	pitch, rhythm, and dynamics have *grammatical* meaning
classically with darkened tone	with ordinary light tone

*Singing without support produces a very weak and "private" sound, almost like singing to oneself. Unsupported singing is practiced in various Western folk traditions and in some non-Western classical styles.

FIGURE 64. *Differences between speaking and singing.*

Very few singers can begin singing out of the blue and hit a given pitch correctly without reference to some previously heard pitch. That pitch may be several octaves away from the one that is to be sung, or it may be at some outlandish, dissonant interval; it may even be the last pitch of the previous song, desperately kept in the head through bows and curtain calls; but, one way or another, it must be there: the composer *must* provide some pitch for the singer at the end of any long rest in the voice part. It is flatly unreasonable to expect a singer to hit any specific pitch accurately after, say, five minutes of indeterminacy or unpitched noises. (The beginning of a piece is an exception to this rule, since the singer can get a note from a pitch pipe while in the wings, or from an instrumentalist while tuning up on stage.)

SPEECH/SONG HYBRIDS

By now it should be clear to the reader that there are numerous and considerable differences between singing with the voice and speaking with it. Figure 64 shows these differences in tabular form. It should be pointed out that ordinary speech is almost never found in any musical context; where spoken dialogue occurs, the supported and focused tones of **stage speech** are used. If genuine ordinary speech is desired, an instruction such as "ordinary speech—do not project or support" will be needed. Many kinds of vocalization intermediate between speech and song exist and are recognized musically, as follows.

1. Rhythmically free singing. This is notated with stemless note-heads and the instruction "in the rhythm of ordinary speech."

2. Rhythmically notated speech. Here the rhythm is controlled by the composer while all other aspects of the sound are produced as in normal speech. It is notated with headless stems and beams.

3. Modulated speech. This resembles rhythmically notated speech, but the positions of

the stems on the staff indicate the general pitch contour of the spoken line. If desired, the rhythm can be left free, but there is no standard notation for that contingency.

4. **Sprechstimme.** The tone quality is halfway between speech and song. In addition, each notated pitch is briefly touched in passing but speech inflections are maintained. Sprechstimme is notated by ordinary notes with X's through the stems. It may be employed in free rhythm, in which case stemless note-heads are used and the X's are placed just above or below them.

5. **Parlando.** This is fully sung, except that the notated rhythms are bent somewhat in the direction of normal speech rhythms; to a lesser extent, the pitches are bent as well. This is the style of singing used in the *recitativo secco* of eighteenth-century Italian opera. It is notated as if fully sung, with the instruction "parlando."

SPECIAL EFFECTS

Voices are second only to woodwinds in ability to produce multiphonics. With the voice, these are produced by attempting to sing simultaneously notes from two different registers. As with woodwinds, it is folly to notate them as chords, since this tells the singer nothing about how to make the sound—in any case, few, if any, singers have enough control to produce multiphonics so precisely and the sound of a vocal multiphonic is even more unitary than that of a woodwind one. Most vocal multiphonics are harsh, gritty affairs, and even the occasional bare octave or twelfth sounds coarse and constricted. One should, as with woodwinds, merely give the main pitch of the multiphonic, together with an indication of the general tone-quality desired. Multiphonics are hard on the throat, and singers should not be required to produce them over long stretches of music. They are easier to produce and easier on the throat when inhaled. An exception is the multiphonic produced by attempting to sing falsetto just a little too low. This sound—produced by many people as a sigh of exasperation—can only be performed on the exhale and is not at all hard on the throat.

A number of devices exist for altering the timbre of the voice in ways similar to the mutes of brass instruments. The **kazoo** is a tube in one side of which is a hole loosely covered by a small membrane. When one inserts the tube into the mouth and sings through it, the membrane rattles sympathetically with the vibration of the air column, making a buzzing sound. It is of course impossible to form bilabial or labiodental consonants while using the kazoo, and the tube suppresses the various vowels rather strongly, so that only three or four distinguishable vowels can be produced through it. The buzzing sound can be stopped simply by covering the membrane with a finger. As an alternative to the usual way of playing the kazoo, the far end of the tube can be covered with one hand while one hums through the nose. In this case the buzzing will stop whenever the sounds [n̪], [ŋ̊], [ɴ], etc.—all of which will sound alike because of the tube—are articulated.

Singing through a cardboard **mailing tube** makes the voice sound covered, distant, and mysterious. The natural resonating frequency of the tube dominates the sound and obscures the vowels.

The **megaphone** is simply a cardboard, plastic, or metal cone that concentrates the voice and projects it forward. In addition to making the voice slightly louder, it increases its "presence" and cuts out a large number of high overtones. The **bullhorn** is an electronic mega-

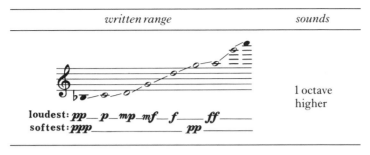

written range	sounds
	1 octave higher

loudest: *pp__p__mp__mf__f____ff____*
softest: *ppp_____pp_____*

FIGURE 65.   *Whistling—vital statistics.*

phone consisting of an amplifier, a very small loudspeaker, and a flared metal cone. Since the device is equipped with a squelch mechanism to keep it from responding to soft background noises, it will only respond when sung or spoken into *forte* or louder, reproducing the sound at levels ranging from *ff* to *fff*. The bullhorn reproduces high and low frequencies very weakly, and thus sounds somewhat like a cheap radio turned up loud. Because of the squelch, plosives become veritably *ex*plosive, and the whole effect is almost luridly apocalyptic.

Finally, one can alter the sound of the voice by singing into a drinking glass, cupped hands, or other cavity. This produces an echo-like timbre in which the resonant frequencies of the cavity are reinforced. If one covers the open mouth tightly with a glass or bottle and then hums through the nose, a different sound results; in this case, the cavity resonance is added to that of the natural cavities of the throat, nose, and chest, adding an additional vowel formant and changing the whole character of the voice, which then sounds thin and nasal—almost as if the singer were inside the bottle. This effect works best when the cavity is fairly large (milk-bottle or wine-bottle size), and if it is large enough (gallon-jug size), one can even sing directly into the bottle through the mouth for a second or two until the air pressure inside it becomes too great.

WHISTLING

Whistling is one of the great unexplored regions of music. Despite the great range and flexibility a practiced whistler can command, very little music has specifically been written to be whistled. For those wishing to give it a try, Figure 65 says virtually all that has to be said. A whistled note has *no* overtones, its timbre being due entirely to its envelope and the slight component of hiss produced by the air as it passes between the lips. In whistling, the stream of air is directed by the top of the tongue downward and outward between the lips, which act exactly like the embouchure hole of the flute. The pitch is determined by the distance between the tongue and the lips. The sound can be varied from a pure, clean whistle, to a hissy or breathy whistle, to colored noise, or all the way to simple white noise (the sound [ʍ̥]).

Whistling can be extremely agile, and good whistlers can execute the most rapid runs and trills cleanly. Large leaps are subject to the same restrictions as for the voice, except that here it is the tongue rather than the vocal cords that must feel the correct position for each note. Articulation in whistling is performed by the glottis, throat, and diaphragm except in extremely rapid figures such as grace notes, when the notes are articulated by the tongue with alternating [dl̥] and [lə̥]. Very clean trills can be produced in this way by some whistlers; others simply move the tongue back and forth rapidly between the two notes of the trill. A tasteful vibrato is impossible in whistling. Some whistlers indulge in a kind of perpetual trill that is supposed to be a vibrato—it sounds awful.

Whistlers, like everyone else, must breathe, but they have an advantage over both singers and wind players in being able to perform easily and convincingly while inhaling as well as while exhaling. The highest and lowest notes of the range cannot be performed on the inhale, nor should one make the mistake of assuming that a whistler can hold a single note or draw out a slur for an indefinite length of time, for the note or slur cannot be held while the breath changes between inhale and exhale.

It is possible to fluttertongue while whistling, but only in the range from (sounding) f^2 to a^3.

There are perhaps one or two people in the world who can whistle and hum two different musical lines simultaneously. It is, however, relatively easy to whistle a tune while humming a fixed note, and vice versa. It is somewhat more difficult, but still within the realm of realistic options, simultaneously to hum and whistle the same tune in strict parallel harmony. The most interesting sound is that produced when the whistle reinforces one of the partials of the voice. Whistling and humming in actual unison (*not* an octave apart) sounds so eerie as to be unsettling. Remember that there is no rule which says that a singer must know how to whistle, and that at least as of this writing far more men than women are virtuoso whistlers.

Musical Examples

"NATURAL" VOICES:

Partch, *The Delusion of the Fury* (Act II)
Weill, *Die Dreigroschenoper*

WOMEN'S VOICES:

Schoenberg, *Herzgewächse*
Maxwell Davies, *Revelation and Fall*
Berio, *Sequenza III*

MEN'S VOICES:

Stravinsky, *Renard*
Henze, *El Cimarrón*
Maxwell Davies, *Eight Songs for a Mad King*

CHILD'S VOICE:

Stravinsky, *Mass*
Xenakis, *Oresteia Suite*
Crumb, *Ancient Voices of Children*

MIXED SINGLE VOICES:
    Stockhausen, *Stimmung*
    Ligeti, *Aventures/Nouvelles aventures*

CHORUS:
    Schoenberg, *Friede auf Erden*
    Stravinsky, *Les Noces*
    Xenakis, *Nuits*

WHISTLING:
    Ives, *Memories* ("A: Rather pleasant")

V

THE PERCUSSION: GENERAL CONSIDERATIONS

ACOUSTICS

The percussion are the most numerous and varied of all instruments, and almost every conceivable type of tone production is represented among them. Nonetheless, all except for a handful of miscellaneous instruments fall within two large organological groups, **membranophones** and **idiophones**. The term "membranophone" corresponds very closely to the ordinary word "drum": membranophones are instruments in which the sound is produced by the vibration of a taut membrane, the **drum head**, which may or may not be affixed to a resonator, or **shell**. In idiophones the vibrating object is a solid block which, unlike a string or membrane, does not need to be pulled taut in order to vibrate.

The acoustics of both membranophones and idiophones are quite complex. As an example, Figure 66 shows the four lowest vibratory modes of a drum head and of a rectangular bar. Note that, although the pattern shown for the drum head is essentially valid for membranophones of all sorts, the rectangular-bar pattern only holds good for those idiophones whose sounding elements are rectangular bars. Idiophones in other shapes behave entirely differently, and with even greater complexity; as a result, there is a tremendous variety of timbre to be found among them.

The partials produced by such complex vibratory patterns are inharmonic, a fact which accounts for several important aspects of percussion sound. The ear can derive only a weak sense of pitch from an inharmonically structured sound, since the upper partials seem to contradict the fundamental rather than reinforce it; many percussion instruments (e.g.,

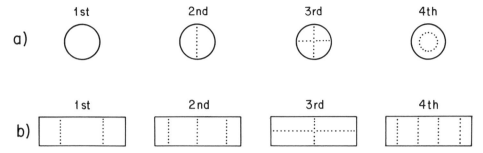

FIGURE 66. *The lower modes of vibration of (a) a drumhead and (b) a rectangular bar. The dotted lines indicate the positions of nodes.*

FIGURE 67. *Lower partials of a rectangular bar tuned to c¹. The frequencies of higher partials depend on the exact dimensions of the bar.*

cymbals, maracas, snare drums) have no definite pitch at all and can only be described as sounding relatively high or low. It has long been traditional to divide percussion instruments into those with and those without definite pitch, but the more one listens to percussion instruments, the clearer it becomes that such a division is untenable. The vast majority of percussion are neither clearly pitched nor clearly unpitched, and can be treated either way by composers. As a general rule, if two instruments, at least one of which is percussion, play at a dissonant interval, the ear interprets the percussion sound as an unpitched noise rather than as a dissonant pitch. The only important exceptions to this rule are the so-called **mallet instruments** (xylophone, vibraphone, and their relatives), the most strongly pitched of all percussion. Interestingly enough, it is these instruments that produce their sound from rectangular bars. Figure 67 shows why these instruments give such clear pitches: the upper partials are so widely separated from the fundamental that they do not conflict with it. Additionally, each bar rests on a pair of strings or felt-covered supports along the nodes of the first partial, so the upper partials are damped. Even with these instruments, however, the lack of reinforcement by harmonically generated partials leaves the pitch so weak that the ear frequently has difficulty in determining in which octave it lies. A great deal of focus can be given to any percussion pitch by doubling the note in some other non-sustaining instrument, such as piano, harpsichord, or plucked strings.

The characteristic shapes of gongs and bells were evolved to make their tonal spectra as harmonic as possible. Two or three partials spaced in approximately harmonic ratios persuade the ear to interpret the whole sound as harmonic, despite the presence of numerous other, clearly inharmonic partials. In fact, the perceived pitch of an instrument of this sort may not even be a part of its tonal spectrum, but a false fundamental supplied by the brain to what it interprets as an incomplete harmonic series.

The most strongly pitched membranophones are the timpani and the boobams. In boobams the long tubular resonator completely dominates the relatively small membrane, which thus acts as a kind of reed to set up truly harmonic vibrations within the tube. In

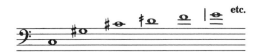

FIGURE 68. *Partials of a drum head tuned to c^0.*

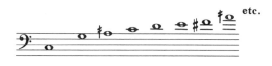

FIGURE 69. *Partials of a timpano tuned to c^0. The lowest pitch is really the second partial.*

timpani the membrane is stretched over a completely enclosed air space, and this displaces the normal drumhead partials (Fig. 68) into a vaguely harmonic pattern (Fig. 69). A small hole often present in the bottom of the shell completely suppresses the weak fundamental, which, if present, conflicts with the "harmonic" upper partials. A comparison of the tonal spectrum of the timpani with the true harmonic series (see Fig. 4) shows the closeness of the approximation and also makes it clear why the timpani give the impression of sounding an octave lower than they really are.

An important determinant of the timbre of an idiophone is the material of which it is made. The vast majority are made either of wood (or a plastic of equivalent resonance), a metal alloy of some sort, or a ceramic such as clay or glass. Each of these three basic materials has characteristic resonance features which lend a certain similarity to the timbres of all idiophones made with that material, regardless of shape or manner of tone production.

PERCUSSION ENVELOPES

With rare exceptions, the percussion are **non-sustaining instruments**, in which the sound, once produced, dies away completely of its own accord unless the sound is repeated. The decay time of a non-sustained sound can theoretically vary from less than a microsecond to half a minute or more; interestingly, the decay times of percussion instruments are not distributed evenly across this range but, rather, are clumped at the two extremes. The majority of percussion sounds decay completely in less than half a second, and most of the remaining instruments have long, smooth decay-times of ten to thirty seconds.

In the matter of envelope—obviously of supreme importance in percussion timbre— the percussion can be divided into three broad groups: those (the majority) in which the instrument is normally struck with some sort of mallet; those in which two approximately equal objects are struck together to produce the sound; and those in which the sound is produced by rattling or scraping. In the first two of these groups, the sound builds up to its attack peak while two objects are in contact with each other; the return of the first complete vibration bounces them apart, and the player's hand follows through on the bounce—that is why the hand and arm movements involved in playing percussion are so quick and precise. Some of the most massive or deep-pitched instruments start very slowly and may have build-up times as long as a quarter of a second; in these instruments the beater is rebounded by a relatively small group of quick-starting mid-range partials that receive most of the energy of the initial stroke, later distributing it among the remaining partials until a stable vibratory pattern is achieved. In the rattling instruments of the third group (which contains rattles of all sorts, ratchets, rasps, and windchimes), the envelope is compounded of numerous individual small clicking or dinging sounds interpreted by the brain as a single complex sound. In ratchets and rasps a more or less continuous sound is produced, with a definite beginning and end; but the overall envelope of rattles and windchimes is a non-sustaining attack and decay pattern similar to that of other percussion; most of the individual small clicks occur almost at the same time, and the ear hears this as the attack peak. Clicks occurring before the peak form the attack pattern, and those occurring after it form the decay. This can be heard very clearly in windchimes, in which each click can easily be identified; the decay pattern of a windchime is simply an irregular series of clicks that gradually decrease in frequency. Note that the loudness of each click also decreases, since the entire system is gradually being drained of its energy.

PERFORMANCE

PLACEMENT OF THE INSTRUMENTS

In the next two chapters we will encounter nearly a hundred different percussion instruments. These instruments can be played singly, but for the most part they are used in mixed groups. The percussionist plays all the instruments in such a grouping simultaneously, as if they were a single complex instrument. The performance characteristics of this large "instrument" depend not only upon the individual percussion instruments of which it is comprised but upon the way they are positioned around the player. In all percussion writing except that which is very easy or heavily indeterminate it is essential that the composer have a definite array of instruments in mind for each percussionist, and if the set-up is particularly large or complex, a diagram of their placement must be provided. The student should attend as many percussion-ensemble concerts and solo percussion recitals as possible, since it is essential to be able to visualize clearly the way percussion instruments can be arranged on a stage and the ways a player must move to "cover" them all when performing.

If the instruments used are few and small, they are placed in a group directly in front of the player; larger arrays are spread out into a semicircle; in extreme cases, the instruments may be arranged in a circle, completely surrounding the player. Mallet instruments, drums, and other instruments with horizontal striking surfaces are wherever possible placed at a level a little below the player's waist. To this end they are attached to adjustable stands or laid on special racks or small towel-covered tables.* Also laid on towel-covered tables, and at this same level, are the "hand instruments"—such as claves or flexatone—which must be picked up and held in order to be played, and any mallets the player will need. Instruments such as gong, chimes, and triangle, which present vertically aligned playing surfaces and are typically suspended from above, are placed at about chest level and generally behind the horizontal instruments (i.e., further from the player). Chimes are suspended from a built-in rack, and special stands are made for gongs and tam-tams, but most of the "vertical" instruments must be suspended from music stands, microphone booms, or coat racks. It is perhaps un-

* A few large instruments (e.g., timpani, vibraphone) have built-in stands of the proper height.

derstandable, in the light of all this, why the percussion section is sometimes referred to as "the kitchen." Indeed, there is a strong analogy between a kitchen and a percussion array, not only in that so many fascinatingly sonorous objects are to be found in the kitchen, but that in a well-designed kitchen the cook is surrounded by stove, sink, and cutting surfaces at waist level, with vertical cabinets and racks ranged above and behind them: in both cases a wide variety of objects large and small have been placed to facilitate the most typical motions of the human arms, hands, and upper body.

In large arrays it may be desirable or necessary to place the "horizontal" instruments in two rows, one behind the other; in this case the instruments further from the player will usually be placed on a slightly higher plane than the nearer ones. It is generally but not invariably desirable in such cases that instruments requiring precise, detailed motions (e.g., mallet instruments) be placed in front of those, such as large drums, that require less precision. Drums in the second row will often have their heads tilted toward the player, making them easier to reach. As a drastic expedient even mallet instruments can be tilted in this way, by mounting them on blocks. A large array can be compacted somewhat by allowing instruments to overlap, so that, for instance, the back half of a timpano may actually be placed *under* a table full of hand instruments, a windchime may be suspended directly over an unused half-octave at the top or bottom of a mallet instrument's range, or the unused bars may even be covered with a towel and used as a table.

It is usual to place sets of identical instruments (e.g., a set of four timpani or of five temple blocks) in a row, with the highest instrument to the player's right—like the notes on a piano keyboard. Such an arrangement is not essential, but it is standard and should be used unless overriding musical considerations favor some other arrangement. It may be desirable to place the instruments in two staggered rows, thus, in order to save space:

Because the player must move about a great deal, percussion instruments are normally played standing. The major exception to this is the **traps**, or jazz drum set, a "prefab" percussion set designed to be played sitting down. The exact makeup of a set of traps is variable, but it will always contain a snare drum, a small double-headed drum, a large tomtom (which may be single- or double-headed), a small, pedal-operated bass drum, at least two suspended cymbals, and a hi-hat (Fig. 70). Note that the suspended cymbals and the smaller drums are all tilted toward the player and that the set-up consists essentially of a row of drums (the highest is on the left, reversing the usual pattern), behind which is a row of cymbals. The small double-headed drum is usually attached to the shell of the bass drum, and there is room there to attach another instrument as well—a cencerro, a woodblock, or another drum or cymbal. The whole system can be further expanded by the addition of, for instance, another bass drum to the left of the original bass drum; two more instruments may in turn be attached to the shell of this drum. In some rock groups the set of traps rivals the most complex "classical" arrays, with tam-tams above and behind the cymbals and a table for hand instruments to one side behind the player—all to be played sitting down!

MOVEMENT OF THE PLAYERS

The position of a traps player in an ensemble is fixed and straightforward, but the motions the music requires of standing players must constantly be kept in mind. The percussionist(s)

FIGURE 70. *A set of traps.*

must be able to make eye contact with the other players or conductor, if any, whenever necessary. Also, it is difficult to play delicately if violent motions of the body are required. An already difficult passage such as

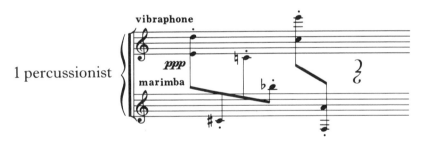

becomes almost impossible if the vibraphone and marimba have been placed at opposite sides of the array. For these reasons the composer must consider very carefully the layout of each percussion array and the positioning of each of these arrays on stage relative to other performers.

There is a strong theatrical component to percussion playing which the composer can ignore only at peril. Any percussion part requiring extensive motion of the player's upper body will take on a dance-like aspect; a player surrounded by a dense, tall array may give the impression of being caged by the instruments or of having erected a protective wall around him/herself; players whose adjoining arrays share an instrument are associated psychologically as strongly as though they were holding hands or tied together with a rope, and if they play that instrument simultaneously, facing each other across its surface, an intense sense of cooperative or competitive endeavor is generated. Most theatrical of all are situations in which a player is required to walk from one array to another or in which instruments must be moved about—pieces calling for a great deal of such movement can become veritable percussion ballets. The dramatic force of all these gestures and situations will be equal to or even greater than that of the musical ideas that necessitate them. If the composer has not calculated the effect of all such procedures theatrically as well as musically, the theater will seem unmotivated, distracting from the music and impeding its flow. This applies even to motions that take place between movements: if a change from one set-up to another is required, the time necessary for the change (up to ten minutes, in extreme cases) must be taken into account, and if the change with all its hectic activity can be woven into the fabric of the piece, so much the better.

Although it is as hard to play percussion well as it is to play any other instrument, the basic technique of striking or shaking is relatively simple, so non-percussionists may be asked to play one or two percussion instruments as well as their own. Parts for such "amateurs" should not include mallet instruments or chimes, nor call for rolls, rapid passagework, or fast changes of mallets. Again, the use of percussion in non-percussion parts is unavoidably theatrical.

NOTATION

The notation of percussion parts has for some time been in a state of flux. In this period of great notational freedom one can of course use any system so long as it makes sense, but it is best to regard the system given here as standard and to depart from it only where necessary for musical or other esthetic reasons. This system constitutes the best and most common modern practice, designed to be easily readable, readily understood, internally consistent, and adaptable to almost any musical context.

UNPITCHED NOTATION

Let us consider first the simple case of a single percussion instrument to which no specific pitch has been assigned. The part for such an instrument is normally written as a rhythm on a single line, thus:

If the instrument is one with a quick decay (e.g., maraca or bongo) no note value greater than the quarter-note should be written—slow rhythms should be notated with alternating notes and rests, as with the last two notes of the above example. On the other hand, note values below the quarter-note should be written so as to be easily read even if they exceed the actual length of the sound. If the example given here were to be played on the claves, for instance, the actual sound would be something like

but the less exact notation is much easier to read. Instruments with longer decays (e.g., cymbals) should be given exactly the desired note values, as with sustaining instruments. If it is desired that a note die away naturally during a rest or while other notes are being played, an

open tie (♩⌣) should be appended to it, with the indication "l.v." (for "let vibrate") below the first of any group of such notes. It may occasionally be necessary to put a cautionary "non l.v." in places where this effect might be expected but is not desired.

Virtually all percussion instruments make use of unmeasured rapid repetition of a note to create the illusion of a continuous, sustained sound. This *roll* or *tremolo* effect is notated with three strokes through the note stem (♩), just like the fluttertongue of winds or the tremolo of strings. The notation "*tr*⌇⌇⌇" formerly used for this effect should be reserved for true trills, as in the following example:

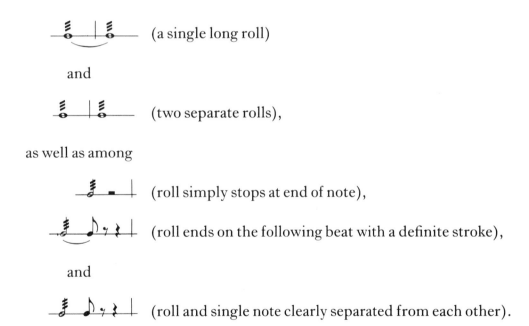

The articulation of rolls must be clearly marked, and distinctions drawn between

(a single long roll)

and

(two separate rolls),

as well as among

(roll simply stops at end of note),

(roll ends on the following beat with a definite stroke),

and

(roll and single note clearly separated from each other).

Dynamics and accents can be used to articulate *within* a tied roll, thus:

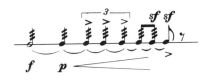

PITCHED NOTATION

So far we have been speaking of a single, unpitched percussion instrument, but suppose a definite pitch is wanted? In this case instead of a single line a regular five-line staff with appropriate clef should be used. The one exception to this is the very simple case of an instrument that plays only one pitch throughout a piece; in this case the pitch may be indicated in the prefatory remarks (or on a tiny staff at the beginning of each line of score), the part itself notated on a single line as if it were unpitched. When more than one pitch is required, a staff must be used. A single staff is used not only for those few percussion instruments that can individually play a wide range of pitches, but for those, such as timpani or bells, that are used in sets; in the timpani example given above, for instance, a single staff is used even though three drums are needed to play the passage. This is the usual way of writing for such instruments, but if the three timpani were located at widely separated locations within the array and served differing musical purposes, then three staves would be necessary. On the other hand, any set of pitched percussion instruments grouped together to provide one note each of a scale from which a single melodic line is to be fashioned may be notated on a single staff,* no matter how heterogeneous the combination. Several of Harry Partch's unique percussion instruments (otherwise outside the scope of this book) display such heterogeneity in their construction.

GROUPED INSTRUMENTS

Homogeneous groups of indefinitely pitched instruments are also notated on staff-like sets of lines, one line for each instrument, arranged from highest (top line) to lowest (bottom line). By way of illustration, if in the timpani example cited above no specific pitches were to be assigned, the passage would be notated thus:

For groups of five or fewer instruments, each instrument should be notated on a separate line, the spaces between the lines not being used. A group of six should be notated on the spaces (not the lines) of a five-line staff, ![staff example], and groups of more than six need both the

---

* Two staves (treble and bass) may be necessary if an extraordinarily wide pitch range is to be covered.

FIGURE 71. *Example of percussion notation.*

lines and spaces of the staff. Ledger-lines should not be used, nor, usually, should staves of more than five lines; in the rare event that a continuum of more than eleven (!) like instruments is required, two five-line staves will be needed, braced together like a piano part. Staves and staff-like configurations of this sort should be used only for unmixed sets of identical instruments graded in pitch.

COMPLETE ARRAYS

Figure 71 shows a sample of notation for a complete percussion array (one player). Note that though the various single lines, staves, and grouped lines are all distinctly separated, the line of music written across them is clearly a single line for a single player. There are no rests on the cymbal line, for instance, because all the cymbal notes are clearly assigned to an overall rhythmic pattern distributed among all the instruments. The meter signatures sprawl across the whole system so that the player will be sure to notice them; dynamic marks are placed directly under the first note they affect; the large quarter-rest in the $\frac{5}{4}$ bar is designed to lead the eye unambiguously from the temple blocks up to the cymbal. The vibraphone has its own notes and rest in this bar for as long as it remains contrapuntally independent of the main line of music, but at the earliest convenient point (third beat) it is notationally reintegrated into the overall rhythmic pattern. The names of all the instruments should be given at the left of each line of percussion score, as here, and the whole part should be braced together at the left.

The positions of the instruments in the score should in general correspond to their positions in the array, with instruments on the player's right appearing at the top of the score and those on the left on the bottom. In the example in Figure 71, for instance, the smallest timpano would probably be directly in front of the player; the other timpani would curve off to the left, with the bass drum at the end. To the player's right would be the tomtoms, and to the right of the tomtoms would be the vibraphone. The tam-tam would be placed behind the timpani, the temple blocks behind the tomtoms, and the cymbal behind the vibraphone. Of course, whatever page order is chosen for the instruments must be adhered to throughout the piece.

There are ways to streamline the rather bulky systems needed for large percussion arrays. First of all, when an instrument is to be silent for several pages of score, its line(s) may be omitted from those pages. Ideally, a blank space should be left to indicate the omission, but this is not absolutely necessary. Suppose in Figure 71 the temple blocks were to fall silent, with their lines omitted and the gap between tomtoms and vibraphone closed: it would be desirable, to avoid confusion, to put a cautionary "(toms)" immediately before the next tomtom note, making it clear that it was not they but the temple blocks that had been omitted. When the temple blocks reenter, an abbreviation such as "tpbl." should be put before their first note.

It is possible to write for two or more different instruments on a single line, if the instruments are used only a few times in the course of a piece and never play simultaneously. Hand instruments in particular can often be notated in this fashion, since many of them must be played with both hands and cannot be played simultaneously with any other instrument; parts for (say) vibraslap, ratchet, and tambourine could all be written together on a single line because of the near-impossibility of more than one of these instruments being played at a time.* If this type of notation is used, the name of the instrument to be played must be given at the beginning of each musical passage on the line.

MULTIPLE PARTS

In pieces with more than one percussion part, the systems for the different players are placed one above another in the score and labeled "perc. I," "perc. II," etc., the brace at the left of each part serving to identify which instruments belong to which player. Note that the positioning of the instruments on the page is entirely a function of who is playing them: if there are four players, each with (among other things) one cymbal, the four cymbals will not be grouped together on the page but will be more or less widely separated, depending on their positions within the players' arrays. If two players share an instrument, that instrument must appear twice in the score.

MALLETS

Percussion instruments are played with a great variety of *mallets* or *sticks* (the two terms are virtually interchangeable). The various types were originally developed for use with certain specific instruments, but the association of mallet-to-instrument is now in most cases tenuous at best, and each instrument can be played with any of a number of different mallets.

The tone quality elicited by a given mallet is almost entirely determined by the size, weight, and hardness of its *head* (the end that strikes the instrument), though one normally speaks of "hard sticks," "light sticks," etc. Generally speaking, small sticks elicit higher frequencies than large ones, as do hard sticks compared to soft ones; hard sticks also produce more attack noise than do soft sticks. Heavy sticks produce louder sounds than light sticks. For ordinary purposes the composer will only need to designate three types of stick: hard, medium, and soft, or heavy, medium, and light. The sticks chosen by the percussionist to fit these categories will depend upon the instrument(s) used and the musical context.

* Under certain circumstances these and other band instruments *can* be played simultaneously (see discussion in chapters VI and VII).

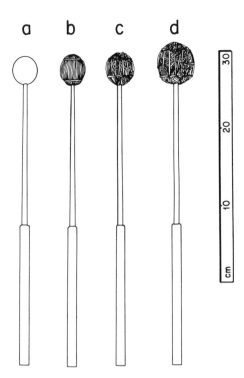

FIGURE 72. *"Rubber series" mallets: (a) unwound rubber mallet; (b) hard wound mallet; (c) medium wound mallet; (d) soft wound mallet.*

RUBBER SERIES MALLETS

It is somewhat annoying that there is no generally accepted term for the most widely used of all percussion mallets, the rubber-headed sticks generally used to play virtually all high and medium-pitched percussion, particularly idiophones. I will use the term "rubber series" to denote these mallets as a group. The heads of these mallets are small rubber balls, ranging from extremely hard to so soft they can be squeezed with the fingers (Fig. 72a). An almost unbroken continuum of these sticks exists between the hardest and softest varieties (one maker, for instance, offers twelve different hardnesses), and there is a parallel series of mallets the heads of which are tightly wrapped in yarn. The yarn of these **wound mallets** (Fig. 72b, c, d) is of a thicker gauge on soft mallets than on hard ones, so the wrapping and the core vary together in hardness. Wound mallets give a gentler attack than the unwound ones and are slightly larger and effectively softer than unwound mallets of equivalent hardness. For an instrument that makes everyday use of these sticks (see the vital-statistics charts in the next two chapters), the indications "soft sticks," "medium sticks," and "hard sticks" are sufficient to denote mallets within the range of winding and hardness normally used with that instrument. To call for an unusually hard or soft mallet or to demand the use of any of these mallets on an instrument with which they are not normally associated it is necessary to fall back on a rather vague terminology derived from the mallet instruments with which the rubber-series mallets were originally exclusively associated. Figure 73 shows how various degrees of hardness can be designated in wound or unwound mallets. The "bell mallet," by the way, is not a mallet for bells but for the "orchestra bells"—i.e., the glockenspiel.

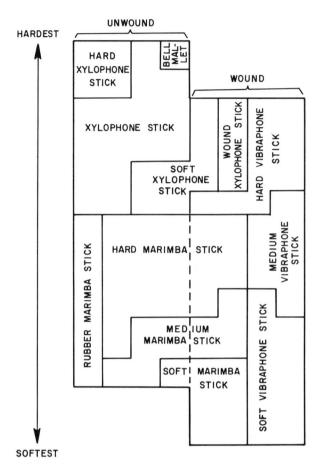

FIGURE 73. *"Objective" names of rubber-series mallets.*
Each block covers the range of sticks, wound and/or unwound, denoted by the term written inside it.

Harder than any of these are **plastic sticks**, which are identical to hard xylophone sticks in weight and appearance but have heads made of phenolic or acrylic plastic rather than hard rubber. Their normal use is in production of harsh, clangorous sounds of almost unbelievable loudness from small or medium-sized metal idiophones, though they can of course elicit soft sounds as well.

FELT STICKS

The sticks used most frequently for large, low-pitched percussion have heads made of felt that are larger, heavier, and softer than the rubber-series mallets; the hardest of these **felt sticks** are a little harder than the softest marimba sticks. Most important among the felt sticks are the **timpani sticks**, available in a continuum of hardnesses out of which the composer need only distinguish hard, medium, and soft (Fig. 74a–c). Softer, larger, and heavier than any timpani stick is the **bass drum beater**, which comes in "heavy" and "light" varieties; many, as in our illustration, have a heavy and a light head at the two ends of a single stick. Most ponderous of all is the **gong beater**, normally used only for large gongs, tam-

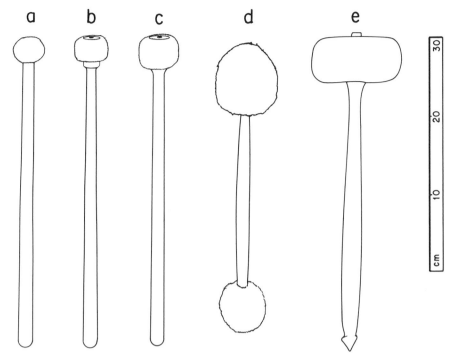

FIGURE 74. *Felt sticks: (a) hard timpani stick; (b) medium timpani stick; (c) soft timpani stick; (d) bass drum beater; (e) gong beater.*

tams, and thundersheets. The important thing about a gong beater is not its softness (some are as hard as a medium timpani stick) but its size and weight.

WOOD AND METAL STICKS

There are rather sketchy wood and metal series of sticks, as well as a few specialized mallets that defy classification. The most common wood stick is the **snare stick** used, as its name implies, mostly with the snare drum. This stick tapers to a very small, light tip which may be carved out of the wood of the shaft or jacketed with plastic. One can distinguish light and heavy snare sticks, but the best way to get a distinctly heavier sound is by using the back end of the shaft, which is considerably thicker and heavier than the tip. The reverse of a timpani stick is of similar weight and in many instances is designed specifically for use as a wooden stick of medium weight. The instruction for reversing these or any other sticks is simply "back of snare [or whatever] sticks." Heavier even than reversed snare or timpani sticks is the **wooden timpani stick,** used on the timpani and other large drums to get a particularly brilliant "drummy" quality. The heaviest "wood" stick is the **chime mallet,** still associated almost exclusively with the chimes; it is actually a small hammer with a cylindrical head made of a rolled-up strip of rawhide, which is more durable than wood and has virtually the same weight and hardness. For "wood" sticks even lighter than snare sticks one may turn to the rattan or plastic backs of any of the rubber-series mallets, which are very light and thin. These produce a sound that is mostly attack noise.

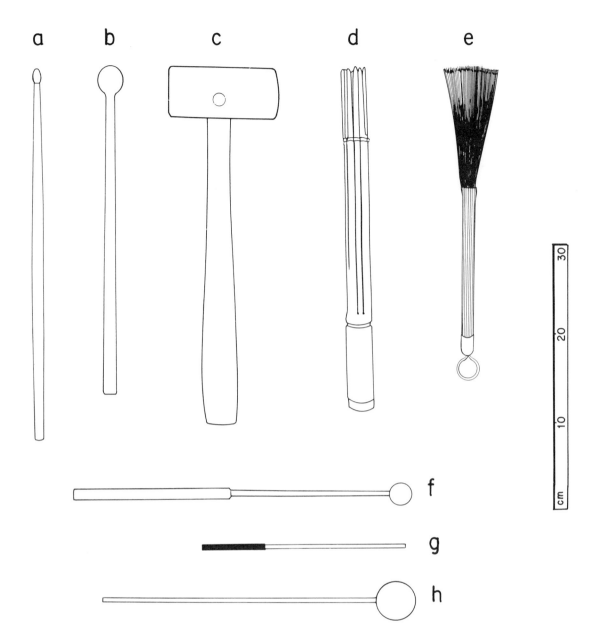

FIGURE 75. *Miscellaneous sticks and mallets: (a) snare stick; (b) wooden timpani stick; (c) chime mallet; (d) switch; (e) wire brush; (f) metal glockenspiel stick; (g) triangle beater; (h) superball stick.*

The hardest sticks of all are those with metal heads. Chief among these are **metal glockenspiel sticks**, the heads of which are tiny balls of spun brass weighing about as much as a rubber-series mallet. These metal sticks give a very light, precise, pinging sound to glass or metal idiophones; they are destructive to drums and wooden instruments unless used very gently. For a very light metal stick actual **knitting needles** made of hollow aluminum have occasionally been used. These produce a sound that is almost all attack noise but somewhat louder and more metallic than that of the reversed rubber-series mallets.

The use of anything heavier than metal glockenspiel sticks is primarily a theatrical gesture. There are the ordinary **nail hammer** and the somewhat smaller **geologist's hammer**, neither of which can be safely used with full force on any but the most simple and rugged of homemade idiophones, and finally the **sledge hammer** (as in, e.g., Berg's *Three Pieces for Orchestra*) which can only be withstood by a massive, flat block of wood or metal and which always makes the percussionist look a bit like a berserker. Since percussion instruments are as a rule both delicate and expensive, none of these hammers should be employed indiscriminately. A specialized metal stick of light weight is the **triangle beater** (Fig. 75g), a simple, headless* metal rod designed to strike from the side rather than the tip. One end of the beater is frequently rubber-jacketed, giving a very weak, muffled sound.

SPECIALIZED STICKS

For very light, swooshing sounds two kinds of **brushes** are available. The older, and now less common, variety is the **switch**, originally—and often still—a bundle of ordinary twigs tied together at one end; for heavy-duty work, switches are made in the form of a wooden cylinder cut lengthwise into strips. Much more common than the switch, and derived from it historically, is the **wire brush**, a fan of thin metal wires. It is incapable of producing sounds louder than *forte*, but can create nuances of great subtlety and delicacy. The switch is a much coarser device than the wire brush, eliciting louder (up to *ff*) and deeper pitches from objects it strikes and containing so much attack noise that it can be used by itself as a hand instrument, producing a soft, dry clatter like a clutched windchime. Both switch and wire brush can be used to produce a continuous, whispery sound from an instrument by rubbing rather than

striking. The notation for this is not quite standardized, but $\overset{\sim\sim}{\rule{0pt}{0pt}}\!\!\int$ is fairly unambiguous. The

notation $\overset{\text{\tiny /}}{\rule{0pt}{0pt}}\!\!\int$ with brushes indicates, as with other sticks, a rapidly repeated striking motion,

and $\overset{tr\sim}{\rule{0pt}{0pt}}\!\!\int$ should be used *only* for true trills. It is occasionally required that mallets of other sorts (especially metal ones) be rubbed across an instrument in this fashion; the notation is the same.

One stick, the **superball stick**, is specifically designed for rubbing rather than striking. Superballs are highly conservative of kinetic energy: when one of them strikes an object, it bounces back with some 90 percent of the speed and power with which it hit. If a hole is drilled into a superball and an ordinary rattan mallet-shaft is stuck into the hole, a mallet is created that will hum when rubbed against various objects. The friction involved in rubbing causes the head of the stick (the superball) to move in minute jerks rather than smoothly; the elasticity of the ball converts this jerking into a regular vibration—i.e., a very rapid bouncing motion. The reader may be familiar with such similar phenomena as the thumb roll of the tambourine or the sound produced by rubbing a wet finger around the rim of a wine glass, but because of its astonishing bounciness a superball stick will hum when rubbed against *anything*—not only drum heads and tam-tams but walls, floors, windowpanes, the bars, sides, and resonators of mallet instruments, any conceivable part of a piano or contrabass, the sole of a shoe. All that is required is that the surface offer some resistance to the ball, for the stick must be pressed down rather firmly to elicit the hum. The ball is so massive and so

* The heaviest triangle beaters are curved into a loop at one end, forming a head of sorts.

elastic that the pitch of the hum (actually a groaning sound very similar to a string drum in timbre) has nothing at all to do with the pitch of the object being rubbed but is simply a function of the pressure and speed with which the ball is rubbed and of the smoothness of the surface against which it is rubbed. The loudness of the sound is also dependent on these factors, ranging between *pp* and *ff*. Of course, if a superball stick is rubbed against an instrument or other naturally vibratory object, the object will be set into vibration by the stick, *at its own frequency and timbre*. Superball sticks cannot be used (except as a theatrical gesture) to strike an instrument; the weight (as heavy as a bass drum beater) and elasticity of the head would cause the stick to bounce repeatedly on every stroke or to fly out of the player's hand.

Another "rubbing" sound is that produced by **bowing**. The contrabass bow employed for this purpose can be used on any idiophone that presents a distinct edge to be bowed—most notably cymbals, gongs, and tam-tams. The sounds produced, which vary considerably, are discussed in Chapter VII, under the headings of the individual instruments. It is recommended that the notation ♩ be used for bowing so that it is possible to differentiate among such effects as:

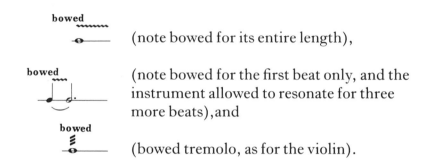

(note bowed for its entire length),

(note bowed for the first beat only, and the instrument allowed to resonate for three more beats), and

(bowed tremolo, as for the violin).

These notations must be accompanied, as above, by the word "bowed" placed immediately before the bowed passage. It may on occasion be desired to indicate downbow ⊓ and upbow ∨ (see Chapter IX).

SPECIAL EFFECTS

Some of the hand instruments can be used as mallets to strike other instruments; maracas and claves are the most useful in this respect. Intriguing and somewhat indeterminate sounds can be produced by dropping or throwing small objects (coins, marbles, dried beans, dice, gravel, BB shot) onto an instrument from above. If they are dropped from high up, or are poured in quantity from a container, they will of course remain underfoot until the end of the piece—unless the clean-up process is made part of the music!

Many subtle and delicate effects can be drawn from most percussion instruments by playing them directly with the hands and fingers. This **finger-style playing** is most useful on rimless, small-headed drums (congas, bongos, dumbegs, etc.), but is of occasional value elsewhere. Most idiophones can be played this way only *mezzo-piano* or softer. The different strokes possible in finger-style playing are produced by (1) the tips of the fingers; (2) the flat of the fingers and side of the thumb; (3) the flat of the hand; (4) the heel of the hand; and (5) the fist. The fist is useful only for getting the loudest possible "hand" sound out of large drums and tam-tams; the various other strokes are covered in the next chapter as part of the discussion of bongos. A special technique is the **thumb roll**, executed by pushing the tip of the thumb across the surface of the instrument. The thumb will vibrate at a very low frequency (the vibration is produced by friction, as with the superball stick) which is not itself heard but which creates a very rapid, steady "roll" sound on the instrument. This effect can be continued indefinitely on loose-tensioned drums—most notably the tambourine, on which the thumb roll is a basic performance technique—but on other instruments it is a very transient phenomenon, more a special kind of attack than anything else. Thumb rolls should

be notated like other "rubbing" effects (♩), with the indication "thumb," "thumb roll," or " ♀ " to be added when necessary as a reminder.

THE INSTRUMENTS

The expansion of the percussion section to its present size and diversity took place so recently that many of the instruments are not yet even approximately standardized. Also, a surprising number of the instruments are not manufactured as such but must be obtained from a variety of unlikely sources or even built from scratch by the percussionist. These uncertainties are reflected in the vital-statistics charts given in the next two chapters.

Most percussion instruments give out only a single pitch; for such instruments the pitch range given is the composite range covered by *all* available instruments of that type. Obviously the upper and lower limits of that range will be quite vague, as will the distinction between "normal" and "extension" tones: it is a matter of the statistical likelihood of finding an instrument of a given type built at a given pitch. Many idiophones are built with no thought of pitch in mind at all, so the distribution is truly random.

Synonyms are listed where necessary, and the more important minor variant instruments are discussed in the text. The nature and origin of each instrument are given in its chart as its **status**, which may fall into one or more of six categories: (1) **standard** instruments built by instrument manufacturers (example: vibraphone); (2) **exotic** instruments, which must be imported from a folk or non-Western music culture (example: tabla); (3) **novelty** instruments built and sold for educational or amusement purposes or as sonorous *objets d'art* (example: shell windchime); (4) **homemade** instruments the percussionist or composer must build from scratch (example: thundersheet); (5) **noisemakers** designed as signaling or warning devices (example: referee's whistle); and (6) **found objects** from kitchen or junkyard (example: brake drums). The "availability" of instruments in the last three of these categories is given only as an indication of how many percussionists *already have these instruments on hand*. For instance, if an instrument is listed as "homemade" and "very rare," this indicates that it will almost certainly be necessary to have one specially built to play any part written for it.

The pieces listed below are meant to serve as musical examples for chapters V through VII of this book. For each piece the number of percussionists involved is given, followed by a list of all the percussion instruments used, including those played by non-percussionists, in the order in which they are discussed here. Infrequently occurring instruments are cited in **bold-face type** so that examples of their use may easily be tracked down. The names of all instruments are given exactly as they appear in the score (translated into English where necessary); when a different name is used in this book, the synonymy is indicated with an equals sign (=). Minor variants of instruments discussed here are designated with the sign of equivalence (≈), and the few instruments not covered here at all are analogized to instruments of similar timbre with the approximation sign (~).*

Milhaud, *L'Homme et son désir*
  (19 players)

    snare drum
    tambourin provençal≈**long drum**
    small double-headed drum
    tenor drum
    bass drums
    tambourine
    sleighbells
    wood castanets
    metal castanets
    slapstick
    triangle
    hammer, with board = **wood slab**
    suspended cymbal
    crash cymbals
    tam-tam
    mouth siren
    wind machine
    whistle

Varèse, *Ionisation* (13 players)

    tarole≈high snare drum
    snare drums
    tambour militaire≈field drum
    side drum = tenor drum
    bass drums
    tambourine
    bongos

    string drum
    maracas
    sleighbells
    güiros
    castanets
    slapsticks
    triangles
    claves
    anvils
    Chinese blocks = woodblocks
    muted cencerros
    suspended cymbal
    crash cymbal = **large Chinese cymbal**
    crash cymbals
    tam-tams
    gong
    chimes
    sirens

Chavez, *Sinfonia India* (5 players)

    timpani
    snare drum
    tenor drum = field drum, or **water gourd**
    bass drum, or tlapanhuehuetl≈very large Indian drum
    Indian drum
    maraca, or clay rattle
    metal rattle

* Such instruments are of limited musical usefulness and are introduced by composers largely as a theatrical gesture.

soft rattle, or tenabari = string rattle made of butterfly cocoons
rattling string = **wooden string rattle**, or grijutian = string rattle made of deer hooves
güiro
rasping stick = wooden rasp
claves
suspended cymbal
xylophone, or teponaxtles≈slit drums

Roldán, *Ritmicas V, VI* (11 players)

timbales de orquesta = timpani
timbales cubanos = **timbales**
bombo = bass drum
bongos
maracas
quijada
güiro
claves
cencerros
marimbula

Harrison, *Canticle No. 1* (5 players)

drums = tomtoms or double-headed drums
tambourine
sistrum
gourd rattle≈maraca
wood rattle
windbell≈glass windchime
morache≈wooden rasp
triangle
woodblocks
dragon's mouths = temple blocks or mokugyos
high bells
bell
large glass bells
clay bells
cowbells = cencerros or almglocken
thundersheet
suspended cymbal
tam-tam
gongs
brake drum

Cage, *Amores* (3 players)

tomtoms = **Indian drums**
pod rattle = **Mexican bean**
wood blocks (not Chinese) = **softwood planks**

Cage and Harrison, *Double Music* (4 players)

sistra
water buffalo bells≈small bells
sleigh bells≈small bells
Japanese temple gongs
cowbells = cencerros or almglocken
thundersheet
large tam-tams
muted gongs
water gong
brake drums

Messiaen, *Chronochromie* (5 players)

suspended cymbal
Chinese cymbal
tam-tam
gongs
chimes
xylophone
marimba

Boulez, *Le Marteau sans maître* (3 players)

frame drum
bongos
cymbalettes≈**jingles**
maracas
claves
cloche double = **agogo bells**
very large suspended cymbal
tam-tams
gong
xylorimba≈xylophone
vibraphone

Berio, *Circles* (2 players)

timpani
tablas≈**small kettle drums**
tomtoms

snare drum
bass drum
tamburo basco = tambourine
bongos
congas
Mexican bean
maracas
wood windchime
glass windchime
sandblocks
güiro
triangles
claves
clapped hands
woodblocks
log drum = slit drum
temple blocks
cencerros
lujon
suspended cymbals
sizzle cymbal
clap cymbals = crash cymbals
finger cymbals
hi-hat
tam-tams
gongs
suspended chimes = chimes
xylophone
marimbaphone = marimba
glockenspiel
vibraphone

Henze, *El Cimarrón* (1 player)

tomtoms
small drum = snare drum
gran cassa = bass drum
bongos
conga
bamboo drums = **boobams**
maracas
chain
bundle of hanging bamboo
    sticks ≈ wood windchime
glass chimes = glass windchime
shell chimes = **shell windchime**
matraca ≈ ratchet

güiro
claves
body percussion
wooden plank = **wooden slab**
metal sheet = **metal slab**
Trinidad gong drum = **steel drum**
    (ping pong pan)
log drums = slit drums
temple bells = Japanese temple gongs
cowbells = almglocken
marimbula
thundersheets
suspended cymbals
tam-tams
crotales
marimba
vibraphone
bird whistle ≈ crow

Xenakis, *Persephassa* (6 players)

timpani or timbales
tomtoms
snare drums
bass drums
bongos
congas
maracas
wooden simantras ≈ **wood rods**
metal simantras ≈ **metal rods**
stones
woodblocks
affolants = small aluminum-foil
    thundersheets
suspended cymbals
tam-tams
gongs
mouth sirens

Crumb, *Music for a Summer Evening*
    (2 players)

tomtoms
bongos
sistrum
maracas
sleighbells
bamboo windchime

glass windchime
quijada
güiro
bell tree
triangles
claves
Tibetan prayer stones≈**stones**
woodblocks
African log drum≈slit drum
temple blocks
Japanese temple bells≈bells
African thumb piano = **kalimba**
thundersheet
suspended cymbal
sizzle cymbal
tam-tams
crotales
tubular bells = chimes
xylophone
glockenspiel
vibraphone
slide whistles

Maxwell Davies, *Eight Songs for a Mad King* (1 player)

tomtom
side drum = snare drum
bass drums
rototoms
tambourine
jingles (= individual sleigh-type pellet-bells) and other small bells
chains
windchimes
football rattle = ratchet

washboard
steel bars = **anvils**
woodblocks
temple blocks
suspended cymbals
foot cymbals = hi-hat
tam-tam
crotales
xylophone
glockenspiel
railway whistle = referee's whistle
bird calls (various)
crow
squeak

Kagel, *Match für drei Spieler* (1 player)

snare drum
bass drum
Chinese paper drum~small Indian drum
Waldteufel≈very small string drum
sistrum
leather and metal dice cups, with dice (~rattles)
sleighbells
ratchets
metal castanets
handbells≈bells
wind-up bell≈electric bell
flexatone
suspended cymbals
sizzle cymbal
crash cymbals
marimba
referee's whistles

VI

THE

PERCUSSION:

DRUMS

The head of a drum is held in place by a hoop that presses it down tightly against the upper rim of the shell. In some drums this hoop forms a raised wooden or metal rim, while in others the hoop lies at or below the level of the head. The distinction is important because it is only on "rimless" drums that the most subtle techniques of finger-style playing (described below in the section on bongos) are possible, while on drums with raised rims there are a number of special "on the rim" playing techniques (discussed in the section on tomtoms).

The hoop is attached to the shell by a number of tension screws or turnbuckles, by means of which the tension on the head is adjusted. The tension must be adjusted evenly all around in order to get a good sound. This process of adjustment is delicate and time-consuming; it is therefore inadvisable to require a drum to change pitch during the course of a performance. Two important exceptions, the timpani and the rototoms, have mechanisms for rapid and accurate alteration of pitch. The upper limit of tension for any drum is the point beyond which there is danger of splitting the head. The lower limit is more vague: below the ordinary level of tension is a rather restricted zone in which the tone becomes tubby, the pitch vague and "scooping" on the attacks, and the dynamic range restricted. Below that, the head ceases to act like a membrane and becomes a sort of parchment thundersheet, producing a sound very much like that made by holding up a piece of paper and tapping it in the middle—but much louder (pp—ff). This interesting sound has been little exploited, if at all.

Drums are normally struck at a point about halfway between the edge and the center of the head. Playing nearer the edge produces a very "brittle" sound full of high partials, while playing exactly in the center produces a rather dull, unresonant thud with prominent fundamental—since most drum shells are much too small to reinforce the fundamental properly, a center stroke will seem less strongly pitched than either a normal or edge stroke. It is important to realize that a change in striking position does not affect the *pitch* of the sound but only its tone color.

The various striking positions are indicated simply by writing "edge" or "center" above the line at the beginning of the affected passage; normal playing position is denoted with the all-purpose abbreviation "nat." or "ord." Where note-to-note changes are required the letters "C," "E," and "N" can be placed above the individual notes, but this practice must be explained to the player in the prefatory material. The word "rim" should not be used, since this indicates that the hoop rather than the head is to be struck. A useful special effect (particularly in rolls) is to move gradually from edge to center or vice versa.

Drums of all sorts except the specialized string-drum and tambourine can be easily and quickly muted or *muffled* with a surprisingly small piece of shammy or a somewhat larger piece of cloth. Either of these can be kept at hand, or even tied to the drum, so that it can be muted or unmuted in a tiny fraction of a second. The effect of muffling is to darken the tone, deaden the attack, and reduce the sense of pitch. Muting is indicated by the expression "muted," "muffled," or "con sord." written above the line, and is canceled with "mute off," "senza sord.," or "nat."

A more extreme kind of muffling can be obtained by damping with one hand while the sound is produced by a stick held in the other. This is most useful as a means of muting individual notes in an otherwise unmuted passage, and in such contexts should be notated as an x above the note, thus: ♩ . It must be remembered that when using hand-muffling the performer must play one-handed, though a stick can be held in the muting hand, ready to use immediately upon returning to normal play.

Hand-damping *after* a note has been played is an integral part of drum technique; it is used to cut off short notes before rests as well as staccato notes, etc. It normally needs no special notation beyond the usual signs of articulation.

Another form of muffling involves holding the stick firmly against the drumhead when playing, rather than letting it rebound. Notes played in this way have a "choked" or "dead" quality. This effect should be notated as an x through the note stem, thus: ♩ . Neither this nor the notation for hand-muffling is entirely standardized, so some explanation should be given when they are used. The advantage of stick-damping over hand-damping is that both hands are free to play, but stick-damped notes can be played no faster than eighth notes at ♩ = 72.

KETTLE DRUMS

TIMPANI

Generically, kettle drums are rimless, single-headed drums in which the shell is completely closed at the bottom. They have a clear, ringing tone and produce a very distinct pitch. The only drums of this type in general use are the **timpani**, large, low-pitched kettle drums whose range can be extended upward by the use of any of a variety of hard-to-find and imprecisely named smaller drums.

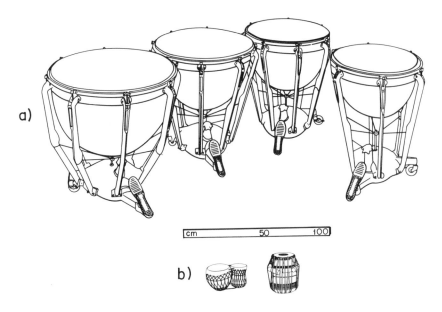

FIGURE 76. *Kettle drums: (a) timpani; (b) small kettle drums.*

Timpani (singular, *timpano*) are among the oldest and most respected of Western percussion instruments, and they remain among the most widely scored of all drums. In its usual form a timpano consists of a parabolic copper bowl (the shell, or **kettle**); sometimes with a small hole in the bottom; the head of the drum is stretched across the top of the kettle. The instrument is permanently attached to a stand (with wheels) that has a pivoting foot-pedal at its base. The pedal is used to adjust the pitch of the instrument by means of a system of rods running either inside the kettle or through the legs of the stand. As the toe-end of the pedal is depressed the pitch rises, and as the heel-end is depressed the pitch falls.* The range of pitches covered by the pedal is only about a fifth; the position of this fifth within the total range of notes available on timpani is determined by the size of the drum and the overall tension to which the head has been adjusted with the tensioning screws around the rim of the drum. Unusually large and small drums are needed for the extremes of the range, and notes below D_0, because they cannot be obtained at optimum tension levels, tend to be less distinct in pitch than the rest of the range. A variety of experimental timpani are now manufactured with a pitch range of a full octave for each drum—the smallest of them can also reach the otherwise unavailable high d^1. These drums have so far not proved very popular with percussionists because small gradations of pitch require great delicacy in adjusting the pedal.

Even on ordinary timpani the position of the pedal required for a given pitch depends on a number of factors, including the weather and how loudly the drum has been played for how long. Because of this uncertainty, the "feel" of the pedal is only an approximate guide to pitch. While a good timpanist can certainly bring the instrument roughly to pitch by feel alone, the intonation of the note will be much better if the player is given a few seconds to adjust the pitch aurally—by bending down to listen while tapping gently on the drum head—before being required to play it. The player does not need silence or even quiet in order to do

* On a few drums this pattern is reversed.

name of instrument	abbreviations	synonyms	range	normal sticks	status	availability
timpani	timp. 	kettledrums	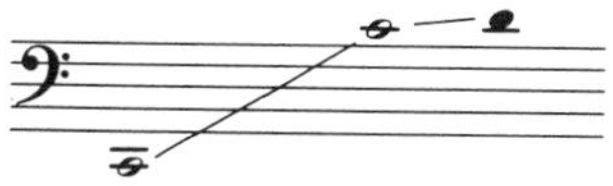 loudest: *fff* softest: *ppp*	timpani sticks (hard, medium, soft, wooden)	standard	common

FIGURE 77. *Timpani—vital statistics.*

this; a trained percussionist can if necessary tune a drum in the midst of an orchestral tutti. It should be clear from all this that the most idiomatic use of the pedal is not as a producer of melodies on a single drum but merely as a tuning device.

Performance Characteristics

Timpani are commonly played in groups of four, particularly when they constitute the player's entire array. The pitches of the four drums should be chosen so that changes in the pitch of any one drum are as few and small as possible. If a part seems to require many and/or exaggerated changes in the pitches of individual drums, it may work better if recast for five or even six drums. On the other hand, four drums should not be demanded for a part that could easily be played on three or fewer. The number of timpani required for the part should be indicated in the list of instruments at the beginning of the score, and it is useful also to give there the range of pitches to be required of each drum. The initial tunings of all the drums should be given at the beginning of their part (see Fig. 78).

In the normal course of events changes in pitch occur rather infrequently. Each change should be indicated in a box above the staff in this fashion: $\boxed{d^0 \rightarrow e\flat^0}$. The exact pitches should be given, not just the pitch class, for $\boxed{g \longrightarrow c}$ does not make it clear whether the pitch is to be raised or lowered. If several drums are to be changed during a single rest, the change-indications should be stacked vertically with that for the highest-pitched drum at the top, thus:

The instruction to change the pitch should be given at the earliest spot in the music at which the change could be made. Whenever possible, changes should take place during rests, but if necessary they can be done while other drums are being played, as in this passage:

FIGURE 78. *Notation used for frequent changes in the pitches of individual timpani.*

Where changes must be made frequently, each new note should be supplied with a Roman numeral to indicate on which drum it is to be played, "I" always indicating the lowest drum. (Figure 78 shows how this is done.) Neither notation is necessary in places where the changes are obvious, as here:

The passage above also shows the timpani glissando, which is notated like any other true glissando (see p. 31). The glissando is, of course, produced with the pedal, and it must be remembered that following the glissando the drum will be at a new pitch unless the pedal is returned to its original position. Upward glissandos are generally the most effective, because the volume of the sound will remain roughly the same, or even increase, throughout the glissando. This happens because tightening the head with the pedal adds to the system energy that acts to counterbalance the normal decay of the sound. In descending glissandos the loosening of the head *subtracts* energy from the system, causing the sound to decay rather precipitously. In glissando rolls the volume level remains constant unless there is a deliberate crescendo or diminuendo. Whenever a drum must change pitch without an intervening rest in that drum, there will be some portamento effect between the notes unless the first note is hand-damped or allowed to die away completely. The combination of hand-damping and retuning can be performed as rapidly as quarter-notes at ♩ = 72; if damping is not desired, the portamento should be notated in the part. The prominence of the portamento—and the consequent need for damping—is reduced if the pitch change is only a half-step or so.

It takes about three seconds for a timpani note to die away completely. Since the decay is initially very rapid, even moderately fast notes (up to, say, eighth-notes at ♩ = 144) can be played clearly without damping, particularly if hard sticks are used. However, at very high speeds the drum sounds will overlap and interfere with each other, the result being a loss in the distinctness of pitch, particularly when the drums are tuned at narrow intervals. A passage such as

will sound very muddy: the *rhythm* will be clear enough, but the pitch will just seem vaguely turbulent, without even a distinct contour. If the notes are more widely separated, like this:

the differences in pitch among the drums will be clear, but the pitches themselves will still be obscured, and the passage could just as well be played on four drums of indefinite pitch. Of course, none of this applies to repeated notes, and a passage such as

will sound perfectly clear.

When not in use, timpani tend to vibrate sympathetically when a neighboring drum is played; this vibration, though not distinctly audible, does somewhat obscure the pitch of the adjacent drum, and for this reason it is desirable to use as few timpani as possible for any given part.

Like most other percussion instruments, timpani are normally played "hand-to-hand," that is, with alternating strokes of the right and left hands, and in the normal course of play one hand crosses over the other from time to time. If the number of drums is small, these cross-overs, even at high speed, will present no problem to the player. However, with five or more drums it is necessary to avoid passages like the following, which would require one hand to reach far over the other:

In practice such awkward cross-overs are often avoided by the use of **double beats**, i.e., two strokes in a row with the same hand. The passage above, for instance, would probably be performed RLRRLR, making it *possible* to play but still rather awkward, since double beats are much easier to perform as repeated notes on one drum. The passage would present no problems at all if its third note were d⁰ instead of f⁰.

It is of course possible to play chords on the timpani simply by striking two drums at once. The chords will not sound very clear unless they consist of bare octaves or fifths; a good way to test in advance the sound of any timpani chord before committing it to paper is to play it on the piano an octave lower than written. For a ponderous and heavy sforzando it may be desired to have a single drum struck simultaneously with both sticks—this should be notated

with double stems, thus: ♪ . Finally, it is possible to play arpeggios and chords of up to four notes by playing with three or four sticks; this is done by holding two sticks between adjacent pairs of fingers. Such pairs of sticks can only be used on adjacent drums. Either of the two sticks can be kept out of the way simply by rotating the wrist.

A number of "advanced" techniques are contained in the following passage:

The first event here is a **double roll**, requiring pairs of sticks in each hand so that both notes will be hit on each stroke of the roll. The next note is also a double roll performed on two drums, initially tuned to the same pitch, that glissando outward while the roll is being played. Note that this maneuver leaves drum III (second from the right) *lower* in pitch than drum II (second from the left). There follow two notes played in the ordinary way, then a two-note chord that must be played with both hands since the drums producing it are not adjacent, then another ordinary note. Throughout these two beats the player must keep the wrists rotated so that only one stick in each hand will strike the drums. The next bar begins with an upward arpeggio requiring two left-hand sticks and one right-hand stick, followed by a downward arpeggio requiring two right-hand sticks and one left-hand stick. After that comes a simple trill played with single sticks from both hands (note that this is *not* the same as the double roll with which the passage began); and finally comes a four-note trill in which the left hand playing drums I and II alternates with the right hand playing drums III and IV. During this trill, drum III must glissando up to B_0, a unison with drum II.

This whole passage is much more exciting to look at than to hear—to get an idea of just how thick and dark it sounds in reality, try it on the piano, an octave down. Those who are interested in exploring further the limits of timpanic virtuosity should study Elliott Carter's *Eight Pieces for Four Timpani*.

Sticks

In the absence of any special indications as to choice of sticks, timpanists will use felt timpani sticks, their hardness depending on the timpanist's perception of the music. These felt sticks, plus the wooden timpani sticks, are normal for the timpani. For a very light, rattling sound, snare drum sticks or even the backs of vibraphone (or whatever) sticks may be used; the timpani cannot be played louder than *ff* with these sticks nor softer than *pp* with any wooden stick. It is also possible to use rubber-series mallets, not for any unique timbre but simply to enable the timpani to be played in conjunction with instruments for which felt sticks would be inappropriate. Again, these mallets are too light to drive the timpani any louder than *fortissimo*, and the unwound mallets (except for the very softest) cannot produce sounds below *pianissimo*. The large felt bass-drum and gong beaters will produce only a weak thud if applied to the timpani, and metal sticks are destructive to drum heads of all sorts. Wire brushes will make the drum speak (no louder than *forte*), but the characteristic slap or hiss of the brush is so much higher in pitch than the drum itself that the effect is of two different sounds. A switch will give a somewhat louder and more unified sound.

Because it has no rim, all the finger-style techniques discussed below under bongos are possible on timpani, but the size of the drum tends to make the various strokes all sound alike, and the width of the head means that either everything must be done very near the edge or the hand must be moved a considerable distance to differentiate between center and edge strokes. Only the most vigorous stroke with the flat of four fingers together can produce even an ordinary *fortissimo* from a system this large.

Special Effects

A rare and not particularly useful effect on timpani (mentioned here for the sake of completeness) is to strike the shell of the instrument, producing a vaguely metallic, not particularly resonant "bonk." The pitch of this sound varies little, if at all, from drum to drum and is not affected by moving the pedal.

Much more intriguing is the use of a timpano as an auxiliary resonator for other instruments. This can be done with any idiophone that has a slow decay and whose resonance is not damped by resting it on the head of the drum—most notably, single cymbals (removed from the stand and rested upside down on the timpano), crotales, and bowl- or cup-shaped bells. The idiophone can be played in the usual fashion and sounds quite normal unless one moves the pedal of the drum while a note is sounding, in which case the timbre of the idiophone will swoop and wobble in a decidedly eerie fashion as the timpano reinforces a chain of pitches running up or down its harmonic spectrum. It is best to use only one instrument on each drumhead, because playing will cause the idiophone to move around a bit and if there were several on one drum they would jostle each other. It is also advisable to avoid the loudest dynamic levels, since a good *fff* whack may knock the cymbal or bell right off the drum. Since the instruments involved are generally light in weight, it is possible to play the timpano on which one of them is resting; the drum will sound somewhat muffled, however, and if it is played louder than *mezzo-forte* the idiophone may bounce or fall off.

It is also possible to use a timpano as an auxiliary resonator for some of the wind instruments—trumpets, flügelhorn, oboe, high clarinets, and soprano saxophone. The instrument must be aimed straight down at the drum, with its bell in close proximity to the drum head, and the drum must be tuned either to the pitch the instrument will play or to a lower octave of that pitch. The woodwinds can only perform this effect on notes that use the entire length of the instrument, i.e., on sax and oboe written $b\flat^0$, and on clarinets written e^0 and b^1. Playing directly into the drum muffles the sound of the instrument, but it also makes the drumhead vibrate sympathetically, adding an odd humming sound to the overall timbre (if the drum is not tuned to the pitch produced by the wind instrument, the sympathetic vibrations do not occur). By moving the bell of the instrument around and tilting it in different directions, changes in the phase and apparent location of the sound can be brought about; these are heard as a puzzling or even disturbing "wobble" in the timbre.

SMALL KETTLE DRUMS

The music cultures of North Africa and Southwest Asia all possess kettle-type drums with clay, wood, or metal shells, mostly far smaller in size and higher in pitch than Western timpani, and these can be used to extend the range of clearly pitched drum notes up to at least f^2. Most of these drums possess a refinement unknown in the West—the thickening or loading of the center of the drum head. This makes the partials of the head completely and truly harmonic; thus these drums have an even richer and clearer tone than the timpani. The clar-

name of instrument	abbreviations	synonyms	range	normal sticks	status	availability
small kettle drums	sm. ktdrs.	clay drums Arab drums	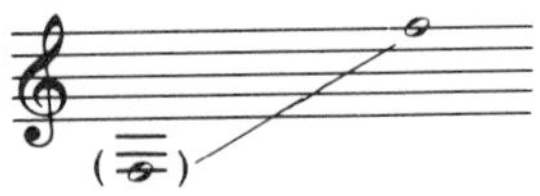 loudest: *fff* softest: *ppp*	variable	exotic	rare

FIGURE 79. *Small kettle drums—vital statistics.*

ity of pitch helps to offset the fact that these small, sometimes even tiny, drums cannot sustain a tone longer than a second or two.

Unlike the timpani, small kettle drums have no built-in stands or foot pedals; most do not even have tension screws. They *can* be tuned (the exact method depending on their construction), but the process is as time-consuming as the hand-tuning of timpani, and composers should therefore limit themselves to one pitch per drum.

Unfortunately, no single, completely unambiguous name is in use for these drums. "Small kettle drums" is the best of the lot, but even this may lead to confusion in the range below c^1, where percussionists may assume that small timpani are intended. The only way to be completely clear is to use a clumsy expression such as "small, kettle-type drums" or "small kettle drums (non-Western)." Of course, each drum has a very specific name in the culture that produced it, but Western composers can ill afford to be so specific, especially since these drums sound so much alike. Most commonly seen is the **tabla** from India, which has a range of about an octave located approximately in the middle of the range given in Figure 79.* The lower limit (f^0) given here for small kettle drums is more or less arbitrary but is justifiable in that *small* drums of lower pitch lack the ringing clarity of tone one looks for in drums of this type.

Small kettle drums must be played with lighter, harder sticks than the timpani—felt sticks (except perhaps in the lowest octave) are no good at all. The best all-purpose mallets are vibraphone sticks (i.e., hard, medium or soft, wound rubber-series mallets). Plastic sticks or (more delicately) snare sticks can be used to produce a brilliant clatter from the drums (at the expense of pitch definition), and it is only with such hard sticks that the *fff* can be attained. The various unwound rubber mallets can be used. These drums are ideal for finger-style playing (indeed, most of them are designed to be so played)—for details, see the section on bongos. A *ppp* can only be obtained with fingers or with very soft sticks.

The material of which the shell of the drum is made has no effect on its sound, and striking the shell will only produce a dry "clack." Because of their small size and lack of resonance, small kettle drums cannot be used as auxiliary resonators.

---

* The tabla's companion drum, the **banya**, is also a kettle drum but produces notes well down in the timpani range. Because of its small size it yields relatively indistinct pitches and has a tone quality like that of a dumbeg or Indian drum.

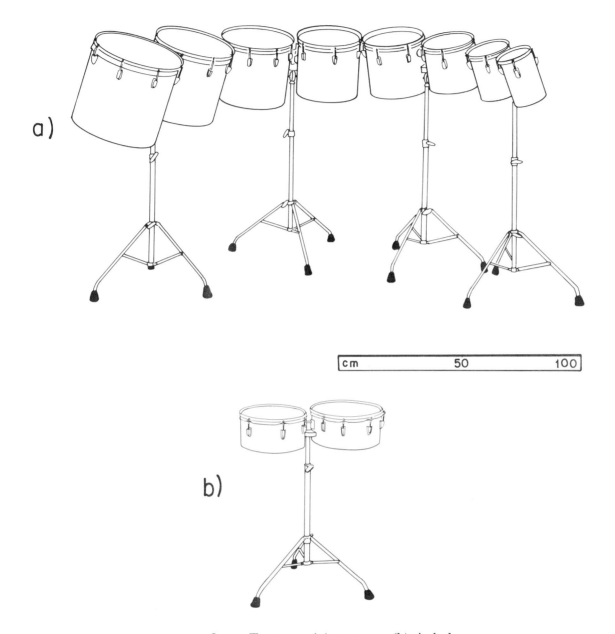

a)

b)

FIGURE 80. *Tomtoms: (a) tomtoms; (b) timbales.*

THE TOMTOM FAMILY

TOMTOMS

A tomtom is a drum that has a cylindrical wooden shell open at the bottom, with a single head and a raised rim. Typically the shell is deeper than it is wide, but this is not necessarily the case, particularly with large drums. The word "tomtom" was for a long time used as a catchall to denote any kind of nondescript drum, and its meaning is still not quite as precise

name of instrument	abbreviations	synonyms	range	normal sticks	status	availability
tomtoms	toms. t.t. 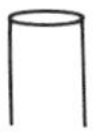	drums	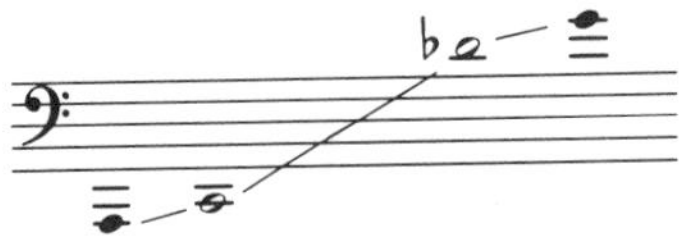 loudest: *fff* softest: *ppp*	variable	standard	ubiquitous

FIGURE 81. *Tomtoms—vital statistics.*

as could be desired. The term is widely used, for instance, to refer to all snareless double-headed drums except the bass drum; furthermore, percussionists will on even the slightest pretext substitute some other instrument for the tomtom. Not only double-headed drums of all sorts (including snare and field drums with snares relaxed) but bongos, rototoms, and timbales have been used in this way.

In fairness, it should be noted that the largest and smallest tomtoms are indeed only marginally different from drums of other sorts. The bongo has been so thoroughly hybridized with the tomtom that the only way definitively to separate small toms from bongos is by the presence or absence of the raised rim, and in a part that does not demand playing on the rim the substitution may be made without offense. In this regard it should be noted that the difference in *sound* between bongos and high tomtoms is entirely a matter of head tension: if the pitch of a high tomtom is raised above about db^1, it will take on the characteristically bright, dry sound of a bongo. At the low end, the largest drums manufactured as tomtoms are capable of descending only to about C_0. Lower notes (down to A_1) are available, but these must be obtained from converted bass drums. The conversion, accomplished by simply removing one head from the bass drum, is complete; a bass drum in this condition *is* a tomtom, no matter what it may have been manufactured to be. Look again at the definition of "tomtom" above; with the exception of timbales (discussed below) any drum bearing the characteristic features of cylindrical shell, single head, and raised rim is a tomtom and should be so called.

Tomtoms are rather weakly pitched and have traditionally been written for as unpitched instruments; nonetheless, pitch is there and can be demanded if desired. The drums are tuned by the usual apparatus of tension screws. Accurately changing the pitch of a given drum takes about half a minute, so one should call for a separate drum for each pitch required. Glissandos, bent notes, and the like *can* be produced on a tomtom by leaning heavily on the drum with an elbow or the heel of one hand, a procedure that both damps the sound heavily and raises the pitch any amount up to an octave for low or medium-pitched tomtoms (but progressively less for high drums; the very smallest tomtoms can only be forced up a fourth, and in no case higher than g^1). *Specific* pitches can be obtained in this way only if the player can hear the note at the end of a preceding glissando or has the opportunity to test it surreptitiously before actually playing it. The heavily damped timbre of these notes is so dramatically different from the normal sound of the drum that it is best that unraised pitches on the same or other tomtoms be hand-damped to ensure uniformity—otherwise the difference of pitch will be lost in the difference of timbre. It must always be remembered, in writing this effect, that the player will have only one hand free to strike the tomtom or any other instrument.

The tone of the tomtom is full and rich. Large toms have timpani-like decays of up to two seconds; smaller ones have progressively shorter decay-times, down to less than half a second for the smallest. The distinctness of individual large drums is blurred in fast passages, just as with timpani. The weak pitch of a tomtom cannot stand up to any competition whatsoever, and in writing for the toms as pitched instruments it must constantly be kept in mind that the sense of pitch will be obliterated not only in low rapid passages and chords of all sorts (except perhaps bare octaves), but even in chords involving other instruments unless the tomtom pitch is doubled by some other, more clearly pitched instrument. Despite the obliteration of pitch, tomtom chords are perfectly effective as *sonorities*, and a combination of high and low drums is clearly heard as such even though the specific pitches are suppressed.

Tomtoms are medium-sized drums, on the average, and a single player can handle with ease a group of as many as eight. For three or fewer, the player will choose medium-sized instruments, and groups of six or more will generally span the entire range. Groups of four or five tend to be skewed toward either the high or the low end of the range, depending on the player's taste, unless the composer has specified "high tomtoms," "medium tomtoms," or the like. Finicky composers may wish to specify the exact pitches of all the drums in order to obtain precisely the desired sonority, even if the drums are then written for as unpitched instruments.

Particularly in large arrays, the smallest tomtoms are often arranged four-in-a-square or three-in-a-triangle rather than lined up in a row as larger drums usually must be. Within such compact groups, all four (or three) drums are equally accessible to both hands and as a result virtually anything may be written without fear that it will be awkward or impossible to play. For drums lined up in the ordinary way, one must pay attention to cross-overs and double beats, as with the timpani.

High tomtoms are normally played with vibraphone mallets, low ones with timpani sticks. For mid-range instruments and for sets of drums covering a broad range, medium or soft vibraphone sticks will be used as "hard sticks" and hard timpani mallets as "soft sticks." It is only with timpani or vibraphone sticks that the drums can be played *ppp*. The backs of snare sticks are the most generally useful wooden sticks; the fronts of snare sticks or plastic mallets provide a crisp, delicate sound for the high drums and wooden timpani sticks a powerful sound for the low drums. Unwound rubber-series mallets also work perfectly well. Wire brushes make a good effect on high or medium tomtoms; on low ones the sound is "divided" as for the timpani. Finger-style playing on drums with raised rims is more or less limited to the tips of the fingers and is most useful in assuring precision at very low dynamic levels.

Playing on the rim is an integral part of the technique of drums with raised rims. This is done with wooden sticks (in a pinch, with plastic mallets or even triangle beaters) and produces a very dry clicking sound, no louder than *ff*. Other kinds of sticks can be used with similar effect to play on the *shell* of the drum. This is one of the most common uses of the switch, for instance. A special effect, for which only wooden sticks are usable, is the **rim shot**. This is performed either by holding a stick horizontally so that it strikes both the rim and the center of the drum or, preferably, by placing a stick with one end on the rim and the other touching the drumhead and then striking that stick with another. Rim shots can be played as softly as *pianissimo*, but their main value lies at the other end of the dynamic scale,

name of instrument	abbreviations	synonyms	range	normal sticks	status	availability
timbales	timbs. tmbls.	(none)	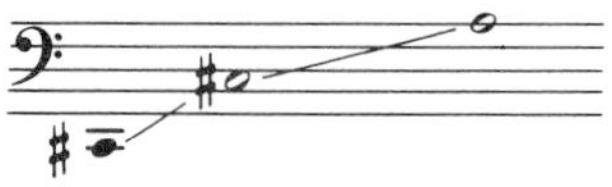 loudest: *fff* softest: *ppp*	back of snare sticks	standard	usually available

FIGURE 82. *Timbales—vital statistics.*

a *ffff* "pow!" attainable in no other way. Rim shots are most effective on small or medium-sized drums but can be performed on even the largest drums.

TIMBALES

Timbales are a specialized variety of tomtom in which the shell is typically—at any rate ideally—made of metal rather than wood; also, unlike most tomtoms, timbales are wider than they are deep. These features serve to emphasize the bright, dry tone of the instrument, a brittle "pam" that is due almost entirely to the very high tension to which the head is usually raised. If the tension is reduced a tomtom-like sound will result, and notes below $c\#^0$ can only be obtained with this sacrifice of timbre. On the other hand, a medium tomtom can if necessary be made to stand in for a timbale simply by raising the tension. Indeed, some drums marketed as "timbales" are utterly indistinguishable from medium tomtoms. Despite their clangorous tone and rapid decay (less than half a second), timbales are no more weakly pitched than ordinary tomtoms and may be written for at specific pitches.

Timbales are made in only two sizes, equivalent to medium tomtoms, and are usually played in pairs. All the types of mallets used on medium tomtoms are also used on timbales, but normally (especially in the absence of any special indication) either reversed snare sticks or special "timbale sticks" of similar weight and diameter will be used; sometimes plastic mallets are substituted. Timbales can be played on the rim just like tomtoms, and the brilliant timbre makes rim shots very effective. Because the tension on the drum is so high, leaning on the drumhead can only raise the pitch about a major sixth.

DOUBLE-HEADED DRUMS

SNARE DRUMS

The most typically Western of all drums are those whose cylindrical shells have at both ends a head with a raised rim. One head is struck in the conventional way, and the enclosed* air space inside the drum communicates strong vibrations to the head opposite. The two heads

* There is, however, always a small hole in the shell to equalize the pressure of air inside and outside the instrument.

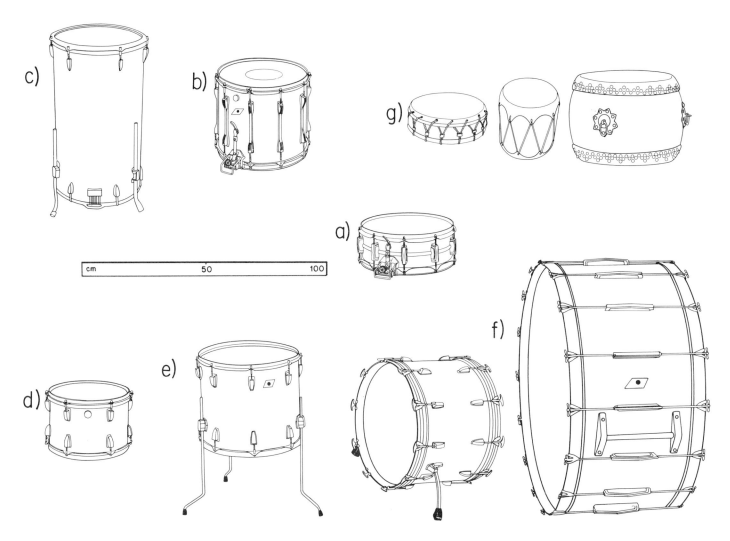

FIGURE 83. *Double-headed drums: (a) snare drum; (b) field drum; (c) long drum; (d) small double-headed drum; (e) tenor drum; (f) bass drums; (g) Indian drums.*

are ordinarily tuned a major second apart (or at some other dissonant interval), so that their combined vibration is genuinely indefinite in pitch. On some of these drums the pitch is made even more indefinite by the addition of **snares**, a number of lightly coiled metal wires stretched across the lower head. These rattle against the head whenever the drum is struck, bringing out so many high partials that the sound becomes an almost unbroken band of white noise. In drums of this type the pitch is determined less by the tension on the drumheads (though this is usually kept high) than by the distance between the snare head and the batter head: the closer the two heads are, the greater will be the number of high partials strongly transmitted to the snare head and the higher the drum will sound. Accordingly, although all these drums have roughly the same diameter, they vary considerably in length. High-pitched ones, much shallower than they are wide, are called **snare drums**, medium-pitched drums of approximately equal height and diameter are called **field drums**, and the low-pitched, deep ones are called **long drums**. In the long drum (and some field drums) the snares are made of gut rather than wire, so that (being more massive) they will respond to somewhat

name of instrument	abbreviations	synonyms	dynamic range	normal sticks	status	availability
snare drum 	s.d. sn. dr.	side drum	_pp(p)–fff_	snare sticks	standard	ubiquitous
field drum 	f.d. f. dr.	parade drum military drum tenor drum	_pp(p)–fff_	snare sticks	standard	common
long drum 	l.d. long dr.	(none)	_pp(p)–fff_	snare sticks	standard	rare

FIGURE 84. _Snare drums—vital statistics._

lower frequencies. The long drum is most commonly called for under the name **tambourin provençal** (or its synonyms **tabor, provençal drum**)—a term which, unfortunately, can denote not only the long drum but a tomtom or tenor drum, with or without a single gut snare stretched across the _batter_ head. Even the term "long drum" is not quite clear and may be misunderstood as a synonym for "tenor drum" unless an expression such as "long drum (with snares)" is used.

The snares raise the pitch of all these drums; even the long drum is moderate rather than low in pitch. The snares can be disengaged ("released," "relaxed") by means of a lever attached to the shell (typically at the top of the instrument where it can easily be reached). With the snares relaxed, the drums are much lower in pitch and quite different in timbre: the snare drum is then medium in pitch, the field drum low, and the long drum very low, and they all sound like tomtoms but without definite pitch and with somewhat quicker decay times (due to the high tension of the heads). When the snares are relaxed the pitch of the drum is governed as much by the tension on the heads as by the depth of the shell, so that one snare drum may sound higher than a second when their snares are engaged, but lower when their snares are relaxed.

If a drum is to play an entire piece with snares engaged, no special direction is necessary, but if it is to play entirely without the snares, then the instrument should be listed at the beginning as, e.g., "snare drum with snares relaxed." The instruction for engaging or releasing the snares is simply "snares on" or "snares off." The snares can be engaged or disengaged with one hand in a fraction of a second. An unavoidable little snapping sound occurs when the snares come in contact with the lower head of the instrument, so they should be engaged at a point in the music when the snap will be covered by louder sounds or at any rate will not be obtrusive.

The snares are so sensitive to any vibration of the snare head that sympathetic vibrations caused by the playing of other instruments nearby will cause them to hiss as loudly as _piano_; for this reason it is best to relax the snares whenever the drum is not being played. The player should do this automatically, but failure to do so is a common fault even among professionals, and the composer cannot go wrong in specifying every occasion on which the snares are to be relaxed.

Snare drums, field drums, and long drums are usually used individually rather than in sets. When used in sets, distinct differences in pitch can be achieved only among a relatively small number of drums: no more than three of each type to a possible maximum of nine drums in this timbre. With snares relaxed the individual drums sound more distinctive, and up to four of each sort may be employed effectively.

With snares engaged the sound of these drums, particularly the snare drum, is very crisp, with decay times of a quarter-second or less. Interestingly, muffling—which can be applied with identical effect to either head—subdues the snare sound as well as the head sound, giving a particularly covered, "dead" effect. Varying the striking position between edge and center produces a slight difference in sound, much more subtle than the effect when the snares are relaxed. Snare sticks are standard for all three drums. Nonetheless, the various tomtom mallets are of use here, too. Vibraphone mallets or hard timpani sticks are particularly useful when the snares are relaxed. When the drum is played *ppp*, the snares will not vibrate; if they *do* vibrate, the volume is automatically raised to *pianissimo*.

Special performance techniques possible only with snare sticks are widely used to make these dry-sounding drums more expressive, and these techniques are useful on drums of other sorts as well, especially those with tight heads. First of all, in producing a roll, each stick is allowed to bounce as it strikes the batter head, making a double repercussion for each stroke of the roll. The roll thus produced is very uniform, smooth, and fine, and can be applied to extremely short notes. The use of grace notes both rolled and unrolled to vary the attack is an integral part of snare drum technique.*

Whether rolled or not, each grace note represents a separate stroke, so that, for instance, the rolled double grace ("closed drag") before the last note of the above example represents two strokes, each allowed to bounce. This bouncing technique is also used for one-handed performance of extremely rapid rhythms. Notes meant to be so played should be grouped together under a slur and each note should be marked with a staccato-dot.

Playing on the rim is somewhat more convincing on snare, field, and long drums than it is on drums of other types, because the clicking "rim" sound is not very different from the normal sound of the drum itself. For some reason, playing on the rim does not cause the snares to vibrate. The rim shot, however, causes *everything*—heads, snares, shell—to vibrate. It sounds like rifle fire and can be as loud as *ffff*.

The wire brush, developed for use with the snare drum, is very useful on field and long drums as well. When they are rubbed the vibration of the snares makes a delicate, smooth hiss; when struck, they make a "chick" sound. The overall effect is of the snares vibrating with little or no attack noise or head sound. Similar effects can be produced with finger-style playing, in which varying the manner or position of striking will have next to no effect as long as the snares are engaged.

* Percussionists speak of "open" and "closed" "flams," "drags," and "ruffs." This terminology is an unnecessary mystification of a really rather straightforward process.

name of instrument	abbreviations	synonyms	dynamic range	normal sticks	status	availability
small double-headed drum	sm. 2-h. dr.	tomtom drum	*ppp–fff*	variable	standard	common
tenor drum	t.d. t. dr. 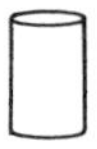	tomtom drum	*ppp–fff*	variable	standard	common
bass drum	b.d. b. dr.	(none)	*ppp–fff*	bass drum beater(s) (light, heavy)	standard	ubiquitous

FIGURE 85. *Double-headed drums—vital statistics.*

A special effect possible on these drums but so far unexploited is playing with snares half-engaged. Each note so played will sound like a "snares off" note accompanied by a long dying rattle from the snares of up to four seconds' duration. This rattle will not occur on notes played softer than *piano*.

The sympathetic vibration of the snares can be exploited by leaving them on while *any* instrument plays nearby at *mf* or louder. The best and most obvious use of this effect occurs when a voice or wind instrument* plays directly into the batter head, which will then respond even to a *pianissimo*.

SNARELESS DOUBLE-HEADED DRUMS

Double-headed drums with raised rims but without snares are found in three varieties. The "small double-headed drum" is an almost invariable component of a set of traps (p. 122). Almost always incorrectly called "tomtom," it is of the same general size, sound, and pitch as a snare drum without snares but has a smaller, looser head. Except for this and the Indian drum (see below), snareless double-headed drums are all quite large; those longer than wide are called **tenor drums**, while those wider than long are called **bass drums**. Size or depth of pitch is not the determining factor here: the small bass drums used in traps are no bigger than the tenor drum used beside them. This tenor drum is usually called the "floor tomtom," and indeed it may be one, since the lower head is not mandatory.

The tenor drum is usually used singly and is made in a rather narrow range of sizes generally intermediate between the field drum and long drum, either of which may be substituted for it (snares relaxed) with impunity. Bass drums are quite variable in size and can be divided into two groups: small ones for use in traps, and much larger ones (often twice the diameter) used in orchestras. Intermediate sizes can be found if necessary, and one occasionally sees a rare "monster drum" dragged out as a (mainly) theatrical effect. With such a range

* See restrictions on woodwinds, p. 147.

it is quite feasible to write for bass drums in groups—though, because of their size, they are usually assigned one-to-a-player. Even without recourse to "monster drums," as many as five bass drums can be used at once with good effect.

It is still considered traditional for the bass drum to be set on its side when it is played; when the instrument is used singly this saves a lot of space. Thus set up, it will normally be played one-handed; passages requiring two-handed playing must be executed with alternate strokes on opposite heads. When the bass drum part is tightly bound to other percussion lines—for instance, when the instrument serves as the lowest of a set of mixed drums—or when a single player must handle more than one bass drum, the drum is usually laid flat like other drums. In any piece in which the position of the bass drum makes a difference, the instrument list should specify "bass drum (standing)" or "bass drum (laid flat)."

Sets of double-headed drums covering a wide pitch range can be formed by using snare drums (snares relaxed) for the highest sounds, field and/or tenor drums in the middle, and bass drums (usually only one) at the bottom.* The performance techniques involved for such a set are exactly the same as for tomtoms, save that since double-headed drums are, on the average, larger and lower-pitched than tomtoms, timpani sticks are virtually mandatory except for special effects. When the bass drum is played by itself, a single bass-drum beater is generally used, assuring maximum power and depth of pitch. For rapid or complex rhythms a pair of soft timpani sticks are used, with virtually the same effect. A barbaric "Ben Hur" sound can be gotten from the bass drum with wooden timpani sticks. In traps, the bass drum is provided with a removable, adjustable, pedal-operated bass-drum beater and the instrument is played with one foot. This pedal beater does not rebound unless the foot is quickly removed—an awkward motion—so the sound is automatically damped with each stroke, producing a precise thud rather than the indefinite five-second boom of a hand stroke. To guarantee this, the bass drum in a traps set is usually heavily muted from inside. Increasingly common are traps with two adjacent pedal bass drums, so that by using both feet a "rolling thunder" trill can be produced. The pedal mechanism is detachable and can be fitted to any bass drum, though it works best on small ones. A drum so used must be set on edge with one head facing the player, making hand strokes awkward (the player must lean down and strike *forward*) but possible.

Two-headed drums (except where snares are involved) can be given the effect of definite pitch by doubling each drum with a single specific note (in the appropriate range) from any non-sustaining instrument. True definite pitch can be obtained by tuning the two heads of a drum to the same pitch, but the resulting sound is virtually indistinguishable from that of a tomtom. Combining the deep, indefinite rumble of a bass-drum roll with a sustained low pitch from some other instrument(s) gives the distinct impression of doubling that pitch at a lower octave.

THE INDIAN DRUM

The Indian drum is a double-headed drum without raised rims. More important, the heads are quite loose and are attached to the shell by tacks or lashings, making the drum difficult, if

* Bass drums are so large that no player can profitably handle more than three, and this to the exclusion of all other drums (unless placed behind the player). Up to five is *possible*, but this would completely surround the player with bass drums and comprise the complete possible horizontal array.

name of instrument	abbreviations	synonyms	dynamic range	normal sticks	status	availability
Indian drum	Ind. dr.	tomtom	*ppp–ff*	variable	exotic, novelty	rare

FIGURE 86. *The Indian drum—vital statistics.*

not impossible, to tune. The drum is usually small and less deep than wide; despite this it is typically as low in pitch as a tenor drum—or lower—because of the looseness of the head. The sound of the drum is typically dark and "tubby" with a rapid decay, and cannot exceed *ff* in loudness. An unambiguous name for this drum is badly needed. The term "Indian drum" is distressingly vague—by no means do all Amerindian drums fall within the limits here described, nor are all drums of this type Amerindian in origin. In Europe, for instance, this type of drum is more likely to be written for under the name "Chinese tomtom."

Indian drums exist in every size from tiny to monstrous, but since the tension on the head of an Indian drum is roughly the same on drums of all sizes, large ones are comparable to the Western tenor and bass drums in both head-tension and timbre. Even small drums tend to differ among each other less in pitch than in timbre: the smaller the drum, the weaker and "deader" the tone.

The weakness and delicacy of tone of Indian drums, together with the absence of raised rims, make them ideal for finger-style playing, and all the techniques discussed below in the section on bongos can be used. Sticks must be light, for example, rubber-series mallets (wound or unwound), snare sticks, or wire brushes.

FRAME DRUMS

THE TAMBOURINE

The shell of a frame drum is so shallow relative to its width that it acts simply as a tensioning hoop for the head without providing any resonance. The tambourine shell is studded with pairs of tiny "cymbals" strung on thin metal rods set vertically across slots cut in the shell; these jingles so completely dominate the instrument that it hardly sounds like a drum at all.

The tambourine, uniquely among drums, is a hand instrument: normally it must be held in one hand while it is being played, which means that time must be allotted for it to be picked up and set down and that while it is being held the player will have only one hand free to play any other instrument. The tambourine is struck with the free hand using the fingertips, the knuckles of the fist, or the flat of four fingers together; the instrument may also be struck against the player's knee. These modes of striking do not differ significantly in timbre; the method used is determined by the dynamics and articulation of the part, and the composer need not specify the form of stroke. Playing near the edge produces a crisp staccato from the jingles, playing in the center a broad tenuto. Here too it is only necessary to specify the articulation, because there is no difference in timbre. The roll on the tambourine can be executed by shaking the instrument, by alternating strokes with the index and ring

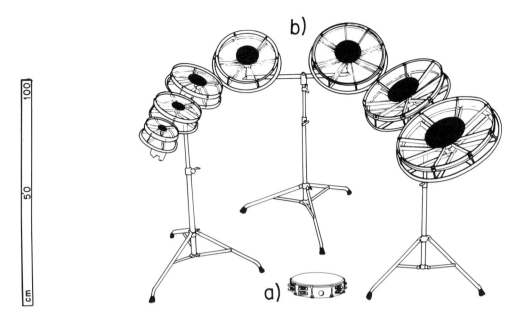

FIGURE 87. *Frame drums: (a) tambourine; (b) rototoms.*

fingers of the free hand, or by performing the **thumb roll** (described on p. 135 above). This last should be notated as a rubbing effect: ♩ . The other two rolls are notated in the usual way: ♪ . The distinction between these notations should be explained in the introduction to any piece in which they occur; alternatively, the precautionary notations "shaken," "fingers," and "thumb" (or the standard thumb sign, ♀) may be placed at the beginning of each roll. The finger and shaken rolls differ more in volume than timbre (the finger roll is softer); dynamics aside, it is not usually necessary to distinguish between them. The thumb roll is, however, quite distinctive in its precision and clarity, and one will generally want to be specific in demanding it. It should be remembered that the thumb roll cannot be performed louder than *ff*.

It is not necessary to strike the head of the tambourine in order to play it. Shaking can be used not only for rolls but for individual notes. The attack will be somewhat vague, and in the *fortissimo* will lack the "pow!" normally contributed by the head. A "normal"-sounding attack—but with no trace of head sound—can be achieved by striking the lower rim of the drum against one's leg or with the heel of the free hand.

All high-quality tambourines are provided with tensioning screws; these do not change the pitch of the instrument (which is entirely determined by the jingles) but serve to tighten the head to the optimum level for the transmission of vibration through the shell to the jingles. Tambourines are made in a wide variety of sizes which, however, differ little if at all in pitch. Large tambourines have more jingles than small ones, though, and thus differ from them in timbre, having a lusher, fuller tone and a somewhat more sluggish attack. For tambourines of different pitches, one must have recourse to the non-Western tambourines of North Africa and Southwest Asia; these sound very much like the Western tambourine (to which they are closely related historically) but many are much lower in pitch. Unfortunately, these instruments are very rare in North America.

name of instrument	abbreviations	synonyms	dynamic range	normal sticks	status	availability
tambourine	tamb.	(none)	$pp(p)$–fff	fingers	standard	ubiquitous

FIGURE 88. *The tambourine—vital statistics.*

Like most hand instruments, the tambourine may be played with both hands. It need only be laid on a cushion, either side up, and played either with the fingers or with sticks. More commonly, though, the tambourine is attached to a stand—unlike a cushion, a stand is adjustable in height, and there is no chance of knocking the tambourine away in *fortissimo* passages. When the instrument is attached to a stand the head is free to vibrate after each stroke, in contrast to either hand-held or cushion playing, in which the head is normally damped. Vibrations of the head will thus decay at natural speed, about half a second, and particularly at low dynamic levels the head will continue to ring after the jingle sound has ceased. The resulting sound is not unitary—it is exactly as if a simple frame drum and a set of jingles were being played simultaneously. At loud dynamic levels this is not a problem, but the only way to get a real tambourine sound out of a suspended tambourine at low volume is either to muffle the instrument or to damp it by hand or stick. The *ppp* is problematic on the tambourine no matter how it is played, for when the head is struck this softly the jingles will not vibrate. The only way to get a *ppp* jingle sound is to tap a single pair of jingles *very* gently.

Only light sticks may be used with a tambourine: vibraphone or marimba mallets are best. Hard xylophone mallets or snare sticks bring out the head sound; with reversed rubber-series mallets the head and jingle sounds will actually be of equal volume. As a special timbre the tambourine may be played with a single stick even when the instrument is hand-held.

Like most other hand instruments, the tambourine can be used to strike another instrument. Obviously, the second instrument must be large (timpano, bass drum, tam-tam). The effect will be as if it were struck with a particularly large and clumsy wooden mallet, and the tambourine will jingle.

ROTOTOMS

Despite their name, rototoms are not tomtoms but frame drums. They are provided with a rotary tuning mechanism at one time widely used in timpani: turning the top of the instrument clockwise raises its pitch and turning it counterclockwise lowers it. Simple frame drums ("hand drums") in the form of jingleless tambourines have existed as long as the tambourine itself; the rototom, introduced in the late 1960s and marketed by Remo, supersedes these drums almost entirely.* While hand drums and rototoms have exactly the same timbre (it would be surprising if they did not), the latter are infinitely more flexible instruments, not only because they can be tuned to specific pitches almost as easily as timpani but because they

* This is reflected in the fact that since 1968 as much music has been written for rototoms as had been written for hand drums in all the preceding centuries.

name of instrument	abbreviations	synonyms	range	normal sticks	status	availability
rototoms	rot. rtms.	(none)	 loudest: *fff* softest: *ppp*	variable	standard	usually available

FIGURE 89. *Rototoms—vital statistics.*

are available in a wide range of sizes (rototoms have a greater overall pitch range than any other drum) and because they are not hand instruments.

Rototoms are made in seven sizes, ranging from 15 to 46 cm in diameter. The exact range of each drum is somewhat variable (depending on the weather, the type of head used, and its age) but each drum can be tuned across a full octave without any distortion of timbre. This range can be expanded to a twelfth or more. The extension pitches outside the octave span (including the overall extension pitches given in Fig. 89) are uncharacteristic in timbre. The low ones are flabby and weak in pitch and the high ones acquire the crisp brittle tone and weak pitch of bongos or timbales.

The tone of the rototoms is similar to that of tomtoms, but a harsh little cluster of high partials gives the tone a certain pungency lacking in tomtoms. The envelopes of these drums are virtually identical to those of tomtoms of similar diameter; one must accordingly watch out for the effects of overlapping decays in the lowest fifth of the range. The writing of chords should be handled as for timpani or small kettle drums; there will be some loss of pitch definition, but above about c^1 even full triads should be effective; dissonances, however, will always seem merely unpitched. Because the pitch is significantly stronger than that of tomtoms but weaker than that of timpani or small kettledrums, rototoms may be written for with equal effectiveness either as pitched or unpitched instruments.

Their relatively small size permits rototoms to be handled by a single player in groups of as many as nine. As with tomtoms, drums in the four smallest sizes can be arranged in a square, allowing complete flexibility in the choice of **hammerings** (pattern of left and right strokes—also called **stickings**). Players (or institutions) are unlikely to own more than one rototom of any given size, so unless one is willing to go to the effort of acquiring extra drums it is probably best neither to write for more than seven at once nor to require two drums of identical pitch range.

Pitch changes on rototoms are not quite as carefree as they are on timpani, since on the rototoms the process requires the use of a hand;* such changes should therefore be used comparatively infrequently. Composers should make use of as many as necessary of the notations used with timpani (pp. 143–44), taking care that all changes are clearly indicated at the appropriate places in the music. As with timpani, single-stroke glissandos are much more effective ascending than descending. Also as with timpani, new pitches may not be perfectly accurate if the percussionist has no chance to fine-tune them before they are played; as an aid in this process, players sometimes mark the perimeter of a drum with masking tape to indicate the position to which it should be turned for a given pitch.

* It is not necessary, however, to put down the stick in that hand.

A detachable pedal tuning mechanism for rototoms has been developed within the past year or so. As we go to press this device is not yet widely distributed, but it certainly seems promising.

The choice of sticks for rototoms is much the same as for tomtoms. The rototoms are of somewhat higher pitch, on the average, so vibraphone sticks are the best all-round mallets to use. Because rototoms have (slightly) raised rims, the use of finger techniques is unfortunately limited. In this area at least, the old hand drums have an advantage—like tambourines, they do not have rims. On the other hand, the various "rim" effects, including the rim shot, can be performed on rototoms.

MISCELLANEOUS DRUMS

BONGOS AND CONGAS

Bongos and congas are rimless drums, open at the bottom, with single, small, very tight heads. In the purest form of both drums, the heavy shells are constructed of vertically aligned wooden slats tapering toward the bottom; bongos are conical, congas fusiform. In actual practice, cost-cutting and hybridization with other drums have resulted in the widespread elimination of slat-type construction and the development of conical congas and completely cylindrical bongos. The best drums of both types retain the original features, which help considerably to establish their distinctive tone qualities. In their Latin-American homeland, congas are made in three slightly different forms called (from largest to smallest) **tumba** (or **tumbadora**), **conga**, and **quinta**. These distinctions have been lost in commercially made congas, not only through hybridization but through the introduction of unclassifiable new varieties, such as the tiny (30 cm tall) congas one occasionally sees in music stores. "Tumba" survives as a vague term indicating a larger-than-average conga and as an even vaguer synonym for a conga of any sort.

As Figure 91 implies, congas differ from bongos not so much in range as in timbre. Both drums have a precise, dry sound that is also somehow pleasingly rich and full. To this quality the conga adds a slightly woody hollowness contributed by the extremely thick head and cavernous interior. The conga has a very quick decay—about a quarter of a second—and this contributes much to the precision and clarity of its sound. The bongo decay takes longer—about half a second—but it is initially very rapid, and all the very prominent upper partials and attack sounds die as quickly as a conga note.

The pitch of these drums is very weak (weaker even than that of a tomtom) but definable enough to be specifically demanded if desired, although both bongos and congas are normally written for as unpitched instruments. Tuning is by means of tension screws. The range of pitches available is quite narrow, partly because the heads must be kept so tight and partly because the drums are made in a very limited variety of diameters. The extension pitches at the bottom of the range are available only at a sacrifice in tone quality—the bongo sounds tomtom-like (indistinguishably so in the case of hybrid, "tomtomoid" bongos) and the conga sounds boomy, almost like a boobam. Leaning on the head will raise the pitch temporarily, as on tomtoms (p. 150). The limits for this are a sixth for congas, a fourth for large bongos, and a minor third for small ones.

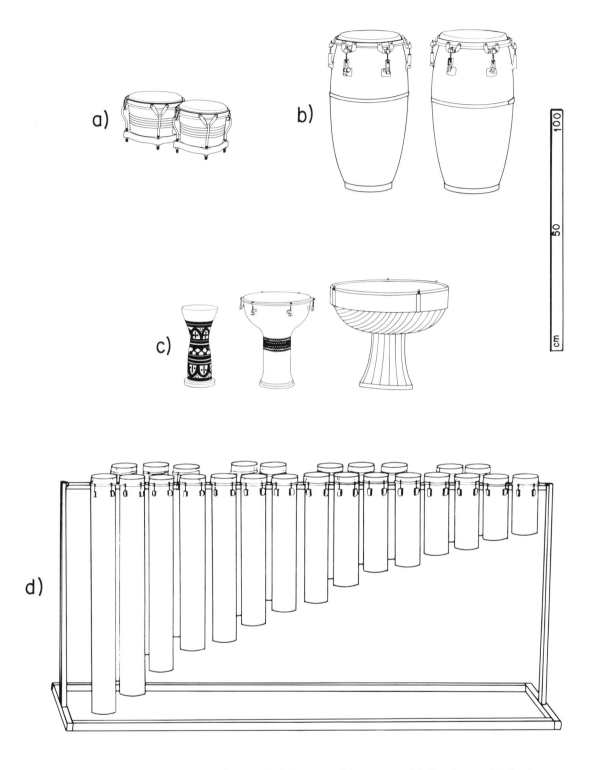

FIGURE 90. *Miscellaneous drums: (a) bongos; (b) congas; (c) dumbegs; (d) boobams.*

name of instrument	abbreviations	synonyms	range	normal sticks	status	availability
bongos		bongo drums	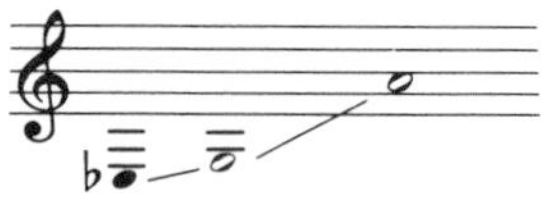 loudest: *fff* softest: *ppp*	fingers	standard	common
congas		conga drums tumbas	 loudest: *fff* softest: *ppp*	fingers	standard	common

FIGURE 91. *Bongos and congas—vital statistics.*

Bongos and congas are traditionally played in pairs, and for finger-style playing this is perhaps just as well. When sticks are used, however, the small diameter of the drums makes it possible for one player to handle many at once; a complete chromatic set covering the entire pitch range of the instrument (fifteen bongos or ten congas) is not out of the question. Such an array would presumably be laid out in two rows, like the bars of a mallet instrument: watch out for cross-overs and double beats!

On congas in particular, playing with the fingers can be grueling—it is not unknown for a drummer to break a hand against the extremely thick, tight head.* Professional conga specialists develop rope-like tendons and thick calluses that protect their hands; "all-purpose" percussionists often wrap their hands and/or fingers with surgical tape when faced with the task of extended, loud conga-playing. On both congas and bongos the tightness of the head coupled with the focusing power of the (it is to be hoped) thick, tapered shell enables the production of a true *fff*, which is not otherwise possible in finger-style playing.

The subtle complexities of finger-style playing have so far eluded attempts to develop a standardized notation. The notations suggested in Figure 92 are designed to be as simple and clear as possible and are consistent with the general system of percussion notation used in this book.

All these techniques are a normal part of bongo playing except the rubbed sounds, the fingernail taps, and the stroke with the heel of the hand, which are special effects. On congas, almost everything is played with the flat of the hand.

It is not necessary to notate every detail of bongo or conga performance—many very successful parts have been written for these instruments in which most or all of the details have been left to the performer. When a whole rhythmic phrase is to be played mostly or entirely with one technique, the part will be easier both to write and to read if that technique is indicated verbally at the beginning of a passage rather than as separate symbols on each note. Verbal indications may also be used to give somewhat less detailed instructions—for

* Lay people are often startled to find that the head of a conga does not yield at all. It is about a millimeter thick, and could not be any thicker without ceasing to act like a membrane altogether.

notation	meaning	sound	*dynamic range*
	center stroke with flat of 4 fingers	ordinary, with a somewhat slapping attack	*ppp–fff*
	edge stroke with the flat of 1–4 fingertips	same, but bright, clear, precise; at high dynamic levels a ringing crack; acoustically homologous to rim shot	*ppp–fff*
	center stroke with fingertip(s)	ordinary, with little attack noise	*ppp–ff*
	edge stroke with fingertip(s)	same, but brighter tone	*ppp–ff*
	stroke with fingernail(s), center	tapping sound	*ppp–f*
	stroke with fingernail(s), edge	same, but more pronounced	*ppp–f*
	thumb stroke, center	sharp thud	*pp–fff*
	thumb stroke, edge	same, but brighter sound; at high dynamic levels a sharp crack	*pp–fff*
	head struck with heel of hand	dull thud, usually with some "scooping" of pitch	*pp–fff*
	head rubbed with finger	moaning or grunting sound	*pp–f*
	thumb roll	moaning or grunting sound	*pp–f*
	head rubbed with fingernail(s) or very lightly with fingers	a fine, light hiss	*ppp–f*
	true roll (flats of both hands)	ordinary	*pp–fff*

Except for the true roll, any of the above can be combined with the following:

notation	meaning	sound	*dynamic range*
	"dead" stroke (damped as it is played)	sound choked off (cannot be combined with rubbed sounds)	—
	stroke damped by opposite hand	sound heavily muffled	—

FIGURE 92. *Suggested notations for finger-style playing.*

name of instrument	abbreviations	synonyms	range	normal sticks	status	availability
dumbegs 	dumbs. dbgs.	darabuccas Arab drums Arabic tablas goblet drums clay drums	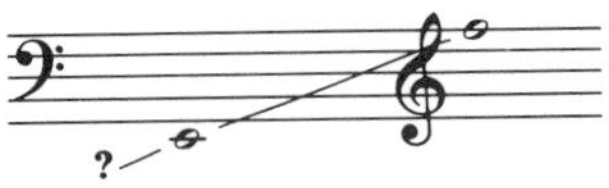 loudest: *fff* softest: *ppp*	fingers	exotic, standard	rare

FIGURE 93. *Dumbegs—vital statistics.*

instance, specifying "fingertips" without differentiating center and edge strokes, or "edge" without indicating whether the flats or the tips of the fingers are to be used. When the two hands are to play complex, independent rhythms it may be necessary to notate them separately, using stems pointing in opposite directions. In extreme cases it may even be necessary to use two separate lines.

Bongos and congas are often played with sticks, particularly when they are included in an array containing other drums. Rubber-series mallets are best—the whole series will work well on congas, while the hard and medium ones are best for bongos. Timpani sticks may be used on congas in a pinch but should be avoided if possible. For wooden sticks the usual choice is snare sticks (either end) on bongos, and wooden timpani sticks or reversed snare sticks on congas.

Both congas and bongos give a satisfactorily wooden "clack!" when struck on the shell with a hard (unwound) stick; soft or wound sticks produce only an anonymous knocking sound. A special effect peculiar to the bongo is use as a rattle, by turning it upside down and dropping in small round objects (dried beans work best), which can then be swished around.

DUMBEGS

It is difficult to say anything with certainty about dumbegs, because neither the name nor the drum is standardized. The drums involved have all the following features in common: (1) a single head, loosely tensioned; (2) no raised rim; (3) a goblet-shaped shell, open at the bottom. The last of these characteristics places them organologically as **goblet drums**, a perfectly satisfactory and well-defined term, adopted, unfortunately, by no one except organologists. Of the names in regular use the least ambiguous and most widespread is **dumbeg**. Even that name is spelled and pronounced in an astonishing variety of ways: I have seen "dumbec," "dumbek," "dombak," "tumbak," "tunbuk," and "dunbak"; most of these are the names of local varieties from various places in the goblet drum's homeland of North Africa and Southwest Asia. "Dumbeg" itself seems to be a strictly Western variant, and is thus legitimate as a general term for all such drums.

As for the actual drums, it sometimes seems as if no two are alike. The shell may be of metal, clay, or wood; the drum may be truly goblet-shaped, or shaped like a vase, or anything in between; the head may be tunable with tension screws, with primitive lashings, or not at all; and the ratios among head diameter, stem diameter, depth of bowl, and depth of stem are completely variable. A few generalizations can, however, be made: (1) Dumbegs manufactured on this continent are almost always equipped with tension screws, have metal shells, and are medium to large in size. (2) The largest dumbegs are made of wood. (3) Small dumbegs usually have clay shells and primitive or nonexistent tuning mechanisms. These small drums, often called **darabuccas** (this term, too, is highly variable in spelling and pronunciation), must be imported. (4) Shape and dimensions tend to vary with the diameter of the head. The larger the drum, the more strongly goblet-shaped it will be, with a *relatively* smaller stem and shallower bowl. The smallest darabuccas are vase-shaped and are almost all stem.

The rareness and variability of dumbegs make it difficult to define their pitch range. The extremes given in Figure 93 represent only the limits of my own experience with these drums. The upper limit of f^2 is almost certainly correct, since drums that produce this note are tiny indeed; E_0 as a lower limit is a cautious guess—lower pitches may well be available.

The best way to describe the tone of the dumbeg is by comparison: it is halfway between an Indian drum and a kettle drum. It is tubby and weak but also very rich, with a weak but definable pitch about as clear as that of a tomtom. The decay time varies, from the largest to the smallest drums, between about three seconds and half a second. In the highest drums, the pitch of the head is reinforced by a **cavity resonance** one or two octaves lower. This cavity resonance is determined by the size and dimensions of the shell, so that whether tunable or not the drum is really built to produce only a single pitch. Despite this, dumbegs are usually treated—both in the West and in their home cultures—as indefinitely pitched drums.

No drum is more clearly specialized for finger-style playing than the dumbeg. The unusual shape of the drum was developed to enable it to be held easily under the arm and played with both hands. The loose head provides the strongest possible differentiation among the sounds of all the different techniques summarized in Figure 92 and permits bending the pitch with relatively little pressure on the head. Even the highest drum can be forced up as much as a fifth (to c^3!) with surprisingly little pressure. The muffling thus produced is less than with other drums, though of course it increases as the pressure is increased. This bending of the pitch is ordinarily produced with the hand that does *not* deliver the stroke: this enables considerable precision and even the production of specific pitches above the "open" note. Both the raised pitch and the muffling should be indicated in the notation, thus:

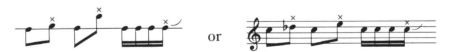

It is also possible to bend a pitch as it is struck; this should be notated as an indefinite upward swoop, thus: ♪ . The drums can be played no louder than *ff* with the fingers.

Dumbegs can, of course, be placed on stands and played with sticks like other drums. The small "darabucca" drums will need sticks like those used for small kettle drums; larger instruments should be treated like tomtoms. Because of the looseness of the head, strokes in *ff* or *fff* will "scoop" in pitch and thus sound "rubbery" to the ear.

Dumbegs show up in scores even more rarely than in reality; there is no dumbeg part in any of our musical examples. For those interested in hearing one, there is a "dumbec" in Terry Riley's *Rainbow in Curved Air*; otherwise, recordings of non-Western music are the best bet.

name of instrument	abbreviations	synonyms	range	normal sticks	status	availability
boobams	bbms. boobs.	bamboo drums	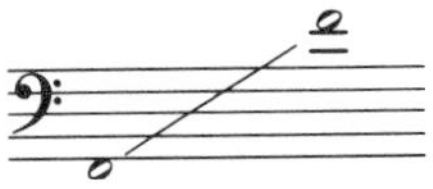 loudest: *fff* softest: *ppp*	wound marimba sticks	standard	very rare

FIGURE 94.   *Boobams—vital statistics.*

BOOBAMS

Boobams are unique among drums in that the pitch is not determined by the head at all but by the dimensions of the shell. Each drum consists of a long tube about 15 cm wide, open at the bottom and with an appropriately small drumhead affixed to the top. Acoustically this system behaves as a stopped pipe, the head acting as a kind of reed to set up vibrations in the enclosed air column, the frequencies of which are determined by the length of the tube. Since each drum produces only a single pitch, it is customary to place groups of them side by side in a specially designed rack, arranged keyboard-fashion like the bars of a mallet instrument. Considering the rarity of boobams and how recently they were invented, there is a surprising unanimity of opinion that their overall range should be that given in Figure 94. A two-octave set of boobams covering this range makes a combined instrument some two and a half meters long, which is about the maximum manageable size. It must be emphasized, however, that the drums are not readily available in such sets of twenty-five. Very few players own boobams: the drums must be rented or borrowed, and naturally only those pitches needed for the specific occasion will be acquired; if these are few, the drums will be simply racked up in a line from lowest to highest just like any other drums. In light of this, it is probably best to indicate at the beginning of the piece what boobam pitches will be required.

The tone of the boobam is a deep, rich boom of great purity that is surprisingly similar to a marimba. What makes the timbre of the boobam unique are the sounds contributed by the head, all of which must be considered attack noise. The tiny head cannot meaningfully be tuned lower than about c^1, so that except at the top of the range the pitch of the head will be higher than that of the tube—increasingly so for lower boobams. The result is a kind of "ghost pitch," somewhere between c^1 and g^1, that doubles a harmonic or privileged frequency of the drum and has a timbre of its own rather resembling a high tomtom. In the highest boobams, where the head is tuned to the actual pitch of the tube, the sound of the instrument is more unitary, resembling a tomtom of unusually clear pitch. The attack sound dies more quickly than the main pitch of the drum but is initially much louder, and in order to keep it as unobtrusive as possible only the softest wound marimba sticks are normally used. Of course, harder sticks can be utilized—even snare sticks and such—but the harder the mallet the more the head sound will be brought out at the expense of the tube sound, particularly for the lower pitches. The head sound is also brought out by playing loudly, and the *fff* (available only from hard sticks) obliterates the main pitch altogether. Because of the different decay times for head and tube (about one-quarter and three-quarters of a second, respectively), boobams sound most effective when played at slow or moderate speed; fast passages,

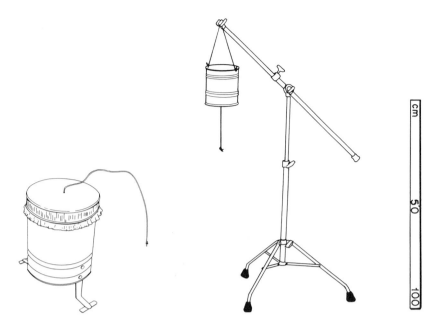

FIGURE 95. *String drums.*

and rolls in particular, will be somewhat unclear in pitch because of the constantly overlapping attack sounds.

The tube-sound of the boobam is the most clearly pitched of all drum sounds. Chords, even full triads, are quite effective, and in the middle part of the range even dissonances will work.

The playing technique for boobams is essentially the same as that for mallet instruments (discussed in Chapter VII). The following exceptions should be noted: (1) glissandos are impossible; (2) when two sticks are held in one hand, the maximum spread is between two drums separated by no more than three others—i.e., in a chromatic set of boobams, the interval of a fifth; (3) hammerings must be very carefully planned to avoid bad cross-overs, as the distance between adjacent notes in a set of boobams is even greater than in a bass marimba.

FRICTION DRUMS

A string drum is just that: a drum with a long string attached to the center of the head. A tiny hole is made in the head, and the string (usually a gut cello or contrabass string) is passed through and knotted underneath the head. The instrument is played by pulling the string taut and rubbing along it lengthwise with a rosined cloth or glove. In its modern form the string drum was originally used only as a theatrical sound-effect, the *lion's roar*, and it is still occasionally encountered under this name.

A real "lion's roar" sound is given out only by the largest string drums. These are usually about the size and shape of an inverted washtub and are firmly attached to a large, flat board.

name of instrument	abbreviation	synonym	dynamic range	status	availability
string drum	string dr.	lion's roar	*p–ff*	homemade	usually available

FIGURE 96. *The string drum—vital statistics.*

The player must put one foot on the board while playing, because in order to put sufficient tension on the string considerable upward pull must be exerted, and the instrument would be lifted off the ground if it were not held down. More commonly seen than these large string drums are medium-sized ones, often made by simply attaching a string to a tenor drum or tomtom. These higher-pitched string drums produce not a lion's roar but a variety of moaning or grunting sounds—more like a Wookie. As these instruments are rarely attached to a base, they must be held down with the player's free hand. High-pitched string drums are only occasionally encountered but are very easily made by poking a hole in the bottom of an empty coffee can and running a knotted string through it; the string is then pulled and rubbed in the usual way. The sound produced is a kind of whoop or squawk, and the fact that the can bottom is not, strictly speaking, a membrane seems to make no difference. Small string drums of any facture can be suspended from any appropriate stand or rack, with the string hanging downward; when the string is pulled the rack automatically holds the instrument in place. Occasionally one sees a particularly elegant medium-sized string drum suspended in this same fashion.

Unlike most percussion, string drums are sustaining instruments and should be notated as such. The pitch is quite definite, but so utterly uncontrollable that the notation of specific pitches would be foolish. Often a note will rise slightly in pitch as it is played, and almost invariably there will be a sudden downward swoop at the end. Dynamics are determined by the pressure with which the string is rubbed.

Usually the string hangs loose when it is not being played. To play the instrument, the percussionist must lean down, grab the string at its base and pull slowly along it, using one hand both to make the sound and to keep the string taut. Suspended string drums eliminate this awkward downward reach. A single note can be played only for about two seconds, though if the player has both hands free a vaguely continuous sound can be produced by continuously pulling along the string hand-over-hand. Both hands must also be free if rapid repeated notes are to be played; for anything faster than eighth-notes at ♩ = 100 the player holds the string taut with one hand and rubs back and forth with the other. By this means one can even produce a roll of sorts. As a special effect the string may be bowed or plucked.

String drums and other friction drums occur worldwide as folk instruments; they all sound much the same. Composers need not concern themselves with any but the ordinary string drum, but two of these exotic friction drums occasionally enter the purview of the Western percussionist. The **Waldteufel** (German: "forest devil") is a Central European toy consisting of a tiny string drum with a loop in the far end of the string, though which one end of a rod is passed. The instrument is held by the rod and whirled round and round, producing sound by friction between the end of the rod and the loop in the string and keeping the string taut by centrifugal force. The **cuica** is a Latin-American instrument that is essentially a bongo, with a wooden rod attached to the center of the lower surface of the head. The player reaches inside the drum to stroke the rod. The sound is a wordless commentary of falsetto whoops suggesting surprise, pleasure, or amusement. A cuica-like sound can be obtained by resting the tip of a snare stick on the head of a bongo or other small drum and rubbing the stick with a rosined cloth or glove—in fact, this technique can be used (with varying timbres) on *any* drum, using any rigid object that comes to a point. The drum will act as a natural amplifier not only of rubbing sounds but of all sorts of minute tapping, scraping, and scratching sounds, raising them from the subaudible range to *pianissimo* or even louder.

VII

THE PERCUSSION:

IDIOPHONES AND

MISCELLANEOUS

INSTRUMENTS

RATTLES

The rattles depicted in Figure 97 have a number of important features in common: all are hand instruments; all produce a rattling sound when shaken; and all are of indefinite pitch and limited dynamic range. Some of them are available in contrasting timbres of wood, metal, and glass, but aside from this distinction the differences in sound among them are almost entirely a matter of envelope.

The envelope of a rattle has two distinct components: the amount of resonance (decay time) of each of the individual clicks of which the sound is composed, and the aggregate pattern formed by these clicks. With a few exceptions these two tend to vary together, so that rattles with a crisp, precise aggregate sound also have a very dry tone, and those with a less precise aggregate sound have a more resonant tone. The majority of rattles can therefore be placed in a line ranging from the very crisp and dry to the very vague and lush, as follows: Mexican bean, sistrum, maraca and related rattles, cabasa and shekere, string rattles, windchimes. Jingles and sleighbells, both of which have very lush timbres comparable to windchimes, have short aggregate envelopes similar to, respectively, the sistrum and the shekere.

SISTRA

The sistrum consists of a frame in the shape of either a tennis racquet or (more usually) a slingshot, across which run one or more rods which pierce the branches of the frame and are

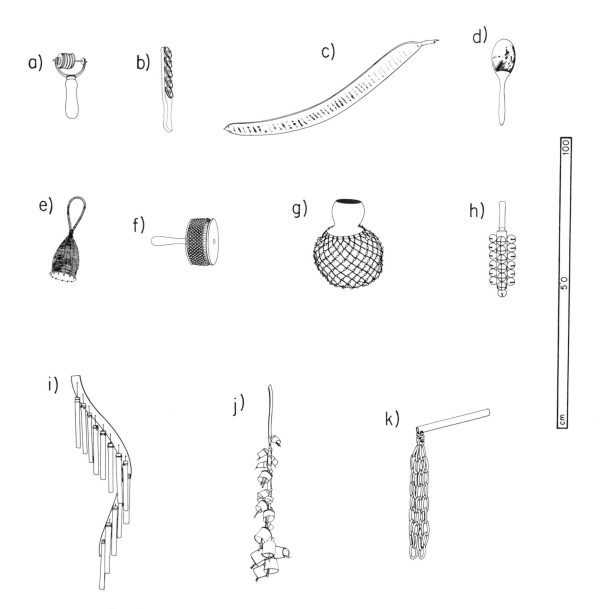

FIGURE 97. *Rattles: (a) sistrum; (b) jingles; (c) Mexican bean; (d) maraca; (e) soft rattle; (f) cabasa; (g) shekere; (h) sleighbells; (i) wooden string rattle; (j) string of jingle bells; (k) chains.*

held in place by it. In the oldest form of sistrum (going back to ancient Egypt and Mesopotamia) there are several crossbars, set loosely in the frame so that they rattle when the instrument is shaken. Most modern instruments have only one bar, firmly attached to the frame but on which are threaded a number of beads or *non-resonant* metal plates.* When the sistrum is shaken, the plates or beads slap together against the frame, giving the instrument its crisp sound.

Sistra with resonant plates are more properly called *jingles*. These are usually seen in the form of a small paddle into one or both surfaces of which one to four nails have been partially

---

* In some exotic sistra the plates are made of wood or other materials, but the sound of the sistrum is in any case so dry that this makes no significant difference in the timbre.

name of instrument	abbreviations	synonyms	dynamic range	status	availability
sistrum	sist. 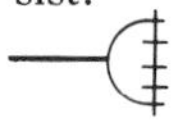	(none)	*pp–f*	homemade, novelty	usually available
jingles	jing.	(none)	*ppp–f*	novelty, standard	usually available

FIGURE 98. *Sistra—vital statistics.*

driven, each nail being threaded with a pair of tiny "cymbals" identical to the jingles of a tambourine. Jingles are also found in the form of a headless tambourine, played exactly like the tambourine (except, of course, for the various head strokes); what such instruments gain in dynamic range they lose in precision and agility.

Both the sistrum and the "normal" type of jingles (note that the name of the latter instrument is always plural) have a very simple playing technique—the instrument is held in the hand and shaken up and down. To all intents and purposes the sound is produced only at the bottom of each downward stroke, and the maximum speed at which either instrument can be played is limited to, say, sixteenth-notes at ♩ = 92. Rhythms of greater speed can be obtained by using two identical instruments, one in each hand. These should be notated together on a single line as one instrument, the choice of right or left for each note being left to the player.

Shaking of both together should be indicated with a double stem, thus: ♪. A good roll can be obtained even from a single sistrum or jingles by holding the instrument vertically and shaking it rapidly back and forth.

Jingles, like tambourines, are almost uniform in pitch. Sistra do vary, but not much: it is probably asking for trouble to demand more than four different pitch levels. Sistra of differing pitches may of course be handled by one player two at a time, in which case they should be notated on two separate lines, or above and below a single line.

Sistra and jingles can be used to strike other percussion, but the surface to be struck should be at least the size of a bongo head. The precise effect produced will vary because sistra differ so much in weight and in the material of which the frame is constructed. Jingles of the ordinary type produce a sound rather like a light wooden stick. Of course, both instruments rattle with each stroke.

TRUE RATTLES

The rattles grouped together here correspond closely to the general public's notion of a rattle: a completely closed hollow vessel inside which a number of small objects are free to, literally, rattle around. By far the most common of these rattles is the **maraca**, an all-purpose rattle of essentially anonymous timbre. Classically, a maraca is a hollow, spherical or ovoid gourd

name of instrument	abbreviations	synonyms	dynamic range	status	availability
Mexican bean	M.b.	pod rattle	*ppp–mf*	found object	rare
maraca	mar.	rattle	*ppp–f*	standard, exotic	ubiquitous
		gourd rattle			
wooden rattle	w.r.	(none)	*ppp–f*	exotic, novelty, homemade	rare
	w. rat.				
glass rattle	g.r.	(none)	*pp–ff*	homemade, novelty	very rare
	gl. rat.				
metal rattle	m.r.	(none)	*pp–ff*	homemade, exotic, novelty	rare
	met. rat.				
soft rattle	s.r.	basket rattle	*ppp–mf*	exotic, homemade	rare
	soft rat.				

FIGURE 99.   *True rattles—vital statistics.*

containing BBs, gravel, or seeds, to which a handle is attached; maracas may also be made of wood or plastic, however. The instrument, like the sistrum, is played by shaking, and it is usually played in identical pairs.

Unlike sistra, maracas are capable of different kinds of articulation: the tone can be made somewhat more crisp and precise by striking the instrument against the palm of the free hand or against a cushion or by tapping it with a finger instead of shaking it. The use of staccato-dots ought to be sufficient indication of this technique, but it is not: add the words "strike against hand" (or "cushion"). The *ppp* can only be obtained in this way, not by shaking.

In addition to the ordinary shaken roll (*piano* or louder), a continuous swishing sound can be produced (*pp–mf*) by holding the maraca loosely downward and swirling it around; this effect should be notated as a rubbed sound, thus: ♩ . Percussionists sometimes perform this effect on the **chocolo**, a gourd, wood, or metal instrument shaped like a bologna sausage. This instrument, also called **ka-me-so**, is identical to the maraca in timbre and is ideal for making such swishing sounds, but is of no use otherwise. A special attack can be produced on the maracas by tapping them against each other; there is no notation for this, so a written instruction must be given.

In order to increase the volume of the maracas, players occasionally tape or tie pairs of them together so that two can be held in each hand. When all four are shaken simultaneously, a true *ff* is produced.

The pitch of a rattle depends mostly on the size of the rattling objects inside it: the bigger the objects, the lower the pitch. All maracas are quite high in pitch, and it is probably not wise to call for more than three separate pitch-levels at a time. The sound of the maraca is deliberately anonymous, not particularly woody, and the high pitch contributes to this effect. It is possible, however, to fashion rattles of only slightly lower pitch with the distinctive tone-qualities of wood, glass, or metal. These distinctions are strongest when the internal rattling objects are of the same material as the shell; thus, a wooden rattle should contain wooden

name of instrument	abbreviations	synonyms	dynamic range	status	availability
cabasa	cab.	cabaca cabaza afuche	*pp–ff*	standard, exotic	rare
shekere	shek.	agbe	*pp–ff*	exotic, standard	rare

FIGURE 100. *Cabasa and shekere—vital statistics.*

beads, a glass rattle (usually made from a closed bottle or jar with a handle attached) should contain glass beads or coarse gravel, and a metal rattle (usually made from a tin can) should contain BBs or ball bearings; the glass and metal rattles are somewhat louder than wooden ones. Rattles of these types (which are unfortunately quite rare) are played exactly like maracas.

Yet another variety is the **soft rattle**, classically fashioned of woven basketry, but occasionally homemade from cardboard. Basket rattles are made in the shape of a maraca, a dumbbell, or a small basket with a built-in handle. The sound of both basketry and cardboard rattles is very crisp and clear, delicate and gentle in a very appealing way. Unfortunately, it cannot exceed *mezzo-forte* in loudness. When swished, a basket rattle "rumbles" a bit because of the ridges formed by the basketry.

Another soft and delicate rattle is the **Mexican bean**, an instrument manufactured by Nature as the seed pod of the flamboyant-tree, *Delonix regia*, an ornamental shade tree originally from Madagascar (not Mexico) but now grown worldwide in tropical regions, including Florida and California. The pod, which resembles those of the related mimosa and locust trees, contains a number of seeds, each loosely enclosed in a separate oblong cavity. The seeds are free to move back and forth across the width of the pod, but only in that direction and for that short distance; it is this which gives the rattle its precision, delicacy, and softness. The instrument can be shaken (*pp–mp*), especially to produce a roll, but sounds best, and has a wider dynamic range, when struck against a hand or cushion.

All the rattles of the maraca group (including the Mexican bean) can be used to strike other instruments (with the same restrictions as for the sistrum). The general effect is that of a very light wooden stick, though the glass rattle may be considerably heavier than the others.

All except the Mexican bean may be suspended from a rack by the handle, to allow them to be struck with sticks of whatever sort and to free the player's hands. They sound much more satisfactory, however, when hand-held.

CABASA AND SHEKERE

In its original form the **cabasa** is very similar to the maraca, except that instead of (or in addition to) being filled with gravel or what-have-you, the gourd is enclosed in a network of large beads. The netting fits rather loosely, so the instrument may be shaken like other rattles, but the more usual way to play it is by holding the net in one hand and the handle of the gourd in the other, twisting in opposite directions to make a grinding sound. The net is usually firmly

name of instrument	abbreviations	synonyms	dynamic range	status	availability
sleighbells	sleighb. 	jingles	*pp–ff*	standard	common

FIGURE 101. *Sleighbells—vital statistics.*

attached to the base of the handle, so the twisting that can be done is limited in extent and the sounds produced are of short duration, comparable to those produced by shaking. The **shekere** is a much larger, deeper-pitched version of the cabasa that is made out of a large calabash, with or without a short handle, enclosed in a network of cowrie shells or large, wooden beads. Figure 97f shows a recently developed commercial variety of cabasa, consisting of a wooden cylinder (with handle) wrapped in corrugated metal and wound spirally with a length of beaded chain. This instrument sounds the same as a traditional cabasa and is played in the same way (the chain acts as the network).

Both cabasa and shekere can be clamped down and then played one-handed by grabbing the netting. They will not rattle satisfactorily if struck with sticks. The cabasa can be used to strike other instruments, provided they are fairly large, but the shekere is much too big.

These rattles have been used very seldom in classical music, and they do not appear in our examples. They are of not infrequent occurrence, however, in Latin popular music. For an example of the use of cabasa, see Jean Barraqué's *Chant après chant.*

SLEIGHBELLS

Sleighbells are a unique kind of rattle consisting of a number of small spherical bells, each enclosing a small metal ball which makes the bell jingle whenever it is moved. Since the ball when at rest is in contact with the metal of the bell, the sound is damped rather quickly. The "orchestral" sleighbells most frequently used by percussionists consist of a thick rod the bottom third of which forms a handle; the remaining two-thirds of the length is lined with four rows of bells, with an additional bell at the very top. Unlike other rattles, sleighbells are not usually shaken but are held in one hand with the bells hanging downward and are tapped on the end of the handle with the palm of the opposite hand. This enables the production of much more precise and rapid rhythms and greater dynamic control than shaking, which is used only in very loud passages and for rolls. The response of the instrument is such that the aggregate decay time varies with the dynamic level, between about an eighth of a second in *pianissimo* to two-fifths of a second in *forte* and louder.

It is almost impossible to move sleighbells without causing some sound, and accordingly players should be allowed either ample time or the cover of a noisy passage whenever the instrument is to be picked up or set down. Similar considerations are involved in using the instrument to strike another: the striking motion will cause the bells to jingle *before* the other instrument is hit. In this regard it should be mentioned that sleighbells are probably the heaviest rattle in the world; when they are used to strike another instrument it is the end of the handle which does the striking, with the effect of a *very* heavy wooden stick.

name of instrument	abbreviations	synonyms	dynamic range	status	availability
wooden string rattle	w.s.r.	wooden: row rattle chain rattle rattling string strip rattle	*ppp–ff*	exotic, homemade	very rare
glass string rattle	g.s.r.	glass: row rattle chain rattle strip rattle	*ppp–ff*	homemade	very rare
string of jingle bells	j.b.	jingles jingle string	*ppp–ff*	homemade, exotic	rare
chains	(none)	(none)	*ppp–ff*	found object	rare

FIGURE 102. *String rattles—vital statistics.*

Orchestral sleighbells cannot easily be suspended and struck with a stick. For this purpose an older form of the instrument is used, in which a single row of bells is fastened to a short strip or loop of cloth or leather. This sort of sleighbells, which has the same sound as the orchestral variety but is somewhat harder to control, is played entirely by shaking and performs quite satisfactorily when suspended and struck. Individual pellet bells can be obtained, ranging from pea-sized to plum-sized, that may be used singly or grouped in batches to form any imaginable configuration: see the discussion below of strings of jingle bells.

Orchestral sleighbells are made with bells of standard size, but in ribbon-type and homemade instruments different pitch levels can be obtained.

STRING RATTLES

String rattles occur in two distinct forms. In one a number of small sonorous objects are tied at intervals along the length of a string, thong, or ribbon so that they rattle against each other when the string is held at one end and shaken. In the other the objects are tied or linked to each other end-to-end to form a chain and a rattle is made by holding three or four such chains together at one end and shaking. The sound produced and the playing techniques involved are the same for both sorts:

(1) Tapping the hand that holds the instrument with the fingers or palm of the opposite hand. This enables the instrument to be played very cleanly and precisely, *ppp–ff*. When playing *pp* or louder it is almost impossible to avoid a second or two of *ppp* rattling from the bottom of the rattle after the note has theoretically stopped. This can be suppressed by resting the bottom of the rattle on a cushion or other non-sonorous object; however, this tends to suppress *all* lateral vibrations of the string, making the rattle sound like such drier types as the cabasa or sleighbells.

(2) Shaking up and down (*pp–ff*). This gives the instrument the "sloshing" attack typical of string rattles, and a decay of about a third of a second, followed by the usual second or so of *ppp* "mumbling."

(3) Shaking back and forth (*pp–ff*). This very strongly emphasizes the "sloshing" nature of the sound. The player can vary the duration of the sound (exclusive of the "mumbling" at the end) from about a third of a second to nearly two seconds. Rolls are performed by lateral shaking and are very continuous in effect.

(4) Dropping the rattle onto a surface from a short height (*pp–ff*). This is a unique "collapsing" sound. The dynamics are controlled by the amount of the string dropped. In order to drop only a small amount, the rest of the instrument must be gradually lowered onto the surface beforehand; this cannot be done without a great deal of *ppp–pp* "mumbling," an interesting sound in its own right. Once the instrument is dropped, raising it will again cause it to rattle, *pp–f*. Unless the surface onto which the rattle is dropped is non-resonant, such as a cushion, it will contribute its own sounds. If the rattle is a heavy chain and the surface is a resonant one such as a metal slab, pail, or tam-tam laid flat, dynamics up to *ffff* can be achieved by dropping the chain from a sufficient height.

(5) Letting the instrument lie in a heap on some surface and agitating it with one hand (*ppp–ff[f]*). This produces a continuous tumbling or crumpling sound with a very clear attack and release. Sounds produced in this way may attain *fff* in loudness if the rattle is heavy and the surface particularly hard and resonant. Notes played in this way should be notated as

rubbed, ♩ , and the notation explained to the player.

(6) If necessary, string rattles can be suspended and struck with sticks, but much of their unique tone quality will be lost.

String rattles vary considerably not only in the way they are put together but in the materials of which they are made. String rattles with a "wooden" sound, for instance, may be made not only of wood but of nutshells, plastic, bone, etc.; "glass" string rattles may be made of clay, stone, or seashells. Metal string rattles are divisible into "lush" and "dry" varieties, depending on the resonance of the objects of which they are made. The only common form of "dry" metal string rattle is **chains**, which have been used as a percussion instrument off and on since the late nineteenth century. "Lush" metal string rattles are made from resonant jingles or little bells and are best called a **string of jingle bells**. The bells are generally either the individual pellet bells mentioned in the previous section or crudely wrought little clapper bells of thin bronze or iron, which can also be used individually or grouped into configurations other than that of a string rattle. Individual bells of either type tend to be pitched somewhere between a^2 and g^4; nonetheless, they are not built with pitch in mind and are often microtonal.

As with windchimes, string rattles of definite pitch are certainly *possible*, but the instruments are invariably constructed so as to be indefinite. Even so, one could with confidence write for up to six string rattles of identical timbre but differing pitch, were they not generally so very rare.

WINDCHIMES

Windchimes—instruments consisting of a large number of identical objects suspended from a common frame in such a way that they will strike against each other when agitated—are clearly a type of rattle. They are treated separately here because, unlike all other rattles, they are not hand instruments; in use they are suspended from above, where they can be struck with a stick (any stick at all—there is no difference in sound) or swept with the hand.

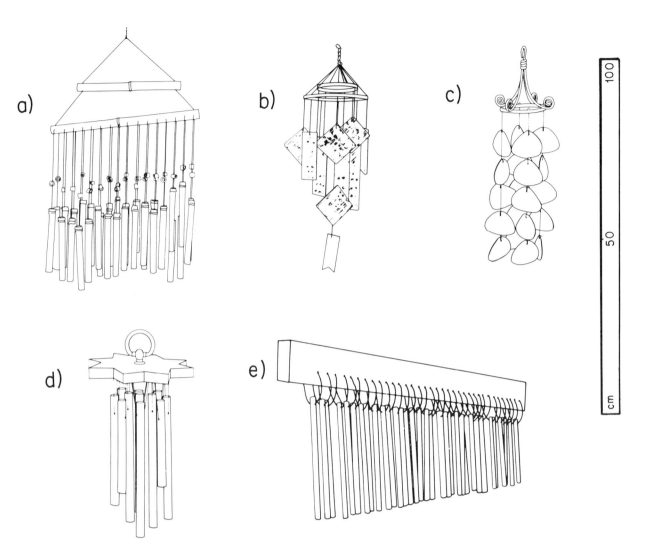

FIGURE 103. *Windchimes: (a) wood; (b) glass; (c) shell; (d) metal; (e) Mark tree.*

As their name implies, windchimes are not built as instruments at all but as decorations to be hung up to tinkle in the breeze. In order to fulfill this function they are built very delicately, with small (i.e., high-pitched) jingles. Four types are in common use: a wooden one, made from short segments of bamboo; one made from little oblong glass plates; one made from flat, usually circular pieces of very thin shell; and one made with four or so tiny brass or steel tubes, acoustically identical to full-sized tubular chimes but much higher in pitch. Wood and shell windchimes are only medium-high in pitch, glass and metal ones considerably higher. The metal windchime is unique in that the little tubes have a long decay time, about three seconds; the jingles of other windchimes, though richly resonant, have quick decays.

Windchimes of each type are surprisingly uniform in pitch-level—it is difficult, if not impossible, to get a variety of pitches in an unmixed timbre. Only the wood windchimes vary significantly in pitch, and then only across a narrow range. This difficulty can be gotten around by various means. First, there is a fairly rare variety of windchime in which the jingles consist of thick, blunt-tipped sea-urchin spines; these sound essentially the same as glass windchimes

name of instrument	abbreviations	synonyms	dynamic range	status	availability
wood windchime(s)	w. windch. wwc.	wood chime(s) bamboo (wind)chime(s)	*pp–f(f)*	novelty	usually available
glass windchime(s)	gl. windch. gwc.	glass chime(s)	*pp–f*	novelty	usually available
shell windchime(s)	sh. windch. swc.	shell chime(s)	*pp–f*	novelty	usually available
metal windchime(s)	met. windch. mwc.	(none)	*pp–f*	novelty, homemade, standard	usually available
Mark tree	M. tr. Mark	chime tree	*pp–f*	standard, homemade	rare

FIGURE 104. *Windchimes and Mark tree—vital statistics.*

(a bit drier) but are a good octave higher in pitch and can be used as an upward extension of the glass windchime. The shell windchime can be used, somewhat less satisfactorily, as a downward extension of the glass one. Shells, sea-urchin spines, etc., are essentially ceramic both chemically and acoustically; in fact, the rare, expensive, and extremely delicate windchimes with jingles made of paper-thin ceramic, sold at craft fairs and fancy boutiques, sound virtually identical to the plebeian shell instruments: in both cases the thinness of the jingles gives them their special timbre. Perfectly satisfactory metal windchimes of lower pitch than those commercially available can be assembled from items available in any hardware store, and especially high or low wooden ones can be constructed with almost equal ease. Large homemade metal windchimes may weigh a kilogram or more; the fact that it would take a hurricane to make such an instrument jingle in the wind is of no concern to percussionists.

The envelope of a windchime is highly indeterminate; it is a statistical assemblage of random clicks rather than a single unified sound. When struck, a windchime will rattle thus for a good five seconds, followed by another five seconds of *ppp* mumbling before coming completely to rest. The attack can be varied considerably in forcefulness and clarity, and composers should feel free to use the various symbols of accentuation to indicate such shadings. A roll can be created by stirring the jingles; remember that when the roll finishes the instrument will continue to rattle for another five seconds or more. A frequently used special effect is the clutching of all the jingles together in a clump between the hands—this makes a loud, very emphatic sound with a definite cutoff; on the wood windchime the sound may be as loud as *fortissimo.* This effect should be indicated by the word "clutch!" written above the staff or by an x through the stem of the note involved (this must be explained to the player). Two or more clutched notes can be written in a row, but at some point the instrument will have to be released, producing the usual five seconds of rattling. Another special effect is to set the windchime tinkling by blowing at it. This gives a very gentle attack and can, of course, be performed while both hands are occupied elsewhere. Pieces have been written in which a small electric fan is set up behind a windchime to provide a continuous background tinkling for a long stretch of time.

name of instrument	abbreviations	synonyms	dynamic range	status	availability
vibraslap	vbslp. vsp.	(none)	*p–ff*	standard	usually available

FIGURE 105. *The vibraslap—vital statistics.*

It is downright dangerous to play a glass windchime loudly with bare hands, and it is probably best that extended *forte* passages on that instrument be played only with sticks.

Windchimes illustrate the current state of chaos in percussion-instrument design and manufacture. Although they have been used almost to the point of cliché in contemporary music, they are still almost exclusively manufactured only as novelties; these novelty instruments, never intended for use in music, are so delicate that as percussion they have a useful life of only about a year. There is no doubt that were they built by percussion-makers to be percussion instruments they would be much sturdier, less prone to becoming hopelessly tangled, and available in a much greater variety of pitches. The very real possibility of windchimes of definite pitch has not yet been explored.

A specialized variety of metal windchime that is now built by at least two percussion manufacturers is the **Mark tree**, a single row of hanging rods or tubes graduated in length and pitch. This instrument was invented in the early 1970s—reportedly by someone whose first name was Mark—and has just begun to become popular in the past few years. It is a virtual substitute for the bell tree (discussed below) and like it is designed to produce a shimmering microtonal glissando when swept lengthwise. Because the sounding elements of a Mark tree are in a single line, they scarcely jangle together at all when the instrument is played, and the effect is thus totally unlike a windchime. Individual elements can be dinged with a triangle beater, but the actual pitch so produced must be left somewhat indeterminate, since it is difficult to pick out a specific chime from the closely packed row. Mark trees are made in at least three sizes of contrasting pitch.

THE VIBRASLAP

The vibraslap is a specialized rattle in which the rattling is caused indirectly, by the vibration of the instrument itself, rather than directly by shaking or striking. The instrument consists of a looped metal rod at one end of which is a large wooden ball and at the other end a very flat, trapezoidal wooden bell; across the mouth of the bell run a number of metal rivets set loosely into sockets top and bottom. The player holds the instrument by the loop in the rod and strikes the ball against the opposite hand, a cushion, or any other resisting object. This causes the ends of the rod to vibrate back and forth, like the branches of a tuning fork, shaking the bell and causing the rivets to rattle in time with the vibrations. The frequency of vibration is in the audible range, but the pitch thus produced is very soft and is completely drowned out by the noise of the rivets—a tight, intense whirring sound with a sharp attack. There is a slightly ominous, menacing quality to the sound, perhaps because it somewhat resembles the buzz of a rattlesnake. The duration of a vibraslap note is a function of its loudness, varying from about a quarter-second in *piano* to a full second in *fortissimo*. The sound is always accented and diminuendo.

The vibraslap, a relatively recent invention, has almost completely replaced the older and now much rarer **quijada**, or **jawbone**, an instrument consisting of the mandible of a donkey, the teeth held loosely in their sockets by strings or springs. The jaw is held near the front and struck sideways against the opposite hand, causing the rami to vibrate and the teeth to rattle. The sound, very close to that of the vibraslap, is a bit softer and more delicate.

Both quijada and vibraslap are heavy instruments and cannot be played swiftly—no faster than eighth-notes at ♩ = 132. A roll can be performed only by shaking the instrument; the sound thus produced cannot exceed *forte*.

The vibraslap can of course be used to strike other instruments, with the effect of a very heavy wooden mallet.

RATCHETS AND RASPS

RATCHETS

The ordinary orchestral ratchet consists of a hand-cranked wooden cogwheel in a common frame with two to four wooden tongues. As the cogwheel turns, it repeatedly pulls back and releases the tongues with a snapping sound, producing a smoothly continuous grinding rattle. Dynamics are controlled by varying the speed with which the cogwheel is turned and, to a certain extent, by varying the pressure of the tongues on the cogwheel with the fingers of the hand holding the instrument. Very soft, short notes may thus come out as single clicks—an effect that is, unfortunately, not completely under the player's control.

The instrument may either be held in the player's hand or fastened to a stand; one hand is of course needed to turn the crank.

It is traditional to notate all ratchet notes, no matter how short, as rolls. Remember that ratchets are in effect sustaining instruments, with a definite end to each note. Individual notes can be very short, but the nature of the ratchet is such that it is impossible to play separate repeated notes faster than about eighth-notes at ♩ = 112.

It is possible, if difficult, to find ratchets at up to three or so different pitch levels.

The **metal ratchet** is listed here as "very rare" only because percussionists seldom own one. The instruments are common enough in five-and-dime stores, where they are sold for use as party noisemakers or *greggers* at Purim. Ratchets of this sort are designed to be held by the handle and whirled around one's head, producing a sound that is continuous but not smooth. This problem can be gotten around by holding the handle and rotating the body of the instrument around it with one finger. The sound of the metal ratchet is genuinely metallic, not only because of the thinness of the metal tongues but because the works of the instrument are enclosed in a light metal box that acts as a resonator. The metal ratchet is softer in dynamics and usually higher in pitch than the wooden kind.

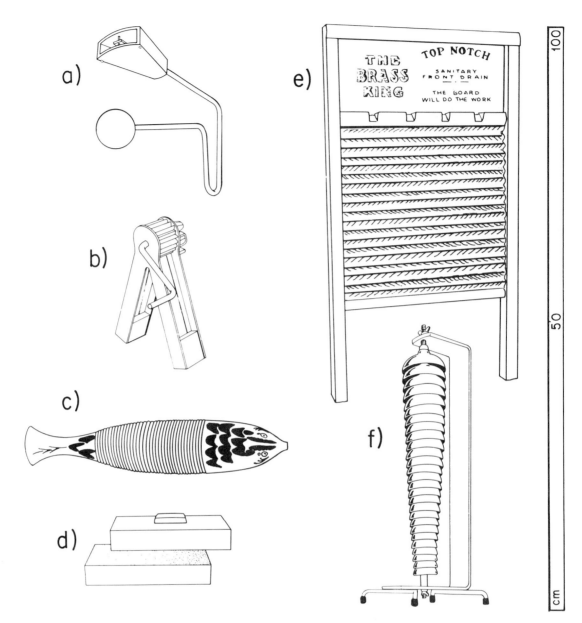

FIGURE 106. *Vibraslap, ratchets, and rasps: (a) vibraslap; (b) ratchet; (c) güiro; (d) sandblocks; (e) washboard; (f) bell tree.*

RASPS

The most commonly employed rasp is the **güiro**, an elongate gourd (or wood carved in a similar shape) with numerous parallel grooves scored in one surface and a hole cut into it elsewhere so that the body of the gourd can act as a resonator. The instrument is cradled in one arm or fastened to a stand, and a stick is scraped across the grooves. A special three-pronged scraper is often used, giving a very fine, delicate scraping sound; however, other thin sticks, such as snare stick, triangle beater, or the reverse of any of the felt or rubber series mallets or of the metal glockenspiel sticks, may be used. The snare stick is particularly effective in bringing out a "woody" quality in the tone.

name of instrument	abbreviations	synonyms	dynamic range	status	availability
ratchet	ratch. 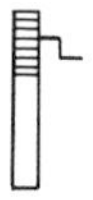	rattle cog rattle	*mf–fff*	standard	common
metal ratchet	met. ratch.	(none)	*mf–ff*	novelty	very rare

FIGURE 107. *Ratchets—vital statistics.*

name of instrument	abbreviations	synonyms	dynamic range	status	availability
sandblocks	sandbl. sbl.	sandpaper blocks	*ppp–f*	standard, homemade	usually available
güiro	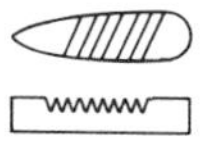	gourd scraper	*pp–ff*	standard	common
wooden rasp	w. rasp	(none)	*pp–ff*	homemade, exotic	usually available
glass rasp	gl. rasp	(none)	*pp–ff*	homemade	very rare
metal rasp	met. rasp	(none)	*pp–ff*	homemade, found object	rare
washboard	wash. wbd.	(none)	*pp–ff*	found object	usually available
bell tree	bell tr.	(none)	*pp–fff*	exotic	rare

FIGURE 108. *Rasps—vital statistics.*

The instrument is normally played with alternate strokes toward and away from the player. The outward stroke (**downstroke**) is slightly more emphatic than the inward one (**upstroke**), and players usually start each phrase or group of notes with one or the other depending on whether the first note has an upbeat or downbeat feel to it. This may lead to an awkward reading if the distribution of notes within the phrase is unusual, and composers may

therefore *occasionally* wish to mark a note as an upstroke () or downstroke (). If two or more notes are to be played in a single stroke (i.e., by starting and stopping the motion of the hand without either reversing direction or starting over from one end of the instrument on each note) they should be grouped under a slur and marked with staccato-dots or tenuto-lines, depending on the effect desired. For instance, the basic samba rhythm popularly associated with the güiro would be notated thus:

All these techniques and notations are derived from the virtually identical usage of bowed strings; for a more detailed discussion, see Chapter IX.

It is occasionally desired that the body of the güiro be struck rather than scraped. Notes played in this way should be indicated with the word "struck" (canceled by "scraped"). For a texture of mixed struck and scraped notes, the former should be written ♪ and the latter

♪ . This must be explained to the player. A roll can be executed on the güiro by scraping rapidly back and forth with a scrubbing motion.

The pitch of a rasp is determined by the width and spacing of its grooves. Güiros tend to be similar in pitch, at the high end of the potential rasp pitch range. A downward extension of the güiro timbre is available with exotic and homemade wooden rasps. The most common of these is the **reco-reco**, which may be made of carved wood, notched bamboo, or a notched cowhorn. It is slightly lower in pitch than the güiro and is frequently used to play "second güiro."* There are numerous other exotic rasps—some consisting of no more than a notched stick—and homemade rasps of similarly simple construction. This whole complex of rasps is best referred to by the general rubric "wooden rasp," a term that can also include the güiro and is recommended for use in pieces in which rasps of different pitch are needed.

Rarely seen but very effective-sounding are homemade rasps of metal and ceramic. The former is best played with a triangle beater or other metal stick, the latter with a glass swizzle-stick (although a triangle beater may be used). All these rasps can themselves be scraped against any object with a definite edge.

There are also three specialized rasps. The **sandblocks** consist of two small, equal pieces of two-by four with sandpaper covering one surface of each block. The sandpapered faces of the blocks are rubbed against each other, producing a very thin, fine hissing—by far the highest-pitched of all rasp sounds. These blocks can also be banged together as a special effect or to add emphasis to the attack. If desired, one of the blocks can be fastened down, leaving the player a free hand. An individual sandblock may also be rubbed against other percussion instruments.

The **washboard** is just that—an old-fashioned scrubbing board. As a rasp it is low-pitched and anonymous in sound, whether the corrugated surface is made of wood, wood covered with metal, or metal alone. Classically, a strap is attached to the top of the board so that it can be hung around the player's neck. There it can be scraped with a stick (wood, metal, plastic, or an unwound xylophone stick) or, more traditionally, played with thimbles worn on the fingers of both hands. In this mode of play ("jug-band style") tapping may be more important than scraping, and the composer may therefore wish to use unadorned notes to signify tapping and to notate scrubbing as a rubbed effect (see Fig. 92).

Finally, there is the **bell tree**, a nested set of actual bells, strung on a rod in order of size. The pitch differences among the bells are microtonal and when an appropriate stick (a metal glockenspiel stick or triangle beater is best) is run along the stack a mysterious-sounding

* Low-pitched tubular wooden rasps of this type are now also made under the name "güiro"; this confusion of names emphasizes the fact that despite differences in appearance all wooden rasps are really the same instrument.

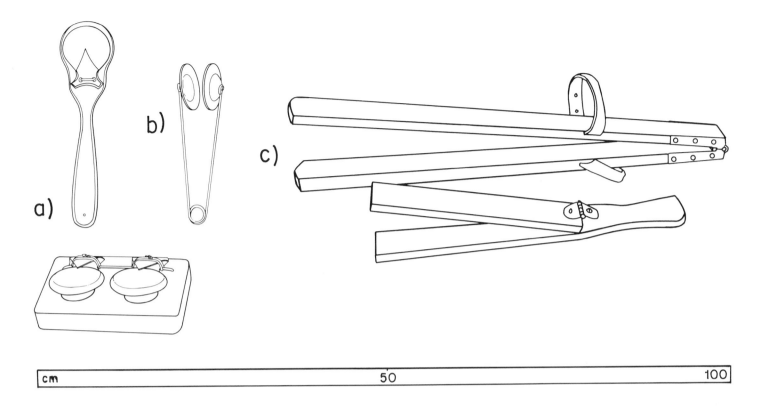

FIGURE 109.   *Castanets and slapsticks: (a) castanets; (b) metal castanets; (c) slapsticks.*

upward or downward glisssando is produced; the sound rings on for five seconds or more. The instrument has, along with the Mark tree (q.v.), been used so heavily in television and movie scores to represent Unknown Powers or The Lurking Presence that its association with the spooky or uncanny carries over into any music, no matter how abstract, in which it is used. The best way to notate the bell tree is to put all the notes on a single line, indicating with

arpeggios whether the glissando is upward (♪) or downward (♪). Short swipes or back-and-forth rolls limited to only some of the bells can be indicated by using notes on, above, or below the line for different pitch levels. The bells are too closely nested to permit picking out individual bells.

CLAPPERS

CASTANETS

Castanets are made in two formats for use under differing circumstances. The more common is a hand instrument consisting of a small wooden paddle to the opposite surfaces of which are hinged two (sometimes four) round, flat clappers. Both the clappers and the paddle are scooped out so that a cavity forms between them when they strike against each other and this increases the loudness and resonance of the sound, which is an extremely clear and precise click. Unlike most rattling instruments, castanets are shaken back and forth rather than up

name of instrument	abbreviations	synonyms	dynamic range	status	availability
castanets	cast. 	(none)	p–$f\!f$	standard	common
metal castanets	met. cast.	(none)	p–$f\!f$	standard	very rare

FIGURE 110. *Castanets—vital statistics.*

name of instrument	abbreviations	synonyms	dynamic range	status	availability
slapstick	slapst.	whip	p–$f\!f$	standard, homemade	common

FIGURE 111. *The slapstick—vital statistics.*

and down. This means that strokes in both directions will produce a strong sound, and therefore the instrument can be played very quickly, including grace-notes, rolls, and so on. The instrument can be used—not very forcibly—to strike other instruments.

The other type of castanets (**table model** or **machine castanets** as opposed to **hand castanets**) is in the form of a small box about the size and shape of a woodblock, with the two clappers set side by side on top of it. The clappers are not only hinged to the box but are provided with springs so that they will return to the raised position after being struck. Table-model castanets are played by striking the clappers, typically with the fingers but occasionally with wound or felt sticks. Harder sticks will work but will produce a lot of distracting attack noise. To play the castanets rapidly the two clappers are struck alternately.

Metal castanets with an appropriately metallic sound are available but have seldom been scored. Formed like a pair of tongs with clappers at the end, they are not shaken, but squeezed together in the hand. Though they can be played quite rapidly, rolls are impossible.

SLAPSTICK

The slapstick is two flat boards hinged together at the bottom. When they are slapped together a sharp snapping sound that resembles the crack of a whip is produced. In commercially made slapsticks, one of the boards is extended beyond the hinge to form a handle. The instrument is played one-handed by shaking it violently downward; at the bottom of the shake the shorter board (which is uppermost) will "run into" the larger one. This process is aided by the spring-loading of the hinge. Slapsticks must be played slowly, with repeated slaps occurring no faster than eighth-notes at ♩ = about 80.

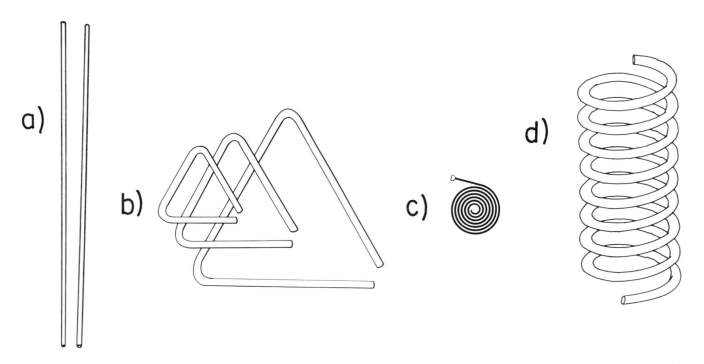

FIGURE 112. *Rods and coils: (a) rods; (b) triangles; (c) clock coil; (d) auto coil.*

Because they depend on spring-loading, commercial slapsticks are all medium to high in pitch. For lower pitches there are homemade instruments, hinged at the bottom (without a spring), that must be held in both hands. These large instruments can be played no faster than quarter-notes at ♩ = 132 but they can be played as softly as *pp*.

The **tap-a-tap** used by Chavez in his monumental *Tambuco* is an interesting variant of the slapstick: it is, in effect, a pair of square, wooden crash cymbals. Since the boards are not hinged together, they have a much wider dynamic range than any slapstick (*ppp–fff*) and are also capable of rubbing effects not possible on slapstick.

Only the smaller, commercial slapsticks can be used to strike other instruments.

RODS AND COILS

RODS

Rods are about the simplest idiophones imaginable: a pair of thin rods of whatever material are held in the hands and struck against each other to produce a weak, dry click. A pair of snare sticks used in this way constitutes a typical set of wooden rods; metal rods tend to be somewhat longer and thinner, glass ones (to prevent breakage) shorter and thicker. Although hand-held

name of instrument	abbreviations	synonyms	dynamic range	status	availability
wooden rods	w. rods	sticks	*ppp–f*	found object, homemade	ubiquitous
glass rods	gl. rods	(none)	*ppp–f*	found object, homemade	very rare
metal rods	met. rods	(none)	*ppp–f*	found object, homemade	usually available

FIGURE 113. *Rods—vital statistics.*

rods can be played very quickly, a true roll is impossible. The rods may be rubbed against each other, *ppp.*

Rods have also been used in other ways. They may be suspended from above (specify **suspended rods**) or mounted upright on a board (specify **mounted rods**); in either case they are struck with hard, light, thin beaters—for example, snare sticks, triangle beaters, knitting needles, or reversed rubber-series mallets. Rods of all sorts are much more resonant when suspended than when held or mounted; suspended metal ones may produce a thin, triangle-like ding instead of a dry click. Suspended rods, because of their tendency to swing back and forth, cannot be played very swiftly, but mounted ones are very stable and all sorts of precise and rapid rhythmic figures can easily be performed, including rolls and (between rods of different lengths) trills. If two such rods are mounted adjacent to each other the trill can be performed with a single stick simply by rattling it back and forth between them. Graded sets of a dozen or more mounted rods have been built by imaginative percussionists, the set then being used as a single complex instrument.

THE TRIANGLE

The triangle is a thickish metal rod bent into the shape of an equilateral triangle and suspended by a string from one vertex so that it can vibrate freely. The instrument was originally hand-held, but nowadays it is almost invariably hung from a stand or rack.

The triangle is normally played with the special metal beater described in Chapter V. Because of the instrument's shape even very fast passages and rolls can be performed one-handed by moving the beater back and forth between adjacent sides of the triangle. To get a *ppp* it is necessary to use the rubber-jacketed reverse of the beater; since not all triangle beaters possess this feature, one should ask for "rubber-jacketed beater." Other sticks that may be used with the triangle are: knitting needle (*ppp–mf*), giving a very tiny, thin version of the ordinary tone with considerable attack noise; reversed rubber-series mallet (*ppp–mf*), which is like the knitting needle, but with a less clear attack; snare stick or other wooden stick (*pp–ff*), creating much woody attack noise; wire brush (*ppp–pp*), or finger (*ppp–pp*).

If the triangle is left free to vibrate, a note will last five seconds or more. A mild vibrato in the tone can be produced by waving a cupped hand back and forth next to the instrument. To get a note of short duration, hand-damping (with the free hand or, in a pinch, with the hand

name of instrument	abbreviations	synonyms	written range	sounds	normal sticks	status	availability
triangles	trgl. tri. 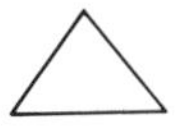	(none)	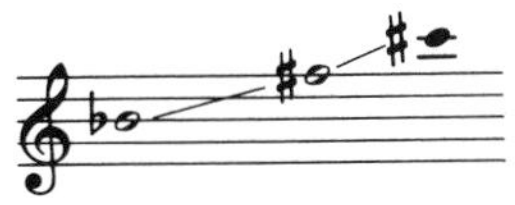	1 octave higher (transposition not standardized) loudest: *ff* softest: *ppp*	triangle beater	standard	ubiquitous

FIGURE 114.   *Triangles—vital statistics.*

holding the beater) is used; this is an integral part of triangle technique, and composers should notate the duration of triangle notes with care. Notes can be **hand-muffled** as well, producing a short, "dead," rod-like sound. Passages to be played thus should be marked "damped" (canceled by "nat." or "ord."); individual notes should be marked with an x ()—a notation which, because it is not yet standardized, must be explained to the player.

Although they possess a weakly definable pitch, triangles are almost always treated as indefinitely pitched instruments. As with many other "indefinitely pitched" idiophones, the pitch range of available instruments is quite small. The pitch of a triangle can be lowered up to a semitone by dipping it in water; the decay time will be slightly shortened and the tone will become a little less tangy. This special tone can be obtained without a drop in pitch by dipping only the lower side of the triangle into the water. For such water effects (including glissandos) the instrument must be hand-held. In writing for pitched triangles the octave transposition must be specified, because there is no standard practice. In fact, the situation among idiophones is so chaotic that it is probably a good idea to specify the octave transposition, if any, of all pitched idiophones whenever they are used. (In my own work I write for all idiophones at actual pitch, using the special clefs described in Appendix I.)

A kind of giant metal windchime can be made by hanging a number of triangles so that they will knock into each other when played.

COILS

Coils, like triangles, are essentially long metal rods thrown into a compact shape. **Auto coils** are thick metal helices used in the suspension systems of automobiles and other heavy machinery. They are massive affairs—each one weighs several kilograms—and as springs they are so stiff that for all percussion purposes they can be counted as rigid. As an instrument the auto coil is suspended from a large, heavy rack with a stout rope or thong and played just like a triangle, which it strongly resembles acoustically. The sound is a bit less tangy with high partials, and a bit quicker to decay, and is a good two octaves lower than the triangle;* it can

---

* Because of the rareness and variability of this instrument I have not given a pitch range. The two I was able to test sounded e^1 and $e\flat^1$, respectively. Others heard on record also seem to lie in the range just above middle C.

name of instrument	abbreviations	synonyms	dynamic range	normal sticks	status	availability
clock coil	 ◎	(none)	*ppp–mf*	light metal glockenspiel sticks	noisemaker	rare
auto coil	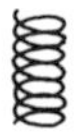 ▒	coil spring coil auto spring	*ppp–ff*	triangle beater(s)	found object	rare

FIGURE 115. *Coils—vital statistics.*

thus serve well as a downward extension of the triangle. It would be interesting to know if the large gap between the pitches of triangle and auto coil could be filled. The auto coil is best played with a heavy triangle beater. Fast rhythms and rolls can be played by moving the beater back and forth between adjacent loops of the coil. A special effect not available on triangle is a rasplike attack performed by running the beater along the length of the coil, striking each loop in turn. This should be notated ♩ and explained to the player; care should be taken to differentiate between the length of time taken by the rasp effect itself and the continued resonance of the instrument after the rasping is completed. Hand-damping is used just as with the triangle. In addition to the triangle beater, the auto coil may be played with a reversed snare stick (better, a wooden timpani stick) or unwound xylophone mallets, which must be paired if a roll is to be performed. A very strong, full sound is produced by the use of a chime mallet, and for the loudest, most brilliant sound possible a nail hammer can be used. Neither of these hammers can be used to produce a roll. There is a great temptation to overestimate the loudness of the auto coil, which, despite its great weight and rugged appearance, cannot produce a true *fff* even with a nail hammer, no matter how hard it is hit. For an example of the use of auto coils, see the fifth ("A la femminisca") of Berio's *Folk Songs.*

Clock coils are altogether different in origin and appearance. They are planispiral rather than helical and are made of metal so thin it could almost be called wire. They are used in grandfather clocks as hour chimes and are designed to imitate the sound of a large, Big Ben type of church bell. Despite their small size and delicacy, clock coils typically have one or two prominent partials well below middle C; however, the perceived pitch of the coil is likely to fall somewhere in the octave above c^1.* Clock coils are very weak in sound, and they must be attached to a resonator (usually a thin-walled wooden box) if they are to be heard at all. Even so they cannot exceed *mezzo-forte* unless they are amplified electronically. The sound of a clock coil is only superficially bell-like; there is always a tangy cluster of high partials unlike any bell's, and the sound can best be described as intermediate between the triangle and the tubular chimes. Although clock coils have a fairly distinct pitch, they are invariably written for as indefinitely pitched instruments, probably because of the difficulty of finding a given specific pitch. Clock coils must be played with pairs of light, hard sticks—metal glockenspiel sticks or triangle beaters. Hard xylophone sticks can be used if necessary. A "rasp" effect like

---

* I was unable to examine enough clock coils to determine their pitch range.

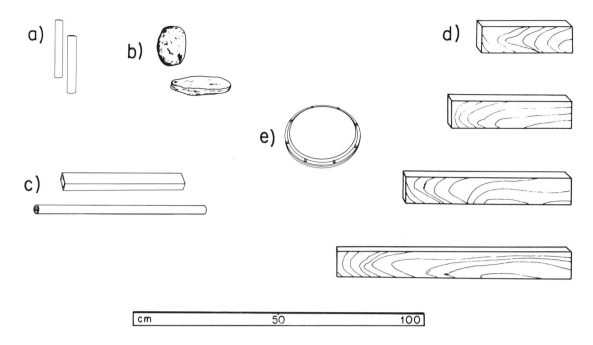

FIGURE 116. *Solid blocks: (a) claves; (b) Tibetan prayer stones; (c) anvils; (d) softwood planks; (e) practice pad.*

that of the auto coil can be achieved by drawing one of the mallets across the diameter of the coil. As an example of the use of clock coils, the reader is referred to the 1942 *Fugue for Percussion* by Lou Harrison.

SOLID BLOCKS

CLAVES AND STONES

Claves are cylindrical blocks of polished hardwood. They are not simply knocked together, like rods; rather, one of them is held loosely cradled between the fingers and thumb of one hand so that the palm of the hand forms a resonating chamber beneath it while the other clave, held firmly in the other hand, is used as a stick to strike it. The sound is a clear, penetrating click of considerable tonal richness despite its extremely rapid decay.

Claves have always been written for as unpitched instruments, but a weak pitch, albeit in a very narrow range, is there to use if desired. Interestingly, the two claves of a pair are seldom of the same pitch and may differ by as much as a third. Since the pitch of the striker clave is not heard, a single pair of claves can be used to produce either of two pitches, playing right-handed for one and left-handed for the other. Since slight adjustments of the hand are necessary to reverse the roles of the claves, alternating pitches should not be required faster than quarter-notes at $\quarternote = 120$. In writing for pitched claves the octave transposition must be specified, since there is no standard.

The usual limit of speed for claves rhythms is the maximum speed with which an object in one hand can be repeatedly struck by an object held in the other. A roll can be performed,

name of instrument	abbreviations	synonyms	written range	sounds	status	availability
claves	clav.	(none)	 loudest: *ff* softest: *pp(p)*	1 octave higher (transposition not standardized)	standard	ubiquitous
stones	(none)	river stones sea stones			found object, exotic	rare

FIGURE 117. *Claves and stones—vital statistics.*

with difficulty, by balancing the striker clave on the thumb and seesawing it rapidly back and forth with the index and ring fingers so that its two ends alternately strike the two ends of the receiving clave. Little dynamic control can be exercised over the roll, which will always come out about *mezzo-forte*.

The only way to get a *ppp* from the claves is to strike a single clave with a wound xylophone stick. Other light, hard sticks can be used instead if necessary, the hard xylophone stick giving the best approximation of normal claves tone. If absolutely necessary, a clave *can* be suspended from above or laid on a table and struck with another clave or with sticks, but the sound will be puny and non-resonant.

More promising is the use of claves as short, heavy wooden sticks to strike other instruments. A particularly interesting effect is to hold a clave sideways, using its full length to produce a small tone-cluster on mallet instruments (q.v.) or chimes.

The name **Tibetan prayer stones** sounds terribly exotic, but in fact these are simply two smooth stones, one flat and one fusiform, such as anyone could pick up in a riverbed or on a rocky beach. The flat stone is held so that the hand forms a resonating cavity beneath it, and it is tapped with the end of the other stone. By varying the size of the cavity beneath the flat stone, as many as six different (indefinite) pitches can be produced. (For convenience, the flat stone may be struck with a metal glockenspiel mallet or triangle beater.)

The name "Tibetan prayer stones" should only be used, if at all, for hand-held stones of this type. Plain "stones" will do for all other purposes, including single-pitch hand-held stones and sets of stones laid on a table to be struck. Ideally, these should be struck with another stone, but plastic mallets, hard xylophone sticks, metal glockenspiel sticks, or (appropriately enough) geologist's hammers may be substituted. The pitch of an unresonated stone depends as much on its shape as on its mass: a boulder may have the same pitch as a pebble. Probably no more than five or six different pitch levels are possible.

ANVILS AND SOFTWOOD PLANKS

Anvils are the closest metal equivalent to claves. Commercially produced anvils are made in the form of a thick oblong bar or tube mounted on a low stand to hold it slightly above the surface of the table on which it must be placed. Homemade anvils are lengths of thick-walled

name of instrument	abbreviations	synonyms	written range	sounds	normal sticks	status	availability
anvils	anv.	metal blocks	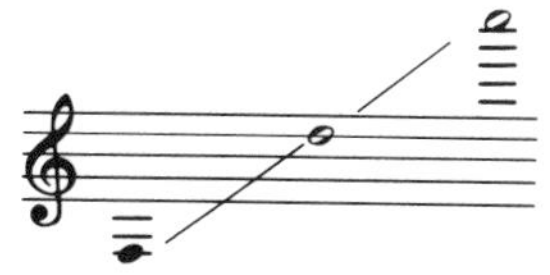 *loudest: fff* *softest: ppp*	1 octave higher (transposition not standardized)	variable	standard, homemade	common
softwood planks	planks	boards beams lengths of wood wood blocks	 *loudest: ff* *softest: ppp*	as written (transposition not standardized)	marimba sticks (hard, medium, soft)	homemade	usually available

FIGURE 118. *Anvils and softwood planks—vital statistics.*

metal pipe a few centimeters in diameter. These can be played like claves, but normally they are laid on a table and struck with sticks, like the commercial type.

Anvils produce a high-pitched, penetrating clink that decays very rapidly but not quite as fast as a claves note. Unlike claves, they have occasionally been written for as pitched instruments, though they are not very strongly pitched and are usually treated as instruments of indefinite pitch. Commercial anvils cover only a very narrow pitch range, but homemade ones are readily available in the range between about d^3 and c^5. Lower anvils can easily be made but are seldom seen, partly because high pitch is the "nature" of the anvil and partly because low ones get rather bulky; the low f^1, for instance, requires a piece of pipe some 120 cm in length. Anvils in the "normal" range can be conveniently grouped together, and a chromatic set covering the entire span can be laid out keyboard-fasion (ideally, on paired supports in a resonating box) to make a sort of mallet instrument about the size of a glockenspiel. A chord played on this "instrument" is heard as a single complex sonority, not as a true chord. Since there is no standard, the octave transposition for anvils must be specified.

Anvils are usually played with metal glockenspiel sticks, though bell mallets, plastic sticks, and hard xylophone sticks are acceptable substitutes. A wound xylophone stick must be used to obtain the *ppp* (light wooden sticks and knitting needles can also play that softly, but they will cause a lot of attack noise). For the loudest, most resonant sound possible a pair of small geologist's hammers may be used. Wooden sticks of whatever weight will produce mostly attack noise.

The glass timbre-equivalent of the anvil is found in **glass bottles**; these are discussed below in the section on bells.

Softwood planks are just that: lengths of ordinary two-by-four laid across paired supports and played with marimba sticks. The sound produced is pleasantly chunky (between marimba and temple-block), with a distinct pitch that composers usually choose to ignore. When pitches are not specified, the planks chosen will almost certainly fall within the range given here as "normal." The extension pitches are quite possible, but require wider or narrower boards than usual. The low extension notes should be played with timpani sticks. Hard sticks may be used to strike the planks, but except for the upper extension pitches they tend to produce an indefinite woody clunk whose pitch varies little, if at all, from plank to plank. Because of the softness and lightness of the wood, softwood planks are considerably larger than marimba bars of equivalent pitch, and no player should be required to handle more than twelve at a time—even fewer, if very low pitches are involved, but perhaps up to sixteen for the uppermost pitches.

BODY PERCUSSION

Anyone can easily experiment with the percussive sounds the body can make. Here are some of the main possibilities:

(1) **Slapping** the side of the stomach or lower chest (*ppp–ff*). The sound will be much fuller and more resonant if one is not wearing a shirt.

(2) **Clapping hands.** Three pitch levels can be produced by clapping palm against palm (low, *ppp–ff*), fingers against palm (medium, *ppp–ff*), or fingers against fingers (high, *ppp–mf*).

(3) **Snapping fingers** (*ppp–f*). A cavity is formed by touching the tips of the fourth and fifth fingers to the base of the thumb. By sliding the third finger suddenly off the tip of the thumb so that it violently strikes the fourth finger, a claves-like snap is produced.

(4) **Stamping** (*pp–ff*). Best with hard-soled footgear. This effect is never as loud as one imagines it to be.

(5) The **cheek-and-finger pop** (*ppp–f*) produced by sticking one finger sideways a very short way into the opposite corner of the mouth, then suddenly bending the knuckle so that the finger tip pops out of the mouth, producing a pop-gun-like sound.

HEAVY SLABS

A slab is a simple, rugged piece of metal plate or a wooden sheet in the form of a large bread board or butcher's block or table top, designed to take the heaviest blows without bending or breaking. Shatter glass, as its name implies, is played in an entirely different way and will be discussed separately at the end of this section. Normally a slab will be set on a towel-covered table, but if (as is not infrequently the case) a sledge hammer is to be used the slab will be put on the floor, usually on a blanket, towel, tarpaulin, or gymnastic mat to keep it from bouncing too noisily when struck; sometimes the floor itself may be hit. The **practice pad** (Fig. 116e), a specially designed cushion resembling the top of a snare drum and used by percussionists to practice drumming at home without disturbing the neighbors, is a more delicate sort of "slab" and will always be set on a table. An odd aspect of slabs is that scores in which they are required—particularly the earlier ones—generally do not mention the instrument at all but call instead for "hammer"; the performer must decide from the nature of the part whether a nail hammer or sledge hammer is intended, and whether the hammer should be struck against a wooden slab or a metal one. The sound produced is extremely dry and muffled; with the sledge hammer a ponderous, thudding quality is added, while with a nail hammer the sounds resemble those produced in carpentry (wood slab) or driving rivets (metal slab). In addition to nail and sledge hammers, slabs may productively be struck with other hard, heavy beaters,

name of instrument	abbreviations	synonyms	dynamic range	normal sticks	status	availability
slab of wood	w. slab	wooden: sheet plank plate board "hammer"	*ppp–fff*	variable	homemade, found object	usually available
metal slab	met. slab	metal sheet metal plate	*ppp–fff*	variable	homemade, found object	usually available
practice pad	pad	soft pad cushion	*ppp–ff*	snare sticks (normal, reversed)	standard	common
shatter glass	shattergl.	pane of glass bottle for breaking breaking glass	*ff*	—	found object	rare

FIGURE 119. *Slabs—vital statistics.*

notably the chime mallet and metal glockenspiel sticks. Snare, plastic, or xylophone sticks *can* be used, but an extremely anonymous sound, apparently all attack noise, will be produced. In writing for sledge hammer, it must be remembered that this beater is extremely ponderous and unwieldy and requires the use of both hands. At lower dynamic levels (i.e., *forte* or *fortissimo*), the hammer can be grasped at or near its head and held a short distance above the slab, allowing the production of repeated notes as fast as eighth-notes at $\flat = 72$; for the *fff* the full length of the hammer must be swung (leave plenty of room in the array!), an action which can be repeated no faster than quarter-notes at $\flat = 58$.

The practice pad is almost always played with light, hard sticks. Snare sticks are usual, but hard xylophone sticks will do as well. The instrument is used in the "lathes" (i.e., "laths") part of Varèse's *Déserts*, designated as "cushion." The sound of the practice pad is a muffled, anonymous thud.

Shatter glass usually takes the form of either a medium-sized pane of glass or a thin-walled bottle, and is played simply by being broken—the pane by chime mallet or nail hammer, the bottle by smashing it over some object. The sound, which is never as loud as one imagines it will be, is mostly produced not by the breakage itself but by the way the pieces fall. For the best sound they should be allowed to fall into a large metal or (better) glass container. The total duration of the sound produced usually varies between one and two seconds.

DRUM IDIOPHONES

WOOD PLATE DRUMS

A wood plate drum is made by removing the head from a tomtom and replacing it with a plywood disk of the same diameter. The instrument is normally played with vibraphone or

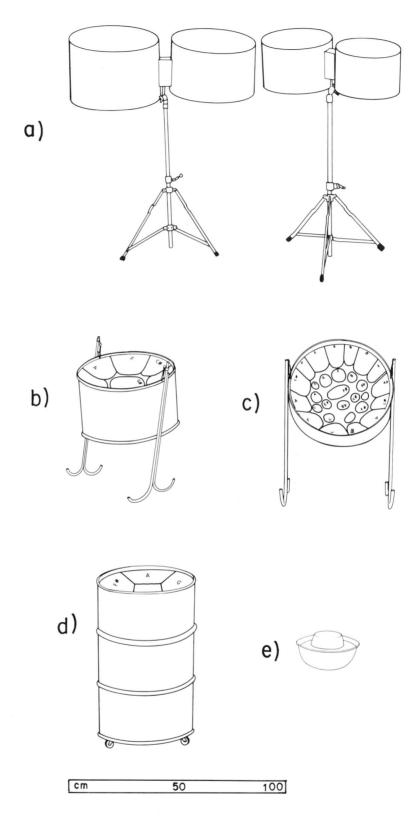

FIGURE 120. *Drum idiophones: (a) wood plate drums; (b) ping-pong pan; (c) cello pan; (d) bass pan; (e) water gourd.*

name of instrument	abbreviations	synonyms	dynamic range	normal sticks	status	availability
wood plate drums	w. pl. dr.	wood drums wooden-headed tomtoms	*ppp–fff*	variable	homemade	rare

FIGURE 121. *Wood plate drums—vital statistics.*

name of instrument	abbreviations	synonyms	dynamic range	normal sticks	status	availability
tin cans	cans	(none)	*ppp–fff*	variable	found object	rare
wastepaper baskets	bask.	(none)	*ppp–fff*	variable	found object	rare
metal garbage cans	garb.	(none)	*ppp–fff*	variable	found object	rare

FIGURE 122. *Metal cans—vital statistics.*

timpani sticks, producing a sound very much like that of a slit drum (q.v.), but more knocking in quality—due to the numerous woody high partials—and with a much less definite pitch. The knocking quality is emphasized by strokes near the rim and partially suppressed by center strokes. Hand-muffling is possible but stick-damping is not. The *fff* can only be obtained with the harder sticks. Even harder mallets than those mentioned can be used—xylophone, plastic, wood, or metal sticks—but these will tend to produce only a high-pitched knocking sound in which pitch differences among different-sized wood plate drums may be lost. At the other extreme, finger-style playing can be used to produce sounds of great delicacy in the range between *ppp* and *mp*. Probably nothing is to be gained from writing for more than four of these instruments at a time. For a piece using wood plate drums, see Stockhausen's *Kontakte* (version with instruments).

METAL CANS

Many "junkyard" instruments, such as the brake drum, produce charming and delicate sounds. In the case of these metal cans, however, a coarse and noisy clatter emerges that is entirely appropriate to their homely origin.

The instruments (the cans are turned upside down and played by striking the bottom) behave quite differently at different dynamic levels. At *mezzo-piano* or softer the sound is somewhat brake-drum–like, with a definable pitch due to one partial outlasting the others. The pitch has little to do with the size of the can, and since all the other partials do their best to obscure it, it is best ignored by composers. At *mezzo-forte* and above the sound becomes an indefinite racket, with all tin cans of whatever size being approximately alike in pitch level but differentiable as a group from wastepaper baskets, which will themselves all be at the same pitch level but differentiable as a group from garbage cans, which will also all be at one pitch level.

It is possible to demand as many as six different tin cans, four wastebaskets, or two garbage cans. These will differ in pitch at low dynamic levels, and at high ones will differ in timbre and thus still be differentiable by the listener.

A wide variety of sticks can be used on these instruments, but best are those that emphasize their clangor: plastic, snare, or xylophone sticks for the tin cans; the same, or wooden timpani sticks for the wastepaper baskets; and wooden timpani sticks, chime mallets, or nail hammers for the garbage cans. For a delicate clicking sound use knitting needles or reversed rubber-series mallets on tin cans and wastebaskets, and snare sticks or metal glockenspiel sticks on garbage cans. A somewhat muffled quality can be produced by using vibraphone or timpani sticks as appropriate for the various-sized cans; these soft sticks must be used if a *ppp* is desired. Surprisingly delicate sounds can be elicited (*ppp–p*) by using the fingers or wire brushes. All these cans can be strongly muffled by hand or stick as for drums; the notation and techniques are the same.

As an auxiliary use, the garbage can may function as a container into which to pour something. The sound produced will be much louder than expected: the dynamic levels produced by various materials are indicated below.

> rubber balls—*ff*
>
> water—*f–ff*
>
> dried beans—*ff*
>
> pebbles or coarse gravel—*fff*
>
> coins, BBs, etc.—*fff*
>
> small stones—*ffff*
>
> heavy link chain, pieces of pipe, large bolts, etc.—*ffff*

A number of small, light objects may be placed in a tin can and swished around or shaken (*pp–ff*) (cf. metal rattles, above).

STEEL DRUMS

Steel drums are among the most tonally flexible and potentially useful of all idiophones, but have been little used outside their Caribbean homeland (they were invented in Trinidad in the early 1940s) because information about them has been hard to find and because there has been next to no attempt to standardize the range of the drums or the pattern of pitches on the surface of each.

The instruments are made from 200-liter oil barrels, 57 cm in diameter; one end of the barrel is cut off and the other is hammered down into a dish shape, with its surface marked off by grooves into a complex pattern of circles and wedges. The grooves serve to isolate acoustically the various wedge-shaped and circular sections so that only the section that is struck will vibrate, and each section can thus be tuned to a different pitch. The pitch names are painted

name of instrument	abbreviations	synonyms	written range	sounds	normal sticks	status	availability
ping-pong pan	p.p. 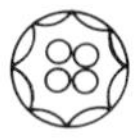	solo-lead pan	 *(notated range)* loudest: *fff* softest: *ppp*	as written	vibraphone sticks (hard, medium, soft)	homemade, standard	rare
cello pans	c.p. 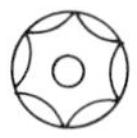	baritone pans	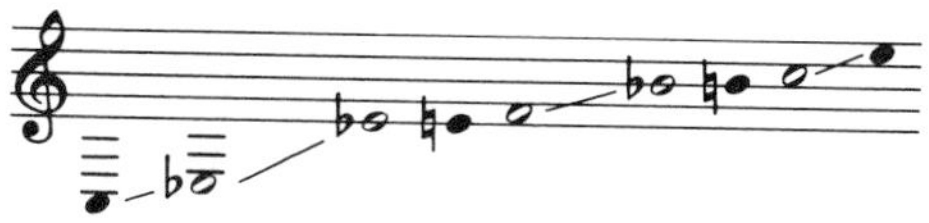 *(notated range)* loudest: *fff* softest: *ppp*	as written	marimba sticks (hard, medium, soft)	homemade, standard	very rare
bass pans	b.p. 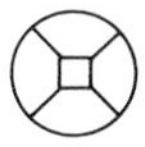	boom pans	 *(notated range)* loudest: *fff* softest: *ppp*	as written	timpani sticks (hard, medium, soft)	homemade, standard	very rare

FIGURE 123.   *Steel drums—vital statistics.*

on each section for reference, since the arrangement of pitches is both chaotic and unstandardized.

The pitch of each section depends on the amount of tension that has been put on it by hammering, but also upon its area; thus, the lower the pitch of the drum, the fewer the notes that can be fitted onto its surface. There are three important varieties of steel drum, differing in range and hence in the numbers of notes which they bear. These are the **ping-pong pan** (soprano range, twenty-five notes),* the **cello pan** (tenor, ten notes), and the **bass pan** (five notes). Cello pans are built and played in pairs, so that twenty notes will be available, and bass pans are built and played in groups of four, also comprising twenty notes. Pans of other sorts exist but are of limited musical usefulness. If a score calls for "steel drum" without any further specifications, a ping-pong pan is understood to be required.

For each type of pan the notes are arranged into a standard pattern of wedges and circles, as shown in Figure 124; the assignment of specific pitches to specific places in the pattern is *not* standard, however, nor is even the choice of pitches to be included in it. The "extension" ranges given in Figure 123 represent the ranges within which all the notes on each type of pan must fall, but the notes of a particular pan can, in theory at least, fall anywhere within that range. For instance, a ping-pong pan may theoretically possess *any* twenty-five notes between b^0 and g^3; in actual practice, however, ping-pong pans almost always have a range of two fully chromatic octaves, and this means that one can confidently assume that all the notes between g^1 and c^3 inclusive will be available on any ping-pong pan. Cello and bass pans are seldom completely chromatic; they sacrifice one or two seldom-used pitches in order to extend the overall range. If the instruments available lack a needed pitch, it is possible to retune a note to provide that pitch in place of some unneeded nearby pitch; this is not, however, a procedure

* Occasionally one may see a ping-pong pan made from an oil barrel of greater than usual diameter; such a pan may have twenty-eight or even thirty-two notes.

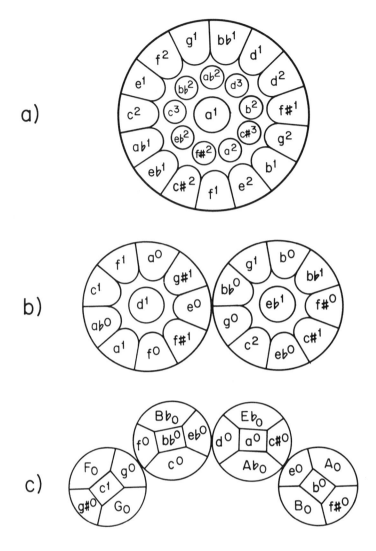

FIGURE 124. *Distribution of pitches on steel drums, as recommended by Seeger: (a) ping-pong pan; (b) cello pans; (c) bass pans.*

to be undertaken lightly, since multiple tunings fatigue the metal and will drastically shorten the useful life of the instrument.

The only readily available source of detailed information on the making and tuning of steel drums is Pete Seeger's *The Steel Drums of Kim Loy Wong.* The tuning system employed in that book is the one shown in Figure 124. Since the vast majority of steel drums are home-made, it is not unreasonable to expect that, at least in the U.S. and Canada, this system will be the most widespread. The apparent chaos in the distribution of pitches in this and all other tuning systems is necessary to minimize the effects of sympathetic vibrations in sections adjacent to the one being struck. There are only one or two small commercial manufacturers of steel drums, and their tuning systems are markedly inferior to Seeger's (for example, involving unnecessary duplication of pitches). Seeger's system has been adopted for this book and is embodied in the "standard" ranges given for the pans in Figure 123.

Steel drums form the core of the popular Caribbean steel band. Like Indonesian game-lans, complete sets of steel drums are usually made, or at least designed, by a single individual, and since in a steel band the instruments are completely self-sufficient, little attention is paid to International Standard Pitch. The pans described by Seeger are in fact pitched a minor third high; the pitches are accordingly reproduced here a minor third above Seeger's notation. Seeger suggests the possibility of tuning higher still, and on the other hand builders equipped with tuning forks sometimes attempt to reproduce Seeger's *notated* pitches, taking the instruments down a minor third, into a region where they do not sound their best. At any rate, classical musicians are most likely to encounter steel drums which, whatever their tuning system, have their notes designated at actual pitch.

As long as the current lack of standardization persists, composers must be very careful in writing for steel drums. The less virtuosic and idiomatic the part, the less likely one is to run up against the quirks and limitations of a particular pan or set of pans; similarly, it is a good idea to limit the number of different notes required, so that even pans of radically different tunings will be able to cover the part. The ping-pong pan is least problematic here, because the chromatic eleventh g^1–c^3 is available on all ping-pong pans and because all notes are on one pan, minimizing the problem of cross-overs.

For performance, ping-pong and cello pans are mounted on special stands (they may instead be hung around the neck by a strap); bass pans are set on the floor on rubber casters or placed as a group on a V-shaped frame with wheels.

The tone of a steel drum contains a large number of *very* inharmonic partials covering a wide range that is about the same for all pitches. The perceived pitch is that of a single prominent partial that tends to lie *above* the others on a ping-pong pan, below the others on a bass pan, and in the middle of the harmonic spectrum on a cello pan. The timbre on all pans is simultaneously richly resonant and coarsely gritty. The instruments sound their best cutting through a mass of other sounds, which will mask the weaker partials and let the main pitch ring through; in exposed passages the pitch of a steel drum is almost swamped by its own competing partials. Even in exposed passages, however, the pitch is strong enough that chords of all types, including dissonances, will be clearly perceived as such, except on the bass pans, on which dissonances and thick harmonies will sound unpitched.

The normal mallets for steel drums are indicated in Figure 123. Harder sticks such as wooden sticks or xylophone mallets can be used, but they will bring out the dissonant partials to such an extent that the instrument will seem unpitched; the same will happen with wire brushes. Metal sticks should be avoided, as they can put the instrument out of tune or permanently destroy its tone. For very delicate passages (*ppp–p*) finger-style playing can be very effective.

Chords of up to six notes can be played on a single pan by holding two or three mallets in each hand (described in detail in the section on mallet instruments, below). Any pair of notes on a single pan can be struck by two mallets held in one hand, but passages in consecutive double notes should move rather slowly unless the composer is dealing with a specific tuning pattern and can gauge the mallet-spread needed for each chord. Chords requiring triple mallets in one hand are more problematic, since certain combinations of notes cannot be taken one-handed; in Seeger's tuning system, for instance, the combination e^1, c^2, g^2 on a ping-pong pan can only be played using two mallets in one hand and one in the other. This is not a problem on a bass pan; the problem there is knowing which notes will appear on a given pan. When both hands are used any combination of notes (even six-note chords) can be played one way or another on a single pan of any type; remember, however, that for cello and bass pans there is no way of knowing whether any two notes will be on the same pan.

name of instrument	abbreviations	synonyms	dynamic range	normal sticks	status	availability
water gourd	wat. g.	water drum	*ppp–ff*	variable	homemade	very rare

FIGURE 125. *The water gourd—vital statistics.*

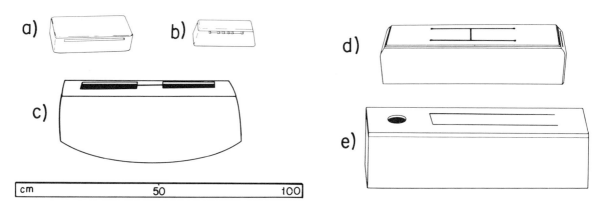

FIGURE 126. *Hollow blocks: (a) woodblock; (b) piccolo woodblock; (c), (d), (e) slit drums (3 types).*

The decay time of a steel-drum note is about two seconds, and articulation is handled much as on the marimba. Rolls and tremolos are used to sustain the sound and to ensure a smooth legato. A special effect unique to steel drums is to sweep a single mallet around the outer circle of pitches on a ping-pong or cello pan, producing a spate of rapid legato notes (no louder than *forte*) in an order determined by the tuning pattern of the pan and the direction in which the sweep is made. Since tuning patterns are essentially indeterminate, this is an indeterminate effect and should be so notated: any reasonable-looking notation will do, but it must be explained to the player.

Our steel-drum example, Henze's *El Cimarrón*, gives only a faint idea of the capabilities of these instruments. Readers are advised also to listen to one or two records of Caribbean steel-band music.

WATER GOURD

This intriguing instrument is made from half of a hollow spherical gourd (or, more prosaically, from a wooden or plastic bowl) floated face down in a bowl of water, so that an enclosed cavity is formed between the gourd and the surface of the water. When the gourd is struck it bobs up and down in the water momentarily, giving a slight wavering quality to the otherwise extremely "dead" and unresonant sound so produced.

Vibraphone or marimba mallets, or even fingers, are best for this instrument, as harder sticks will produce mostly attack noise and softer ones almost no sound at all.

In addition to the optional part in *Sinfonia India*, Chavez has written for water gourd in his *Tambuco*. A metal equivalent of the water gourd can be made using a bell (see below). For glass, use a Florence flask: the differences in timbre are slight, in technique, none.

name of instrument	abbreviations	synonyms	written range	sounds	normal sticks	status	availability
woodblocks	wbl.	Chinese blocks	  loudest: *fff* softest: *ppp*	1 octave higher (transposition not standard-ized)	xylophone sticks (hard, medium, soft); snare sticks	standard	ubiquitous

FIGURE 127. *Woodblocks—vital statistics.*

FIGURE 128. *Cross-section of a woodblock.*

HOLLOW BLOCKS

WOODBLOCKS

Woodblocks are made from oblong blocks of hardwood undercut top and bottom with deep slots that act as narrow resonating chambers for the thin shelves of wood above them (Fig. 128). Each woodblock therefore makes two separate notes (which may not be of the same pitch), but only one of these—depending on which side is up—is accessible at a time. Woodblocks are normally laid flat on a towel-covered table (or clamped to a stand) and are struck with hard, light beaters to produce a sound that is very crisp and dry but a bit more resonant than that of claves. Normally, unwound xylophone sticks (*pp–fff*) will be used. Wound mallets (*ppp–ff*) are used to produce a gentler attack and fuller sound. Snare sticks are also frequently used, producing the "ricky-tick" sound associated with early jazz. Heavier wooden sticks will produce a somewhat fuller sound, while reversed rubber-series mallets (*ppp–f*) will make a very delicate, dry, and brittle sound. Metal sticks should not be used, as they will damage the instrument, and felt sticks will not make the instrument sound. For very soft (*ppp–p*), subtle playing, fingers can be used, as can wire brushes (though not very effectively).

Woodblocks are almost always treated as instruments of indefinite pitch, but a weak pitch is present which can be exploited if desired. The octave transposition is not standardized. The upper extension tones given in Figure 127 are provided by **piccolo woodblocks**. These sound the same as regular woodblocks and are played in the same way, but are built somewhat differently, being trapezoidal in cross-section and producing only one note rather than a choice of two.

A single percussionist can easily handle a dozen or more woodblocks. Up to six can be struck at once using multiple-mallet techniques.

name of instrument	abbreviations	synonyms	written range	sounds	normal sticks	status	availability
slit drums	sltdr. slit dr. 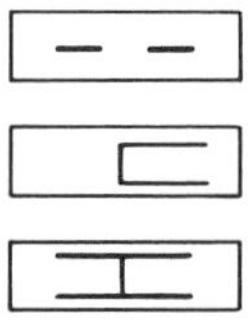	wood drums log drums	 *(musical staff)* loudest: *ff(f)* softest: *ppp*	as written	variable	standard, homemade, novelty, exotic	usually available

FIGURE 129. *Slit drums—vital statistics.*

SLIT DRUMS

Although slit drums are closely related to woodblocks in structure, they are quite different in sound, being not only much lower in pitch but delivering a considerably warmer and more sustained sound with a somewhat more definite pitch. In fact, slit drums are written for at specific pitches as often as not. As Figure 129 shows, the instruments are obtained from a motley variety of sources, and, as might be expected, there is little standardization in their appearance—though, fortunately, the sound and the manner of playing are quite similar for all. The three most common forms of slit drum are shown in Figure 126c, d, and e. The first of these is highest and delivers the clearest pitch; it and the second type produce two notes from each "drum"; the third type (generally lowest in pitch) gives only one note. The second and third types are played by striking the tongue(s) formed by the slit in the top of the box; the first type is played by striking the two sides of the instrument near the slit.

The sound of a slit drum is a pleasant, slightly mysterious "boomp" resembling that of the marimba but less clearly pitched, and decaying in about one second. Because of the relatively long decay, rolls on the slit drum have some of the genuinely sustained quality of low marimba rolls. Slit drums give the impression of being an octave lower than their actual pitch.

Slit drums can be played equally effectively with marimba mallets, vibraphone mallets (especially for high notes), or timpani sticks (especially for low notes). The *fff* requires a hard stick and will be mostly attack noise. A similarly noisy sound is elicited with the use—at any dynamic level—of xylophone mallets or other very hard sticks. Metal sticks should never be used, as they will damage the instruments. Soft timpani sticks should be used only in emergencies, as they produce no special timbre and cannot make the instruments sound louder than *forte*. Delicate, mysterious sounds (*ppp–p*) can be made with the fingers.

A single player can handle up to five slit drums with ease—this may give anywhere from five to ten different notes, depending on which type(s) of slit drum is used. By holding two mallets in one hand a player can strike two notes at once on the same or adjacent drums. Remember that there is no fixed relationship between the pitches of a two-note slit drum: they may be a minor second apart, an octave apart, or anything in between.

Despite the relatively strong pitch, slit-drum chords will not sound as such, except for bare octaves and fifths.

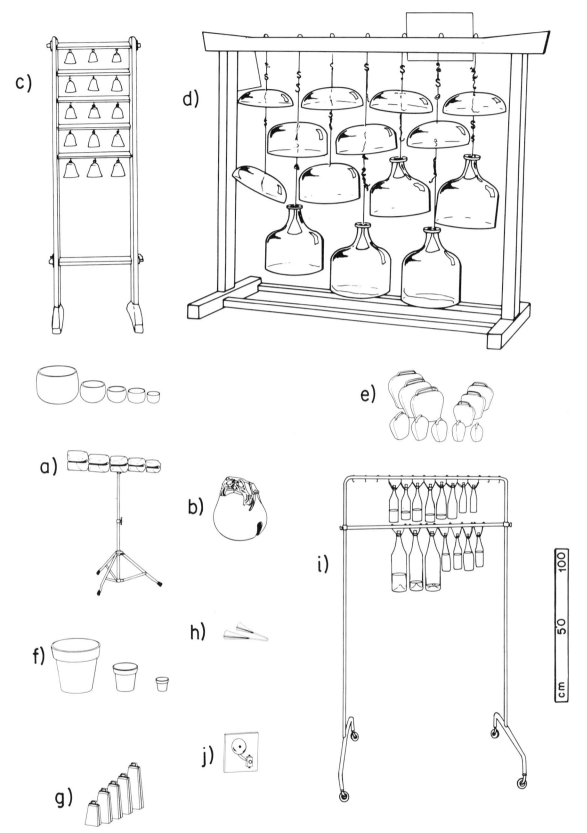

FIGURE 130. *Bells: (a) temple blocks; (b) mokugyo; (c) bells; (d) glass bells; (e) almglocken; (f) flowerpots; (g) cencerros; (h) agogo bells; (i) glass bottles; (j) electric bell.*

name of instrument	abbreviations	synonyms	written range	sounds	normal sticks	status	availability
temple blocks	tpbl. 	Chinese temple blocks dragon's mouths	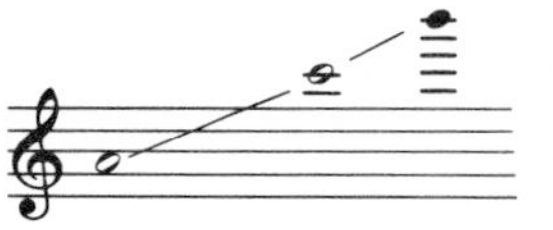 *loudest: fff* *softest: ppp*	as written (transposition not standard-ized)	variable	standard	common
mokugyos	mok.	mokubios wooden drums dragon's mouths wooden fish Buddhist slit drums	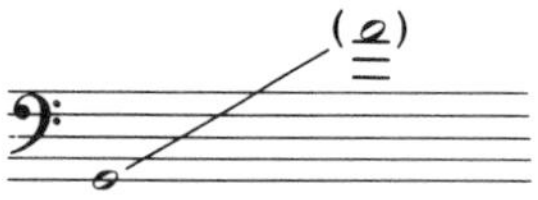 *loudest: ff(f)* *softest: ppp*	as written (transposition not standard-ized)	variable	exotic	very rare

FIGURE 131. *Temple blocks and mokugyos—vital statistics.*

BELLS

TEMPLE BLOCKS AND MOKUGYOS

Those familiar with temple blocks may be surprised to see them included here among the bells—but they truly are bells, in structure if not in sound. The rounded shape and cavernous interior of these wooden bells gives them a distinctively hollow, clucking tone that is instantly recognizable. The temple blocks are a Western version of the Chinese **mu yü**, and many manufacturers go so far as to imitate the traditional Chinese practice of carving the bells to form stylized dragon's heads and lacquering the design in red and gold. Others simply preserve the basic shape of the instruments, lacquering them in plain red or not at all.

Temple blocks normally come in sets of five, filling a (roughly) pentatonic octave. These are mounted on a special rack, either five in a row or in two rows, three below and two above. The instrument has always been considered of indefinite pitch but, as with woodblocks, a weak pitch is there to be exploited if desired. Like slit drums, temple blocks give the impression of being an octave lower than they really are.

When played with unwound xylophone mallets, plastic sticks, or reversed snare sticks, temple blocks have a hard, precise sound that suits them for the task of forming a downward extension of the woodblock sound, although the temple blocks will always sound a bit too rich, with too long a decay, to be identified as woodblocks. More appropriate to the temple blocks are vibraphone or marimba sticks, which emphasize the instrument's rich hollowness and give a subtler attack. Felt sticks will make the instrument sound only weakly, and metal sticks are potentially damaging. Fingers may be used, *ppp–p*.

In recent years composers have become interested in extending the range of the temple blocks downward by using large imported instruments of the mu yü type. The name for these is **mokugyo**, after the Japanese equivalent of the mu yü. In Western usage the term implies any temple block of particularly large size and thus can be applied not only to the Japanese mo kugyo but also the mu yü and the monstrous Korean **mo ko**. These instruments may be in

name of instrument	abbreviations	synonyms	written range	sounds	normal sticks	status	availability
bells	 (bell symbol)	(none)	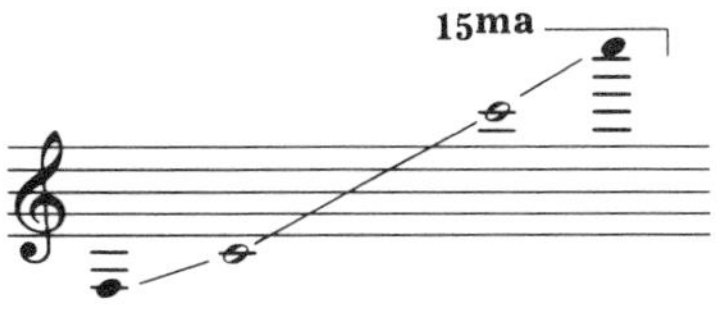 [staff notation, up to **15ma**] loudest: *ff(f)* —— *ff* —— softest: *ppp* ——	as written (transposition not standardized)	variable	exotic, novelty, found object, standard, noisemaker	usually available
glass bells	gl. bells	musical glasses glass bowls	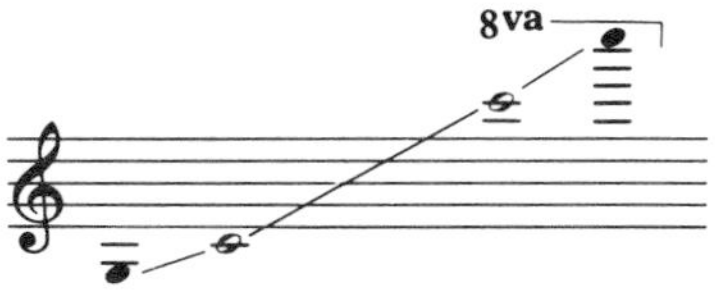 [staff notation, up to **8va**] loudest: *ff* softest: *ppp*	as written (transposition not standardized)	variable	found object, novelty	rare

FIGURE 132. *Bells—vital statistics.*

typical temple-block shape or may take the form of an ornately carved fish or bird; the sound and playing technique are the same in all cases. Of the many synonyms in use, one should particularly avoid "mokubio"; this looks like a mere spelling variant but is actually the name of an altogether different Japanese instrument resembling the Western woodblock.

Soft marimba mallets or heavy timpani sticks must be used on mokugyos—or even special extra-heavy beaters of medium hardness, such as are used with the bass marimba. For a drier, knocking quality—and to obtain the *fff*—chime mallets may be used.

Examples of the use of mokugyos are rare. The "wooden drums" part in Varèse's *Déserts* was probably conceived for mokugyos, but available recordings do not reflect this. For an unambiguous mokugyo part, see Barraqué's *Chant après chant*, and also listen for the mokugyo in recordings of Buddhist liturgical music.

TRUE BELLS

Although bells are among the oldest and most familiar of percussion instruments, they have been little scored, due to continuing confusion in both terminology and construction. The pitch of a bell is a direct function of its size and an inverse function of its thickness; also, up to a point, thick-walled bells will be proportionately louder than thin-walled ones. Church bells, which are so loud that their sound can reportedly kill at close quarters, are of necessity very thick-walled, and in order to keep the pitch reasonably low the bells must be of monstrous size. Since even a c^1 church bell weighs several tons, many composers have unjustifiably assumed that bells of any kind are impractical for concert use. Fortunately, there exist a wide variety of small, thin-walled bells (Fig. 130c) that are entirely suitable for the concert hall. These bells vary considerably in construction but fall into two basic types: "ordinary" bells, which are suspended from above, and bowl-shaped bells, which are placed on a towel-covered table.

"Ordinary" bells are suspended from a rack, either in a single line or in two rows with the sharps above and the naturals below. Clappers—if present—are normally removed or immobilized.

Bowl-shaped bells ("cup bells") may be actual bowls selected for their sonority, but real bells—mostly exotic—are also made in this form. **Japanese temple bells** in particular are prized for their beautiful tone. Large ones (below c¹) are often called **temple gongs**. Cup bells of any sort cannot be played louder than *ff* without danger of knocking them over, but in partial recompense for this limitation of dynamic range they are susceptible to a variety of special effects impossible or difficult to perform on "normal" bells. First of all, cup bells are ideal for use with timpani in the auxiliary resonator effect described on p. 147. Also, the pitch of a cup bell can be lowered* up to a fourth by pouring water into it; this can be done to adjust the pitch or to produce a downward glissando. The water will not affect the tone of the bell but will shorten its decay time somewhat. Cup bells can even be floated in a bowl of water; when struck, the bell will bob around, causing the pitch to wobble.

Water effects are possible with "ordinary" bells but are subject to considerable limitations. A bell must be individually hand-held and tilted so that part of the rim is always above water. By dipping the bell in the water the pitch can be lowered up to a major sixth. Upward and downward glissandos can be performed in this way (remember that the bell must already be in the water if an upward glissando is to be played). If the entire rim is below the water but air remains within the bell, it will behave like a water gourd, producing a very dull "thok" with a slight metallic quality; this effect is perhaps better done with an almglocke (see below).

The number of bells a single player can handle depends on their size. For chromatic sets of bells, the limits are roughly as follows:

$$f^0–c^1 \text{ (8 bells)}$$
$$c^1–c^2 \text{ (13 bells)}$$
$$c^2–c^4 \text{ (25 bells)}$$

The twenty-five-bell limit should probably be observed even for the tiny bells at the top of the range. High-pitched bells are frequently written one or two octaves below their actual pitch; such an octave transposition must be specified; otherwise it would be well to include a cautionary "actual pitches" when listing the pitches of the bells needed for a given piece.

Because they are found in such a wide range of pitches, it is difficult to make general statements regarding the choice of mallets for playing bells. Figure 133 presents the various possibilities in tabular form. Additionally, delicate and gentle sounds can be made (*ppp-p*) with wire brushes or with the fingers. Neither of these should be used above about c⁴.

Where necessary, a single-stick roll can be performed on any sort of bell—except a temple block or glass bottle—by rattling the stick back and forth across the mouth of the instrument.

The "true" bells we have been discussing have long decays, of some six seconds (decreasing to three seconds at c⁵ and one second at c⁶), but are normally played "l.v."; all damping should therefore be carefully indicated. As a special effect a bell can be damped as it is played (⌐) to produce a short-lived, "dead" sound.

Bells can be bowed, *p–ff*, with a brilliant, singing tone. By using very light pressure a *ppp* whisper can be produced. Bowed passages should proceed very slowly, as bowing normally requires a rather contorted position and careful, heavy motions on the part of the player, and because the sound starts quite slowly. Even more slow-starting (several seconds) is the deep humming sound which can be elicited from Japanese temple gongs by rubbing around the

---

* It is important to remember that dipping an idiophone in water or pouring water into it *lowers* the pitch, because the resistance of the water forces it to vibrate more slowly.

	Very low bells	A wide range of bells	Very high bells
Brightly metallic bell sound, *pp–fff*	heavy triangle beaters geologist's hammers	triangle beaters	light triangle beaters
Somewhat more delicate, *pp–fff*	metal glockenspiel sticks light triangle beaters plastic sticks hard xylophone sticks	metal glockenspiel sticks	knitting needles
"Normal" sound, *pp–fff* (= "hard sticks")	soft xylophone mallets	medium xylophone mallets	bell mallets plastic sticks
Gentle but precise attack, *ppp–fff* (= "medium sticks")	medium unwound marimba sticks	hard unwound marimba sticks	soft xylophone mallets
Gentle, vague attack (ideal for rolls) *ppp–ff* (= "soft sticks")	soft vibraphone mallets	medium vibraphone mallets	hard vibraphone mallets
Rustic, vaguely woody attack, *pp–fff*	reversed snare sticks chime mallets	reversed snare sticks	snare sticks
Light, clicking attack, *ppp–ff*	snare sticks knitting needles	reversed rubber-series mallets snare sticks	reversed rubber-series mallets

FIGURE 133. *Choices of sticks for bells.*

edge with a soft beater. As a special effect a bell can be shaken mouth-up, with small objects (e.g., dried beans or BBs) in it.

Glass bells are usually found objects, for example, carboys, salad bowls, rice bowls, or crystal goblets. Playing techniques are much the same as for metal cup bells. The sound of glass bells is delicate and ethereal; they must be played gently, to avoid breakage. Their pitch can be lowered by as much as a fourth by adding water. Bowls can be floated if desired; goblets can be held in the hand and gently shaken, and if they are partially filled with water the pitch will wobble very satisfactorily. Glass bells are more readily bowed than metal ones, producing a sound that is both painful to hear and breathtakingly beautiful. For an example of bowed glass bells, see the "God Music" section of Crumb's *Black Angels*. Fine crystal goblets can also produce a smooth, steady hum when rubbed around the edge with a wet finger. Because of the relatively low density of glass, glass bells tend to be larger than metal bells of the same pitch and should therefore be used in smaller numbers. As usual, the octave transposition is not standardized.

"SEMI-DRY" BELLS

The various metal and ceramic bells used by percussionists can be classified according to the overall contour of the decay pattern. All bells have essentially exponential decays in which most of the partials (the **strike tone**) drop to nothing in a very short time while a few low partials (the **buzz tone**) hang on far longer.* In the bells we have just been discussing, the strike tone lasts for a full second or longer, and in some of these bells the strike tone and buzz tone are identical.

In almglocken and flowerpots the strike tone dies in about half a second, and the ear interprets the whole sound as somewhat "dead" or "dry" despite the fact that the buzz tone

---

* The perceived pitch of a bell may be that of the strike tone, that of the buzz tone, or some other pitch—perhaps even one not actually present in the bell's harmonic spectrum.

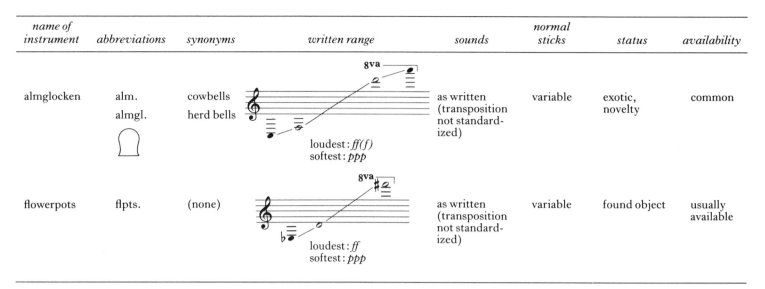

name of instrument	abbreviations	synonyms	written range	sounds	normal sticks	status	availability
almglocken	alm. almgl.	cowbells herd bells	loudest: *ff(f)* softest: *ppp*	as written (transposition not standardized)	variable	exotic, novelty	common
flowerpots	flpts.	(none)	loudest: *ff* softest: *ppp*	as written (transposition not standardized)	variable	found object	usually available

FIGURE 134. *"Semi-dry" bells—vital statistics.*

will ring on for one to five seconds (almglocken) or one-half to three seconds (flowerpots). The nature of the sound is such that composers can use or ignore the buzz tone as suits their fancy, confident that it will not usually get in the way of a series of sixteenth-notes, but that when needed to flesh out a half-note it will be there to do the job. However, the buzz tone cannot be depended on in dense, *fortissimo* passages, since it never exceeds *forte*; conversely, rapid passages in *pp* or *ppp* may sound a bit muddy unless hard sticks are used, because of the relative weakness of the strike tone at such low dynamic levels. In slower passages, hand-damping can eliminate the buzz tone where it would prove obtrusive.

Even irrespective of envelope these "semi-dry" bells are quite similar in timbre: very lush and pleasant (with, in the almglocken, a slightly hollow quality), and quite different in effect from both the clear brilliance of "real" bells and the harsh clangor of cencerros and bottles.

Almglocken are genuine cowbells—or souvenir imitations thereof—from Central Europe. For use as percussion instruments their clappers are removed and they are suspended in groups like "ordinary" bells or mounted horizontally like temple blocks. Flowerpots are seldom called for as such, but are used to play parts written for "clay bells." Real clay bells are made as novelty items, but ordinary red clay flowerpots are actually superior as musical instruments because they are alike in structure, composition, and tone and are available in a great variety of sizes. They may be suspended, bell-fashion, using the convenient hole in the bottom, or they may be set upright and played like cup bells.

The sticks used with almglocken and flowerpots are much the same as those used with traditional bells; metal sticks are seldom used because they obscure the pitch of the bells (particularly low ones) by bringing out numerous high partials at the expense of low ones. The maximum number of bells that should be assigned to any one player varies, as with traditional bells.

An almglocke can be water-dipped like a traditional bell, with the same major-sixth maximum lowering, and can also produce the "metal water-gourd" effect. Water effects are impossible with flowerpots because of the difficulty of hand-holding them and because of the hole in the bottom.

name of instrument	abbreviations	synonyms	written range	sounds	normal sticks	status	availability
agogo bells	agogos 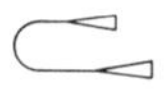	(none)	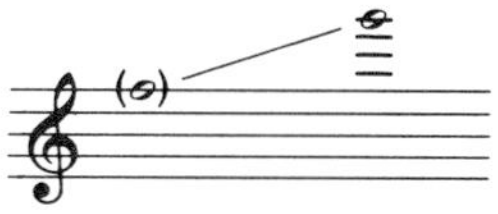 loudest: *fff* softest: *ppp*	as written (transposition not standardized)	variable	standard, exotic	usually available
cencerros	cenc. 	cowbells goat bells sheep bells metal blocks	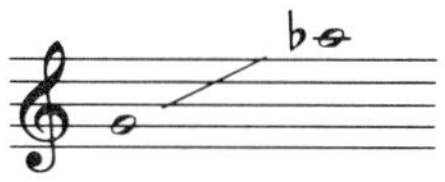 loudest: *fff* softest: *ppp*	as written (transposition not standardized)	variable	standard	ubiquitous
glass bottles	bottles 	(none)	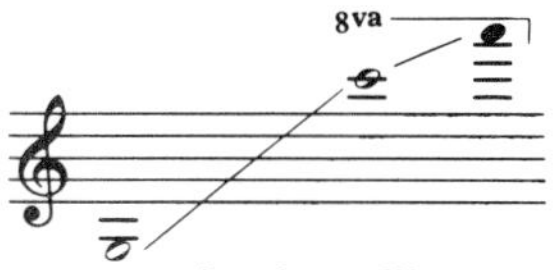 loudest: *fff* softest: *ppp*	1 octave higher (transposition not standardized)	xylophone sticks (hard, medium, soft); metal glockenspiel sticks	found object	rare

FIGURE 135. *Dry-sounding bells—vital statistics.*

Bowing an almglocke generally produces a squawk unrelated to the instrument's official pitch. Bowing a flowerpot is a chancy proposition at best, and when—if—it does speak, the sound will also be a squawk.

Almglocke and flowerpot alike can be used as rattles in the manner described for traditional bells.

Both instruments may be used with a timpano as an auxiliary resonator (p. 147). The almglocke will be slightly muffled (no buzz tone) because it must be laid on its side.

Two particularly important and virtuosic parts for almglocken (inaccurately called "cencerros" in both cases) have been written by Messiaen in his *Couleurs de la cité céleste* and *Et exspecto resurrectionem mortuorum.*

DRY-SOUNDING BELLS

Cencerros, agogo bells, and glass bottles represent the dry side of the bell family. The strike tones of these bells decay to nothing in a quarter-second or less; the buzz tone is either nonexistent (most bottles) or lasts a mere three seconds. The buzz tone of cencerros and agogos is usually considered a nuisance, and when the bells are set up (they are mounted horizontally, like temple blocks) they are often lightly muted with cloth to eliminate this buzz. Composers sometimes specify this themselves, as it is by no means universal practice; in any case, both bells are normally used in rackety musical contexts in which the buzz tone cannot be heard.

All these bells are coarse and clangorous in tone and weak in pitch. Cencerros and agogos are traditionally treated as indefinitely pitched instruments; whatever tradition may be said to exist for bottles has them played at specific pitches, though they are, if anything, *less* well defined in pitch than the metal bells. In fact, the tone of bottles is generally so harsh and short-

name of instrument	abbreviations	synonyms	dynamic range	status	availability
electric bell	el. bell elec. bell	doorbell	*ff*	noisemaker	usually available

FIGURE 136. *The electric bell—vital statistics.*

lived that it makes as much sense to call them glass anvils as glass bells. Despite their vast differences in appearance, cencerros and agogos are virtually identical in timbre and have an ultimate common ancestor in the agogo-like bells of West Africa. The high-pitched commercial agogos are used as an upward extension of the rather limited cencerro range. Doubtless lower agogos can be found, but since the ubiquitous cencerro occupies this range they are superfluous.

Cencerros—and, in recent years, agogo bells—are extremely common in rock and jazz. The cencerro may be attached to a stand as part of the traps, but more likely will be used as a hand instrument; the agogos are always hand instruments in this context. In a classical context, on the other hand, both types of bells are mounted on stands or (cencerros) laid on a towel-covered table. It is for use as hand instruments that agogo bells come attached in pairs to a shared U-shaped handle. A hand-held cencerro is simply cradled in the hand, muffled just enough to eliminate the buzz tone. Further muffling ($\overset{\times}{\r}$) can be accomplished by squeezing a little tighter.

In popular music both bells are played with reversed snare sticks, and these are probably the best all-round sticks. If desired, however, any of the various sticks for other medium-high bells can be used here too. Remember that soft or wound sticks will emphasize the buzz tone at the expense of the strike tone. Water and rattle effects have exactly the same potential and limitations on these bells as on the almglocken. Bowing a cencerro produces a squawk; agogos are too narrow-mouthed to bow effectively.

Glass bottles are suspended by the neck (i.e., mouth upward) from a rack and played only with hard sticks. Their raucous clinks can be tuned by adding water (the maximum the pitch can be lowered varies from as little as a perfect fourth to as much as a major thirteenth, depending on the shape and thickness of the bottle). The pitch of a bottle is a function of its size only up to a certain point: the low g^1 given here was not obtained from a monster terrarium bottle, but from a medium-sized, flask-shaped wine bottle filled with water—the terrarium bottle (empty) gave only $b\flat^1$, and a not very satisfactory one at that. At the other extreme, the c^5 is given by many bottles of pill-bottle or spice-bottle size. Smaller bottles will not produce a pitch, but bottles about that same size made of thick-walled fancy crystal can produce tones as high as a^5.

THE ELECTRIC BELL

An electric bell is a small, dome-shaped bell enclosing an electric motor that drives a repeating clapper. The bell is played by pressing the button to turn it on and releasing it to turn it off—

this can be done with either finger or foot. The bell has a definite pitch, but since the repetition rate of the clapper is itself in the audio range, the sound is more likely to be heard as unpitched. Closely related to the electric bell are its spring-driven (clock alarm) and hand-cranked (old-fashioned doorbell) ancestors, and also the **electric buzzer**, in which the clapper strikes a plastic or pasteboard casing instead of a bell. All notes for these instruments are best notated as rolls.

METAL TONGUE INSTRUMENTS

SANSAS

The kalimba and marimbula belong to the **sansa** family of instruments, in which the sound is produced by plucking or striking any of a group of metal tongues that are held firmly down against a pair of support bars (the **bridge** and the **bearing bar**) by an overlying **pressure bar**. The vibrations of the tongues are transmitted through the bridge to the hollow **body** of the instrument, which acts as a resonator to amplify the sound to audible levels. The pitch of each tongue is inversely proportional to its free length in front of the bridge.

The original homeland of the sansas is sub-Saharan Africa. African sansas may have anywhere from seven to twenty-six tongues, with ten being the most common. The arrangement of pitches is basically diatonic or pentatonic, and the range seldom exceeds two octaves. The highest and lowest pitches one is likely to encounter are roughly d^3 and G_0. If desired, the instrument can be tuned to standard Western pitches by adjusting with a pliers the distance each tongue projects beyond the bridge.* The tongues are arranged fanwise—in either one of the patterns shown in Figure 139, or in a combination of the two—but often one or two tongues will be "out of order." In the second of these patterns, the tongues in the back row are bent slightly upward to make them more accessible to the fingers. Note that, at least in the single-row pattern, adjacent tongues produce pitches a third or (pentatonic sansas) a fourth apart, and that three adjacent tongues usually produce a major or minor triad.

Those sansas in which the body consists of a plain flat board are meant to be played inside a gourd resonator, to amplify their otherwise weak and puny sound. Some sansas have a small, asymmetrically placed hole in the body that, when repeatedly covered and uncovered by a finger, creates a very delicate, expressive vibrato; this vibrato is strongest in the middle of the instrument's range and does not affect the highest and lowest notes at all.

Authentic African sansas invariably have **brays**, usually in the form of light metal or raffia rings, attached to the tongues behind the bridge. When a note is played the bray on that tongue rattles, giving the sound a strong buzzy quality and making it a bit louder than it would otherwise be.

Sansas can be played either of two ways: most commonly, by cradling the instrument in both hands and plucking with the thumbs (whence "thumb piano"), or, alternatively, by holding the instrument with thumbs underneath and plucking with the other fingers. The latter method is capable of greater speed and contrapuntal virtuosity than the former but is harder to learn and does not allow use of the vibrato hole. The spacing of the tongues is such

---

* Retuning, an arduous and tricky process, cannot be undertaken in the middle of a piece.

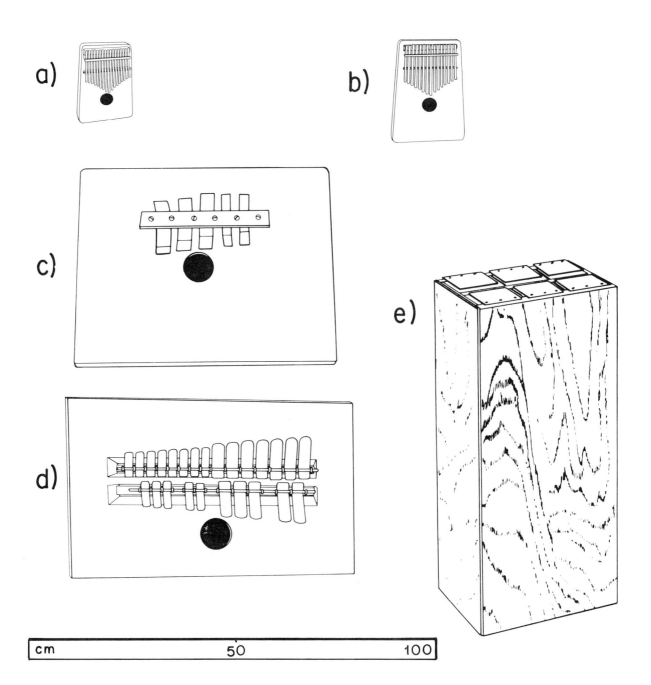

FIGURE 137. *Metal tongue instruments: (a) treble kalimba; (b) alto kalimba; (c) marimbula—traditional; (d) marimbula—commercial; (e) lujon.*

that a pair of adjacent tongues can be simultaneously plucked by one finger; obviously, this too is easier when playing with thumbs.

Because no two sansas are likely to have the same combination of pitches, composers are faced with a problem similar to the one posed by steel drums—the more specific one's demands, the less likely it will be that an appropriate instrument can be found. The best bet is to write either for ten indefinite pitches (assume they're laid out as in Fig. 139a), or for a smaller number (six or seven) of specific diatonic or pentatonic pitches in mid-range. A way out of the

name of instrument	abbreviations	synonyms	written range	sounds	normal sticks	status	availability
treble kalimba	tr. kal.	sansa mbira thumb piano	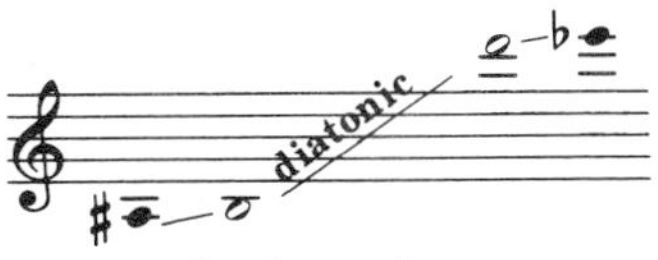 *diatonic* — loudest: *sfmp* softest: *ppp*	as written	fingers	novelty	usually available
alto kalimba	alt. kal. akal.	sansa mbira thumb piano	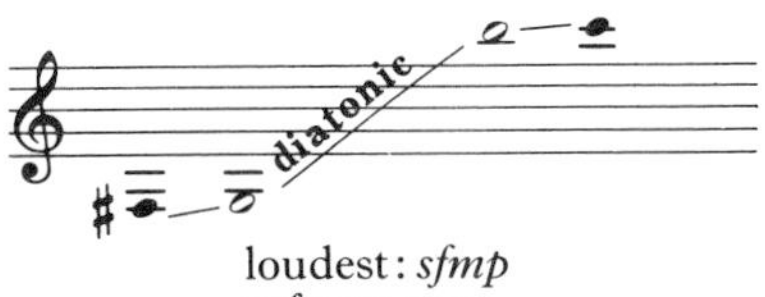 *diatonic* — loudest: *sfmp* softest: *ppp*	as written	fingers	novelty	usually available
marimbula	mbla.	(none)	**commercial** 	as written	vibraphone sticks (hard, medium, soft)	standard	very rare
			traditional 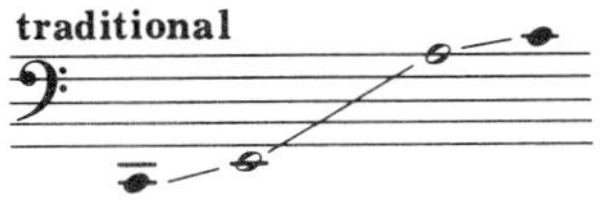 — loudest: *sfmp* softest: *ppp*	as written	marimba sticks (hard, medium, soft)	exotic, homemade	rare

FIGURE 138. *Kalimbas and marimbulas—vital statistics.*

dilemma is presented by the **kalimba,** a sanitized, Westernized sansa without brays whose sole virtue is that it is also standardized. This novelty instrument comes in treble (i.e., soprano) and alto sizes, each with seventeen diatonic tongues arranged as in Figure 139a and covering the range shown in Figure 138.* The hardwood body of a kalimba is solidly constructed and the instrument may weigh more than a traditional sansa twice its size. There are two vibrato holes: by covering one of them while vibrating with the other, the range of pitches affected by the vibrato is shifted downward. The sound of the kalimba is very gentle, sweet, and delicate, reminiscent of a music box—this is not surprising, since music boxes are also plucked-tongue idiophones. Because of the heavy body and absence of brays the tone is somewhat thin and characterless compared to that of a traditional sansa.

The decay time of a kalimba note is about three seconds, on a traditional sansa only about two. The instruments are normally played without damping, so that if notes are to be stopped short some specification such as "non l.v." or the use of staccato-dots will be needed. Muffling—performed by laying one thumb across the tongues in the space between the bridge and the pressure bar—drops the decay time to about half a second and thus emphasizes the "plucked" quality of the sound. Each thumb covers only half the tongues, and notes from opposite sides of the instrument have to be muffled by opposite hands—an awkward procedure. The instrument is held entirely by the hand doing the muffling, since the other hand must leave its normal position and reach across to the "wrong" side of the instrument, plucking with the index finger.

* The instruments are built in G major but may be tuned to any key.

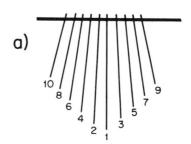

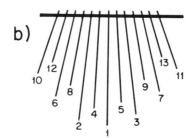

FIGURE 139. *The two basic patterns for the tongues of a sansa.*

Two special effects are available on sansas, including kalimbas. One of these is a swipe *across* all the tongues with a fingernail, producing a harp-like down-and-up "glissando" (actually a **rip**) when performed slowly, an arpeggiated tone cluster when performed quickly. The following notations are suggested; they will be instantly understood without explanation.

A **tambour** effect can be obtained by tapping the body of the instrument with a finger or thumb. The sound of this may be as loud as *piano*, but there will be a *ppp* resonance of the tongues as well. By tapping in different places—left vs. right side of the instrument, or directly onto the vibrato hole(s)—several different pitches can be made to stand out of this hazy tone cluster.

The bass member of the sansa family is the *marimbula*, a Cuban instrument with—usually—seven diatonically tuned tongues. The tongues are considerably wider and stiffer than those of other sansas, and though they can be plucked, they are best played by striking with soft sticks. The instrument, too large to be hand-held, must be placed on a table. There are no brays and no vibrato hole. The range of the commercially manufactured chromatic marimbula (see Fig. 137d) unfortunately lies so much higher than that of the traditional marimbula that it is in effect a different instrument. Among our musical examples the Roldán

name of instrument	abbreviations	synonyms	written range	sounds	normal sticks	status	availability
lujon	(none)	(none)	𝄢 [written range staff notation]	as written	vibraphone sticks (hard, medium, soft)	homemade	rare
			loudest: *ff* softest: *ppp*				

FIGURE 140. *The lujon—vital statistics.*

Ritmicas require a traditional marimbula, while Henze's *El Cimarrón* requires the commercial type. The marimbula is much weaker in pitch than most sansas and should probably not play chords.

THE LUJON

The lujon is a tall oblong box open at the top and divided vertically, like a soda-bottle carton, into six compartments in two rows of three each. The top of each compartment is almost covered by a thin, rectangular plate of aluminum attached to the box along one side. When struck, these plates vibrate like the tongues of a marimbula, the compartments acting as resonators, to produce a pleasant "thunk" of moderately defined pitch. There is no standardization in the choice or pattern of lujon pitches, so composers have generally treated the instrument as if it were unpitched. Since the pitch is relatively weak, this is certainly not inappropriate; if specific pitches are really necessary, the possible range is given above. Remember, only six pitches are possible per instrument; the lujon can be tuned, but neither as easily nor as extensively as a sansa. Its decay time is only about a second.

Vibraphone sticks should be used on the lujon whenever possible. Hard timpani sticks or unwound marimba mallets may be used in a pinch, but xylophone mallets or other hard sticks will produce only a strong click of attack noise at the expense of the fundamentals of the plates, making them all sound alike.

THE MUSICAL SAW

The musical saw is a novelty instrument in the form of a saw without teeth. Unlike all other percussion, this instrument must be played sitting down; the player holds the "handle" of the saw between the knees, holding the other end in one hand. By flexing the instrument to a greater or lesser extent, higher or lower pitches can be produced when the instrument is struck or bowed with the free hand. A much larger type also exists, designed to rest on the floor, with a handle at the upper end that is grasped in one hand and used to flex the instrument while it is struck or bowed with the other hand. This floor-model instrument (manufactured by Carroll Sound, Inc.) may be played standing.

Traditionally, the musical saw is played with a bow. It is extremely tricky to play, and one who can play a simple melody at moderate speed in tune and without squeaking must be

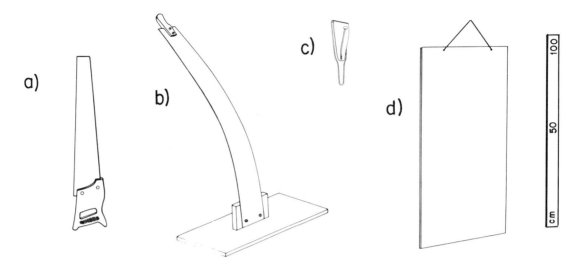

FIGURE 141. *Warped sheet instruments: (a) musical saw—lap model; (b) musical saw—floor model; (c) flexatone; (d) thundersheet.*

name of instrument	abbreviations	synonyms	written range	sounds	normal sticks	status	availability
musical saw	saw	(none)	**lap model** / **floor model** / loudest: *ff* softest: *ppp*	1 octave higher (transposition not standardized)	bow	novelty / standard	rare / very rare

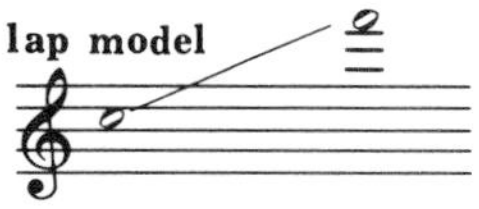

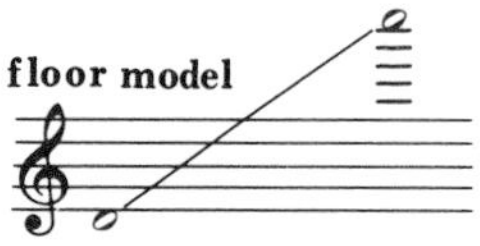

FIGURE 142. *The musical saw—vital statistics.*

counted a virtuoso. Individual pitches cannot usually be picked out "from scratch" but must be started out of tune and rapidly adjusted. Succeeding pitches are approached by portamento, and this, combined with the instrument's high pitch and ethereal tone (reminiscent of audio feedback), makes for a decidedly unearthly effect. The rare floor-model instrument is somewhat easier to control, since it is larger, and in the upper part of its range notes can be picked out as individual upper partials (by bowing closer to or further from the handle at the top) with little or no change in the flexion. Very few percussionists have acquired enough of the difficult bowing technique of either lap or floor model to play any but the most indeterminate passages, preferring wherever possible to use a mallet. A vibraphone stick is best for this, as it deemphasizes the prominent inharmonic "strike tone." Harder sticks may be used, but even with a vibraphone mallet this initial clank makes the pitch of the instrument considerably less definite than when it is bowed. Since a struck note dies away in about a second, there is little opportunity to correct a faulty pitch after it has started—though, again, after the first note of a passage a fair degree of accuracy can be maintained by the use of portamento. On a

name of instrument	abbreviations	synonyms	written range	sounds	status	availability
flexatone	flex.	(none)	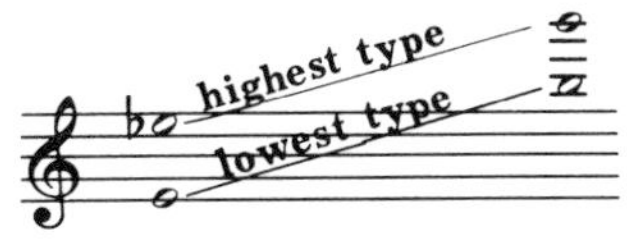 highest type / lowest type loudest: *ff* softest: *pp*	1 octave higher (transposition not standardized)	standard	common

FIGURE 143. *The flexatone—vital statistics.*

floor-model instrument, striking only elicits the first partial, and the range is hence restricted to sounding d²–b². These notes are brought out by striking near the base of the saw. Striking closer to the handle produces an increasingly pitchless clank. Whether a musical saw (of either type) is bowed or struck, the unavoidable imprecision of pitch can be disguised by vibrato. For an example of musical-saw writing, see the third movement of Crumb's *Ancient Voices of Children*. Crumb's intention that this difficult instrument be played as an "extra" by the mandolinist is flatly unreasonable.

THE FLEXATONE

The flexatone is a hand instrument, an adaptation of the musical saw to the requirements of the concert percussionist. It consists of a triangular blade of spring steel attached at the base to the branches of a Y-shaped frame. The top of the triangle extends into a small metal tab that is held down by the thumb while the other fingers hold the handle of the frame; by pressing the tab downward with the thumb, the triangular blade is flexed to a greater or lesser degree, yielding various pitches (just as for the musical saw).

Attached to the tab are two thin, flexible rods with little pith balls on their free ends. When the instrument is shaken, the two balls alternately strike opposite sides of the triangular plate, producing the sound. Normally, therefore, flexatone notes are really rolls, and they are traditionally notated as such. Individual non-repeating notes can be produced by holding back one of the pith balls with the index finger, but only at low dynamic levels (*pp–mf*), since when the instrument is shaken strongly even the single remaining ball is likely to "repercuss." It is difficult to control the motion of the pith ball precisely, so passages in single notes are best kept to a slow or moderate tempo—unless, of course, the rhythm is to remain indeterminate. Switching from single notes to rolls is slightly awkward, so the two techniques should be confined to separate musical passages.

The pitch range of the flexatone has never been standardized (Fig. 143 gives the highest and lowest types usually encountered). The range of a given flexatone is usually a twelfth but may be as little as an octave. As may be imagined, it is difficult to maintain a steady pitch on the flexatone while it is being shaken; furthermore, initial pitches are even harder to pinpoint than they are on a musical saw. For all these reasons, flexatone pitches are best left somewhat indeterminate: analog notation without clef will give precise contours without requiring the

name of instrument	abbreviations	synonyms	dynamic range	status	availability
cricket	crick.	(none)	*mf*	novelty	rare

FIGURE 144. *The cricket—vital statistics.*

name of instrument	abbreviations	synonyms	dynamic range	normal sticks	status	availability
thundersheet	thunder. th. sh.	thunder machine metal sheet	*ppp–fff*	variable	homemade	common

FIGURE 145. *The thundersheet—vital statistics.*

player to hit and maintain any specific pitch. Nonetheless, specific pitches can be obtained, provided one is willing to put up with some imprecision. Players do, for instance, manage to make a fairly convincing job of Schoenberg's unrealistic flexatone writing in the *Variations* (Op. 31), *Moses und Aron*, and the *Kol Nidre*.

THE CRICKET

The cricket is a small toy made of two pieces of metal, one of which serves as a prop and resonator while the other is a piece of spring steel that is flexed back and forth to make the sound. The instrument is held between the thumb and index finger of one hand, and each time the free ends of the two pieces of metal are pinched together a cricket-like click is produced by the spring as it flexes. Upon releasing, another click is produced as it unflexes; thus, any musical use of the cricket *must* contain an even number of notes.

A lower-pitched relative of the cricket, called the **wobble-board**, made a brief appearance around 1960 but has not been seen since. Its bumptious "poit!" is a sound well worth resurrecting.

THE THUNDERSHEET

The thundersheet, a suspended piece of sheet metal, is shaken by hand or struck with sticks to produce a rumbling and/or crackling "thunder" noise. Those used to produce realistic thunder effects for the stage are huge—three meters or more in height—and are struck with a gong beater. Ordinary thundersheets are much smaller (50–150 cm) and higher in pitch; the term "thundersheet," unmodified, refers to instruments of this size. To get an unusually large one, it is necessary to specify "very large thundersheet" or even "largest possible thundersheet." At the other extreme small, high-pitched ones can be made from metal foil: specify "small foil thundersheet." These small instruments cannot exceed *ff* in loudness.

Thundersheets may be either struck or held at the top and shaken. The wave produced by shaking takes about two-thirds of a second to propagate the length of the sheet, and the instrument will rumble for about that long. Repeated shaking faster than sixteenth-notes at $\quad\downarrow$ = ca. 76 will produce a continuous rumble instead of discrete notes. When struck, the thundersheet behaves quite differently, producing a sharp crack that decays in only a third of a second. Bass-drum beaters or timpani sticks are generally used, although vibraphone mallets will do at low dynamic levels. For the loudest possible dry-sounding crack a chime mallet or nail hammer may be used, and plastic sticks or hard xylophone mallets will create equally loud rolls. Foil thundersheets are best struck with the fingers, since anything heavier may tear them. The reader can easily experiment with the behavior of thundersheets using an ordinary sheet of paper, which acts very similarly when shaken or struck.

Ordinary, medium-sized thundersheets may be bowed, producing a grating squeal like that of a bowed tam-tam.

CYMBALS

SUSPENDED CYMBALS

Suspended cymbals are the simplest and most common cymbals; indeed, the word "cymbal," unmodified, implies an instrument of this type. It is a rigid, slightly curved disk of spun brass with a raised **dome** in the center through which runs a small hole by means of which the instrument is bolted to an adjustable stand (Fig. 146a, b, c).* Cymbals are manufactured in sizes varying between 20 and 65 cm in diameter, and in seven gauges of thickness (paper-thin, thin, medium-thin, medium, medium-thick, thick, extra thick). Compared to a thick cymbal, a thin one has a more rapid attack and produces more and higher partials; it will be distinctly higher in overall pitch than a thick cymbal of the same diameter. Compared to a small cymbal, a large one will have a longer decay (up to fifteen seconds for the longest, as opposed to about five seconds for the smallest) and a slightly broader dynamic range at the loud end of the scale: a crescendo roll on a large cymbal can approach *ffff*. Large cymbals are also lower in pitch than small ones, but the difference is not as dramatic as might be expected; in fact, the difference in pitch between the largest and smallest cymbals of a given thickness is usually not as great as the difference in pitch between the thickest and thinnest cymbals of a given size.

Additional variety is provided by **sizzle cymbals** and **Chinese cymbals**. Sizzle cymbals, typically large and thin, are provided with brays, either small rivets attached loosely to the cymbal through holes in its rim, or a pair of metal boxes, partly open at the bottom, attached by rods to the top of the stand and containing ball bearings that rest lightly on the surface of the cymbal. The brays bring out high partials—making the tone a virtual hiss—and lengthen the cymbal's decay time.

Chinese cymbals differ from ordinary suspended cymbals (sometimes called **Turkish cymbals** in contradistinction) mostly in having a strongly demarcated dome and a slightly turned-up rim and in being made of a lighter alloy. Formerly available only from the Orient, they are now increasingly being manufactured by Western makers. Their basic timbre is the

---

* Since the exact center of the cymbal is a node for all partials, clamping it at that point does not damp it or otherwise affect the tone.

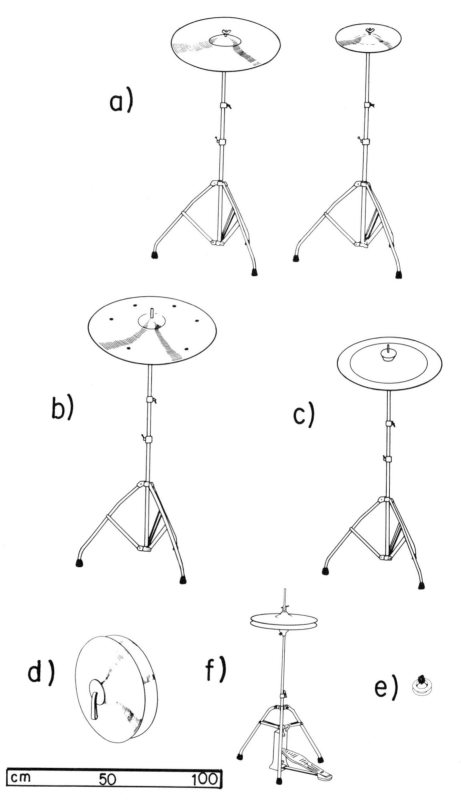

a)

b)

c)

d)

f)

e)

cm   50   100

FIGURE 146. *The cymbal family, I: (a) suspended cymbals; (b) sizzle cymbal; (c) Chinese cymbal; (d) crash cymbals; (e) finger cymbals; (f) hi-hat.*

name of instrument	abbreviations	synonyms	dynamic range	normal sticks	status	availability
suspended cymbal	sus. cym. susp. cymb. ⏌	ride cymbal Turkish cymbal cymbal	*ppp–fff*	variable	standard	ubiquitous
sizzle cymbal	siz. cymb.	crash cymbal	*ppp–fff*	variable	standard	common
Chinese cymbal	Ch. cymb. ◡⌒◡	(none)	*ppp–fff*	variable	standard, exotic	usually available

FIGURE 147. *Suspended cymbals—vital statistics.*

same as that of other cymbals, but the sound decays exponentially rather than linearly,[*] dropping to a very low level (*pp*, from a loud stroke) in only about two seconds. Chinese cymbals are made in a relatively small range of sizes and thicknesses. Meaningful distinctions of pitch can be made among as many as six ordinary cymbals but no more than four Chinese cymbals or two sizzle cymbals—in fact, sizzle cymbals are usually written for singly. For an example of a piece featuring multiple Chinese cymbals, see Cage's *First Construction in Metal*.

Playing technique is the same for all these cymbals. They are most frequently played with vibraphone sticks, but almost any other kind of stick except chime mallets, metal hammers, gong beaters, or bass-drum beaters can be used to good effect. Snare sticks are normally used to play the cymbals in a traps set, giving a very precise attack and enabling clear production of rapid rhythmic patterns that would become blurred if played with softer sticks. Other hard sticks share this property, and metal sticks produce a brittle, pingy attack. For a smooth, steady roll, soft sticks are essential. Playing gently (*pp* or softer) near the rim with soft sticks brings out a very low partial (the fundamental?), which, however, does not seem to be closely related to the instrument's size or thickness. Delicate sounds can be produced by the fingers (up to *mezzo-piano*) or by wire brushes (ditto). A single-brush roll can be executed by sticking the edge of the cymbal right into the bundle of wires, dividing it into two bunches; the brush is shaken up and down, causing the two bunches of wires to strike the top and bottom of the cymbal alternately. Similar one-handed rolls can be made with other kinds of sticks by holding two sticks in one hand, with one above the cymbal and one below it.

There is a tendency for repeated notes on a cymbal to crescendo, as left-over vibratory energy from each stroke is added onto that from the stroke following; for this reason crescendos are easier to control and more characteristic of these instruments than are diminuendos. Without hand- or stick-damping sudden drops in dynamic level are impossible, although sudden upward jumps in loudness are entirely characteristic.

Hand-damping is an important part of cymbal playing, and any well-written part will indicate very clearly the durations of all notes and whether or not they are to be allowed to vibrate beyond the next attack. If a sudden drop in dynamic level is desired, the preceding

[*] Actually, all idiophones decay exponentially; what is meant here is that the decay time is considerably less even than that of an ordinary cymbal, with a rapid initial drop-off to *pp* followed by a much smoother decay from *pp* to silence.

name of instrument	abbreviations	synonyms	dynamic range	status	availability
finger cymbals	fing. cymbs. fing. cym.	(none)	*pp–ff*	standard	usually available
crash cymbals	 crash cym. crash cymbs.	cymbals hand cymbals	*pp–fff*	standard, novelty	common

FIGURE 148. *Crash and finger cymbals—vital statistics.*

loud note will have to be damped immediately before the soft note is played; since players are frequently sloppy about the performance of such passages, the notation of this articulation with a *luftpause* (') or "railroad tracks" (//) is advisable. **Muffling** by hand ( ) or stick ( ) is also quite possible and very effective, giving a dull, choked sound. Short, staccato notes are often muffled simply to get them short enough: it takes very heavy muffling indeed to get the decay time of a cymbal down below a quarter of a second.

Special effects include the following:

1. Playing on the dome. This gives a more rapid decay, a reduced dynamic range (usually no louder than *ff*), and, most important, far fewer partials than the normal sound—one could probably assign a pitch to this sound, but as the observable pitch is quite weak and bears little relation either to the average pitch-level of the instrument or to the low "edge" pitch mentioned above, it is probably better ignored.

2. "Rubbed" effects produced by bowing (a teeth-grating squeal), scraping along the edge of the cymbal with a screw rod (a harsh, rasping sound), and running the end of almost any light, hard object—including, of course, any of the hard sticks—rapidly from the center to the edge of the cymbal (a bright-sounding zing that works best with metal: a triangle beater, for instance).

3. Laying the cymbal (*sans* stand) upside down on a timpano for the wawa effect described on p. 147. The instrument rests on its dome, and though it is liable to tip over and touch the timpano at the edge, this seems to present little obstacle to "normal" playing and timbre.

CRASH CYMBALS

Crash cymbals are the ordinary paired cymbals of nineteenth-century orchestral music, and finger cymbals are a miniature version of these. The cymbals are strapped loosely to the player's hands (finger cymbals are usually strapped to the thumb and index finger of one hand) and clashed together in a glancing blow. For soft or delicate passages the crash cymbals may be lightly touched together at just one point along the edge.

Crash cymbals vary from medium-sized to very large. They are traditionally used—even in contemporary music—in an essentially colotomic fashion, i.e., playing isolated single notes to punctuate cadences or slow repeated notes once per beat or once per bar. Since they are heavy and unwieldy, they cannot be played much faster than eighth-notes at $\quarternote = 120$.

Finger cymbals, only a few centimeters in diameter, can be played as fast as one can repeatedly clap together the thumb and index finger. They are still occasionally confused with **crotales** (q.v.). Crash-type cymbals intermediate in size between finger cymbals and ordinary crash cymbals are hard to find—instruments in this 9–25 cm range seem to be made only as toys or educational instruments of rather inferior quality—but they do exist. They are played like ordinary crash cymbals but can be played up to twice as fast because they are so light in weight.

The roll on crash cymbals is performed by rubbing the two plates together in a circular motion. This is traditionally notated ♪, like other rolls. The "rubbed" notation, ♩, should be reserved for the **strisciato**, an effect produced by starting with the plates in contact with each other and sliding them rapidly apart to produce a delicate "zing." The word "strisciato" should accompany this effect wherever it is notated. Both roll and strisciato can be performed on finger cymbals only if they are strapped to the index fingers of both hands.

Among the special effects pertaining to the crash cymbals is one that produces what is perhaps the most hideously unpleasant sound in all music: the plates are held at right angles to each other and ground slowly together by rotation—with what effect may well be imagined. More useful—and certainly kinder—is the use of one crash cymbal to strike another (large, flat) instrument, e.g., gong, tam-tam, timpano, or bass drum. In striking a drum, the cymbal will vibrate only weakly—no louder than *forte*—no matter how hard the drum is hit. A single crash cymbal may also be dangled horizontally and played like a suspended cymbal. This was a common practice prior to the introduction of suspended cymbals, but there is no great point in it anymore. A single crash cymbal (held vertically) may also be dipped in water up to half its depth while it is vibrating; this produces a strong downward glissando.

Damping and muffling, and the proper and consistent notation of these, are as important for crash cymbals as for suspended ones. Short notes are damped by pulling the plates back against the sides of the chest. Muffled notes (♩) are produced by striking the plates directly together and leaving them in contact. As a special effect, the plates may be clapped together in this way but then immediately separated and allowed to ring normally. No fixed notation exists for this effect, but the sound is essentially of the *sforzando-piano* type, with a loud, ponderous attack followed by a much weaker continuation of the sound. Finally, a note may be stopped by bringing the vibrating plates into gentle contact with each other, causing a quickly decaying, irregular, rattling sound as if an insect were caught between them.

THE HI-HAT

The hi-hat is a unique development of the crash cymbals for use in traps sets. It is best played sitting down but can be played standing if necessary. It consists of a pair of small cymbals attached to a stand in such a way that the depression of a foot pedal at the base of the stand clashes them together. The instrument is sometimes also struck—traditionally with snare sticks—and notes in *ppp* must be so played.

A tremendously subtle variety of sounds can be elicited from the hi-hat but no standard notation has been developed for it; whatever notation is used must be explained to the player. The notation I use in my own work—and which I strongly recommend—uses two lines for the instrument. Notes on the upper line are played with the plates open (pedal up), and those on the lower line are played with the plates closed (pedal down). All notes are played with sticks except those preceded by a slur, thus:

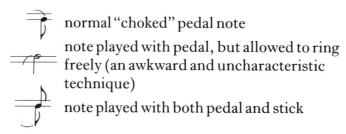

normal "choked" pedal note

note played with pedal, but allowed to ring freely (an awkward and uncharacteristic technique)

note played with both pedal and stick

Much of the expressiveness of the hi-hat is gained by varying with the foot the pressure on the closed plates: the higher the pressure, the more dry and quick-decaying the sound will be. Staccato notes, especially soft ones, are sometimes played on the upper surface of the top plate with the tips of the snare sticks and the pedal tightly closed, producing a "ricky-tick" sound, but usually the hi-hat is played with the *side* of the stick striking the *edge* of the plates. This enables production of varying articulation, from staccato to tenuto, depending on the loudness and the foot-pressure, and also assures that strokes made with the pedal up will be properly full and resonant. Strokes on the open cymbal with the tips of the sticks sound rather thin. All this can be notated on the lower line using ordinary signs of articulation:

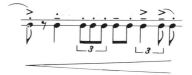

As a special effect, the pedal may be half-closed (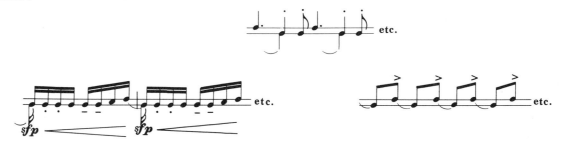) so that the plates rattle randomly together when struck.* Below are three typical hi-hat patterns frequently used in popular music:

* If one is willing to sacrifice most of the instrument's characteristic techniques, it is possible to adjust the hi-hat so that the pedal will not completely close the plates even when fully depressed, permitting easy and accurate production of this half-closed sound.

name of instrument	abbreviations	synonyms	dynamic range	normal sticks	status	availability
hi-hat	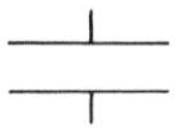	pedal cymbals foot cymbals	*ppp–fff*	snare sticks	standard	common

FIGURE 149. *The hi-hat—vital statistics.*

It is of course possible to play the hi-hat with any of the full range of sticks used on suspended cymbals, but snare sticks give the greatest expressive range.

GONGS AND TAM-TAMS

Gongs and tam-tams are frequently confused even by composers, for both are heavy metal disks with bent-back rims, suspended vertically by a cord running through two holes in the rim. The tam-tam, however, is essentially a downward extension of the suspended cymbal, with a flat or gently curved surface and no trace of definable pitch, while the gong typically has a raised **dome*** in the center and is of definable pitch. Gongs are available in a wide variety of sizes, timbres, and appearances, for differing musical purposes. At one extreme are instruments without domes, indistinguishable in appearance from tam-tams. These have a very weak pitch† and are used, usually singly, to play gong parts in which pitch would be obtrusive. Except for these, all gongs have the characteristic raised dome, and in many the bent-back rim is considerably deeper than that of a tam-tam; some gongs are as deep as they are wide. The shape of a gong governs its timbre, and the instrument is tuned as it is made by adjusting the size and depth of the dome. On some gongs the pitch of the instrument is brought out by striking the dome, while striking the main part of the instrument creates a sound more like that of a tam-tam, in which, however, the main pitch is still prominent. The extent of the difference between these two sounds depends on the exact construction of the gong, and the more loudly a gong is struck the more like a tam-tam it will sound. Finally, there are gongs that produce a beautiful, rich pitch no matter where they are struck and that sound like tam-tams only when hard sticks are used on the flat portion of the surface. Both tam-tams and gongs are normally struck just off-center; striking near the edge brings out the higher partials at the expense of the lower ones. If a gong is to be struck on the dome this must be specified.

Both tam-tams and gongs are available in a tremendous range of sizes, varying from as little as 18 cm in diameter to as much as 150 cm. The medium-large sizes—ca. 45–100 cm (for gongs C_0–c^1)—are most characteristic and most frequently encountered. To get an unusually large or small tam-tam it is necessary either to give the dimensions desired or to use some such expression as "very small tam-tam" or "giant tam-tam," since "large," "medium," and "small" are usually construed as lying within the narrower limits. Gongs of any size can of course be specified by pitch.

Gongs and tam-tams of medium size or larger are almost invariably played with a heavy gong-beater. These instruments are so massive that the sound takes an appreciable time to

* Percussionists often use a much less dignified term for this protuberance. We shall stick with "dome."

† The pitch *is* there, though. Even these gongs sound quite different from tam-tams.

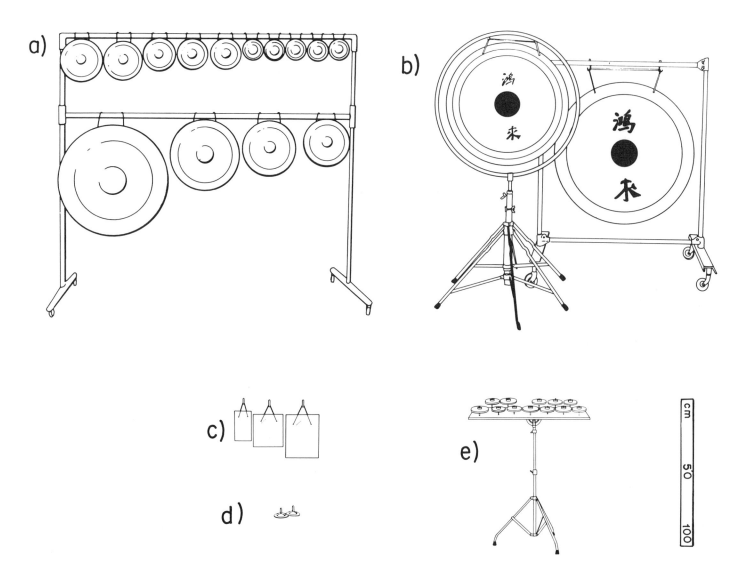

FIGURE 150. *The cymbal family, II: (a) gongs; (b) tam-tams;*
(c) bell plates; (d) crotales—hand type; (e) crotales—mallet type.

bloom following each stroke, creating a splash of sound that is most prominent if the note is struck cold or is much louder than the note preceding. The decay time may exceed thirty seconds. Smaller instruments have proportionately quicker attacks and decays; thus, the smallest tam-tams behave and sound very much like thick cymbals of similar diameter, while high-pitched gongs behave rather like bells. Instruments of small or very small size (gongs: above about f^0) are played with timpani sticks, and medium-sized ones (gongs: down to about A_0) can be so played as well. Very small instruments (gongs: above about c^1) can be effectively played with vibraphone mallets. These can be used on larger instruments, but not at the highest dynamic levels, and only with an increasing emphasis on high partials; nonetheless, vibraphone mallets are preferred for "on the dome" playing of all but the largest gongs. Xylophone sticks, chime mallets, plastic sticks, and metal sticks (except hammers, which will damage the instruments) can be used to get a brilliant, stinging attack from gongs and tam-

name of instrument	abbreviations	synonyms	written range	sounds	normal sticks	status	availability
gongs	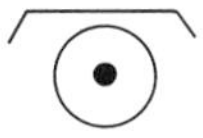 ⊙	(none)	 𝄢 ... 𝄞 loudest: *fff(f)* softest: *ppp*	as written	variable	standard	common
tam-tams	tam tamt.  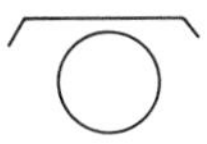	(none)	dynamics: *ppp–fff(f)*	—	gong-beater	standard	common

FIGURE 151. *Gongs and tam-tams—vital statistics.*

tams of all sizes, and these or vibraphone sticks are necessary whenever any kind of rapid rhythm is desired, since with softer mallets the individual tones tend to blur indistinguishably.

Repeated notes on a gong or tam-tam tend to accumulate vibratory energy, as cymbals do, and are thus more suited to crescendo than diminuendo. When—as often happens—a very loud note on a large instrument must be struck cold, the percussionist will usually set the instrument vibrating with a (hopefully, unheard) *ppp* stroke beforehand, so that all the energy of the main stroke increases the volume rather than dissipating itself in overcoming the inertia of the resting metal. Similarly, a true *ffff** is possible on a large gong or tam-tam only as the culmination of a crescendo.

Damping and muffling may be even more important on gongs and tam-tams than on cymbals. Notes on small instruments can be stopped by grasping the edge firmly with one hand; larger instruments are increasingly difficult to stop, and large or very large ones must be literally embraced with both arms and clasped firmly to the player's body for up to half a second. Stick-damping is only effective on small instruments, though on large ones it can shorten the decay time by up to two-thirds. For those gongs in which the pitch is concentrated in the dome, damping the dome alone will eliminate the main pitch while allowing the tam-tam–like edge resonance to continue undisturbed, while *gently* damping the edge will eliminate this resonance without disturbing the main pitch (strong edge-damping stops the entire sound). Careful edge- or center-damping can also be used to eliminate the highest or lowest partials from an ongoing tam-tam sound.

The muffling of a gong or tam-tam is obviously a problematic affair. Small ones can be muffled by being laid flat across, e.g., a pair of towel-covered sawhorses. If a medium-sized gong or tam-tam is laid face down on a timpano, it will not only be muffled but will have access to the timbre-modifying effect of the drum's pedal. Muffling a gong produces a particularly pleasant effect since the dome tone is only minimally altered.

* In fact, a large tam-tam in a small hall can cause severe and permanent hearing damage if it is not handled carefully.

name of instrument	abbreviations	synonyms	written range	sounds	normal sticks	status	availability
bell plates	bell pl.	(none)	 [musical staff notation] loudest: *fff* softest: *ppp*	as written	heaviest possible gong-beater	standard, homemade	very rare

FIGURE 152. *Bell plates—vital statistics.*

The bowing and scraping effects described for suspended cymbals are equally effective on gong or tam-tam and produce very similar sounds. A special "rubbed" effect, a continuous zinging sound, can be produced by running a hard stick (particularly a triangle beater) circularly around the surface of the instrument. Moving the butt end of a wood-handled stick slowly across the surface produces indeterminate squawks resembling the sound produced by bowing. Both gongs and tam-tams continue to sound very impressive even when dipped in water. The pitch can be lowered (not raised!) as much as an octave in this fashion, and various glissandos can be produced. Since the instrument to be dipped must be hand-held, only small or medium-sized instruments should be used. Remember also that the resistance of the water shortens the decay time of the sound to an increasing extent the greater the depth to which the instrument is dipped.

The tam-tam has so many partials arrayed so densely that a large tam-tam can act as a kind of reverb unit for any instrument played into it, producing a thin metallic ghost of the original timbre about four dynamic levels softer. As might be expected, high notes are resonated more effectively than low ones. In writing for gongs or tam-tams their large size, long decay, and cumbersome playing technique must be considered. Particularly when the instruments are large, it is folly to write any kind of rapid figuration, not only because of the difficulties involved in hitting the (of necessity widely spaced) instruments in time, but because the resulting sound would just be a muddle. Moreover, when hit strongly, the instruments are liable to swing back and forth and may even topple the stand to which they are attached.

BELL PLATES

Bell plates were invented to play the inordinately low-pitched bell parts written by many composers around the beginning of the twentieth century. They are about the size of gongs of equivalent pitch but are typically rectangular and quite thick—hence very heavy. Because of their great mass they are normally played with the heaviest possible soft beater—either a heavy gong-beater or specially padded metal hammers. They can also be effectively played with chime mallets. When notes below about a^0 are struck *fff*, the tone breaks into a cluster of high partials more reminiscent of a domeless gong than of a bell, and light, hard sticks will also make the tone somewhat snarly, but otherwise the bell imitation is very good. The bell tone is elicited by striking one or two particular spots near the center of the plate; strokes elsewhere (especially anywhere near the edge) produce, again, the "domeless gong" sound. Almost the

name of instrument	abbreviations	synonyms	written range	sounds	normal sticks	status	availability
crotales	crot. 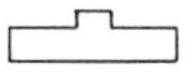	antique cymbals	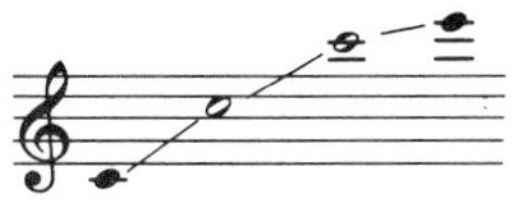 *(musical notation)* loudest: *fff* softest: *ppp*	1 octave higher (transposition not standard-ized)	metal glockenspiel sticks, bell mallets	standard	common

FIGURE 153. *Crotales—vital statistics.*

only example so far of composition for bell plates as such is the last movement ("Tombeau") of Boulez's *Pli selon pli.*

CROTALES

Crotales are, proportionally, the thickest of all cymbals. The thickness eliminates large numbers of high partials, giving the crotales a clear, ringing pitch and a timbre best described as intermediate between glockenspiel and triangle. To a certain extent they can be considered an upward continuation of the bell plates, but they are even clearer in pitch.

Crotales exist in two forms. The older and now rarer type is a pair of very thick, high-domed finger cymbals. Because of their weight they are held in opposite hands rather than on two fingers of one hand. The two cymbals may be tuned to the same pitch or a minor second apart; in the latter case the intent is to give them an indefinite pitch, a prime example of the principle that percussion dissonances tend to sound merely unpitched. These "unpitched" crotales are used to play parts in which no pitch is specified and which are otherwise suitable for hand crotales; they are also often used to play finger-cymbal parts. All hand crotales are played by holding them horizontally and tapping them together edge to edge. Obviously, a single player can only handle one pitch at a time, but with "unpitched" crotales the specific pitches of the two individual cymbals can be brought out either by damping the unwanted pitch after the stroke or by striking only one of them, suspended cymbal fashion, with a glockenspiel mallet.

Much more common are crotales in the form of a disk on a short central stem that is pierced by a threaded hole. A group of crotales of different pitches are attached in keyboard order to screw rods on a flat board, making a single compound instrument. Thus arrayed, the crotales are played like a mallet instrument; broadly speaking, they *are* a mallet instrument. The range of such a set of crotales has become increasingly standardized as the one octave c^3–c^4; pitches outside this range are now rare. It is generally understood that parts for the crotales should be written an octave below actual pitch, but complete agreement on this point has not yet been reached, part of the problem being that crotales give the impression of sounding an octave higher than they really are.

Crotales are played with metal glockenspiel sticks or, for a coarser sound, with bell mallets. Other sticks that can be used if necessary are plastic mallets, xylophone sticks, or triangle beaters. Tiny, delicate sounds with much attack noise can be elicited by snare sticks or knitting needles. For the *ppp* hard vibraphone sticks are best; other options at this low dynamic level are wire brushes or even fingers.

Playing techniques are like those for mallet instruments, discussed below; glissandos, however, are impossible. Two or three mallets can be used in each hand and the full octave can be stretched one-handed. The decay time for the individual crotales is about five seconds; since crotales are normally allowed to vibrate freely, all damping should be indicated carefully. If desired the sound may be muffled by hand or stick, producing a dry, anvil-like clink.

Crotales, like other cymbals, may be bowed or scraped. The very beautiful bowed sound gives the instrument's main pitch rather than the indeterminate squawk typical of other cymbals. Remember that bowing must be done slowly and with care and that the "white key" and "black key" notes must be bowed on opposite sides of the board. An individual crotale can be hand-dipped in water with a resultant drop in pitch of up to a whole step (with drastic shortening of decay time), but a special suspension system must be rigged for it, since it normally hangs horizontally rather than vertically. Finally, a crotale may be rested stem downward on a timpano for the "wawa" effect discussed in Chapter VI, or a very subtle vibrato can be produced by shaking a cupped hand up and down above a vibrating crotale.

CHIMES

THE CHIMES

Chimes, like bell plates, were originally devised to play parts written for bells, but they have long since established themselves in their own right. Despite its plural name, this is a single instrument consisting of eighteen long metal tubes of uniform diameter and thickness suspended in a special rack in keyboard order, with the sharps hung behind and a few centimeters higher than the naturals. Individual chimes are easily removed from the rack (not during performance, though!) and can be hung separately in any pattern desired. The extension pitches indicated in Figure 155 are sold as individual tubes, and when used they must be hung separately from the rest, since the rack holds only the traditional eighteen chimes.* Unlike true mallet instruments, the chimes is a "vertical" rather than a "horizontal" instrument: the tubes are struck at the top, at the level of the player's head.

The rack in which the chimes are hung is provided with a **sustain pedal** which, like that of the piano, allows the tubes to vibrate freely when it is depressed and damps them when it is released. Unlike the piano pedal, however, this sustain pedal can easily be locked down so that the player's foot need not stay glued to the pedal for every "l.v." Hand-damping is also used in chime playing, in passages where some notes of a chord are to be stopped but others allowed to ring through. Notes struck without the pedal down produce a strongly muffled clank. When necessary, individual tones may instead be hand-muffled.

Chimes are normally played with—what else—chime mallets, but other sticks may be used as well, most notably the rubber-series mallets. Of these, xylophone sticks, bell mallets, and plastic sticks give an increasingly raucous and clangorous tone, while vibraphone and marimba sticks give a delicate and gentle one. These soft sticks must be used whenever a *ppp* is desired; conversely, they cannot be used to produce the *fff*. Other sticks that can be used are

* Rarely, one encounters a rack of twenty chimes, including the high f♯² and g².

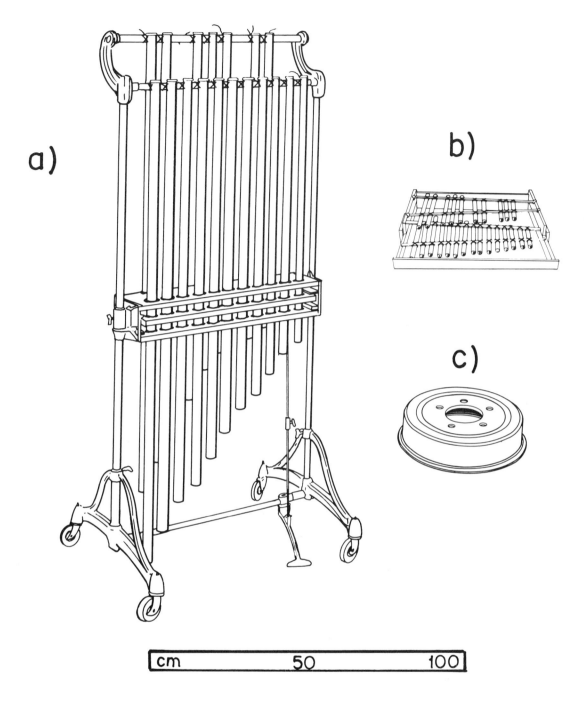

FIGURE 154. *Chime instruments: (a) chimes; (b) metal tubes; (c) brake drum.*

snare sticks, knitting needles, and metal glockenspiel sticks, all of which give a weak tone with much attack noise; snare sticks and knitting needles are limited to dynamics of *ppp–ff*. Fingers or wire brushes can be used to produce sounds of a mysterious and very delicate character no louder than *pianissimo*. When rubber-series mallets or metal glockenspiel sticks are employed, multi-mallet techniques can be used (see the section below on mallet instruments). The maximum one-hand stretch easily covers the entire eighteen-note range of the chimes. Chime mallets are much too heavy and short-handled for multi-mallet performance, but the long,

name of instrument	abbreviations	synonyms	written range	sounds	normal sticks	status	availability
chimes		tubular bells	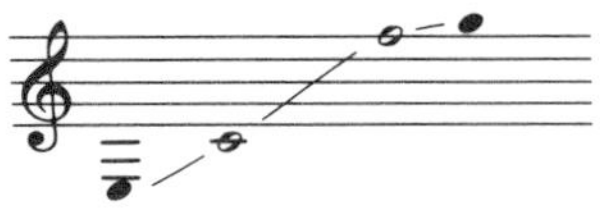	as written	chime mallets	standard	common

loudest: *fff*
softest: *ppp*

FIGURE 155. *Chimes—vital statistics.*

cylindrical head can be turned sideways to strike two adjacent tubes simultaneously. A special technique possible only with snare stick or knitting needle is a one-handed trill, executed by inserting the stick between two adjacent tubes and rattling it back and forth.

Like the mallet instruments, chimes produce a so-called "glissando" (actually a rip) if a stick is run along the row of tubes so that it strikes each in turn. This should be notated either note-for-note with a slur or like the key rip of woodwinds (p. 31). Remember that because there are two rows of pipes the glissando must consist either of all sharps or all naturals and that a glissando on the sharps must be very rapid if it is not to sound ragged (because of the gaps in that row of tubes). Also, unless the glissando is played on muffled tubes each note struck will continue to ring as the others are played, making the effect more like an arpeggiated tone-cluster than a real glissando. It is traditional for the note at the end of a glissando to be struck separately with the opposite stick; if this is not desired, it must be indicated by notating a slur over the entire glissando right to the last note, rather than ending the slur just before this note (see p. 243).

Chimes may with difficulty be bowed, but they will produce only an indeterminate squawk. An individual chime may be hand-dipped in water, but practical considerations (the great depth of water necessary for the total immersion of a chime) require that any water-mediated glissando not exceed a half-step below the chime's "dry" pitch.

METAL TUBES

There used to be a mallet instrument called the **tubaphone** whose sounding elements were thin metal tubes. This instrument is, alas, no longer made, but individual metal tubes are of not infrequent occurrence in percussionists' *armamentaria* and are easily enough prepared by cutting thin piping to the required lengths. Percussionists who do make such tubes often make complete diatonic or chromatic sets of them and line them up in keyboard order on paired supports in a wooden tray, like a glockenspiel, to make a sort of homemade tubaphone. Since no two of these homemade instruments are of identical compass, however, it is best for composers to think in terms of individual metal tubes grouped together ad hoc and played like a mallet instrument. It is unusual to find tubes pitched lower than (sounding) c^2, because of the unwieldy length of tubing required for lower notes. Nonetheless, Lou Harrison, for instance, has used tubes sounding as low as a^0—up to 64 cm in length.

Tubes have an exceptionally sweet and pure tone, without either the brilliance and clangor of the glockenspiel or the cool impersonality of the vibraphone. The sound decays in three

name of instrument	abbreviations	synonyms	written range	sounds	normal sticks	status	availability
metal tubes	tubes	(none)	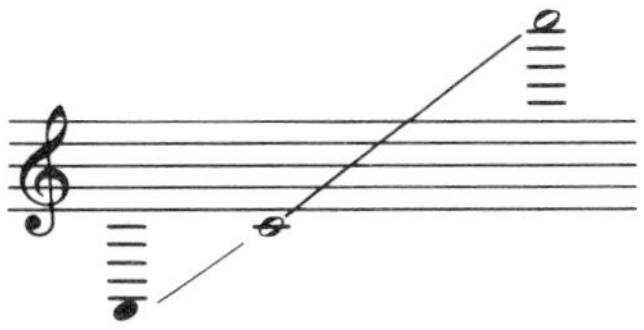 *(musical staff)* loudest: *fff* softest: *ppp*	1 octave higher (transposition not standardized)	xylophone sticks (hard, medium, soft)	homemade	rare

FIGURE 156. *Metal tubes—vital statistics.*

name of instrument	abbreviations	synonyms	written range	sounds	normal sticks	status	availability
brake drums	brake dr.	(none)	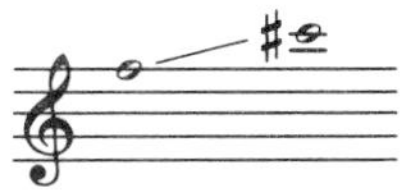 *(musical staff)* loudest: *fff(f)* softest: *ppp*	as written (transposition not standardized)	variable	found object	common

FIGURE 157. *Brake drums—vital statistics.*

to five seconds, depending on the exact type and size of tube used. Playing on a set of tubes involves almost exactly the same techniques as playing a glockenspiel (q.v.), except that somewhat softer sticks (xylophone mallets) should be used. Glockenspiel sticks or triangle beaters can be used when a particularly hard or brilliant sound is desired, and snare sticks can be employed for soft, rackety sounds with much attack noise. Wound sticks or even fingers will be needed for the *ppp*. Multi-mallet technique is entirely appropriate, and though the width of the tubes varies considerably from instrument to instrument, a one-hand stretch of up to two full octaves should always be possible. Tubes can be bowed, but produce only an anonymous squeal of indeterminate pitch.

BRAKE DRUMS

The brake drum is the classic junkyard instrument. Easily obtained, richly resonant, and amazingly consistent in timbre from one to another, it is hard to imagine how this gift of the auto industry could be improved upon as a musical instrument. Acoustically, the brake drum is essentially a squat, heavy chime whose irregular shape gives it a decay time of only about half a second. Brake drums are pitched (in a surprisingly narrow range), but several prominent conflicting partials obscure the main tone,* and composers almost always leave the pitch indeterminate.

* Different people may perceive different pitches from one brake drum, and perception of the matter may vary depending on such factors as the acoustics of the room, what sticks are used, and what other instruments are playing.

The "drums" are laid on a sturdy table (they weigh several kilograms each) and are traditionally played in groups of four or six. Xylophone or bell mallets, metal glockenspiel sticks, or plastic sticks are normally used—the harder the louder, as usual: wound sticks are needed for the *ppp*. Using multi-mallet technique with any of these sticks, up to four brake drums may be struck at a time, or two at a time one-handed. Other possible sticks—with which, however, multi-mallet technique is impossible—are chime mallets, geologist's hammers, and nail hammers, the last two of which can reach *ffff*—a dynamic level that should not often be inflicted on defenseless audiences. For special effects wire brushes may be used (*pp–ppp*), or switch (slightly louder), fingers (*ppp* only), or light wooden sticks or knitting needles (*forte* or less— much attack noise). Finally, a brake drum may be scraped with a file or screw rod.

MALLET INSTRUMENTS

THE XYLOPHONE FAMILY

A mallet instrument is a set of tuned rectangular bars laid out in keyboard order across paired supports (usually thin rope) in a trapezoidal frame. In all except the glockenspiel the tone of each bar is reinforced by a tubular resonator hanging from the frame below it and tuned to the pitch of the bar. The frame has legs (with wheels) to hold it at a convenient height for playing.* The glockenspiel has no resonators and no legs: the body of the instrument is a flat box in which the bars lie and which acts as a collective resonator for all of them, and the instrument must be laid on a stand or table to be played.

The bars of a mallet instrument are thinned from below toward the center. This emphasizes the fundamental and in most instruments alters the harmonic spectrum so that the second partial lies exactly two octaves above the fundamental. Each bar together with its resonator forms a self-contained acoustical unit, i.e., even if a given bar is used as the lowest note on one instrument and an identical bar is used as the *highest* note of another instrument, the sound of the two bars will be identical.

This is particularly important for the xylophone family, mallet instruments with bars made of wood.† Though there are some slight differences in the construction of these three instruments (the xylophone uses harder wood than the others and has bars of equal width, while in the others the bars are graduated in width as well as length), where the ranges overlap they are virtually identical in sound. A c^2 (sounding), for instance, played on the xylophone sounds the same as one played on the marimba, provided the same mallets are used for both. The striking difference between the dry, cutting, sardonic tone of the xylophone and the lush, warm, rather vague sound of the marimba is largely due to the mallets used. The choice of mallets is governed by the ranges of the instruments, since soft sticks cannot play high notes efficiently and hard sticks do not sufficiently bring out the fundamentals of low notes. Thus the range of each instrument does govern its timbre—but only indirectly.

* The apparently symmetrical arrangement of the resonators of many mallet instruments is created by a false front of fake resonators. The real resonators are of logarithmically decreasing length. On the bass marimba the longer resonators are doubled back under the instrument, which would otherwise have to stand a meter and a half above the ground.

† In many xylophones and some cheap marimbas the bars are made of a special plastic of equivalent resonance.

FIGURE 158. *Mallet instruments: (a) xylophone; (b) marimba;*
(c) bass marimba; (d) glockenspiel; (e) vibraphone; (f) lithophone.

name of instrument	abbreviations	synonyms	written range	sounds	normal sticks	status	availability
xylophone	xyl. 	(none)	 loudest: *fff* softest: *ppp*	1 octave higher	xylophone sticks (hard, medium, soft)	standard	common
marimba	mar. mmba. 	marimba-phone	 25 % loudest: *fff* softest: *ppp*	as written	marimba sticks (hard, medium, soft)	standard	common
bass marimba	bs. mar. bs. mmba.	(none)	 loudest: *ff(f)* softest: *ppp*	as written	variable	standard	very rare

FIGURE 159. *The xylophone family—vital statistics.*

The sticks normally used for xylophone and marimba are summarized in Figure 73. Soft marimba sticks can only make the xylophone speak very softly, while hard xylophone sticks (as well as the still harder sticks associated with the glockenspiel) damage the soft wood of the marimba bars and are therefore never used. It is entirely possible to make a xylophone sound like a marimba and vice versa; for this purpose one should simply specify "very soft sticks" (or "vibraphone sticks") for xylophone → marimba, and "very hard sticks" for marimba → xylophone. The bass marimba ideally uses special mallets that are even softer, larger, and heavier than soft marimba sticks, but regular marimba sticks will do. In general, composers should specify only soft, medium, or hard sticks. No single type of stick can cover the complete dynamic range of these instruments, since only wound sticks can produce the *ppp* and, at least above c^3, only hard, unwound sticks can produce the *fff*.

For special effects certain other sticks can be used on these instruments. Tapping with the fingers produces a very delicate, exotic effect, *piano* and softer (and above about c^2 no louder than *pp*). Wire brushes may also be used, with similar dynamic limitations, but except on the bass marimba each brush stroke will hit two or more adjacent bars (because of the width of the fan of wires). Snare sticks can be used, up to *forte* (reversed snare sticks up to *fortissimo*) in passages where a very dry sound with much attack noise is wanted.

The xylophone family is more highly standardized here than in Europe, where the range of the xylophone is still quite variable and where one frequently runs across a hybrid instrument called the **xylorimba** (almost unknown on this continent), whose highest note is c^5 and whose lowest may be c^1, f^0, or c^0. The low A_0 extension of the marimba, a recent and largely American phenomenon, is gradually becoming more widespread. The ranges of the marimba and xylorimba are so large that it is appropriate to use sticks of different hardness for passages at their lower versus their upper ends.

Virtuoso percussionists are capable of playing any of the mallet instruments with great rapidity and accuracy even in the most angular and irregular passages. Composers must nonetheless beware of boxing the player into an impossible corner with passages such as this:

which requires a rapid double-beat over a leap of a ninth, or this:

which requires for the ab^2 either a similarly awkward double-beat or a cross-over in which the left hand must pull out from under the right and shoot back over it to hit a high note on the back row of bars, all in the space of a thirty-second-note. The problem is not so much the octave cross-over, though this is in itself rather awkward, but the fact that the preceding cross-over has put the player's hands in a position from which it is impossible to get to the ab^2 in time. Such "tangled" cross-overs should be avoided even when they cover much smaller intervals. Where tangling of the hands is not involved, cross-overs are no problem, though of course the larger the cross-over, the more cautiously the player must proceed.

The decay time of notes on the wooden mallet instruments increases exponentially as the scale is descended, so that while notes on the xylophone and in the upper part of the marimba's range are very crisp and dry (even with soft sticks), those at the bottom of the marimba, and on the bass marimba, last so long as occasionally to require hand-damping. The note c^3, for instance, rings for about a quarter-second, while c^2 lasts half a second, c^1 one second, c^0 two seconds, and C_0 a full four seconds. In the lower part of the range the attack becomes increasingly sluggish, and rapid passages below about c^1 are increasingly likely to sound blurred. Choice of sticks is very important in this range: hard,* unwound sticks cut through the long individual resonances to bring clarity and precision to even the most rapid low-pitched passages—this, however, at the expense of pitch definition; soft, wound mallets produce an almost imperceptible attack, so that, for instance,

Allegro

played with soft mallets will seem more like a single, regularly throbbing sound than four distinct notes, while a roll will sound genuinely continuous and a trill will sound like a continuous chord. Whatever the choice of sticks, articulation should be handled with care: particu-

---

* I.e., hard marimba sticks, not xylophone sticks.

larly below f⁰, hand-damping will be needed for all staccato notes, for short notes followed by rests, and for passages in consecutive eighth- or even quarter-notes when particular clarity is desired; and whenever damping is used the player's agility is of course limited. Slow staccato notes can be damped as they are played by light stick-muffling. Heavy muffling by hand ( ) or stick ( ) can be used as a special effect even at the top of the xylophone range; as usual with muffling, the sound produced is very "dead" and relatively weak in pitch.

One of the most important features of mallet-instrument playing is **multi-mallet technique**, which allows the performer to play chords of up to eight notes by holding up to four mallets in each hand. In multi-mallet playing the hand is held palm downward as a loose fist. The sticks emerge from between the bases of the fingers. By tilting the wrist the "extra" stick(s) can be held out of the way so single notes can be played.

For most purposes it will not be necessary to have more than two sticks in each hand, and except where absolutely necessary this number should not be exceeded, since with three or four mallets per hand the player's flexibility is greatly hampered. With only two sticks in the hand, the angle between the sticks can by changing the configuration of the fingers be quickly and easily changed from nearly 180° to nearly 0° (or anywhere in between), enabling the performance of all sorts of chords and intervals, while with three or four sticks in the hand such changes of angle are limited in scope and difficult and uncertain of execution. Even with two sticks it is best for the most part to write intervals that are parallel or nearly so. A passage such as

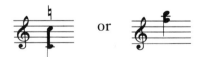

is impossible even in moderate tempo, though at slow speeds (say, ♩ = 60) it is tricky but possible.

On the xylophone the *average* maximum interval stretch between the outermost sticks held in one hand is a thirteenth.* On the marimba, which has bars of varying width, the situation is more complicated. From the low A₀ one can stretch upward about a ninth; this increases to a tenth at e⁰, an eleventh at e¹, and a twelfth at c². It is probably best not to exceed a seventh on the bass marimba.

When three or four sticks per hand are used, all changes of angle should be allowed plenty of time, for the player will probably have to adjust the positions of the sticks with the opposite hand, and if both hands must hold three or more sticks, the process can be as clumsy as putting on a watch while wearing mittens. With four sticks per hand the two middle sticks will always be spaced evenly between the other two. Such four-stick playing is most useful for the production of tone-clusters such as

or

---

* The maximum depends upon the size of the player's hands and the length of the sticks and is thus quite variable.

of up to eight notes. Since the sharps on the wooden mallet instruments are raised above the naturals, the three or four mallets in each hand must play all natural or all sharp notes—otherwise the middle mallets might make contact with no bar at all or with the wrong one. The second of the two tone clusters given above, for instance, must be taken this way:

Because of the possibilities opened up by multi-mallet playing, all rolls and trills should be carefully and accurately notated. Particularly to be avoided is the bad habit of writing

 when is intended.

All mallet instruments are capable of glissandos (so called—actually rips) produced by running a single stick along one row of bars. This is notated as a rip, and one should distinguish between

in which the note following the glissando is separately attacked, and

in which it is not. Glissandos on the back row will tend to sound ragged because of the irregular spacing of the bars there. Other things being equal, it is best for upward glissandos to be executed by the right hand, downward ones by the left.

A special technique related to the glissando is to slide a stick off a bar in the back row down onto an adjacent bar in the front, thus making relatively easy passages such as

which would otherwise be almost impossible.

By holding a finger strongly across the middle of a bar which is then struck with the opposite hand it is possible to produce **harmonics** on the marimba and bass marimba. These harmonics, which can be produced only on bars pitched g^2 or lower, sound two octaves above the fundamental pitch of the bar. The fundamental is not completely eliminated, and the sound is almost like a negative photograph of the normal sound, with the relative prominence of the first and second partials reversed. The harmonic decays in about half the time of the ordinary note. Harmonics should be notated at the pitch of the fundamental (not that of the harmonic), with the usual little circle above the note to indicate "harmonic," thus:

This notation should be explained to the player, since some composers notate the perceived pitch, as for woodwind or string harmonics.

It is possible to use a bow on these instruments, producing a strong, clear pitch *pp–ff* on any note from (sounding) c⁴ down, and a *ppp* whisper from a⁴ down. The louder, full sound is slow to speak and clumsy to produce, so bowed passages must move very slowly. Remember, too, that sharps and naturals must be bowed on opposite sides of the instrument.

Two special noises that should be mentioned are that produced by striking the body of the instrument (typically at one end), and that made by using the resonators as a kind of rasp. The former is a dull click or thunk, the latter a rackety sound in which the presumed "pitch" of the individual resonators plays no part.

THE VIBRAPHONE FAMILY

The vibraphone family consists of those mallet instruments whose bars are made of metal. The family is somewhat less homogeneous than the xylophone family, and the highest and lowest types (glockenspiel, bass metallophone) lack the damper pedal and vibrato mechanism that are characteristic of the vibraphone proper; the glockenspiel even lacks resonators.

The decay time of the metal bars is quite long—five seconds for the glockenspiel, seven seconds for the others—and to control this duration the vibraphone is fitted with a **damper pedal** analogous in its operation to that of the piano. Notes played with the pedal depressed sound for their complete natural duration. Unlike the chimes pedal, the pedal of a vibraphone cannot readily be locked down (though for special purposes it can be *weighted* down with a cinderblock, a brake drum, or what-have-you), nor does it completely choke the sound of notes played while it is undepressed: such notes die very quickly (about a quarter-second) but otherwise sound completely natural, and short or rapid notes are thus normally played without pedaling. True muffling must be accomplished by hand or stick, as with other mallet instruments. By the use of **half-pedaling** and other subtleties of execution, vibraphonists can produce articulation as varied and sophisticated as that of any sustaining instrument, and detailed writing such as this:

which would be simply affectation in, say, a marimba part, is entirely appropriate to the vibraphone. Even an "fp" is possible. The notation for pedaling is "l.v. ‿‿‿⌐" (or "ped. ‿‿‿⌐") placed below the staff, the end of the half-bracket indicating the point at which the

name of instrument	abbreviations	synonyms	written range	sounds	normal sticks	status	availability
glockenspiel	glock. glsp. G	orchestra bells	*(musical notation)* loudest: *fff* softest: *ppp*	2 octaves higher	metal glockenspiel sticks (heavy, light) bell mallets	standard	common
vibraphone	vib. vibr. vibes V	vibraharp	*(musical notation)* loudest: *fff* softest: *ppp*	as written	vibraphone sticks (hard, medium, soft)	standard	common
bass metallophone(s)	bs. met.	(none)	*(musical notation)* loudest: *ff(f)* softest: *ppp*	as written	variable	homemade	very rare

FIGURE 160. *The vibraphone family—vital statistics.*

pedal is to be released.* If the pedal is to be held down for some time the indication is "l.v. (sempre)," with a short half-bracket (⌐⌐) placed separately at the end of the passage. Details of pedaling should generally be left to the player; composers should give pedaling indications only in places where the required use of the pedal is not implicit in the notes. In this regard one should especially bear in mind that rapid legato runs will normally be performed with the pedal down; such a passage will not seem blurred provided the pedal is released the instant the texture thins or slows. The following passage displays the way in which the pedal is normally used.

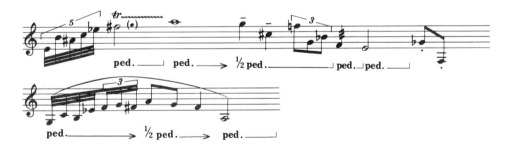

In contrapuntal passages hand-damping must occasionally be used in conjunction with the pedal. For example, if a single long note is to be held while several shorter notes are played beneath it, the pedal must be held down for the long note and each of the shorter notes

* "Ped." indicates specifically that the pedal is to be depressed, while "l.v." indicates simply that the notes are to be sustained beyond their notated value, without specifying how.

be individually hand-damped. The use of a cautionary "non l.v." by the notes to be damped is generally a good idea, since composers have been known to write

when

was intended. Of course, such a "pyramid" of notes should be notated this way:

The vibraphone also has a unique vibrato mechanism (from which it gets its name). Each resonator has poised at its top a metal disk that blocks it off almost completely. All the disks in each row of resonators are strung together on a single rod and the two rods are attached to a small electric motor that rotates them (and the disks) synchronously, so that all the resonators at once are alternately opened and closed by the rotating disks. This in turn causes a gentle fluctuation in the loudness of the notes. The motor that drives the disks can easily be turned off, and when on can be varied in speed (on all good vibraphones) between two and eight pulses per second. In the absence of any special indications, the vibraphone will be played with the motor on, at a vibrato speed chosen by the player. It is possible to turn the motor on or off or to change the vibrato speed while playing—even while a note is still sounding—if the player has a hand free to manipulate the dial on the motor.

The vibrato mechanism was originally devised to mitigate the vibraphone's very cool, "objective" tone. The glockenspiel is distinctly more brilliant and ringing in quality, even when played with soft sticks, because its bars are thinned on the under side considerably less than on other mallet instruments, so the second partial does not reinforce the double-octave of the fundamental but instead lies at a dissonant interval.

The only way to extend the range of the vibraphone family below the traditional lower limit of f^0 is through the use of some sort of homemade bass metallophone.* There is of course no hint of standardization in the construction or range of these instruments, and it is best, since they are so rare, that composers build or at least design their own as needed. Generally speaking, it is inadvisable to exceed the range of one chromatic octave. Notes in this range—particularly below F_0—are often built as individual bar-and-resonator units without a common frame. Especially below C_0, the great size of the individual bars may mandate that the player actually stand *between* the middle pair of a group of no more than eight bars. Such low bars must be played with gong beaters. The resonators of notes below about G_0 will be

* A handful of vibraphones are now made with a four-octave compass, descending to c^0, but even if this range were to become standard over an octave's worth of potentially useful notes would still not be incorporated into any commercially available instrument.

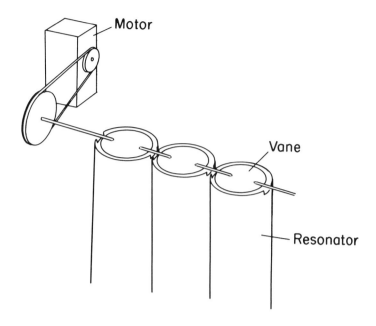

FIGURE 161. *The vibrato mechanism of the vibraphone.*

quite tall, and if they are not doubled back (a sophisticated piece of carpentry) the percussionist may have to stand on a riser. The thinning of the bars of a bass metallophone is beyond the reach of all but the most skillful and well-equipped do-it-yourself instrument maker, so the sound will be considerably richer and fuller than that of the vibraphone—almost gong-like, in fact. The major experimenter with bass metallophones at present is Lou Harrison, whose "Western Gamelan" includes bars as low as A_1.

As Figure 73 shows, vibraphone sticks are invariably wound. Unwound sticks will only be used when they are specifically requested by the composer; they not only give a sharper attack but also bring out the instrument's weak upper partials, making the tone somewhat gritty (soft unwound mallets) or harshly jangling (e.g., xylophone mallets or plastic sticks). With soft wound sticks the attack may be almost imperceptible and repeated notes may blur together into a single pulsating sound. This effect can be used deliberately to give the impression of a vibrato conflicting with that produced by the motor, as in this example, which will be heard as a four-against-five pulsation:

The glockenspiel has its own array of special sticks, all very hard and traditionally differentiated by weight. Metal sticks are the most commonly employed, rubber and plastic sticks being used when a harsher, more cutting tone is desired. Snare sticks, knitting needles, wire brushes, or fingers can be used on all these instruments to produce the usual delicate special effects.

All members of the vibraphone family except the glockenspiel can be bowed, producing a very beautiful, sweet sound. Remember that, as for the marimba, bowed sounds are cum-

name of instrument	abbreviations	synonyms	written range	sounds	normal sticks	status	availability
lithophones	lith.	stone chimes	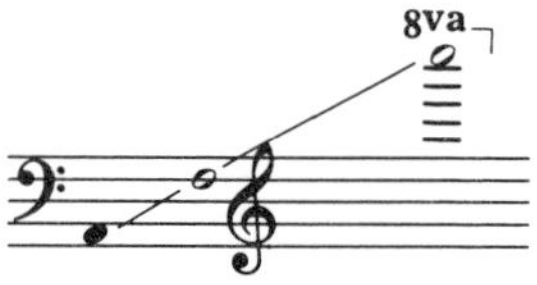 *(musical notation)* loudest: *fff* softest: *ppp*	as written (transposition not standardized)	variable	homemade	very rare

FIGURE 162. *Lithophones—vital statistics.*

bersome to play and slow of speech, and that sharps must be bowed on the far side of the instrument, naturals on the near side. With the pedal down, a bowed note will continue to ring on for its normal seven seconds after the bowing has stopped, and the distinction in sound between a note bowed for its full length and one bowed only at its beginning should be borne in mind.

Performance techniques on these instruments are virtually the same as for the xylophone family. Maximum one-hand stretches for multi-mallet playing are two octaves plus a second for the glockenspiel. Professional-quality vibraphones have bars of graduated width, giving maximum stretches of a ninth from f^0, a tenth from g^0, an eleventh from d^1, and a twelfth from a^1 up. On the vibraphone the rear row of bars lies in the same plane as the front row, so triple- and quadruple-mallet chords can make use of notes in both rows,* and "diagonal" glissandos (starting on a sharp and ending on a natural, or vice versa) can be produced.

Harmonics are performed just as they are on the marimba and can be gotten from any bar pitched f^2 or lower. A special effect unique to the vibraphone is the **bent tone** produced by holding a mallet very firmly against a bar at one of the nodes of the first partial (i.e., the places where the bar rests on its supports), striking the bar with the opposite hand, and while the tone is ringing moving the mallet (still under great pressure) away from the node toward the center of the bar. The result is a true downward glissando of up to a semitone, coupled with a considerable shortening of the decay time. On most instruments this effect cannot be produced above about c^2.

As with the xylophone family, some rather useless noises can be made by striking the end of a vibraphone or using its resonators as a rasp.

LITHOPHONES

Lithophones—mallet instruments with stone bars—remain experimental curiosities despite the potential they present for the development of a third family of mallet instruments to contrast with the existing wood and metal types.†

* For such a chord, the interval distance between the three or four sticks in the hand will be less than in an all-naturals or all-sharps chord, for the hand must be turned in at an angle if notes in both rows are to be struck.

† An additional possibility, at present totally unrealized, would be a **vitriphone**, with glass bars. Such an instrument would sound similar to the lithophone but would have a purer tone and a long decay approximating that of metal.

The sound of a lithophone is quite rich (the bars are not thinned), with a clinking, glassy attack even when soft sticks are used. The decay time averages about one second (longer for low pitches, shorter for high ones) but may be much shorter, depending on the type of stone used and the exact shape of the bars. The pitch range given in Figure 162 is not that of any one instrument but is, rather, the total range within which lithophones have been built. Individual lithophone bars are considerably larger than wood or metal ones of the same pitch: bars below c^0, for instance, are over a meter in length and a three-octave instrument giving f^0–f^3 is as large as a marimba with low A_0 extension. Sticks and performance techniques are essentially the same as for other mallet instruments. As with the bass metallophone, it is best to compose for lithophones only on a "build as you write" basis. Existing parts for lithophones can be found in works by Orff (e.g., *Antigonae*) and Robert Erickson (*Cardenitas*).

MISCELLANEOUS INSTRUMENTS

WIND MACHINE

The wind machine is, like the string drum and the thundersheet, a theatrical sound effect. It consists of a large wooden barrel with widely spaced slats that is mounted in a frame and rotated with a handle (much like a lottery drum). An ordinary tarpaulin is draped over the barrel, and as the barrel moves beneath it a turbulent whooshing sound is produced which does indeed closely resemble wind. Pitch and volume vary together (like real wind) and are a function of the speed with which the barrel is rotated. As with sirens (to which the wind machine is related) only the dynamics, not the pitch, should be notated. Also siren-like is the instrument's great inertia, which prevents it from playing any sort of articulated rhythm; instead, it plays individual (usually long) notes of fluctuating dynamic contour.

FRICTION SQUEAKS

The squeak (another sound effect) is a wooden handle stuck tightly into a hole in a wooden board. Depending on the speed with which the handle is turned, various creaking or squeaking noises are produced. Pitch and timbre vary with the dynamic level and, as with other such instruments, only the dynamics need be notated. Quite rapid rhythms can be produced by pushing the handle back and forth, rather like a ratchet.

The friction birdcall consists of a solid, rosined wooden or metal cylinder nested in a hollow wooden or pasteboard one. When the two parts of the instrument are ground together (by rotating the inner cylinder while the outer one is held steady) an irregular, very bird-like twittering or chirping is produced. Dynamics are governed by the pressure with which the hand forces the inner and outer cylinders to rub together. Pitch is fluctuating and uncontrollable. As with the squeak, rapid rhythms can be produced if desired.

Both these instruments are normally held in one hand and played with the other, but if necessary they can be fastened down and played one-handed.

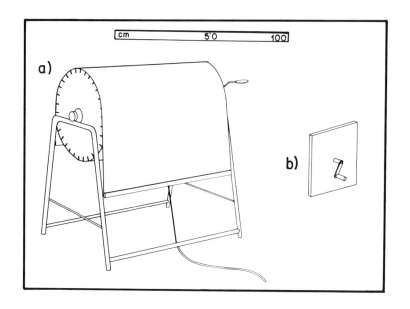

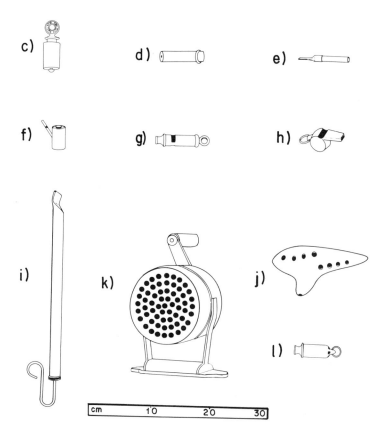

FIGURE 163. *Miscellaneous "percussion": (a) wind machine; (b) squeak;
(c) friction birdcall; (d) crow or duck call; (e) razzer; (f) water whistle; (g) signal whistle;
(h) referee's whistle; (i) slide whistle; (j) ocarina; (k) siren; (l) mouth siren.*

name of instrument	abbreviations	synonyms	dynamic range	status	availability
wind machine	wind	(none)	*ppp–ff*	homemade	rare

FIGURE 164. *The wind machine—vital statistics.*

name of instrument	abbreviations	synonyms	dynamic range	status	availability
squeak	(none)	(none)	*ppp–ff*	homemade	very rare
friction birdcall	birdcall	(none)	*ppp–mf*	noisemaker	rare

FIGURE 165. *Friction squeaks—vital statistics.*

name of instrument	abbreviations	synonyms	dynamic range	status	availability
crow	(none)	duck call fox call (etc.)	*p–f*	noisemaker, novelty	very rare
razzer	(none)	Bronx cheer party buzzer	*pp–f*	novelty	very rare
water whistle	w. whis.	bird whistle nightingale (etc.)	*pp(p)–ff*	noisemaker	rare
signal whistle	sig. whis.	whistle police whistle (U.K.)	*ppp–ff*	noisemaker	rare
referee's whistle	ref. whis.	whistle pea whistle police whistle (U.S.)	*p(pp)–fff*	noisemaker	usually available

FIGURE 166. *Whistles and buzzers—vital statistics.*

WHISTLES AND BUZZERS

A number of simple-minded, one-note woodwinds are traditionally assigned to the percussion, though heaven knows *anyone* can play them. The crow is a simple wooden tube with one or more organ-type or harmonica-type metal reeds in it. In various incarnations (not strictly speaking synonymous, but so treated here) it is used to imitate the sounds of crows, pheasants, ducks, and other raucous birds, and even the yap of a fox. The simple cawing

name of instrument	abbreviations	synonyms	written range	sounds	status	availability
slide whistle	slide whis.	swanee-whistle	 *(musical notation)* loudest: *mf—f ——— ff ——* softest: *ppp —— pp —— p —*	as written (transposition not standard-ized)	novelty	usually available

FIGURE 167. *The slide whistle—vital statistics.*

sound (resembling that of an oboe or bassoon reed played by itself) can be modulated into a variety of squawks and quacks by shading the far end of the tube with one hand.

In the razzer the "reed" is a pair of flat rubber lips attached to the far end of the tube. The sound produced by this party noisemaker is adequately described by its alternate name of "Bronx cheer."

The true whistles (including the slide whistle and ocarina, discussed separately below) work on the principle of the recorder (q.v.), in which air is blown through a narrow channel that directs it against a sharp edge built into the body of the instrument. The signal whistle is the simplest of these, but it usually embodies two or three whistles of different pitch sharing a common mouthpiece; the tone of the instrument is heard as a single complex hoot. The common referee's whistle contains a little pith ball that rattles around when the whistle is blown, causing the tone to flutter. This fluttering does not occur at dynamic levels below *piano*. The water whistle, as its name implies, contains water, and this causes the pitch to burble in a very pleasant, bird-like fashion. The burbling does not occur in *ppp*.

THE SLIDE WHISTLE

The slide of a slide whistle is a lubricated, movable plug manipulated by a handle. The instrument is thus a stopped pipe, with a hollow, hooty tone. The range given is for the most commonly seen type of metal slide whistle—31 cm long exclusive of the slide. These are simply stamped out of sheet metal, and since the lip of the tone hole is not bevelled, the tone produced is quite breathy, especially at the top of the range. More sophisticated construction is found in the little plastic slide whistles sold as toys, and these have a better tone, but are distressingly short-lived, with a useful life of less than a month.*

The very small distance between adjacent notes on the slide whistle precludes complete intonational accuracy and, as with the flexatone and musical saw, composers must be willing to put up with much swooping and after-the-fact pitch correction, particularly on the first note of a passage. Nonetheless, scalewise passages can, with practice, be played with considerable accuracy even without intervening glissandos.

* These plastic slide-whistles are of course quite variable in pitch range, but few or none can descend below f^2. On the other hand, their better-designed tone-hole enables them to overblow (at the twelfth, of course) and thus to attain pitches up to an octave or more above the highest first-partial note.

name of instrument	abbreviations	synonyms	written range	sounds	status	availability
ocarina	(none)	"sweet potato"	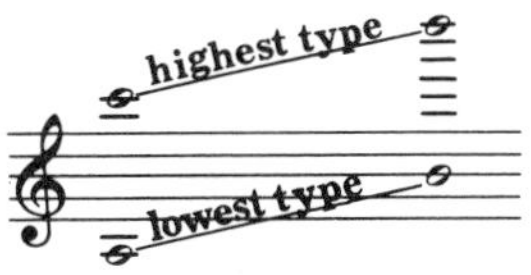 highest type / lowest type loudness: *mp*	as written (transposition not standardized)	novelty	rare

FIGURE 168. *The ocarina—vital statistics.*

name of instrument	abbreviations	synonyms	dynamic range	status	availability
siren	 (symbol)	(none)	*pp–ffff*	noisemaker	rare

FIGURE 169. *The siren—vital statistics.*

THE OCARINA

The ocarina belongs to the family of **vessel flutes**, a group in which, unlike other woodwinds, the body of the instrument is essentially globular rather than cylindrical. Acoustically such an instrument has no overtones and thus has a very pure, "objective" tone much like that of a person whistling. Also, theoretically at least, the fingerholes in the instrument affect the pitch not according to their position but solely according to their size and the number left open—in reality, the ocarina is not globular but egg-shaped, and the position of the holes does have some bearing on the pitches they produce.

Fingering systems and range vary tremendously among ocarinas. There may be anywhere from eight to ten fingerholes, but the range is almost always a major ninth lying somewhere between the limits given in Figure 168. The most commonly encountered range is (sounding) c^2–d^3; the lowest ranges are very rare.

Formerly ocarinas were made with considerable care, in a wide variety of sizes and with special tuning mechanisms, but the instrument is now little more than a toy, and much shading and fork-fingering is needed to play one in tune. Where such sophistication is desired the instrument should be assigned to a recorder player, who will know best how to deal with it; but perhaps the most reliable procedure is simply to treat the instrument as a generator of up to ten or so indeterminate pitches, as Lou Harrison does in his *Canticle No. 3.*

THE SIREN

The kind of siren used in music is the old-fashioned hand-cranked kind sometimes called a "civil defense siren." Ambulance and police sirens are either driven by the car engine or (more recently) are electronically produced sounds with a tone different from that of a true

name of instrument	abbreviations	synonyms	dynamic range	status	availability
mouth siren	(none)	(none)	*pp–ff*	standard	usually available

FIGURE 170. *The mouth siren—vital statistics.*

siren. As might be imagined, the hand-cranked siren is of little and decreasing use to the world at large, and the time may soon be upon us when works like Varèse's *Ionisation* will have to be performed with substitutes, museum pieces, or "historical reconstructions."

The sound-producing element of a siren is a heavy, hollow metal cylinder with numerous evenly spaced lengthwise slots. This is encased in another cylinder, also slotted. The inner cylinder is rotated by means of the attached handle; each time its slots coincide with those in the outer cylinder, a puff of air is produced. The regular spacing of the slots ensures the regular timing of the puffs, which, taken together, form a sound of a specific frequency. The pitch and dynamics of a siren are direct functions of the speed with which the handle is turned.

The inner cylinder of a siren is very heavy and thus has tremendous inertia which must be overcome both in starting and stopping. It is impossible to start a siren abruptly at a high dynamic/pitch level, and the sudden stopping of a high, loud sound is only possible on sirens with thumb brakes—now almost impossible to find. The pitch of a siren, though very clear, is impossible to control with any accuracy, and they are accordingly treated as unpitched instruments. Siren parts of necessity consist of a succession of individual long notes, each beginning with a crescendo and ending with a diminuendo.

THE MOUTH SIREN

Probably, many people have heard the "whee!" of a mouth siren without realizing what it was. These tiny sirens, driven by the player's breath, are much higher-pitched than "real" sirens and have none of the fearsome majesty of sound associated with the parent instrument. Unlike ordinary sirens, the sound of a mouth siren can be cut off abruptly at a high dynamic level simply by stopping the breath, for air must be forced through the instrument if it is to make a sound. This abrupt cutoff does not stop the cylinder (or disk) from rotating but merely stops the sound; this enables the production of passages of genuine rhythmic interest that would be impossible on an ordinary siren—for example,

Note that passages must begin with a crescendo (which may, however, be extremely rapid), and that leisurely alternation of crescendo and diminuendo remains basic to this instrument despite its rhythmic flexibility.

VIII

THE

KEYBOARDS

GENERAL CONSIDERATIONS

Except for a handful of percussion, all the instruments we have discussed so far fall neatly into groups related both by acoustics and by playing technique. The various keyboard instruments, however, are related to each other only by playing technique; numbered among them are idiophones (celesta), stringed instruments (piano), woodwinds (organ), and electronic instruments (ondes martenot). The keyboard mechanism so dominates this acoustic miscellany that, with certain exceptions, all keyboard music looks much alike on the page, and music written for one instrument can be played on another with surprisingly little distortion of the musical content*—indeed, prior to the eighteenth century composers made little or no distinction among the keyboard instruments.

TECHNICAL DISTINCTIONS

The major acoustic distinctions to be made among keyboard instruments are that between sustaining and non-sustaining instruments and that between those which are **touch-sensitive**—i.e., those in which the loudness of the notes is governed by the force with which the

* This is not to condone such substitutions, however. The practice of playing harpsichord music on the piano or of treating virtually *all* music as legitimate grist for organ or piano transcriptions is in questionable musical taste at best.

	sustaining	*touch-sensitive*
celesta	no	yes
keyboard glockenspiel	no	yes
toy piano	no	yes
piano	no	yes
electric piano	no	yes
clavinet	no	yes
accordion (etc.)	yes	no
organ	yes	no
electric organ	yes	no
melotron	yes	no
performance synthesizer	yes	no
ondes martenot	yes	yes
harpsichord	no	no
clavichord	no	yes
hurdy-gurdy	yes	no

FIGURE 171. *Keyboard instruments classified by sustaining power and touch sensitivity.*

keys are struck—and those which are not. The above table (which for the sake of convenience includes three "early" keyboard instruments discussed in Chapter XIII) shows how these features are distributed among the keyboards.

It will be noted that almost all keyboards that are touch-sensitive are non-sustaining, and vice versa. As might be imagined, there are substantial differences in playing technique between these two groups of instruments, differences that can be generalized as "piano technique" versus "organ technique" and are discussed below under the headings for those two most important of all keyboards.

Non–touch-sensitive instruments are typically supplied with a variety of **stops** by means of which the instrument can take on a variety of different timbres. Each stop usually affects the whole keyboard and has not only its own timbre but also a specific loudness and even pitch: many stops sound not at written pitch but in some other octave. In the organ, where the idea of stops first originated and where it is most highly developed, stops are found giving pitches as much as three octaves above or below the keyboard pitch, and there are non-octave stops whose function is to add a strong third, fifth, or even seventh partial to the tone of an ordinary stop used simultaneously. The terminology for the various octaves is based on the fact that the note C_0 on the organ (its lowest keyboard pitch) requires an open pipe about eight feet (two and a half meters) long; thus any stop that sounds at actual pitch is said to be an "eight-foot" (8′) stop. If the stop sounds an octave above keyboard pitch, it is a 4′ stop, if two octaves higher a 2′ stop, etc.; if it is an octave *below* keyboard pitch it is a 16′ stop, and so on. The organ's non-octave stops get fractional numbers: a twelfth above keyboard pitch (third partial) is 2⅔′; two octaves plus a major third above keyboard pitch (fifth partial) is 1⅗′; two octaves plus a flat minor seventh above keyboard pitch (seventh partial) is 1⅐′.

The various stop pitches are called **registers**; one speaks of, for instance, "the 8′ register" or "the 4′ register." There may be many stops in each register, and the name of each stop says something about its timbre—for example, "flute stop" or "harp stop." The art of combining and contrasting stops is called **registration**.

Keyboard instruments are enough alike in technique that doubling is fairly easy, particularly where similar conditions of sustention and touch-sensitivity prevail. The organ, accordion, and ondes martenot require performance techniques that players of other instruments cannot be assumed to have mastered,* but players of these three instruments are often, though by no means always, able to double on piano and other "ordinary" keyboards. Any pair of non-sustaining keyboards, as well as electric organ, performance synthesizer, and melotron, may be set next to each other at right angles, the lowest note of one instrument adjacent to the highest of the other, so that the player can rapidly and easily shift from one to the other or even play them simultaneously.

With the exception of a few specialized electronic instruments, keyboard instruments are **polyphonic**; that is, many different notes can be played simultaneously, enabling the production of chord progressions and counterpoint on a single instrument. This is achieved by providing each note with its own separate string, pipe, bar, or what-have-you, so that when the key governing that note is depressed, the note will sound no matter what other notes may be needed simultaneously. One consequence of this is that, all else being equal, the greater the number of notes sounded simultaneously the louder the sound will be. Acoustic interference takes its toll and the effect is much more subtle than might be imagined, but the varying of texture to obtain nuances of volume is a vital part of sensitive keyboard writing, particularly for instruments that are not touch-sensitive. Basically, a chord of eight notes will sound a little less than one dynamic level louder than a single note played with the same force.

FINGERINGS

The only limits on polyphonic playing are the number, spacing, and dexterity of the player's fingers. Since the arrangement and width of the individual keys are standard for all keyboards, the following chart, which shows the average maximum stretch between the various fingers of one hand, is valid for keyboard instruments of all sorts. Note that left-hand configurations are mirror images of right-hand ones, so that the thumb normally plays the lowest note of any right-hand grouping and the highest in a left-hand one.

In addition to the ordinary stretches charted above, the thumb can be turned under the other fingers, reaching as much as a fifth beyond the second finger. While this turning-under of the thumb is awkward and seldom used in chords, it is absolutely essential to the smooth and rapid playing of scales and scale-like patterns, where the thumb reaches under and beyond two, three, or four other fingers to continue the scale beyond the range of five notes. Observe that (1) the left-hand fingerings are essentially a mirror image of the right-hand ones; (2) the fifth finger is seldom used in such passages (it is employed much more frequently in chords and leaping passages, such as broken octaves); and (3) the thumb is turned under—or, what amounts to the same thing, the rest of the hand is rotated over the thumb—only when the

---

* This is also true of the harmonica, which does not even have a keyboard and is in this chapter only for want of any more appropriate location.

	Stretch From Finger			
	1	2	3	4
5	M 10th	M 7th	M 6th	aug. 4th
4	M 9th	m 6th	perf. 4th	
3	m 9th	aug. 4th		
2	M 7th			

FIGURE 172. *Limits on spacing of intervals and chords on a keyboard instrument: average maximum stretch between pairs of fingers on one hand, where all fingers are positioned over the keys.*

thumb strikes a white key, and preferably the note F or C (right hand), E or B (left hand). Indeed, the whole fingering pattern is arranged around the favorable positioning of the thumb, which is almost never used to strike a black key in scalewise passagework (since it is shorter than the other fingers, in order for it to strike a black key the hand must be either rotated outward or placed far back on the keyboard). In chords and leaping figures, however, the thumb plays black keys as often as any other finger.

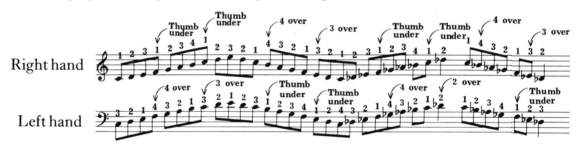

Broken chords and leaping passages are generally fingered as if the notes they contained were to be played simultaneously as a chord:

Among instruments of the piano type there is some flexibility in this regard; see the discussion of the piano, below.

There is almost no limit to the agility of keyboard music. Passages requiring large or awkward movements of the hands must of course be written with some caution, and rapid repeated notes (usually played with alternate fingers of one hand) are difficult, though possible; but performance standards for pianists at least are currently so high that feats of incredible virtuosity have become almost commonplace.

NOTATION

Music for a keyboard instrument is generally notated on two staves, braced together at the left of each line of music, and with the bar lines, if any, running through the complete double staff.

258 MODERN INSTRUMENTS

Notes played by the right hand are generally written on the upper staff, those played by the left hand on the lower staff; however, the two staves are usually also assigned different clefs, and where the assignment of hands is simple and obvious it is entirely normal to assign high notes to the upper staff and low notes to the lower one, regardless of how they are to be played:

Indeed, notes of more than three ledger-lines are to be avoided between the staves. In complex passages, nonetheless, and especially when the hands must overlap or even cross, composers should keep the two hands on strictly separate staves, even though, for instance, a bass clef may be required for the upper staff and a treble clef for the lower. Despite these precautions it will *occasionally* be necessary to specify verbally which hand is to play, particularly when one hand enters before the other and in an uncharacteristic range. This is done by simply writing the letters "L.H." or "R.H." at the beginning of the passage in question.

Crossed-hand passages are usually so obvious from the notation that no special instruction is necessary, but when the two hands overlap in the same range great care must be taken to see that they don't get tangled up. Basically, in such a situation one hand must lie above and behind the other, and that hand should generally be the one that has to use more fingers and to play more black keys. Often it does not matter which hand is on top; and all other things being equal, if one hand is "on the scene" before the other, that hand will take the lower position. On occasions where the relative position of the hands is important to the playability of the passage, the notes to be played by the top hand should be marked "sopra" (Italian: "above"), or those for the lower hand marked "sotto" ("below"). It may also be wise to indicate the fingering of one or both parts if the passage is particularly sticky—determination of the best fingerings requires access to a keyboard but no particular ability as a keyboardist.

Tricky and deceptive-looking passages in general, as well as dense counterpoint and oddly spaced chords, will benefit from an *occasional* indication of fingering. This should be kept to the absolute minimum, and it should be remembered that in indicating the fingering of a single note, that of a great many succeeding notes may well be implied by simple logic. Fingering is indicated with the Arabic numerals 1–5 for the five fingers of the hand, placed immediately above the notes indicated. If a change of fingers is required while a key is kept depressed, this is indicated with a curved line, thus: ⌢, indicating in this case that the note is to be struck with the second finger, and the third finger then substituted while the key is held down. All the notes of a chord should be fingered, not just one or two. The figures are usually stacked above the chord in the same order as the notes they affect, but they may be placed to the left of those notes instead. When the thumb is to play two notes at once (see below), a bracket is used to show that the single figure 1 is to be applied to two notes:

A number of special notations applied to chords should be mentioned here. The **arpeggio**, in which the notes of the chord are struck one after another in a rapid sweep, is indicated with a vertical wavy line to the left of the chord affected. Normally the notes are played from

lowest to highest, but with arrowheads it is possible to differentiate downward (↓) from up-

ward (↑) arpeggios. Some composers use a straight vertical arrow (↑) to indicate a rapid arpeggio, reserving the wiggly line for a more leisurely, romantic effect. A vexed question of keyboard notation is what to do about arpeggios in which the notes are struck in a less traditional sequence, the usual solution being to indicate the order as a series of grace notes individually tied to the chord itself:

Sometimes the word "arpeggio" is added to make sure the effect is properly played (grace notes are usually played more slowly than the notes in an arpeggio). One defect of this notation is that it requires a sharp-eyed and slightly paranoid player to discover the last note in the sequence—in this case, d^2—since that note is usually simply written into the chord and its presence may not be at all obvious.

The distribution of the notes of a chord between the two hands is usually made clear by their assignment to one or the other of the two staves or by their grouping on two note-stems. Where this is not feasible (generally in chords consisting of whole notes or other stemless note-forms) the distribution of the notes may if necessary be indicated with a half-bracket:

o
o
o o o o
o o o o   or   o o o o
o   o o o o
o

Harmonically, a **tone cluster** is any chord consisting entirely of seconds, but on keyboard instruments the term implies not so much a harmony as a playing technique in which notes are struck in some way other than with the tips of the fingers. The smallest "tone cluster"—usually not considered as such—is that produced by using the side of the thumb to play two adjacent white or black keys; this technique is so traditional that one simply writes the required notes and lets the player deduce the fingering. Only for such unusual configurations as

will it be necessary to provide a fingering. Larger tone clusters, performed with the flat or side of the hand or with the whole forearm, have a special notation of their own, consisting of a

heavy black line linking the two outermost notes of the cluster (♪) or, for open note-heads, the "open" equivalent of this notation ( ). If the cluster consists entirely of white keys, a natural sign is placed *above* the cluster, and if it consists entirely of black keys, a sharp is placed there. All-white or all-black clusters of less than a sixth in width are played with the side of the hand, loosely curled into a fist for the smaller intervals. This is usually called "playing with the fist," but the image called up of a pugilistic attack on the defenseless keyboard is of couse totally inaccurate. "Mixed" tone clusters such as

with the heel of the hand playing white keys while the side of the fifth finger plays black ones, are also possible, but these should be written out in full, as here, and the direction "with fist" added. Fully chromatic tone-clusters a sixth or less in width are played with the flat of the hand (or of the fingers, held together) held normally. The thumb is not really needed for this, and may play its own note outside the cluster:

Tone clusters of all sorts a seventh or an octave in width are played with the flat of the hand held sideways. All sorts of "mixed" tone clusters are possible in this mode, but it must be remembered that all the black keys must form a single coherent group, as must all the white keys; a cluster with, for instance, white keys at top and bottom and black keys in the middle cannot be played this way. Some possible "mixed" clusters—and suggested notations for them—are shown below.

Tone clusters greater than one octave in width are performed with a combination of the side of the hand and forearm. Those between a ninth and two octaves wide are somewhat awkward, and chromatic clusters (performed by jamming the arm and hand into the angle at the front of the black keys) may miss a few black keys at the elbow end of the cluster. Double-octave clusters are performed with the hand turned aside, and since the hand is not used, the fingers can pick out single notes (*not* chords) as much as an octave beyond the wrist end of the cluster. Clusters of more than two octaves require the hand again; the maximum width of cluster is three octaves (larger ones are performed with both arms, up to six octaves). "Mixed" clusters are possible, as described above, and by bending the wrist various complex combinations can be achieved—the composer should derive these by direct experimentation. In general, though, white keys should be grouped at the elbow end of the cluster. It might be thought that a large, double-arm cluster must be very loud, but in fact it is usually only a little more than one dynamic level louder than a single note played with equal force. Nonetheless, the loudest sounds possible on any keyboard instrument are these double-arm clusters.

The keyboard **glissando**, performed with thumb or index finger, is really a key rip, as with the mallet instruments, and should be notated as such. It can only be done on the white keys, though the glissando may begin and/or end with a black key.

The position of keyboard instruments in a score is not quite standardized. In orchestral or other large scores they are usually found between percussion and strings, though keyboard idiophones are often buried among the percussion, and members of the organ, accordion, and ondes martenot families may appear almost anywhere, including top or bottom. In chamber music, keyboard instruments almost invariably appear at the bottom of the score, though, again, "light" instruments such as the celesta or accordion may appear elsewhere.

KEYBOARD IDIOPHONES

KEYBOARD GLOCKENSPIEL AND CELESTA

The term "keyboard percussion" is normally used to refer not to the instruments here at issue but rather to those which in this book are called "mallet instruments": the xylophone, vibraphone, and so on. The celesta and keyboard glockenspiel have traditionally been numbered among the percussion, however, and are often included in percussionists' arrays, though there is nothing in percussionists' training that would enable them to play these instruments, both of which are virtually identical in technique to the piano, described below.

The sound-producing elements in the celesta and keyboard glockenspiel are rectangular metal bars like those of the vibraphone and glockenspiel. These are struck by small hammers that work like the hammers of a piano but in appearance resemble small, light, rubber-series mallets.

The keyboard glockenspiel sounds almost exactly like the ordinary glockenspiel, and its main value lies in its ability to play polyphonically. In light of this it is somewhat surprising to find that most parts for the instrument are largely monophonic—indeed, many parts are written on a single staff. The celesta differs from the vibraphone in having a considerably more delicate tone but it is just as cold and impersonal, and of course it lacks the vibraphone's vibrato. As with other idiophones, the lack of harmonic upper partials in the sound of these instruments makes chords into single sonorities rather than identifiable collections of pitches, and the ear often has great difficulty in determining the octave in which a given note lies; this is particularly true in rapid, disjunct passages.

Both celesta and keyboard glockenspiel are, of course, touch-sensitive and non-sustaining. The sound, particularly in the lowest notes, dies away rather more rapidly than that of a piano. Both instruments are provided with a system of dampers and a damper pedal, just like the piano;* because of the massiveness of the bars, however, the dampers are only partially effective, and a truly sharp staccato is impossible. The massiveness of the bars also precludes piano techniques that depend on sympathetic resonance. There is no equivalent to the piano's other two pedals, and no easy access to the interior.

---

* Some keyboard glockenspiels do not have these features.

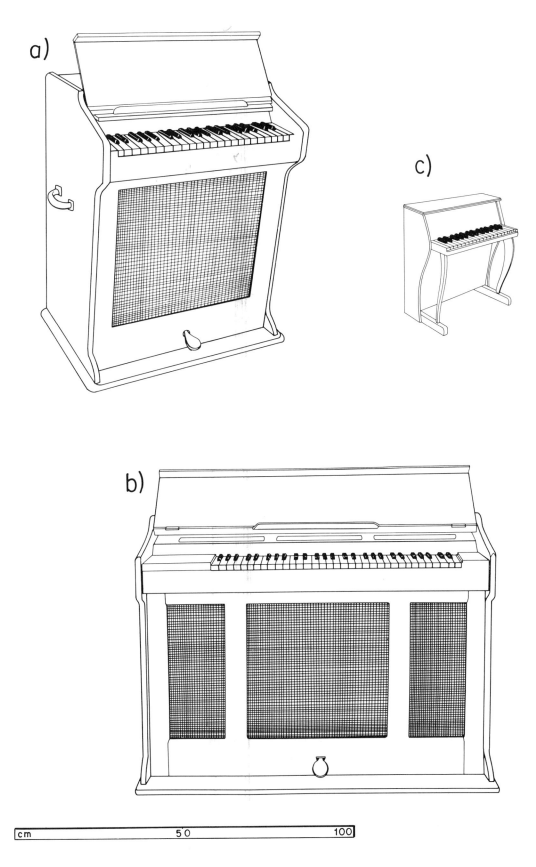

FIGURE 173. *Keyboard idiophones: (a) keyboard glockenspiel; (b) celesta; (c) toy piano.*

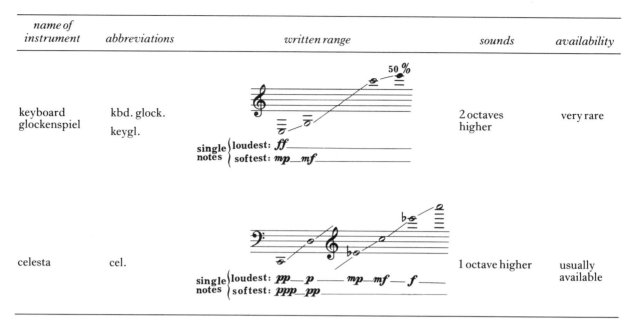

name of instrument	abbreviations	written range	sounds	availability
keyboard glockenspiel	kbd. glock. keygl.		2 octaves higher	very rare
celesta	cel.		1 octave higher	usually available

FIGURE 174. *Keyboard glockenspiel and celesta—vital statistics.*

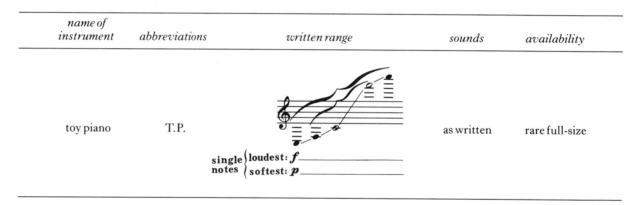

name of instrument	abbreviations	written range	sounds	availability
toy piano	T.P.		as written	rare full-size

FIGURE 175. *The toy piano—vital statistics.*

The touch on these instruments is somewhat lighter than on the piano but is almost unbearably sluggish, so that dynamics, particularly at the soft end, are hard to control. It will be observed that both have very narrow dynamic ranges, a consideration of which composers are all too often forgetful. If the keyboard glockenspiel were not so rare, the two instruments would ideally be used as a pair, the celesta for soft passages and the keyboard glockenspiel for loud ones; in fact, a duplex instrument, with both actions in one case and a double keyboard, could easily be made—but no one so far has done so.

THE TOY PIANO

The toy piano is not really a piano at all. Its sound is produced from thin metal rods clamped to a frame and thinned at the clamped end to improve their tone, a gentle, bell-like chiming with a very prominent partial a major thirteenth above the fundamental. The rods are struck with hammers resembling those of the piano, and the **action** (the mechanism connecting the keys to the hammers) is a simplified version of piano action. Unlike the piano, the entire action—keys, hammers, and all—is made of "sturdy molded plastic," and because of this and various other corners cut in the manufacture of what is after all a toy, the action is loose (making dynamics hard to control) and very noisy. The typewriter-like clatter of the keys must be counted part of the instrument's sound—and no unpleasant sound it is.

The toy piano has no dampers and no damper pedal, so each note dies away naturally as it is struck. Fortunately for the clarity of the sound, decay is initially very rapid, and the tone dies away completely in only about four seconds. The pitch is actually more focused than that of the celesta, but the inharmonic partials make it hard to decide in which octave a note lies.

Jaymar, the most serious maker of toy pianos, manufactures eight sizes ranging from a single-octave diatonic model to one with 49 keys covering four full chromatic octaves—quite impressive for a toy. Figure 175 gives the ranges of the three largest sizes: c^1–f^3, f^0–f^3, and c^0–c^4, all completely chromatic. Notes above f^3 are somewhat flabby and "dead." The instruments are frequently out of tune—usually sharp—when purchased, but can be brought to pitch by filing down or building up the offending rods.

Toy pianos are, of course, built to be played by small children. Though the keys are of regulation width, the instrument itself is very low and must be set on a riser if an adult is to play it.

The dynamic range is, if anything, even narrower than here given.

MUSICAL EXAMPLES

KEYBOARD GLOCKENSPIEL:
> Messiaen, *Chronochromie*

CELESTA:
> Webern, *Five Pieces for Orchestra*, Op. 10
> Messiaen, *Turangalîla symphonie* (6th mvt.)
> Stockhausen, *Refrain*

TOY PIANO:
> Cage, *Suite for Toy Piano*
> Crumb, *Ancient Voices of Children* ("Todas las Tardes en Granada")

THE PIANO

BASIC FEATURES OF THE INSTRUMENT

The piano (now called "pianoforte" only in the most stiffly formal contexts) is, in its modern form, a product of the late nineteenth century—a genuinely *industrial* product built around a heavy metal frame cast in a foundry and designed to withstand for years some twenty tons of pull placed on it by the strings running across it. In no other instrument is this amount of

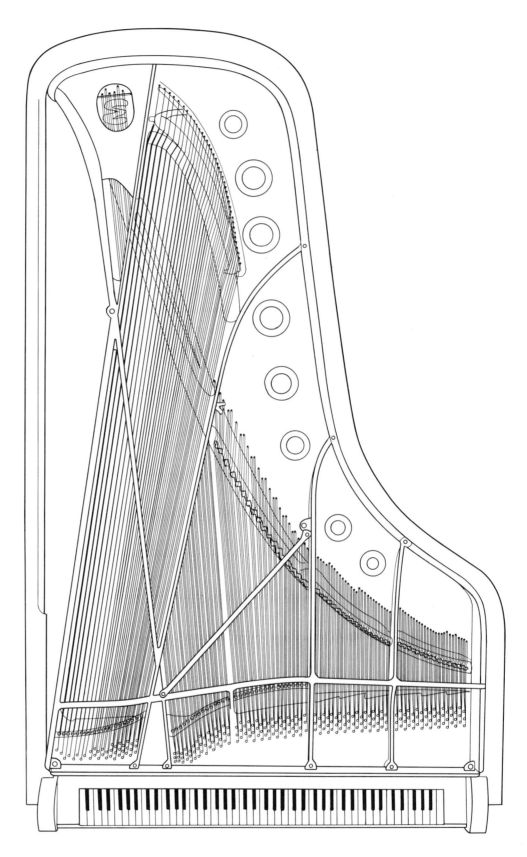

FIGURE 176. *Full-size grand piano with cover removed, seen from above.*

MODERN INSTRUMENTS

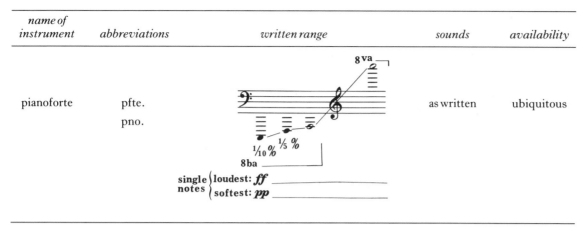

name of instrument	abbreviations	written range	sounds	availability
pianoforte	pfte. pno.		as written	ubiquitous

FIGURE 177. *The piano—vital statistics.*

internal tension even approached. In addition, the action is immensely complex, and the combination of great weight, dangerously high tension, and complexity means that merely to tune the instrument, let alone the kind of minor repairs other instrumentalists are used to doing on their own, requires the services of a specially trained technician.

Pianos are built in two formats: the **grand piano**, in which the strings, frame, and sound-board lie in the horizontal plane, oriented from front to back; and the **upright piano** (further subdivided—in order of decreasing height and tone quality—into the **full upright**, **studio upright**, **console upright**, and **spinet**), whose strings, frame, and soundboard are aligned vertically. Grand pianos are far superior to uprights, and only grands are used in concerts. Upright pianos are generally used only for study, practice, and home entertainment.

The range of the piano is among the most standardized of all instruments. The extension tones shown in Figure 177 are extremely rare, and would not even be worthy of mention were it not for the fact that they appear in pianos by Bösendorfer, generally considered to be the finest in the world. When played by themselves these extra low tones have an indescribably weird sound reminiscent of ring-modulation. Even when not used, the sympathetic resonance they provide helps to give the Bösendorfer its extraordinarily full, rich tone in the low bass. (Needless to say, composers should write these notes only as optional extras, if at all.)

Everybody knows that the sound of a piano comes from strings and that the strings are struck by hard felt hammers; the details are less widely known. In order to keep the dynamic range as high and as uniform as possible throughout the compass of the instrument, notes in the upper part of the range (usually from $B\flat_1$, F_0, or $B\flat_0$ up) are triple-strung, i.e., there are three unison strings, struck by the same hammer, for each note. Notes below this down to about F_1 or $F\sharp_1$ are double-strung, and only the lowest notes are single-strung. Pianos of the highest quality tend to have more strings than average, with a greater number of triple-strung notes than usual.

The action of the piano is designed so that there is never any direct mechanical connection between the player's fingers and the strings; the hammer is not pressed against the string, but is simply launched toward it, so that it bounces off the string and immediately falls back, allowing the string to vibrate freely. If a piano key is depressed very slowly and carefully, its hammer will not come in contact with the string at all.

Each note is provided with a felt **damper** that is automatically raised off the string when the key governing that note is depressed and falls back in place when the key is released, thus stopping the sound. The piano's highest notes have no dampers, for they are relatively weak in volume and die away quickly. The highest dampered note typically may be anywhere from eb^3 to g^3, generally falling higher on good pianos than on mediocre ones.

The piano is equipped with three pedals used as aids in expression. Of these, the right-hand pedal is by far the most important. It is called the **damper pedal**, and when depressed it raises all the dampers from all the strings, thus allowing notes to ring on after the keys are released, either for their complete natural duration (some twelve seconds, on the average), or until the pedal is released. The use of this pedal, a fundamental part of piano technique, is described in detail below.

The left-hand pedal is called the **soft pedal**, and when depressed it shifts the whole action—including the keyboard—to the right (rarely, left), so that the hammers strike only two of each set of three strings, and only one of each set of two. Single-strung notes are unaffected. This does make the sound softer, but only very slightly; more important is the effect on the tone, which becomes subtly more gentle and rounded. This pedal is not usually used for distinct contrasts of volume and timbre but, rather, as an aid to expression at low dynamic levels. This is described below in more detail. On most upright pianos the soft pedal is provided with an altogether different mechanism, whereby the rail against which the hammers lie when at rest is pushed closer to the strings, thus decreasing the distance between hammers and strings. The main effect of this is to diminish the dynamic range.

The middle or **sostenuto pedal** is relatively seldom used. When it is depressed, any dampers already raised will not fall back. It thus acts like a selective damper pedal, letting individual notes or chords chosen by the player ring on for as long as the pedal is depressed but allowing other notes to be played staccato. A passage such as the one below

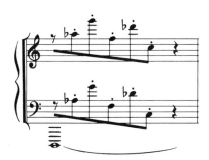

is impossible without the middle pedal. This passage would be played by first striking the D_1, then depressing the middle pedal while the key was still held down, then releasing the key and playing the high notes. The middle pedal was only introduced toward the end of the nineteenth century and is still not a completely standard feature. Very fine pianos are still to be seen— mostly in Europe—with only two pedals, but as more and more pieces requiring its use are written, the middle pedal is bound to become universal—at least on grands—in the near future. Only a handful of uprights have a genuine sostenuto pedal of the sort just described. Many have only two pedals, and on others the third pedal is a functionless dummy; most common is a middle pedal that works exactly like the damper pedal save that it affects only the bass part of the range, usually from c^0 down.

In the normal course of play the damper pedal is depressed for each chordal or harmonic entity, that is to say, in accordance with the harmonic rhythm of the piece. Only soft and detached or intricately contrapuntal passages are generally played without pedal. The pedal is usually depressed *after* the keys are struck; the added sympathetic resonance from the unplayed strings causes the sound to bloom and is in large measure responsible for the flexibility and expressiveness of the piano despite its percussive means of tone production. In moving from chord to chord (or sonority to sonority, texture to texture) the pedal is released just as the new chord is being struck and then immediately depressed again. In detached playing the pedal is of course released much sooner. If a chord is preceded by a rest the pedal can theoretically be depressed before the chord is struck, but this is in fact only done where a particularly broad and resonant tenuto or sforzando is desired.

ARTICULATION AND PEDALING

Articulation on the piano is differentiated with both fingers and pedal. The continuum between staccato and legato can be expressed with the fingers alone, as can the various types of accent, simply by varying the touch; but the pedal is also involved in these differentiations: staccato notes are usually played without pedal, for instance, and accented notes, unless they are quite fast, are usually pedaled separately for each accent, even if the harmony does not

change. Portato () on the piano means specifically that the notes are to be played with

staccato touch but legato pedaling, and the staccato-tenuto ( ) is often similarly interpreted to imply staccato touch combined with tenuto pedaling. Similar considerations lie behind such apparently contradictory notations as

The indication "fp" is usually realized by pedaling the indicated note or chord but then releasing the pedal while continuing to hold the key(s) down; the sudden removal of sympathetic resonances gives the effect of a sudden drop in volume, though the actual change in loudness is quite small.

A basic feature of piano writing is the production of varied textures through the use of broken and arpeggiated chords in all manner of patterns. These patterns are seldom of direct melodic interest, being used almost solely as a textural device. The underlying harmonic or melodic information buried within the pattern is articulated with the pedal and by bringing out specific notes with the fingers. Anyone interested in transcribing for piano music written in other media, or vice versa, must remember this aspect of piano style, which makes note-for-note transcription undesirable and often impossible. Even those who feel above such activities (and it should be borne in mind that music-theater works require piano-vocal scores as a matter of practical necessity) would do well to compare, for instance, Mussorgsky's original *Pictures at an Exhibition* with Ravel's orchestral transcription of it, or the Chaconne from Bach's D-minor violin partita with Busoni's piano transcription. Much can be learned about the nature of piano style from such study.

The constant use of the damper pedal gives pianists a certain flexibility in the fingering of broken and arpeggiated chords, for with the pedal down it is possible to put together groups of notes that could not be struck simultaneously. Chords such as

for instance, which do not quite lie under the hand, can be played simply by moving the hand across the keys while arpeggiating the chord with the pedal down. Careful composers provide such combinations with an arpeggio sign, as above, but this is frequently omitted, the implication being "play the notes as close to simultaneously as possible." It is also possible by this means to play arpeggiated chords containing many more notes than there are fingers to play them. Sometimes large chords that cannot be taken in one swipe are divided into a single practicable chord with an immediately preceding grace-note chord containing the notes left over at top and/or bottom. With such grace notes (unlike the arpeggio) pianists often take their time, even introducing *tempo rubato* to accommodate them.

For an unusual phrasing or to create an extended blur of sound the composer will occasionally need to specify exactly how the damper pedal is to be used. The symbol for the use of this pedal is " 𝄟 " written beneath the staff, with " ✳ " indicating its release. These ornate notations are increasingly being replaced with the simpler and more modern-looking "ped." and "⌐_____⌐," as used on the vibraphone. If the pedal is to be held down for more than one line of music, the expression "ped. (sempre)" should be used. If several notes or chords are to be pedaled separately one after another, it is traditional to mark each one "ped." without the closing asterisk or half-bracket.

A subtle technique used by pianists in certain styles and occasionally specified by composers is **half-pedaling** (symbol: "½ ped."). With the pedal thus half-depressed, neighboring sonorities blur lightly into each other but, because the dampers are slightly in contact with the strings, the notes die away just a second or two after the keys are released. Half-pedaling only works perfectly on a first-rate piano in excellent condition whose action has recently been regulated. In most cases some notes will ring on much longer than others, and half-pedaling should thus only be used in thick or dense passages where a great many notes sound at once and where there are frequent changes of harmony. A special effect related to half-pedaling and sometimes given the same name involves releasing the keys and then immediately depressing the pedal before the sound has been completely damped. The remaining sound continues as a filtered echo of the original notes, *pp* or *ppp*. A suggested notation for this effect is:

The damper pedal is useful even for the damperless notes in the upper part of the range, for the sympathetic resonance from the unplayed lower strings adds considerable body to these generally weak and ephemeral tones. Indeed, the only way to get a convincingly long-lived tone from the top octave is to strike the notes (preferably *forte* or louder) with the damper pedal down; after the loud attack (mostly attack noise) the note's main pitch will whistle on inside the piano, *p* or softer.

The soft pedal is used by pianists in conjunction with the damper pedal mostly as a way of varying the attack in soft or gentle passages. Composers should specify this effect (with the words "una corda" written above or below the staff) only when the soft pedal is to be held down for at least a few notes in a row.

The sostenuto pedal (also called "third," "middle," or "Steinway" pedal) should be specified wherever it is needed, for, as we have seen, a passage such as the one given on page 268 might be played with the damper pedal depressed throughout. Unfortunately, there is no standard notation for the sostenuto pedal; the term "sostenuto" in a piano score has only its ordinary meaning. Notations that have been used include "sos. ped.," "ped. III," "ped. II," and a variety of specially designed symbols.

When a single key or group of keys is depressed silently or is held down after the sound has completely died away, the sympathetic resonance of those strings will continue to be brought out by the playing of other notes. To be specific, notes above the pitch in question that double an upper partial of the silent note will ring on in a ghostly *ppp* of sympathetic resonance; conversely, notes below the silent pitch that have the pitch for one of their upper partials will cause the silent note itself to ring in a similar ghostly fashion. The sostenuto pedal is very useful for this effect because it can be used to sustain the silent pitch(es), leaving the player with both hands free. If a note is to be depressed silently the player must be allowed time to do so slowly and with care. On some pianos (e.g., Baldwins) it is virtually impossible to depress the keys silently.

SPECIAL EFFECTS

The sympathetic resonance of the piano strings can also be used in conjunction with other instruments. By singing or by playing any hand-held instrument directly into the piano, *forte* or louder, a distant *pp* or *ppp* echo will be elicited, giving back not only the pitch of the note played but to a certain extent its timbre as well. Of course, the damper pedal must be depressed to achieve this effect, and the piano's lid must be removed or completely raised.

The piano is a fairly powerful instrument, and for chamber music the lid is "put on the short stick," which holds it only a few centimeters open. The instrument is not ordinarily played with the lid completely closed, but that is certainly an option: the tone becomes somewhat muffled and "dead" and significantly softer than usual, so that with the additional aid of the soft pedal a true *ppp* can be produced.

A significant aspect of twentieth-century piano technique is the direct manipulation of the instrument's interior. The highly diverse techniques involved are categorized below. The reader is advised to refer periodically to Figure 176 for a better understanding of this material. The figure shows a full-size Steinway grand, seen from above; smaller instruments and those by other makers have a slightly different arrangement of metal bars and different numbers of strings and dampers. These differences are reflected in the variability of the playing restrictions imposed on the techniques here discussed. Many of these techniques require the player to stand, making pedaling and normal (on the keys) playing awkward, and many require the piano lid to be completely open or, preferably, removed altogether. The instrument's music rack must also often be removed, creating the problem of where to put the music. All of this, of course, and almost all of what follows apply only to grands. Interior work is very limited and difficult on uprights.

Sounds Made by Plucking, Striking, or Sweeping with the Hands

1. *Plucking the strings.* In the lower part of the range (at least up to d^1, and up to $c\#^2$ or higher on full-sized grands) the strings can be plucked in the space between the dampers and the tuning pins. The chief advantage of this is that the player need not stand up in order to pluck the strings. For all higher notes the player must stand up and pluck the strings beyond the dampers or (for damperless strings) beyond the crosswise metal bar. The sound of the plucked string, a brilliant ping reminiscent of the harpsichord, cannot exceed *forte* in loudness. Below the $c\#^2$–d^1 limit a gentler, richer sound can be obtained by plucking near the middle of the string. The player must stand up to do this.

In order to get a normal sound the dampers of all strings to be plucked must be raised. If they are not, a dry, dull "plunk" results.

It is difficult for the eye to pick out one note from another among the piano's many strings, so plucked notes must almost always be marked with bits of masking tape or the like in advance of performance, and even then plucking should be restricted to isolated single notes or groups of only a few notes, preferably close together in pitch. If the pitch is left indeterminate the strings can of course be plucked with much more freedom.

2. *Muting the strings.* This is done by pressing a fingertip against the string at one end. Notes below b^1, c^2, or $c\#^2$ (depending on the piano) are muted at the end of the string nearest the player; this can be done sitting down. Above this limit notes with dampers must be muted at the far end, and those without are muted just beyond the crosswise metal bar (capotasto bar) that forms a bridge for them—all this requires that the player stand.

To produce a sound, muting must be combined with plucking or (more usually) normal keyboard playing with the free hand. Muted notes decay in about half their normal time and sound dark and sombre compared to ordinary piano tone. Similar to muting is the complete **choking** of the sound by pressing a finger against the string(s) anywhere except at its extreme ends. When a choked note is struck by the hammer, a dull thunk, heavy in attack noise, results. Both muting and choking can be applied to a note that is already ringing.

3. *Harmonics* are produced exactly as on other stringed instruments (see Chapter IX) by lightly touching a node of the appropriate partial. Harmonics of any pitch up to about sounding e^3 can be produced on any string, and the second partial is obtainable up to somewhere between $c\#^4$ and f^4 inclusive (from strings pitched an octave lower) depending on the quality of the piano. The node for the second partial is too far away to reach from the keyboard below about D_0 (fundamental pitch).

Because the bass strings of the piano overlap the strings immediately above them, certain harmonics on the overlapped strings are not available. The bass and treble divisions of the piano are usually separated either at $B\flat_0/B_0$ or E_0/F_0; harmonics are not possible on the two notes immediately above the break. On the next two notes only the fifth and higher partials are available, on the next two after that the fourth partial is available but not the second or third, and on the next three to five all partials but the second can be played. Harmonics tend to sound cool, impersonal, and a bit mysterious—increasingly so for high partials. The higher the partial the more strongly the note's decay will be reduced and its dynamic level lowered. All harmonics must be played from a standing position, and all require that the damper pedal be depressed.

4. *Sweeping the fingers or fingernails across the strings* to make a glissando. This effect, which can be produced as loudly as *fortissimo* (particularly in the bass range), can be done with or without raised dampers; it sounds very dry if the dampers are not raised. If only selected dampers are raised (by depressing keys silently or with the sostenuto pedal) the notes in question will emerge strongly from the glissando and will ring on long after it has died. The extent of a swept glissando is limited by the lengthwise, crosswise, and diagonal metal bars inside the instrument. Any extensive glissando requires skillful alternation of the hands if it is not to sound discontinuous when crossing these bars. This is particularly true of the smooth, full-toned glissando produced by sweeping the strings on the far side of the dampers where, it will be noticed, the two notes immediately above the bass/treble break cannot be gotten at all. The more snarly glissando produced on the near side of the dampers is trouble-free in the bass, but since the dampers, crosswise bar, and pinblock crowd in on each other in the treble one must switch from the front to the back end of the strings somewhere between d^1 and $c\sharp^2$.

5. *Scraping the wound bass strings lengthwise.* The rasping sound produced (up to *fortissimo*) with the fingernails may be contrasted with a gentler, windy sound made by stroking with the fingertips, no louder than *piano*. The pitch of these scraped notes is exactly four octaves above the fundamental pitch of the note scraped. Most pianos have wound strings up to E_0 (small "baby grands" may have wound strings up to $B\flat_0$). The four notes immediately above the bass/treble break can be effectively scraped only in front of the dampers, so long notes (which require scraping a considerable length of string) should be avoided for those pitches.

Strings Struck, Swept, or Scraped with Percussion Sticks or Other Devices

Particularly common and effective is the use of a bass-drum beater to strike all the lowest strings at once, producing a deep, full boom as loud as *fortissimo*. These percussion techniques, as well as the finger techniques just discussed, can be performed by a non-pianist standing in the bend of the instrument, provided somebody or something presses down the damper pedal. A person standing in the bend of the piano cannot reach the part of the strings that lies between the dampers and the tuning pins but can produce the same effects at the opposite end of the strings, *except in the octave above the bass/treble division*, in which the far ends of the strings are covered by overlapping bass strings. Indeed, the four notes immediately above the break will be completely or virtually unavailable to a person beside the piano.

Bowing

C. Curtis-Smith has worked out a means of bowing the piano using multiple lengths of nylon fishing line threaded under or between groups of strings. This effect may be heard in virtually any of his recorded works with piano and can be studied in detail in the preface to his *Rhapsodies* (1973).

Striking or Knocking the Frame of the Piano

This is done with the knuckles or with percussion mallets. When the damper pedal is depressed, these sounds will ring on, *pp* or *ppp*, inside the instrument.

The Prepared Piano

This term denotes the insertion of various objects into the piano for the purpose of altering the tone when it is played either normally or with any of the techniques described above.

1. *Tack piano*. The hammers of a grand piano should be left strictly alone: they are vital to the tone quality of the instrument and can easily be damaged. The well-known device of sticking thumbtacks in the hammers to create a jangly, honky-tonk sound should be inflicted only on battered old uprights inured to such indignities.

2. *Light flat or round objects laid loosely on the strings;* for example, paper, aluminum foil, an aluminum pie plate, coins, marbles, rulers, or small sticks of wood. The sounds produced are rattling and indeterminate, since the object(s) are bounced around by the vibration of the strings and sooner or later fall off altogether onto the frame or soundboard.

3. *Objects inserted between the strings*. Held in place by the strings between which they are inserted, these objects do not move during play. The objects most suitable for such use are bolts of various sizes (with or without nuts), golf tees, small rubber erasers, coins, or strips of plastic such as collar tabs or a small, flexible ruler. Highly varied and interesting sounds can be produced by such means, ranging from a more or less muted version of ordinary piano tone to sounds resembling idiophones played with soft sticks: almglocken, cencerros, muted gongs, even temple blocks and slit drums. The exact effect produced must be determined by experimentation (bear in mind the variable positioning of the bass/treble break and the variable stringing layouts of different pianos), but certain general categories can be distinguished: (a) light objects serving only to mute or choke the piano tone; (b) heavier objects that add significantly to the mass of the strings, lowering their pitch and drastically altering their timbre; (c) objects inserted between strings of different pitches, linking them together as a single vibrating body of indefinite pitch; and (d) objects—such as a loose nut held in place with a bolt—inserted loosely enough to rattle when the string is played but not otherwise affecting the tone.

Several objects may be inserted at different points along the length of the same pair of strings, and for triple-strung notes the right + middle pair of strings may be prepared differently from the middle + left pair, or one string may be left completely unprepared. By using the soft pedal (eliminating the left-hand string) the timbre of such a note may be radically altered.

One final word about "piano interior": despite its rugged metal frame and heavy strings the piano is a delicate instrument—particularly the hammers, dampers, and strings—and great care must be taken not to damage it. The hammers and dampers should not be touched, and the strings, unlike those of a violin, guitar, or harp, are not designed to be touched and tend to corrode if handled frequently* or roughly. Preparations that require the strings to be forced visibly apart should be avoided, and it is a good idea to wipe the strings with a dry cloth after each performance, rehearsal, or experimental session in which they are touched.

* With half a century of "piano interior" masterpieces behind us it is high time something was done about this: it is ridiculous for piano makers to continue pretending that such considerations have nothing to do with their craft.

A handful of "quarter-tone pianos," with two keyboards pitched a quarter-step apart, were built in the early twentieth century. These experimental instruments were not successful, but quarter-tone piano parts continue to be written from time to time. These are invariably played on a pair of pianos set next to each other at right angles, one tuned a quarter-step lower than the other. The "detuned" piano must be tuned *down* the quarter-step, for tuning it up may cause the instrument to literally and very dangerously collapse or explode from the increased tension. Tuning a piano down a quarter-tone removes hundreds of kilograms of tension from the frame; this is hardly good for the instrument, but it is at least not dangerous to life and limb. Because of the deleterious effects of detuning, the quarter-tone instrument is always a cheap upright.

MUSICAL EXAMPLES

PIANO:

Ives, Piano Sonata no. 2 ("Concord")
Stravinsky, *Les Noces*
Varèse, *Déserts*
Messiaen, *Turangalîla symphonie*
Stockhausen, *Klavierstück IX*
Cage, *Sonatas and Interludes*
Crumb, *Music for a Summer Evening*

ELECTRIC KEYBOARDS: NON-SUSTAINING

THE ELECTRIC PIANO

We now arrive at the first of many "electric" instruments to be discussed in this book, and it is necessary at this point to define some terms. "Electric" instruments are divided into two types: **electronic** instruments, in which the sound is the result of an oscillating voltage created by purely electronic means (more about this in Chapter X), and **electromechanical** instruments, in which a very soft sound created by non-electronic means is electronically amplified.

Electric pianos may fall into either of these categories. Generally the electromechanical ones are superior. The sound of these comes from small metal tines resembling the reeds of an accordion or harmonica and which are themselves called "reeds." These are struck with small hammers working like those of the piano, and the tiny sound produced is amplified electronically.

All electromechanical and some electronic pianos are touch-sensitive; those that are not are considered inferior instruments. With fingers alone the player can govern only about four dynamic levels—which four are determined by a volume control knob above the keyboard. This knob is sometimes replaced by a foot pedal that is not spring-loaded, so that a volume level once chosen will remain even if the player's foot is needed elsewhere. The volume control expands the instrument's overall dynamic range to the limits of human sensitivity and endurance, *ppp–ffff*; similar huge dynamic ranges are characteristic of all "electric" instruments.

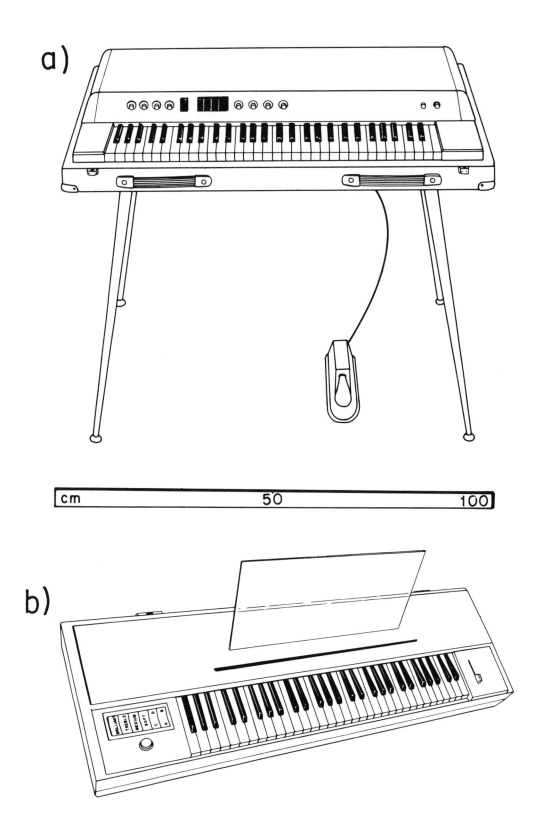

a)

cm 50 100

b)

FIGURE 178. *Non-sustaining electric keyboards: (a) electric piano; (b) clavinet.*

name of instrument	abbreviations	written range	sounds	availability
electric piano	elec. pno. el. pno.	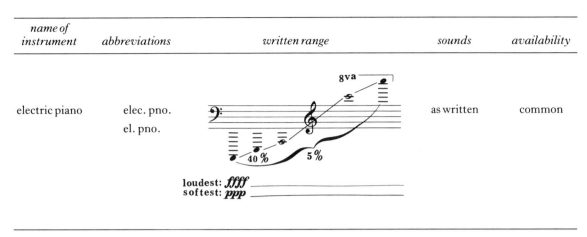	as written	common

FIGURE 179. *The electric piano—vital statistics.*

Some electromechanical pianos have a damper pedal ("sustain pedal") like that of a real piano but others do not, and no electronic piano has one.

The most important thing to bear in mind about the electric piano is that it is *not* a debased form of pianoforte but an entirely separate instrument with its own distinctive timbre. Like most electrical instruments it has an extremely rich, rather coarse tone that is best served by thin harmonizations and widely spaced contrapuntal lines. The very full tone makes a damper pedal somewhat supererogatory, for the thick chords and stylized rhythmic patterns of traditional piano music would probably come across on the electric piano as impenetrable murk.

The notes of the electric piano sustain about as long as equivalent pitches on the ordinary piano. By adroit use of the volume control a note can be sustained rather longer than usual, be made to stay at full volume throughout most of the decay, or even be increased in volume after it has been struck.

Electric pianos are usually provided with one or two tone-control knobs, like the treble/bass knobs on an amplifier. Except for such impressionistic instructions as "bright tone" or "dark tone," manipulation of the timbre is best left to the player. As with other electrical instruments, the electric piano can be coupled to all kinds of tone-modifying devices such as vibrato, reverb, and fuzz-tone. These are discussed in Chapter X.

THE CLAVINET

There are a number of **electric harpsichords** on the market, some under fanciful trade names. Most have the normal harpsichord range of F_1–f^3, though some are missing a fifth or octave at the bottom of the range. The instrument may be electronic or electroacoustic and is a remarkably good imitation of real harpsichord timbre, though it is by no means close enough to fool a careful or sophisticated listener. Some electronic pianos, organs, and performance synthesizers have this sound available as a stop. The electric harpsichord is used in a number of Beatles songs ("Lucy in the Sky with Diamonds," "Because"), and can also be heard in Terry Riley's *A Rainbow in Curved Air.*

A more distinctive instrument is the **clavinet** (Hohner's trade name for its patented electric clavichord). The ordinary clavichord is an extremely soft instrument totally unsuited

name of instrument	abbreviations	written range	sounds	availability
clavinet	clvnt. clav.	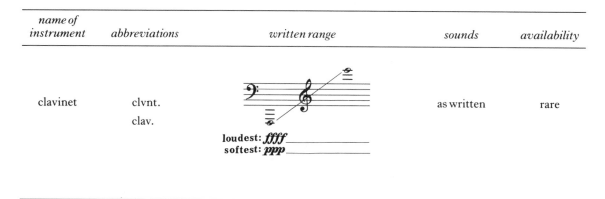	as written	rare

FIGURE 180. *The clavinet—vital statistics.*

for ensemble work; the clavinet, on the other hand, has the enormous dynamic range of most electric intruments and a tone quality more reminiscent of the electric guitar than of its parent instrument.

The mechanism of the clavinet is virtually identical to that of the clavichord,* each key being a simple lever that presses a **tangent** against a string. The tangent remains in contact with the string as long as the note sounds, acting both to produce the sound and as a bridge determining the sounding length of the string. When the key is released the string is automatically damped by muting material resting against the unused portion of the string behind the tangent. This gives the sound an incredibly quick cutoff that gives the clavinet much of its air of crispness and precision—a feature it shares with the clavichord. An incredibly brittle staccato is available, and it is even possible to play a trill staccato, each note clearly separated from its neighbors.

Because the fingers are in direct mechanical connection with the strings throughout the duration of each note, the clavinet is the most expressive of the modern keyboards. By varying the pressure on the key *after* the note is struck, it is possible to produce a delicate vibrato, or bent tones up to a quarter-tone above the pitch initially sounded. The vibrato is ineffective in chords and is best applied to single melodic lines. It is not a standard technique, and since it can only be applied to slow-moving or static passages—preferably to individual notes—the instruction "vibr. ⌐⌐⌐⌐⌐⌐⌐⌐" should be written above the staff wherever vibrato is desired, the half-bracket indicating for how long the effect is to be applied.

Only three dynamic levels can be differentiated by touch alone (four, if full advantage is taken of the contrast in loudness between full chords and single notes), but a volume control knob like that of the electric piano gives the clavinet the tremendous overall dynamic range characteristic of "electric" instruments in general. The instrument is provided with six "stops" (really treble/bass filter pre-sets) and a "muting slide" to control its timbre; with these the tone can be inflected across a range bounded by an approximate "electric-piano" sound at one extreme and a "harpsichord" sound at the other. As with the electric piano, the details of their use are best left to the player.

* See Chapter XIII for details.

MUSICAL EXAMPLES (FROM THE POPULAR LITERATURE)

ELECTRIC PIANO:
Paul Simon, "Congratulations"
Herbie Hancock, "Steppin' in It"

CLAVINET:
Stevie Wonder, "Keep on Running"

FREE-REED INSTRUMENTS

HARMONICAS

The harmonica is not a keyboard instrument, but its affinities and playing technique make it fit more comfortably into this chapter than elsewhere. It is closely related to the melodica and accordion, both unquestionably keyboard instruments; furthermore, it is a somewhat polyphonic instrument capable of playing chords, and its notes are lined up left-to-right in an essentially keyboard-like fashion.

The harmonica, melodica, and accordion constitute a family of **free-reed** instruments.* Unlike the **beating reeds** of woodwind instruments and most organ reed stops, a free reed lies in a slot through which it is free to vibrate (Fig. 183). Air passing through the slot sets the reed vibrating, and the resulting pitch is entirely a function of the reed's mass, length, and flexibility—there is no governing air column. A free reed thus constitutes a very compact acoustical system, and a great many can be fitted into a very small space. A harmonica may contain sixty-four reeds in an instrument only twenty cm long and four cm deep.

Without a controlling air column the pitch of a beating reed will rise as the air pressure is increased, while a free reed will remain stable. Free-reed instruments can thus produce a range of dynamics by varying the air pressure—unlike the organ, in which each reed stop has a single fixed dynamic level.

The mouthpiece of a harmonica is pierced by a row of holes each of which typically has access to at least two reeds of different pitch, one of which sounds on the exhale (**blow notes**) and the other on the inhale (**draw notes**). Harmonicas are made in an astounding variety of types, including "blow only" varieties, 8' + 4' octave-sounding models, and celesting ("tremolo") models, but all are variants on three basic patterns.

* The oldest and most respectable Western member of this group is the **harmonium** or reed organ. Though many old examples of this instrument are, at this writing, still to be encountered, only a handful of trivialized and decadent instruments continue to be manufactured, and the instrument seems to be slipping quietly into extinction. There are numerous important early twentieth-century parts for the harmonium, and should it despite appearances stage a comeback, the interested student may wish to consult Schoenberg's *Herzgewächse* for a notion of its capabilities.

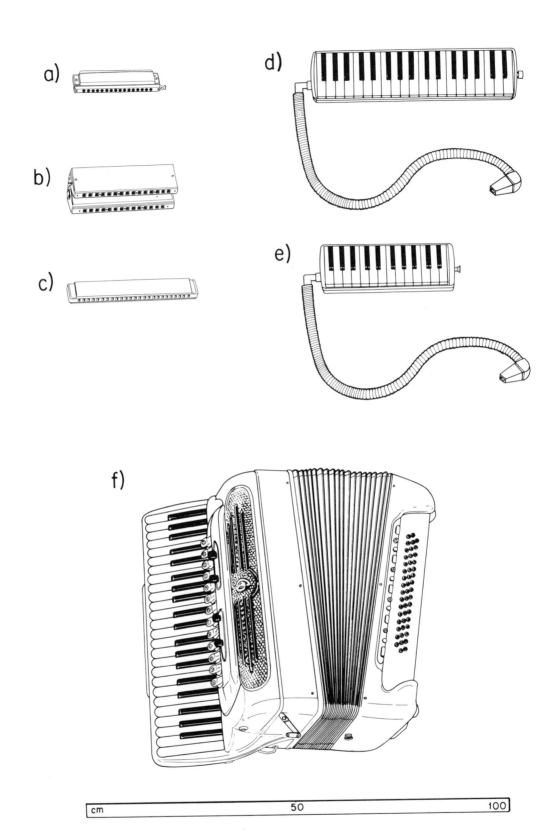

a)

b)

c)

d)

e)

f)

cm   50   100

FIGURE 181. *Free-reed instruments: (a) chromatic harmonica; (b) double bass harmonica;*
(c) bass harmonica; (d) melodica; (e) melodica bass; (f) accordion.

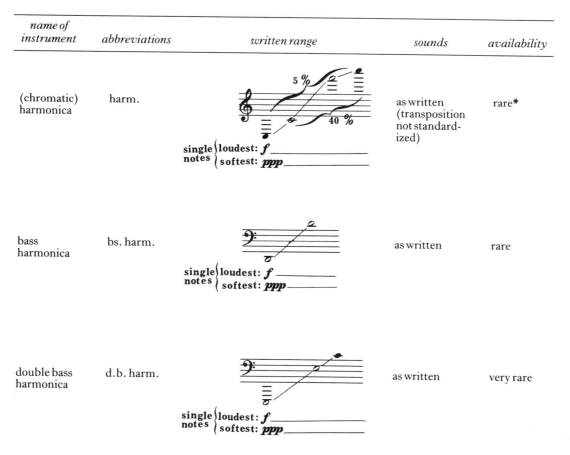

name of instrument	abbreviations	written range	sounds	availability
(chromatic) harmonica	harm.		as written (transposition not standardized)	rare*
bass harmonica	bs. harm.		as written	rare
double bass harmonica	d.b. harm.		as written	very rare

* It may be startling to see an instrument that can be found by the dozens in any music store described as "rare," but the reader must bear in mind that "availability" as defined here is not that of the instrument itself but of competent players with formal music training.

FIGURE 182. *Harmonicas—vital statistics.*

The **diatonic** (or "**marine band**") **harmonica** typically has ten holes giving the following notes:

Notice that f¹, a¹, and b³ are missing. This pattern can be found transposed into every major and minor key.

Chromatic harmonicas are fitted with a slide mechanism that enables production of four tones from each hole instead of two. When the slide is pushed in it gives access to a different set of reeds, and when released automatically shifts back to the "out" position. In **Koch-type** chromatics the diatonic pattern is preserved, and pushing the slide in yields the same pattern transposed up a half-step. With this pattern the notes f♯¹, a¹, a♯¹, and b³ remain

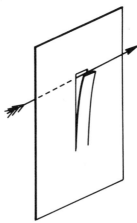

FIGURE 183. *A free reed; arrow shows direction of air flow.*

unavailable. **Fully chromatic** harmonicas use a different pattern, and will as likely as not have twelve holes rather than ten. Some even have sixteen holes (see Fig. 182). This

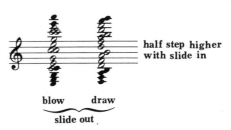

pattern is the most useful for all but the most invincibly tonal material. Both Koch-type and fully chromatic harmonicas exist in versions transposed down to a^0 or $b\flat^0$ and up to d^1, e^1, f^1, or g^1, but composers are advised to stick to the c^1 model, which is both the most common and most useful.

The harmonica is played with the mouth covering four adjacent holes at a time. When playing a monophonic line, the tongue covers the three left holes, so that air enters only the hole furthest to the right. For purposes of harmonization, the tongue may uncover any or all of the three blocked holes (provided all unblocked holes are adjacent) and may do so in an independent rhythm while note(s) from the right-hand hole(s) are being sustained:

(Note that in the above passage the second f^2 must be played as an $e\sharp^2$, i.e., a "blow" with the slide pushed in.)

Aside from this refinement, breathing and tonguing are much as they are on traditional woodwinds. For notes to be played legato they must be either all blow notes or all draw notes. The slide presents no obstacle to legato playing; in fact, it may be used to produce a trill. Large skips cannot be played completely legato but, as on the trombone, a very convincing "fake" is possible.

Blow and draw can be alternated very rapidly—as rapidly as one's diaphragm can alternate exhale and inhale—but notes so alternating must always be detached. Despite the use in play of both inhale and exhale, the player must occasionally take a breath.

name of instrument	abbreviations	written range	sounds	availability
melodica	mel.	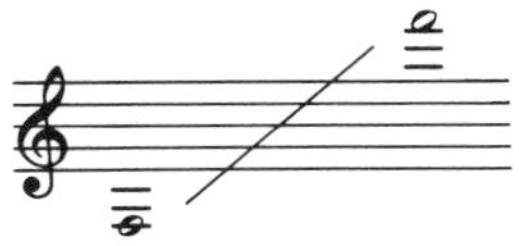 *(staff notation)* single notes { loudest: *f* / softest: *ppp*	as written	usually available
melodica bass	mel. bs.	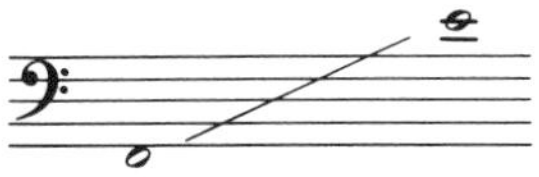 *(staff notation)* single notes { loudest: *f* / softest: *ppp*	as written	very rare

FIGURE 184. *Melodicas—vital statistics.*

Vibrato on the harmonica, when desired, is made by fluttering the left hand back and forth at the bottom of the instrument (where the tone emerges), alternately obscuring and releasing the sound. A different kind of vibrato can be made by moving the tongue back and forth in the mouth.

Skilled players can bend the pitches of the notes by overblowing (or "overdrawing") beyond the reeds' capacity, and/or by partially blocking holes with the tongue. If done carefully this drives them slightly flat and *lowers* the volume; if forced too hard, however, the reeds will simply stop vibrating. Bent tones are easier and more idiomatic on diatonic harmonicas than on chromatic ones. Draw notes can be bent up to a whole step at the bottom of the range, but not at all at the top. On chromatic harmonicas, blow notes can be bent up to a half-step throughout the range (most easily in the middle), while on diatonic ones these notes can be bent up to a whole step at the high end, but only a quarter-step at the low end.

Among the various specialized harmonicas the most interesting and worthwhile are the **bass harmonica** and the **double bass harmonica**. Both have blow-only holes and no slide. On the bass harmonica the notes are simply arranged from left to right in chromatic order; the double bass harmonica is a duplex instrument (see Fig. 181) with the naturals on the lower half and the sharps on the upper, both in keyboard order. Obviously, both bass and double bass harmonicas are intended to be strictly monophonic, though they can if desired play small tone-clusters.

MELODICAS

The melodica is a breath-driven keyboard instrument. In order for a note to sound two conditions must be satisfied: air must be passing through the instrument, and a key must be depressed. The mouthpiece of a melodica lies at the left end of the keyboard, so that normally the instrument is held directly in line with the player's mouth, allowing only the right hand to play the keys. The left hand is used to hold the instrument. However, there are available a special

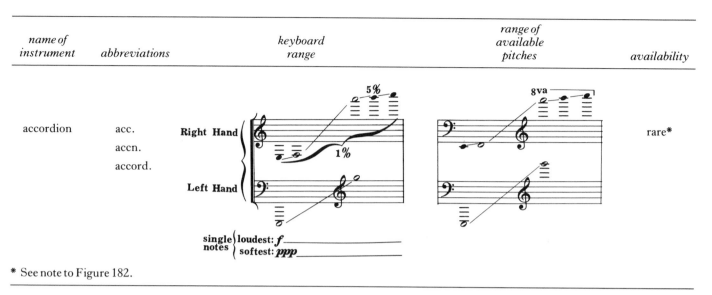

name of instrument	abbreviations	keyboard range	range of available pitches	availability
accordion	acc. accn. accord.			rare*

* See note to Figure 182.

FIGURE 185. *The accordion—vital statistics.*

stand and a long, flexible mouth tube, which together enable the instrument to be set crosswise in front of the player, like ordinary keyboard instruments, so that both hands can be used.

Unlike the harmonica, the melodica is completely polyphonic and is hence a somewhat more useful instrument. Its tone is virtually identical to that of the accordion, but the expressivity and capacity for rapidly repeated notes provided by breath as opposed to bellows makes the melodica worthwhile in its own right. Though David Bedford's *Music for Albion Moonlight* is so far virtually the only piece to specify a melodica, the instrument has been increasingly used in the performance of pieces with indeterminate instrumentation—most notably by Christian Wolff.

The melodica's keyboard technique is essentially that of the organ, but notes can be articulated by the tongue as well as with the fingers. The tongue is generally used only for rapid repetition (including fluttertongue), accents, and sforzandos.

The pitch range given in Figure 184 is that of the largest, "professional" melodica. The smaller sizes, which have tiny ranges, are of little use musically. There is a **melodica bass** (not "bass melodica"), but it is rarely seen.

THE ACCORDION

The accordion is unique in having completely different keyboards for the right and left hands. These are aligned vertically, with the highest pitch of each keyboard at the bottom and the lowest at the top.

Between the two keyboards is a large, flexible **bellows** that supplies the instrument with wind. Each note is provided with two identical sets of reeds, one speaking as the bellows collapses and the other speaking as it expands. Articulation with the bellows is very similar to that of bowed string instruments (see Chapter IX): a slur indicates that all notes beneath it are to be taken not only legato but, of necessity, in one motion of the bellows; portato (⌢♪ ♪ ♪) and related notations indicate articulation with the bellows rather than the fingers; and the symbols ⊓ and ∨ above notes may be used to indicate the beginning of compression and expansion strokes, respectively.

Unlike bowing, however, motion of the bellows is never rapidly alternated. Normal detached articulation is provided by the keys, as on the melodica; the bellows is used to articulate only portato and accented notes and those that must emerge gradually from silence. An air valve operated by the left thumb enables the player to move the bellows silently from one extreme to the other in about half a second, if desired, so that, e.g., two long compression strokes may follow one another without an intervening expansion stroke.

A single stroke of the bellows can last about as long as a clarinet note played at comparable volume. Where necessary as an aid to proper phrasing, an apostrophe—analogous to the "breath mark" of winds—may be used to indicate the place in the music where the bellows are to be reversed. While it is impossible to continue a note completely smoothly while reversing the bellows, it is possible, as with bowing, to approach very close to such continuity.

The keyboard for the right hand is of the ordinary sort, and the right-hand technique is identical to that of the organ. The left hand, however, uses a **button keyboard**, a very compact diagonal grid of pushbuttons in which many more notes lie directly under the hand than on a traditional keyboard.

There are three competing types of arrangement for the left-hand buttons. The vast majority of accordions are still made in the **Stradella system**, outlined below, in which the left hand is tied to the playing of common chords and tonal bass lines. In the Stradella system four of the six buttons in each diagonal row give out chords, fully voiced across as many as five octaves. The last two buttons in the row look in the chart as if they produce single notes, but they do not; rather, they produce the entire pitch class over three to five octaves.

						C^0
					C^7	
				Cm		F^0
			CM		F^7	
		E		Fm		$B\flat^0$
	C		FM		$B\flat^7$	
		A		$B\flat$m		$E\flat^0$
	F		$B\flat$M		$E\flat^7$	
		D		$E\flat$m		
	$B\flat$		$E\flat$M			
		G				
	$E\flat$		etc.			

FIGURE 186. *The Stradella system of accordion basses and chord buttons. The pattern is given as seen from the front, i.e., with the bellows at the left. For the player this is reversed.*

It will be readily seen that the Stradella system is unsuited to any kind of sophisticated music-making. Its deficiencies are ameliorated somewhat in **free-bass** accordions, in which the two left-hand buttons in each row do give out single pitches, but for serious musical purposes a **chromatic free-bass** accordion is essential. Here the buttons are arranged in only three vertical rows and give out single pitches only, as shown below.

```
                    E
      F                          F♯
                    G
      G♯                         A
                    A♯
      B                          C
                    C♯
      D                          D♯
                    E
      F                          F♯
                    G

                   etc.
```

FIGURE 187. *Pattern of left-hand buttons on a chromatic accordion. The pattern is given as seen from the front, i.e., with the bellows at the left. For the player this is reversed.*

Note the economy of this pattern: minor seconds run diagonally downward to the (viewer's) left, major seconds right, and minor thirds straight up and down. Because there are three rows of pitches instead of two, the total pitch range covered is greater in this system than in others; it is this wide range that is given in Figure 185. The compact arrangement of buttons allows the fingers to stretch across much greater intervals than on a traditional keyboard, so that despite the fact that the thumb is not normally used and that the left hand, holding the instrument, cannot twist about with as much facility as, say, a organist's, almost any imaginable configuration of pitches within the range of two octaves can be played. The average maximum stretches are shown below. The thumb is included in these calculations because it *can* be used if the player unorthodoxly slips the hand forward around the side of the instrument. Chords requiring the thumb should be given some preparation time, since bringing the thumb forward is an awkward maneuver.

Stretch From Finger

	1	2	3	4
5	3 8ves	2 8ves	1 8ve	tritone
4	2 8ves + tritone	10th	tritone	
3	2 8ves + 3d	6th		
2	2 8ves			

To Finger

A finger can push down two adjoining buttons simultaneously (the fingering should be given where this is needed), and tone clusters up to two octaves wide can be produced with the flat of the hand.

A tiny but growing minority of accordionists play chromatic free-bass instruments. These are the "classical" accordionists—often dedicated and highly trained professionals—interested in something more than the endless round of polkas and "Lady of Spain" that is the lot of the Stradella-system player. Composers should do these people a favor and stick to the chromatic instrument in their writing. In fairness it should be mentioned that **combination instruments** exist, in which there is either a chromatic free-bass system adjoined by the usual five rows of chord buttons, or else "stops" to switch the left hand from Stradella to chromatic and back again.

Most accordions have four **ranks** (complete sets)* of reeds available to the right hand. Two of these right-hand ranks are at 8′ pitch, one is at 4′, and one is at 16′. The two 8′ ranks are different in timbre and are called "flute" and "clarinet," respectively. The "flute" tone is not at all flute-like but is, rather, the normal reedy accordion sound; the "clarinet" is a more rich and fruity tone. Most of the possible combinations of the four ranks are provided by twelve stops (traditionally called **registers**), each of which is denoted by a symbol placed above the staff.

$$\ominus \quad \text{flute} = \text{flute } 8'$$

$$\ominus \quad \text{clarinet} = \text{clarinet } 8'$$

$$\ominus = 2 \times 8'$$

$$\ominus = 4'$$

$$\ominus = 8' + 4'$$

$$\ominus = 2 \times 8' + 4'$$

$$\ominus = 16'$$

$$\ominus = 8' + 16'$$

$$\ominus = 2 \times 8' + 16'$$

$$\ominus = 8' + 4' + 16'$$

$$\ominus = 4' + 16'$$

$$\ominus = 2 \times 8' + 4' + 16'$$

Those registers in which a single 8′ rank is combined with the 16′ and/or 4′ ranks use the flute in preference to the clarinet. Unlike the stops of an organ, only one accordion register can be engaged at a time, so combinations such as "clarinet 8′ + 4′ " are unavailable. $\ominus$ is called forth by a long pressure bar below the keyboard—like the space bar of a typewriter—worked

* In this case actually double sets, since each rank must be provided with both pressure and suction reeds.

by the heel of the hand. The other eleven registers appear as pushbuttons above the keyboard and require a free finger for their operation. The four solo registers, and those in which both 8′ ranks are present, are unambiguous in pitch, ⊖ giving a particularly full, sombre effect and ⊖ a particularly brilliant one. With ⊖, ⊖, ⊖, and especially ⊖ it will be somewhat unclear which octave is the main one and which the auxiliary. Whenever a true *fortissimo* is desired ⊖ should be used, since only with the aid of all four ranks can the instrument compete even with ordinary woodwinds in this respect.

Stradella-system accordions may have up to ten registers for the left hand, attempting to make up in sonority what is all too clearly missing in the way of pitch. Chromatic accordions have two left-hand ranks; these two ranks can be permutated in only three possible ways, symbolized as follows:

$$\ominus = 8' \qquad \ominus = 4' \qquad \ominus = 8' + 4'$$

These three registers are replicated up and down the left side of the instrument so that all can be easily reached at any point without moving the hand. Their timbre is calculated to fit in equally well with both right-hand timbres, and their volume is set so that a single left-hand rank will balance one or two right-hand ranks, while ⊖ will balance three or four right-hand ranks.

Whatever registers are used, the notation should stick to keyboard (i.e., 8′) pitch, any octave transposition being sufficiently indicated by the register symbol.

Musical Examples

HARMONICA (FROM THE POPULAR LITERATURE):
   Bob Dylan, "I Dreamed I Saw St. Augustine"
   Herbie Hancock, "Steppin' in It"

BASS HARMONICA (FROM THE POPULAR LITERATURE):
   Paul Simon, "Papa Hobo"

DOUBLE BASS HARMONICA:
   (no example)

MELODICA:
   Bedford, *Music for Albion Moonlight*

MELODICA BASS:
   (no example)

ACCORDION:
   Berg, *Wozzeck* (Act II, scene 4)
   Hindemith, *Kammermusik No. 1*
   Del Tredici, *Vintage Alice*
   Nordheim, *Osaka-Music Dinosauros*

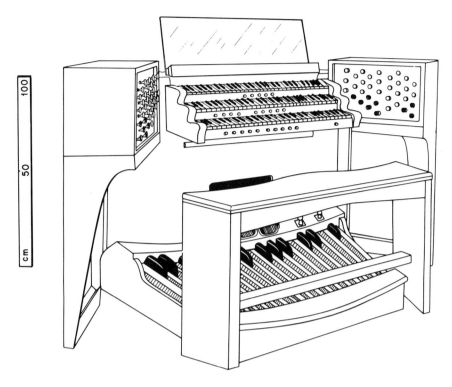

FIGURE 188. *A typical organ console.*

THE ORGAN

The organ is with justice called the king of instruments, for it is the largest, most complex, and arguably the most versatile of all. Its overall pitch range is a staggering nine octaves covering the entire gamut of musically useful frequencies; its dynamic range approaches that of an electronic instrument; and its variety of timbres is exceeded only by the studio synthesizer.

BASIC FEATURES OF THE INSTRUMENT

No two organs are alike, for each must be designed to fit, architecturally and acoustically, the room in which it is installed. Installing an organ in a building is comparable in effort and expense to adding a new wing; and moving an organ, like moving one's household, requires taking everything apart and putting it back together again in the new location, all arranged differently and perhaps completely redesigned.

The organ's great complexity and variability have proved daunting to many composers, and by far the greatest proportion of the organ literature has been written by people who were themselves organists. It is hoped that the following presentation will be of aid in dispelling some of this mystery and confusion.

The keys, stop-knobs, and other controls of an organ are located on a **console** (Fig. 188) which, unlike the rest of the instrument, is often movable and may even be stored in a closet when the organ is not in use. A typical organ console has three **manuals** (keyboards for the

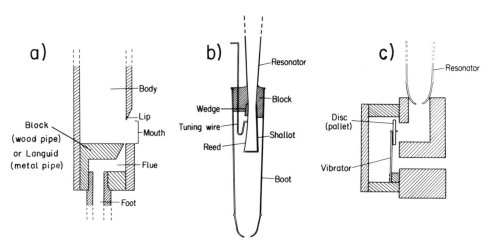

FIGURE 189. *Diagrammatic sagittal sections of organ pipes: (a) flue pipe; (b) reed pipe; (c) diaphone.*

hands), each with the five-octave range given in Figure 190, stacked one above the other. For the feet there is a **pedal** keyboard of two and a half octaves; this is just like any other keyboard, with black and white keys arranged in the usual pattern, but the keys are of course very large so that they can be played with the feet. No modern organ lacks a pedalboard and no organ has more than one, but the number of manuals varies. An organ with two manuals is considered small (single-manual instruments are almost always historical reconstructions and will not be further considered here), while large organs have four or even five.

Each of the manuals, and the pedal as well, controls its own distinct group of stops known as a **division** of the organ. The stops in a division are designed to complement and blend with each other, and each division is conceived with a particular musical purpose in mind. The divisions of a three-manual organ are called (starting with the top manual) **swell**, **great**, **choir**, and **pedal**. The great division (or **great organ**, as it is called) is the most important in any organ, containing the most commonly used, all-purpose stops.

The pipes of the **swell organ** are always **enclosed** in a **swell box** fronted by Venetian shutters which can be opened and closed by means of a **swell pedal** (also called **swell shoe**) located above the pedalboard and operated by the player's right (usually) foot. The swell box gives the organ its only real powers of crescendo and diminuendo, and that across only two dynamic levels: *mp–f*, say, or *pp–mp* or whatever, depending on the loudness of the stops being used at the time.*

Divisions other than the swell may be enclosed in whole or in part. On a few organs all divisions are enclosed, but this is almost universally frowned upon since enclosure, even with the shutters fully open, causes the sound to blend and resonate in a way that, while tonally attractive, tends to weaken the clarity of individual melodic lines. Generally, each enclosed division or partial division is provided with its own swell shoe. Swell shoes are not spring-loaded, and once set in a given position will stay put until a change is needed.

The **choir organ** mostly contains accompanimental stops designed more for smooth and well-blended harmony than for clear melody. It is often but not always enclosed. The **pedal organ** is specialized for the performance of bass lines and of *cantus firmus* in all registers. Its

* The difference in loudness seems greater than it really is, however, because when the pipes are obscured by closing the shutters the sound becomes not only soft but *distant*.

stops are centered around 16′ rather than 8′ pitch, so that, for instance, there will usually be a stop sounding at 5⅓′—i.e., the third partial of 16′. The pedal division usually also contains a few full-toned soloistic stops at 4′ and/or 2′ pitch, to play mid- and high-range *cantus firmus* lines.

If an organ has only two manuals they are swell and great. If there are more than three manuals, the "extras" are at the top, above the swell manual. The fourth manual is usually called **solo** and its division mostly contains rather loud, self-sufficient stops that are indeed intended to carry a single melodic line accompanied from another manual. The solo organ is usually enclosed. If there is a fifth manual its division may have any of a wide variety of names, depending on what specialized function has been assigned to it. Usually it will be some sort of **antiphonal division**, its pipes placed at a distance from the rest of the organ. If the fourth manual is not a solo, it too may control an antiphonal division whether or not a fifth manual is present. Antiphonal divisions are frequently the great, swell, and/or choir divisions of a preexisting small organ cannibalized to augment a larger successor. Among specially designed antiphonal divisions, perhaps the most common are the **celestial organ**, specializing in loud stops, and the **echo organ**, specializing in very soft ones (usually enclosed). Echo, celestial, solo, and numerous other specialized divisions, antiphonal or not, may also appear as **ancillary divisions** on a medium or large organ. Ancillary divisions, of which there are seldom more than two or three, are not attached to any particular manual but are available to all by means of **couplers**. Couplers—which look and act exactly like stop knobs or tiles—also link the various manuals to each other and to the pedal; when the coupler "pedal to great" is drawn, for instance, all the stops of the pedal organ become available for use on the great manual, but not vice versa. For the reverse effect, the "great to pedal" coupler is used. Couplers for most or all possible combinations of manuals (and pedal) are generally present; those linking the pedal and the other manuals to the great are *always* available. Couplers may be drawn together in any combination.

The stop controls of the organ are located to the right and left of the manuals (see Fig. 188) and take the form of draw-knobs or rocking tiles, each imprinted with the name and register of the stop it governs. The stop controls for each division are typically grouped together. Normally, drawing or releasing a stop requires that the appropriate hand be free for at

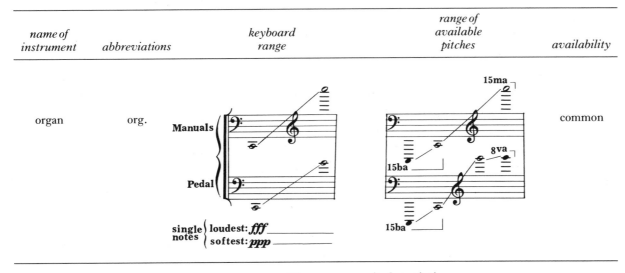

name of instrument	abbreviations	keyboard range	range of available pitches	availability
organ	org.			common

FIGURE 190. *The organ—vital statistics.*

least half a second, and changing a complicated combination of stops may require the use of both hands for up to four seconds.

Fortunately, however, the process of adding, subtracting, or changing stops is made considerably easier by the use of **pistons**, which are present on all medium and large organs. A piston is a pushbutton which when pressed automatically draws any prearranged combination of stops (including couplers and/or tremulant, if desired) while releasing all stops not needed for that combination; the player can thus draw and release many stops at once by pressing a single button. To make things even easier, the pistons are scattered all over the console in handy places—above and/or below each manual, in the keyjambs, above the pedals—so that one will always be within easy reach (a quarter-second) of each hand and each foot.

Related to the pistons is the **crescendo pedal** (or **shoe**), a non–spring-loaded pedal resembling the swell pedal. When rocked forward it gradually brings on *all* the stops (with the exception of célestes, percussions, and tremulant—see below) in a smoothly graded series, with a crescendo effect that can cross the instrument's entire dynamic range. When rocked back it releases these stops in reverse order, leaving (at the extreme position) only the stops the player had drawn beforehand. If the loudest, fullest possible sound is desired ("full organ"), the crescendo pedal will be rocked all the way forward.

THE STOPS

There are hundreds of different kinds of organ stops; needless to say, no organ possesses all or even most of them. The stops are classified into eight or so groups based on their timbre and the way in which they are constructed, and examples of each of these groups are found on all but the very smallest organs.

All but a specialized handful of stops are either **flue stops** (Fig. 189a) or **reed stops** (Fig. 189b).

Flue pipes produce their sound exactly as a recorder does: a jet of air (supplied by a rotary electric blower) emerges from the flue, whence it is directed across the mouth of the pipe toward the sharp edge of the pipe's upper lip. The "air reed" thus produced is set into vibration just as in the flute, and sets up a standing wave in the pipe, the frequency of which is determined by the pipe's length and whether or not it is blocked off ("stopped") at the top. If the pipe is stopped it sounds an octave lower than otherwise and gives forth only odd-numbered partials. The tone of a flue pipe begins with a pronounced **chiff** of high-pitched inharmonic sounds as the standing wave builds up and stabilizes. In soft-sounding pipes of low pitch the chiff may be considerably louder than the steady tone.

A clear majority of organ stops are flue stops. These are further subdivided into **foundations**, **flutes**, and **strings**. This division is based on the degree of harmonic development of the stops, the strings having many and strong upper partials, the flutes having few and weak ones, and the foundations lying somewhere in the middle.

The foundations, as the name implies, are the most important stops in the organ, and at least some will be found in every division of the instrument. These are the stops with the typical "organ" sound, full, smooth, and rich, and they are often used by themselves. But they are also designed to blend with and support every other timbre on the organ without destroying the individuality of those timbres. This is particularly true of foundations at other than 8′ pitch. A basic point of organ registration is the varying of timbre and dynamics through the addition of stops that double upper partials of a stop already drawn, and most of this work is done with foundation stops. Generally, the higher the register of a given stop the softer it will be, so that it will blend with a stop of lower pitch rather than competing with it. When one or more high-pitched stops are added to an 8′ stop of any sort, they will, without destroying the basic timbre, *brighten* the tone quality, *increase* the loudness, and *clarify* the attack (because high pipes speak more quickly than low ones). Addition of 16′ and/or 32′ stops also increases the loudness but the tone then becomes ponderous and heavy. If such a stop is loud enough it will be heard as the fundamental, the 8′ stop then being heard as the second or fourth partial.

The most important foundations are the **diapason chorus**, found complete in the great and pedal organs and perhaps in other divisions as well. These stops are usually named as follows:

Name	*Pitch on the Manuals*	*Pitch on the Pedal*
contra (or double) diapason, or diapason	16′	32′
diapason or principal	8′	16′
principal or prestant	4′	8′
nasard	$2\frac{2}{3}'$	$5\frac{1}{3}'$
principal or superoctave	2′	4′
tierce	$1\frac{3}{5}'$	$3\frac{1}{5}'$
larigot	$1\frac{1}{3}'$	$2\frac{2}{3}'$
twenty-second	1′	2′

All these are standard features of almost any organ. Rarer stops in this series are:

Name	*Pitch on the Manuals*	*Pitch on the Pedal*
resultant	32′	64′
contra (or double) diapason	32′	—
subquint	$10\frac{2}{3}'$	$21\frac{1}{3}'$
terz or third	$6\frac{2}{5}'$	$12\frac{4}{5}'$
quint	$5\frac{1}{3}'$	$10\frac{2}{3}'$
tenth or gross tierce	$3\frac{1}{5}'$	$6\frac{2}{5}'$
septième	$1\frac{1}{7}'$	$2\frac{2}{7}'$
twenty-ninth*	$\frac{1}{2}'$	1′

*The $\frac{1}{2}'$ register is more likely to appear as a flute stop, under some such name as *campana* or *sifflöte*.

Of these, the quint and twenty-ninth (or its flute-stop equivalents) are not uncommon on medium-sized organs; the others are generally found only on large organs, and it is a rare instrument indeed that possesses them all.

Stops that sound at pitches other than 8' or one of its octaves are called **mutations**. These stops reinforce various non-octave upper partials of 8' stops and stops in other octaves, as the table below shows. Mutations are not in fact used for partials above the eighth. This is not to say that a 64' and a 1⅐' stop would never be drawn simultaneously, but only that if they were (and this would require a coupler because it is unlikely to the point of impossibility that both would be in the same division) they would both—together with numerous other stops—be in the service of reinforcing 8' or perhaps 16' pitch. All this of course applies only to "normal" registration: if one wants each key to sound two discrete notes five octaves plus a flat minor seventh apart then there is nothing for it but to draw resultant 64' + septième 1⅐' and damn the consequences.

Partial Number	Fundamental Pitch				
	64'	32'	16'	8'	4'
3	$21\frac{1}{3}'$	$10\frac{2}{3}'$	$5\frac{1}{3}'$	$2\frac{2}{3}'$	$1\frac{1}{3}'$
5	$12\frac{4}{5}'$	$6\frac{2}{5}'$	$3\frac{1}{5}'$	$1\frac{3}{5}'$	
6	$10\frac{2}{3}'$	$5\frac{1}{3}'$	$2\frac{2}{3}'$	$1\frac{1}{3}'$	
7			$2\frac{2}{7}'$	$1\frac{1}{7}'$	
10	$6\frac{2}{5}'$	$3\frac{1}{5}'$	$1\frac{3}{5}'$		
12	$5\frac{1}{3}'$	$2\frac{2}{3}'$	$1\frac{1}{3}'$		
14		$2\frac{2}{7}'$	$1\frac{1}{7}'$		
20	$3\frac{1}{5}'$	$1\frac{3}{5}'$			
24	$2\frac{2}{3}'$	$1\frac{1}{3}'$			
28	$2\frac{2}{7}'$	$1\frac{1}{7}'$			
40	$1\frac{3}{5}'$				
48	$1\frac{1}{3}'$				
56	$1\frac{1}{7}'$				

The pitch of a mutation stop is not tempered, but tuned perfectly to the appropriate harmonic of 8' pitch. If, for instance, one were to draw the larigot 1⅓' on one manual and a soft 8' stop on another, depressing the c^1 key on the first and the e^3 key on the second, one would expect a unison at e^3 to result; but in fact the two e^3's would beat strongly against each other because of the difference between the equal temperament of the keyboard itself (as reflected in the 8' e^3) and the just intonation of the larigot rank as a whole relative to 8' pitch. The unfortunately rather rare septième 1⅐' is particularly interesting, for if it were unorthodoxly to be used as a solo stop it would produce nothing but quarter-tones—otherwise unavailable on the organ without special tampering.

No stop ascends above sounding c^6, and those of less than $2'$ pitch **break back** to a lower octave rather than pass this limit. A $\frac{1}{2}'$ stop, for instance (see the example below), breaks back twice as the scale is ascended,

so that the stop actually sounds at $1'$ pitch in the octave from (written) $c\#^2$ to c^3 and at $2'$ pitch from $c\#^3$ to c^4. When a mutation breaks back it no longer doubles a partial but, rather, a privileged frequency one or two octaves lower; at these giddy altitudes it seems to make no difference.

At the other end of the scale, $64'$ stops break back in their *lowest* octave, so no pitch below C_2 is ever produced. The one exception to this is the stop called *resultant*, which also happens to be the most commonly found $64'$ stop. The resultant sounds simultaneously two ranks of diapason or flute pipes a fifth apart, the lower rank being at $32'$ pitch. If the stop is well designed and the building acoustics are favorable, one hears a powerful difference tone (the "resultant") at $64'$ from the interaction of the two ranks. From the pedal low C_0 this stop plays both C_2 and G_2 but is heard (or, rather, felt) simply as C_3—a frequency of only 8 Hz.

The resultant is an example of a **compound stop**, in which a single stop-knob gives simultaneous access to two or more ranks of pipes. The most important compound stops are the **mixtures**, which lie at the opposite end of the scale from the resultant, since the ranks of a mixture are tuned to produce a balanced cluster of high partials—up to the sixteenth in some examples.* A large mixture *may* contain an $8'$ rank—or even a $16'$ or $32'$ one, as some pedal mixtures may contain up to eighteen ranks of pipes—but it is characteristic of all mixtures that they are intended to be drawn in combination with appropriate octave-sounding stops. If drawn alone a mixture stop produces an audible chord of independent pitches rather than a blend of unobtrusive harmonics. Individual mixture pipes, unlike those of ordinary stops, may ascend as high as c^7, but most or all of the ranks in a mixture break back one or more times in a staggered pattern. This feature is purposely designed to give notes in different parts of the keyboard slightly different timbres—the sort of thing we take for granted in ordinary string and wind instruments but which would be virtually absent from the organ without mixtures. These slight timbral differences allow each line of complicated polyphony to emerge with the utmost clarity.

* The thirteenth, fourteenth, and fifteenth partials are never present, and the seventh, ninth, and eleventh are rare.

Common stop-names for various types of mixture are *cymbal, fourniture, acuta, sesquialtera,* and *plein jeu.* A compound stop related to the mixture is the **cornet**, which differs, however, in that its partials are so balanced that it can—indeed, should—usually be used as a solo stop giving a unified, very rich sound. Cornet ranks break back only where absolutely necessary. The individual ranks of both mixtures and cornets always consist of flue pipes, usually of the foundation variety.

Moving on from the foundation stops we come to the **flute stops**. These are subdivided into **open**, **stopped**, and **half-stopped** flutes. Stopped flute pipes are covered at the top and sound rather hooty; acoustically they are **stopped pipes** (for a discussion of which see Chapter II). The cover of a half-stopped pipe is pierced by a smallish hole; these pipes are somewhat harsh and penetrating in timbre. Most open flutes produce a sound much like that of the recorder; the reader can experiment with the sounds of stopped, half-stopped, and open pipes by playing on a recorder mouthpiece while blocking off the bottom of it (partially, completely, or not at all) with one hand.

Open flutes are by far the most common (typical stop-names: *blockflöte, spitzflöte, hohlflöte, waldflöte, orchestral flute, tibia*), occurring across a wide range of both dynamics and pitch: open flutes may be pitched anywhere from 32′ to ½′—including all the common mutation pitches, though the ordinary foundation-type mutations work perfectly well with most flute stops. The softest of all organ stops, the *ppp vox angelica* 8′, may be either an open flute or a foundation. Unfortunately, this and the few other *ppp* stops are generally available only on large organs.

Stopped flutes (*gedeckt, bourdon, quintadena,* etc.) are generally quite soft—never louder than *forte.* They occur at all pitches from 64′ to 1′, including the most common mutation pitches.

Half-stopped flutes (*rohrflöte* and other names beginning with "rohr-") are the least common type, though almost any organ will have at least one such stop. They are found within a dynamic range of *p* to *mf* and at pitches between 16′ and 2′. The rare *rohrquint* 5⅓′ and *rohrnasat* 2⅔′ are the only half-stopped mutations.

Acoustically, flute stops differ from foundations in having a less well-developed harmonic spectrum. At the opposite extreme are the **string stops**, whose name derives—rather imaginatively—from their very bright, zingy tone. String stops are less common than either flutes or foundations; almost all are named after stringed instruments, the major exception being the *salicional,* the most useful and common of all string stops.* Strings are built at a wide variety of dynamic levels, and at pitches from 32′ to (rarely) 2′, including all the more common mutations—though, again, the ordinary foundation mutations serve string timbre perfectly well.

A specialized type of compound stop called **céleste** is usually made from string ranks. A céleste consists of two otherwise identical ranks tuned a few Hz apart so that they beat together, making a very pleasant, gentle vibrato. Célestes are usually soft (*mezzo-forte* or softer) and are almost invariably of 8′ pitch. Because the low difference tone that makes the vibrato effect is difficult to elicit at low pitches, célestes descend only to c^1, g^0, or c^0, breaking back below that pitch.

---

* On the other hand, the group of stops beginning with "geigen-" (German: "violin-") are not string stops at all, but foundations.

The most common céleste stop is the *voix céleste*, usually made from salicional pipes. Some specialized célestes have more than two ranks, the idea being to create not a vibrato but the slight turbulence characteristic of massed instruments playing in unison. Foundation and flute célestes also exist, usually with a slower vibrato than a string céleste: the most common foundation céleste is called *unda maris* (Latin: "wave of the sea"). There is no such thing as a reed céleste.

Each pipe of a **reed stop** (Fig. 189b) enlcoses in its base (or **boot**) a single metal reed that beats against the opening in a **shallot**, the whole system resembling a clarinet reed and mouthpiece. Unlike the clarinet, however, a reed pipe's pitch is governed entirely by the reed itself: the "pipe" ascending above the boot is actually a **resonator**, governing the timbre but not the pitch.

Reed stops are divided into three groups: **chorus reeds**, **semichorus reeds**, and **imitative reeds**. All of the organ's *fff* stops are chorus reeds. Almost always loud—never softer than *mezzo-piano*—chorus reeds have a brilliant, blaring tone and are all named after brass instruments, with the important exception of the low-pitched *bombarde* stops. They are found at pitches from (rarely) 64′ to 4′. Reed mutations are very rare; those that do exist are chorus reeds designed to reinforce the upper partials of the loud 16′ or 32′ *contra bombarde* or *tuba* stop, usually as part of an ancillary **bombarde organ** division.

Semichorus reeds are characterized by short resonators that only slightly mitigate the naturally buzzy tone of the reed: in German these stops are collectively called the *Schnarrwerk*. They are mostly rather soft, never louder than *forte*; the *vox mystica* 8′ is a *ppp* semichorus reed found on some large organs. All octave-sounding pitches from 32′ to 1′ are represented among these stops, which are generally named after Renaissance and medieval instruments (the *gemshorn*, however, is a foundation stop and the *bombarde* is a chorus reed). An important exception is the common *vox humana* 8′, which sounds just barely enough like a human voice to be vaguely disquieting in effect.

The **imitative reeds** are mostly products of the nineteenth century, when the organ was conceived of as a sort of keyboard orchestra. These stops represent attempts to imitate the sounds of orchestral reed instruments, all of which are represented on one organ or another. The two basic timbres, oboe/bassoon and clarinet,* are each represented in a variety of pitches and timbres; clarinet imitations, for instance, include (*orchestral*) *clarinet* 8′ or 16′, *bell clarinet* 8′, *basset horn* 8′, and *major clarinet* 8′ or 16′. The oboe/bassoon group includes octave-sounding stops ranging from *contra bassoon* 32′ to *octave oboe* 4′. The most deliberately imitative stops generally have the word "orchestral" in their names. In addition to the imitative reeds there are imitative flutes, strings, and chorus reeds, but none of these sounds so distinctive as the imitative reeds.

A few miscellaneous stops do not fit into the scheme outlined above. The **diaphone** (Fig. 189c) is reed-like in its mechanism, but instead of a thin reed the vibrator is a solid block called **a pallet**. Diaphones are voiced to sound like foundation stops and are used to give a true *ff* or even *fff* foundation tone at 16′, 32′, or even 64′ pitch, where a flue stop could not play so loudly. Although the diaphone is acoustically unique, musically it is just another foundation stop.

* There exist *saxophone* and *contra saxophone* stops, but these are found only on rather decadent large organs.

Most organs contain one or more **percussions**, which are actual percussion instruments built into the organ and struck by pneumatically driven hammers when a key is depressed. The only percussion commonly found in new organs is the *chimes*, an ordinary two-and-a-half-octave set of tubular chimes built into the instrument and serving more of a ceremonial than a musical function. The old theater organs originally built to accompany silent movies contain a wide variety of percussions—everything from xylophone to piano to castanets—and in Europe even the most respectable Baroque organ is likely to feature a rotating, jingling *Cymbalstern* or twittering *nightingale*.

Finally, there is an important "stop" that makes no sound at all—the **tremulant**. This device produces a fluctuation in the air supply so that a vibrato is imparted to all the stops. Every organ has at least one tremulant, and many have several of different speeds and/or in different divisions. As might be imagined, the tremulant is not traditionally used in combination with a célesting stop. When this is done, the two conflicting vibrati produce an uneven, turbulent sound.

It will readily be seen from the foregoing that organ registration is an art as complex and demanding as all the rest of instrumentation put together. The extent to which composers ought to specify the registration of their organ music has been—deliberate indeterminacy aside—a vexed question for a long time.

Most of the literature runs to one or the other of two extremes. Some composers prefer to leave everything up to the organist—a procedure which, though admirably trusting, is an invitation to disaster, particularly if one is working in an unfamiliar idiom. Others, especially those who are themselves organists, specify everything in great detail; the disadvantages to this are, first, that one must have access to an organ in order to be certain of the sounds produced, and, second, that the great differences among individual organs make such detailed specification only partially applicable to any organ other than the one at which it was composed.

The reader is advised to avoid both these extremes and to register according to these principles: (1) specify only those stops and registers that are meant to be clearly heard, leaving the player to adjust the balance and blend with subsidiary stops of his or her own choice; and (2) avoid specifying any but the most common stops by name, using instead the general designations listed below. These, combined with the register in feet and the indicated dynamic level, will give the organist all the guidelines necessary to choose appropriate stops on any organ:

> foundations
> flutes
> stopped flutes
> rohrflöte
> strings
> chorus reeds
> semichorus reeds
> oboe (8′ or 4′) or bassoon (16′ or 32′)
> clarinet
> mixture(s)
> céleste
> tremulant

Surprisingly little has been done in the way of developing contemporary special effects for the organ. The only such effect that has been used is **switching off the electric blower** (this can be done from the console). The effect produced is one of combined diminuendo and downward glissando, with various little squeaks and toots as the flue pipes produce whistle tones (p. 30) just before dying away. The composite sound is rather like a bagpipe deflating, especially if reed stops are involved.

Two possible special effects that have so far remained unexploited are the **special tuning** of a stop and **rearranging pipes**. All organ pipes can be tuned, but only reed stops can be adjusted easily enough (with their tuning wires) to make it worth a composer's (or performer's) while to retune even one rank for a special effect (microtones, unconventional temperament, etc.). As mentioned above, the septième 1⅐′ (if present) produces quarter-tones without retuning. An equally intriguing possibility is to mix the pipes from two or three different ranks (no lower than c^1—deep pipes are increasingly large and heavy) to produce a "stop" in which different notes have more or less radically different timbres and/or dynamic levels.

NOTATION

Organ music is written on three staves. The lowest staff bears the pedal part; notes played by the hands are written on the upper two staves in the usual fashion. These upper staves do *not* represent separate manuals. Of course, if the two hands play simultaneously on separate manuals, their parts will be segregated on the same two staves, but the situation must be clarified by specifying the manuals involved either by name or with Roman numerals, "I" representing the lowest manual. Changes of manual by both hands together should also be indicated in this way.

All registration instructions are written immediately above the staff or staves they affect, possibly with a brace or half-bracket if more than one staff is affected. All the stops in a new combination should be listed together in a vertical stack, with both name and register given for each.* If one or more stops are to be added or subtracted from an existing combination, the name of each stop is preceded by a + or − , respectively.

The organ and other sustaining, non–touch-sensitive keyboards have substantially different finger technique from that of the piano. The normal articulation of successive tones on the organ is legato, whether or not a slur is written, and in order for the necessary smooth connection to occur each finger must remain on its key to the very last possible instant. To aid in this process two techniques are used that would sound weak and awkward on a touch-sensitive instrument: first, a finger may slide off a black key directly onto an adjacent white key, and second, the thumb may "walk" off a white key onto any adjacent key, white or black, by bending and unbending the knuckle. In addition, organ fingering requires a great deal of substitution, as here:

* The name comes first: "diapason 8′," not "8′ diapason." Of course, no register is given for mixtures, couplers, or tremulant, though in organ specifications the number of ranks in a mixture is given as a Roman numeral, e.g., "fourniture IV."

Composers must be careful not to exceed the fingering possibilities of the instrument; even

such an easy-looking passage as:  is impossible to play legato.

In detached playing, of course, these limitations do not apply. Notes are detached in organ music only at the ends of phrases or where specifically marked by the end of a slur, a staccato-dot, a tenuto line, or an accent.

The pedals are played with heel and toe of both feet. Substitution (of heel for toe or vice versa, or of one foot for the other), sliding with the toe from a black key to any adjacent key (black or white) and "walking" one foot across the keys with alternating toe and heel are all integral parts of this technique. Black keys are always played with the toe. Trills and rapidly repeated notes must be taken with alternate feet.

When playing a single line the two feet working together can play with great rapidity if desired, and even when each foot handles a separate line surprisingly rapid motion is possible. Since each foot can play two-note chords of a second or third, or tone-clusters up to a minor sixth in width, slowly moving polyphony of up to four independent parts is possible, though difficult:

Most organists would regard such a passage as a bit perverse, and composers should write this sort of thing only where absolutely necessary.

The example above also illustrates the symbols used for designation of pedaling patterns. These are as follows:

Λ = toe

U = heel

Λ– U , U –Λ = substitution of heel for toe (toe for heel) in one foot

Λ↘Λ , Λ↘U , U↘Λ , U↘U = substitution of left toe or heel for right toe or heel (notated above staff)

Λ↗Λ , Λ↗U , U↗Λ , U↗U = substitution of right toe or heel for left toe or heel (notated below staff)

Λ – Λ = slide toe off first note directly onto second

Indications for the right foot are placed above the pedal staff; those for the left foot are placed below it. Pedaling, like fingering, should only be specified where absolutely necessary for the clarification of a tricky or deceptive passage.

MUSICAL EXAMPLES

ORGAN:

> Janáček, *Glagolitic Mass*
> Hindemith, *Kammermusik* No. 7
> Varèse, *Ecuatorial*
> Messiaen, *Les Corps glorieux*
> Kagel, *Improvisation ajoutée*

ELECTRIC RELATIVES OF THE ORGAN

THE ELECTRIC ORGAN

Like the electric piano, the electric organ is not simply a debased form of its parent instrument but an independent musical entity with its own characteristics.

The electric organ is an extremely variable and ill-defined instrument, and in order to comprehend its vagaries it is necessary to consider the hypothetical ideal—the "essence," if you will—around which are clustered its various real forms. This archetypal instrument is an electronic imitation, not of the ordinary organ as described above, but of the theater organ of the early twentieth century. These organs were short on mixtures and mutations, possessing instead a great variety of soloistic 8′ stops, running to extremes such as the *tibia clausa*—a *fortissimo* stopped flute with virtually no upper partials—and the *kinura*, a semichorus reed so buzzy it has been compared to "a bee in a bottle." There were also many imitative stops and numerous percussions, and almost everything was enclosed.

All these features are carried over into electric organs, even though pipe organs are no longer designed in this way. The basic appearance and operation of an electric organ are the same as those of a pipe organ, but all sounds are produced electronically.* In place of swell and/or crescendo pedals there is a **volume pedal** covering the entire dynamic range of the instrument. This gives the electric organ considerably more dynamic flexibility than a pipe organ.

It is an unfortunate fact that the vast majority of electric organs made today are unadulterated junk. Everyone has seen these tiny, gadget-ridden, musically useless plastic toys in the salesrooms of "piano" dealers, where they are sold in large numbers to the naïve—but one should not on this account write off the electric organ altogether, for fine instruments continue

---

* Some early electric organs—now highly prized—were electromechanical, but all currently made are electronic.

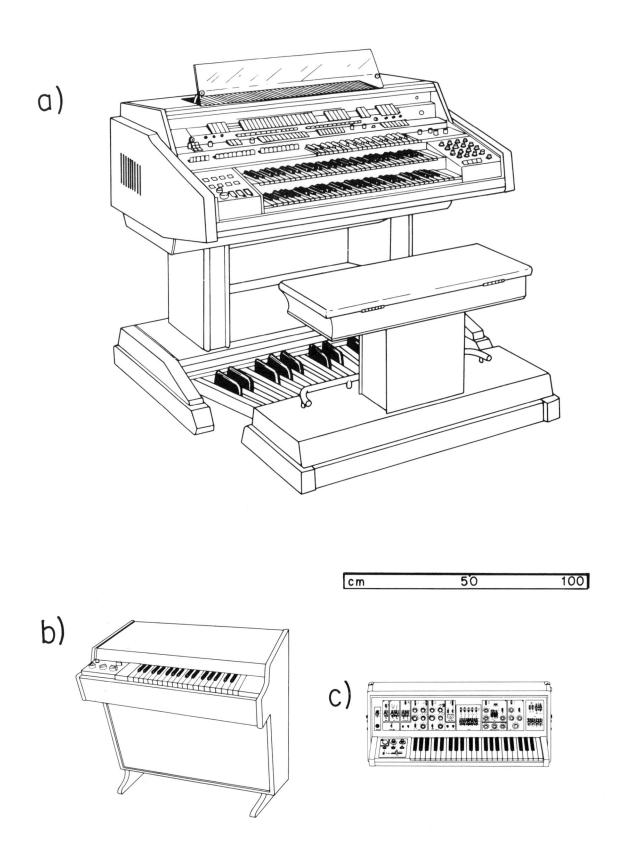

cm 50 100

FIGURE 191. *Sustaining electric keyboards: (a) electric organ;*
(b) melotron; (c) performance synthesizer.

name of instrument	abbreviations	keyboard range	range of available pitches	availability
electric organ	elec. org.			common

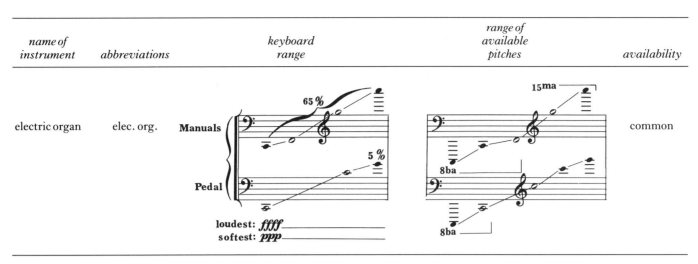

FIGURE 192. *The electric organ—vital statistics.*

to be made. Some of these, intended for use where a pipe organ would be desirable but would not fit the space and/or budget allotted, have up to five manuals and a great many stops; it is interesting that even these "respectable" organs have numerous theater-organ–type stops.

The more typical electric organ—the sort used by jazz and rock groups—is a much smaller instrument, with only two manuals and a smaller keyboard range than the pipe organ, especially in the pedals, which seldom exceed two octaves. Some cheap models have no pedals at all. Most electric organs have no pistons, though there may be "presets" giving the more common combinations. All have couplers, but few have any ancillary divisions.* Only the 8′ series of mutations are likely to be present, and they perhaps only on one manual. There is always a tremulant—often of variable speed—and there may be a **reverb** and/or a **sforzando** tab as well. Many older electric organs were built with a **Leslie** attachment—a raised, rotating loudspeaker that sprayed the sound around the room, causing subtle shifts of phase in the echoes. Recent instruments have a purely electronic **phaser** instead. The schlockier varieties of electric organ are provided with **repetitions** that give a repeated attack (at variable tempo) for as long as each key is held down. Some repetitions apply only to the percussions, but some will affect any stop. Some of the percussion repetitions give specific dance rhythms (tango, polka, etc.). For many years the repetitions had no use except among the musically illiterate, but they are now to be heard quite frequently in popular music.

There are at least two percussions in any electric organ. These most frequently include snare drum, castanets, bass drum, tambourine, wood block, marimba, vibraphone, chimes, piano (i.e., *electric* piano), and/or harpsichord, though almost any imaginable percussion instrument or plucked string can be found in one organ or another. These non-sustaining sounds are made electronically, and if indefinitely pitched will produce the same sound from every key, just as on a theater organ. A "snare drum" stop, for instance, produces a little "biff" of white noise of exactly the same pitch and timbre from each key.

* When there is one, it is for the purpose of keeping traditional and theater stops out of each other's way.

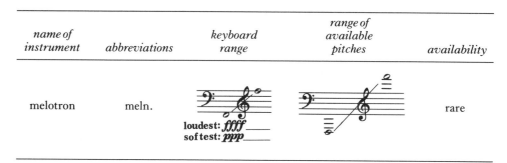

name of instrument	abbreviations	keyboard range	range of available pitches	availability
melotron	meln.			rare

FIGURE 193.   *The melotron—vital statistics.*

The tone of the electric organ, as of the theater organ before it, tends toward the extremes of a mysterious, detached coolness on the one hand and an overbearing lushness on the other—usually both in the same instrument.

There are on the market many electric-organ hybrids—with the electric piano, with the performance synthesizer, with the accordion (the "bellows" acting as a volume control), and so on. None of these instruments is very worthwhile. Competition with the performance synthesizer has led to the introduction of all sorts of unusual and even bizarre timbres. Many of these are quire attractive, but in the constant succession of new brands and models an experimental stop can easily become obsolete before it has even reached the awareness of the musical public.

THE MELOTRON

The melotron takes the principle of the imitative stop to its logical conclusion. Each note on this instrument is produced by a short piece of tape with the sound of a flute (4'), violin (4'), and cello (16') recorded on it on three separate tracks which the player can select by means of a three-position switch. Notes below the range of the instruments recorded are produced through electronic manipulation of notes an octave higher. There is only one manual and no pedals. Only one timbre can be played at a time, though it is possible to switch from one to another in mid-note. Because of the limited length of the tapes, no single note can exceed eight seconds in duration (but the **orchestron**, a recently invented variant, can sustain tones indefinitely). Loudness is controlled by a knob above the keyboard.

Despite its almost obscenely imitative nature, melotron music still has an odd, electronic flavor to it both because the dynamics are unrelated to the original loudness of the instruments recorded and because the attacks are missing from the tapes, so that while a realistic legato is possible, detached notes have a purely electrical onset.

In addition to the three standard "stops," tapes can be purchased giving brass (8') or choral (8', on the sound [ɑ]) timbres, and various others are available from time to time.

THE PERFORMANCE SYNTHESIZER

Performance synthesizers differ from the studio-type synthesizer in that they are seldom modular, have all circuitry governed by switches and potentiometers rather than patch cords, are

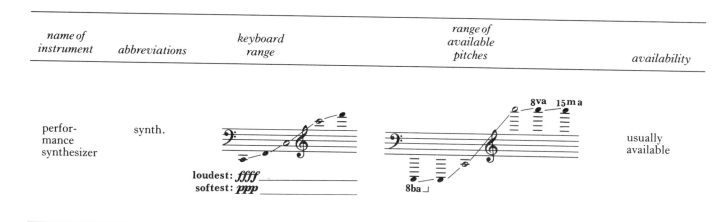

name of instrument	abbreviations	keyboard range	range of available pitches	availability

FIGURE 194. *The performance synthesizer—vital statistics.*

small enough to be portable, and are much more limited in the number and variety of sounds they can produce. Certain digital performance synthesizers rely so completely on stored "live" sounds that they are in effect digital melotrons. The superiority of such an instrument to the conventional melotron is obvious, and indeed "analog" melotrons seem to be on the way out. (Detailed information on synthesizer functions and terminology is given in Chapter X.)

A "typical" performance synthesizer (hard to define because this instrument is extremely variable) produces most of its sounds from a single oscillator and is thus monophonic: if two keys are depressed simultaneously only the lower will sound. There will be only one manual and no pedals.

The timbre of the oscillator is governed by a number of "stops" usually resembling electric-organ stops in both name and tone quality. It is important to remember that even at this far remove the model for, say, a "string" or "brass" stop is usually the equivalent *organ* timbre, not the orchestral one. There may be an "organ" stop giving a diapason-like tone. There will always be at least one 16′ and one 4′ stop; many synthesizers have 32′ and/or 2′ capacity, and on some the pitch of the whole instrument can be independently adjusted up or down by any amount.

In addition to these electric-organ–like features there are distinctive "synthesizer" characteristics:

1. One or more high- or low-pass filters with variable band-width.

2. Separate controls governing attack and decay times. The attack may be varied between near-instantaneity and a long, slow crescendo of some ten seconds; the decay starts immediately upon completion of the attack and is similarly variable. The decay may be switched off altogether, leaving a continuous tone like that of the organ. Any decay pattern will be cut off instantly by release of the key.

3. On some synthesizers it is possible to link the filter to the attack/decay mechanism, giving the rather silly "bwee" attack popularly associated with synthesizers.

4. Many have an auxiliary oscillator, with independent pitch and volume controls, used to create complex sounds or two-part parallel harmony. There may also be a ring-modulator.

5. There is usually a portamento control by means of which the speed of the oscillator's shift from one keyboard pitch to the next can be varied, enabling the production not only of portamento *per se* but also glissandos of any length and speed.

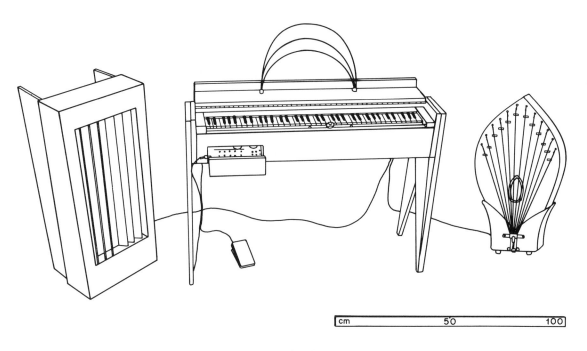

FIGURE 195. *Ondes martenot.*

6. Sequencers, often multistage and sometimes involving a digital memory, are increasingly to be seen.

Finally, a variety of additional devices may be present, most frequently including reverb, phaser, and/or vibrato units.

Increasing numbers of **polyphonic** synthesizers are now being made, capable of playing two, four, eight, ten, sixteen or more parts, depending on how many oscillators there are. Some have a separate oscillator for each key. Polyphonic synthesizers seldom have pitch variability (except, of course, that provided by the keyboard itself and by the octave transpositions of some of the stops) and have a limited range of preset timbres. In fact, were it not for the separate attack and decay controls most of these instruments would be indistinguishable from electric organs, since all the other "synthesizer" features are suppressed or severely restricted. Some instruments have both a single monophonic "stop" of independently variable pitch and timbre and several polyphonic ones that are more restricted.

The performance synthesizer is really a hybrid between the studio synthesizer and the electric organ. All degrees of hybridization exist, ranging from near-studio models to electric organs with added "synthesizer stop." There are also specialized performance synthesizers such as bass-range **pedal synthesizers** and **drum** and **guitar synthesizers** designed to be played by percussionists or guitarists rather than keyboard players. The **lyricon** is a newly invented woodwind synthesizer designed to be played by a clarinet or sax player, and the even newer **EVI** ("electronic valve instrument") is designed for brass players.

The digital synthesizer, still on the drawing board when the first draft of these pages was written, is now very much with us. The microelectronics revolution has thrown the electronic keyboard industry into a state of chaotic experiment and innovation from which it is unlikely to emerge as long as the size and cost of component circuits continue to decrease by—as

Scientific American puts it—"a factor of two every eighteen months." Not only performance synthesizers but electronic organs, pianos, and harpsichords (to say nothing of combination forms that may be as bizarrely hybrid as griffins) are constantly appearing with new sounds, new gadgets, new capabilities—and in more and more cheap and compact forms.

The new performance synthesizers may be wholly or partly digital (see Chapter X). Software for these instruments (meaning, in most cases, nothing more than a variety of pre-packaged timbres) relies on floppy discs, or tape cassettes like those used in home video games. Most have no interface capability at all. The main effect in any event has been to make available uncannily accurate imitations of massed strings, brass, etc., as well as sound effects such as surf, helicopters, and so on. Digital drum synthesizers come full circle in that realistic drum and cymbal (traps) sounds are obtainable from them.

The problem with all this attractive technology is that new models grow obsolete and die as fast as they are born. When work on this book was begun in 1976, one of the most popular polyphonic synthesizers was the Arp String Ensemble; but by the time we started production in 1983 Arp had gone out of business. Anyone unwise enough to have written idiomatically for that particular synthesizer five years ago has now got a problem—and this example could be multiplied endlessly. Performers may well revel in wave upon wave of new toys, but composers will just have to sit back and wait until the waters subside.

MUSICAL EXAMPLES

ELECTRIC ORGAN:
> Stockhausen, *Momente*
> T. Riley, *A Rainbow in Curved Air*
> Reich, *Four Organs*

MELOTRON (FROM THE POPULAR LITERATURE):
> The Beatles, "Strawberry Fields Forever"

PERFORMANCE SYNTHESIZER (FROM THE POPULAR LITERATURE):
> Herbie Hancock, "The Traitor"

THE ONDES MARTENOT

The ondes martenot is an electronic keyboard instrument of tremendous artistic sophistication and expressivity. In this respect it is light-years ahead of the other electronic keyboards, which whatever their other merits are utterly incapable of subtlety. The sound of the ondes—produced by the (electronic) heterodyning of two ultrasonic oscillators—is extremely rich and attractive, reminiscent of the violin or the voice and as expressive as either.

The instrument is monophonic (if several keys are depressed simultaneously only the lowest will sound), and the keyboard is normally played by the *right hand only*. The left hand works a set of controls (Fig. 196) governing timbre, dynamics, and articulation. The latter two functions are controlled by a large rectangular button that gives increased loudness in

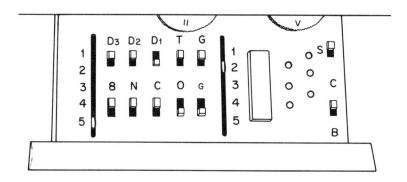

FIGURE 196. *Ondes martenot—controls for the left hand.*

response to increased pressure—thus, the ondes is touch-sensitive. In order for a sound to be produced a key must be depressed and at least minimal pressure applied to this expression button. While maintaining steady pressure on the button it is of course possible to differentiate everything between staccato and legato by means of the keys alone, but for accents, swells, and the numerous unnotated subtleties of dynamic expression this does not suffice, and normally the **expression button** will be struck separately for each detached note, acting in this regard rather like the tongue of a wind player. For the rare passage so disjunct that both hands are required on the keyboard, the ondes is equipped with a volume pedal like that of other electronic keyboards.

In order to keep such passages to a minimum, the left hand is provided with six **transposition buttons** immediately to the right of the expression button. From front to back these six buttons shift the pitch of each key by a quarter-step down, a quarter-step up, a half-step up, a whole step up, a major third up, and a perfect fifth up. They are additive in combination—like the valves of a brass instrument—so that the fifth and sixth buttons, for example, raise the keyboard pitch by a major seventh when used together.

The front two transposition buttons are of course used for the production of quarter-tones. The remaining buttons serve to extend the effective stretch of the right hand, enabling it to negotiate leaps of up to two-and-a-half octaves without shifting position. Since a single motion of the hand can be used in striking both the expression button and the transposition buttons, the latter are particularly suited to the production of grace notes, and that is indeed their main function in most musical contexts.

The microtonal resources of the ondes martenot are not restricted to the transposition buttons. Each right-hand key can be moved slightly to the left or right to produce vibrato and bent tones up to a quarter-tone above or below normal pitch; the keys are spring-loaded to return to their normal position when released. In addition there is a movable **ring** used for glissandos. The ring is attached to a thin rope running in front of the keyboard; moving the ring (into which the right index finger is inserted) winds and unwinds the rope inside the instrument, producing variations in pitch corresponding to the position of the ring. The notes of the equal-tempered scale are labeled just beneath the rope, so specific pitches can be accurately pinpointed with this mechanism. The transposition buttons can be used in conjunction with the ring.

A switch at the right front of the control drawer governs the choice of keyboard (position C, standing for the French "clavier") or ring (position B—French "bague"). Since the right

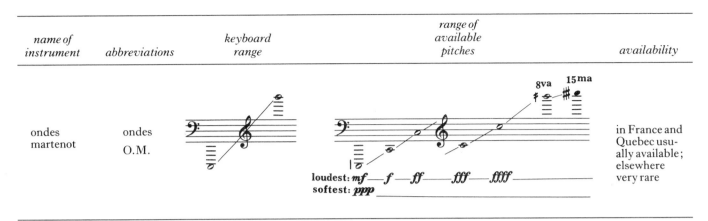

name of instrument	abbreviations	keyboard range	range of available pitches	availability
ondes martenot	ondes O.M.		loudest: *mf* — *f* — *ff* — *fff* — *ffff* softest: *ppp*	in France and Quebec usually available; elsewhere very rare

FIGURE 197. *The ondes martenot—vital statistics.*

hand is perfectly capable of playing the keyboard while the index finger is in the ring, the switch from keyboard to ring and back can be quite fluid, limited only by the left-hand excursion necessary to shift the B/C switch.

On the front of the instrument is a switch governing the register of the keyboard (and ring). The ondes' two registers, an octave apart, are simply called "high" and "low," and cannot be designated in feet because the two are considered equal in importance. All notes are written *at actual pitch* no matter which register is used. The "keyboard range" given in Figure 197 is that of the low register, chosen for notational convenience, though the high register is if anything more often used. There is no timbral difference between the registers. The transposition buttons can be used to extend the range upward beyond the top of the upper register to a surprising c ♯ 6 (Fig. 197). This top note requires the simultaneous use of five of the six buttons, making the manipulation of the expression button somewhat awkward. Many older ondes martenots still in use have only the two quarter-tone transposition buttons, and accordingly cannot ascend beyond b ♯ 4 (they can produce indeterminate pitches up to about e^5, however). On the other hand, these same old instruments have a very coarse tuning knob that can *lower* the range of the keyboard as a whole by any amount down to the subsonic range. This low-note capability has been abandoned because those notes are weak and unconvincing—they are not even very clearly pitched.

The ten switches to the left of the expression button control the timbre and distribution of the sound. Those marked "D_1," "D_2," and "D_3" ("diffuseur"—French for "loudspeaker") are speaker outputs. D_1 is the ordinary timbre of the instrument. D_2 engages a spring-based reverb unit built into the speaker. D_3 is an auxiliary output which may feed to a separate speaker placed at a distance (for antiphonal effects), or can be used to interface the ondes martenot with other electronic devices (see Chapter X). D_3 can also be used with either of two older speakers whose production has recently been discontinued. One is a plate-type reverb unit (former D_2), and the other (former D_3, illustrated) encloses the speaker cone in a complete sound-box with sympathetic strings running across it, front and back. Neither of these speakers can match D_1 (or the new D_2) in power, and the old D_3 is reportedly cranky and difficult to maintain. Its beautiful and distinctive timbre, resembling D_1 played into a piano interior, is well worth preserving, however, and old "palms" are likely to remain available for many years.

The remaining seven switches control the timbre of the output signal. They are designated as follows:

$$\begin{aligned}
\text{T} &= \text{tutti} \\
\text{G, g} &= \text{gambé ("stringy")} \\
\text{O} &= \text{ondes (basic timbre)} \\
\text{C} &= \text{creux ("hollow")} \\
\text{N} &= \text{nasillard ("nasal")} \\
\text{8} &= \text{octaviant (prominent second partial)}
\end{aligned}$$

The strength of the second partial in "8" is governed by a slider to the left of the switches. The other slider (on the right) controls the prominence of the "gambé" sound, but only when "g" (not "G") is engaged. In combination these seven "stops" interact in complex and subtle ways, so their detailed use is best left to the player; nonetheless the primary designations "hollow," "nasal," etc., can be given just as they might be on any other instrument.

On the far right side of the control drawer, just above the C/B switch, is one final switch, marked **S** (for "souffle"—breath). When engaged, this switch adds a component of white noise to the tone. The intensity of the white noise relative to the main pitch is governed (on a scale of I to V) by a dial placed just behind the switch. When S alone is engaged, without any of the other timbre switches, white noise alone is produced.

The other dial (behind T and G) controls the blend of speaker outputs when D_1 is used simultaneously with D_2 and/or D_3. The scale of this dial is marked 0 to V; in position 0 only D_1 will sound, while in position V only D_2 (and/or D_3) will be heard.

A final refinement is a **knee lever** below the keyboard, which when pushed to the side gives progressive removal of the sound's harmonic train. On the most recent model this has been replaced by a foot pedal of equivalent function.

MUSICAL EXAMPLES

ONDES MARTENOT:

> Messiaen, *Turangalîla symphonie*
> Varèse, *Ecuatorial*

IX

THE

STRINGS

GENERAL CONSIDERATIONS

The acoustics of a vibrating string were partially discussed in Chapter I. It should be further noted here that the pitch of a string is a function not only of its length but of its tension (direct relationship) and mass (inverse relationship).

ACOUSTICS

Even the most massive string presents so little surface to the air that its tone is extremely soft. In order to bring it up to audible levels the string is either amplified electronically, or, more usually, coupled acoustically to a thin, flat **soundboard**. In the harp the strings are in direct contact with the soundboard, but in virtually every other non-electric string instrument each string passes over a narrow **bridge** at one or both ends before its point of attachment. The string is pressed firmly against the bridge, which picks up the string's vibrations and transmits them to the soundboard on which it stands.

The soundboard has several hundred times the surface area of the strings to which it is coupled, and is thus capable of transmitting the sound to the air much more efficiently than the strings themselves. To achieve even more amplification the soundboard usually forms one wall of a complete wooden box, whose cavity defines an enclosed air space capable of vibrating in sympathy with the soundboard. The enclosed air communicates with the outside air via one or more holes in the box.

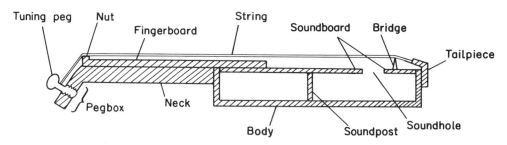

FIGURE 198. *Diagrammatic sagittal section of a string instrument with fingerboard.*

A string may be set vibrating by striking (cimbalom), plucking (guitar), or bowing (violin); only bowing provides a sustained sound. The tone quality may be varied by activating the string near its middle, at one end, or somewhere in between; this is discussed in more detail under the separate headings for individual instruments.

The strings of a string instrument may be made of metal, gut (made from the outer intestinal lining of sheep, not cats), or nylon. The mass of a low string is increased by a **winding** of fine wire around the central core.

The strings of each instrument are tuned to specific, standard pitches, but unorthodox tunings (called **scordatura**) can be used. Typically, scordatura for any string may run up to a major second above the standard tuning or a perfect fourth below it without seriously affecting the timbre of the instrument. This is least problematic and most effective with gut strings. Scordatura cannot be imposed more than a second above the standard tuning without risk of snapping the string, but a gut string may be dropped as much as an octave for special effects. Extreme lowering of this sort produces an increasingly muffled tone quality, decreased sustention of tone, and lowered dynamic range. A very slack string is quite likely to rattle against adjacent strings, the soundboard, or the fingerboard, especially at high dynamic levels. (The possibilities of scordatura are not reckoned in the ranges given for the instruments in the vital-statistics charts.)

PERFORMANCE CHARACTERISTICS

In the harp, the cimbalom, and the string keyboards there is a separate string for each note, but in the guitar and violin families the strings are few in number and run along a **fingerboard** at the far end of which the tuning pegs are located. The **pegboard** or **pegbox** is set at a slight angle to the fingerboard so that the strings are automatically pressed down against the far end (the **nut**) of the fingerboard (see Fig. 198). By pressing the string firmly against the fingerboard with a finger of the left hand, the player can shorten its vibrating length, thus raising its pitch by any desired amount.

The left thumb is usually held at the back of the instrument's neck and is thus not ordinarily involved in this **stopping** of the strings. For indicating fingerings the remaining fingers are numbered one to four, starting with the index. Figure 199 shows how, by using only the few available strings tuned in fourths or fifths, these four fingers can play all the notes in the range of several octaves without shifting the position of the hand along the neck. Note that on small (high-pitched) instruments such as the violin or mandolin the relationship between fingerings

	0	g^0	d^1	a^1	e^2
	0		Pitch of Open String		
Finger	1	ab^0, a^0	eb^1, e^1	bb^1, b^1	$f^2, f\#^2$
	2	a^0, bb^0, b^0	$e^1, f^1, f\#^1$	$b^1, c^2, c\#^2$	$gb^2, g^2, g\#^2$
	3	$b^0, c^1, c\#^1$	$gb^1, g^1, g\#^1$	$db^2, d^2, d\#^2$	$ab^2, a^2, a\#^2$
	4	$db^1, d^1, d\#^1$	$ab^1, a^1, a\#^1$	$eb^2, e^2, e\#^2$	$bb^2, b^2, b\#^2$

VIOLIN

	0	E_0	A_0	d^0	g^0	b^0	e^1
				Pitch of Open String			
Finger	1	F_0	Bb_0	eb^0	$g\#^0$	c^1	f^1
	2	$F\#_0$	B_0	e^0	a^0	$c\#^1$	$f\#^1$
	3	G_0	c^0	f^0	bb^0	d^1	g^1
	4	$G\#_0$	$c\#^0$	$f\#^0$	b^0	eb^1	$g\#^1$

GUITAR

FIGURE 199. *Fingerings for notes in first position on the violin and guitar.*

and notes is essentially diatonic, while on larger (lower) instruments such as the guitar or cello the relationship is chromatic.

Of course, the hand can be shifted up the neck, transposing the whole pattern upward by various intervals. Each discrete unit of distance shifted is numbered as a **position**, that closest to the nut being **first position**—shown in Figure 199. Shifting up a step would put the hand in **second position**, up two steps **third position**, and so on. The key to good string-writing is to keep the notes as much as possible "under the hand," i.e., within the range reachable by the fingers without shifting, and where shifts must be made to keep them generally small. Where large shifts must be made the music cannot move with quite as much agility, though so high are current playing standards, particularly on the violin, that feats of great virtuosity are frequently achieved.

The amount by which a string's sounding length must be shortened to produce a given rise in pitch is a function of the length of the string, and as one goes higher and higher on the string the distance between adjacent scale steps becomes shorter and shorter. This can be seen clearly in the arrangement of frets on the neck of a guitar. As an example consider a rise in pitch of one octave. This requires reducing the sounding length of the string by one-half, and accordingly the player's finger must be put down exactly in the middle of the string. To rise another octave half the *remaining* length must be removed, i.e., only *one-quarter* of the whole, and jumping yet a third octave would require shortening the string by only another eighth. Theoretically, then, one could produce infinitely high pitches by using increasingly small lengths of string; in practice, however, the limit is determined by the shortest length at which the string will vibrate.

The practical significance of all this is that the higher one goes on a string the greater the pitch interval across which one's fingers can reach without shifting. But since the individual pitches are closer together high on the string, it is more difficult to play strictly in tune up there; this is particularly a problem on the violin.

It will be noticed that, unlike wind instruments, strings do not make use of upper partials to extend the range but use the first partial exclusively. This makes their timbre much more uniform throughout their range than that of a wind instrument. Only the open-string notes stand out, for these are slightly more brilliant and robust than stopped notes. Isolated upper partials can be obtained from a string, but these are used strictly as a special timbral effect, not as a range extension. These **harmonics** are obtained by *lightly* touching a node of the appropriate partial. Harmonics of an open string are called **natural harmonics** and those produced from a stopped note are called **artificial**.

On instruments of the guitar or violin type, the position of the nodes can be described in terms of the pitch that would be produced if the string were stopped, rather than lightly touched, at that point. The relationship among fundamental pitch, node position, and harmonic produced is shown in Figure 200. Note that there are two graded series of nodes—one approaching the nut, the other approaching the bridge and corresponding in position to the spots where the same pitches would be produced by stopping as fundamentals. Between these the higher partials have a number of additional nodes which are, however, seldom used.

FIGURE 200. *Harmonics* theoretically *generatable from the note* c^0.

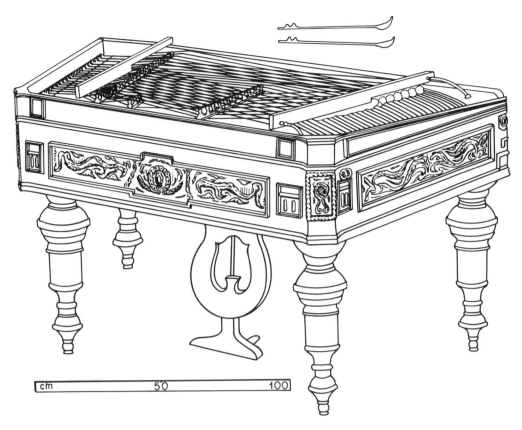

FIGURE 201. *The cimbalom and its beaters.*

THE CIMBALOM

The cimbalom is a Hungarian popular instrument that is extremely rare in North America and would find no place in this book had it not been used in two major works by Stravinsky and in a variety of other compositions, mostly Eastern European.

It belongs to the large group of instruments known as **zithers**, in which there are numerous strings running across a large soundboard and which have no neck—the piano and harpsichord are also zithers. Zithers in which the strings are struck with mallets are called **dulcimers**, and the cimbalom is a highly developed dulcimer with a large range and a sustain pedal.

Except for the optional low D_0 and C_0, every note on the cimbalom is at least triple-strung. The higher notes may be quadruple- or even quintuple-strung.

In order to preserve a compact layout and yet keep the pitches clearly enough separated for accurate play, the strings are run across a complex system of five bridges (Fig. 203). Some of the strings passing each bridge run over it in the normal way, while others pass *under* it and are thus inaccessible to the player at that point. By running alternate courses (a **course** is any set of strings running closely adjacent to each other and meant to be played simultaneously) over alternate bridges, the player is given access to neighboring pitches on alternate sides of the instrument. The reader can visualize how this works by interlacing the fingers of his/her hands and looking at them from above.

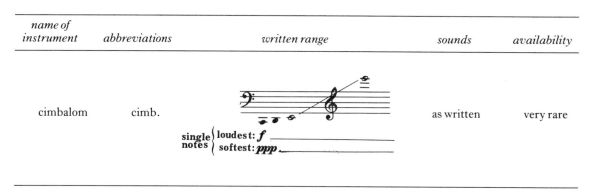

name of instrument	abbreviations	written range	sounds	availability
cimbalom	cimb.		as written	very rare

FIGURE 202. *The cimbalom—vital statistics.*

In the upper part of the instrument's range a single course may produce as many as three different notes by being strung over several bridges. For instance, the highest (rearmost) course runs from the hitchpins on the left up to the center-left bridge, producing a♭², then across to the center-right bridge, making b♭², and finally from there down to the tuning pins on the right, giving e³. The second course starts with a brief unused portion rising from the hitchpins to the left bridge; the course then passes to the left-center bridge, giving c³, but it is strung *beneath* this bridge and beneath the center-right bridge as well, so the portion between these bridges is also unused. The course then rises from the right-center bridge to the right one, giving e♭³, and from there is attached to the tuning pegs.

Except for the notes just mentioned and the note b♭², the strings are not actually held down by the bridge(s) they pass beneath; rather, they run freely through a hole in the bridge, which therefore does not demarcate their sounding length. The sixth course, for example, runs straight from the hitchpins up to the right bridge, bypassing the center-left bridge and giving only the single note e♭¹.

It will be noted that this method of stringing produces a rather disorderly arrangement of pitches, particularly in the upper part of the range.

The cimbalom is capable of agility equaling or surpassing that of any mallet instrument, to which it is similar in technique. It is played with a pair of special sticks that are somewhat shorter and lighter than rubber-series mallets. Each stick is held between the thumb and middle finger and steadied above by the index finger. The heads of the sticks are long and thin, enabling the player to strike two adjacent courses simultaneously. The interlacing of the courses results in different tones being adjacent at different places along each single course; thus, by striking in one or another place e♭¹ (for instance) can be made to sound simultaneously with e♭², d³, d♭¹, g², or b♭¹. Since there are two sticks, a large variety of three- and four-note chords are available by this means. Multi-mallet playing *may* be possible but does not appear to have been attempted. The traditional grip for cimbalom sticks plus the fact that the instrument is usually played sitting down may make multi-mallet playing difficult or unrewarding.

Both wound and unwound sticks are available, the wound ones being usual. An additional timbre variation can be achieved by striking very near the bridge. This produces a snarly, spitting tone rich in upper partials and is designated by the term **sul ponticello**, also used for other string instruments. This term may if necessary be abbreviated to "pont."; it is canceled by the expression "ord." or "nat."

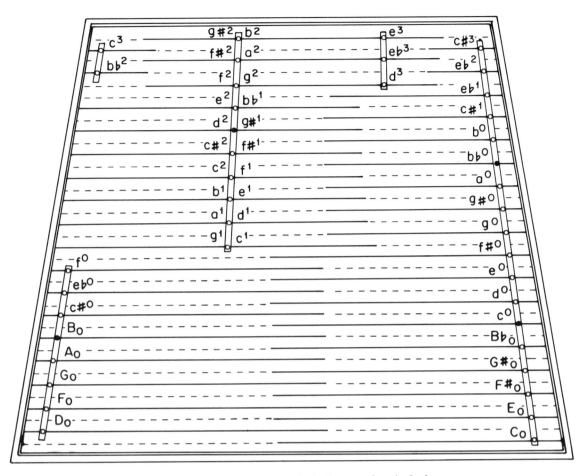

FIGURE 203. *Layout of pitches on the cimbalom.*

The tone of the cimbalom is bright and harpsichord-like, with a distinctive pinging attack. The sustaining power of the instrument is intermediate between marimba and harpsichord. The sustain pedal functions and is used identically to that of the vibraphone. The damper bars do not affect the notes e♭², g², a², b♭², b², c³, c♯³, and e♭³.

Cimbalom music may be notated on one or two staves, whichever is clearer and more convenient.

MUSICAL EXAMPLES

CIMBALOM:
  Stravinsky, *Renard*
  Boulez, *Eclat*

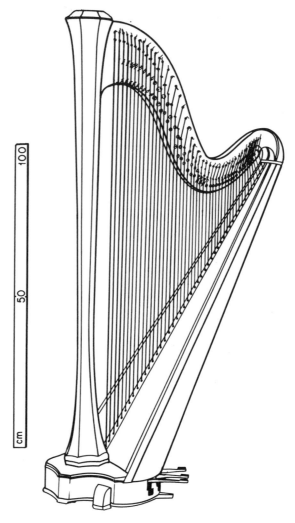

FIGURE 204. *The harp.*

THE HARP

The harp is unique in that it is strung perpendicular to the soundboard. As may well be imagined, this arrangement is very inefficient acoustically, and the harp is thus the softest of all the standard orchestral instruments. It compares well in volume with such instruments as the harpsichord, acoustic guitar, and bass flute, and must be scored carefully when combined with anything louder—even a light voice or a violin.

THE PEDALS

The strings of the harp are tuned diatonically, i.e., seven strings in each octave. Chromatic tones are obtained with a mechanical stopping action controlled by seven pedals (Fig. 205). Each pedal governs an entire pitch-class, so that the pedal furthest to the left controls all the D

MODERN INSTRUMENTS

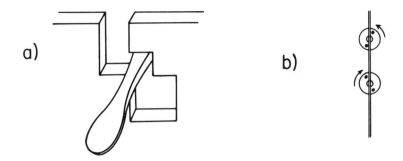

FIGURE 205. *Details of harp mechanism: (a) a pedal; (b) string with forks.*

strings, the second from the left all the C strings, and so on (from left to right the order is D, C, B, E, F, G, A). Each pedal moves in a stepped slot, the steps enabling the pedal to be left in any of three positions. In the uppermost position all notes in the pitch-class governed by the pedal will be flat, in the middle position they will be natural, and in the lower position they will be sharp.

Each string is provided with a pair of rotating disks (mounted on the "neck" at the top of the harp), each with two prongs. The string is tuned to the flatted note; when the pedal is depressed to the middle position the upper **fork** rotates just enough so that its prongs firmly stop the string, shortening its length and raising its pitch a half-step to the natural position. When the pedal is depressed further, the lower fork also rotates and the string is raised another half-step.

Note that all the strings are tuned to give flat notes: that is why the harp is often described as being tuned "to the key of C♭ major." This is just a technical detail, however; it is best to think of the harp as tuned to the "white key" notes of the keyboard, the pedals giving flat notes when raised and sharp ones when depressed. The low C_1 and D_1 strings are not provided with forks and are thus unaffected by the C and D pedals. On some harps the high g^4 is also unalterable. These strings can be tuned sharp or flat in advance, but if this is done they must of course remain that way throughout the piece. Though such special tunings of these strings are not at all unusual or unorthodox the player should be forewarned whenever they will be required.

The three left-hand pedals are operated by the left foot, the four right-hand ones by the right foot. The middle (E) pedal may if necessary be taken by the left foot, and that foot may even reach over to the F pedal in a pinch (though this is clumsy), while the right foot can make a similarly awkward reach over to the B pedal. In an emergency, one foot can shift two pedals simultaneously; the foot must be turned sideways to do this and the two pedals so moved must both end in the same position—both flat, both natural, or both sharp.

The spelling of all notes and chords in a harp part should reflect the way they are played, even when this results in illogical-looking formulations such as the following:

name of instrument	abbreviations	written range	sounds	availability
harp	hp.	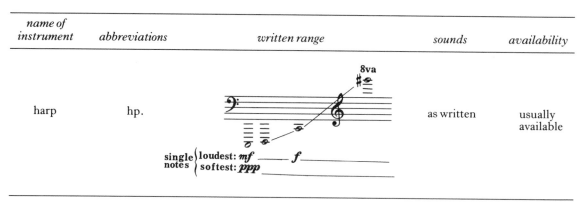	as written	usually available

FIGURE 206. *The harp—vital statistics.*

At the beginning of a piece and at each subsequent major change in the configuration of the pedals, the complete configuration should be given. The best way to do so is by means of a diagram like this:

This is a schematic representation of the actual positions of the pedals; pedals shown on the horizontal line are in the natural position, those above it are flat, and those below it are sharp. The pedals are indicated left to right just as they appear on the harp, and the vertical line divides the three left pedals from the four right ones. As given, then, our diagram indicates the disposition Db, C#, B#, Eb, Fb, G♮, A♮, the one needed to play the passage shown above. An older notation would be simply to list the pitches by name as we have just done, but the schematic diagram is much more compact and, for a harpist, more quickly and easily read.

Whenever an individual pedal or two must be shifted during the course of a piece, the new pitch should be given below the double staff, as below. When two pedals must be shifted simultaneously, the right-hand pedal should be notated above the left-hand one, as in the example.

The pedals can be operated swiftly and silently, but highly chromatic music is not idiomatic for the harp. A part like the one in Schoenberg's *Herzgewächse*, while it is possible to play and even musically effective, is not written so much for the harp as in spite of it.

It is not traditional on the harp to shift the pitch of a string while it is vibrating, but the effect has become quite common of late. It should be notated as a portamento, thus:

but it must be emphasized that the sound produced is not a portamento but a simple slur.

It is even possible to make a half-step trill with a pedal; such trills should be carefully distinguished from ordinary ones by some special notation, since harp trills are usually performed by alternately plucking adjacent strings. There is no standard notation, but the following will be instantly understood and is recommended:

FINGERING AND ARTICULATION

Harp music is notated on two staves, just like piano music, and, as with piano music, notes for the right hand are placed on the upper staff, notes for the left hand on the lower staff (with exceptions as noted on p. 259). The instrument rests on the player's right shoulder and the hands pluck the strings from opposite sides so that either hand can play in any part of the range at any time without getting tangled up with the other. Because the instrument is placed slightly to the right the two hands approach the strings at different angles, the left reaching straight forward while the right is bent fairly sharply at both elbow and wrist. This difference leads to differences in playing technique in certain situations. It is awkward for the right hand to reach the bass strings, and below G_0 it should be assigned nothing more elaborate than isolated single tones.

Traditionally, neither little finger is used because they are too short to reach the strings when the hands are held in their normal positions. But if the hand is twisted around a bit the little finger *can* be used, and harpists now increasingly are using the fifth fingers in certain passages that are simplified thereby. The use of these fingers will always remain exceptional and specialized, however, and composers, unless they are very familiar with the vagaries of harp fingering, should leave the details of their use up to the player. It is worth bearing in mind, however, that it is possible for one hand to play five notes at a time, provided they are all on adjacent strings.

The chart below shows average maximum two-finger stretches for the harp. Scales are fingered ascending (4)3214321 and descending (1)2341234 in either hand.

Stretch From Finger

To Finger	1	2	3
4	12th	8ve	7th
3	11th	7th	
2	9th		

The maximum duration of a harp tone is about half a second at the top of the range, three seconds in the middle, and six seconds at the bottom. All notes are normally allowed to ring on indefinitely, except when followed by a rest or in places where there is a strong drop in dynamic level, marked change of harmony, texture, etc., or (with the exception noted above) when the pitch of a string must be changed with its pedal. There is seldom much need for damping at the top of the harp's range, where the sound is always delightfully clear, crisp, and brittle, but in the middle and lower registers the overlapping resonances make for an unavoidable muddiness of rhythm and blurring of harmony unless there is frequent damping. All of this is normally left up to the harpist, who at the very least will "clear" the harp of unwanted bass resonances from time to time by damping all the lower strings simultaneously with the flat of one or both hands. Such clearing may be called for specifically by notating the symbol ⊕ above the staff at the appropriate spot; if any notes (in any part of the range) are to ring past that point, this must be explicitly indicated with ties or some other notation.

To produce a staccato, a harpist must damp each note separately, using the index finger of the right hand or the base of the left thumb, a technique known as **"sons étouffés"** (French: "damped tones"). A staccato so produced can be played as fast as sixteenth-notes at ♩ = 92 in either hand (a bit slower for leaping or chordal passages in the right hand).

As a special effect individual strings may be muted by pressing against the string near the neck with fingers of the left hand and playing only with the right, or they may be muffled completely by pressing with fingers, the flat of either hand, or a whole forearm near the middle of the strings. Neither technique is traditional, and both will have to be explained. The following notations are recommended: for muting, ; for muffling, .

Normally the harp is plucked with the tips of the fingers near the middle of the strings. This gives the full, gentle, but rather colorless tone characteristic of the harp. The tone may be modified in two ways:

1. By plucking near the soundboard. This makes the instrument sound much like a classical guitar; it is designated by the expression "près de la table" and is canceled by "pos. nat."

2. By plucking with the fingernails, which makes for a rather pingy attack and snarly tone quality. It is designated by the symbol ⌣ placed above the note. If a group of notes are affected, a half-bracket of the appropriate length should follow the symbol, and if a long passage is to be played thus it should be marked " ⌣ (sempre)" and canceled by "nat."

It is usual for all chords on the harp to be slightly arpeggiated, the standard arpeggiation symbol being used only where a more leisurely effect is intended. If a chord is to be sounded without any arpeggiation at all, a bracket should be placed by it, thus: .

The harp's glissando—actually a rip and so notated—is performed by drawing a finger across the row of strings. The thumb is normally used for descending glissandos, the index finger for ascending ones, but for a glissando with the fingernail this pattern is reversed. Multiple glissandos can be performed with up to three fingers of each hand ascending and four descending (with fingernails, one ascending and three descending). It is possible, though unorthodox, for a finger or thumb of the same hand to trail lightly behind the glissando, damping each note immediately as it is played. If this effect is desired it must be specified verbally.

A venerable technique, now a cliché, involves the maximum use of enharmonic unisons (e.g., E♭ + D♯) in the pedals so that the harp glissando gives out not a complete scale but a pentatonic scale, diminished seventh chord, or dominant ninth chord. Enharmonic unisons are also useful in reinforcing the power of single notes:

and for rapid repetitions of a note:

Tremolos are usually performed by this means, but a single-string tremolo is also possible (by shaking a finger back and forth across the string). This should be notated as a tremolo, while the two-string tremolo should be written as a trill.

SPECIAL EFFECTS

The **tuning key glissando** is an unorthodox effect that produces a genuine glissando rather than a rip. The harp's metal tuning key is held firmly against the string and slid along it; the relatively great mass and hardness of the tuning key effectively stops the string at whatever point it is applied, and sliding it produces a glissando, in the same way that bottleneck technique does on the guitar. Specific pitches can be obtained by marking the affected string with bits of masking tape. The lowest pitch that can be so produced on any string is a whole step above its open (flat) pitch, and to get even this the tuning key must be held in the left hand right up against the sharp fork, for only on that side of the harp is that portion of the string available. The tuning key can also be used to produce microtones, otherwise available only through scordatura.

Application of the tuning key shortens the decay time of a string by a factor of one-half, so glissandos must be rapid. The highest pitch obtainable (and it can be gotten even from the lowest bass strings) is about g^4. Nonetheless, the highest string on which a glissando is practicable is the g^3 string. Above this the tuning key may still be placed against the middle of the string (though it cannot effectively be slid), and when so placed it produces a note an octave higher than usual, thus extending the harp's compass up to a surprising g^5. Notes so produced decay extremely rapidly.

A tuning key glissando can be produced on two adjacent strings at once by sticking the key between them at an angle, so that both are stopped. The key can also be rattled back and forth between a pair of strings, which will alternate stopped and open pitches. This should be notated as a trill between the two open strings, with the stopped pitches given as small note-heads in parentheses and an instruction such as "trill with tuning key."

Note that the action of applying the tuning key to a string effectively stops that string to the appropriate pitch; the stopping forks, which lie above the tuning key, will have no effect as long as the key is in contact with the string. If, on the other hand, the tuning key is applied to the string below the point where it is plucked, the forks will retain their usual power, but the sound will be a faint, disembodied ppp, since the key will separate the vibrations of the string from the soundboard.

Foremost and most traditional of special effects on the harp are **harmonics**. In ordinary practice these are produced one-handed, on the second partial only, and notated with the usual small circle above the *fundamental* pitch (not the pitch of the harmonic), thus sounding an octave higher than written. In the right hand the string is plucked by the thumb while the side of the index finger touches the node; in the left hand the string is also usually plucked by the thumb, but the node is touched by the opposite edge of the hand itself. While only one harmonic at a time is possible for the right hand, up to three at a time (within the range of a sixth) or even, uncomfortably, four (on adjacent strings) can be produced with the left.

The sound of the harmonics is softer than usual, distant, ethereal, and impersonal. Harmonics are weak and somewhat tricky on the wound bass strings (G_0 and lower), and on the lowest two strings they can only be produced two-handed (i.e., touching the node with one hand while plucking with the other)—a technique so unorthodox it must be explained to the player. The highest possible harmonic is d^4, played on the d^3 string.

The third, fourth, and fifth partials can be obtained as harmonics (up to the f^2, c^1, and c^0 strings, respectively), but they are not traditional and must be explained. The following notation is recommended:

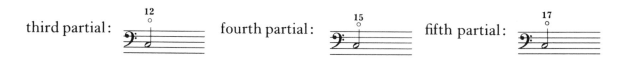

These higher partials are even more denatured in tone than the second, and in the bottom octave all fifth-partial harmonics must be taken two-handed. The third and fifth partials can be used as transposing devices to produce pitches that would otherwise be obtainable only by moving the pedals. It is possible by this means, for instance, to produce a chromatic scale without moving the pedals, or an "impossible" chromatic tone cluster.

Other special effects on the harp include:

1. Plucking a string in the plane of the harp so that (in *forte*) it rattles against its neighbors. This can be done up to $c\sharp^1$ and is notated thus:

2. A very similar effect can be produced up to g^2 by holding a pedal halfway between two positions so that the affected strings rattle against the prongs of the half-engaged fork. Recommended notation:

3. Yet another buzz can be produced by holding the tuning key (less reliably, a fingernail) right next to the string.

4. Plucking the harp with a guitar pick or other plectrum.

5. Striking the strings with a snare stick or knitting needle or flicking them with a fingernail. With the stick or knitting needle a trill can be produced by inserting the stick between

two strings and rattling it back and forth. Tone clusters up to a tenth in width can be produced by slapping the strings (not in the top octave) with the flat of the hand, and an octave-wide tone cluster glissando can be created by sliding the hand across the strings.

6. A whistling or tearing sound produced by sliding the fingers or fingernails along the length of one of the wound bass strings.

7. A vibrato produced by pressing repeatedly against the top of the string with the left thumb while playing normally with the right hand. In the two octaves above c^1 bent tones of as much as a half-step can be produced by this means.

8. Preparing the harp by threading it with a ribbon or strip of paper (see the Crumb example cited below).

9. Tapping the soundboard with fingertips, knuckles, fingernails, or a marimba stick; striking with the tuning key (or other object) the metal plate that covers the right side of the neck; or rattling about in the soundhole or along the row of tuning pegs.

10. Making a subdued racket with the pedals. This last is more a theatrical than a musical effect, since it makes the player look like the recipient of a double hotfoot.

MUSICAL EXAMPLES

HARP:

Falla, *Psyché*
Chavez, *Sinfonia de Antigona*
Varèse, *Offrandes*
Berio, *Sequenza II*
Crumb, *Ancient Voices of Children*

ACOUSTIC GUITARS

The term "plucked strings" does not usually include either the harp or the harpsichord, but is used only with reference to those plucked-string instruments that also have a distinct neck and fingerboard.

Of the many varieties in general use in North America all but the banjo, ukulele, and mandolin are called guitars. The large and varied guitar family can be divided into acoustic versus electric types.

The three important varieties of acoustic guitar are very similar in construction and technique; they have differing timbres, however, and are used for differing musical purposes. All have six courses, tuned as given in Figure 208, and a fingerboard inlaid with raised **frets** that aid the player in producing stopped notes securely and accurately, and give these notes much of the resonant fullness of open-string notes.

The **classical guitar** has nylon strings, giving it a delicate, refined tone. The body intersects the neck at the twelfth fret. The term "guitar," unmodified, refers to this instrument in any classical-music context.

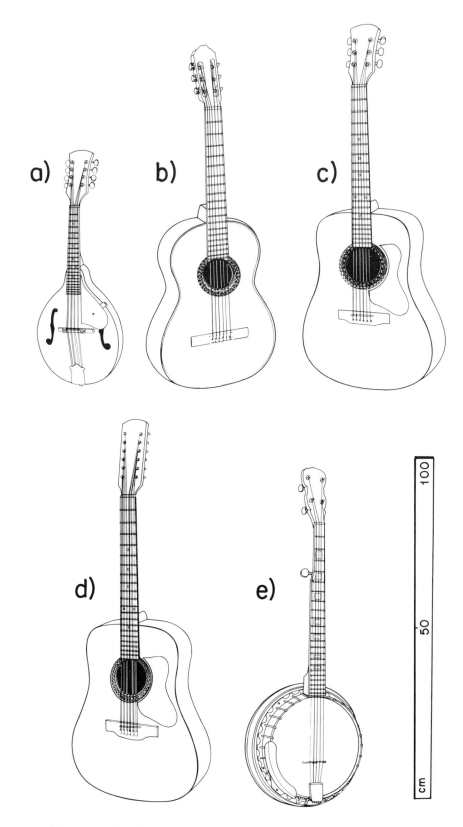

FIGURE 207. *The acoustic guitar and related instruments: (a) mandolin; (b) classical guitar; (c) folk guitar; (d) twelve-string guitar; (e) five-string banjo.*

name of instrument	abbreviations	written range	tuning	sounds	availability
guitar	guit.	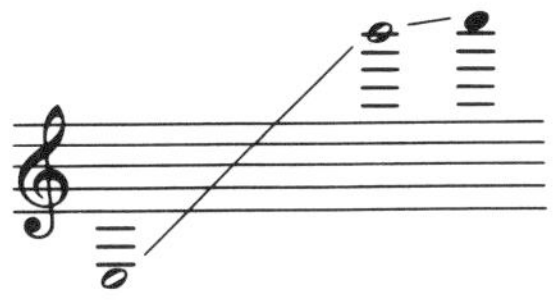		1 octave lower	classical: common folk: ubiquitous 12-string: common

single notes { loudest: *mf* _____ softest: *ppp* _____

FIGURE 208. *The guitar—vital statistics.*

The **folk guitar** has wire strings, with a narrower neck and shorter body than the classical guitar. The body intersects the neck at the fourteenth fret. This is the standard "acoustic guitar" of popular music, and it has a brighter and more penetrating tone than the classical guitar.*

The **twelve-string guitar**, as its name implies, has geminated strings, the lower three courses being tuned in octaves $(8' + 4')$, the upper three as unisons. The two strings in each course lie very close together and are plucked simultaneously. The strings are of metal; the large body intersects the broad neck at the twelfth fret. The instrument is designed to give a particularly full, rich sound and is typically used to provide chordal accompaniments in popular music.

Guitars of all sorts are held on the player's lap (or hung from a strap around the neck) with the instrument's neck to the left. In this playing posture the lowest string is in the highest position, i.e., closest to the player's head.

RIGHT HAND TECHNIQUE

The classical guitar is plucked with the nails of the first four fingers of the right hand. Scalewise passages are usually played with alternating index and middle fingers or, in more rapid passages, index and ring fingers. For very rapid repeated notes (even tremolos) the index, middle, and ring fingers are all used in rapid alternation. In polyphonic playing the different fingers will usually pluck different strings, the thumb always being lowest whenever it is used and the ring finger highest.

Two types of stroke are used. The **rest stroke**, in which the finger after plucking the string comes to rest against the neighboring string (the next higher string for the thumb, the next lower for the other fingers), is capable of considerably more speed and power than the **free stroke**, in which it does not. The free stroke is, however, essential for polyphonic playing and all other situations where adjacent strings must sound at the same time. In poly-

* The **dobro** is a folk guitar with a partly metallic body and a correspondingly twangy, metallic sound.

phonic playing (up to three fully independent parts or four partly independent ones) the fingers never cross each other.

Any chord of more than four notes, as well as any other perceived by the guitarist as essentially homophonic in function, will be strummed (i.e., very rapidly arpeggiated) with the thumb. For the maximum possible force the same thing can be done by flicking across the strings with the backs of the nails of all the other fingers together; this last is a specifically flamenco technique, and must be specified. Degrees of arpeggiation are indicated on the guitar as follows:

$$\text{[}\ \genfrac{}{}{0pt}{}{}{}\quad = \text{non arpeggiato}$$

$$\uparrow\ \text{or}\ \downarrow\quad = \text{rapid strum in the indicated direction}$$

$$\updownarrow\ \text{or}\ \updownarrow\quad = \text{leisurely arpeggio in the indicated direction}$$

In the slow arpeggio each note is plucked separately by a different finger. In the absence of any special indication the guitarist will play a mixture of strummed and unarpeggiated chords.

Tremolo chords can be played by strumming rapidly back and forth across the strings with all the fingers in a loose rotary motion. This too is a special flamenco technique called

rasgueado and such tremolos should not only be notated as such, e.g., $\dag$, but should bear the cautionary indication "rasgueado" as well, especially since guitarists tend to read such

notations as wide trills (the so-called "fingered tremolo"), thus for  playing

. Composers should not perpetuate this confusion of notation and terminology, but should write a tremolo where a tremolo is desired and a trill* where a trill is desired.

A greater variety of right-hand techniques are used on the folk and twelve-string guitars than on the classical guitar. There is no reason that any of the techniques described below could not be used on classical guitar, but they are non-traditional there and must be specifically requested when desired. Folk and twelve-string guitars may be played in the standard classical manner just described; or they may be plucked with the flesh of the fingers (which gives a more blurred, indistinct attack); or with a single **flat pick** held between the thumb and index finger and giving a powerful, strong tone though capable of playing only single melodic lines and strummed chords; or with a **thumb pick** attached directly to the thumb and used in the same way, with or without the aid of the other fingers, which may or may not be supplied with **finger picks**. Thumb and finger picks are essentially large, powerful artificial fingernails and are designed to give the loudest and strongest possible tone to this soft and delicate instrument.

* Those unwilling to untraditionally use the notation ♩ for trills more than a second in width should use the older ‖ which, however clumsy and illogical it may be, has at least the virtues of unambiguity and traditional approval.

The basic left-hand fingering pattern for the guitar is shown in Figure 199. Average maximum stretches along one string are as follows:

Stretch From Finger

From the first fret			1	2	3
	To Finger	4	perf. 4th	m3^d	M2nd
		3	M3^d	m3^d	
		2	m3^d		

Stretch From Finger

From the seventh fret			1	2	3
	To Finger	4	perf. 5th	perf. 4th	m3^d
		3	aug. 4th	m3^d	
		2	perf. 4th		

Stretch From Finger

From the twelfth fret			1	2	3
	To Finger	4	m6th	perf. 4th	perf. 4th
		3	perf. 5th	M3^d	
		2	aug. 4th		

To find the maximum interval stretch on two different strings, simply add together the single-string maximum and the interval between the open strings. It must be remembered that these stretches are maximums and hence rather awkward. Normally there will be only one fret between adjacent fingers in any fingering combination—anything more is considered an **extension**.

In gauging the possibility or difficulty of a given chord the following two rules should also be taken into account: (1) a higher finger (in number) will never stop a lower fret than a lower finger (e.g., the middle finger will never stop a lower fret than the index finger does); and (2) when two or more fingers stop strings at the same fret, the lowest-numbered finger will take the lowest string, and so on up in order. There are a few exceptions to this rule, but they are not important for the composer to know.

It is possible to lay the index or little finger flat across several strings at once, stopping all of them; this is called a **barre**. Any number of strings may be involved, but all must be adjacent. A **full barre** of four or more strings must include the first (e^1) string. A **partial**

barre of two or three strings entails the complete muffling of the next higher string above the barre unless another finger stops that string at the same or a higher fret. Needless to say, any strings stopped above the barred fret will not be affected by the barre. In folk and twelve-string guitar-playing a barre-like configuration is used to prevent unwanted strings from vibrating: the tip of a finger stops a string in the normal way while damping one or two higher strings. This allows the strumming of chords such as this: [chord notation] whose notes would otherwise have to be plucked separately. There is no reason this technique could not be used on classical guitar—it is just not traditional.

A full barre cannot be made above the point where the neck meets the body of the instrument. Partial barres can be made up to the highest complete fret (the last fret or two frequently serve only the e^1 string).

On folk guitar the left thumb is frequently used to stop the E_0 string, thus enabling the player to stop up to five of the instrument's six strings simultaneously with different fingers. When the thumb is used it must be no more than one fret above or below the index finger. The necks of classical and twelve-string guitars are too wide for this technique to be of any real use.

A totally unorthodox technique for use in compositional emergencies involves bringing the whole hand around the neck so that (as on the cello) the thumb can stop a string—enabling huge stretches (an augmented fourth from the first fret, a minor sixth from the seventh fret) and sonorities such as [notation] which would otherwise be impossible to produce. If used, this technique requires about a half-second rest for the player to get the hand in position. But one should ask if the whole thing is really necessary; the example given above, for instance, could be played in the ordinary way just by transposing it down a whole step and using the open A_0 string.

NOTATION

Where necessary, guitar fingerings can be indicated as follows: the fret number is designated with a Roman numeral, fingers are numbered with Arabic numerals (0 signifies an open string), and circled Arabic numerals denote the strings (① being the highest string and ⑥ the lowest). Fingering should be indicated only to clarify a tricky or deceptive passage or where a special tonal effect is desired, e.g.: [notation] as opposed to [notation] . It will seldom be necessary to specify more than one of the three variables, since when one is known the other two usually follow logically.

Popular music uses a variety of special tablature notations for the guitar, of which the commonest is a stylized picture of the neck of the instrument with dots indicating the placement of the fingers: [diagram] .

The lowest string is at the left, and the heavy line across the top represents the nut. The curved line connecting two dots denotes a barre; the "x" indicates that the A_0 string is not to

be played. This particular configuration produces an F-major chord:  . Diagrams
of this type are used in popular-music **lead sheets**, in which the melody is written out in full
while the (guitar) harmony is simply indicated with chord names written above the staff.
Fingering diagrams are in the main only given for unusual chords or for unorthodox voicings
of ordinary chords.

The fingers of the right hand are indicated by the letters p (or ♀), i, m, and a, respectively. These notations will seldom be needed by composers, save for an occasional p to clarify
accentuation and phrasing.

ARTICULATION

It is traditional for guitarists to leave all notes ringing indefinitely unless they are marked
staccato or followed by a rest—or until either the string or finger involved is needed for another note. The decay times of the open strings of the guitar vary from four seconds for the
highest string to eight seconds for the lowest. Stopped tones last from two seconds (on the e^1
string) to six seconds (on the E_0 string). Very high notes may ring for as little as one and a half
seconds.

All this must be borne in mind by anyone writing for the guitar, for guitarists use the
overlapping sounds of individual notes much as a pianist uses the sustain pedal, to make the
sound fuller and to bring out the harmonic rhythm; but they do so automatically, *according
to what the composer has required of the left hand.* If the music is written in such a way that
frequent awkward or *harmonically* pointless changes in the configuration of the left hand are
required, it will sound hesitant and gawky no matter what the player does. Furthermore, one
of the foundations of guitar technique is the use of overlapping single notes to make counterpoint out of what is notated as a disjunct monophonic line; the slight differences in timbre of
the different strings aid in this. This is even the case in flat-pick folk style, though admittedly
not as much as in other idioms. As an example of this technique, here is a standard pattern
used in popular music, as it might be notated (here with fingerings added):

and as it would sound:

The effect is of two quite distinct outer parts plus two somewhat less well-differentiated inner voices.

Articulation on the guitar is normally detached and tenuto, with slurs frequently used simply as phrasing indications, but the instrument is capable of a true legato—within certain limitations. An upward slur is produced by fingering a note, plucking it, and then stopping the already vibrating string with another finger at a higher fret; for a downward slur the string is stopped at both pitches simultaneously (only the higher will sound), then the higher finger is lifted. If the fingers are moved in the normal way in slurring, there will be a drop of about two dynamic levels between the note plucked and the note slurred; to keep up the volume the player makes subtle use of the techniques of **hammering-on** and **pulling-off**. In the upward slur the second note is stopped with a sudden, percussive hammering motion, while in the downward slur the upper finger delicately and glancingly plucks the string as it is lifted off. By these means a legato passage can be continued indefinitely in *pp* or *ppp*—but all slurs can contain only four different pitches (five, if an open string is used) since all notes must be produced on one string and without moving the hand along the neck. The only exception to this is the *glissando* (actually a rip, and so notated) produced by sliding a single finger along the string without lifting it. Minor-second slurs produced by this means are notated as portamentos (); other slurs are notated in the normal fashion, and composers are urged to use this notation only where a true legato is desired.

Trills on the guitar are normally produced legato and should therefore be short except in *pp* or *ppp*. Long trills will wherever possible be played on two strings by alternate plucking, as will trills greater than a second in width. If there is any doubt, the way in which a trill is to be played can be specified by indicating the string(s) on which its notes are to be played:

Hammering-on and pulling-off can be used as special effects in their own right, and when so used are produced more forthrightly than when they are used as aids in the production of legato. Hammering-on can be done no louder than *piano* unless the string involved is already vibrating. The sound, as might be expected, is delicate and percussive. The notation

is recommended but will have to be explained. Pulling-off can be performed as loudly as

mezzo-forte and always has a pingy, *sul ponticello* timbre (see below). The notation, may have to be explained.

Staccato notes can only be played slowly on the guitar since each note must be damped separately, either by hand or by slightly lifting the left-hand finger if the note is a stopped one.

Notes may be muffled ( ) with the base of the right hand as they are plucked (this effect is rather inappropriately called "pizzicato") or damped out entirely with unused left- or right-hand fingers laid loosely on the strings.

The vertical Bartók-pizzicato of the violin family is possible on the guitar: the string, held between two fingers, is pulled vertically and allowed to snap back against the finger-board. The standard notation for this is $\uparrow$, but as it is not a common technique on the guitar it may have to be explained.

The tuning of the guitar gives it a marked propensity for the key of E, in which the open strings can be used to great advantage to make the sound of the instrument particularly full and rich. While music in other keys—or in no key—can be quite effectively played on the guitar as it stands, folk and twelve-string players frequently make use of scordatura to bring this richness to other keys; a common "D-tuning," for instance, is D_0, A_0, d^0, $f\sharp^0$, a^0, d^1. These players also make frequent use of a device called a **capo** (short for "capotasto"—Italian for "master fret") which when strapped around the guitar neck (this can be done in a few seconds) acts as an artificial nut, clamping the strings down firmly at that fret and effectively transposing them all upward. Of interest to composers is the fact that these "artificial" open strings sound more thin, ringing, and brilliant—mandolin-like—than the unaltered ones, and more so the higher the fret at which the capo is attached. This can be heard clearly at the beginning of the Beatles' "Here Comes the Sun," where the acoustic guitar with capo at the fifth fret stands out prominently. There is no reason that a capo could not be used on a classical guitar to produce a similar effect—it is just not traditional. Capos are seldom used above the seventh fret.

The detached, precise tone of the guitar demands transparent textures and well-spaced harmonies, particularly in the bass. A little experimentation with simple chord fingerings will show that the guitar's tuning system is engineered to provide such spacings easily and naturally.

When melodic lines move by leap, especially in broken chords, the guitarist will endeavor to find a single *chord* fingering—or as few such as possible—covering the necessary notes so that the left hand can be held steady while the right hand plucks various strings. This is especially important in polyphonic writing, which the player's left hand will treat as a simple progression of chords while the polyphony is articulated by the right hand. Composers should therefore keep to a minimum the number of times in which awkward shifts are required of the left hand. The best progressions allow the player to keep one or more fingers stationary, shifting the other fingers around them.

The tone of the guitar can be altered by varying the place at which the strings are plucked. Plucking near the bridge (*sul ponticello*—usually written out in full, but if necessary abbreviated "pont.") produces a pingy, snarling sound reminiscent of the harpsichord. Plucking near or over the fingerboard (**sul tasto** or **sulla tastiera**) yields a particularly thick, smooth tone. Playing exactly in the center of the string (*molto sul tasto*) makes the sound extremely sweet and pure.

Natural harmonics on the guitar are available from the second to ninth partials inclusive. Partials above the sixth are tricky; they require a second or two of preparation time and must be plucked *sul ponticello*. They are most easily produced on the e^1 string. Harmonics up to the sixth can be barred. Natural harmonics can if necessary be produced by the right hand alone on the second, third, and fourth partials, and two simultaneous harmonics can be played thus if they are made at the same node on adjacent strings.

Artificial harmonics are produced on the guitar by stopping with the left hand while plucking and touching the node with the right. They are normally produced singly and only at the second partial, but the third and fourth partials can be used, and two-note artificial-harmonic chords can be played provided the notes are on adjacent strings and their nodes are right next to each other. Artificial harmonics must be played slowly and are difficult or impossible to produce from notes stopped above the twelfth fret. Artificial and natural harmonics may be combined with each other and with regular notes in chords.

The sound of harmonics is delicate and impersonal, but the full complement of plucked attack noise gives them a somewhat sforzando character at all dynamic levels. They are also softer than regular notes. All these characteristics become more marked the higher the partial used. Natural harmonics should be notated like any other guitar notes (i.e., an octave above their actual pitch) with the usual little circle above the note to indicate that it is a harmonic. The exact choice of node and so on should be left to the player. Artificial harmonics should be notated on long stems with the stopped pitch indicated as a small note-head in parentheses, thus: . This is also a useful notation when natural harmonics at the unusual seventh or ninth partials are to be played: . As this example shows, natural harmonics extend well above the highest stopped note. The following very high notes are available (actual pitches):

Artificial harmonics cannot be played this high.

Six high quarter-tones are available as seventh-partial harmonics, but microtones are available in other ways as well. The most conventional of these is the use of **bent tones** produced by pushing or pulling the string sideways with the stopping finger, raising the pitch by as much as a semitone. The next higher string will be prevented from vibrating unless it too is "warped" in this way. Bent tones are most easily produced on the folk guitar, on which the low E_0 string can be warped up as much as a whole step. The guitar's **vibrato** is produced similarly, but by a *lengthwise* shaking of the left hand. It is normally used only in slow-moving, emotional passages and should probably be specified where desired. Neither bent tones nor vibrato can be produced on an open string.

SPECIAL EFFECTS

Bent tones are normally used to inflect a pitch that starts or ends normally. Solid microtones are best obtained either by scordatura (remember, though, that each string tuned to a microtone will give microtones *from every fret*) or by **bottleneck technique**. For bottleneck playing the guitarist wears a rigid metal, glass, or plastic tube around the left index finger or little finger. This tube stops the strings *without depressing them against the frets*, thus enabling easy production of true glissandos and microtones of all sorts. The tube can, of course, only be used in barres, but some flexibility is given by the other left-hand fingers, which are used normally. Bottleneck playing is a folk-guitar technique that is perfectly usable on the other types of guitar. It must be specified whenever it is desired.

A very recent innovation of much promise is the development of guitars with interchangeable fingerboards. These fingerboards have various arrangements of frets so that different scales and temperaments can be produced. Among the various fingerboards being manufactured are those with twenty-four equal-tempered notes to the octave, twelve-note just intonation, twelve-note mean-tone tuning, and Harry Partch's nineteen-note justly intoned scale.

Special effects on the guitar are largely limited to tapping the instrument with the side of the thumb, the knuckles, or the back of a fingernail (using the tip would damage the instrument's finish) of the right hand. Most traditional of these effects is the **tambour**, in which the guitarist taps either the bridge or the bottom ends of the strings with the side of the thumb. This produces a drum-like percussive sound in which the pitches of the strings will be clearly heard. Composers should indicate whether they wish the strings to be damped out by the left hand and whether it is the strings or the bridge that is to be tapped. The strings will also vibrate (though very weakly) when the body of the instrument is tapped. The *tambour* can be as loud as *forte*, other tapped sounds no more than *mezzo-forte*.

A tearing or squawking sound can be made by running the fingers or fingernails lengthwise along any of the three wound bass strings. A bit of this occurs inadvertently during hand shifts in normal play.

For the "snare-drum effect" the player twists two strings together with the left hand so that they buzz delicately against each other when plucked. The sound is more reminiscent of a clock-coil or sansa than of a snare drum, particularly in *sul ponticello*. The pitches of the strings will be about a half-step higher than one would expect them to be. Once the strings are twisted together the fingers not involved in the twisting can be used to stop higher pitches in this sound (one finger can stop both pitches simultaneously), and the twisting finger itself can be slid toward the nut as far as the third fret—below the third fret this effect cannot be produced.

Soft, bell-like sounds of indeterminate pitch can be obtained by plucking the strings behind the nut. Finally, the instrument can be **bowed** with a cello or contrabass bow. Since the bridge is flat rather than curved only the outer (e^1 and E_0) strings can be bowed separately.

MUSICAL EXAMPLES

CLASSICAL GUITAR:

Britten, *Nocturnal*
Webern, *Drei Lieder*, Op. 18
Boulez, *Le Marteau sans maître*
Henze, *El Cimarrón*

name of instrument	abbreviations	written range	tuning	sounds	availability
mandolin	mand.	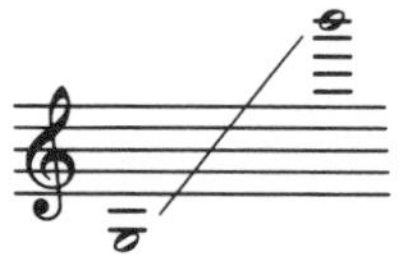		as written	usually available

single notes { loudest: *f* ——— softest: *pp* ———

FIGURE 209. *The mandolin—vital statistics.*

FOLK GUITAR: (FROM THE POPULAR LITERATURE):
    Paul Simon, "Peace like a River" (two tracks)
    Joni Mitchell, "Little Green" (capo 3d fret)
    The Incredible String Band, "Astral Plane Theme"

TWELVE-STRING GUITAR (FROM THE POPULAR LITERATURE):
    Leo Kottke, "Easter and the Sargasso Sea"
    Jefferson Airplane, "Embryonic Journey"

THE MANDOLIN

The mandolin is not, strictly speaking, a member of the guitar family, but it is used in both classical and popular music as a "soprano guitar."* It is placed *above* the guitar in scores where both appear. It has eight metal strings in four unison courses, tuned exactly like a violin; in fact, most mandolin players are also violinists. The lowest pair of strings is wound. The distance from nut to bridge on the mandolin is a couple of centimeters longer than on the violin, but the basic fingering pattern (Fig. 199) and maximum stretches (Fig. 220) are identical to those on the violin. Chord fingering and other left-hand techniques such as barre, hammering-on, and pulling-off are as for the guitar. Folk mandolinists use the left thumb to stop the g^0 strings (only in chords, not for individual notes); they also, though rarely, use a capo. Bent tones, while possible on the mandolin, are hard to do and very small in width. Bottleneck technique is possible on the mandolin, but unorthodox. The snare-drum effect is impossible.

    The double metal strings of the mandolin are calculated to give the loudest, most brilliant, and longest-lasting sound possible from this small instrument, and the mandolin is accordingly slightly louder than the guitar, with a very bright, cheerful, tinkling tone. But the sustaining power of the mandolin is very weak, not exceeding three seconds even for the open strings, so the instrument is much more monophonic—or, rather, homophonic, since chords can be played—than the guitar. An appearance of polyphony can be produced by writing in the broken style described above for the guitar.

    * Much more like a "soprano guitar" in actual construction is the **ukulele**, a tiny instrument with only twelve frets and four strings, tuned g^0, c^1, e^1, a^1. This instrument is now treated as little more than a toy, and indeed its small range, softness, lack of sustaining power, and unimpressive plunky timbre render it of doubtful value musically.

name of instrument	abbreviation	written range	tuning	sounds	availability
banjo	ban. bjo.	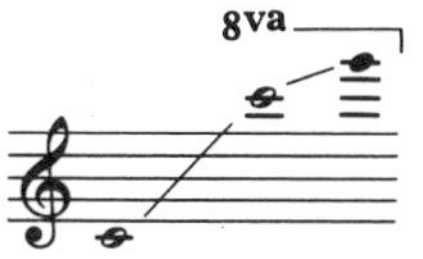 single notes loudest: *ff* softest: *pp(p)*		1 octave lower	usually available

FIGURE 210. *The banjo—vital statistics.*

Both folk and classical mandolinists play with flat pick only; all notes are played with the pick, and chords are rapidly strummed.

To make up for the lack of sustaining power, classical mandolinists in particular make extensive and systematic use of tremolo to produce the effect of a sustained sound for long notes and legato passages. All tremolos must be notated by the composer (the notation is ♪, as for other instruments).

Harmonics, both natural and artificial, are produced as on the violin; *sul tasto* and *sul ponticello* effects can be produced but have not such strikingly different tone qualities as they do on the guitar or violin.

MUSICAL EXAMPLES

MANDOLIN:

> Schoenberg, *Variations for Orchestra*, Op. 31
> Stravinsky, *Agon*
> Crumb, *Ancient Voices of Children*

THE BANJO

The banjo is the loudest non-electric string instrument; it is equivalent in power to the clarinet or even the saxophone. In full chords the *fortissimo* can approach *fff*; contrast this to the guitar and mandolin!

The body of a banjo is a structurally complete frame-drum (q.v.), complete with tension screws (called "brackets"). The neck sticks out sideways from the frame and the bridge is placed on the parchment or plastic **head**, which acts as a very efficient soundboard. This, combined with the instrument's thin, high-tension strings (only the lowest is wound), gives the banjo its ability to play loudly.

Banjos are made in three slightly different varieties. Of these by far the most common and versatile is the **five-string banjo**. The fifth string is a high-pitched **drone**, not intended to be stopped; nonetheless it runs along the fretboard like the other strings and can be easily stopped at any fret. It is attached, with its own nut, at the fifth fret, and its open pitch is in most tunings the same as the pitch given by the first string when stopped at that fret.

The **plectrum banjo** and **tenor banjo** have no drone string. The plectrum banjo is otherwise identical to the five-string instrument, but the tenor banjo is more distinctive in that it has a slightly shorter neck, very high string tension, and a low **action** (i.e., the strings lie very close to the fretboard). These features give it a marginally more brilliant, ringing, and wiry tone than the five-string or plectrum banjos, and make the *ppp* (easily obtained on the other instruments) virtually impossible.

The tuning given in Figure 210 is the most common of many five-string banjo tunings. Other common tunings are "open G tuning" (written g^2, d^1, g^1, b^1, d^2) and "open D tuning" (written a^2, d^1, $f\sharp^1$, a^1, d^2). A useful variant of open G tuning raises the first string to written e^2, allowing the instrument to be played with guitar fingerings. Tenor banjos are frequently tuned to written c^1, g^1, d^2, a^2, which allows easy doubling by a violist or cellist.

Banjos almost always have twenty-two frets. The upward extension tones in Figure 210 are made available by tuning the first string higher than written d^2, or the fifth string higher than written g^2. Maximum left-hand stretches are charted below.

From the first fret

Stretch From Finger

To Finger	1	2	3
4	aug. 4th	M3d	M2nd
3	perf. 4th	m3d	
2	M3d		

From the seventh fret

Stretch From Finger

To Finger	1	2	3
4	m6th	perf. 4th	m3d
3	aug. 4th	m3d	
2	perf. 4th		

From the twelfth fret

Stretch From Finger

To Finger	1	2	3
4	M7th	m6th	M3d
3	perf. 5th	M3d	
2	aug. 4th		

The banjo's left-hand technique (though not the fingerings) is identical to that of the folk guitar, and most banjoists play the guitar as well. Because the tenor banjo's strings lie so close to the fingerboard, it can produce bent tones only by pushing, not pulling.

On some banjos the tuning pegs for the second and third strings are adapted for use as **Scruggs pegs**. With these, a flick of the wrist automatically raises the pitch of a string by a pre-set amount, adjustable between a half-step and a whole step. When the peg is rotated back the string returns to its original pitch. This enables nearly instantaneous retuning (compare "open G" and "open D" tunings), and the pegs can also be used to produce elegant and powerful bent tones on the open strings.

The banjo's acoustically sensitive head and shallow body make for explosive attacks and quick decays: five seconds for the open strings, two to four for stopped notes, decreasing to less than half a second at the end of the fingerboard. As a result, banjo stylings feature simple homophony or broken-style pseudo-polyphony, the latter being especially characteristic of the bluegrass music with which the five-string banjo is closely associated. The open strings are used as much as possible, which is why they are so often tuned to the notes of a major or minor triad. The banjo is picked with the first three fingers of the right hand, using either the fingertips, fingernails, or (loudest and most common) finger picks. Sometimes the remaining fingers are used to pluck a four- or five-note chord without strumming (as they often are on the guitar), but usually they are held lightly against the drum head to steady the hand. The right fifth finger can also be used to **mute** the instrument by laying it along the bridge. Chords are often strummed with a flick of the index finger or of all the fingers together (except the thumb), but this is not possible with finger picks. Tremolos are played with alternating fingers, as on the guitar.

Banjo players make frequent use of the capo. When the capo is used the fifth string may be retuned or it may be hitched around a screw the player has set into the fingerboard expressly for this purpose. There also exist special fifth-string capos which affect only that string.

Natural harmonics are available up to the fifth partial on all banjos. Five-string and plectrum banjos can reach the eighth partial, but only in the "bridge series" of harmonics (Fig. 200). Artificial harmonics are produced and notated as on the guitar.

In slow passages or on individual long notes it is possible to produce a **vibrato** by varying the pressure exerted on the drum head by the right fourth and fifth fingers, but vibrato is normally produced guitar-fashion. Resting the right wrist on the drum head will partially damp the resonances of notes played immediately before—the effect is like that produced by releasing the sustain pedal of the piano while continuing to hold down the keys. Pressing heavily on the head with the right wrist causes the pitch to bend downward about an eighth of a step. One can tap the head directly, producing a bongo-like sound.

As another special effect, very high notes of indeterminate pitch can be obtained by plucking the strings behind the bridge. Plucking behind the nut is not very effective.

MUSICAL EXAMPLES

BANJO:
Thomson, *The Plow That Broke the Plains*
Crumb, *Night of the Four Moons*

(FROM THE POPULAR LITERATURE):
Earl Scruggs, "Randy Lynn Rag"

ELECTRIC GUITARS

In an electric guitar, in place of the soundhole are one or more **magnetic pickups** that respond to the position of the instrument's metal strings, converting their motion into a changing electric voltage which is then amplified and sent to the loudspeaker, whence it emerges as sound. The body of the instrument is in most cases completely functionless acoustically, and hence may, and does, take on just about any shape, some of which are quite bizarre. The body may intersect the neck at the fourteenth fret or be cut away around the neck so that the left hand may reach even the last fret with complete freedom.

Anyone who plays electric guitar can play acoustic guitar and vice versa, for the basic technique of playing the electric instrument is identical to that of the folk guitar (described above). The only important exception is in the matter of bent tones, which can be very widely inflected on the electric guitar: up to a minor third above the "rest" pitch even at the first fret, and up to a perfect fourth from the fifth and higher frets. The player can control the pitch quite accurately and even produce bent-tone melodies by varying the pull on a single note:

In extremely bent tones the string is pulled or pushed so far that all the other strings in that direction get bunched together and are unusable as long as the bending persists.

Many electric guitars are provided with a **wiggle bar** in the form of a long handle operated by the right hand, which when pushed bends the pitch of all the strings uniformly. Some of these can bend the pitch either way, but others can only bend it downward. In any event, there is virtually no limit on the degree of downward bending—though if the pitch is bent more than about an octave down the strings become too loose to vibrate effectively, so the note decays very rapidly.

All good electric guitars have two or—less frequently—three separate pickups placed in slightly different positions. A pickup near the bridge will "hear" the strings in that position, where the upper partials are strongest, whereas one near the base of the neck will "hear" the strings where these partials are weakest; the former yields a harsh, jangling timbre, while the latter yields a smooth, almost muffled tone. The pickups are accordingly designated "treble" and "bass" (and "middle"). Mounted on the body of the guitar are separate tone controls (like the treble/bass knobs on an amplifier) for each pickup and a master volume-control knob for the whole instrument. Most two-pickup instruments have a separate volume knob for each pickup. The amplifier into which the instrument is plugged of course has its own tone and volume controls. Without recourse to the volume controls the player can differentiate only three dynamic levels on the instrument's strings.

The coarse and powerful tone of the electric guitar is utterly unlike that of the acoustic guitar—even its harmonics can cut like daggers (cf. Buffalo Springfield's "For What It's Worth"). This timbre demands the very thinnest of scoring, and the electric guitar seldom plays chords. Its genius is for melody, pure and simple; and with its great sustaining power and capacity for bent tones it is far superior to the acoustic guitar in this regard.

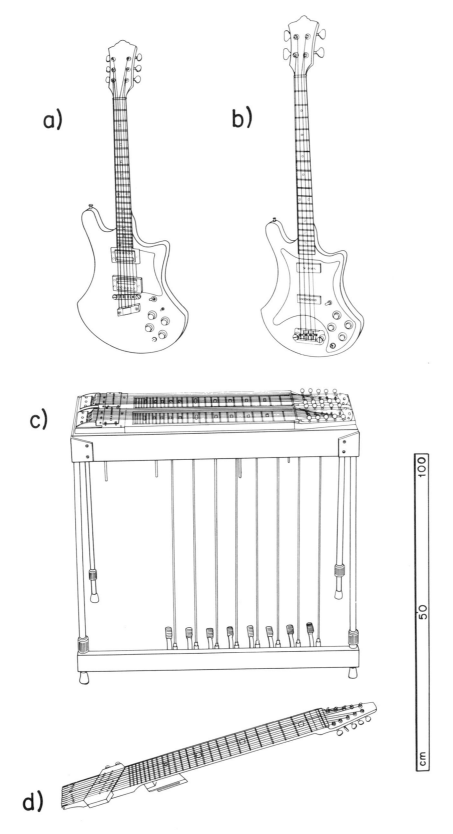

FIGURE 211. *Electric guitars: (a) electric guitar; (b) electric bass guitar; (c) pedal steel guitar; (d) Chapman stick.*

name of instrument	abbreviations	written range		tuning	sounds	availability
electric guitar	el. guit. elec. guit.	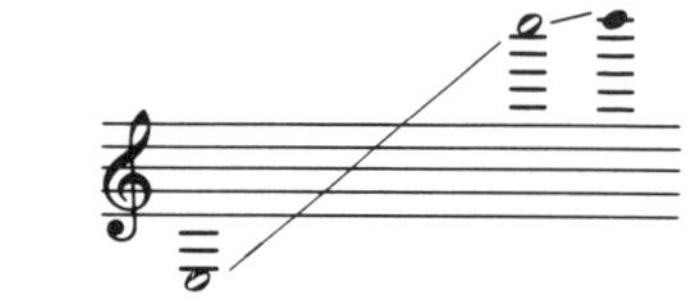 *(written range notation)* loudest: *ffff* softest: *ppp*		*(tuning notation)*	1 octave lower	ubiquitous
electric bass guitar	el. bs. elec. bs.	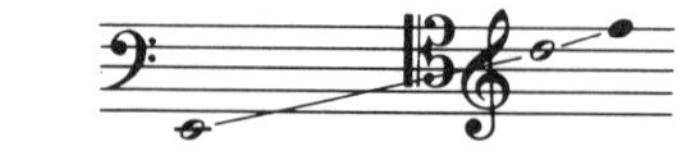 *(written range notation)* loudest: *ffff* softest: *ppp*		*(tuning notation)*	1 octave lower	common

FIGURE 212. *Electric guitars—vital statistics.*

An **amplified acoustic guitar**, whether the amplification be via air mike, contact mike, or even magnetic pickup (see Chapter X), does *not* sound like an electric guitar but retains its own nature, albeit somewhat distorted. Electric and amplified acoustic guitars are used side by side in popular music, and the distinction must be borne in mind when studying this repertoire. Also, some electric guitars (mostly those with hollow, wooden bodies) can be made to sound "merely" amplified by proper adjustment of the various tone controls, and under such conditions may well play full chords or even polyphony. **Electric twelve-string guitars** and **electric mandolins** are invariably of this type; indeed, many of these are so well designed acoustically that they may satisfactorily be played without amplification.

A number of electronic tone-modifying devices are traditionally used with the electric guitar. These include fuzz tone, reverb, vibrato, wah-wah pedal, and, recently, phaser as well. All these are discussed in detail in the next chapter. Fuzz tone in particular is so closely associated with the electric guitar that many people think of it as the instrument's normal timbre. In addition to its unique timbre, however, the fuzz box gives the player access to a variety of feedback phenomena that are otherwise available only in *ffff* with an overdriven amplifier. Most important is the ability to *sustain any note indefinitely*, merely by adjusting the controls properly and "aiming" the guitar at the loudspeaker so that its output will reinforce the vibration of the strings. **Feedback** pure and simple involves a similar reinforcement of one or more upper partials—often producing a multiphonic-like effect—of any vibrating string. If the guitar is brought close enough to the speaker these squealing or squawking sounds start even if no string has been plucked. The pitch(es) of feedback are dependent on the acoustics of the strings, speaker, and hall as well as on the electronic vagaries of the amplifier and/or fuzz box, and hence cannot be predicted or specified in detail. Once produced, however, the sound can be controlled by varying the orientation and position of the guitar relative to the speaker.

Even without the fuzz box the electric guitar's great powers of sustention allow the right hand to leave off plucking the strings and come to the aid of the left hand in legato passages. Thus, the right index finger can make a full barre *above* the left hand, acting as an "instant capo." Alternatively, the right hand can finger notes near the end of the fingerboard while the left hand stays near the nut, the two together producing a highly jagged but perfectly legato line.

As a special effect the flat pick may be scraped along any of the wound bass strings, producing a rasping glissando howl of indefinite pitch. Another special effect unique to the electric guitar is the use of the flat pick to cut off each note almost immediately after it has been plucked by one of the fingers holding the pick. This sound is not merely staccato but has a choked, chirping offset as the pick briefly articulates a high harmonic while cutting off the note.

The recently invented **E-bow** is an electronic device, held in the right hand, that sets up a magnetic potential opposite to that of the pickup. When it is held just above a string the combined effect causes the string to vibrate. The E-bow, as its name implies, is thus really an electronic bow, enabling the production of very smooth attacks and indefinitely sustained tones with full control of crescendo and diminuendo.

The **electric bass guitar** (or "electric bass") is essentially identical to the electric guitar in its performance techniques, and almost everyone who plays this instrument can also play guitar.

Electric basses have two pickups with the usual separate tone controls. The neck is slightly longer than that of the guitar and the instrument is accordingly slightly less agile. Maximum stretches are as follows:

From the first fret

	Stretch From Finger		
To Finger	1	2	3
4	M3^d	m3^d	M2nd
3	M3^d	M2nd	
2	m3^d		

From the seventh fret

	Stretch From Finger		
To Finger	1	2	3
4	aug. 4th	M3^d	M2nd
3	perf. 4th	M2nd	
2	M3^d		

	Stretch From Finger		
	1	2	3
To Finger 4	m6th	M3d	m3d
To Finger 3	aug. 4th	m3d	
To Finger 2	perf. 4th		

From the twelfth fret

Bent tones up to a major second in width can be produced (up to a major third on the low E_1 string). Harmonics can be produced up to the eighth partial except on the E_1 string, on which only the second, third, and fourth partials are available.

Some electric basses are fretless and can therefore produce true glissandos and microtones without bending, scordatura, or bottlenecking. Their tone resembles an amplified pizzicato contrabass.

Increasingly to be seen are **double-neck electric guitars**, instruments with two parallel necks attached to one body—usually either six-string and twelve-string, or six-string and electric bass. The two necks have completely independent pickups and knobs for tone and volume.

Finally, the rare **electric sitar** should be mentioned. This is an ordinary electric guitar—with the usual complement of six strings, twenty-one frets, and two pickups—in which the strings pass over a flat metal block that acts as a bray when they are plucked, reproducing to an uncanny degree the characteristic nasal twang of the Indian sitar. The electric sitar also has thirteen **sympathetic strings** (with their own pickup) designed to enhance the sitar effect.

MUSICAL EXAMPLES
(FROM THE POPULAR LITERATURE)

ELECTRIC GUITAR AND ELECTRIC BASS GUITAR:
Neil Young, "Cowgirl in the Sand"
The Beatles, "I Want You (She's So Heavy)"
Jefferson Airplane, "The House at Pooneil Corners"

name of instrument	abbreviations	written range	sounds	availability
pedal steel guitar	ped. st. p.s.g.	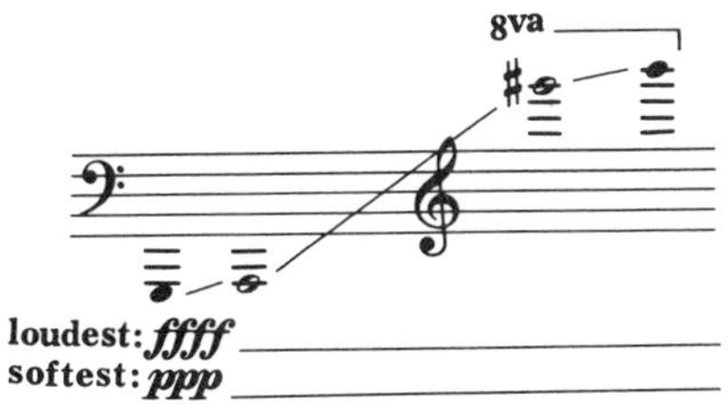 *(music notation, written range; loudest: ffff, softest: ppp)*	as written	rare

FIGURE 213. *The pedal steel guitar—vital statistics.*

THE PEDAL STEEL GUITAR

The pedal steel guitar is a guitar in name only, for it resembles its parent instrument neither in construction nor performance. It is, nonetheless, a descendant of the acoustic guitar, and the relationship between these instruments ought to be understood.

An extreme form of bottleneck technique on the acoustic guitar involves laying the instrument flat on a table or on the player's lap, tuning it to some "open" (i.e., triadic) tuning, and sliding a heavy bar along the neck to differentiate pitches; this technique is called "Hawaiian guitar," and at one time there were guitars specially made to play in this style (cf. Weill's *Dreigroschenoper*). An electric Hawaiian guitar—often with built-in legs—is called a "steel guitar," and when this instrument was given a greatly augmented number of strings plus a set of pedals for changing their pitches (harp fashion) it became the modern pedal steel guitar, or "pedal steel" for short.

The pedal steel exists in two forms. One has two parallel necks each provided with (typically) ten strings, eight pedals for the left foot, and two levers, operated by the right knee, that also function as pedals. The other type has only one neck (usually with twelve strings), seven pedals for the left foot, two right-knee levers, and three left-knee levers.

Each string on a pedal steel guitar runs over and is attached to its own rotatable metal **bridge finger**. The bridge fingers are attached to the pedals, and when a pedal is depressed it rotates all the bridge fingers to which it is attached, lowering or raising the pitches of the strings by changing their tension. Note that this is not the same mechanism as the stopping action of harp pedals; if a pedal is depressed while a string it governs is vibrating there will be a short but clear glissando to the new pitch.

The connection of strings to pedals is almost infinitely changeable and adjustable by the player (though this is time-consuming and requires that the instrument be turned upside down). On any good pedal steel each string can be attached to *at least* three pedals simultaneously—two to raise the pitch and one to lower it. Each pedal can also be attached to several strings at once, with the same or different effect on the pitch of each. The extent to which depressing the pedal changes the pitch is freely variable from nearly nothing up to a minor

| | L. Knee | | | L. Foot | | | | | | | R. Knee | |
	←	↑	→	1	2	3	4	5	6	7	←	→
e^1											$-d^1$	
g^1					$+g\#^1$							
f^1												
d^1								$-c\#^1$			$+e\flat^1$	$-c^1$
$b\flat^0$	$-a^0$			$+c^1$		$-a^0$			$+c^1$			
g^0		$-f\#^0$			$+g\#^0$				$+a^0$			
f^0			$-e\flat^0$				$-e^0$					
d^0						$-c^0$		$-c\#^0$			$+e\flat^0$	
$B\flat_0$				$+c^0$								
G_0		$-F\#_0$							$+B_0$			
$E\flat_0$							$+E_0$		$-D_0$			
$B\flat_1$							$+C_0$		$-G_1$			

FIGURE 214. *Single-neck pedal steel guitar—standard copedant (B♭6 universal tuning).*

third in either or both directions. On double-neck instruments the first three (leftmost) pedals affect the rear neck and the other five affect the front one; the knee levers can be attached to either neck.

Diagrams showing the effect of each pedal are called **copedants**. These are laid out like the ones in Figures 214 and 215. The pedals are simply numbered across the top from left to right and the knee levers are designated by arrows showing the direction in which the knee must move to activate the lever. The far left column of a copedant gives the tunings of all the strings, listed from back to front. The tuning of the pedal steel guitar is as variable as that of other popular string instruments, but there are standard tunings—and, for that matter, standard copedants—for pedal steels of both the double- and single-necked varieties. These standard tunings and copedants are given in Figures 214 and 215.

In addition to the wide variety of pitches available from the open strings and from the pedals in whatever configuration, flexibility and inflection are available from the player's left hand, which stops the strings with the heavy, bullet-shaped metal bar or "steel" that gives the instrument its name and is used much like a bottleneck on a guitar. The bar is held, rounded end forward, between the thumb and middle finger, with the index finger lying on top of it to steady it. It is long enough to cover nine strings but can cover fewer by being placed so that it only partially overlaps the set of strings, sticking out beyond them on one side or the other. The bar is normally removed from the strings only when the open strings are used; otherwise it is slid from one position to the next. The bar is really a movable nut; its weight and hardness allow it to stop the string much more cleanly than the player's fingers could, and the result is that stopped notes sound just like open notes. The instrument has the bright, full, "open-string" sound throughout its range, which—again, because of the precision of the bar's action—is huge: a full three octaves above the pitches of the open strings.

Note that the bar is essentially a transposing device: the pattern of available pitches is established by the tuning of the strings, modifiable by the use of the pedals, and that pattern—including any pedal modifications—is transposed upward by the use of the bar.

		L. Foot								R. Knee	
		1	2	3	4	5	6	7	8	←	→
Rear Neck (E9 Tuning)	f#^{1}										
	e♭^{1}									−d^1	
	g#^{1}		+a^1								
	e^1			+f#^{1}							
	b^0	+c#^{1}		+c#^{1}							
	g#^{0}		+a^0								
	f#^{0}										
	e^0									−e♭^{0}	
	d^0										
	B$_0$	+c#^{0}									
Front Neck (C6 Tuning)	g^1					+g#^{1}					
	e^1						+f^1				
	c^1							+d^1			−b^0
	a^0				+b^0			+b^0			
	g^0					−f#^{0}					
	e^0						−e♭^{0}				
	c^0								+c#^{0}		
	A$_0$				+B$_0$						
	F$_0$					+F#$_0$			−E$_0$		
	C$_0$					+D$_0$			−A$_1$		

FIGURE 215. *Double-neck pedal steel guitar—standard copedants.*

The pedal steel guitar is provided with a fretboard, but the strings lie well above it and do not come in contact with it even under the weight of the bar: it serves only as a visual aid to the correct placement of the bar. Microtones, glissandos, bent tones, and other pitch inflections are all child's play with the bar; indeed, systematic use of glissando and portamento from both bar and pedals is a major feature of pedal-steel style. The bar is also used to produce a vibrato that is typically applied on a note-by-note basis, blooming separately on each pitch after it has been struck.

Special bars are used to modify the timbre. A bar with one flat side is used to get an electric sitar sound (use of the flat side produces this effect; when the bar is turned over it produces a normal sound), and a wooden bar is used to produce a very realistic imitation of a banjo.

The player's right hand is held parallel to the strings, which are plucked by thumb and finger picks. Usually only the first three fingers of the right hand are used, but all five may be.

The decay time of the open strings is about seven seconds, decreasing to five seconds at two octaves above open pitch, and to three seconds at the top of the range. Notes are normally allowed to ring for their full duration, but unwanted resonances are damped from time to time (generally corresponding to changes in the harmony) by the side of the right hand and little finger. Muting or total muffling can also be produced by this means. Placing the bar on the strings always produces some sound; sliding it along otherwise silent strings produces a *pp* glissando. When other notes are ringing this sound is masked, but occasionally the player will want to damp the strings while moving the bar.

Sul tasto and *sul ponticello* can be differentiated on the pedal steel guitar, but there is only one magnetic pickup.

As mentioned above, the pedals are all operated by the left foot. The first three pedals are the most important, and these (or any other group of three) can be manipulated by rocking or rotating the foot without moving the heel. Two adjacent pedals can be depressed simultaneously with the toe, and up to four at once can be depressed by turning the foot sideways. The pedals and knee levers are all spring-loaded, that is, they automatically return to their normal position as soon as they are released by the foot or knee. Half-pedaling—to get a pitch change less than that for which the pedal is set up—is tricky but is in fact used from time to time. The pedal action is unfortunately rather noisy, so frequent rapid pedaling should be avoided.

In actual play it is frequently desired to change all the strings *except* the one(s) affected by a given pedal, and this is accomplished by moving the bar so that it contradicts the change imposed by the pedal. Players are actually able to hold the pitch of a string smoothly constant while it is being "fought over" by bar and pedal this way.

The right foot controls a **volume pedal**, as well as on/off buttons and control pedals for any electronic tone modifiers (vibrato, fuzz tone, etc.) that are being used in conjunction with the pedal steel. In traditional pedal steel style the volume pedal is used with great subtlety not only to control the overall dynamic level but to produce crescendos and swells on individual notes and even to inflect the attack. The volume pedal also allows notes to be sustained at a steady loudness for most of their decay time. Sometimes the player will drop the volume pedal to zero to eliminate the weak glissando produced by sliding the bar along silent strings. The fingers can produce a range of three dynamic levels without moving the volume pedal.

Natural harmonics on the pedal steel guitar are articulated with the side of the left little finger (i.e., with the bar raised off the strings). Artificial harmonics are articulated with the right ring fingertip or knuckle or with the side of the hand and are plucked with one of the other right-hand fingers. The seventh partial is the highest obtainable. Harmonics cannot be produced higher than the instrument can otherwise go (b^4).

The pedal steel guitar is fertile ground for special tonal effects, so far largely unexploited.

1. The wound bass strings (usually the lowest four on each neck) may be scraped lengthwise.

2. The instrument may be "prepared," piano fashion. Remember: the bar cannot slide past an obstruction; if the preparation is left of the bar it will probably have no effect on the sound; and the portion of the string immediately above the pickup must vibrate if anything at all is to be heard.

3. Various amplified tapping and scratching sounds can be made with the fingers on the pickup itself.

4. Unamplified (*ppp*) sounds can be obtained by plucking to the left of the bar.

5. The bar may be placed diagonally across the strings. This reduces the number of strings it can cover, as follows:

Number of Frets Between
Front and Back of Tilted Bar

Position of Rear of Bar		9	8	7	6	5	4	3	2	1
	3d fret								7	9
	6th fret							3	8	9
	9th fret						3	6	9	9
	12th fret						5	7	9	9
	15th fret					4	7	8	9	9
	18th fret				5	6	7	9	9	9
	21st fret	5	5	6	7	7	8	9	9	9

Maximum Number of Strings
Covered

6. The strings may all be bowed together.

7. Finally, the strings may be struck with a snare stick, triangle beater, or other light, thin stick. When the strings are struck right above the pickup this effect is straightforward, but when struck elsewhere one must take into account the fact that the stick stops the string, bar-fashion, for the moment that the two are in contact, and that there will therefore be a squeaky little "grace note" before each note so struck, its pitch varying inversely with the distance of the striking point from the pickup. The duration of the "grace note" can be varied by varying the mode of attack and will even be the only note produced if the stick is kept in contact with the string after each note struck.

MUSICAL EXAMPLES
(FROM THE POPULAR LITERATURE)

PEDAL STEEL GUITAR:
  The Grateful Dead, "The Dire Wolf"
  Crosby, Stills, Nash, and Young, "Teach Your Children"

THE CHAPMAN STICK

The Chapman stick ("stick," for short) is a very recent outgrowth of the electric guitar. Available only since 1974, it has been steadily gaining in popularity and is likely to be a permanent addition to our instrumental resources. The designation "very rare" for this instrument must be considered only temporary.

All notes on the stick are produced by hammering-on. Since the instrument is not plucked, the right hand is free to articulate pitches just as the left hand does. The two hands approach the fingerboard ("touchboard," in Chapman's terminology) from opposite sides— as on a woodwind—so the fingering pattern for the two is identical, rather than opposite as on a keyboard. The maximum stretches are the same as those of the electric bass.

As Figure 216 shows, the stick has ten strings divided into treble ("melody") and bass divisions of five strings each. The lowest string in each division is in the middle of the finger-

name of instrument	abbreviations	written range	tuning	sounds	availability
Chapman stick	stick	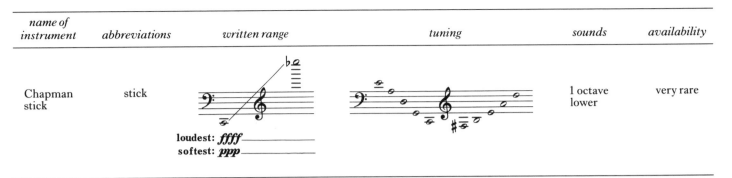		1 octave lower	very rare

loudest: *ffff* _____
softest: *ppp* _____

FIGURE 216. *The Chapman stick—vital statistics.*

board; this enables both hands to play together in mid-range without getting in each other's way. Note that the third and tenth strings are unisons, the second and ninth an octave apart, and the first and eighth two octaves apart.

Either hand can play any string, but as a rule the left hand plays the bass strings and the right hand the treble. Since the right hand spends most of its time around the twelfth fret and the left up near the nut, a well-separated treble/bass texture results:

It should be emphasized, however, that either hand can play with ease at any fret. Note that in normal play both hands reach across most of the fingerboard; when they are to play in the same region of the neck or to pass each other, they must be kept out of each other's way. This is best done by having them reverse roles, i.e., temporarily assigning treble to the left hand and bass to the right.

Because of the great width of the fingerboard the thumbs are not used. The barre is possible but clumsy and seldom desirable.

The strings of the stick run very close to the fingerboard so that articulation can be as light and easy as possible. The attack can be varied from sforzando to legato, and five dynamic levels can be differentiated by the fingers alone. Despite the unique playing technique the onset of individual tones in detached playing much resembles the plucked sounds of the ordinary electric guitar. Production of the legato requires alternating fingers or, at low volumes, a slide. Chords, since they are not strummed, tend to be keyboard-like in effect.

A velvet damper runs beneath the strings between the nut and the first fret and acts like the damper felt of a clavichord or clavinet, stopping the tone instantly when the finger is removed from the string; and like the clavichord and clavinet the stick is capable of an incredibly crisp and brittle staccato, even in trills and rapid runs.

The open strings are played by ordinary plucking. Because of the damper these notes reverse the usual pattern, being *less* brilliant and resonant than the stopped notes. The open strings are seldom used except for the lowest, whose pitch is available no other way.

The tone of the stick is considerably more delicate than that of most electric guitars; it approaches the quality of an amplified folk guitar. The bass and treble divisions have separate pickups with independent volume controls and *separate output*, so that if desired the output of the two divisions may be routed to separate speakers. Since this involves separate amplifiers as well, the two divisions can be assigned contrasting tone qualities.

Fuzz-tone, wah-wah, and other effects can be used with the stick just as with other electric instruments; they all, however, tend to coarsen the tone and reduce the expressivity of the instrument, undermining the unique and impressive polyphonic potential that is the stick's raison d'être.

The behavior of the strings, in terms of vibrating duration, capacity for bent tones, and so on, is the same as that of the electric guitar and electric bass. *Sul tasto* and *sul ponticello* effects are obviously out of the question, as are natural harmonics; but artificial harmonics (attacked with one hand, the node touched with the other hand) are produced very easily.

Stick parts are best notated, piano-fashion, on two staves, one for each hand.

MUSICAL EXAMPLES
(FROM THE POPULAR LITERATURE)

CHAPMAN STICK:
King Crimson, "Sartori in Tangier"
"Elephant Talk"

THE VIOLIN FAMILY

The violin and its relatives are the only modern Western bowed string instruments. The bow, held in the right hand, is drawn across the strings, creating a continuous, sustained sound by friction between the hair of the bow (from the tails of specially bred horses) and the string. This friction is aided by the presence of sticky **rosin** rubbed onto the bow hairs by the player as part of the warm-up process each time the instrument is played.

The members of the violin family are as alike as the members of any woodwind family, but they are normally thought of as completely separate instruments. This is largely because their fingerboards have no frets, and in order to play in tune the player must learn through practice the exact stretches for all intervals in all parts of the fingerboard; in switching from one member of the family to another one must completely reinterpret the proprioceptive cues from the left hand in order to play in tune. The doubling violin/viola is not uncommon, however, and occasionally a cellist picks up a violin and as a joke starts playing the Dvořák cello concerto—roughly in tune.

All members of the violin family have curved bridges and fingerboards so that the bow can be used on the middle strings individually. All have four strings and all except the contrabass are tuned in fifths. All have a full, rich, singing tone. The violin and cello are particularly strong and bright in timbre, while the viola and contrabass (whose bodies are not quite big enough to resonate their lowest pitches properly) sound smoother and more velvety. All sound brighter, more focused, and more intense in their higher reaches. As usual, the open strings produce a stronger, richer sound than stopped notes.

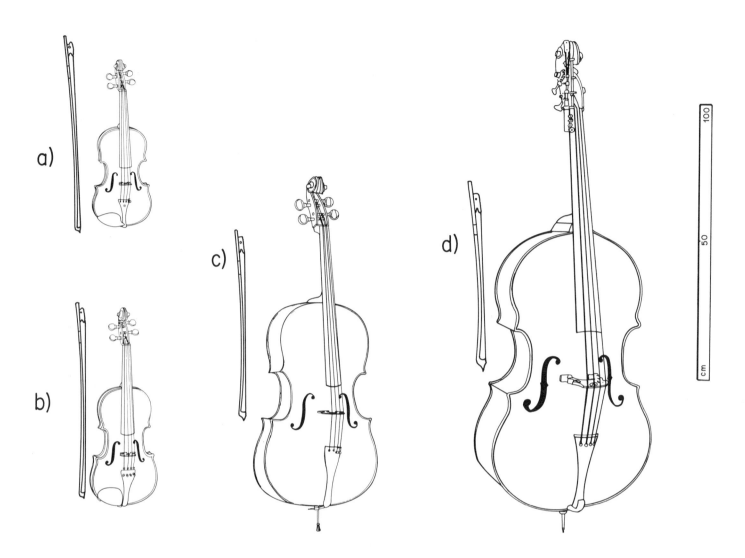

FIGURE 217. *The violin family: (a) violin; (b) viola; (c) violoncello; (d) contrabass.*

In writing for these instruments it must be borne in mind that they are soft. Their most comfortable dynamic level is *mezzo-piano*, and their *fortissimo* is barely worthy of the name—it certainly cannot compete with the *fortissimo* of the clarinet or saxophone.

It is also worth remembering that playing standards differ considerably among the different members of the family. Standards of violin playing are currently higher than for any other instrument except the piano; those for viola and cello are also high but not as spectacularly so, while contrabass playing standards—though they are rising—are the lowest of any major instrument: many *professional* players cannot even consistently play in tune.

A word about terminology: "violoncello," like "pianoforte," is now used only in contexts of extreme formality. The spelling " 'cello" (with an apostrophe) has become somewhat archaic and is fast losing ground to plain "cello." The contrabass is known under a great many names in English; in order of decreasing respectability these are "contrabass," "bass viol," "bass violin," "string bass," "bass fiddle," and "bull fiddle." All are commonly abbreviated to "bass" in ordinary conversation. The term "contrabass" is actually the least commonly em-

name of instrument	abbreviations	written range	tuning	sounds	availability
violin	vln. vn.	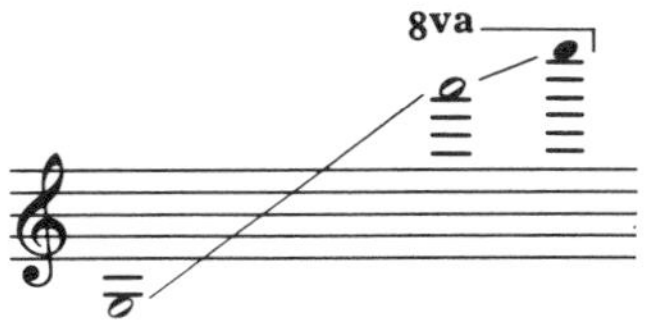 loudest: *ff* softest: *ppp*		as written	ubiquitous
viola	vla. va.	 loudest: *ff* softest: *ppp*		as written	common
violoncello	vcl. vc.	 loudest: *ff* softest: *ppp*		as written	ubiquitous
contrabass	cbs. cb.	 30 % loudest: *ff* softest: *ppp*		1 octave lower	common

FIGURE 218. *The violin family—vital statistics.*

ployed of these expressions, but it is increasingly preferred both by contrabassists and composers, because this is the name of the instrument in all European languages other than English.

Unlike the other members of the family, the contrabass varies a great deal in size, in construction, and even in technique. Most have four strings tuned in fourths from low E_1 (written an octave higher), but fully one-third of the literature for the instrument descends to C_1 and many contrabasses are built or modified to reach this note. Some of these are **five-string contrabasses** with a C_1 string added to the usual four; other players simply retune their E_1 down to C_1 when the need arises. Most common, however, is the **low C_1 extension**, which can be built in or added to an ordinary bass. The extension is just that: extension of the fingerboard past the nut to a point just beyond the top of the scroll. The lowest string passes over this extension and then back down to its tuning peg. The player does not directly stop the extended portion of the string, but rather makes use of four keys, just like woodwind keys, that stop the string mechanically for the notes E_1, Eb_1, D_1, and Db_1, the levers for which

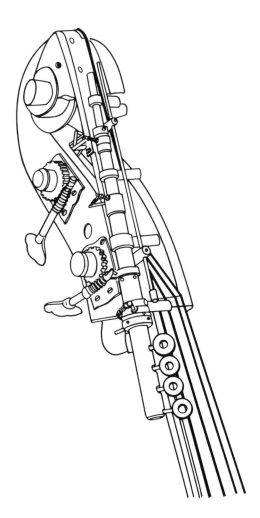

FIGURE 219. *Detail of low C₁ extension mechanism for the contrabass.*

are placed in a row at the level of the nut. By means of a lever behind the neck the player's left thumb can lock down the E₁ key, turning the C₁ string back into an E₁ string. Reversing this lever unlocks the E₁ key again, and most "machine basses" also unlock automatically whenever the E♭₁ key is depressed. The "machine" can be frightfully noisy, but it is nonetheless the preferred method of reaching C₁ because a machine bass can still play passages such as

that require an open E₁ string and those such as

that would be very clumsy on a five-string instrument because of the E₁ string intervening between the C₁ and A₁ strings. Composers are advised, should they descend below E₁ in their contrabass writing, not to make parts so idiomatic for one type of bass that they cannot be played on another. It should also be borne in mind that soloists (as opposed to orchestral players) usually prefer to use a small contrabass without the extra low notes; some even use a very small instrument tuned a whole step higher than usual, though such a cello/bass hybrid seems rather pointless.

The violin and viola are held perpendicular to the player's body with the bottom of the instrument tucked between chin and left shoulder. With the help of an attached chin rest the instrument is held firmly in position by chin and shoulder alone (players frequently develop a "violin hickey" and take to wearing scarves), so that the left hand is freed from the need to support the instrument. The cello and contrabass are held vertically and supported off the floor by an adjustable **endpin** emerging from the bottom of the instrument. The difference in playing posture means that to a violinist or violist the lowest string is at the player's left, while on the cello or contrabass the lowest string is on the right. This affect only the practice of bowing, for violinists and violists twist the left hand around the back of the neck so that the fingerboard is approached from the left side of the instrument (i.e., the player's *right*) just as it is on the cello, contrabass, or any other necked string instrument. The violin and viola are held such that the sound tends to be directed toward the player's right; therefore, in pieces where the spatial arrangement of the performers is important composers should avoid positioning these players in any way that places the audience to their left.

LEFT HAND TECHNIQUE

The basic fingering pattern for the violin was given in Figure 199; that for the viola is the same, though of course a fifth lower in pitch. The patterns for cello and contrabass are as follows:

Pitch of Open String

Finger	C_0	G_0	d^0	a^0	
0	C_0	G_0	d^0	a^0	
1	$C\#_0, D_0$	$G\#_0, A_0$	$e\flat^0, e^0$	$b\flat^0, b^0$	
2	$E\flat_0$	$B\flat_0$	f^0	c^1	CELLO
3	E_0	B_0	$f\#^0$	$c\#^1$	
4	$F_0, F\#_0$	$c^0, c\#^0$	$g^0, g\#^0$	$d^1, d\#^1$	

Pitch of Open String

Finger	E_1		A_1		D_0		G_0		
0	E_1		A_1		D_0		G_0		
1	F_1	$F\#_1$	$B\flat_1$	B_1	$E\flat_0$	E_0	$G\#_0$	A_0	
2	$F\#_1$	G_1	B_1	C_0	E_0	F_0	A_0	$B\flat_0$	CONTRABASS
4	G_1	$G\#_1$	C_0	$C\#_0$	F_0	$F\#_0$	$B\flat_0$	B_0	

The contrabass pattern requires some explanation. There are two separate columns of notes for each string because the half-step difference between the columns requires an actual shift of the hand—not a simple extension of one finger as it would on the other bowed strings—and repeated shifts are required in order to play any scale. Note also that the large stretch between adjacent half-steps on the contrabass leaves room for only three notes within the compass of the hand, so that the third finger is normally not used—though certain patterns of notes do require its use.

For both cello and contrabass the fingering pattern changes in higher positions. In these **thumb positions** the left thumb is brought around to the front of the neck (not around the back, since the body of the instrument intervenes) and used, along with the other fingers, to stop notes. In thumb positions the fourth (i.e., little) finger is not used because bringing it into position to stop a note below the thumb would force the intervening fingers far over to the side where they could not reach the strings. In thumb positions (which begin in about fifth position on the cello and seventh position on the contrabass) the fingering pattern becomes fully diatonic, as on the violin.

The thumb may if desired be used in lower positions if an unusually large stretch is required (see chart of maximum stretches). Its use in such cases should be designated by the conventional "thumb" symbol, ♀.

The chart below gives the average maximum left-hand inter-finger stretches for all members of the violin family. These maximums should be consulted whenever there is any doubt as to the feasibility of any chord (called **multiple stop** on these instruments) or artificial harmonic.

It is worth noting here that it is possible to stop notes beyond the end of the fingerboard, simply by pressing hard on the string. In Figure 218 the note produced on the highest string at the end of the fingerboard is given as the uppermost note of the "normal" range, while the highest note beyond the fingerboard is shown as the top of the upward extension range. Intonation is very tricky in these high notes, particularly on the violin and viola.

BOWING

The **bow** is held at its right end, the hand grasping it from above with the thumb on one side and the other fingers opposite it. True to form, the contrabass is a partial exception to this, for those players who use the so-called **German bow** (as opposed to the regular **French bow**) hold it underhand, gamba fashion (see Chapter XIII).*

The player's bowing arm is held well out from the body and the bow is moved mostly from the elbow. In ordinary detached playing the direction of motion of the bow is alternated with each note. Strokes in which the hand moves away from the instrument (**downbow**) are marginally more powerful than those in which the hand moves toward the instrument (**upbow**), and players automatically start each passage with an upbow or downbow depending on whether its first note falls on a weak or strong beat or division of a beat.

In some cases the bowing pattern will have to be reversed halfway through a passage, or

---

* Unlike a gamba bow, however, the German bow's power stroke is the downbow, just as with the French bow.

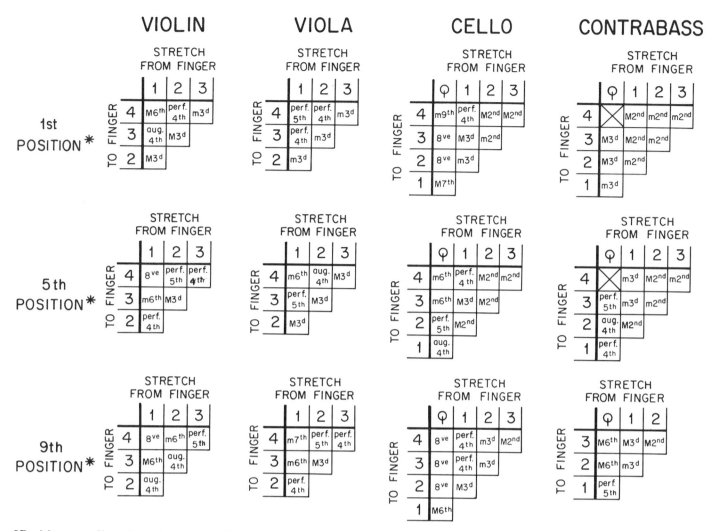

*Positions are diatonic and represent the position of the first finger or thumb. Thus, in first position the first finger is placed a major second above the pitch of the open string; for fifth position it is placed a major sixth up, and in ninth position a major tenth up.

FIGURE 220. *Maximum single-string interval stretches between all pairs of fingers in different positions on members of the violin family. Violin figures are also valid for mandolin (q.v.).*

the whole passage may require unorthodox bowing, in which case the composer may wish to indicate the proper bowing with signs for upbow (V) or downbow (⊓), thus:

It must be emphasized that it is not essential for the bowing pattern to correspond with the metrical accentuation in every detail. In three-quarter time, for instance, the normal alternation of upbows and downbows frequently produces "reversed" bars:

STRINGS 357

but the difference in weight of upbow and downbow is so subtle that no need would be felt to break the alternation.

Players can normally be trusted to work out the best bowing pattern for themselves. In deciding whether to introduce a break in the bowing pattern the composer should be aware that the production of two downbows or two upbows in a row requires the lifting and repositioning of the bow so that the first note in any such pair will always be at least somewhat staccato. Such repeated upbows and downbows can be used to give a breathless or stomping quality to the music.

For bowed instruments the slur indicates specifically that all the notes included thereunder are to be taken in one stroke of the bow. The maximum time that can be allotted to a slur (or to a long single note) before the player runs out of bow varies from about three seconds in *fortissimo* to *at least* thirty-five seconds in *ppp*. The figures are somewhat shorter for the contrabass than for the other members of the family. Players are adept at changing the direction of the bow almost imperceptibly if need be, and composers frequently write extremely long notes and slurs with the caution "change bow imperceptibly." In orchestral writing, slurs and long notes can be held indefinitely by the simple expedient of having the different players in the massed section change bow at different times; this they will do automatically whenever circumstances demand it. The **tremolo**, performed by rapidly alternating the direction of the bow and notated with three lines through the stem of each note affected, can be used to continue a tone or slur indefinitely but is more usually employed as a timbral effect. One should distinguish carefully between (a continuous tremolo) and (two separately attacked tremolos).

All slurs must be between notes on the same or adjacent strings, and if the left hand is required to shift more than one position between two slurred notes there will be an audible portamento between the notes. Thus on the violin, for instance, a slur such as can only be performed with an audible glide. Note that on the cello, where a^0 is an open string, this same slur could be made without a shift and hence without a glide.

The notations , , and indicate that the notes are to be played, respectively, staccato, tenuto, and separated by rests, but without alternating or repositioning the bow between notes. The notes are separated by merely stopping the bow and starting it up again in the same direction. Note that is not the same as ; the latter implies that the bow is to be picked up and "started over" for each separate note, whereas the former indicates that the bow is simply to stop between notes without being repositioned.

The effect of this **portato** bowing is a genuine connectedness among the notes despite their clear and complete detachment. The intent of these notations when applied to other instruments of other sorts is precisely the imitation of this portato sound.

The whole question of bow articulation has been the subject of unforgivable mystification by violin pedagogues, who have applied a battery of conflicting and imperfectly defined French and Italian terms to every conceivable motion of the bow. The limited usefulness of this terminological apparatus is reflected in the fact that no two string players, string teachers, orchestration texts, or organologists will agree as to the exact meaning of all these terms or even how many discrete phenomena are being labeled. However, it is necessary to know something of bow articulation in order to write intelligently for these instruments, and, unfortunately, the existing confused proliferation of terms is all we have to work with.

The most important distinction is that between bowing "**on-the-string**" and "**off-the-string**." In playing on-the-string (**alla corda**) the bow is not lifted between notes, and when it stops it forcibly stops the vibration of the string before starting the next note. This is the normal articulation of detached notes at slow and moderate speeds and of the tenuto at all speeds. Ordinary detached, on-the-string playing is pretentiously and unnecessarily referred to as *détaché*, and the tenuto portato is equally unnecessarily called *louré*. The sharp staccato

(𝅘) is performed on-the-string, acquiring its pointedness from the fact that the notes are individually cut short by stopping the bow—a technique called **martellato**, which is usually also used to differentiate ˄ from ˃ . The notation ˙ is usually taken to imply an unaccented staccato alla corda.

Ordinary staccato is almost always played off-the-string, that is, the bow is lifted from the string following each note. At slow and moderate speeds this is done note by note, the bow being physically lifted by the player's arm after each stroke (**spiccato**); at higher speeds (or in isolated short notes) the bow is literally bounced off the string (**saltando**). For a particularly connected effect or at very high speeds, the bow is allowed to bounce repeatedly of its own volition (**jeté**—French for "thrown"; the Italian equivalent *gettando* is almost never seen), the speed of the bouncing (which can be increased or decreased at will) being controlled by the pressure with which the player holds the bouncing bow against the string. Most authorities maintain that the *jeté* is to be used only for rapid staccato portato. Some do not distinguish *saltando* from *jeté* at all, and the distinction is admittedly fairly academic. At any rate, the *jeté* can be used to make a **spiccato tremolo**, notated 𝅘 .

The vexed question for bow articulation is what to do with rapid passages marked neither staccato nor tenuto. All other things being equal, a player will perform a loud, vigorous, or muscular passage on-the-string, and a soft, delicate, or precise one off-the-string. If the composer has a preference and the solution isn't obvious from context, the passage should be marked *alla corda* or (for want of a general term for off-the-string playing) *spiccato* or *saltando*.

Whether a passage is played on- or off-the-string, the bow will always be lifted from the string following the last note before a rest. If the note in question is an open string it will continue to vibrate softly for a second or two after the bow has been lifted. If this effect is desired it should be indicated with the usual "l.v." and/or slur-to nowhere (⌐) notations, but usually it is *not* desired, and one cannot depend on the players to damp the open string automatically, despite the obtrusiveness of this sound, e.g., at the end of a piece. To make sure an open note is damped after the bow is lifted a good stiff "non l.v!"—exclamation point and all—will be needed.

Except for the *martellato*, stopping a note dead in its tracks by choking it off with the

bow must be counted a special effect. Since notations such as $\overset{\prime}{\circ}$ or ♩ ♩ ♩ will not be understood, it is best to indicate this effect with "railroad tracks" (//) and the instruction "choked release."

Aside from the vagaries of articulation, the timbre of the instrument can be altered in several ways by changing the manner of bowing:

1. Bowing near the bridge, **sul ponticello** (abbreviated *pont.*)—a snarling, glassy sound. Many players (particularly cellists) overdo this and end up with some high partial instead of the fundamental.

2. Playing near the fingerboard, **sul tasto** or **sulla tastiera**—a dull, heavy sound that cannot be produced louder than *mezzo-forte* and must be bowed *flautando* (see below).

3. Playing with just the edge of the bow hairs, **flautando**—a delicate, flute-like tone that cannot be produced louder than *mezzo-forte*.

4. Playing exclusively near the grip end (**frog**) of the bow, **al tallone**—fierce, biting attacks and coarse tone, applicable to short notes and tremolos only.

5. Playing exclusively near the tip of the bow, **sulla punta d'arco**—delicate, tentative attacks and wispy tone, applicable to short notes and tremolos only.

6. Playing with the wooden part of the bow, **col legno**. The on-string and off-string versions of this are very distinct and are nowadays specified separately. In **col legno tratto** the bow is turned sideways and drawn across the strings so that both hair and wood are used; this produces a very coarse tone. In **col legno battuto**, the more usual kind, the bow is turned upside down and the wooden part alone is bounced on the strings, producing a distinct, woody click with each attack.

All these techniques are invoked with their Italian names and canceled with "nat.," "ord.," or "modo ord." With obvious exceptions, it is possible to use these devices in combination. All are quite traditional and have been in use since the seventeenth century.

Contemporary, non-traditional bowing effects include:

1. Bowing behind the bridge—four squeaks of indeterminate pitch.

2. Bowing the tailpiece of a cello or contrabass or the endpin of a cello. This produces a vaguely pitched, string-drum-like sound at about Bb_0 on the cello and B_1 on the contrabass.

3. Bowing *behind* the fingers of the left hand (violin and viola must be held cello-fashion to do this). The sound is very thin and gamba-like, *pp* or *ppp*. The pitch is a function of the distance between the finger and the nut and is thus the inverse of the pitch produced on

the other side of the finger. Only the note an octave above the open string yields the same pitch on both sides of the finger.

4. **Underbowing**, i.e., the use of too little bow pressure to make the note speak. A *pp–ppp* hiss is produced, very slightly colored by the fingered pitch.

5. **Overbowing**, i.e., the use of too much bow pressure. This makes a very harsh grating or squawking sound, colored by the fingered pitch. Privileged-frequency "undertones" a fourth, octave and/or eleventh *below* the fingered pitch may be produced, but these are extremely difficult to control with any accuracy.

PIZZICATO

A traditional and widely used technique is the **pizzicato**, in which the strings are plucked rather than bowed. For any extensive or complicated pizzicato passage the bow is put aside (this takes about half a second), but individual pizzicato notes can be played while still holding the bow. Pizzicato and bowed notes can be alternated about as rapidly as eighth-notes at ♩ = 120, but this is very awkward.

Pizzicato is invoked with the instruction "pizz." and canceled with "arco."

Stopped pizzicato notes on the violin and viola decay with great rapidity; the open strings ring softly for a second or two. On the cello and contrabass, open strings ring for two to three seconds and stopped notes in the lowest octave of each string ring for one-half to one and a half seconds. Within these time limitations slurs and glissandos can be performed in pizzicato just as on the guitar.

Pizzicato can be played at great speed by alternating fingers or by plucking back and forth with one finger. Pizzicato chords are generally strummed, guitar-fashion, and should be provided with arrows or arrowed arpeggio-signs to indicate the direction of the strum. Cellists and contrabassists use the thumb for upward arpeggios, the index finger for downward ones. For extensive strummed passages a violinist or violist will hold the instrument guitar-fashion; back-and-forth strumming can then be done with the thumb and index finger held together. A passage of this sort (even on cello or contrabass) should be specifically marked "alla chitarra."

A pizzicato chord to be plucked simultaneously rather than strummed should be marked with a bracket, e.g., ⌈𝄞 , and the instruction "non arp."

Pizzicato may be performed *sul ponticello* or *sul tasto* if desired, just as with bowed notes. For a particularly stinging attack, the string may be plucked with the fingernail rather than (as is usual) with the flesh of the finger. This effect provides a useful intermediary between the normal sound and that of the snapped pizzicato described below. If desired, it must be called for with the expression "coll'unghia."

Two specialized forms of pizzicato are in use. The **left-hand pizzicato**, indicated with a plus sign above the affected note, is plucked by any free left-hand finger—ideally but not necessarily as a pull-off from the previous note. The sound is rather thin and somewhat *ponticello*, but the main effect is one of informality, since left-hand plucking is often used by players to check their intonation while tuning up, and hence tends to carry this association.

Left-hand pizzicato can be used simultaneously with bowing on the same or another string. Cellists and contrabassists frequently use a subtle left-hand pizzicato to aid in the attack of a loud, low bowed note. Left-hand pizzicato with the fingernail is impossible, since players must keep the nails of the left hand very short.

The **snapped**, **vertical**, or **Bartók pizzicato** is performed by pulling the string vertically and letting it snap back against the fingerboard with a snapping or slapping sound. This effect does not work for very high notes or in *ppp*. It is notated with the symbol ↋ above the note. (Observe that the reverse of this symbol, ♀ , means "stopped by the (left) thumb"; the two must not be confused.)

As an unorthodox pizzicato effect a guitar-type flat pick may be used and the instrument played *alla chitarra*. **Hammering-on** is occasionally used (especially by cellists) to aid in the attack of a bowed note. By itself it is usable but very weak—*pp* or less—and tends to produce pitches from the portions of the string on *both sides* of the finger, though this can be suppressed. A louder hammered-on sound can be produced unorthodoxly by wearing thimbles on the fingers of the left hand.

CHORDS

Normally the members of the violin family are monophonic instruments, but chords of up to four notes (**double**, **triple**, and **quadruple stops**) can be played, subject to certain limitations. For the left hand the limitations on pitch choices can be derived easily from the charts of maximum stretches given above. All else being equal, the easiest multiple stops are those in which the lowest-numbered finger used stops the lowest-pitched string used, and so on up in order. Remember that any slur requires either lifting or depressing a finger, use of a previously unused string, or a shift of the hand. Because of the curved bridge, quadruple stops must be arpeggiated (the four notes cannot be sounded simultaneously) and it is usually impossible to sustain triple stops for any great length of time. The limitations are as follows: on violin and viola, triple stops can be fully sustained in *forte* or louder, or for an instant in *mezzo-forte*, but at softer dynamic levels triple stops must be arpeggiated; on cello, triple stops can be attacked simultaneously in *forte* or louder, but only two of the notes can be sustained; and on the contrabass all triple stops must be arpeggiated.

Triple and quadruple stops are frequently written as if they were to be fully sustained, but this is just a convention. The player will hit all the notes and then sustain only two (usually the top two) or, where possible on violin and viola, three. If one of the notes involved is an open string it will be allowed to vibrate and can still contribute to the chord even when it is no longer bowed. Where arpeggiation is necessary it will be performed very quickly, unless the arpeggiation sign, implying a more leisurely approach, is appended. Arpeggiation will be from bottom to top unless otherwise specified.

In orchestral writing, care must be taken to distinguish multiple stops from divided sections. The term "divisi" should be rigorously appended whenever a section is to be divided and "unis." used when it is to reunite, while multiple stops should be bracketed, e.g., 𝄚 , if there is any doubt as to their meaning.

Arpeggiated and broken chords of all kinds are whenever possible fingered in the left hand as if they were multiple stops, the different notes being articulated by moving the bow from string to string. In writing passages of this type composers should always bear in mind the exigencies of the left hand and try to keep each separate *gruppetto* within the limits of what can be grasped by the left hand without moving.

Trills are usually performed in the obvious way, by repeatedly stopping and unstopping a note with one finger, but wide trills (often confusingly called "tremolos") can be performed with the bow by alternating strings. The rapid alternation of two strings, especially when used as a timbre effect, is known as **bariolage**. Frequently advantage is taken of the difference in timbre between stopped and open versions of the same pitch, as in this violin example from Bach:

Double stops on nonadjacent strings are possible by calling for—and explaining—either of two unorthodox techniques. The two outermost strings can be bowed simultaneously by turning the bow upside down and pressing it up against the strings from underneath. This technique is very difficult to control, requires considerable preparation time, and can only be performed slowly. A potentially much more useful technique that has, however, not yet (1984) been used in any composition is simply to push one of the middle strings down out of the way at the very end of the fingerboard and then bow the two strings adjoining it. The open strings and all natural harmonics that lie within reach of the other left-hand fingers may be played in this way, and by playing slightly *sul ponticello* one may play thus with one of the two strings stopped, even near the end of the fingerboard. In the region near the bridge where true *sul ponticello* is played, the pushed-down string rises up high enough to be bowed and the "disjunct" double-stop is not possible. On all members of the violin family except the cello it is possible to push down *both* middle strings and play on the outer two strings (open strings and natural harmonics only), *mezzo-piano* or softer.

TONE AND EXPRESSION

The four strings produce slightly different timbres, which composers occasionally exploit by specifying the string on which a given passage is to be played. The lowest string in particular yields a fuzzy, covered tone compared to the others. Strings may be named either by letter (violin: G, D, A, E—analogously for the others) or by Roman numerals, I designating the highest string. Passages to be played on a given string are marked "sul G" or "sul IV," etc. String numbers (without the "sul") are also used to clarify the fingering of unusual multiple stops and harmonics.

A distinct vibrato is ordinarily applied to every note long enough to bear it. The vibrato is created as on the guitar, by shaking the left hand so that the fingers stopping the strings rock back and forth, creating a slight waver in pitch. If it is not desired the instruction "senza vibr." must be used. Vibrato is not normally applied to harmonics or open strings, though it can be if desired. On an open string the vibrato is produced by placing a finger on the nut and shaking the hand as usual.

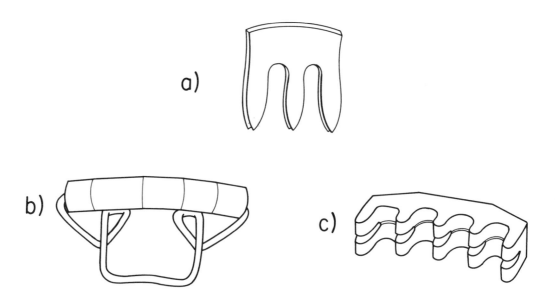

FIGURE 221. *Violin mutes: (a) traditional type; (b) newer style; (c) practice mute.*

Mutes are made for all members of the family. The ordinary mute exists in two forms. Both are slipped onto the top of the bridge, where they function by adding mass to the bridge and thus decreasing the efficiency with which it transmits vibrations to the soundboard. The older and still more common variety (Fig. 221a) is kept aside (on the music rack or in a vest pocket) when not in use, and requires about a second to be picked up and put in place, and another second when it is put aside. The newer variety (Fig. 221b) remains attached to the strings between bridge and tailpiece and can be slid up onto the bridge in less than half a second. The two types have the same effect.

The mute decreases the volume of the instrument only very slightly, but it makes the timbre gentle, velvety, and distant, as though the instrument were being played behind a closed door.

The **practice mute** (Fig. 221c) is essentially a heavy, metal version of the older type of ordinary mute. It reduces the maximum volume to *piano* and gives the instrument a tiny, thin, very distant sound.

On the violin family instruments, **harmonics** have the usual distant, denatured quality and low dynamic level. Limitations on natural harmonics are as follows.

Violin: possible on the e^2 string up to the sixth partial; on the a^1 string up to the seventh partial; on the d^1 string up to the eighth partial; on the g^0 string up to the ninth partial.

Viola: possible up to the ninth partial on all strings.

Cello: possible up to the twelfth partial on all strings. Nodes for partials above the sixth lie so close together that the player cannot reasonably be asked to pounce on any of them from far away.

Contrabass: possible on the G_0 string up to the sixteenth partial; on the D_0 and A_1 strings up to the fourteenth partial; and on the E_1 (or C_1) string up to the tenth partial. Nodes for partials above the eighth lie so close together that the player cannot reasonably be asked to pounce on any one of them from far away.

The high partials on any of the instruments are much more secure when played from nodes near the bridge rather than from equivalent nodes near the nut—unless the player has metal strings (instead of the usual wound gut), in which case it doesn't matter. Few players know or feel at ease with the "extra" nodes between the bridge series and the nut series (see Fig. 200).

A special effect (available on all members of the family and first exploited by Stravinsky) is the natural-harmonic "glissando" produced by sliding a finger down or up the string along the nodes of the bridge series or nut series of harmonics, usually starting with the third or fourth partial. The weak "extra" nodes in the middle do not speak during this progress, so a truly glissando-like curve of pitches is produced:

On cello and contrabass the pitch of a natural harmonic can be bent upward by "warping" the string sideways, guitar-fashion. On the cello the pitch may be raised as much as a quarter-step by this means, while on the contrabass harmonics can be raised an entire half-step.

Artificial harmonics are produced by stopping a string with one left-hand finger and touching the appropriate node with another finger of the same hand. On violin, viola, and cello the second to fifth partials are usable for artificial harmonics (subject, of course, to limitations of stretch—Fig. 220), though the fourth is by far the most frequently used. On the contrabass the third to sixth partials are available where the stopped note lies an octave or more above the pitch of the open string, but the third to eighth partials are available from stopped notes below that. On gut-strung contrabasses artificial harmonics are impossible when the stopped note lies less than a fifth above the pitch of the open string. On all the members of the family the upper pitch-limit for artificial harmonics is the same as that for ordinary stopped notes.

A natural harmonic should be notated as if it were an ordinary note, but with the usual little circle above it to indicate that it is a harmonic. Contrabass harmonics, like other notes, should be notated an octave above their sounding pitch. Bent harmonics require some sort of clarification.

Artificial harmonics are notated in a three-tiered system that gives the stopped note, the location of the node, and the resulting pitch on one stem with differently formed note-heads, thus:

An historically older and still more common practice reverses this notation, giving the stopped note with an ordinary note-head and the sounding pitch with a small, parenthetical note-head unattached to the stem. The notation used here is to be preferred because it places the emphasis where it belongs—on the pitch produced.

Since instruments of the violin family have no frets, **microtones** are a simple matter in theory, but, particularly high in the range, they are often difficult to place accurately. The gap between quarter-tones is so narrow that on the violin adjacent quarter-tones cannot be played with adjacent fingers above first position but must be distinguished by rocking (not even sliding) one finger slightly forward or back. The same is true for the viola above third position. Nonadjacent quarter-tones are of course no problem in this respect. On contrabasses with low C_1 extension the quarter-tones below E_1 can be played by sticking the left hand into the machine and manipulating the C_1 string directly; this is of course very awkward and no kind of legato or glissando is possible.

Aside from this, all members of the family have almost unlimited possibilities of true glissando (see p. 31). Formerly, the normal practice was for any glissando that started or ended low in the range to cross strings, thus sounding somewhat discontinuous; today most players know to keep the whole glissando on one string if at all possible. Composers for their part should not write glissandos that exceed the range of an individual string. This one, for instance, is impossible:

Among contemporary special effects not mentioned so far are scraping a string lengthwise with bow or fingernails, possible on all strings except the violin's (unwound) top e^2; and tapping the body of the instrument with fingers, knuckles, or the wood of the bow.

MUSICAL EXAMPLES

VIOLIN:

Ravel, *Tzigane*
Bartók, Sonata for solo violin
Messiaen, *Quatuor pour la fin du temps*

VIOLA:

Hindemith, *Kammermusik* No. 5
Boulez, *Le Marteau sans maître*
Feldman, *The Viola in My Life*

VIOLONCELLO:

Messiaen, *Quatuor pour la fin du temps*
Schoenberg, Cello Concerto (after Monn)
Xenakis, *Nomos alpha*

CONTRABASS:

Prokofiev, Quintet for winds and strings, Op. 39
Crumb, *Madrigals* (Books I, IV)
Chihara, *Logs*

STRING QUARTET:

Bartók, String Quartet No. 4
Cage, *String Quartet in Four Parts*
E. Brown, String Quartet
Crumb, *Black Angels*

ADDITIONAL EXAMPLES

STRING ORCHESTRA:

Bartók, *Divertimento*
Chavez, Symphony No. 5
Xenakis, *Syrmos*

FULL ORCHESTRA:

Hindemith, *Symphonie Mathis der Maler*
Stravinsky, *Le Sacre du printemps*
    Agon
Janáček, *Sinfonietta*
Bartók, *Bluebeard's Castle*
Webern, *Six Pieces*, Op. 6 (original version)
Messiaen, *Chronochromie*
Ligeti, *Atmosphères*

X

ELECTRONICS

GENERAL CONSIDERATIONS

Before even getting down to basics it is necessary to consider just what the nature and function of this chapter is to be. Electronic music is universally taught as a subdiscipline of composition, not of performance; and as instrumentation surveys are also largely aimed at the composer a discussion here of electronic music might seem a duplication of effort.

That this chapter has nonetheless been included is the result of the following considerations:

1. The ability to study and analyze a piece of electronic music ought not to be dependent on the taking of a special course in the subject any more than the study of the orchestral literature, say, should be dependent on the taking of a course in conducting.

2. Hands-on experience is, theoretically at least, no more of a necessity for composition in the electronic medium than in any other.

3. Courses in electronic music tend to concentrate largely or solely on tape music, glossing over the important interface between electronics and "acoustic" instruments.

This chapter's scope and contents are determined by these considerations.

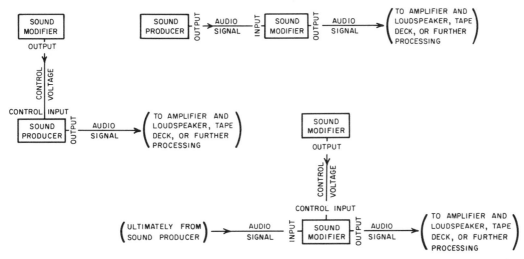

FIGURE 222. *Relationships between sound-modifying and sound-producing devices.*

BASIC PRINCIPLES

The vast majority of electronic devices are not sound *producers* but sound *modifiers* that must be used in conjunction with some sound source, which is as likely as not to be non-electronic.* If the sound source is non-electronic its sound must be converted into an electric signal—usually by means of a microphone, but occasionally in some other fashion. The electric signal changes in intensity in proportion to the intensity of the original audio signal; changes in air pressure become changes in voltage. If the sound source is electronic, it produces varying voltages "from scratch."

The electric signal representing the sound is then processed and altered by whatever sound-modifying devices are being used, then fed to an amplifier and loudspeaker, where it is converted back into sound.

Some sound-modifiers produce a **control voltage** that governs the behavior of the sound producer itself or of some other sound-modifier, while others act directly upon the audio signal, which is fed through them. The basic possibilities are diagrammed below in Figure 222. Note that every device has an *output* and that outputs are invariably linked to *inputs* of other equipment.

The intensity of the effect of most devices (e.g., the loudness of an amplifier or the pitch of an oscillator) is governable by a built-in **potentiometer** which may take either the familiar rotating dial form or that of a lever which is slid back and forth in a straight line (**sliding pot**).

The output of any piece of equipment can be sent to several different places simultaneously by means of a **multiple**, a simple circuit in which one incoming signal becomes four or more identical outgoing signals without any alteration. Any electronic music studio will have several multiples—they are frequently built into synthesizers and mixer boards.

A **mixer** is the opposite of a multiple, in that it is designed to take a number of different audio signals and unite them into one. To do this without distortion requires circuitry considerably more sophisticated than that of a multiple. Any mixer worthy of the name is provided

---

* Tape music produced entirely from non-electronic sound sources is known as **musique concrète.**

with separate volume controls for each input, and two, four, or eight separate outputs to which any of the inputs can be routed by means of switches. Large mixers frequently also have built-in reverb units (q.v.) that can be applied to any incoming or outgoing signal.

SCORING

The scoring of electronic music varies considerably from composer to composer and piece to piece. Compositions for tape alone are seldom scored, and if they are the score is likely to take the form of a book-length description of every process used in the production of the tape. Where a tape is combined with instruments the tape part may be omitted from the score altogether save for indications of the starting and stopping points of the individual tape segments ("cues"), or there may be a graphic score conveying in a general way the sense of the material on the tape but impossible to interpret fully without hearing the tape. Such scores may contain ordinary musical notation where appropriate.

The line of score representing the tape may be placed at the top or bottom of the score or immediately above the percussion. The real-time manipulation of live instrumental sounds should be indicated verbally as adjuncts of the specific instrumental lines affected. If one device is used to modify several different instruments its instructions should be placed at the top or bottom of the score or just above the percussion.

THE STUDIO SYNTHESIZER

In Chapter VIII we saw that the performance synthesizer is essentially a specialized type of electric organ. The studio synthesizer, though it superficially resembles the smaller performance instrument, is adapted to many more different and varied musical functions. It is too big and expensive, too cumbersome in its operation to be of much use in live performance, though small studio synthesizers are occasionally so used. Its real destiny is to be used in combination with the tape recorder for the production of **tape music**, in which the time taken for detailed revision of the connections among its numerous components will not hold up the show.

Like organs, no two studio synthesizers will be exactly alike, for synthesizers are **modular**. Just as an organ may have just about any combination of a large variety of stops, so a synthesizer has numerous discrete **components** of separate and well-defined function. The components may be arranged in various ways relative to each other, and new ones may be added as long as there is room for them in the cabinet—and even beyond, if new cabinetry is built or acquired. The Moog synthesizer illustrated in Figure 223 resembles other studio synthesizers in its basic appearance—a keyboard in front with an impressive-looking array of components rising behind, with their knobs, switches, and sockets for inputs and outputs— but other brands of synthesizer, and even other Moogs, may be quite different in detail.

Most of the components of which synthesizers are made had existed as independent entities for years before the synthesizer was invented. What makes a batch of components into a synthesizer is their *standardization*, whereby all are designed to the same electrical and electronic tolerances, with uniform controls (note how similar all those knobs are) and identical connecting devices. Stereo buffs are well aware that there are at least six mutually exclusive

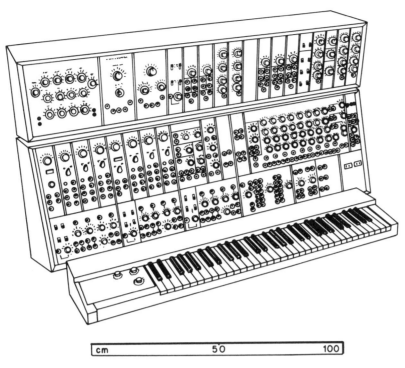

FIGURE 223. *A typical Moog studio synthesizer.*

ways to attach a wire to a piece of electronic equipment for the purpose of connecting it to another piece of equipment; in a synthesizer all connections ("**patches**") are made in one and the same way, greatly simplifying and speeding up the connecting ("patching") process.

On Moog synthesizers, for instance, all inputs and outputs are in the form of sockets built to receive the type of plug known as a **phone jack**. All that is necessary to hook up the various components is a quantity of electric wire ("cable") of various lengths, tipped by phone jacks at both ends; either end of any of these wires ("**patch cords**") may be plugged into any other socket within its reach. Of course not every possible patch makes sense—patching one input to another, for example, is pointless. Common patches may be built into the synthesizer and engaged with the flick of a switch. The input and output sockets of some synthesizers are arranged together in a tight grid on a **patch panel** so that the patch cords can be very short and unobtrusive. The designer of an electronic music studio will usually link the synthesizer to the tape decks, mixer board, and other equipment by means of a master patch panel governing the whole studio.

It cannot be emphasized too strongly that the studio synthesizer is not intended to be used alone. Unlike the performance synthesizer, its strong point is the processing of sounds, not their generation, and many of the components produce the most musically worthwhile results when applied to sounds originating outside the synthesizer. To this end all synthesizers have a **line input** for signals from a tape recording or a phonograph record, and almost all have a **mike input**—with the necessary preamplifier built in—for microphones.

The actual sound-generating resources of the synthesizers are relatively unimportant; in fact, there are really only two, oscillators and white-noise generators. An **oscillator** does exactly what its name implies—it creates an oscillating voltage. If the frequency of the oscillator lies in the audio range, then the voltage will make a sound when fed into a loudspeaker.

name of waveform	graph of waveform	harmonic spectrum	timbre
sine wave		pure tone (fundamental only)	like whistle or recorder: cold and colorless
sawtooth wave		second partial ½ as loud as fundamental, third partial ⅓ as loud as fundamental, fourth ¼, fifth ⅕ (etc.)	like muted brass: very bright and buzzy
square wave	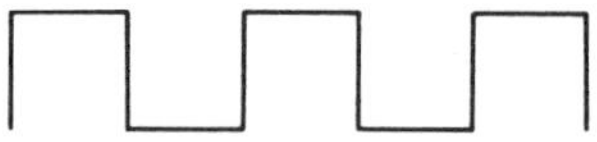	odd partials only ("stopped pipe"); relative loudness of partials as for sawtooth wave	like crumhorn: rich and buzzy, slightly hollow
pulse wave		all partials present at equal volumes	like model-airplane motor: very coarse buzz
ramp wave		intermediate between sawtooth and triangle	like sawtooth wave, but less bright and buzzy
triangle wave		second partial ¼ as loud as first, third partial ⅑, fourth ¹⁄₁₆ (etc.)	like sine wave, but warmer, less impersonal

FIGURE 224. *Oscillator waveforms.*

The wave-form produced by an oscillator is harmonic, that is, its partials lie in the harmonic series (Fig. 4), just like those of a wind or string instrument. The various oscillator waveforms are listed and described in Figure 224. Unless each has its own output, a multiposition switch is used to select among the various waveforms. Sine, square, and sawtooth waves are to be had from just about any oscillator; the other types are less common. On many oscillators all gradations between pulse wave and square wave are available by means of a dial (the "symmetry control"). Others have a similar dial-controlled continuum of ramp waves between the extremes of sawtooth and triangle.

Oscillators are strictly monophonic, producing only one pitch and one waveform at a time. Any decent synthesizer will be provided with a minimum of four oscillators, and usually more. The pitch of an oscillator can be governed by external controls (including other oscillators), and is adjusted in range by a **frequency vernier** dial covering two or three octaves, and usually also by a rotary switch that moves by octave leaps from well below the audio range up to the vicinity of c^5. External control, which takes place through a separate control input, is so important that the full term "voltage-controlled oscillator," or **VCO** for short, is often applied to an oscillator with this type of control. It was the development of voltage control for oscillators that made synthesizers possible.

Oscillator outputs themselves are used not only as audio signals but as control voltages. In the latter capacity they are most valuable at subsonic frequencies. For example, a sawtooth wave of 2 Hz frequency applied to another oscillator as a control voltage will produce from that oscillator a series of repeated upward glissandos, each half a second long; the width of the glissando can be adjusted by controlling with an amplifier the amplitude of the slow sawtooth wave (see below). If that sawtooth wave were patched into the control input of an amplifier, the result would be a series of repeated half-second crescendos affecting whatever sound is being amplified. If an oscillator output of audible frequency is used as a control voltage, the result is a more or less severe distortion of the controlled sound into a bell-like or multiphonic-like timbre in which the frequency of the controlling oscillator is heard as a prominent (usually inharmonic) partial. The waveforms of most synthesizer oscillators become distorted at very low frequencies, and below about 1 Hz the distortion will be distinctly audible in controlled audio signals. Large, expensive oscillators can be obtained from science-oriented electronics firms, having essentially distortion-free waveforms from as low as one-quarter Hz or less and ascending several octaves into the supersonic range. Virtually all other synthesizer components are also manufactured independently in large, expensive, very high-quality forms, and electronic music studios may acquire half a dozen or so of these items, hooking them all into a master patch panel so that they can be used easily with the synthesizer.

As implied in the foregoing discussion, the control input of an oscillator governs the pitch of the oscillator as a function of the incoming voltage—the higher the voltage the higher the pitch.

The only other type of audio-signal producer found in synthesizers is the **white-noise generator**, which produces a constantly fluctuating random voltage containing all frequencies. The sound is the same as that which accompanies the "snow" (its video equivalent) on a blank television channel. On some synthesizers a **pink-noise** generator will be found instead—pink noise being a form of white noise in which equal energy is found in all octaves. It is much lower-pitched than white noise and sounds a bit like distant thunder. A few also produce **random noise**, white noise of subsonic frequencies used as a control voltage.

The **amplifiers** on a synthesizer (usually four or more) are really **attenuators**, in that they *reduce* the strength of the audio signal rather than increasing it. The volume ("gain") of the amplifier is adjusted by a potentiometer running from zero up to the full volume of the incoming signal; more to the point, its governance can be turned over to a control voltage, the amplifier reading an increase in the control voltage as an increase in gain. As with oscillators, the voltage-control feature is the most important aspect of these devices, so much so that they are formally referred to as "voltage-controlled amplifiers," or VCAs for short, to distinguish them from a **power amp** of the sort found in a home stereo system.

A **filter** is a device that allows only certain frequencies to pass through it; it can be thought of as an electronic mute. Filters may be divided into four types: **high-pass filters**, which reject all frequencies below a certain **cutoff frequency**; **low-pass filters**, which reject all frequencies *above* the cutoff frequency; **band-pass filters**, which allow through only a narrow band of frequencies; and **band-reject filters**, which reject only a narrow band. All except the rare band-reject filter are found on most synthesizers.

The rejection of frequencies beyond cutoff is not absolute. The rejection is more complete and efficient the further beyond the cutoff one goes, but even well beyond the cutoff frequency a little sound will get through. The abruptness and completeness of the rejection—the **slope** of the filter—is governed by a potentiometer, as is the location of the cutoff frequency on high- and low-pass filters. The location of the cutoff frequency is also subject to voltage control (the higher the control voltage the greater the range of frequencies excluded). Some band-pass filters have variable band-width, in others the whole band can be moved up and down the frequency spectrum, and either or both of these parameters may be subject to voltage control; but usually band-pass filters are found banked together in groups of eight to twelve, their fixed bands overlapping slightly and among them covering the whole frequency spectrum (the highest and lowest of such an array are really high- and low-pass filters). In a filter bank of this sort the *amplitude* of each band (but not its width or location) is independently adjustable.

Filters must be thought of as *timbre* modifiers since each individual partial of the input will be passed or rejected separately. There is generally no point in using a low-pass filter on any sound whose fundamental lies above the filter's cutoff frequency, but on a high-pass filter the fundamental of a harmonic timbre can be completely filtered out *and will be resupplied by the ear* so that the pitch of the sound will not seem to change, though its timbre will become increasingly thin and tinny, like a cheap radio. A filter really provides an artificial *formant* to the sound (see the discussion of formants in Chapter IV).

The treble and bass controls on a power amplifier (or radio or phonograph) are really high- and low-pass filters, and a little experimentation with these will give a good idea of the effects produced by filters in general, though those on a synthesizer are capable of much stronger and more marked effects.

The **reverb unit** may be thought of as a sort of filter. The timbre it produces is essentially a sort of echo but, unlike true echoes, reverberation does not copy the envelope of the original sound—the incoming sound is not *repeated* but is merely given a thin, ghostly *extension* that gives the illusion of space around the sound source or of distance between it and the listener. Reverb units (which are often built into mixer boards as well as synthesizers) are provided with a potentiometer governing the relative strength (mix) of the main signal and its reverberation.

The **keyboard*** of a synthesizer generates a control voltage which when patched into the control input of an oscillator governs its pitch according to which key is pressed. The keyboard can theoretically also be used to produce a graded series of loudnesses, degrees of filtration, or whatever, but there is not really much point in doing so. The range of a large studio synthesizer's keyboard has been pretty well standardized at five octaves, C to C. Smaller, portable synthesizers have smaller keyboards of two and a half to three and a half octaves (see the discussion of performance synthesizers in Chapter VIII).

This description of the keyboard applies to its appearance only, for not only can its scale be transposed up or down any amount (by adjusting the oscillators and a **range** dial on the keyboard itself), but the **scale** (i.e., the difference in pitch between adjacent keys) is also adjustable: the range of the keyboard as a whole may be reduced to as little as one octave or expanded to as many as seven or eight. Theoretically, the keyboard remains equal-tempered whatever its range or scale, but in practice the upper end of the scale tends to compress near the upper end of the oscillator's range.

Besides the potentiometers governing scale and range, there is one for **portamento**, which controls the rate at which the keyboard switches from one pitch to the next. When this control is set at zero, the change is virtually instantaneous; at higher settings there will be portamento between the notes, at still higher ones glissandos of increasing duration are produced, until at maximum setting it may take thirty seconds or more for the oscillator to slide from one pitch to the next. The keyboard acts not only as a control voltage but as a **trigger** and timing device, so that depressing a key not only specifies the pitch of the oscillator but starts it

* Buchla synthesizers have a button keyboard like an accordion left-hand keyboard; all others have the ordinary piano-type keyboard.

oscillating as well, and releasing the key stops it. On most systems the triggering aspect can be overridden so that if desired the oscillator will continue to sound (at the previously determined pitch) even after a key is released, and will not stop until it has been unplugged or turned off manually.

The keyboard is monophonic, that is, only one key at a time will produce a sound. If the keyboard is patched to more than one oscillator, unisons or strict parallel harmony will be produced. A few now have **duophonic** keyboards that can produce two pitches (but no more) at once.

Most synthesizers possess a **linear controller** in addition to the keyboard. This is a metallic ribbon that gives a continuum of voltages according to where it is touched. It is used for glissandos and such, but its main value is as a control voltage for amplifiers, filters, and other non-pitch devices where a sliding scale is more useful than the discrete values of a keyboard. Like the keyboard, it gives increasing voltage from left to right and is a trigger as well as a control voltage. Unlike the linear controller of an ondes martenot (Chapter VIII), there is no visual guide to the location of pitches, so it is difficult to find precise pitches on it when it is used to govern an oscillator.

The **envelope generator** is normally used in conjunction with the keyboard and an oscillator to give a "realistic" envelope to the individual notes as opposed to the bare on/off quality of sounds controlled by the keyboard alone. It may, however, be applied to any audio signal and be controlled by any kind of electronic triggering device. The envelope generator produces a control voltage that is usually patched into a VCA, where it controls the loudness of the audio signal coming through the amplifier, as follows.

When the key (or other trigger) is depressed the amplitude of the sound rises from zero to an attack peak and then moves from there (usually by descent) to a steady-state volume; when the key is released the amplitude drops from steady-state back to zero. The *relative* amplitudes of attack peak and steady-state volume can be adjusted to any degree, and either one may be zero, but the *absolute* loudness of the resulting sound is dependent on the volume of the unprocessed audio signal, which is also the maximum volume that can be attained.

The time required for the sound to build up to the attack peak, for its drop (or further climb) to steady state, and for its final decay are all independently variable by potentiometers from about a microsecond up to thirty seconds or more. Releasing the key causes the decay to start even if the attack pattern is not yet complete; similarly, depressing the same or another key will interrupt an ongoing decay with a new attack pattern, starting not at zero but at the volume presented by the decaying tone. Slurring (i.e., proceeding from one pitch to the next without intervening attack or decay) is possible simply by not releasing the first key until the next has been depressed.

When the attack times are very rapid, the timbre of the sound is affected. With a steady-state volume of zero, for instance, and the shortest possible attack pattern, a sine tone will sound like a woodblock or claves. As the attack length is increased the sound becomes first like a templeblock, then a xylophone, then a marimba, then a vibraphone. Note that to achieve the effect of a non-sustaining instrument the steady-state volume must be set at zero.

On most synthesizers the number of envelope generators equals the number of oscillators. By mixing (summing) the outputs of two differently calibrated envelope generators, complex envelopes (e.g., with two separate attack peaks) can be produced.

By patching an envelope generator into a filter or oscillator rather than (or in addition to) a VCA, attack and decay patterns involving changes of timbre or pitch can be produced.

The **sequencer** is a producer not so much of timbre as of rhythm: it is used to set up rapid sequences of *different* sounds without the tedious recording and tape-splicing process that would otherwise be required. The sequencer consists of a battery of eight or more* control voltages, each with its own output and each regulated by its own potentiometer. These control voltages may each be applied to any device in the synthesizer that has a control input, and thus among them they are able to produce a wide variety of effects.

Coupled with the battery of control voltages, sometimes as a separate component, sometimes built in, is a **timing pulse generator** that sets off the control voltages one after the other in a non-overlapping series. The amount of time allotted to each output is independently variable by potentiometers and can itself be subject, if desired, to voltage control—even from one of the sequencer's own outputs. The timing pulses can also be controlled manually by pushing a button to produce each pulse.

The sequence of timed control signals can be made to stop at any point in the series or to endlessly return from that point back to the beginning of the series, producing an ostinato sequence of sounds. The repeat may be literal or may if desired call forth a *different voltage* from each output, these voltages governed by a second bank of potentiometers which together comprise the second **stage** of the sequencer. From the end of the second stage the pattern may stop, return to the beginning of the first stage, or go on to a third stage governed by a third bank of potentiometers. Some sequencers have a fourth stage; in any case, one has the option at the end of the last stage of either stopping or going back to the beginning of the first stage and running through the whole pattern over and over again until the sequencing is stopped manually. The multistage arrangement greatly expands the capacity of the sequencer: an eight-position, three-stage sequencer, for instance, can produce up to twenty-four different sounds before stopping or repeating.

A sequencer can move from sound to sound with tremendous rapidity, even moving faster than the ear can follow so that the sequence of sounds is heard as a more or less continuous burble.

ADDITIONAL FEATURES

All the foregoing are standard features of virtually all studio synthesizers. Other components exist which may or may not be found in any given synthesizer, or may be purchased as separate pieces of equipment.

Among the most important of these is the **ring-modulator**. A ring-modulator takes two different audio-signal inputs and converts them to a single output containing all the combination tones (summation and difference frequencies) generated by the heterodyning of the two inputs, but with the inputs themselves removed. The resulting sound is very clangorous and complex, strongly resembling woodwind multiphonics.

The ring-modulator produces its most valuable effects when one of the inputs is an ordinary instrumental or environmental sound and the other is an oscillator tone (sine wave is best) of fixed pitch. Under these conditions the output will be recognizable as a transformation of the "natural" input and will be markedly different in quality as the "natural" input moves from one pitch to another, for the ring-modulator in effect *converts harmony into timbre*; it can thus

---

* Eight is the usual number, but sequencers are available with up to 256 separate outputs.

be a very powerful compositional tool. The best results are obtained when the output is then mixed with one or both of the input sounds.

Similar in effect to the ring-modulator is the **frequency shifter**, which differs in that its output contains *only* the summation tones or *only* the difference tones from the two inputs, the choice being made by means of a switch.

The **phase shifter** (**phaser**, for short) delays the incoming audio signal very slightly and then recombines it with the undelayed input. The two combined signals are more or less out of phase with each other, and the phenomenon of interference (see Chapter I) eliminates all frequencies (that is, individual partials) that turn out to be wholly or mostly opposite in phase.* These frequencies are all integral multiples (i.e., harmonic partials) of the lowest of them. The phaser is thus really a **comb filter**, eliminating certain specific frequencies scattered across the whole audio spectrum. Since the eliminated frequencies fall into a harmonic sequence, the effect is as if a sound were *subtracted* from the input—and that is the way it is heard. The extent of the output delay can be varied, thus altering the set of eliminated frequencies.

Phasers are much more common in performance synthesizers than in studio models.

A **waveform clipper** flattens out the waveform at top and bottom, as if the peaks and troughs were cut off flat. The result is a decrease in amplitude coupled with a change in timbre in the direction of a square wave. With square and pulse waves the amplitude will be decreased without any change in timbre. The extent of the clipping is governed by a potentiometer.

An **envelope follower** tracks the amplitude (not, strictly speaking, the envelope) of an audio signal and converts it to a control voltage. This device is most useful when applied to an instrumental or environmental sound, for the amplitude of a synthesizer-generated sound can usually be taken straight from the envelope generator.

Similar in function is the **frequency follower**, which tracks the fundamental or most prominent frequency of an audio signal and converts it to a control voltage.

The **vocoder** is really a sort of "timbre follower." It contains two separate banks of band-pass filters that are applied to a pair of audio inputs, breaking down the tonal spectrum of each into half-octave units. The outputs from one filter bank are fed into the control inputs of a bank of envelope followers and VCAs, which together govern the amplitude of the outputs from the opposing filters. The result is that no frequency is stronger in the second signal than it is in the first, and the timbral characteristics of the first signal are therefore to some extent imposed on the second.

The various components of a vocoder can be patched together every which way so that, e.g., the highs of one signal can be put in charge of the lows in another, but the device is at its best when used "straight." The output of a "scrambled" vocoder usually sounds much like that of a ring-modulator, and the result simply isn't worth the effort involved.

A **spatial locator** distributes the final audio signal among two or four (rarely eight) tape channels or loudspeakers. With two channels the apparent location of the sound can be made to appear anywhere on a line between the two speakers; with four speakers arranged in the corners of a room the sound can be made to move around anywhere within the plane in which the speakers lie. It is technically possible to get full three-dimensional motion with four speak-

---

* Technically, phasers of this sort are called **flangers**, while phasers *sensu stricto* produce the same effect by other means.

ers arranged in a tetrahedron, but rooms and halls being the shape they are, this is usually achieved by the use of eight speakers arranged in a cube.

A one-dimensional (two-channel) spatial locator is controlled by a sliding potentiometer, a two-dimensional (four-channel) one with a **two-dimensional potentiometer** or "joy stick," whose appearance and motions resemble those of an automobile floor gearshift. A **three-dimensional potentiometer** is a large, clumsy, and expensive device, and in most music requiring more than four channels the motion of the sound is produced with a combination of simpler devices.

Finally, two "visual aids" should be mentioned. The **oscilloscope** displays the shape of any waveform fed into it; the **frequency counter** gives a numerical read-out in Hertz of the frequency of the input signal. These devices are of use when the characteristics of an unheard or unhearable signal must be precisely gauged and adjusted.

THE COMPUTER AS SYNTHESIZER

A distinction must be drawn between computer *composition*, in which the computer is used to select and order sounds and/or to print out a score, and computer *sound synthesis*, in which the computer creates and modifies sounds directly. It is only the latter that concerns us here.

Ordinary electronic instruments, including the synthesizer, are **analog** devices, that is, the variations in air pressure that comprise a sound are represented within the instrument as analogous variations in voltage. The oscilloscope trace of an oscillating voltage is exactly the same as the graph of the sound waves produced by sending that same voltage to a loudspeaker.

The computer, on the other hand, is **digital**. Its output consists of a series of numbers which must be electronically decoded to be useful. The numbers are expressed in the extremely simple **binary** form,* using only the digits "1" and "0," represented within the machine by positive and negative electric currents, respectively. Note that the *quantity* of the current is irrelevant and that information can be stored on tape at great density and processed (both mechanically and electronically) at very high speeds without "noise" (information loss) becoming a problem. The speed of individual computer operations is measured in nanoseconds, i.e., in *billionths* of a second.

Because the computer's output is essentially a code, the meaning of that output can be whatever the operator desires. A great many common procedures and the basic mechanisms for telling the computer what to do are encoded in standardized ways and these meanings are stored permanently in the computer's memory; a person wishing to operate a computer must learn an appropriate **computer language** governing these processes.

The output of a computer may be recorded for storage directly on magnetic tape, or on disks, or it may be decoded into some human-readable form such as a typewriter printout, a pen-and-ink graph or drawing produced by a **plotter**, or a video display.

For sound-producing purposes the computer's output is fed to a **digital-to-analog converter** (DAC), which produces a fluctuating voltage in response to instructions from the computer: the bigger the number sent by the computer at any instant, the larger the voltage

* For those who have forgotten how binary (base-2) numeration works, each power of two is represented by the figure "1" in different positions, thus: $\frac{1}{4} = .01$, $\frac{1}{2} = .1$, $1 = 1$, $2 = 10$, $4 = 100$, $8 = 1000$, etc. The numbers from 1 to 8 are binarily notated as 1, 10, 11, 100, 101, 110, 111, 1000.

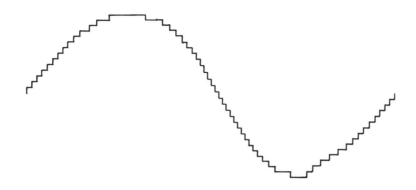

FIGURE 225. *Computer-generated approximation of a sine wave.*

produced. Since the output of the computer consists of discrete numbers generated at regular intervals, the resulting voltage is stepped rather than smoothly graded (Fig. 225). In practice, however, the numbers controlling the voltage are produced at so high a rate that the effect is of smoothly continuous changes in voltage. The rate at which the computer puts out numbers (the **sampling rate**) is specified by the programmer. At a sampling rate of 32,000 samples/ second (i.e., twice 16,000 Hz—the upper limit of audibility) the tiny irregularities become inaudible because they represent partials too high to be heard. For most purposes a sampling rate of 25,000 samples/second is quite sufficient, as tones above 12,500 Hz seldom enter into any musical context even as upper partials.

It is important to remember that the computer does nothing on its own but only responds to instructions from outside. In making a sound (or rather, in sending sound-producing information to the DAC) the computer is responding to a **program** prepared by one or more people. Each separate digital output must be specified, but the instructions for any repetitive operation can be stored in the computer's memory as a **subroutine** and referred to as a unit whenever necessary. For example, any waveform need only be described once and that description stored in the memory; then when a sound using that waveform is needed, one need only direct the computer to the **address** in the memory where the waveform is stored. Simple mathematical operations applied to the waveform will then give the note its proper pitch, amplitude, and duration.

Quite a few standardized programs have been developed to aid in the production of computer music. Many of these are available commercially in **software packages**, prerecorded on disk or tape for immediate use. A program of this sort automatically sets up the computer to do all or most of the things a synthesizer does, storing the various processes— including the standard waveforms—in the memory. In some systems a special extra memory chip or PROM ("programmable read-only memory") covers this same ground in hardware form. In either case the user's own program can then get right down to the business of making music—specifying pitch, amplitude, duration, and timbre in fairly ordinary terms, or making and storing special subroutines for use in the specific work at hand.

For an ordinary microcomputer, user-generated programs must be entered on the typewriter-like keyboard of the now-familiar **VDT** or **CRT** ("video display terminal," "cathode ray terminal") with which they are equipped. More sophisticated systems may have **graphic inputs** enabling the computer to "read" graphed analog notation or even ordinary musical notes.

An **analog-to-digital converter** (ADC) is the computer's equivalent of line and mike inputs. With this device any sound, live or on tape, can be encoded digitally and processed by the computer. In this way "real" sounds can be manipulated by the computer or even stored in its memory.

While a microcomputer can be used in live performance, typically by programming two rows of VDT keys to serve as a music "keyboard," its use in such a context is clumsy and limited. Rather, these devices excel in the production of **computer-generated tape music**. To make such a piece, the whole thing (or a substantial portion of it) is programmed in advance. The program is then run, and the resulting music is monitored as it comes from the DAC. There will be small errors in almost any new program, which will need to be **debugged** one or more times before it is perfect.

Compared to analog synthesizers, computers give much more accurate and reliable results throughout the range of human perception and endurance. Computer-generated tape music is immediately distinguishable from analog tape music by its uncanny clarity and cleanness. More important is the computer's ability to do *more* than a synthesizer. In fact, *anything that can be described mathematically can be performed by a computer.*

In this respect the potential of computer sound synthesis is limited only by the imagination of the composer. Among the things that can be done with a computer—and by no other means—are: a realistic Doppler shift for a sound that moves from one loudspeaker to another; reverb in imitation of the qualities of sound at any distance or distances from the listener, in any real or imagined acoustic space; timbres halfway between, say, xylophone and soprano voice, or any other combination of real or unreal timbres; and transposition of the pitch of a taped or live input without affecting duration or timbre.

With a computer no tape manipulation is needed, since all those techniques (described below) can be performed digitally with much greater flexibility, reliability, and control than with a tape deck. A computer can be used, for instance, to give a delayed replay of a live sound without any of the restrictions involved in tape delay.

DIGITAL SYNTHESIZERS

A **digital synthesizer** is in essence nothing more than a microprocessor interfaced to a music keyboard of the sort used in analog synthesizers. The compactness and portability of all such units is tending to blur the distinction between performance and studio synthesizers, but for the time being that distinction remains valuable—see Chapter VIII.

The most sophisticated, studio-oriented (and expensive) digital synthesizers incorporate a complete VDT and have the ability to interface with such other hardware as a modem (for signal transmission along telephone lines), plotter, or printer. Even on these instruments, however, the standard synthesizer waveforms and such other traditional functions as envelope generation and filtration can be independently accessed with switches above the music keyboard—just as in an analog instrument. In fact, some digital synthesizers are operationally indistinguishable from analog instruments, except that no digital synthesizer needs patch cords.

The most conservative instruments are simply analog synthesizers with digital controls. In these, the microprocessor acts merely as a super-sequencer and programmable patch panel.

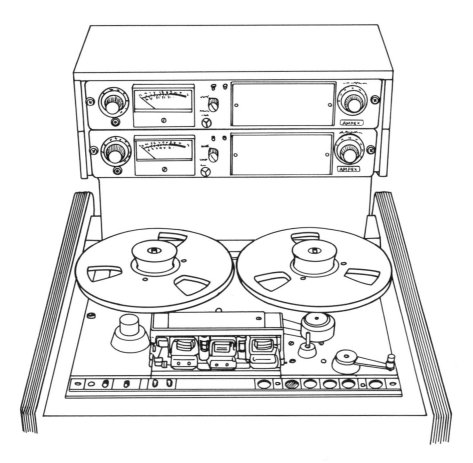

FIGURE 226. *Studio-type reel-to-reel tape deck.*
The protective cover over the tape heads has been removed.

THE TAPE DECK

In tape music the tape deck is an active sound-modifying agent in its own right. For such purposes an open, reel-to-reel tape deck, allowing full access to the tape, is essential. The tape moves from left to right past three **tape heads**: erase, record, and playback, in that order. When a tape is played, the playback head "reads" the tape as it moves past, setting up a voltage equivalent to the amount of magnetism on the tape at any given point. In recording, the erase head clears the tape and the record head then lays down new material coming in from microphone, turntable, synthesizer, or whatever, magnetizing the tape in amounts equivalent to the incoming voltage. If the person doing the recording wishes to monitor the tape while it is being recorded, the tape deck's monitor switch is placed in the "tape" position, engaging the playback head so that the sounds just recorded can be heard immediately. If the monitor switch is placed in the "source" position, the incoming signal is heard instead.

Tape decks are equipped with a set of buttons or a multi-position switch governing the motion of the tape. Record and playback both use the ordinary "play" or "forward" speed; the controls also have "stop," "fast forward," and "rewind" settings used strictly to manipulate the tape. In these modes the tape is lifted away from the tape heads and can neither record nor play back. Professional tape decks are equipped with a further setting of great value for the production of tape music. In this "edit" mode the tape is stopped but the reels can be moved freely by hand; furthermore, the playback head is turned on so that one can hear the tape while manipulating it. This enables a given sound on the tape to be lined up precisely with the playback head: the spot can then be marked with an adhesive **signal dot** and moved back opposite the record head so that recording of new material can begin at exactly the place desired.

The ordinary "stop" control does not halt the tape instantly, and if the tape is stopped in mid-sound there will be a perceptible swoop in pitch (downward in playback, upward in recording) as the tape decelerates. The same thing happens in reverse if the tape is started in the middle. Both effects can be avoided by the use of the "instant stop" setting found on some tape decks. However, normal usage is wherever possible to start and stop recording or playback at places where the source and/or tape are silent.

Professional tape decks are **half-track** machines, in which half the width of the tape is used for each of two stereo channels. A tape made on such a machine has only one side; if turned over it will play back the same material backward and with the channels reversed. It is possible to get two sides of material on a half-track tape, but only by recording on just one channel. When the tape is turned over, the unused track can then be filled with new material. Volume controls for the unused channel must be turned to zero in both recording and playback. If both channels were played back simultaneously one would be heard going forward while the other went backward.

In addition to professional, half-track tape decks, an electronic music studio is likely to have at least one high-quality nonprofessional machine that records on four tracks. Particularly valuable is a **quarter-track quad** tape deck, which can record and play back either two sides of stereo or one side of quadraphonic tape, depending on how the controls are set.

On any tape recorder it is possible to record on one channel while playing back on another. It is not possible to add new sounds to a tape track that is already recorded,* but it is possible to add new sounds to old by recording on a separate track and then **mixing down** the resulting stereo tape. This is done by playing both channels into a mixer and combining them into a single output, which is then recorded on one track on another tape deck.

The synchronization of new material with a track already recorded requires the use of the **sel sync** ("selective synchronization") switch, which makes the recorder play back *through the record head,* so that the sounds on the prerecorded track will be heard as they pass the record head and will thus synchronize exactly with sounds recorded through that head at that instant.

In order to make use of the sound-modifying capabilities of tape decks, it is necessary to have at least two of them—one to produce the effect and one to record the result. Here are the possibilities:

1. **Speed variation.** A professional tape deck can be run at either of two speeds: 38 cm/sec. or 19 cm/sec. If a tape recorded at 19 cm/sec. is played back at 38 cm/sec. it will sound twice as fast and an octave higher, in thin, "Munchkin" timbres. The reverse process will produce sounds twice as slow and an octave lower than recorded, with clumsy, grumbling timbres. Either effect can be doubled (quadrupled, octupled) by simply repeating it; for example recording a tape at 19, playing it back at 38 and recording the result at 19 on another deck, then playing the new tape at 38 will give an end result four times as fast and

---

* But see the discussion of tape echo below.

two octaves higher than the original. Non-professional tape decks play at 19 and 9½ cm/sec., and if one of these is used such an effect can be achieved directly, by recording at 9½ and playing back (on a professional machine) at 38.

The motors on most professional tape decks keep their speed constant by adjusting to the steady frequency of the incoming alternating current. By adding a special, heavy-duty oscillator to the system, the speed of the motor can be varied indefinitely between the 19 cm/sec. and 38 cm/sec. extremes. Voltage-control applied to the oscillator allows the tape speed to be controlled by an outside signal, for example, from a synthesizer.

In the "edit" mode the reels can be turned by hand, producing an irregular, generally low-pitched playback of whatever is on the tape.

2. **Backward playback.** As mentioned above, a half-track recording can be reversed simply by turning it over. On some tape decks it is possible to run a tape backward without flipping the reel, and in "edit" mode a tape may be run backward by hand, albeit slowly and irregularly. Backward sounds generally have a very characteristic envelope, with vague onset and very sharp release, that is immediately recognizable as "backward." Synthesized sounds with a similar envelope will also sound "backward" even if they are not.

Backward playback can easily be combined with speed variation.

3. **Tape delay.** This effect is produced by recording on one track, playing it back immediately, and recording it on the other track. The distance between the playback and record heads will cause a delay between the original signal and its duplicate, equal to 0.175 seconds at a tape speed of 19 cm/sec. or half that at 38 cm/sec. Longer delays can be achieved by repeating the process across a number of tracks on several tape decks and monitoring only the last track recorded. With two quadraphonic decks at 9½ cm/sec. the total delay across the eight tracks would be $8 \times (2 \times 0.175)$ seconds or 2.8 seconds. If the various intermediate tracks in such a scheme are also monitored one will get a series of overlapping echoes (in this case, eight) each of which can be separately controlled in volume. If filtration and reverb are applied at each stage a genuine echo effect will be produced.

A more interesting and easily produced echo effect can be created by mixing the delayed sound with the continuing live material and recording both on the original track. Since the delayed sound will be repeatedly played and recorded, played and recorded, one gets an endlessly repeating **tape echo** that, depending on the record and playback volume settings, will either gradually die away, stay the same (with very gradual distortion due to information loss from the repeated recording), or get gradually louder until a continuous howl of **feedback** (see the discussion below under Live Electronics) is produced.

Delays and echoes even longer than 2.8 seconds can be produced by stringing the tape from the feed reel of one deck to the take-up reel of another, and then recording on the first and playing back on the second, so that record and playback heads may be separated by a meter or more.

4. **Cutting and splicing.** A tape may literally be cut apart and put back together using a special splicing tape. The splice itself is virtually inaudible. By cutting and splicing one can do such things as remove the attack from a sound or put together bits of tape recorded at different speeds and/or in opposite directions.

5. **Tape loops** are produced by splicing together the ends of a short length of tape. When played back, the material on the tape will simply repeat endlessly as the loop goes round and round.

All of the techniques above can be used in live performance—even splicing, which can be done silently in only about thirty seconds. Nonetheless, the most common use of the tape recorder in live performances is as the passive presenter of a prerecorded tape. Such a tape may be divided into **cues**, that is, separate taped segments connected by spliced-in colored **leader**. The performer starts the tape at the correct point in the score, stops it at the leader, and sets up the next segment while waiting for the next cue to appear in the score.

LIVE ELECTRONICS

Just as some of the equipment already discussed can be used in live performance, so all of what is described below can be used to make tape music.

The soul of live electronics is **amplification**. The amplifier used is a power amp that truly increases the power of the signals it receives.

In live electronics one must face the problem of what to do with the unaltered live sounds, which of course go out into the air "plain" whether or not they are also subjected to electronic modification. There are only a limited number of solutions to this problem:

1. Impose a tape-mediated delay between the unaltered sound and its electronic avatar.
2. Deliberately exploit the simultaneous sounding of the "raw" and processed sounds.
3. Drown out the live sounds with the altered sounds.
4. Use live sounds so tiny they cannot be heard.
5. Place the live performers out of hearing of the audience, piping in only the processed sounds.

All five alternatives require microphones of some sort and thus an amplifier as well. The ordinary sort of microphone is an **air mike**, picking sounds up from the air just like the human ear. Air mikes are available that pick up sounds only from the front (**unidirectional** or **cardioid**), from front and rear (**bidirectional**), or from all directions (**omnidirectional**). It must be remembered, however, that no sound comes exclusively from one direction and that even a unidirectional mike pointed directly away from the sound source will pick up its echoes from that direction—admittedly at a much lower level.

Though ideal for recording purposes, air mikes are of limited usefulness in a live situation. By far their most common use is for simple amplification. In almost every acoustic space this is limited to just *one dynamic level* above the unamplified sound. If greater amplification is attempted, **feedback** will result, whereby the mike will pick up the amplified sound, amplify it further, pick it up again, and so on, so that within a fraction of a second nothing is coming from the speakers but an *ffff* electronic howl on one pitch, usually one of the resonant frequencies of the room. If a microphone is aimed directly at a loudspeaker to which it is connected, feedback will result, even in a totally silent space. Feedback has been deliberately exploited as a musical effect but as it is injurious to both ears and loudspeakers it is best avoided—especially since it can easily be imitated with a synthesizer.

A very recent development promises to go a long way toward eliminating feedback as a problem. It is a device that transposes the pitch of the amplified sound by an (inaudible) fraction of 1 Hz. With the live and amplified sounds at different pitches, they no longer reinforce each other and feedback is much less likely to occur.

For drastic amplification or for picking up the sound of one instrument to the total exclusion of other sounds however loud, a **contact mike** must be used. As the name implies, a contact mike is attached directly to a vibrating surface, picking up the sound from the surface itself rather than from the air. Ordinary contact mikes may be attached to percussion instruments or to the soundboard of a stringed instrument or of a stringed or idiophonic keyboard. For voices a cup-shaped **throat mike** is strapped to the larynx. For winds and free-reed keyboards an attachment specifically designed for the instrument in question must be acquired, while for organ there is nothing. On brasses it is usually easier simply to point a unidirectional air mike right up the bell. On a complexly resonant object such as a tam-tam a contact mike will produce different timbres depending on exactly where it has been attached.

Because it picks up elements of the sound that normally do not reach the audience, contact amplification of an instrument makes it sound very coarse and gritty. Contact mikes are best used to pick up sounds produced *piano* or softer and amplified two dynamic levels or so, so that the original sound is completely buried. Among the most interesting applications is the use of the mike to pick up sounds that are too tiny to be heard under any other circumstances. Everyone has had the experience of finding fascinating sounds in a vibrating object held right next to the ear; the contact mike makes such sounds available to an audience sitting at a distance.

A specialized "contact mike" is the **phonograph cartridge**, which responds to the vibrations of any thin object stuck into it, for example, a toothpick, the end of a Slinky, or a piece of wire.

Magnetic pickups like those used in electric guitars (q.v.) are made for use with mandolin, folk guitar, the various members of the violin family, and the piano. Only the guitar, mandolin, and violin types can be considered common. All, predictably enough, produce an amplified sound that is "electric" in quality—very strong, rich, and full, but somewhat coarse.

A loudspeaker **transducer** is the opposite of a microphone, converting electricity into sound instead of vice versa. Normally, transducers are attached to loudspeaker cones, but they can be used independently to set vibrating any objects to which they are attached—like contact mikes in reverse. The object in question will add its own acoustic characteristics to the output of the transducer.

If the object is very massive and/or naturally non-resonant, the resulting sounds may be only subaudible, in which case a contact mike may be used to raise the volume to audible levels. The most thoroughgoing use of transducers so far is in David Tudor's *Rain Forest*.

Many devices found as components of synthesizers are frequently used independently for live electronics. Among the most frequently employed are filters, mixers, reverb units, oscillators, ring-modulators, and (in popular music) phasers.

There remain to be discussed a number of electronic devices used mainly in popular music.

Vibrato, like reverb, is frequently built into the amplifiers used by electric guitarists and is also available as a separate unit. The vibrato produced is one of amplitude and is variable in intensity and frequency.

The **fuzz box** imposes a gritty distortion on the tone and makes the second partial often as loud as or even louder than the fundamental. This is in imitation of the effect produced by overdriving a power amp; the fuzz box makes this sound available under controlled conditions and without the damage to ears and equipment that can result from overdriving. On most models the strength of the effect is adjustable.

The **wawa pedal** controls the cutoff frequency of a built-in low-pass filter. The "wa-wa" sounds produced by this means are analogous to those produced on brass instruments with a harmon mute. Some wawa pedals double as volume pedals, and the two effects may be linked.

The **voice box** is an intriguing device with strong potential for classical-music applications. It consists of a small loudspeaker completely enclosed in a box, the sound being allowed to emerge only through a long plastic tube. The performer silently mouths various vowels around the end of the tube, imposing their formants on the emerging sound, with a remarkably speech-like effect.

Echo units provide a delayed repetition of sounds played through them. Most are in fact tape-delay devices containing a small tape loop, but analog and even digital units are increasingly to be seen. These purely electronic devices are capable of extremely short delays giving the effect of unison playing, and the digital ones can produce extremely long delays as well.

The **chorus** is a related effect in which several tiny delays are produced to give the effect of a massed unison ensemble.

The **octave divider** is a simplified version of the frequency follower. It transposes incoming sounds up or down by any round number of octaves. This rather rare device can be heard used to great effect throughout Frank Zappa's album *Uncle Meat*.

All these gadgets and others as well can be controlled with a set of foot-operated on/off switches. There is no reason such switches could not be used in connection with classical live electronics, but usually they are not. As we go to press, expanded-capability, multi-function digital versions of all these "effects-boxes" are becoming available.

MUSICAL EXAMPLES

TAPE MUSIC:

Stockhausen, *Hymnen*
Babbitt, *Philomel*
L. Hiller, *Electronic Sonata*
Lansky, *Six Fantasies on a Poem by Thomas Campion*

LIVE ELECTRONICS:

Stockhausen, *Mantra*
                Mikrophonie I
Johnston, *Casta**

PART TWO

Early Instruments

In Modern Reconstructions

XI

INTRODUCTION TO EARLY INSTRUMENTS

The distinction must be drawn at the outset between early instruments as they *were* and as they *are*. Although standards of authenticity are continually rising, it is doubtful that modern reproductions will ever altogether give up modern materials or be built in numbers proportional to their historical use. The harpsichord, for example, was for most of its history a four-octave instrument with only one or two ranks of strings, but it is unlikely that such instruments will ever form more than a minority of modern harpsichords or that plastic quills will ever be abandoned in favor of authentic crow feathers. Furthermore, modern "early" instruments come with far fewer variants than their historical models. This is particularly true of medieval instruments, of which historically there were probably no two exactly alike.

Performers of early music will find in this chapter a practical guide to the instrumentation of that music, which its composers have left indeterminate, but in general we are concerned here not with the history of instruments or instrumentation but only with modern forms and uses. The instruments here discussed are *modern* copies, used in modern realizations of early music and also, increasingly, for *new* compositions. Once the old instruments were reintroduced, it was inevitable that composers would start to put them to new uses. Part Two of this book is therefore largely aimed at the composer and arranger, not the scholar and historian. It is important to remember that the instruments are here described in their modern state: for example, not one of the woodwind fingering charts in Chapter XII agrees in every particular with historical fingering patterns.

Many early instruments never had music written specifically "for" them, so it is impossible to cite specific musical examples of their use. Readers are urged to consult one of the recorded guides to medieval and Renaissance instruments in order to learn the sounds of the individual instruments, and then to listen to some appropriately performed ensemble music, chansons, or the like to hear how those instruments fit into a musical context.

As the current early-music boom continues it is virtually certain that all these instruments will be made in ever-more-authentic versions and in forms representing all stages of their histories. It is just as certain that they will all rapidly became more widely available, especially those here designated "rare" or "very rare."

Finally, let it be observed that the special effects described for these instruments, as well as most of the wind-instrument "extension" ranges, are for the benefit of modern composers and are *not* to be used in performances of early music. It has proven impossible for me completely to delineate all the special effects of which these instruments are capable; much experimentation remains to be done. The upward extension ranges for strings mostly reflect individual instrumental differences in number of frets and/or length of fingerboard.

It is customary in speaking of early instruments to use a three-tiered system: Renaissance, Baroque, modern. This terminology is deceptive, in that the instruments do not in fact coincide with the musical periods in any pat way. With the important exception of the violins and viols, "Baroque" instruments belong not to the Baroque period as such (1600–1750), but to the eighteenth century, including the Classic period: the stretch from 1660 to 1715 saw the first appearance of the "Baroque" forms of flute, recorder, oboe, bassoon, rackett, horn, harpsichord, clarinet, and piano, and all but recorder and rackett were still being used in very similar forms in 1800.

The Baroque forms shade off gradually into the modern, of which they are direct ancestors. This book ignores the Baroque flute, oboe, bassoon, organ, brass, and percussion (as well as the early clarinet and piano) as being too much like their modern descendants to be of much interest to composers. It also ignores such early instruments as tromba marina and panpipes, which were probably never used in any serious musical context.

INSTRUMENTATION
OF EARLY MUSIC

The instrumentation of early music is left to custom and to the performers. Not every possible choice is historically believable, musically viable, or in good taste, and the following is an attempt to provide some general guidelines. Of necessity in a book of this sort, the presentation can be neither very scholarly nor completely exhaustive; it is, however, a reliable practical guide for the vast majority of the music of the period, based on the best current understanding of the practice of those times.

Above all it is necessary to avoid anachronism. For each instrument discussed in the following chapters, approximate dates are given for its appearance and disappearance from Western art music. Note that these are not dates of invention and extinction. Many instruments spent their earliest or latest days either as folk instruments or as amateur household items, with no more relevance to the art music of their time than the ukulele, autoharp, and bugle have today.

Gregorian chant. The division of this music into solo and choral chants is well understood and widely documented. Women's voices would have been used only in convents, and then only sometimes. Only three instruments are known to have been accepted in medieval churches: the organ, the organistrum, and small sets of bells. All should be used sparingly and conservatively in this repertoire, the organ and organistrum in strict unison with the chant. The use of bells should be strictly colotomic, marking off phrases or verses with a single stroke. Bells are specified in certain liturgical contexts, particularly in the Sarum rite, and to be on the safe side they should probably be used only in those places. Reasonable pitch choices would be to double the pitch sung at the moment when the bell is rung or to ring the final or dominant note of the mode of the chant.

Secular monophony. Any and all instruments of the time* may be used in heterophonic accompaniment of the sung line. The melody is sung by a soloist, though occasionally two people may sing in dialogue. It is probably unwise to use more than four or five instruments in such a song.

Medieval dances. Any combination of instruments may be used. Monophonic dances should be performed heterophonically.

Early organum. Performed by two solo male singers, unaccompanied.

Notre Dame organum. The *tenor* is sung by a small number of singers, massed or *alternatim*, with or without organ or organistrum doubling. The duplum and (if present) triplum and quadruplum are solo lines. Male voices only.

Polyphonic conductus. Solo male voices (*not* choral). Instruments *may* double discretely. Avoid percussion and drones.

Motets (thirteenth century). Each line may be taken by any *solo* male voice or instrument of the appropriate pitch, or by voice and instrument in unison or at the octave. "Normal" practice is to sing all texted parts (with or without instrumental doubling) and use instruments for untexted lines. If an untexted line is sung, solmization syllables are used. Instruments should be of contrasting timbres. Shifting or changing instrumentation in midstream is generally not in good taste, nor is the use of percussion or drones.

Polyphonic songs (to 1450). Same as thirteenth-century motets.

Mass movements, etc., before 1400. *Solo male voices only*, possibly with organ doubling. This includes Machaut's *Messe de Notre Dame*. The earliest composer whose liturgical polyphony may legitimately be sung chorally is Ciconia.

Motets (fourteenth century). Solo male voices. Untexted *tenor* may be played or sung. Discrete instrumental doubling of other lines acceptable. Avoid drones and percussion. Do not shift or change instruments during the course of a piece.

Abstract instrumental music (to 1450). Heterogeneous ensembles, usually one to a part. No percussion or drones. If octave transposition is used, all lines must generally be treated the same; do not, e.g., read one line at 4′ while others are at 8′.

Renaissance masses, motets, mass movements, etc. (except those of Spain, Northern Italy, and Southern Germany). Small chorus (men and boys) *a capella*. *A capella* repertoire may legitimately be performed by a "whole" (unbroken) instrumental consort, but not *together* with voices or in broken consorts. Such mixed ensembles were occasionally used at the time but do not represent the best practice, as the music is certainly not conceived for mixed timbres.

Instrumental ensemble music, 1450–1520. Generally one to a part, and without changes during the course of a piece. Mixed timbres still usual, but they should be chosen to blend well with each other, and "whole" consorts are generally acceptable. Keyboards and other chordal instruments may play continuo-like chord progressions. Percussion should be

---

* Except the large and positive organs, which were found only in churches.

used only in dance music, and there only occasionally, for boisterous numbers. The fifteenth-century *basse danse* repertoire was typically played by an ensemble of two shawms and slide trumpet, the latter taking the *cantus firmus*. In non-dance instrumental music, voices may take any or all of the lines, using solfège syllables.

Chansons, 1450–1520. These differ from earlier songs in that instruments should blend well with each other and with voices. No percussion.

Frottole. As above. If there is only one singer, (s)he should take the superius, the other parts going to instruments.

Instrumental ensemble music, 1520–1600. The standard is to use "whole" consorts of instruments from the same family, though this is not absolutely inflexible. Cornetts and sackbutts consort together. The curtal can be used as the bass for any group of winds. Polychoral pieces should use contrasting consorts in each choir. A piece may be played by a 4' or 16' consort, if that is found to work musically, but do not perform at 2' or 32'.

For particularly splendid performances, especially of Northern Italian or Southern German repertoire, double consorts (unison or octave) may be used and may even alternate to create terraced dynamic effects. In that same repertoire, especially toward the end of the century, a keyboard or plucked string instrument may be added to each choir in a *basso seguente* role and the bass line may be reinforced.

English ensemble music of this period is almost all conceived for viol consort, though other whole consorts may be used instead.

Shawms, schryari, rauschpfeiffen (all of which consort together and with brasses), as well as citterns and rebecs, should be reserved for dances and other music of distinctly popular character. Percussion should be added only to boisterous dance performances.

Abstract ensemble music (canzone, ricercare, fantasias, In Nomines) may be *sung*, using solfège syllables.

Part-songs, 1520–1600. Generally *a capella*, and one to a part. Women's voices are accepted in this repertoire at least by the end of the century and probably much earlier. Those madrigals and other part-songs intended for festival or ceremonial use were performed chorally, sometimes with instrumental reinforcement. English madrigals may if desired be accompanied by lute and/or bass viol or curtal.

Masses, motets, etc., in Northern Italy, Southern Germany, and Spain. The "Venetian" style of Northern Italy and Southern Germany allows, even favors, the use of instruments in sacred choral works. Starting roughly with the works of Lassus and Andrea Gabrieli, instruments may be used in any polychoral work (except those of expressly penitential or sombre character), and in single-choir works intended for festive or pompous occasions.

Each choir should be assigned to either voices or instruments, though individual vocal lines or an entire vocal choir may be instrumentally doubled if this seems appropriate. The choirs should be balanced in loudness unless contrasting dynamic effects seem clearly intended. Instrumental choirs may be composed of mixed groups of instruments, but all those in one choir should be of basically similar sound and volume. Non-sustaining instruments should be used only to double a part already assigned to a sustaining instrument or voice. All parts of one, several, or all choirs should be doubled by one or two organs as a *basso seguente*, and any or all bass lines instrumentally reinforced—particularly by curtal or sackbutt. No percussion, citterns, or loud reeds (shawms, etc.) should be employed.

Spanish church music of the period used instruments in a somewhat different fashion. Here all parts should be sung and instruments be used only to double, but the instruments most frequently used were a flamboyant ensemble of sackbutts and shawms. Even quiet or subdued works would be likely to have a curtal doubling the bass line.

Early keyboard music. Many pieces specify the instrument required, or it is possible to deduce this from external or internal evidence. Where this is not the case, the piece may legitimately be played on any keyboard instrument of the time. Pieces with a sacred *cantus firmus* are almost always intended for organ. Baroque works based on dances are for any keyboard *except* the organ; however, earlier pieces of this type might well be played on regal or chamber organ.

Continuo lines: orchestral. The bass line is played by a section of cellos doubled at 16' by a section of contrabasses.* Whenever reeds or brass are playing, a bassoon should be added to the continuo—even if there is a separate obbligato bassoon part—for the duration of the passage in question. The bassoon alone accompanies reeds or brass *soli.*

In concertos the *soli* passages are accompanied by a single cello on the bass line; thus also in recitative.

The chord instrument should be organ for sacred works and any others intended for church performance and harpsichord in all other cases.

Continuo lines: non-orchestral. The bass instrument should usually be of the same family as the melody instrument(s): bassoon for oboe, cello for violin, etc. For flutes use gamba, for recorders use gamba or (prior to about 1720) bass recorder at 4' pitch. For low-pitched solo instruments (bass voice, viola, cello, bassoon) a contrabass at 16' may be an appropriate continuo bass. For cornetts or horns use cello or curtal (later bassoon) continuo.

Choral sections of sacred vocal works may be supported by curtal (= bassoon), sackbutt (= trombone) or (in French works) serpent. The sackbutt (together with regal) is also used as continuo for demonic or underworld characters in early operas, and perhaps to support an ensemble containing obbligato sackbutt parts. Solo voices, where no obbligato instruments are present to give a clue, should be supported by cello or gamba on the bass line.

Pre-orchestral operas and related genres (monodies, sacred concerti, etc.) use a great variety of chord instruments. The various continuo-lutes were most popular, but harpsichord, positive organ, harp, and bandora were also used; the regal was used with sackbutt in demonic and underworld scenes. Harpsichord is favored for instrumental chamber combinations. After about 1660 the harpsichord is preferred for all secular music, the organ for sacred. The lute remains, up to about 1720, the traditional accompaniment for solo voices in pieces containing no obbligato instrumental lines beyond the continuo.

It is not absolutely necessary to use two instruments on the continuo line, but the use of a single instrument should be sparing and well-motivated musically. The single instruments best adapted to complete continuo playing are the continuo lutes (which can bring out the bass line on their own) and the gamba (which can to a certain extent play chords).

---

* If an obbligato cello line has been written, only contrabasses play the continuo.

POSITION OF EARLY INSTRUMENTS
IN MODERN SCORES

There is of course no standard arrangement, but the old instruments should be kept near their modern counterparts.

The following order is suggested:

recorders

flutes

shawms

oboes

rauschpfeiffen

schryari

crumhorns, kortholt, etc.

clarinets

saxophones

racketts, sordunes

curtals

bassoons

cornetti

brass

percussion

keyboard idiophones

piano

clavichord

harpsichord

organ

dulcimer

psaltery

harp

lyres

citterns

lutes

guitars

viols

rebecs

fiddle

liras

viola d'amore, baryton

violins

hurdy-gurdies

XII

EARLY

WINDS

AND

PERCUSSION

THE RECORDERS

It is entirely appropriate that our discussion of early instruments begin with the recorder, the best known and most widely played of all. The recorder could be described as a breath-blown organ flue pipe with fingerholes. Air passing through the narrow windway is directed across the **mouth** of the recorder against the edge of the wooden **lip**, producing sound exactly as in an organ pipe.

The recorder exhibits a number of properties that we will find over and over in early woodwinds. First, it is very soft—as becomes immediately apparent when it is combined with modern instruments. Second, individual notes scarcely can be varied in loudness at all. To get different dynamic levels it is necessary to play in different parts of the range, as the instrument increases markedly in loudness as the scale is ascended. Composers *should not indicate dynamics in any recorder part*, as the player has virtually no control over them. Twentieth-century composers—including Hindemith and Berio—have consistently misunderstood this and have regularly scored dynamic indications for recorder that are pure fantasy in terms of the instrument's capabilities. Players simply ignore such markings.*

---

* The dynamic markings in Baroque recorder parts are "faked" by means of varied articulation and vibrato. This is entirely within the period's understanding of dynamics but does not, of course, correspond to modern concepts.

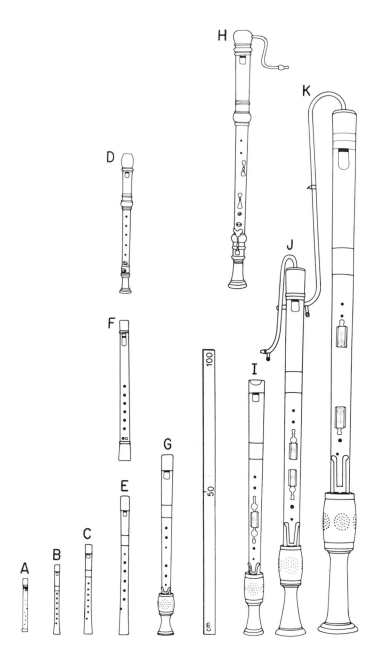

FIGURE 227. *Recorders: (a) garklein; (b) Renaissance sopranino; (c) Renaissance soprano; (d) Baroque alto; (e) Renaissance alto; (f) medieval alto; (g) Renaissance tenor; (h) Baroque bass; (i) Renaissance bass; (j) great bass; (k) contrabass.*

For all early woodwinds it is necessary to watch out for fingering difficulties. Note that many notes require fork-fingerings, and that a number of trills are awkward or impossible to perform.

The fingering chart given is for alto recorder. To be applied to other sizes of recorder it must in many cases be transposed, for though recorders are built in F and C they use only octave transpositions: thus the low C of garklein, soprano, tenor, and great bass recorder is fingered like the low F of sopranino, alto, bass, and contrabass.

name of instrument	abbreviations	approximate dates of original use	written range	sounds	availability
garklein Floetlein	gkl.	until 1650	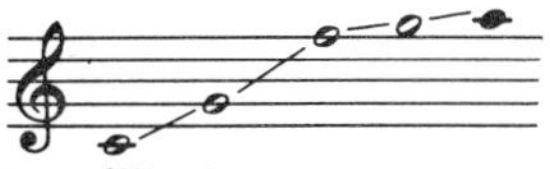 loudness: *pp—p—mp*———	2 octaves higher	very rare
sopranino recorder	snrec.	Baroque 1660–1750	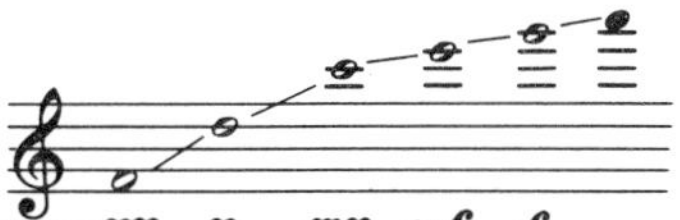 loudness: *pp—p—mp mf—f*	1 octave higher	common
		Renaissance until 1690	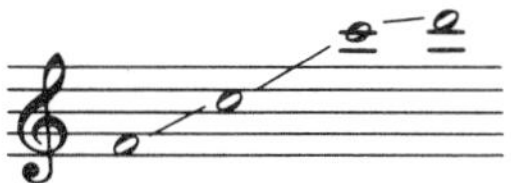 loudness: *pp—p—mp*———	1 octave higher	very rare
soprano recorder	srec.	Baroque 1660–1750	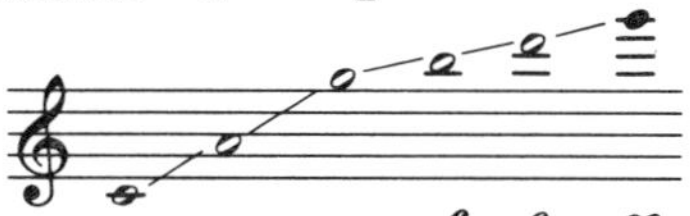 loudness: *pp—p—mp mf—f—ff*	1 octave higher	ubiquitous
		Renaissance until 1690	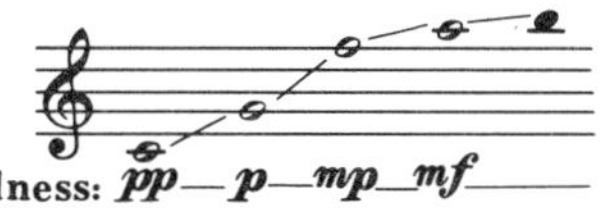 loudness: *pp—p—mp mf*	1 octave higher	rare
alto recorder	arec.	Baroque 1660–1750	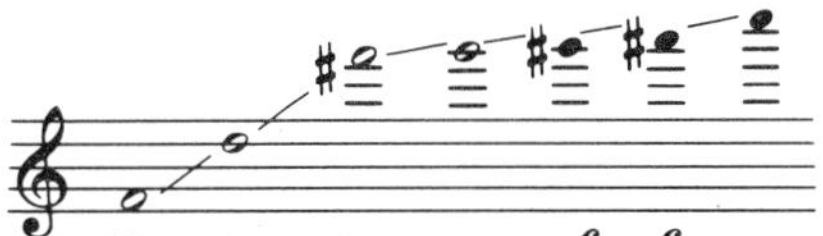 loudness: *pp—p—mp——mf—f*———	as written	ubiquitous
		Renaissance until 1690	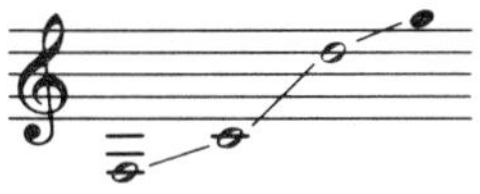 loudness: *pp—p—mp*———	1 octave higher	rare

FIGURE 228. *The recorder family—vital statistics.*

The lowest two chromatic tones are produced by half-hole fingerings, and composers must be careful about their use. A passage such as this is very awkward to play:

but this is not:

On most tenor recorders the low c^1 is reached by means of a key, and the $c\sharp^1$ is impossible. All lower recorders are provided with a similar key for the bottom note, and the lowest chromatic

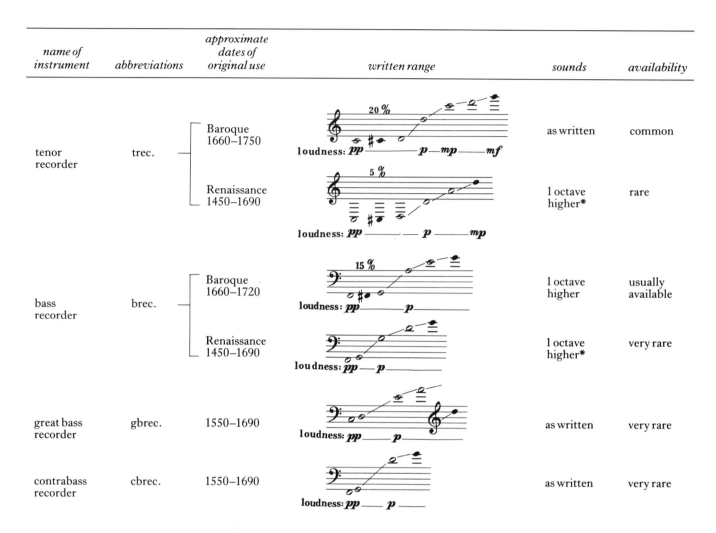

name of instrument	abbreviations	approximate dates of original use	written range	sounds	availability
tenor recorder	trec.	Baroque 1660–1750		as written	common
		Renaissance 1450–1690		1 octave higher*	rare
bass recorder	brec.	Baroque 1660–1720		1 octave higher	usually available
		Renaissance 1450–1690		1 octave higher*	very rare
great bass recorder	gbrec.	1550–1690		as written	very rare
contrabass recorder	cbrec.	1550–1690		as written	very rare

* Renaissance tenor and bass recorders read at actual pitch when serving as superius and altus of an 8′ consort, while the great bass recorder may read at 4′ when playing continuo or serving as bass to a 4′ consort.

The recorder family—vital statistics, continued.

tone is unavailable except on those bass recorders provided with a special (and ahistorical) key for the $f\sharp^0$. Some bass recorders are provided with up to four or five other keys as well, but this does not affect the fingering or availability of notes.

Recorders are made in **Renaissance** and **Baroque** patterns, of which the Baroque is far more common. The lower register of Renaissance recorders has a fuller tone than the Baroque type, with much more "presence" and a distinct, organ-like chiff of attack noise, but this strong lower register is gained at the expense of range at the upper end. There are also slight differences in fingering—on Renaissance recorders the low register fork-fingerings (on alto $b\flat^1$, b^1, $c\sharp^2$, $e\flat^2$) have only one finger put down beyond the open hole. The Renaissance instruments

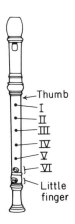

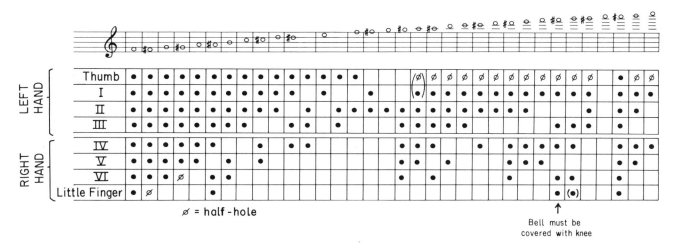

FIGURE 229. *Fingering chart for Baroque alto recorder.*

provide a much stronger and more believable bass, and the two lowest sizes of recorder are strictly Renaissance types.*

The tiny garklein (which at least one maker has been unable to resist calling a "mini-prino") is also a strictly Renaissance form. It is of dubious value in early music (it appears to have been a "gimmick" instrument, as the sopranino saxophone is today), but today's composers may be interested in it because of its incredibly high tessitura.

Any modern pieces written simply for "recorders," without qualification, will be played on Baroque instruments; and the term "recorder," similarly unqualified, refers to the Baroque alto, the most common and important size. Renaissance recorders must thus be specified when their use is desired. Composers wishing to have both the organ-pipe fullness of the low Renaissance types and the range and flexibility of the higher Baroque instruments may combine the two without fear, as they blend well together.

* Great bass and contrabass recorders have been made in the Baroque pattern, but these instruments are not only historically invalid but virtually useless musically.

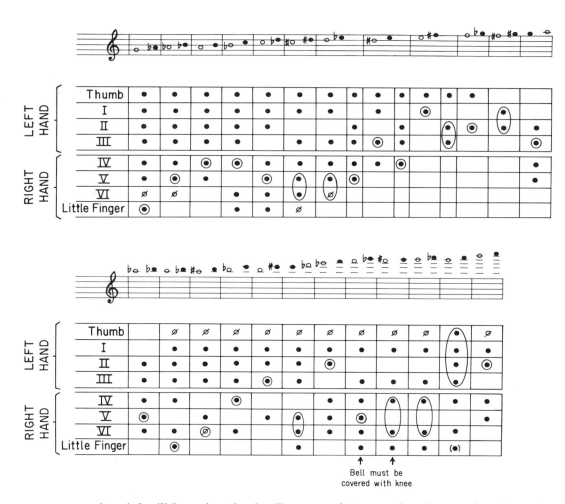

FIGURE 230. *Special trill fingerings for the (Baroque alto) recorder: the complete fingering shown produces the open note; when the circled fingers are raised, the filled note is produced.*

It will be noted that several of the recorders read in different octaves in their Renaissance and Baroque incarnations. This reflects their differing musical uses: the Renaissance types in an SATB 4′ consort, the Baroque types as soloists with A and T at 8′, S and Sn at 4′.

There is, by the way, a confusion of terminology with regard to the sizes of recorder, the British and Americans using conflicting names for some sizes, as follows:

American	*British*
soprano	descant
alto	treble
great bass	quart bass
contrabass	great bass

One or two builders are now making **medieval recorders** in sopranino, soprano, and alto sizes. Instruments of this type were used up to about 1500; Renaissance recorders appeared around 1485. The tone of these instruments is unusually delicate and whistle-like, resembling that of the various Western folk recorders. The upper register in particular is much lighter than that of either the Baroque or Renaissance type. Interestingly, the medieval recorder has as great a range as the Baroque form, including even the upper extension tones.

The tone of recorders—even (if they are well made) the highest and lowest varieties—is beautifully sweet, clear, and delicate. The instrument is played with extremely low breath pressure but at high air volume, so frequent breaths are necessary, particularly for the larger sizes. A vibrato is available if desired.

Tonguing (including double-tonguing and fluttertonguing) is as on the flute. Special effects include breathy playing, over- or underblowing (these affect both pitch and timbre), multiphonics (more easily performed than on the flute), and humming while playing. Microtones are possible and easy above a♭¹ on the alto recorder or the equivalently fingered pitch (A♭, E♭) on other recorders. Glissandos can be played very smoothly except across the register breaks and can go right to the bottom of the range, even where the lowest note has a key.

Because of the low breath pressure, cyclic breathing is very difficult, but it is possible if the player blows into the windway through pursed lips.

MUSICAL EXAMPLES

RECORDERS:

Schmelzer, Sonata a 7 flauti (SSAATTB)
Telemann, Sonata in C, from *Der getreue Musikmeister* (A)
Handel, "Augeletti che cantate" from *Rinaldo* (SnAA)
Hindemith, Trio for recorders (SAA or SAT)
Berio, *Gesti* (A)
Wolff, *Electric Spring No. 2* (AT)

GEMSHORNS

A late and specialized variety of medieval recorder is the **gemshorn**, primordially a signal instrument fashioned from the horn of a chamois. A considerably larger horn is needed to make a musically useful instrument, and in its fully developed form the gemshorn was made from a cow or ibex horn, usually (today almost invariably) the former. In this state the instrument flourished from roughly 1375 to 1540. Modern gemshorns are available in soprano to bass sizes—the bass probably should be used only for music post-1450.

Because the bore of a gemshorn is so wide at the top and completely closed off at the bottom, the instrument is somewhat ocarina-like in its acoustics. The tone is very beautiful, covered, slightly hooty, and a bit louder than even the Renaissance recorder. Gemshorns overblow only irregularly and inconsistently, *approximately* two octaves above the fundamental; the practical compass of the instrument is thus limited to the lower register alone, though indeterminate overblown notes can be used as a modern special effect. The bass gemshorn is reportedly able to ascend to sounding a¹—presumably using a completely open fingering for that note.

THE TABOR PIPE

The **tabor pipe** is another specialized variety of recorder, designed to be playable with one hand. This is accomplished by making the bore very narrow, as in a brass instrument, so that a

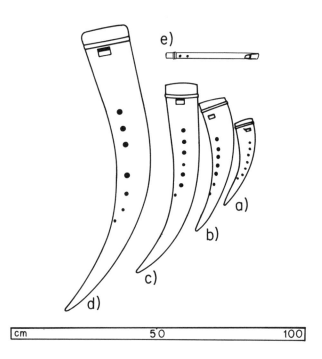

FIGURE 231. *Recorder relatives: (a) soprano gemshorn; (b) alto gemshorn; (c) tenor gemshorn; (d) bass gemshorn; (e) soprano tabor pipe.*

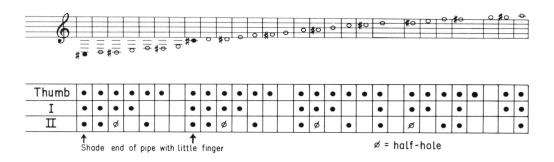

FIGURE 232. *Fingering chart for soprano tabor pipe (the instrument sounds two octaves higher).*

variety of high partials lying close together can be produced easily, while the fundamental is weak and not normally played. The player uses the free hand to play the tabor drum (q.v), and this pipe-and-tabor combination was used for dance music. In modern terms it is intriguing to think of someone playing tabor pipe with one hand and percussion or keyboard with the other.

In addition to the ordinary soprano in D, whose range and fingering are given above, there is an alto in G (non-transposing).

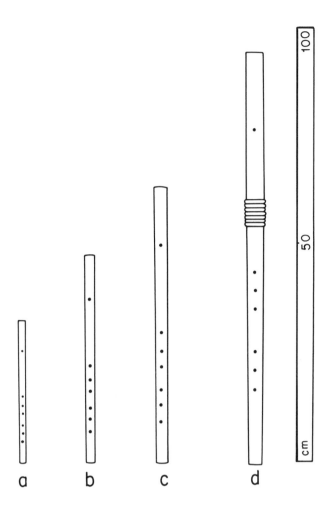

FIGURE 233. *Renaissance flutes: (a) soprano; (b) alto; (c) tenor; (d) bass.*

RENAISSANCE FLUTES

Renaissance flutes are too much like the modern flute to be of much interest to composers—in fact, they sound more "modern" than Baroque flutes do—but they are included here for the sake of completeness and as an aid to students of early music.*

The tenor is the most important member of the family and is the direct ancestor of the ordinary flute of today. Note that in the Renaissance the flute was a 4′ instrument. It is worth comparing Figure 235 with the modern flute fingering chart (Fig. 14) and with the recorder chart (Fig. 229). The underlying similarity of woodwind fingering patterns is much more clearly apparent among these keyless early instruments than among their modern successors.

The Renaissance flutes sound distinctly less full and more breathy than modern flutes. Articulation and special effects are virtually the same in the two types.

* The Baroque flute—with a tapering bore and a key for low $d\sharp^1$—was introduced around 1680 and almost immediately replaced the older type.

name of instrument	abbreviations	approximate dates of original use	written range	sounds	availability
soprano Renaissance flute	sRfl.	until 1580	 loudest: *p* – *mp* – *mf* – *f* ___ softest: *pp* ___ *p* – *mp* – *mf* ___	1 octave higher	very rare
alto Renaissance flute	aRfl.	until 1680	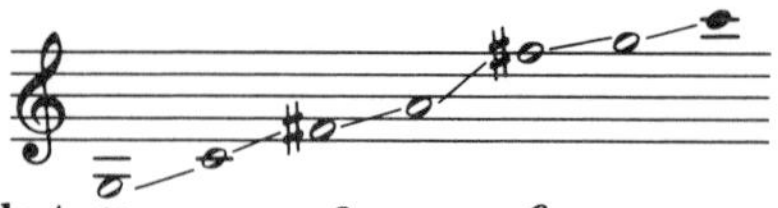 loudest: *p* – *mp* – *mf* ___ *f* ___ softest: *pp* ___ *p* – *mp* – *mf* – *f*	1 octave higher	rare
tenor Renaissance flute	tRfl.	until 1680	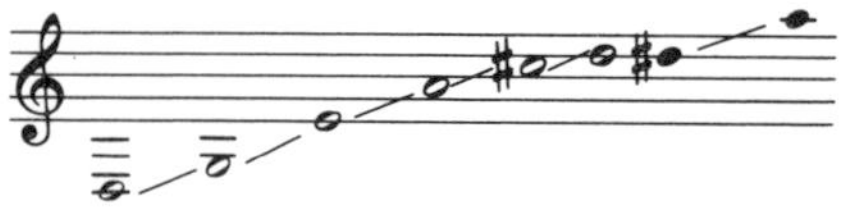 loudest: *p* ___ *mp* – *mf* – *f* ___ softest: *pp* ___ *p* – *mp* ___ *mf*	1 octave higher	rare
bass Renaissance flute	bRfl.	until 1680	 loudest: *pp* ___ *p* – *mp* ___ *mf* ___ softest: *pp* ___ *p* – *mp* ___	1 octave higher	very rare

FIGURE 234. *Renaissance flutes—vital statistics.*

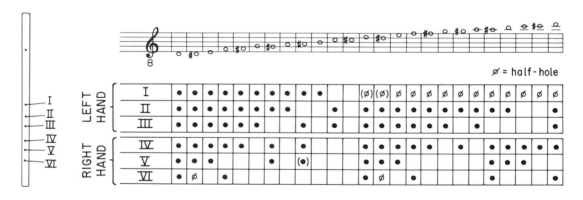

∅ = half-hole

FIGURE 235. *Fingering chart for tenor Renaissance flute.*

MUSICAL EXAMPLES

RENAISSANCE FLUTE:

Morley, *The First Book of Consort Lessons*, No. 12: "Goe from my window" (T)
Schütz, *Symphoniae Sacrae*, Pt. I, Nos. 7–8: "Anima mea liquefacta est"/"Adjuro vos, filiae Jerusalem" (TT)

THE SHAWMS

The shawms are ancestors of the oboe family but differ from them considerably in function, appearance, and sound. Shawms were, at least after the Middle Ages, primarily band instruments, performing roughly the same musical function as that of the saxophones today. Like saxophones they are loud instruments, designed to carry well outdoors and to compete with brasses on a more or less equal footing.

The tone of a shawm is brilliant, blaring, and nasal, almost out of control. The lowest notes on any of them are wall-rattling honks. The fierce tone is initiated by a distinctive quacking attack when notes are tongued. In order to get the strongest possible sound the lips do not control the reed directly: they are instead pressed against a wooden **pirouette** at the top of the instrument. The pirouette, resembling a brass-instrument mouthpiece, serves to hold the lips firmly against the base of the reed, supporting it but not damping it, since the blades of the reed are almost entirely within the player's mouth. Played thus, there is little control over dynamics, which may be varied only between *forte* and *fortissimo* throughout the range, the lowest notes being the loudest. On bass and great bass shawms there is no pirouette,* and the reed is taken directly between the lips as in oboes and bassoons, giving a range of controlled dynamics roughly parallel to that of a saxophone but narrower at all points in the range.

As can be seen from Figures 237–39, the shawm has an inflexible fingering system best suited to diatonic music. The thumb hole is present only in the soprano and sopranino sizes, but the fingerings are not significantly different on the lower sizes, save that the $c\#^1$ (on the tenor—on the alto it would be $f\#^1$, on bass $f\#^0$, etc.) is a problematic "fake" or may not be available at all, and the d^1 (again, on the tenor) is available only in the upper-register fingering.

Except for sopraninos and some sopranos, the right little-finger note is governed by a key, making the chromatic note immediately above impossible to produce (see fingering chart). The lower extension tones for alto and tenor and the equivalent three bottom notes on bass and great bass are produced by additional keys for that finger and for the right thumb. The extended alto and the *unextended* tenor are sometimes referred to as **nicolo** shawms, while the extended tenor is often called **basset**, particularly in England.

If we ignore the downward extensions, the lowest notes of the various shawms are f^1, c^1, f^0, c^0, F_0, and C_0—a much more rational pattern than Figure 237 at first appears to show. As usual with early winds, all are non-transposing instruments, and the fingering chart must therefore be transposed to F for sopranino, alto, and bass shawms.

All the keywork on any shawm is enclosed in a protective, pierced wooden barrel called a **fontanelle**. This is analogous in function to the little metal baskets built over certain low saxophone keys and is indicative of the rough handling historical shawms were expected to endure. The "swallowtail" design of the keys on these and other early woodwinds reflects the fact that they all could be and were played *with either hand uppermost*. Everyone today plays with the left hand uppermost, but the **swallowtail keys** are retained as a gesture to tradition.

Despite the inflexible fingering system, shawms are capable of microtones above e^1 on the soprano (or the equivalent pitch on other sizes) and glissandos down to d^1 or the equivalent. Multiphonics are considerably fewer than on modern double-reed instruments.

---

* At least one major modern builder leaves the pirouettes off all sizes of shawm, but this ahistorical practice is unlikely to persist much longer.

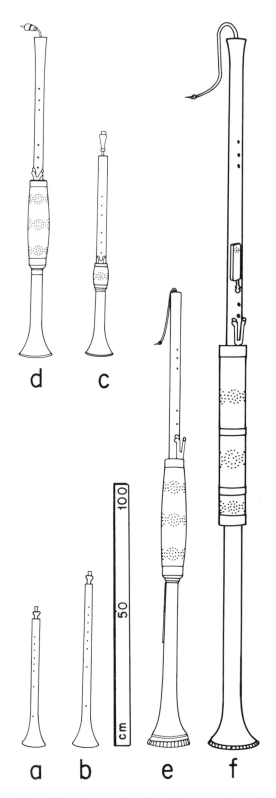

FIGURE 236. *The shawm family: (a) sopranino; (b) soprano; (c) alto; (d) tenor; (e) bass; (f) great bass.*

name of instrument	*abbreviations*	*approximate dates of original use*	*written range*	*sounds*	*availability*
sopranino shawm	sn. shawm	1200–1670	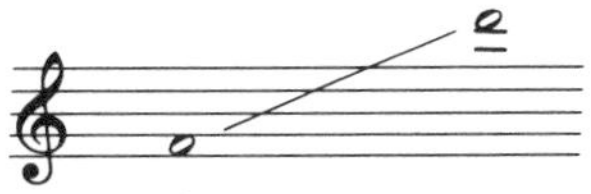 **loudness: *f/ff***	as written	very rare
soprano shawm	s. shawm	1300–1670	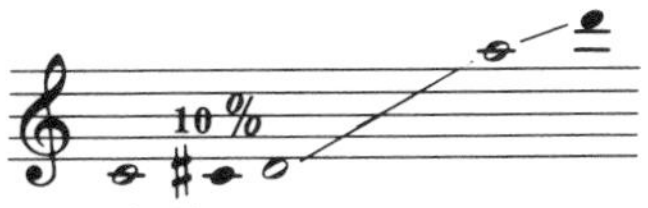 **loudness: *f/ff***	as written	rare
alto shawm	a. shawm	1325–1670	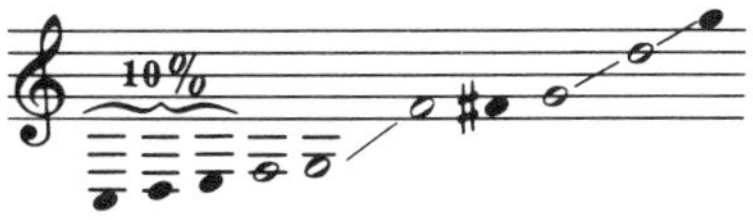 **loudness: *f/ff***	as written	rare
tenor shawm	t. shawm	1360–1670	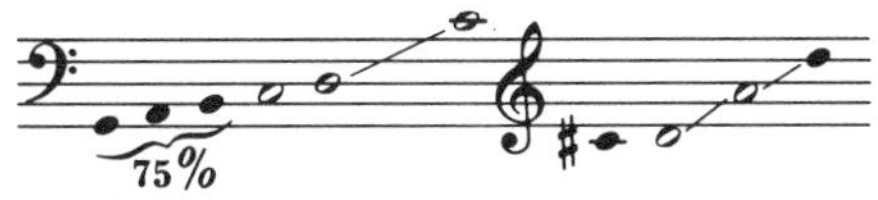 **loudness: *f/ff***	as written	rare
bass shawm	b. shawm	1450–1670	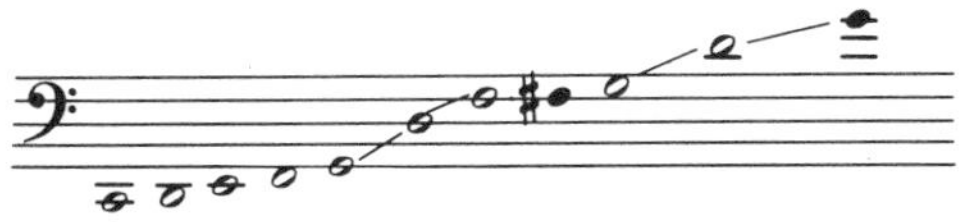 **loudest: *ff*** ——— **softest: *f*** ——— ***mf–mp*** ———	as written	very rare
great bass shawm	gb. shawm	1550–1670	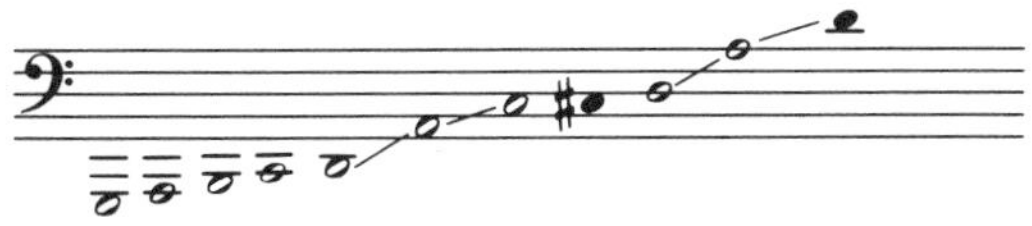 **loudest: *ff*** ——— **softest: *f*** ——— ***mf–mp*** ———	as written	very rare

FIGURE 237. *The shawm family—vital statistics.*

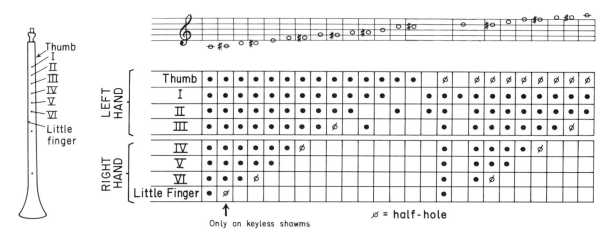

FIGURE 238. *Fingering chart for soprano shawm.*

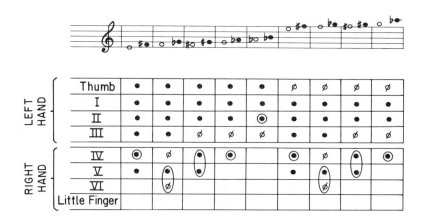

FIGURE 239. *Special trill fingerings for the soprano shawm: the complete fingering shown produces the open note; when the circled fingers are raised, the filled note is produced.*

BASSANELLI

The Baroque oboe, introduced around 1655, very quickly displaced the shawm all over Europe. There were several earlier attempts to create a soft-toned, expressive shawm, of which the most important was the **bassanello** (1575–1625). Originally made in sizes corresponding to unextended tenor, bass, and great bass shawms, bassanelli are among the very few Renaissance instruments that have not yet been revived.

MUSICAL EXAMPLES

SHAWMS:

    Schein, "Hosianna dem Sohne David," from *Opella nova* (TTB)
    Wernick, *Songs of Remembrance* (S)
    Kagel, *Musik für Renaissanceinstrumente* (SATB)

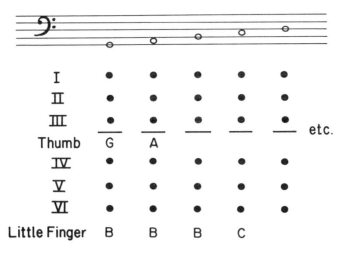

FIGURE 240. *Extension tones for tenor shawm.*

BAGPIPES

Bagpipes are of course still with us as folk instruments, but in the Middle Ages (to about 1400) they were used in all kinds of music, especially monophonic. Modern players of this repertoire use any of the dozens of modern folk bagpipes—the most prominent of many instances where modern folk instruments are used for the performance of medieval music.

Complete delineation of all the kinds of bagpipes would take a book in itself, and is clearly outside the scope of this one, but a brief discussion is merited.

Air from the bagpipe-player's mouth is used to inflate a leather bag, and air from the bag (which is kept under pressure by the player's left arm) flows continuously through the various reed pipes attached to it. The melody pipe is called the **chanter**. It does not overblow and seldom exceeds the range of a ninth. Also attached to the bag may be one or two **drone pipes** giving the note two octaves below the chanter's keynote, and the fifth or octave of that.

The chanter has a conical bore and double reed; the drones have single reeds and cylindrical bores.

Much of the variety in modern bagpipes postdates the Middle Ages. Such things as bellows-blown pipes, cylindrical or single-reed chanters, overblowing chanters, and triple drones did not exist in medieval bagpipes; the earliest bagpipes had no drones at all. Single drones first appeared in the mid-thirteenth century and double ones in the fourteenth.

The fingering pattern for the chanter varies, but it basically resembles that of the recorder's lower register, save that  is usually only a half-step below

The next-to-lowest note, the keynote of the chanter, may sound anywhere between g^1 and c^2.

The tone of a bagpipe is a brilliant and raucous *fortissimo* designed to be heard outdoors. At the beginning of a piece the sound is started by suddenly pressing the bag, and at the end it is stopped by just as quickly releasing it. It is possible, though difficult, to do these things without a swoop in pitch. Articulation in the normal sense is impossible during the course of a piece, but articulation of a sort is produced by introducing numerous grace notes.

THE CRUMHORNS

In the crumhorns we see a number of features found in no modern woodwind. First of all, it is a **reedcap instrument**, that is, the reed is completely covered by a removable cap with a hole in the top through which the player blows (Fig. 244). The player's lips do not touch the reed.

The crumhorn—unlike any modern instrument—combines a double reed with a cylin-

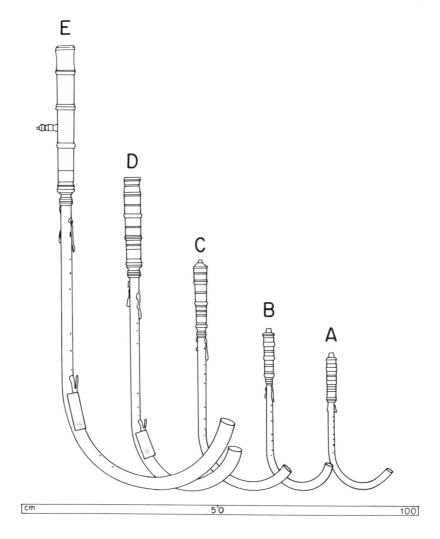

FIGURE 241. *Crumhorns: (a) soprano; (b) alto; (c) tenor; (d) bass; (e) great bass.*

drical bore. The instrument's delicate buzz has therefore some of the liquid quality of the clarinet, but buzziness is the main impression. The cylindrical bore requires that the base of the reed be no narrower than the bore itself, so crumhorns have a very narrow bore coupled to an unusually large reed. The buzzy tone-quality reflects the dominance of the reed in this system. Dynamic inflections are totally impossible on any reedcap instrument, and reedcap instruments of all types have a somewhat explosive attack, rather like the way a person with a stuffy nose says "d" or "b."

Since the bore of the crumhorn is narrow, the tone holes are mere pinholes, and half-hole fingerings are impossible. Crumhorns and other cylindrical double-reeds are played with unusually high breath pressure but low air volume.

The crumhorn does not normally overblow. Its fingering system is to all intents and purposes that of the Renaissance recorder's lower register. The lowest two chromatic tones are missing. Almost all modern crumhorns have one or (more usually) two ahistorical upward-extension keys for the left thumb and first finger. On alto crumhorn these give g#^{1} (thumb key), a^1 (front key), and b♭^{1} (both keys). Bass and great bass crumhorns take the lowest note with a key, and are occasionally fitted with downward extensions. Such an extension may take either of two forms: there may be three extra keys for the right thumb and little finger, as with the low shawms (q.v.), or there may be only one extra key (for the little finger), which may be pre-set to give any *one* of the three possible extra low notes.

The crumhorn is the foremost example of an instrument in which increasing authenticity is actually reducing its value to the modern composer. In the 1960s virtually all crumhorns were equipped with both upward extensions, and about fifty percent of the basses and great basses had shawm-type downward extensions; furthermore, the two missing chromatic tones were universally available via recorder-like double fingerholes. Some crumhorns are now made without *any* upward extension, and the authentic alto in (non-transposing) g^0—a tone higher than the usual modern alto in f^0—is now available from several makers.

Two or three good multiphonics can be gotten from a crumhorn. The tiny fingerholes make glissandos somewhat tricky, but they are possible. Quarter-tones can be had from (on alto) f♮^{1} up. Notes can be inflected in pitch by varying the breath pressure—increasingly so as the scale is ascended, so that while the lowest note cannot be bent at all, the highest can be varied across a major second or more. The position of the "true" note within the inflection range varies from instrument to instrument and depends also on the adjustment of the reed.

With various combinations of instrument and reed, very low breath pressure will produce overblowing to the third partial, a multiphonic, or a privileged-frequency "undertone" a fourth below the usual pitch. All these phenomena are difficult to control and are limited to the lower part of the range.

CORNAMUSES

The **cornamuse** is a special variety of crumhorn, straight in profile and with a plugged bell. The plug mutes the instrument, making it considerably less buzzy but not much softer. The lowest note emerges from a set of small holes pierced in the sides of the bell. When the plug is removed the cornamuse sounds exactly like a crumhorn. Fingering pattern and sizes are as for the crumhorn. Dates of original use are about the same, but cornamuses seem to have become extinct earlier—around 1625. All modern cornamuses are provided with two upward-extension keys, but the low sizes never have any downward extension. The extremely rare great bass cornamuse (not illustrated) probably did not exist historically.

The mysterious **douçaine**, of which no examples or illustrations survive, was presumably an ancestor (unplugged? uncapped?) of the cornamuse; it existed from about 1275 on.

MUSICAL EXAMPLES

CRUMHORNS:

Schein, Padovana for crumhorns, from *Banchetto musicale*
Kagel, *Musik für Renaissanceinstrumente*

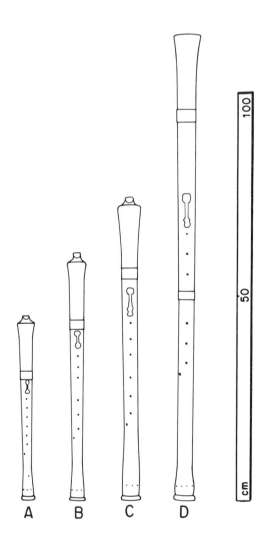

FIGURE 242. *Cornamuses: (a) soprano; (b) alto; (c) tenor; (d) bass.*

name of instrument	abbreviations	approximate dates of original use	written range	sounds	availability
soprano crumhorn	scrum.	1530–1635	 80% ... loudness: *mp* *mf*	as written	rare
alto crumhorn	acrum.	1450–1635	 80% ... loudness: *mp* *mf*	as written	rare
tenor crumhorn	tcrum.	1450–1635	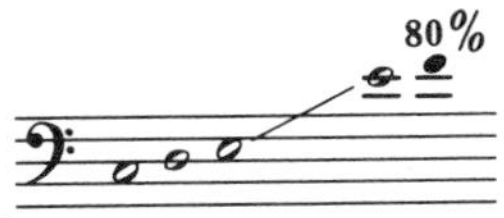 80% ... loudness: *mp*	as written	rare
bass crumhorn	bcrum.	1450–1635	 80% ... 5% ... loudness: *p* *mp*	as written	rare
great bass crumhorn	gbcrum.	1550–1635	 80% ... 5% ... loudness: *p* *mp*	as written	very rare

FIGURE 243. *The crumhorn family—vital statistics.*

OTHER REEDCAP INSTRUMENTS

KORTHOLTS

The **kortholt** was a short-lived experimental instrument of which we would know nothing had Praetorius not figured one in his *Syntagma musicum*. The bass kortholt is probably more common now than it ever was historically, and the higher sizes are purely conjectural.

The kortholt is essentially a cornamuse with its bore extended and bent back like that of a curtal or sordune (q.v.). As with the latter instruments, both parts of the bore are housed in one piece of wood, and the extra low notes (in the bass kortholt, those below F_0) are taken with the thumbs. The remaining notes are fingered as on the crumhorn.

Not surprisingly, these instruments sound exactly like cornamuses.

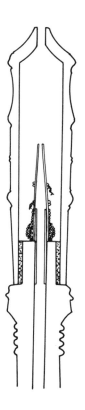

FIGURE 244. *Diagrammatic section of the top of a crumhorn, showing reed in place inside reedcap.*

RAUSCHPFEIFEN AND SCHRYARI

The **rauschpfeifen** and **schryari** comprise two related families of loud reedcap instruments. The schryari, with its narrow cylindrical bore and tiny fingerholes, is best thought of as a very loud, blaring crumhorn, while the rauschpfeife has a conical bore and is essentially a reedcap shawm. Both can be considered as musically more or less interchangeable with the shawm. Their sound is a brilliant, bagpipe-like skirl.

The rauschpfeife is the only reedcap instrument that overblows. It became extinct in Germany (its homeland) around 1550, but apparently lived on in France, for a modified form (in ATB sizes) crops up there in the seventeenth century under the name **hautbois de Poitou**. The rauschpfeife fingering system closely resembles that of the recorder; the only important difference is that low G♯ (sopranino and alto) is a fork-fingering rather than a half-hole. All tenor and some alto rauschpfeifen are provided with a key for the lowest note.

The tenor schryari also has such a key, and both alto and tenor schryari are provided with upward extension keys for left thumb and first finger—these were the inspiration for similar keys put on modern crumhorns. The soprano schryari has a plugged bell, like a cornamuse, to balance its volume with the lower sizes. The schryari was apparently limited to Germany throughout its lifetime.

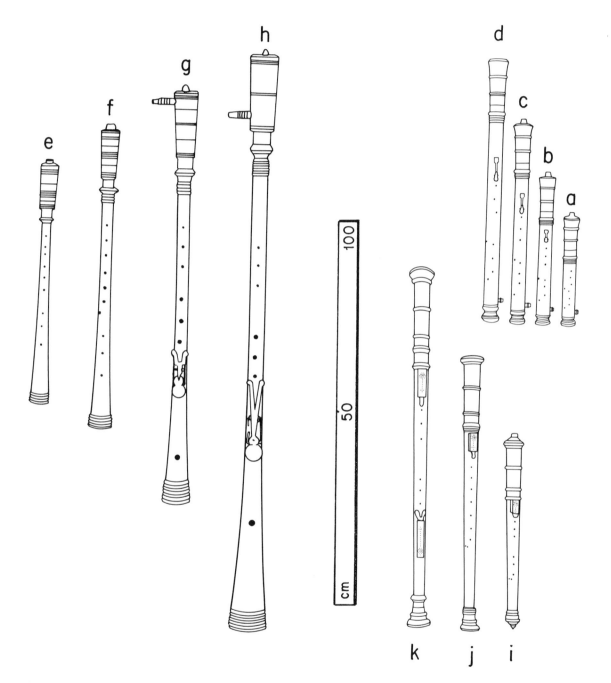

FIGURE 245. *Other reedcap instruments: (a) soprano kortholt; (b) alto kortholt; (c) tenor kortholt; (d) bass kortholt; (e) sopranino rauschpfeife; (f) soprano rauschpfeife; (g) alto rauschpfeife; (h) tenor rauschpfeife; (i) alto schryari; (j) tenor schryari; (k) bass schryari.*

name of instrument	abbreviations	approximate dates of original use	written range	sounds	availability
soprano kortholt	skt.	—	 loudness: *mp*	as written	very rare
alto kortholt	akt.	—	 loudness: *mp*	as written	very rare
tenor kortholt	tkt.	—	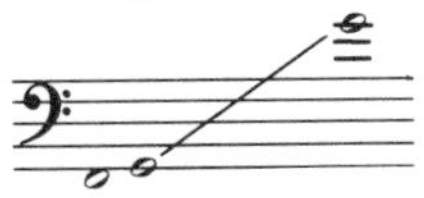 loudness: *mp*	as written	very rare
bass kortholt	bkt.	1600–1640	 loudness: *mp*	as written	rare

FIGURE 246. *The kortholt family—vital statistics.*

THE CURTALS

The bass curtal is the direct ancestor of the bassoon (compare the fingering charts), to which it is very similar in playing technique. It differs from the modern instrument not only in being virtually keyless but in that both channels of the bore are housed in a single piece of wood. The curtals are even softer and more veiled in tone than modern bassoons, and many are provided with a removable pierced cap for the bell to ensure that even the lowest notes will have this quality.

The Baroque bassoon was introduced around 1670, but the older instrument continued in use for another half-century. It is important to realize that early and mid-seventeenth century "bassoon" parts are intended for the curtal.

The two highest members of the curtal family sound rather like muffled English horns. They formed part of an SATB 8′ consort of curtals, used indoors in place of shawms—the Baroque oboe superseded them in this function. The contrabass curtal was never more than an experimental curiosity, but it did exist and was used.

The lowest three chromatic tones are weak and awkward on the curtal as originally designed. About half of all modern curtals are provided with one or two extra keys and a tone hole for the left little finger to make these notes easier to produce.

The curtal has multiphonics in as much profusion as the bassoon, and easily produces microtones and glissandos from G_0 to f^0 (on the bass curtal) and also from g^0 up.

name of instrument	abbreviations	approximate dates of original use	written range	sounds	availability
sopranino rauschpfeife	snrausch.	1500–1550	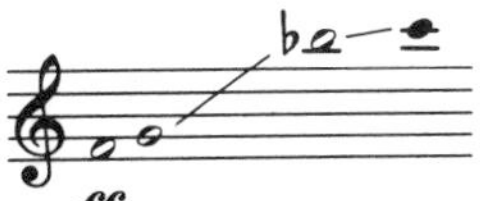 *(written range notation)* loudness: **ff**	as written	very rare
soprano rauschpfeife	srausch.	1500–1550	 *(written range notation)* loudness: **ff**	as written	very rare
alto rauschpfeife	arausch.	1500–1550 (–1670)	 *(written range notation)* loudness: **ff**	as written	very rare
tenor rauschpfeife	trausch.	1500–1550 (–1670)	 *(written range notation)* loudness: **ff**	as written	very rare
alto schryari	aschr.	1535–1650	 *(written range notation)* loudness: **ff**	as written	very rare
tenor schryari	tschr.	1535–1650	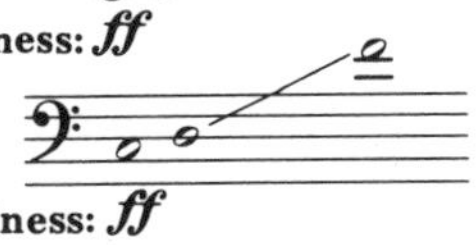 *(written range notation)* loudness: **ff**	as written	very rare
bass schryari	bschr.	1535–1650	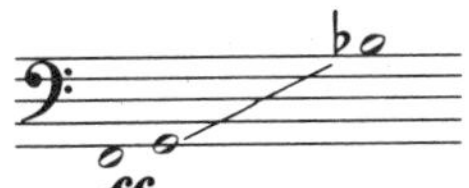 *(written range notation)* loudness: **ff**	as written	very rare

FIGURE 247. *Rauschpfeifen and schryari—vital statistics.*

MUSICAL EXAMPLES

CURTALS:

Schütz, *Symphoniae Sacrae*, Pt. I, Nos. 16–17: "In lectulo per noctes"/"Invenerunt me custodes civitatis" (TBB)

Domini est terra, SWV 476 (TBBBGb)

Schmelzer, Sonata "La Carolietta" (1669) (B)

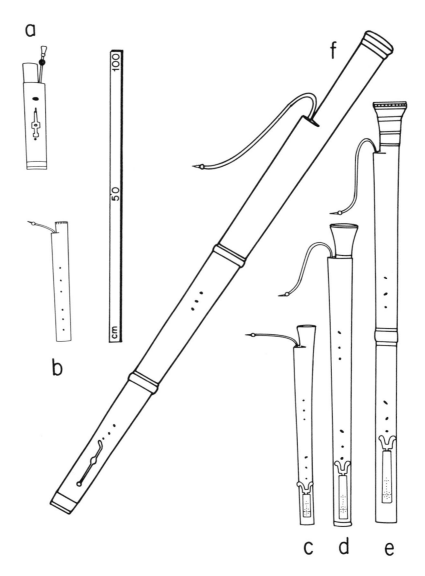

FIGURE 248. *Curtals: (a) soprano; (b) alto; (c) tenor; (d) bass; (e) great bass; (f) contrabass.*

THE RACKETTS

The rackett is surely one of the strangest creations of the human brain. It is a cylindrical-bored double-reed instrument, but the bore is folded back on itself *eight times* to make nine short, parallel bores housed in the same piece of wood. The large reed on its staple is inserted into the top of the central bore; the tiny instrument is held in both hands, as a squirrel holds an acorn, and in play looks more like some sort of elaborate bong than a woodwind.

There are tone holes for all ten fingers—two rows of four on the front of the instrument and two thumbholes on the back. There are also two further tone holes closed by the middle joints of the index fingers. The lowest note does not emerge from a bell, but from a larger-than-usual tone hole or group of holes at the lower left of the back of the instrument.

name of instrument	abbreviations	approximate dates of original use	written range	sounds	availability
soprano curtal	scurt.	1540–1670		as written	very rare
alto curtal	acurt.	1540–1720	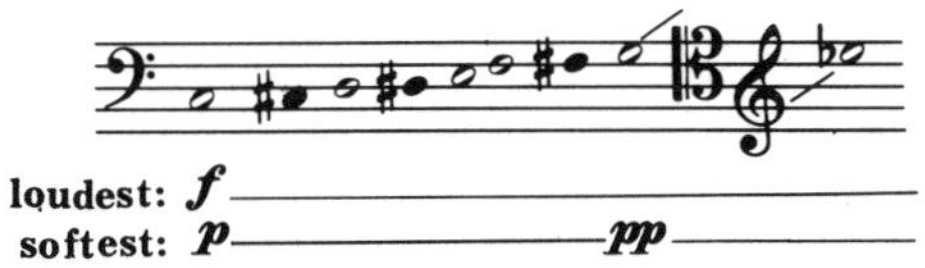	as written*	very rare
tenor curtal	tcurt.	1540–1720	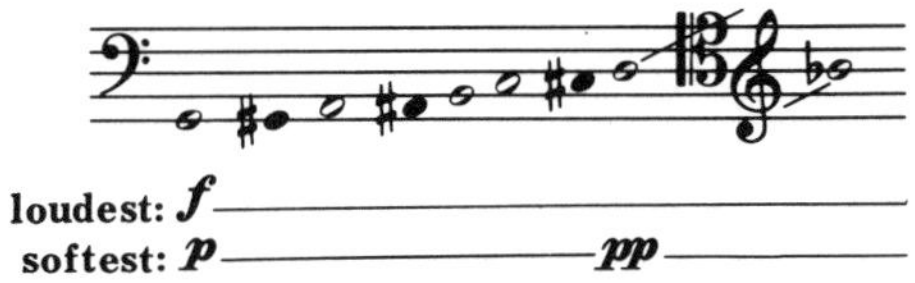	as written*	very rare
bass curtal	bcurt.	1540–1720		as written*	rare
great bass curtal	gbcurt.	1540–1720		as written*	very rare
contrabass curtal	cbcurt.	1575–1720	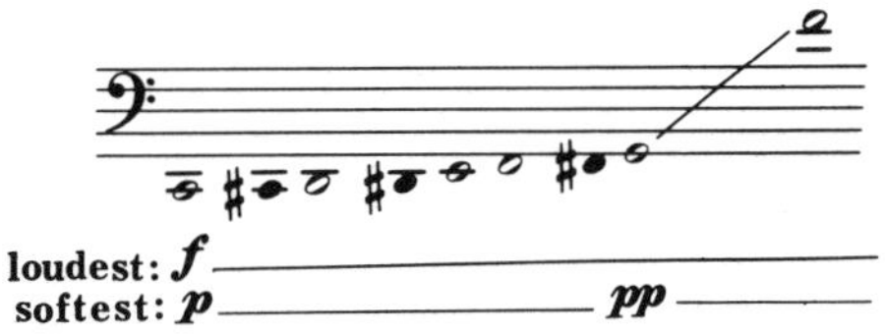	1 octave lower	very rare

* In the sixteenth century these four sizes were used together as a 16′ consort, playing notes an octave lower than written.

FIGURE 249. *The curtal family—vital statistics.*

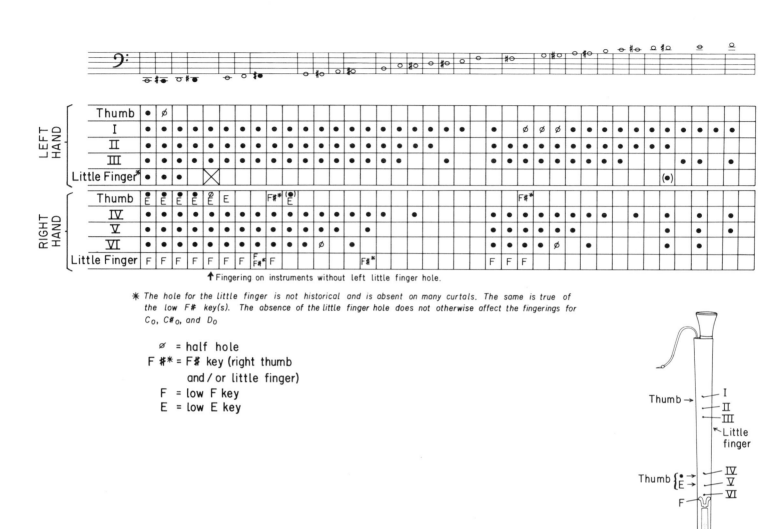

FIGURE 250. *Fingering chart for the bass curtal.*

The rackett is played with a pirouette (p. 405), but unlike the shawm it is not very loud. Indeed, it sounds much like a crumhorn, though not quite so buzzy and without the explosive reedcap attack.

The rackett's clumsy fingering system is best suited to the performance of diatonic music at moderate tempos.

There are four sizes of rackett, which were used together as a 16′ consort during the instrument's brief Renaissance career. Designations for the various sizes are a source of confusion; in addition to the T/B/Gb/Cb system used here, they are referred to elsewhere as tenor, bassett, bass, and great bass.

Exactly how racketts were used in the seventeenth century remains a bit of a puzzle. As there is next to no music for them, it must be assumed that they were employed as substitutes for the curtal. That was certainly the case with the eighteenth-century **Baroque rackett**, which is sometimes even called "rackett bassoon." The Baroque rackett is only superficially

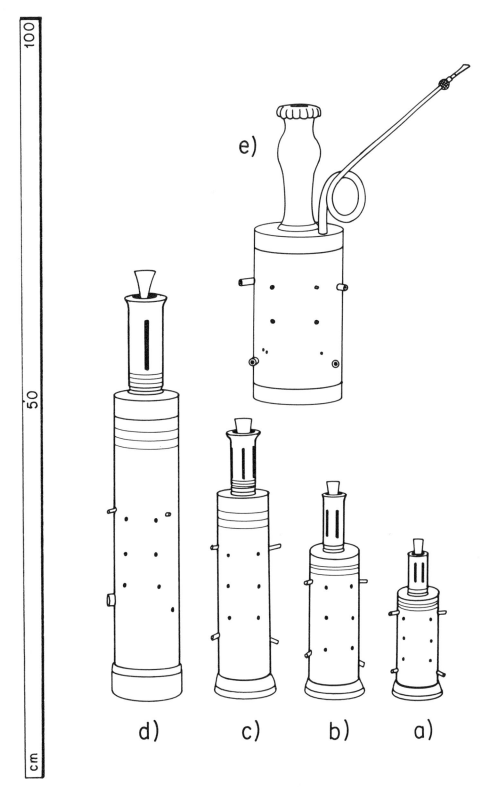

FIGURE 251.   *Racketts: (a) tenor; (b) bass; (c) great bass; (d) contrabass; (e) Baroque.*

name of instrument	abbreviations	approximate dates of original use	written range	sounds	availability
tenor rackett	track.	1575–1650	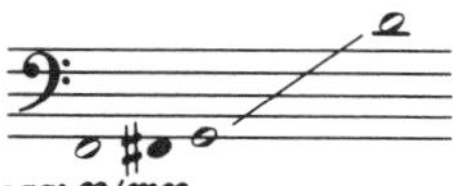 *(musical notation)* loudness: **p/mp**	as written*	very rare
bass rackett	brack.	1575–1650	 *(musical notation)* loudness: **p/mp**	as written*	rare
great bass rackett	gbrack.	1575–1650	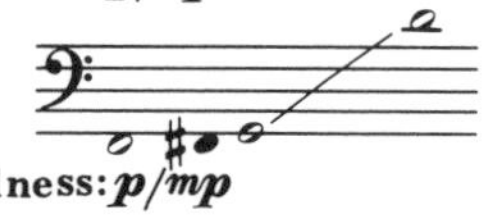 *(musical notation)* loudness: **p/mp**	1 octave lower	very rare
contrabass rackett	cbrack.	1575–1650	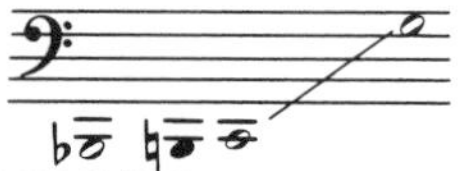 *(musical notation)* loudness: **p/mp**	1 octave lower	very rare
Baroque rackett	rack.	1690–1750	 *(musical notation)* loudest: **f** _____ softest: **pp** _____	as written	very rare

* When playing as part of a 16′ consort these instruments are notated an octave higher.

FIGURE 252. *The rackett family—vital statistics.*

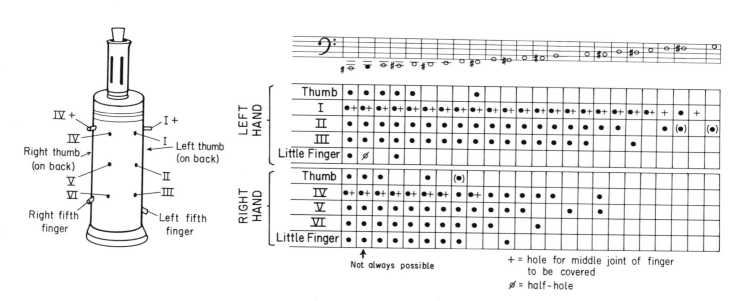

FIGURE 253. *Fingering chart for the Renaissance bass rackett.*

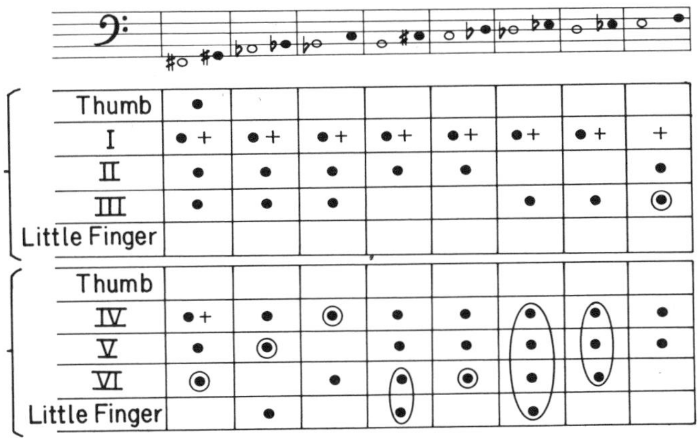

FIGURE 254. *Special trill fingerings for the Renaissance bass rackett: the complete fingering shown produces the open note; when the circled fingers are raised, the filled note is produced.*

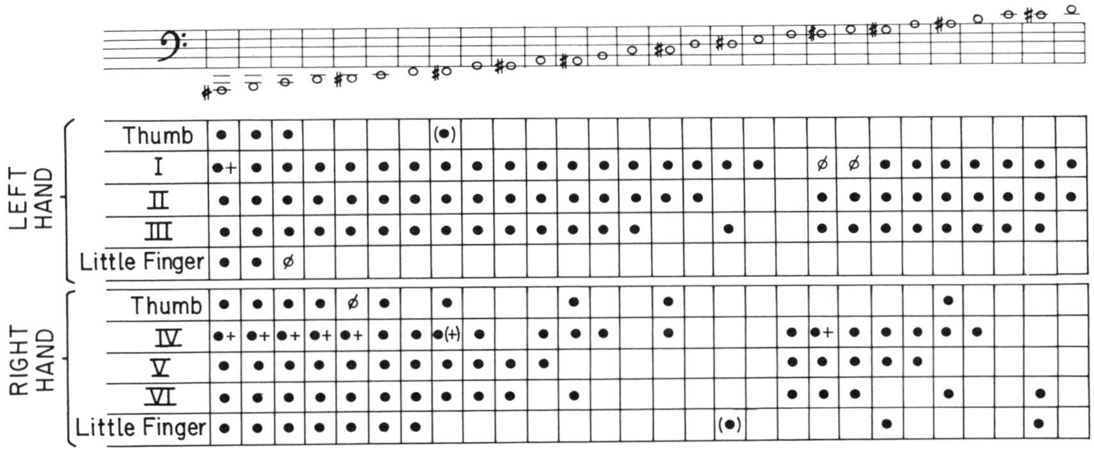

FIGURE 255. *Fingering chart for the Baroque rackett.*

similar to the Renaissance instrument, for its bore is conical and has ten sections rather than nine. The reed is directly controlled, and the direction of the bore is reversed: it starts with a bassoon-like crook inserted at the upper left and ends with a bell emerging where the reed and pirouette would be on a Renaissance rackett. The fingering system (Fig. 255) is even loonier than that of a Renaissance rackett; note, however, that the Baroque rackett overblows, unlike its Renaissance counterpart. The tone holes for the little fingers and for the middle joints of the index fingers are set at the end of little metal tubes called **tétines** (French: "nipples"). Some modern makers have retroactively added these to the Renaissance rackett.

The tone of the Baroque rackett is very similar to that of the Baroque bassoon.

Glissandos can be played on both types of rackett across any part of the range that does not involve opening or closing a *tétine*. The instrument has such a hard time just making the half-steps that individual microtones are largely out of the question.

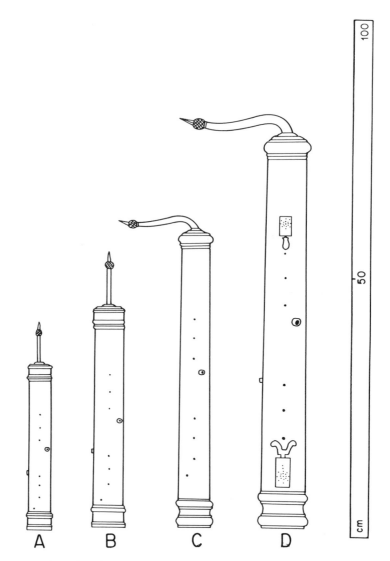

FIGURE 256. *Sordunes: (a) tenor; (b) bass; (c) great bass; (d) contrabass.*

THE SORDUNES

The most recent Renaissance wind instrument to be resurrected is the sordune, so christened by its chief modern maker (Wood), since there is no original English name. "Sordune" is a reasonable extrapolation from Italian "sordone" and German "Sordun" and is in fact the name of an organ stop imitative of this instrument.

The sordune can be thought of either as a capless kortholt or a cylindrical curtal: it has a lip-controlled double reed and a doubled-back cylindrical bore. The tone is reported to be intermediate between rackett and curtal; the dynamic range is probably something like *pp–mf* throughout the compass.

Like the rackett, the sordune has fingerholes for all ten fingers plus the middle joints of

name of instrument	abbreviations	approximate dates of original use	written range	sounds	availability
tenor sordune	tsord.	1580–1625		as written	very rare
bass sordune	bsord.	1580–1625		as written	very rare
great bass sordune	gbsord.	1580–1640		as written	very rare
contrabass sordune	cbsord.	1580–1625		1 octave lower	very rare

FIGURE 257. *Sordunes—vital statistics.*

the index fingers. The fingerings are much more normal than a rackett's, however, the "extra" tone holes being closed only for the lowest notes, thus:

great bass sordune
$\begin{cases}\end{cases}$
F_0—add right little finger
E_0—add right thumb
D_0—add middle joint of right index finger
C_0—add left little finger
$B\flat_1$—add middle joint of left index finger

Wood uses the British system of nomenclature for his sordunes, labeling them tenor, quart bass, bass, and great bass. The instruments illustrated are by Theatrum Instrumentorum. They are slightly more authentic than Wood's, with the tenor pitched a whole step higher. This workshop labels the sordunes SATB, and points out that even the higher sizes ought to read at 16'—as they certainly ought when used in consort.

At this point let us sort out the varieties of early reed instruments in tabular form:

	Conical Bore	Cylindrical Bore
Capped Reed	Rauschpfeife	Crumhorn, Cornamuse Kortholt Schryari
Pirouette	Shawm	Rackett
Fully Exposed Reed	Curtal	Sordune

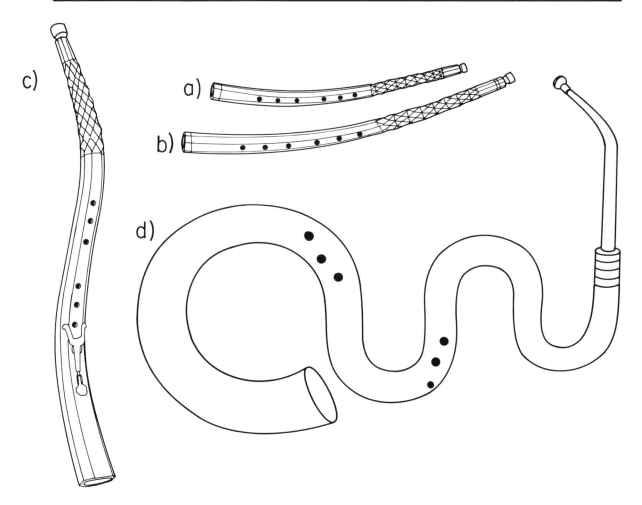

FIGURE 258. *The cornett family: (a) cornettino; (b) cornett; (c) tenor cornett; (d) serpent.*

THE CORNETTS

The instruments of the cornett family are classified organologically as **fingerhole horns**—instruments combining the "lip-reed" embouchure and cup mouthpiece of a brass instrument with the fingerholes and short, wide bore of a woodwind. Their hybrid nature is emphasized further by the fact that they are made of wood (or, nowadays, of plastic).

Renaissance technological limitations required that these curved instruments be carved out in two mirror halves, which were then glued together and bound in black leather. Modern ones, especially those made of plastic, are not infrequently produced in one piece.

The removable mouthpiece (also wooden or plastic) is in a special form called an **acorn cup**. Mouthpieces more closely resembling those of trumpets are also made for the benefit of modern players, most of whom come to the cornett from some modern brass instrument. The small diameter of cornett and cornettino mouthpieces makes it most comfortable to play them slightly to one side of the mouth, where the lips are thinner; again, modern brass players find this hard to deal with and often keep the instrument exactly centered.

name of instrument	abbreviations	approximate dates of original use	written range	sounds	availability
cornettino	cttno.	until 1750	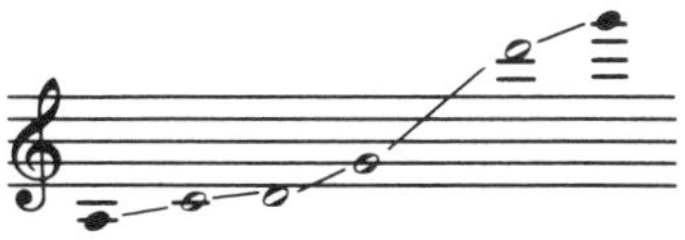 loudest: *mp—mf—f—ff* softest: *pp*	as written	rare
cornett	ctt.	until 1750	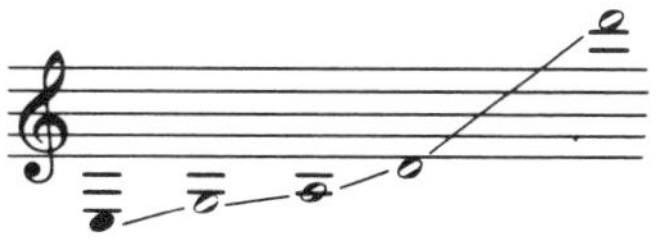 loudest: *mp—mf—f—ff* softest: *pp*	as written	rare
tenor cornett (lysarden)	tctt. (lys.)	1500–1750	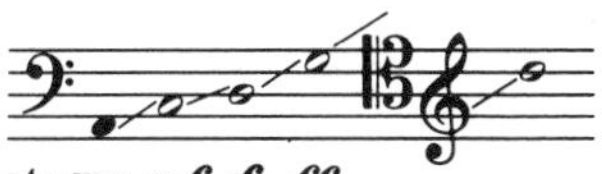 loudest: *mp—mf—f—ff* softest: *pp*	as written	very rare
serpent	serp.	1590*–1850	 loudest: *f—ff* softest: *pp*	as written	very rare

* Experimental bass cornetts were occasionally being made as early as 1570.

FIGURE 259.   *The cornett family—vital statistics.*

The short, wide bores of the cornett family give them a woodwind-like emphasis on the lowest two partials, which are used to make different-sounding upper and lower registers, with a brief altissimo register at the top. The lips dominate this system even more than they do in ordinary brasses. The modern canard about this family, that any note can be played from any fingering, is not true, though it certainly seems that way to beginners. Nonetheless, any note can be lipped up as much as a minor second and down a third or more. The lowest three notes are indeed all played with the same fingering,* and accordingly cannot be slurred to each other without at least a little portamento.

The fingering pattern of the serpent is extremely variable, and no two instruments—even by the same maker—respond in exactly the same way. There is therefore no fingering chart given here for it, but the basic pattern is the same as for the other members of the family. The serpent is pitched an octave lower than the tenor cornett.

The downward extension tones shown in Figure 259 are produced by lipping down the lowest note even further. They have the same weak and flabby quality as the privileged-fre-

* Most, but not all, tenor cornetts are provided with a key for the right little finger which gives a stable low c[0]. In the absence of this key the low d[0] is lipped down, as usual.

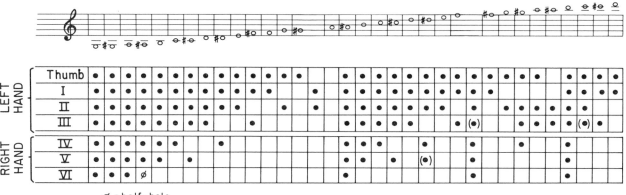

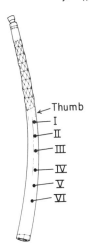

ø = half-hole

FIGURE 260. *Fingering chart for the cornett.*

quency pedal tones of trumpets and should be used only as a special effect except on the serpent, where they are much stronger—they are mentioned as possibilities even in nineteenth-century serpent methods.

Other avant-garde effects possible on these instruments are glissandos (very smooth and easily controlled, except across the register break), microtones (easily produced, but impossible to pinpoint at high speeds), and multiphonics. These last are produced with the lips, brass-fashion, and are all harsh and gritty; the "interharmonic" type of triadic brass multiphonic is not possible. Production of multiphonics is aided by fingering, but, unlike the woodwinds' fingerings, that of the cornetts does not even approximately govern the frequencies produced.

The serpent's curves are purely fanciful; that of the cornett reflects its early medieval origins as a pierced animal horn. Note that the fingerholes of the tenor cornett run along the spine of the S-curve, while on the other three instruments they are set into the side of the curve. The cornett and cornettino curve off to the player's right; the tenor cornett is held between the player's knees with the bell pointing out and down; and the serpent is held sideways with the bell at the player's right (curving down and to the left). There is, by the way, a movement afoot, largely in England, to revive the delightful old name **lysarden** (i.e., "lizard") for the tenor cornett—a name that aptly fits its shape and (quite coincidentally) parallels that of the serpent.

The cornett proper has several variant forms. The **straight cornett** was originally, and is now, a cheap version of the instrument, turned on a lathe from a single piece of wood and not

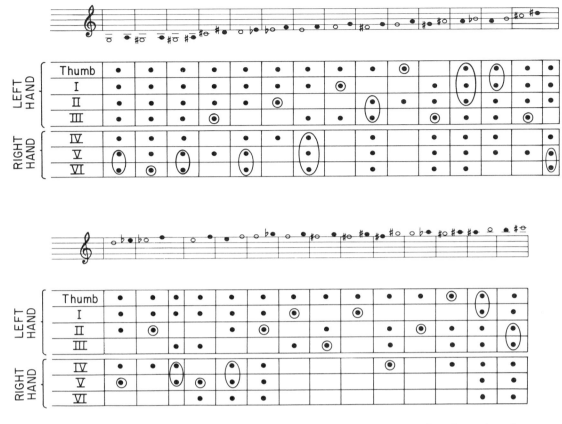

FIGURE 261. *Special trill fingerings for the cornett: the complete fingering shown produces the open note; when the circled fingers are raised, the filled note is produced.*

leather-covered. Also fitting this description is the **mute cornett**, which in addition has the mouthpiece carved into the body of the instrument rather than being detachable. This feature makes the tone even more gentle and delicate than that of the ordinary cornett. The ordinary cornett is said to be "in G" on the basis of its fingering pattern; a few cornetts are made a tone lower, in (non-transposing) F, but mute cornetts are only in G. (This contradicts historical practice, in which mute cornetts were apparently built at the lower pitch more often than not.)

Despite numerous assertions to the contrary, the tone of the cornett is really quite trumpet-like, particularly in the upper register. The overall effect is, however, considerably more delicate and expressive than the trumpet, and the dynamic range is that of a woodwind. The lower register is characterized (particularly from f¹ to a¹) by a not unpleasant hoarse quality that is less trumpet-like in effect. In terms of tonal beauty, flexibility, and expressiveness, the instrument fully merits the voluminous praise heaped upon it by early-seventeenth-century writers, and is much more suitable for chamber music than any brass instrument.

The cornettino sounds even more trumpet-like than the cornett. It does not have much literature of its own, but is mostly used to play high-lying cornett parts.

The tenor cornett (or lysarden, if you prefer) sounds somewhat covered and hoarse throughout its range—though, again, there are differences between the registers. The covered and hoarse quality is even stronger in the serpent, the sound of which somewhat resembles a trombone played with a bucket mute. The lower register is very clumsy and awkward-sounding at high speeds, but the upper can be very agile.

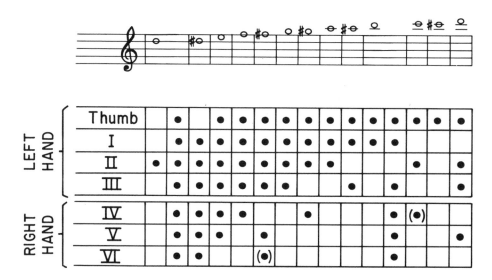

FIGURE 262. *Fingering chart for the cornettino, upper register.*
The lower register duplicates the cornett fingerings, but gives notes a fourth higher.

Throughout the Renaissance and Baroque periods the cornett family was not played as a unit; rather, a cornett and/or cornettino used for high parts would be accompanied by sackbutts on the lower lines. The tenor cornett was occasionally substituted for alto sackbutt in such groups but does not ever seem to have been the instrument of choice. The serpent was from the first a continuo instrument, used in French choirs to support not cornetts but voices. There it remained throughout the seventeenth century; during the eighteenth it gradually became a band instrument (cf. the original scoring of Handel's *Music for the Royal Fireworks*) and in the nineteenth even appeared in the orchestra from time to time.

Starting in the 1780s some serpents were made in bassoon shape, under the name **serpent bassoon** or **Russian bassoon.** Russian bassoons made of metal (1800–1850) are called **bass horns**;* the bass horn in turn became the **ophicleide** (1817–1880), which had eleven keys and a fingering system that was different from the others. At each stage of this evolution the tone became louder and more tuba-like, but not strongly enough to prevent the replacement of all of them by the tuba itself. Except for the true serpent, none of these instruments is manufactured today, though there are plenty of old bass horns and ophicleides around, gathering dust. A modern use of ophicleides is Henze's *The Raft of the Medusa.* The "tuba" parts in Berlioz's *Symphonie fantastique* are really for ophicleides, as are the "tuba" lines in many other early-nineteenth-century orchestral works. The Heinrich example cited below uses ophicleide and serpent side by side in parts of differing character.

MUSICAL EXAMPLES

CORNETTINO:

Schütz, *Symphoniae Sacrae*, Pt. III, No. 3, "Wo der Herr nicht das Haus bauet"
Schmelzer, Sonata a 8 duobus choris, from *Sacro-profanus concentus musicus* (1662)

---

* Do not confuse this with the modern *baritone horn.*

CORNETT:

    G. Gabrieli, Sonata No. 18 (a 14), from *Canzoni e Sonate* (1615)
    Monteverdi, Sonata sopra "Sancta Maria ora pro nobis," from *Vespers* (1610)
    Schmelzer, Sonata "La Carolietta" (1669)
    Kagel, *Musik für Renaissanceinstrumente*

TENOR CORNETT:

    (no example)

SERPENT:

    Anon. (Pleyel?), Feldparthie "Chorale St. Antonii" (formerly attrib. Haydn)
    Heinrich, *Manitou Mysteries**

EARLY BRASSES

Unlike many early woodwinds, all the early brass instruments have direct modern descendants that sound much the same as their forebears. They are thus not of much interest to modern composers and are cited here only for the sake of early-music performers.

The valveless trumpet and horn are very ancient but were used only for signals, fanfares, and so on until circa 1600 and 1700, respectively. Of more interest to modern composers than to early-music performers is the **Baroque mute**. This mute, made of wood with a narrow channel through it, is equivalent in effect to the stopping mute of the (modern) horn, raising the pitch of the instrument by a whole step, reducing the dynamic level, and making the timbre very stuffy and distant. There is no reason why mutes of this type could not be made for modern trumpets and trombones, even for tubas, and they would certainly provide an interesting "new" timbre.

The earliest brass instrument to be used for truly musical purposes was the trombone, or, rather, its ancestors the slide trumpet and sackbutt. The slide of the S-shaped slide trumpet is a simple straight tube which is located between the mouthpiece and the body of the instrument. In order to play it the left hand must hold the mouthpiece steady while the right moves the rest of the instrument back and forth. Because the slide is a single straight shank instead of the long U-shape of the trombone, the distance between adjacent slide positions is twice what it is on the latter instrument, allowing for only four positions within the reach of the arm. Several notes at the bottom of the range are therefore missing, as Figure 266 should make clear. Note that the slide trumpet, at least the modern version, is built in C.

Initially the slide trumpet was played in the bottom two octaves of its range, as a proto-sackbutt. It took the *cantus firmus* in fifteenth-century *basse danses* and was used in other music as well. With the appearance of the sackbutt the slide trumpet was moved to the back burner, appearing now and then as a clumsy substitute for the tenor sackbutt but barely

---

* The orchestral works of A. P. Heinrich (1781–1861) are currently available only on microfilm from the Library of Congress. Study of their brilliant and unorthodox orchestration well repays the effort of finding them. The serpent part in *Manitou Mysteries* probably represents the peak of the literature for that misbegotten instrument.

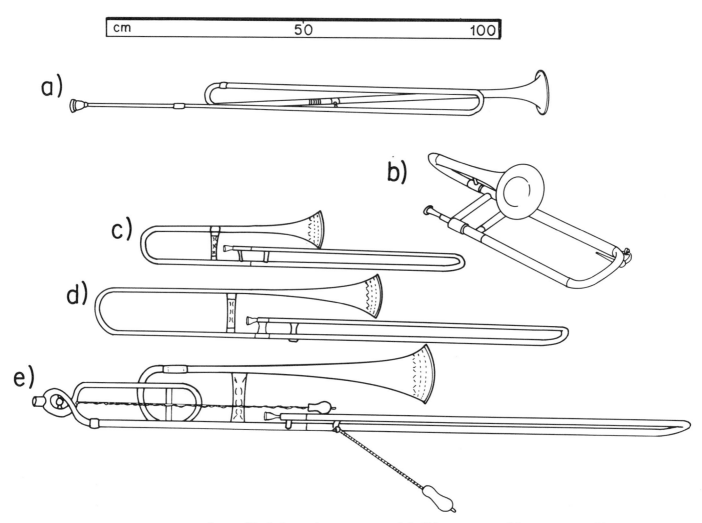

FIGURE 263. *Early brass instruments: (a) slide trumpet; (b) soprano sackbutt; (c) alto sackbutt; (d) tenor sackbutt; (e) bass sackbutt.*

surviving the sixteenth and seventeenth centuries. In the eighteenth century it returned to brief prominence again, as a *trumpet* substitute playing in the *upper* two octaves of its range, where the clumsiness of the slide is not so obtrusive and where it provides a number of notes missing from the natural harmonic series.

The three main sackbutt sizes are direct ancestors of the simplex alto, tenor, and bass trombones of the nineteenth century, from which they differ only in details. Their narrow bores and small bells (modern trombonists call them "ice-cream cones") give the sackbutts a mellower tone and easier high register than the trombone.*

The evolution of these instruments was not only slight but so gradual that it is impossible to draw a hard and fast line between the last sackbutts and the first trombones. A convenient division year is 1785, the low point of trombone history. Modern sackbutts are based largely on seventeenth-century models.

* The highest notes of the slide trumpet are possible because its bore is narrower still. The valveless trumpet (of which, remember, the slide trumpet is only a slight modification) had a much narrower bore than modern trumpets, being in effect a soprano horn.

name of instrument	abbreviations	approximate dates of original use	written range	sounds	availability
slide trumpet	slide trp. slide tr.	1400–1750		as written	very rare
soprano sackbutt	ssack.	1690–1785	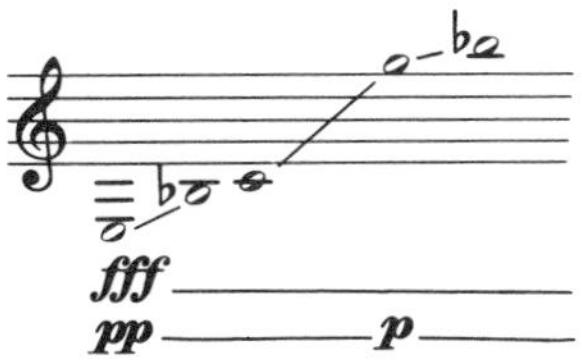	as written	very rare
alto sackbutt	asack.	1450–1785	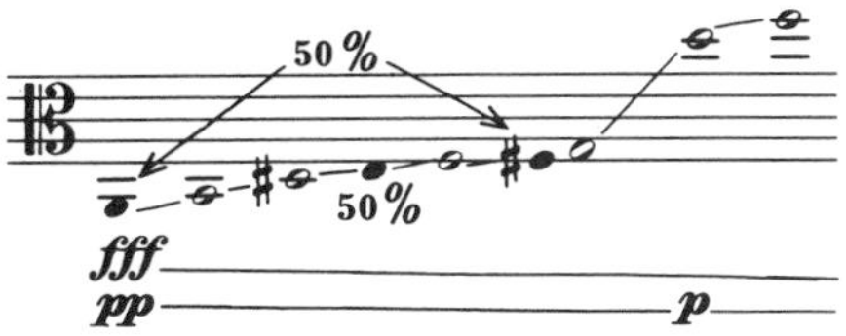	as written	rare
tenor sackbutt	tsack.	1450–1785	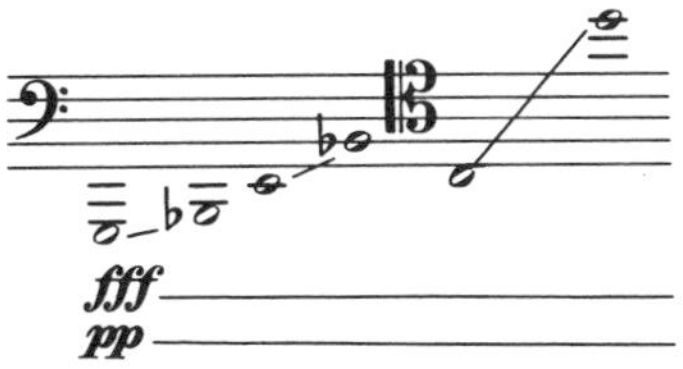	as written	rare
bass sackbutt	bsack.	1500–1785		as written	rare

FIGURE 264. *Sackbutts and slide trumpet—vital statistics.*

The tenor sackbutt is built in non-transposing B♭ and the bass in E♭, with a tuning slide adjustable down to D;* a few basses are built in F/E, a tone higher. Note that the bass sackbutt is provided with a pivoting handle that enables the slide to be extended the full seven positions, not just six as in later bass trombones. Alto sackbutts are made in both F and E♭, and this difference accounts for the competing "extra" notes shown in Figure 264. The soprano sackbutt in B♭ (never called "sackbutt" historically) was—with rare exceptions—used only to double the soprano voices in German chorales.

* Tuning down to D makes the E_0 available but takes away the $E♭_0$.

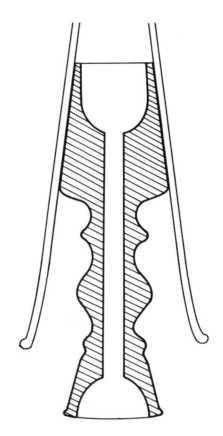

FIGURE 265. *Diagrammatic longitudinal section of a Baroque trumpet mute in place.*

FIGURE 266. *Chart of slide positions for the lower register of the slide trumpet.*

The sackbutt is often used anachronistically in modern performances of fourteenth-century music. While the substitution of tenor sackbutt for the very rare slide trumpet does no great violence, there is only the flimsiest evidence that even the latter instrument existed prior to 1400, nor does the sackbutt's tone fit the angular, gothic spirit of the *Ars nova*. What evidence we have seems to indicate that even in the fifteenth century these instruments were used only for dance music.

MUSICAL EXAMPLES

SACKBUTTS:

G. Gabrieli, Sonata No. 18 (a 14), from *Canzoni e Sonate* (1615) (3A, 6T, B)
Schütz, *Symphoniae Sacrae*, Pt. I, No. 13: "Fili mi Absalon" (AATB)
Schmelzer, Sonata "La Carolietta" (1669) (T)
Kagel, *Musik für Renaissanceinstrumente* (ATB)

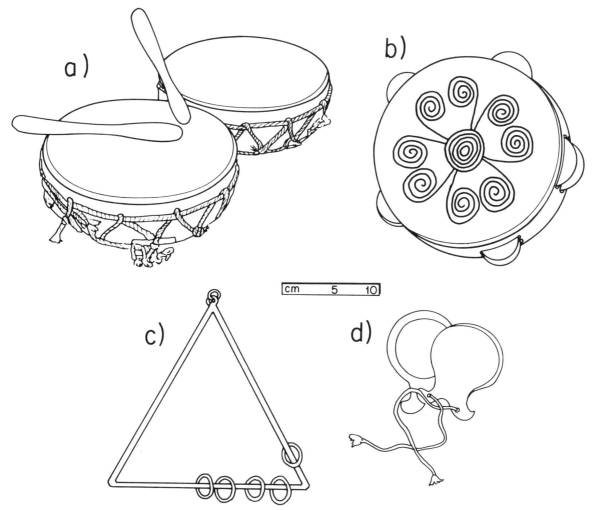

FIGURE 267. *Early percussion instruments: (a) nakers; (b) timbrel;*
(c) Renaissance triangle; (d) early castanets.

EARLY PERCUSSION

The golden age of percussion is right now. There is scarcely any older type of percussion instrument that does not have a close modern equivalent, and early percussion cannot be of much interest to the modern composer.

Twentieth-century enthusiasm for highly varied rhythms and timbres has led to an insupportable overutilization of percussion in performances of early music—a distortion as bad in its way as the varied dynamics and "corrected" harmonies applied to that music by nineteenth-century editors.

A large variety of percussion instruments are known to have existed in the Middle Ages and Renaissance, but only a handful would have been used in the surviving music of those times. The early forms of snare, bass, and tenor drums, as well as the timpani, were exclusively military instruments, used for signaling and to keep time on the march. Numerous other instruments were used only in folk music or were simply noisemakers. Only the following eight types appear to have had any use in art music, and then only in the limited contexts specified in Chapter XI.

Nakers (1250–1500) are a type of small kettledrum, sometimes provided with a snare. They are played in pairs, with short, bulbous wooden sticks—never, authentically, with the fingers. Their pitch is much less clear than most such drums and is completely undefined on instruments with a snare.

The **tabor** (–1650) was always used conjointly with the tabor pipe (discussed above in the section on recorders) in dance music. The modern *tambourin provençal* is a tabor, but the instrument may take other forms, often much shorter and flatter but always with one or more gut snares across the batter head.

The **timbrel** (–1650) is a tambourine. Its numerous jingles are of hammered brass and may take the form of pellet bells. There may also be a snare across the head. All these features are found in certain modern Near Eastern tambourines, which may reliably be used as timbrels. The brass jingles give the instrument a dry, rustling timbre quite unlike the lush jingling of a modern tambourine.

Renaissance triangles (–1810), more varied in form than modern ones, were often trapezoidal. More important, there were three metal rings (five, after 1600) strung along the instrument's lower beam, and these gave it a strong, jangling sound. Since all three varieties are closed (to prevent the rings from falling off), the brilliant tang of the modern triangle is absent. Note how long such instruments remained in use. The triangle in Mozart's *Abduction from the Seraglio* should be of this type.

Up to a diatonic octave of small **bells** were occasionally used liturgically during the Middle Ages, but apparently not in any other music.

Crotales, in their hand-held form, and smallish, thin **crash cymbals** were in use at least occasionally throughout the period. The former were the more common up to the beginning of the seventeenth century.

Finally, **castanets**, in the tricky-to-use two-piece form in which they still exist as folk instruments, were used (in Iberia only) from about 1200 on.

Even reasonably authentic modern reconstructions of any of these instruments are very rare, but the temptation to substitute modern forms or to use folk or toy instruments should be resisted.

XIII

EARLY

KEYBOARDS

AND

STRINGS

EARLY STRINGED KEYBOARDS

THE HARPSICHORD

Of all the early instruments resurrected in this century, only the harpsichord has found a secure and permanent place in contemporary music. Indeed, most people are unaware that it was ever extinct. The instrument's standard modern form is modeled on a very late phase of its historical development, when it had expanded to its largest range and greatest timbral variation—at the sacrifice of volume and fullness of tone.

The strings of a harpsichord are plucked by **quills** set in **jacks** that rest freely on the ends of the keys. The speed or force with which a key is depressed in no way affects the loudness of the resulting tone. Each quill is mounted on a spring-loaded, pivoting **tongue** so that it can slide quietly back past the string when the key is released. This action is not entirely silent, and the release of a large chord that has been allowed to die away is accompanied by a delicate, pattering thud as the jacks fall back into place; in most musical contexts, however, this is not a problem. The subliminal ticking of each attack and release is an integral part of harpsichord tone and is particularly apparent in the highest part of the range (cf. the end of Ligeti's *Continuum*). The basic tone is extremely brilliant and pingy, even snarly in the bass. This extremely high harmonic development means that for the harpsichord, unlike the piano, thick chords can be written in the bass without loss of clarity.

Each jack is provided with a damper that stops the vibration of its string when the key is released. There is no damper pedal. Undamped vibrations die relatively quickly, in a range

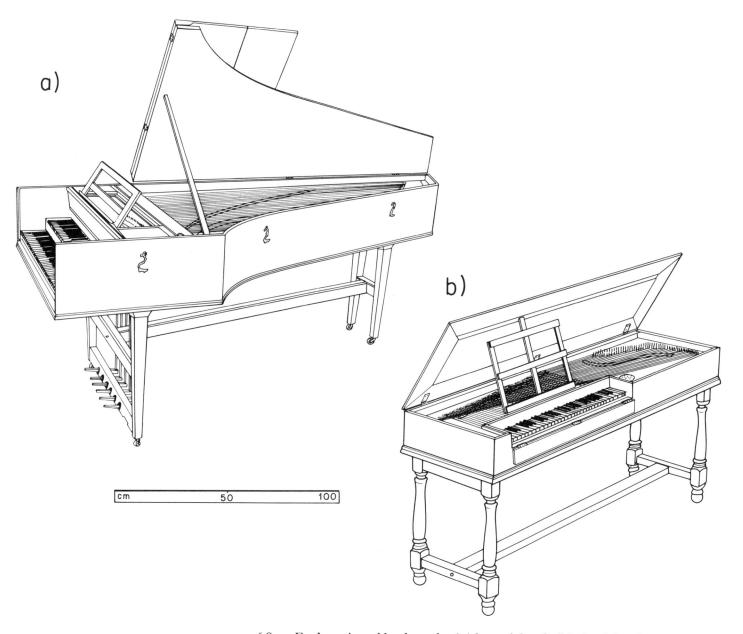

FIGURE 268. *Early stringed keyboards: (a) harpsichord; (b) clavichord.*

from about five seconds at the bottom of the instrument to less than half a second for the highest 4′ tones.

The timbre and dynamics of the harpsichord are varied, like those of the organ, by means of varied registrations; these are controlled by pedals, operated by both feet, that move in stepped slots so that, like harp pedals, they can be locked into position. The organization varies a great deal from one harpsichord to another, but a typical instrument will have something like the following.

On the lower manual: three ranks of strings, giving 8′, 8′, 4′, each governed by a pedal. The two 8′ ranks have slightly different timbres and dynamic levels. The three ranks are used in varying combinations to give *individual* dynamic levels from *pp* to *mf*.

name of instrument	abbreviations	approximate dates of original use	keyboard range	range of available pitches	availability
harpsichord	hpsi. hpschd. hpd.	1400–1815		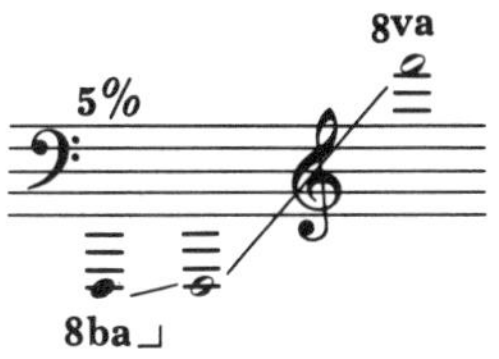	common

FIGURE 269. *The harpsichord—vital statistics.*

On the upper manual: a single 8′ rank of strings (governed by a pedal) which may be **muted** either by engaging another pedal or by means of a button above the keyboard that must be drawn or slid by a free hand. The mute is known as the **buff stop** or **harp stop**. The muted tone decays very rapidly, is much less bright than the ordinary harpsichord sound, and is dominated by the instrument's attack noise. It sounds more like a classical guitar (with someone knitting along in time) than a harp.

There will always be a **coupler** for the two manuals, engaged either by pedal or by shoving in or pulling out some one of the manuals themselves. The coupler is mostly used to bring all four ranks of strings together for the *mezzo-forte*.

In addition to all this, there may be other, less standard stops, each with a pedal. Most common of these is the **lute stop**, which gives a snarly *sul ponticello* effect by plucking one or another of the 8′ ranks near the ends of the strings. A few large harpsichords have a ponderous 16′ rank of strings (lower manual), and there may be a rare **peau de buffle** stop in which the use of special leather quills tones down the attack noise. Finally, there may be a second 8′ rank of strings on the upper manual.

The various dynamics specified above refer to single notes only; as with any other keyboard instrument, the greater the number of notes sounding together the louder the sound will be. A good, strong *forte* can be had from the instrument when a full, chordal texture is employed together with full registration. The *fortissimo*, however, is unavailable even in large tone-clusters—which, by the way, give hardly any sense of pitch, sounding more like a delicate and domesticated crash of surf than anything else.

Unlike an organist, a harpsichord player has a modicum of touch control over the dynamics of the instrument. Normal practice with the harpsichord, as with the harp, is to *slightly* arpeggiate every chord, and the speed with which this is done affects the perceived dynamic level: the faster the arpeggiation the louder the effect. A chord will only be struck non arpeggiato to give the impression of a sforzando. Varied arpeggiation is also used to give the impression of legato, tenuto, etc.

Increasingly, harpsichords are modeled after specific historic states of the instrument. Those based on pre-eighteenth-century instruments have no pedals, a four-octave keyboard (usually C_0–c^3),* only one to three ranks of strings, and usually just one manual. "Decadent"

---

* The $C\sharp_0$, $E\flat_0$, $F\sharp_0$, and $A\flat_0$ may be missing and the remaining keys organized into a **short octave** whereby the "E_0" key gives C_0, "$F\sharp_0$" gives D_0, and "$G\sharp_0$" gives E_0.

late-eighteenth-century types may have every gadget already described plus swell shutters, a "bassoon" stop of parchment laid across the strings, or other items, but the trend is generally away from such overloaded instruments.

Like the piano, harpsichords are built in different formats. An upright harpsichord is a **clavicytherium**, an oblong or trapezoidal one is a **virginal** (or **virginals**) if strung cross-wise, a **spinet** if strung diagonally. The terms "spinet" and "virginal(s)" were used at various times and places to refer to the harpsichord in general; on the other hand, the term "harpsi-chord" has been used as a specific designation for the ordinary, wing-shaped "grand" form of the instrument.

The virginal is of special interest because it seems to be nearly as old as the "grand" harpsichord and because most models have a very sweet, beautiful tone—not at all brilliant or pingy—due to the strings being plucked near the center instead of toward one end. Virgin-als have a four-octave range, one manual, and a single 8′ rank of strings sounding *piano*.

In performing early music on the harpsichord one must bear in mind the capabilities of instruments built at the time the music was written. The earliest harpsichords had a single 8′ rank of strings. Varied registration (8′, 4′, buff and lute stops) became available around 1580, but changes in registration were effected not by pedals but by moving the keyboard or the jack rail, or by hand-operating a slider or button, or by pressing a knee lever; such changes could thus only be made between movements, not during the course of play. Double manuals were also introduced at this time but appear to have been used only for transposing. Double, non-transposing manuals appeared around 1700, and pedals were added in the late eigh-teenth century. *Peau de buffle* and 16′ stops should only be used for post-Baroque music. The harpsichord ended its days accompanying the recitative in operas; it is seldom appropri-ate to use the harpsichord for keyboard music written after about 1785.

For modern special effects the harpsichord is much less flexible than the piano. Only the uppermost rank of strings is accessible to direct manipulation or "preparing," and which rank that is varies from instrument to instrument. Plucking a string will produce a muffled "thunk" unless its key is depressed—and it is impossible to depress a key silently unless all stops have been disengaged.

On the other hand, the instrument is much more adaptable to special tunings than is the piano, since its individual ranks are single-strung rather than triple-strung and the strings are under much less tension than those of a piano. The upper manual, for example, could easily be tuned a quarter-tone flat, so that between the two manuals twenty-four notes to the octave could be obtained.

Musical Examples

HARPSICHORD:

J. S. Bach, *Brandenburg Concerto No. 5.*
Rameau, *Pièces de clavecin II* (1724)
D. Scarlatti, Sonatas K. 420 and 421
Falla, Concerto for harpsichord, flute, oboe, clarinet, violin, and cello
Ligeti, *Continuum*

The clavichord is at once the simplest and the most expressive of keyboard instruments. Each key is a simple lever at the far end of which is an upright metal blade called a **tangent**. When the key is depressed the tangent rises up and strikes the string, *remaining in contact with it* and acting not only as a tone producer but as a bridge dividing the string into two acoustically separate portions. The left-hand portion of the string (they run crosswise, as in the virginal) is prevented from vibrating by a damper felt running past it, and the note is produced only by that portion of the string lying to the right of the tangent. When the key is released the damper felt—now in acoustic communication with the vibrating part of the string—instantly damps the sound, giving the notes a characteristically crisp release. This crispness gives the clavichord great clarity of line, even at very high speeds, and enables the production of unbelievably sharp staccatos, even staccato trills.

Because the tangent imparts its energy at the (acoustic) very end of the string the resulting sound is very soft, but it has a high degree of harmonic development. The clavichord's extreme softness restricts it to use as a solo instrument played for the performer's own enjoyment or for, at the most, about twenty people in a space no bigger than the average living room. The instrument can play in ensemble with voice, recorder, bass flute, harp, guitar, or lute, but in every case as a distinctly unequal partner. True equality of ensemble could be obtained only if the clavichord's partner were percussion (specifically, idiophones) played finger-style—needless to say, this is a strictly modern option.

Played by itself, to oneself, the clavichord's softness is psychologically transformed into an ordinary dynamic range. This is reflected in the traditional dynamic notation for the instrument, which corresponds to reality roughly as follows:

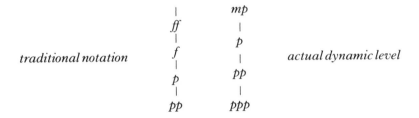

In this scheme the levels *mf* and *mp* are hardly ever used. The clavichord is played with an extremely light touch, and the key dip is only a few millimeters. Because of this it is possible to play up to five parallel "glissandos" (i.e., key rips) in each hand—an interesting effect that has never to my knowledge been exploited.

All surviving historical clavichords are double-strung—that is, each tangent strikes a pair of strings—to augment the volume and fill out the tone. Some are even triple-strung in the bass. Despite this, as many as half of the clavichords built today are single-strung and, therefore, sound rather thin and puny.

The clavichord's high harmonic development means that, as with the harpsichord, thick chords in the bass do not lose clarity. Tone-clusters, however, do not have the white-noise pitchlessness of harpsichord clusters. The tone of the clavichord is best described as intermediate between harpsichord and lute. Notes last about as long as they do on the harpsichord. The "lute" aspects of the tone are due to the fact that the player's finger remains in direct mechanical contact with the string throughout the duration of each note, with a resulting expressiveness of tone that is unknown in any other keyboard save the clavinet, the clavi-

name of instrument	abbreviations	approximate dates of original use	keyboard range (written & sounding)	availability
clavichord	clav.	1350–1795	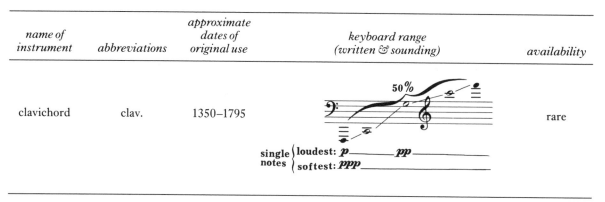	rare

FIGURE 270. *The clavichord—vital statistics.*

chord's electric offspring. One can even make a vibrato by varying the pressure on the key after the note is struck. This vibrato is usually referred to by its old German designation,

Bebung, and was originally indicated thus: ⌐ . There is no reason why modern writers should not substitute the modern expression "vibr."

Bent tones can also be produced, a quarter-tone or more above the unbent pitch (up to a half-step in the bass of many instruments), though it must be stressed that the bending occurs only after the attack. If secure, steady quarter-tones are desired, the instrument must be retuned, as it easily can be (downward only).

Further modern effects are possible—striking, sweeping, or plucking the strings (a dull "thunk" markedly lower in pitch than the equivalent ordinary note), or sweeping a chord after its keys have been (slowly and carefully) depressed silently, or "preparing" the strings, piano-fashion—but none of these seems very worthwhile.

The larger range given in Figure 270 is that of the clavichord at the peak of its development in the late eighteenth century. Clavichords built to earlier patterns will have smaller ranges—usually the four octaves C_0 to c^3. Many of these are of a type known as **fretted clavichords**. Such instruments have *more than one key for each string* (or course of strings). This is possible because the tangents act as bridges, and one string or course can thus be used to produce several different pitches. In a fretted clavichord notes using the same string(s) cannot be played simultaneously, as only the highest will sound. Such "forbidden" chords are usually minor seconds in distant tonalities (C and D♭, D♯ and E, F and G♭, A♯ and B), though occasionally three notes will play from one string (for instance C♯, D, E♭) making a "forbidden" major second.

Fretted clavichords are often so small and light that they can be easily carried under one's arm.

MUSICAL EXAMPLES

CLAVICHORD:

>C. P. E. Bach, Sonata No. 4 from *Achtzehn Probe-Stücken in sechs Sonaten* (W. 63/4)
>>(Many "clavier" works not specifically requiring the clavichord are primarily conceived in terms of that instrument. See, for example, J. S. Bach's *Chromatic Fantasy and Fugue* in D minor, BWV 903, or Haydn's sonatas nos. 31–33, Hob. 46, 44, and 20.)

In its modern form the organ is an instrument that has actually evolved backward; since about 1920 organ building has concentrated on the revival of eighteenth-century stops and divisions in instruments of otherwise modern pattern. Because of this, many modern organs are perfectly suitable for the performance of even the oldest organ repertoire, provided that the organist uses appropriate registration.

There is no room here to go into a detailed history of organ design and registration, which every organist must study in some detail if organ music of varied times and places is to be rendered convincingly. The following is a brief outline.

The earliest organs (descended from the still earlier Greco-Roman **hydraulos**) are of the type known as **positive** or **chamber organs**—small, movable but not portable instruments with one manual and no pedals. Medieval organs had flue pipes only and were fixed in timbre and dynamic level, without separate stop controls. They did, however, have several ranks of pipes, and thus sounded as what would now be called a *cornet* stop.

Around the beginning of the fourteenth century the organ began to grow, and by 1425 instruments as monstrous as any built today were being made, with up to three manuals (after ca. 1360) and/or pedals (after ca. 1300). The pedals were mere pulldowns, and the extra manuals were added only to extend the range upward and/or downward—the instrument could only play "full organ," often, after the addition of reed stops in about 1400, a very loud "full organ." The much softer positive organ remained in use side by side with its giant offspring.

Introduction of separate stops for contrasting loudness and timbre occurred in both positive and "great" organs around 1450. At first this simply involved building contrasting divisions of pipes for each manual; a bit later, stop knobs were introduced; and by the beginning of the sixteenth century the organ had achieved essentially its modern form. The swell box and crescendo pedal are eighteenth-century inventions associated with the rise of the Classical style, and almost all imitative stops are of nineteenth-century origin.

The positive organ became a secular instrument and survived until the late eighteenth century as a continuo instrument. It has now been revived, as have slightly larger chamber-type organs with pedals. A positive organ per se never has ranks of lower than 16' or higher than 2' pitch, and has a keyboard of limited range, usually F_0 or C_0 to a^2 or c^3. It will typically have four or five stops, possibly including one 8' semichorus reed.

There is a *forte* semichorus reed of unbelievably snarling tone called the **regal**, and from roughly 1460 to 1720 there was a type of positive organ, also called "regal," provided *only* with that timbre.* The regal's single keyboard has the same sort of range as a positive organ's, and the instrument may be provided with 4' and/or 16' stops. Many models have a removable cover that can be placed over the reeds to reduce their loudness—rather like an organ swellchamber.

Finally, there is the medieval **portative organ**, a genuinely portable organ with a single rank of 4' flue stops that is usually an open metal diapason. This instrument is held in the lap

---

* It is difficult to imagine for what it could have been used in its last half-century—perhaps as a continuo instrument at dances and outdoors?

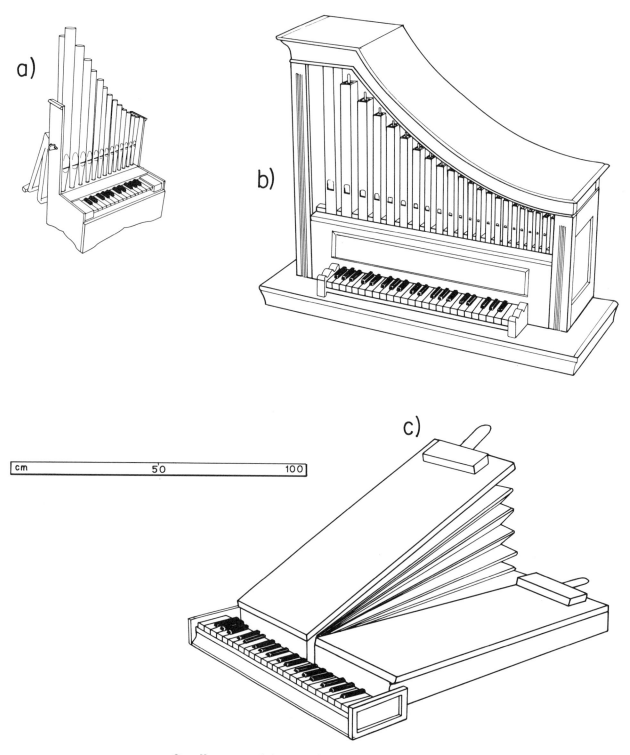

FIGURE 271.   *Small organs: (a) portative organ; (b) positive organ; (c) regal.*

name of instrument	abbreviations	approximate dates of original use	keyboard range	range of available pitches	availability
portative organ	port.	1250–1500	 loudness: *p* ____	sounds 1 octave higher	rare
positive organ	pos.	–1785	 50% single notes { loudest: *ff* ____ softest: *pp* ____	 8va	very rare
regal	reg.	1460–1720	 50% *f* ____		very rare

FIGURE 272. *Early organs—vital statistics.*

at right angles to the player's body; the right hand plays the keys while the left works the bellows (all other organs require an assistant to pump the bellows, or else an electric blower). Because of the angle at which the right hand must be held, chords and polyphony are awkward, and the portative organ is therefore a monophonic ensemble instrument. Theoretically at least, the thumb could be used for drones, though usually only the index and middle fingers are employed in playing.

The range of modern portatives has been virtually standardized at c¹–c³, reading, of course, an octave lower for virtually all medieval music.

MUSICAL EXAMPLES

REGAL AND POSITIVE ORGAN:
Monteverdi, *Orfeo* (Act IV)
Kagel, *Musik für Renaissanceinstrumente*

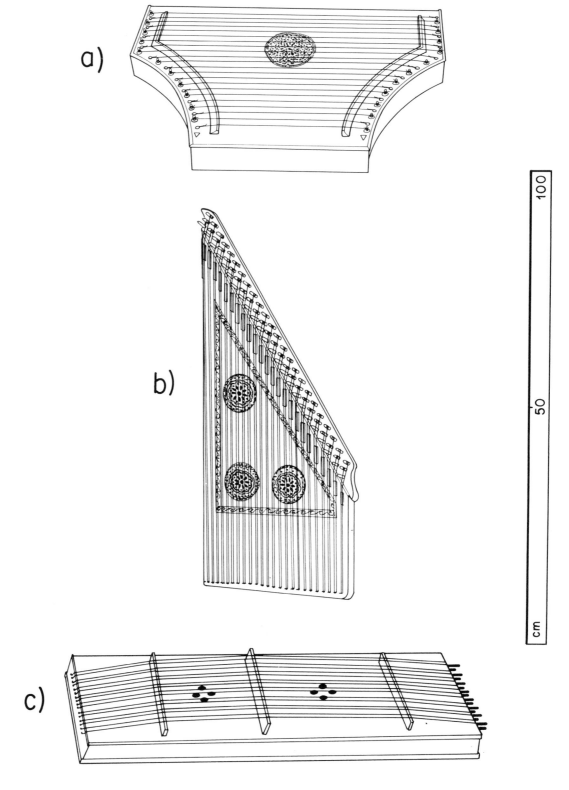

a)

b)

c)

100

50

cm

FIGURE 273. *Psalteries and dulcimer: (a) "pig's head" psaltery; (b) medicinale; (c) dulcimer.*

PSALTERIES AND DULCIMERS

The psaltery and dulcimer are the keyboardless ancestors of the harpsichord and piano, respectively. They belong to the organological category of **zithers**—neckless instruments in which the soundboard underlies the full length of every string. Both are now and have always been highly variable instruments. The essential difference between the two is that a psaltery is plucked while a dulcimer is struck with short, thin wooden beaters resembling those of the modern cimbalom—itself a very advanced sort of dulcimer.

Psalteries can be either held across the chest and plucked directly by the fingers of one hand (with or without wire finger-picks) or with a single feather plectrum, or laid flat on a table and plucked with a pair of feather plectra. They vary a great deal in form, being rectangular, symmetrically trapezoidal (with or without incurved "pig's head" sides), or wing-shaped (a type known as the **medicinale**). The wire strings, in ten to seventeen courses, could be singly or multiply strung, the latter more and more prevalent in the later development of the instrument. The range varies from a diatonic tenth to an octave more than that, still diatonic, upward from a^0, c^1, f^1, or g^1. In the late fifteenth century chromatic psalteries were occasionally made, covering a similar range with up to twice as many courses, single-strung.

The dulcimer, always laid flat, was typically a symmetrical trapezoid, often with a bridge down the middle dividing the strings into two unequal portions to double the number of available notes. Like the psaltery, the dulcimer is wire-strung; typically, there are three or four strings in each course. The range is usually smaller than that of the psaltery—a diatonic octave, tenth, or twelfth upward from c^1, f^1, g^1, or c^2.

Thus for instruments of reasonably authentic pattern; unfortunately, a majority of the psalteries and dulcimers made today are unacceptably inauthentic. One sees such things as late (folk-instrument) dulcimers with multiple bridges and interlaced courses, or little artsy-craftsy psalteries with no relationship to any real instrument ancient or modern.

It will be noted that both psaltery and dulcimer are quite high-pitched; presumably they were played at 4′ pitch. Unlike the psaltery, the dulcimer appears always to have been predominantly a popular instrument—strictly so after about 1500—and it should probably only be used for dance music and the like. Both instruments became folk instruments during the course of the sixteenth century. The psaltery and the dulcimer both have a very attractive, delicate, tinkling tone, the latter with a slightly spitting percussive attack. The sound decays very quickly, lasting little more than a second even at the bottom of the range.

name of instrument	abbreviations	approximate dates of original use	range	availability
psaltery	psalt. ps.	1100–1500	variable loudest: *mp* softest: *ppp*	rare
dulcimer	dulc.	1400–1500	variable loudest: *mp* softest: *ppp*	very rare

FIGURE 274. *Psaltery and dulcimer—vital statistics.*

There was a gut-strung psaltery in the shape of a right triangle, held and played like a harp, which Sybil Marcuse has labeled **rote**, though this term is more commonly used to designate the medieval bowed lyre. As no other name has been advanced for the instrument now in question, however, "rote" it must be, at least for the nonce. Because the soundboard get in the way of the right hand, only the left hand can pluck the strings of this instrument; the right is used to support it. "Rotes" were made psaltery-sized, but also in bigger varieties; a large modern "rote" would probably descend to c^0. The range is, once again, variable, but is usually two diatonic octaves.

EARLY HARPS

The medieval and Renaissance ancestors of the modern harp differ from it quite strikingly in tone, due to the presence of **bray pins** set in the soundboard next to the strings. The buzzing of the strings against the brays gives both the medieval and Gothic (i.e., Renaissance) harps a brittle, nasal twang that is, though not indelicate, most unharplike to modern ears. Furthermore, medieval harps are strung in wire rather than gut, giving the instrument a bit of the tinkling sound of a psaltery. Gut strings were used on a minority of harps starting in the late fourteenth century, and the Gothic harp is usually but not invariably gut-strung; harps were occasionally wire-strung as late as the eighteenth century. The brays give these instruments a clarity of line not found in the blurred tones of modern and Baroque harps.

The range (and hence the size) of medieval harps was and is highly variable: as few as six strings to as many as twenty-five (three and a half octaves), with ten to seventeen strings being usual. The range, whatever it is, presumably fits within the standard medieval gamut of G_0 to e^2. Fifteenth-century Gothic harps had a similarly small and variable range, but by the sixteenth century the range had more or less standardized at F_0–a^2, with some instruments giving C_0–e^2 and a few giving the combined range of both types.

Early harps are diatonic instruments, without the elaborate mechanism of forks and pedals that gives chromatic capability to modern harps. It was apparently commonplace for medieval harpists to retune while performing. Renaissance players did this much less often, but they did at least occasionally press a finger against a string to raise its pitch a half-step.

Baroque "double" and "triple" harps, usually brayless (invariably so after 1625) and with two or three parallel or interlaced sets of strings to give a complete chromatic range, first appear around 1550. They sound much like modern harps. As part of the experimentation leading to the Baroque harp, there was a brief vogue for the **Irish harp**, a folk instrument that had been following its own line of development since the Middle Ages and would continue to do so up to the nineteenth century. During its brief moment of glory as an art-music instrument it had brayless metal strings and was chromatic from c^1 up. This Renaissance Irish harp is played with the fingernails (grown long for the purpose) and is reported to sound much like a virginal.

The vast majority of modern "early" harps are nothing of the kind. Small in range, strung in gut (or, rather, nylon), neither medieval nor Gothic in form and built *without brays*, such instruments are in fact modeled, directly or ultimately, on Scottish and Irish folk

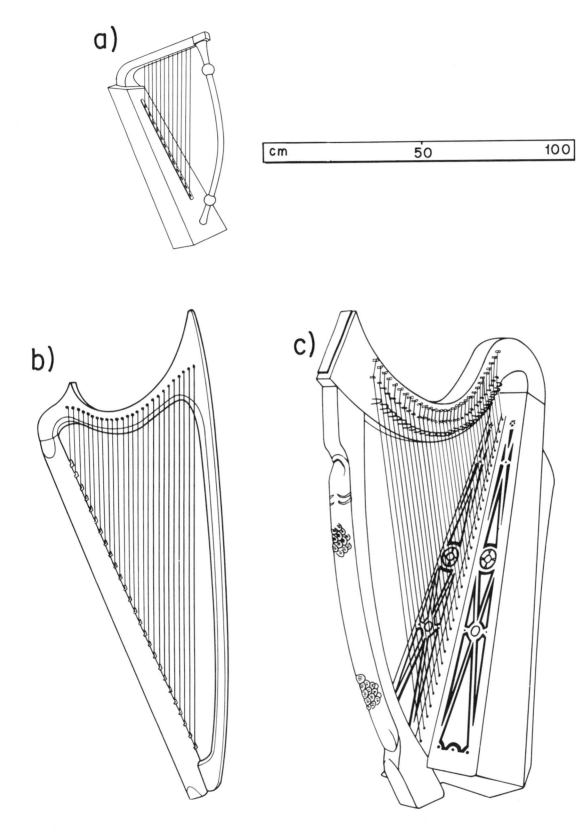

a)

b)

c)

cm   50   100

FIGURE 275. *Early harps: (a) medieval; (b) Gothic; (c) Irish.*

name of instrument	abbreviations	approximate dates of original use	written range	sounds	availability
medieval harp	med. hp.	until 1450	variable single {*mp* loudest notes {*ppp* softest	as written	very rare
Gothic harp	Gth. hp.	1400–1625	 single } loudest: *mf* notes } softest: *ppp*	as written	rare
Irish harp	Ir. hp.	1580–1625	 DIATONIC CHROMATIC single } loudest: *mf* notes } softest: *ppp*	as written	very rare

FIGURE 276. *Early harps—vital statistics.*

harps of the nineteenth century. Cute as they may look and sound (Lou Harrison has written very effectively for this type of harp), they are not even remotely like the true Renaissance or medieval harp. Fortunately, there are a few makers of more authentic instruments.

THE MEDIEVAL LYRE

Organologically a lyre is a stringed instrument whose soundbox has a **yoke** consisting of two upward-extending **arms** linked across their ends by a **crosspiece**. The strings run from the crosspiece to the opposite end of the body. On fully developed medieval lyres (i.e., after ca. 1000) the whole thing is in one piece, or built to look as if it were.

Historically these instruments were extremely variable in form, size, number and tuning of strings, and manner of playing. The modern resurrection of the lyre has only just begun and is proceeding very slowly, despite the great importance of the instrument in the twelfth and thirteenth centuries. So far only a handful of makers build lyres, and these lyres (especially those designated "crwth" or "crowd") are often based on post-medieval folk lyres.* The following discussion is based on what is known of actual medieval lyres and presumably will correspond with modern reality once the reconstruction of these instruments gets underway in any serious fashion.

The size may vary from cello-sized to violin-sized—possibly representing three distinct types—with the majority viola-sized or a bit larger. The pitch of a string would then theoretically lie somewhere between G_0 and e^2 (the medieval gamut), most likely between c^0 and a^1.

* It does seem, however, that "crwth" is likely to become the standard modern English name for this instrument.

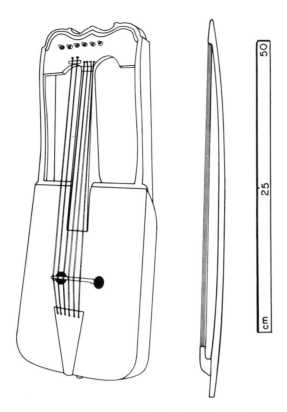

FIGURE 277. *Medieval lyre, with bow.*

name of instrument	abbreviations	approximate dates of original use	range	tuning	availability
(bowed) lyre (crwth)	(none)	−1400	variable loudest bowed: *f* loudest plucked: *mf* softest: *ppp*	variable	very rare

FIGURE 278. *The lyre—vital statistics.*

Unlike Classical and early medieval lyres, the high-medieval lyre was normally bowed, with an arcuate bow resembling that of the fiddle. The strings therefore run parallel to each other, rather than fanning out from the bridge as on earlier lyres. The strings usually number three or four, though there may exceptionally be as many as nine; at any rate, all but one of the strings are drones. The melody string is stopped by reaching through the yoke from behind (below) and pressing *sideways* against the string with either the tips of the fingers or the backs of the fingernails. This is true even of those lyres in which the strings are backed by a "fingerboard" running between the crossbar and the top of the body. Sometimes the hand reaches around the instrument to the front, instead of through the yoke.

All the drones must be sounded at once, since the bridge is flat. On waisted or narrow-bodied lyres the bow can be tilted so that only the melody string sounds, but on wider specimens all strings must be sounded at once. The instrument was quite frequently played pizzicato—a survival of its former non-bowed status—though probably not alternating pizz. and arco within a single item of music.

The tone of a bowed lyre resembles that of a hurdy-gurdy, though not so thin nor with the squeak of articulation noise that begins every hurdy-gurdy note.

THE LUTES

Most of the stages of the lute's long and complicated history are now represented by modern instruments. It is probably best to start not at the beginning but in the middle, with the Renaissance lute, the most common type available today. This is an instrument with eleven gut strings (nowadays usually nylon) arranged in six courses; the uppermost string (the **chanterelle**) is single while the others are geminated. The lowest three courses usually are octave pairs of strings (i.e., 8′ + 4′), but practice varies from player to player and some or all of these may be unisons instead. The neck is provided with eight frets, and the range and tuning are those shown as "normal"—in white notes—at the top of Figure 280. The frets on a lute are usually not inlaid metal but gut (or nylon) tied around the neck. Such frets can be moved to produce unusual scales or temperaments. This is a painstaking and time-consuming procedure, however, and some players may object to it.

The basic playing techniques for both left and right hand are essentially identical to those of the classical guitar—at least as far as the composer or arranger need be concerned—and the left-hand interval stretches are identical as well. Note that when the lute is tuned one step higher (as it not infrequently is) the lowest five courses have exactly the same pitches as the *highest* five courses of the guitar. The rather low tension of lute strings means that harmonics are trickier to get than on the guitar, and nothing above the fifth partial should be attempted.

The tone of the lute is slightly more delicate, focused, and precise than that of the guitar, with a considerably higher harmonic development. Typically, rapid melodic figuration will be picked out on the highest string, with the lower strings either strummed chordally or working together in interlocking counterpoint like that of guitar music, but independent melodic material can be played on any string.

Unlike the guitar, the lute is notated at actual pitch—at least, lutenists prefer it thus—and may be written on two staves if necessary. Actually, lute players are usually happiest with **lute tablature**. Music for lute and other plucked strings was almost invariably notated in tablature throughout the Renaissance and Baroque periods, and any accomplished player will know how to read it. Different tablatures were used at different times and places, but all have certain features in common; the type described below (French lute tablature) is the one most frequently used in early music and is of the greatest potential value to a composer or arranger who wishes to intabulate new music for the instrument.

In tablature a staff of six lines is used: the lines represent the lute's six courses, with the lowest at the bottom. Notes are designated on the staff by lower-case letters of the alphabet standing for the fret at which the string in question is to be stopped; "a" designates the open string, "b" the first fret, and so on. The *combined* rhythm of all notes is indicated separately

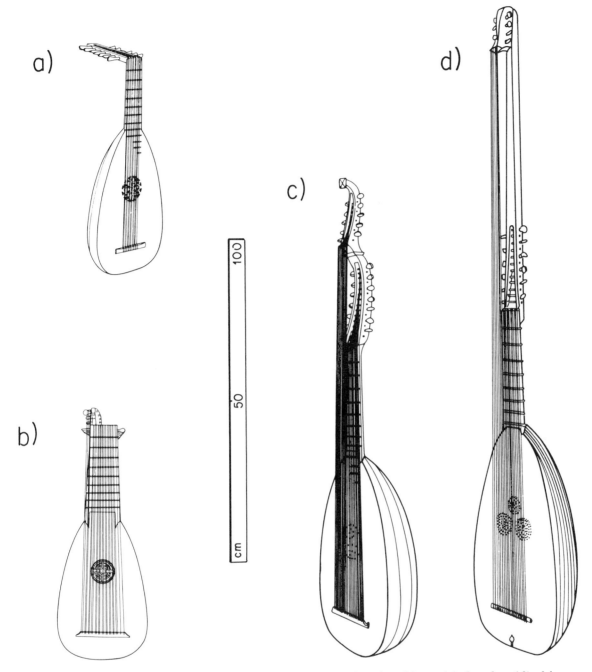

FIGURE 279. *The lute family: (a) 6-course lute; (b) theorboed lute; (c) theorbo; (d) chitarrone.*

above the staff. Out of this combined rhythm the counterpoint is automatically dissected by the assignment of specific notes to specific strings and the general rule that notes be held as long as possible. Figure 281 is an example of how this works in practice. Dynamics and expression marks can be applied to tablature just as to ordinary notation. The principles of this tablature can be applied to any plucked instrument with a fretted fingerboard, even such modern ones as electric guitar and banjo. For such purposes the Spanish tablature may be preferable; in this system numbers instead of letters are used to designate the frets, with "0" being the open string and "1" the first fret.

name of instrument	abbreviations	approximate dates of original use	range (written & sounding)	availability
(Renaissance) lute	(none)	1200–1630	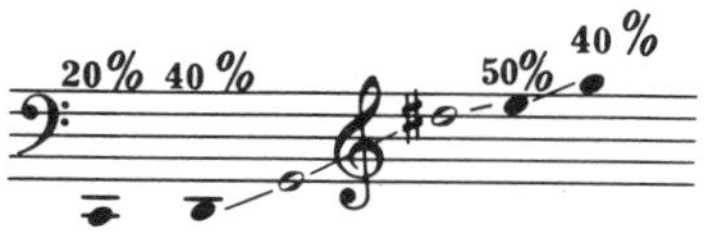 single notes: loudest: *mp*; softest: *ppp*	usually available
Baroque lute	lute	1595–1760	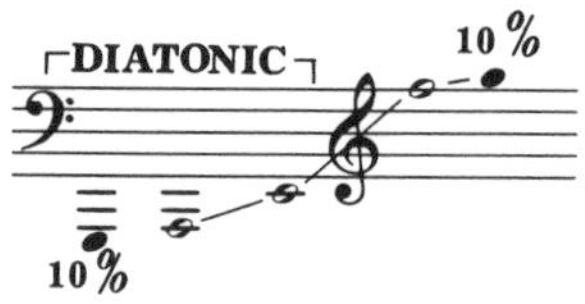 single notes: loudest: *mp*; softest: *ppp*	very rare
theorbo	theo. thrb.	1580–1740	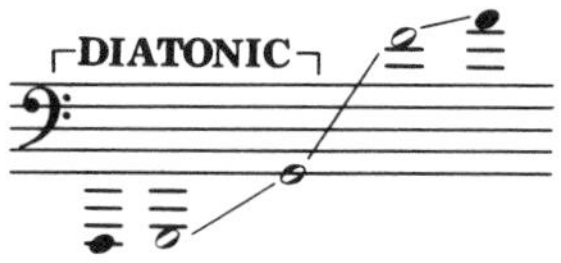 single notes: loudest: *mp*; softest: *ppp*	very rare
chitarrone	chit.	1580–1655		very rare

FIGURE 280. *The lute family—vital statistics.*

Even during the sixteenth century variant lutes existed with extra frets and/or extra bass strings. On lutes with a longer neck than usual, the neck has nine frets. On such instruments the space between the first and second fret is equivalent to that between the nut and the first fret on shorter instruments. Whether provided with a ninth neck-fret or not, many lutes have a number of short frets (usually four) set into the **belly** (= soundboard) of the instrument and usually serving only the top one or two courses. By pressing the string against the soundboard it is possible to play notes even beyond the last fret (however many there may be) up to at least $b\flat^2$, but these "extra" notes die almost at once and sound very dead.

In addition to the ordinary six-course lute, lutes with seven to ten courses were in use throughout the high Renaissance, becoming more and more common as the Baroque period approached. The additional courses (always double-strung) were usually tuned as follows:

7-course lute	D_0
8-course lute	F_0, E_0; or F_0, $E\flat_0$
9-course lute	F_0, $E(\flat)_0$, D_0; or F_0, $E(\flat)_0$, C_0
10-course lute	F_0, $E(\flat)_0$, D_0, C_0

All these extra courses could be fingered, but except for the seventh course it was usual to play them simply as open strings. Furthermore, the Renaissance lute was also made in small

name of instrument	tuning

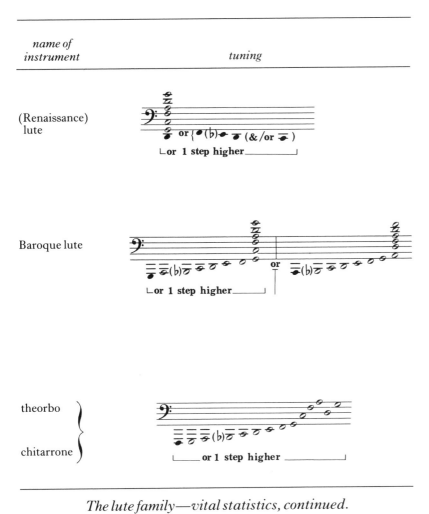

The lute family—vital statistics, continued.

(treble) and large (bass) varieties tuned, respectively, a fourth higher and a fifth lower than usual, but these have scarcely been revived yet.

In the Baroque period the ordinary "tenor" lute was expanded even further to make it suitable for continuo playing. A diatonic series of single or double (8′ + 4′) couses was added, bringing the total number of courses to twelve or thirteen. The lowest several of these did not run over the fingerboard and were usually attached to a separate pegbox on an extension of the neck (see Fig. 279), in which case the instrument was called a "theorboed lute" or "archlute." The dividing point between on-board and off-board courses is highly variable; a given lute may have anywhere from six to eleven on-board courses, with the rest being off-board. Whatever the arrangement, it is not usual to finger any of the courses below the sixth; these **diapasons** are merely plucked with the right thumb as open strings. The tuning of the diapasons varies with the key of the piece to be played. In fact, the tuning of the whole Baroque lute was and is highly variable, the three tunings given in Figure 280 being simply the most common and important. At least one seventeenth-century writer complained that lutenists had to spend half their lives retuning, and the situation must have been similar to that prevailing among folk guitarists today.

FIGURE 281. *A sample of lute tablature and its transcription.*

In tablature the diapasons are notated thus:

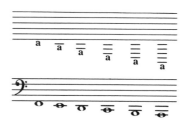

FIGURE 282. *Intabulation of diapason strings.*

In addition to the ordinary Baroque lute, there were two very large lutes designed specifically for continuo purposes. The **theorbo** and **chitarrone** differ somewhat in appearance but are tuned and fretted the same. In fact, since intermediate types were built, it is not at all clear that they are not really a single type. There are thirteen or fourteen courses—usually six on-board and seven or eight off-board. These can be double-strung 8′ unisons throughout, double-strung throughout with octave-sounding diapasons, double-strung on-board courses with single-strung diapasons, or single-strung throughout—particularly on theorboes of early pattern. If the diapasons are octave-sounding, the sixth and perhaps fifth and fourth courses may be so as well. The first course is often single-strung.

The large size of these continuo lutes is calculated to give them the fullest, most resonant, and longest-lasting bass notes possible. Sometimes these instruments, or at least their diapasons, are even strung in wire.

The maximum stretch from index to little finger is only a major third from the first fret, so any kind of scalar passagework requires frequent shifts of the hand up and down the neck. In addition, the first two courses are tuned an octave lower than they are on the lute.

The combination of specialized features found in continuo lutes suits them to the production of relatively slow-moving chord progressions with a firm bass rather than to the intricate counterpoint and rapid melodies of the ordinary lute—though such music can, within limits, be performed on the lower instruments.

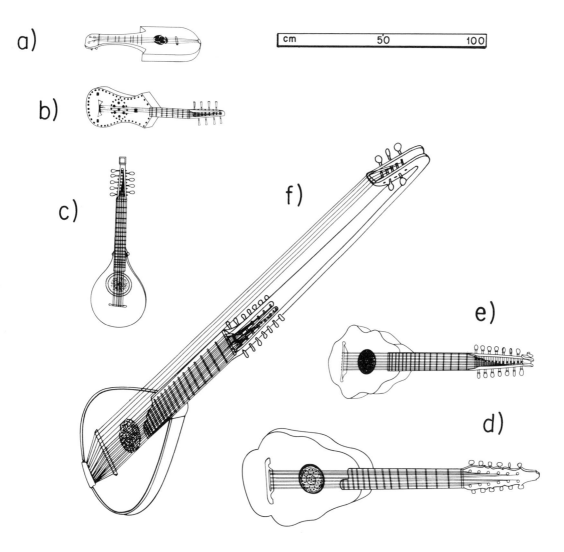

FIGURE 283. *The cittern family: (a) citole; (b) "gittern"; (c) cittern;*
(d) bandora; (e) orpharion; (f) ceterone.

The **medieval lute** in its earliest form had only four courses, tuned c^0, f^0, a^0, d^1 (i.e., the middle four of the later lute); it had no frets, and it was played with a plectrum. It could be single- or double-strung. The chanterelle existed at least sporadically from very early on and becomes standard by 1400. The sixth course first appears around 1460 and becomes standard by 1500. Around 1400 four frets were added to the neck, increased by mid-century to the usual eight. Note that the range of notes available from each string remains the same no matter what the number of frets. Between 1450 and 1500 the plectrum gradually fell into disuse.

Though one or two makers claim to build medieval lutes, the earliest style of lute generally available today is a mid-fifteenth-century type with five courses and eight frets. For an earlier type of lute, players use a restrung Arabic *'ūd*, which resembles the medieval lute very closely in most respects. The tone is quite different from that of the Renaissance lute, being very plunky and short-lived. The medieval lute was essentially a monophonic ensemble instrument and did not historically indulge in counterpoint.

The **mandora**, a soprano lute ancestral to the mandolin, appears around 1270 under the name **gittern**. It originally had three or four strings tuned an octave above the medieval lute, had no frets, and was played with a plectrum. The instrument acquired frets (nine of them) on roughly the same schedule as the lute. Renaissance and Baroque mandoras *occasionally* had five or six courses tuned lute-fashion (but an octave up), *occasionally* had geminated strings, and were *occasionally* played with the bare fingers. The mandora was quite highly thought of up to about 1600; in the seventeenth century its prestige declined steadily and at the low point (1700 or so) it was replaced by the mandolin, which has been slowly regaining the long-lost esteem of its ancestor. Very few modern builders have turned to the mandora, and there is apparently only one who makes a Renaissance type. One maker's "tenor" and "bass" varieties can presumably be used as medieval lutes.

Another virtually unrevived lute is the medieval **long-necked lute**, an instrument of approximately the proportions and range of a banjo, with three or four metal strings tuned variably and a long, fretted fingerboard. This instrument, played with a plectrum, was in use in art music up to about 1400, after which it became first a popular instrument (under the name **colascione**) and then a folk instrument. Modern musicians use Middle Eastern equivalents such as the Syrian *tanbura*. Their tone is twanging and plunky, and a good notch louder than the lute.

MUSICAL EXAMPLES

RENAISSANCE LUTE:

Des Prez/Spinacino, *La Bernardina*
Dowland, *Forlorn Hope Fancy*
Morley, *The First Book of Consort Lessons*, No. 12: "Goe from my window"

BAROQUE LUTE:

D. Gaultier, *La Rhétorique des dieux*, Suite II in A
J. S. Bach, *Suite* in E minor for lute, BWV 996
F. J. Haydn, *Cassation* in C for lute, violin, and cello
(arrangement of string quartet Hob. III, 6)

THEORBO:

W. Lawes, *The Royal Consort*, Suite No. 2 in D minor

CHITARRONE:

Monteverdi, *Orfeo*

THE CITTERNS

The cittern differs from the lute in being flat-backed and wire-strung. It is played with a plectrum and has inlaid (and therefore unmovable) frets. The strange **reentrant** tuning reflects the use of individual open strings as drones accompanying whatever string is taking the melody—though the instrument is far from being limited to such accompaniments.

In the Middle Ages the term **citole** was used very broadly to designate any flat-backed, fretted instrument with four strings. Instruments of this type were ancestral to the guitar as

name of instrument	abbreviations	approximate dates of original use	range (written & sounding)	tuning	availability
citole	ctl.	until 1350	 single notes { loudest: *f* / softest: *pp*		very rare
cittern	cit. ctn.	1500–1650	 50 % ... 5 % single notes { loudest: *f* / softest: *pp*	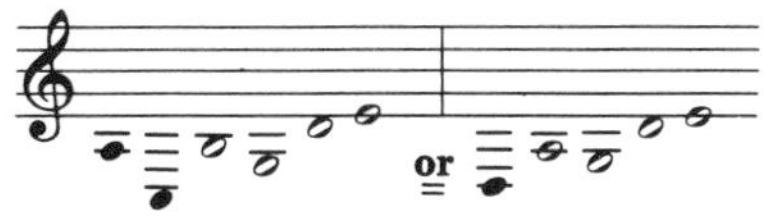 or	very rare
bandora		1562–1670	 single notes { loudest: *f* / softest: *pp*		very rare

FIGURE 284. *The cittern family—vital statistics.*

well as the cittern, and until recently the guitar-like varieties (which started appearing around 1250) were incorrectly referred to as "gitterns," a term that actually designates the medieval mandora (q.v.). This has led to the production of two distinct types of modern citole reproductions (Fig. 283a, b), both quite authentic, which actually represent extreme forms of a single medieval instrument. Now that the terminology has been straightened out, we may expect to see intermediate forms produced as well.

The "gittern" type of citole differs from the cittern type in several important respects. In the cittern type the strings are of metal, the tuning is reentrant, and the frets are arranged diatonically to produce the gapped range shown in Figure 284. On the d^1 string, for instance, only the following notes would be available: d^1, e^1, $f\sharp^1$, g^1, a^1, b^1, c^2, d^2, and e^2. The tone is remarkably similar to that of a banjo, though not as loud, penetrating, or aggressive.

The so-called "gittern," on the other hand, is gut-strung and produces a more guitar-like sound, albeit one that is short-lived, plunky, and somewhat muffled. The tuning is not reentrant (it is likely to be something like d^0, g^0, b^0, e^1) and the frets are not diatonic. The range is therefore not gapped and is usually a fourth lower than that given in Figure 284. Its maximum volume is only *mp*.

The citole was quite well thought of throughout the Middle Ages, but in the fifteenth century its prestige declined rapidly until it became a rare folk instrument. Sometime in the later part of that century it was transformed into the double-strung, finger-plucked Renaissance guitar (q.v.) and the **cittern**, also double-strung but retaining the use of the plectrum.

This latter instrument had as many different forms and tunings during its history as did the lute, but the vast majority of modern citterns are of the ordinary four-course variety. The cittern never completely regained the esteem formerly accorded the citole, and except for the brief period from 1575 to 1615 or so its acceptance in art music, though real, was grudging and tentative—like the electric guitar today or the classical guitar in the nineteenth century. It should accordingly be kept out of serious ensemble music, except for that composed during the period cited.

The tone of the cittern, though short-lived, is considerably more delicate than that of the citole; it is halfway between mandolin and lute in quality. The cittern's small size gives it a maximum stretch, from index to little finger, of a tritone from the first fret.

Several attempts were made at devising a bass cittern, of which the most important was the **bandora**, invented in 1562 and almost immediately popular. The bandora (or pandora) has six double courses tuned more like a lute than a cittern (a bandora designed to be tuned *exactly* like a lute is called an **orpharion**). The lowest two courses are octave-sounding and the others are unisons. Its tone is beautifully rich, full and resonant, suited for music of dignity and solemnity. It sounds almost like a virginal but with a bit more twang, because of the geminated strings. Maximum stretch from the first fret is a perfect fourth.

Another type of bass cittern is the **ceterone** (1590–1625), which resembles the chitarrone in appearance as well as in name. Originally a highly variable instrument, modern copies tend to reproduce one particular surviving specimen with seven double on-board courses and five single off-board ones. The upper courses are tuned cittern-fashion; the instrument as a whole descends to D_0 or C_0 and ascends to b^2. It sounds (surprise!) like a bandora.

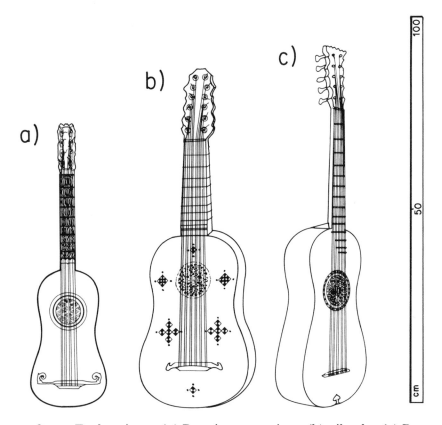

FIGURE 285. *Early guitars: (a) Renaissance guitar; (b) vihuela; (c) Baroque guitar.*

Musical Examples

CITTERN:

Holborne, Galliard for cittern and bass, from *The Cittharn Schoole* (1597)
Morley, *The First Book of Consort Lessons*, No. 12: "Goe from my window"

BANDORA:

Dowland, Galliard, from the *Braye bandora MS*
Morley, *The First Book of Consort Lessons*, No. 12: "Goe from my window"

EARLY GUITARS

As string instruments go, the guitar has been remarkably conservative throughout its long history. Some medieval citoles were even more guitar-like in appearance than the one shown in Figure 283b; modern reconstructions are distinctly guitar-like in sound as well, though this may be due partly to retrospection on the part of the builders.

Renaissance and Baroque guitars are double-strung instruments, plucked directly with the fingers and normally reading from tablature. The Baroque instrument sounds much like the modern one, if slightly lute-like. Its two lowest courses may be tuned as 8′ unisons, 8′ + 4′ octaves, or 4′ unisons. The high-pitched Renaissance guitar sounds rather like a coarse-

name of instrument	*abbreviations*	*approximate dates of original use*	*written range*	*tuning*	*sounds*	*availability*
Renaissance guitar	guit.	1450–1650	or a 4th or 5th higher 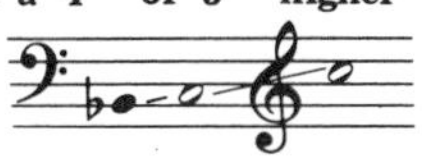 single notes { loudest: *mp* softest: *ppp*	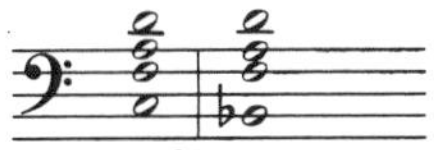 or └or a 4th or 5th higher┘	as written	very rare
viheula	vih.	1500–1590	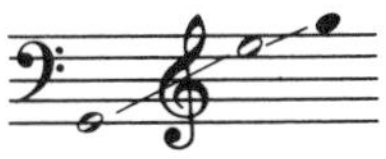 single notes { loudest: *mp* softest: *ppp*	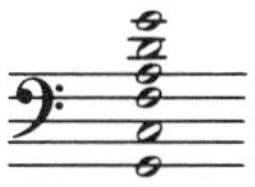	as written	very rare
Baroque guitar	guit.	1550–1750	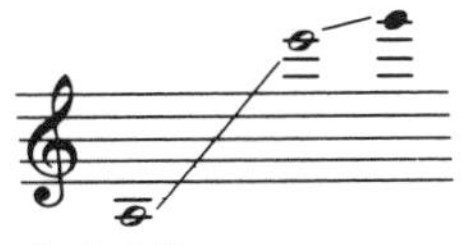 single notes { loudest: *mp* softest: *ppp*	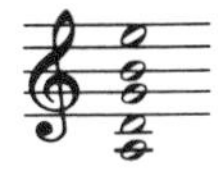	1 octave lower	very rare

FIGURE 286. *Early guitars—vital statistics.*

toned soprano lute; its tones last far longer than one would expect at this high pitch. The lowest course is octave-strung; the uppermost is usually an ungeminated chanterelle.

Throughout the Renaissance and Baroque periods the guitar was immensely popular but not as highly esteemed as the lute, and its literature is more limited.

The **vihuela** is a guitar strung and tuned like, and sounding almost exactly like, a lute. Historically its use was restricted to Spain, where it was substituted for the lute and shared the lute repertoire.

All these early guitars have movable, tied-on, gut or nylon frets.

MUSICAL EXAMPLES

RENAISSANCE GUITAR:

Mudarra, Pavana III, from *Tres libros de musica* (1546)

VIHUELA:

Milan, Fantasia XI, from *El Maestro* (1536)

THE VIOLS

Early bowed instruments were usually developed by the application of the bow to some pre-existing plucked type. We have already seen this with the lyre. It may help to keep these instruments straight if the equivalencies are laid out here in tabular form.

original plucked instrument	bowed adaptation
lute	viol
gittern	rebec
citole	fiddle

The relationship between lute and viol can be clearly seen in their joint possession of movable, tied-on, gut or nylon frets and of six gut strings tuned in an identical pattern (compare the lute tuning to that of the tenor viol). The neck of a viol is fitted with seven frets, but the fingerboard extends well beyond the last fret, and thus in the upper part of the range glissandos and microtones can be played.

The treble, alto, and tenor viols are not held under the chin but are rested on the player's knee (whence **viola da gamba**, i.e., "leg viol"). The bass is held between the knees, cello-fashion, but without an endpin; and the great bass—or **violone**, as it is more widely known—rests directly on the floor, where it may be positioned between the legs or played standing. Since the term "bass viol" is frequently used to designate the modern contrabass, the true bass viol is frequently referred to by the Italian term "viola da gamba" or simply "gamba," indeed, all members of the family are frequently designated as "gambas." Similarly, the term "violone" has been used for all sorts of low-pitched bowed strings, so to be certain of getting this instrument the complete expression "violone da gamba" must be used.

Viol technique differs from violin technique mostly in the matter of bowing, for the viol bow is held palm-upward, and may be gripped in front of the frog rather than directly at it.

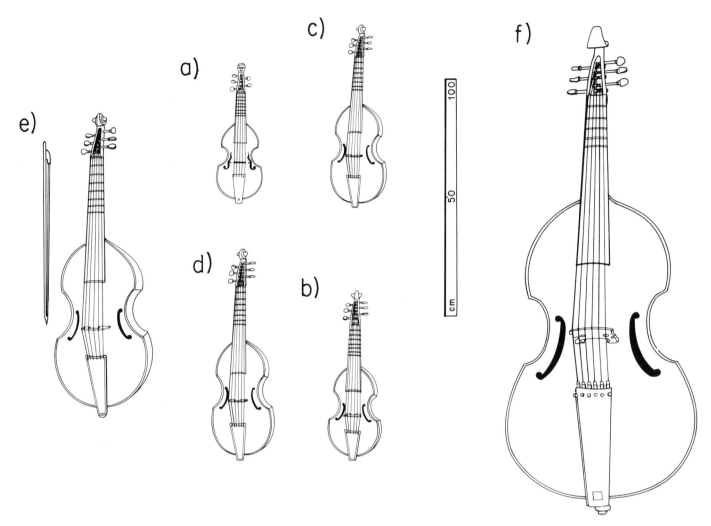

FIGURE 287. *The viol family: (a) pardessus de viole; (b) treble viol; (c) alto viol; (d) tenor viol; (e) bass viol; (f) violone da gamba.*

The right middle finger is held against the bow hairs, aiding in their tensioning and giving the player direct control over this variable from moment to moment. The underhand bowing makes the upbow into the power stroke; viol bowing patterns are thus the reverse of violin ones.

The **pardessus de viole**, a very late addition to the family, never formed part of the viol consort but was used (in France only) as a violin substitute. Note that it usually has only five strings.

The tone of all the viols is weaker, thinner, and more nasally zingy than that of the violin family. Equally important is the relatively slow, gentle attack, which gives viol articulation a relaxed, almost laid-back sound totally in contrast to the aggressive, muscular attack of loud violin or cello playing.

The bridge of a viol is flatter than that of a violin, and as a result triple stops can be fully sustained as softly as *piano*, and in *forte* even a quadruple stop can be sustained. Quintuple and sextuple stops are not infrequently written, but these must be arpeggiated; however, the

name of instrument	abbreviations	approximate dates of original use	range (written & sounding)	tuning	availability
pardessus de viole	p.d.v. pard.	1680–1780	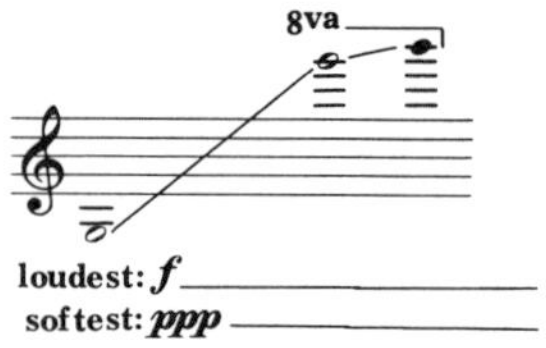 loudest: _f_ softest: _ppp_	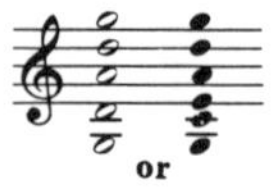 or	very rare
treble viol	tr. v. tr. gamb.	1480–1690	 loudest: _f_ softest: _ppp_		rare
alto viol	a.v. a. gamb.	1480–1690	 loudest: _f_ softest: _ppp_		very rare
tenor viol	t.v. t. gamb.	1430–1690	 loudest: _f_ softest: _ppp_	 or 1 step higher	rare
bass viol (viola da gamba)	b.v. vdg. gamb. bs. gamb.	1480–1760	 5% loudest: _f_ softest: _ppp_		usually available
violone da gamba	vne. vne. d.g.	1550–1690	 loudest: _f_ softest: _ppp_	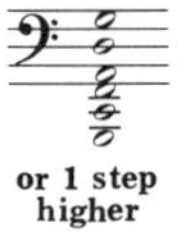 or 1 step higher	very rare

FIGURE 288. *The viol family—vital statistics.*

precision afforded by the frets makes stopped notes on a viol much more resonant than those of equivalent violin-family instruments, and particularly in the lowest sizes a tone will if allowed ring on quite strongly after the bow is released. Similarly, the pizzicato is much more resonant and long-lasting than in the violin family—a more satisfactory sound altogether. All the special bowed and plucked effects used on members of the violin family can be used on viols.

TENOR VIOL

Stretch From Finger

From the first fret

To Finger	1	2	3
4	aug 4th	M3d	M2nd
3	M3d	M2nd	
2	m3d		

VIOLONE

Stretch From Finger

From the first fret

To Finger	1	2	3
4	M3d	m2nd	m2nd
3	m3d	m2nd	
2	M2nd		

Stretch From Finger

fifth fret

To Finger	1	2	3
4	perf. 5th	perf. 4th	m3d
3	perf. 4th	m3d	
2	m3d		

Stretch From Finger

To Finger	1	2	3
4	M3d	M2nd	m2nd
3	m3d	M2nd	
2	M2nd		

FIGURE 289. *Maximum single-string left-hand interval stretches for tenor viol and violone.*

Maximum left-hand stretches for the bass viol are virtually identical to those for the cello, and on the treble viol they are only slightly less than on the viola. The pardessus has easier stretches than the violin, with maximums a half-step greater for each perfect fifth of reach. The alto viol maximum stretches are less than the viola's to the extent of a half-step in each tritone of (viola) reach (i.e., if a violist can barely reach a tritone, then the alto-viol player can only reach a fourth). Maximum stretches for the tenor viol and violone are shown above. Because of their playing posture, all the viols can make use of thumb positions, though this was seldom, if ever, done historically.

The ordinary consort of viols consists of one or two each of trebles, tenors, and basses in various combinations. The so-called alto viol, used occasionally to play second-treble lines, is virtually useless musically—it was never common historically and is unlikely ever to be so in the future.

All the viols are higher-pitched instruments than one would guess from their size: the bass viol plays in a distinctly higher tessitura than the cello, while the treble normally plays in the range of the violin, not the viola. At certain times and places it was apparently the practice to play even higher on all the viols, taking music on two tenors, bass, and violone that would be perfectly playable on two trebles, tenor, and bass.

The bass viol was—at least from the beginning of the sixteenth century—the most important instrument of the family and the one most often employed as a solo instrument. In the seventeenth century it was made in three slightly different varieties (all now once more available) for differing musical purposes. The normal instrument is the **consort bass** used in ensemble and continuo playing. The **division viol**—built slightly smaller, to make the left-hand stretches easier—is designed for solo playing of improvised variations ("divisions"), while the **lyra viol** (smallest of all) specialized in the performance of full chordal textures, both as soloist and as a continuo instrument, and was usually written for in tablature, making use of a wide variety of special tunings. It must be emphasized, however, that all types of music can be played on *any* bass viol; lyra-viol music can be played on a consort bass, for example. Finally, it should be mentioned that bass viols of a late French pattern are provided with a seventh string, tuned to A_1.

MUSICAL EXAMPLES

VIOLS:

Morley, *The First Book of Consort Lessons*, No. 12: "Goe from my window" (TrB)
W. Lawes, *Six-Part Consort Suite No. 1* in C minor (TrTrTTBB)
 Suite No. 2 in C for two division viols and organ
 Suite No. 2 in G minor for three lyra viols
Gibbons, Fantasias a 3, from *Musique for the greate dooble bass* (TrBVlne)
Schütz, *Erbarm dich mein, o Herre Gott*, SWV 447 (TrTTB)
Rameau, *Pièces de clavecin en concert*, concert II (B)
Pousseur, *Madrigal II* (B)

THE VIOLA D'AMORE AND BARYTON

The viola d'amore and baryton are offshoots of the viol family, provided with a set of wire **sympathetic strings** in addition to the ordinary, bowed, gut ones. The sympathetic strings lie beneath the bowed ones, running under the fingerboard and through a hole at the base of the neck so that for half their length they run *in back of* the neck. They do not, of course, pass over the bridge but run through it, under it, or beside it to independent points of attachment.

The viola d'amore is bowed overhand, and its tone is intermediate between viol and violin—a gentle, silvery variant of ordinary violin tone. The baryton sounds more gamba-like, and may be bowed either underhand or overhand. The sympathetic strings of both instruments add a subtle, blurred halo of reverberation that is much more apparent live than in recordings (where the ear has difficulty separating this resonance from the acoustic reverberation of the recording studio).

The viola d'amore has seven sympathetic strings, usually tuned in unison with the bowed strings. The tuning given in Figure 291 is the most common, but numerous other accordaturas have been used and it is a good idea to specify the tuning of the viola d'amore in any piece in which it is used.

The term "viola d'amore" pre-dates the instrument itself by at least twenty years; it was originally used for a sort of wire-strung violin. With the baryton the reverse is the case, since bass gambas were occasionally provided with sympathetic strings at least as early as 1616. It would therefore not be inappropriate to use a baryton as a continuo instrument in early-seventeenth-century music or even to employ it in the division-viol and lyra-viol repertoire.

The baryton would be virtually forgotten today had it not been used in numerous important compositions by Haydn. The tuning given here is only one of many historical tunings, but it is the one used by Haydn and is thus universal today. Unlike those of the viola d'amore, the numerous sympathetic strings of the baryton are so arranged that they can be

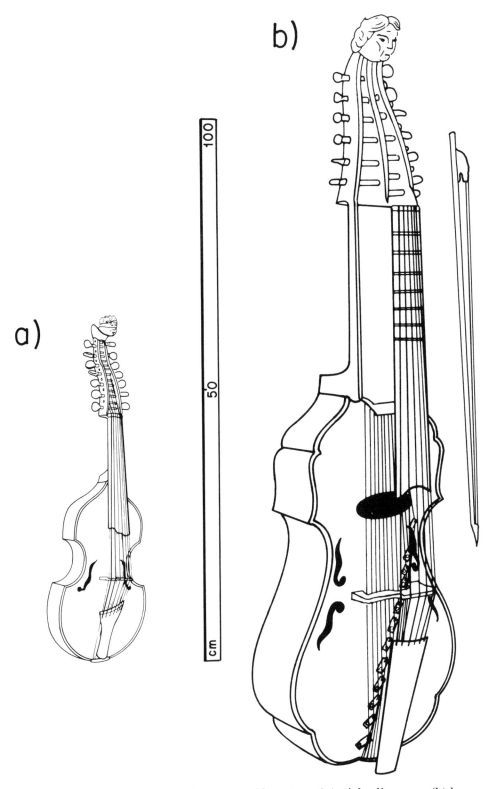

FIGURE 290. *Viola d'amore and baryton: (a) viola d'amore; (b) baryton.*

name of instrument	abbreviations	approximate dates of original use	range (written & sounding)	tuning	availability
viola d'amore	vda. vla. d'am.	1700–1785			very rare
baryton	brt. btn.	1650–1785			very rare

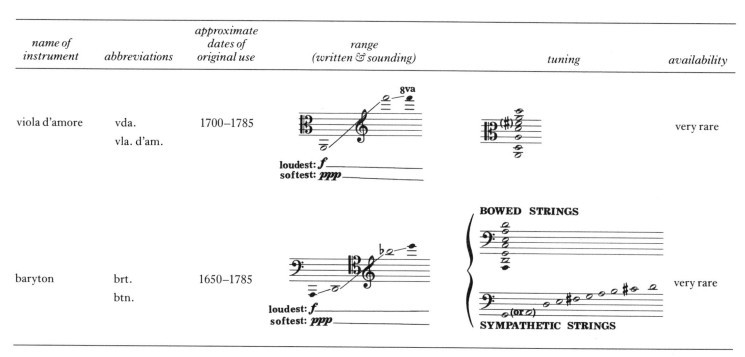

FIGURE 291. *Viola d'amore and baryton—vital statistics.*

plucked by the left thumb behind the neck. Their number and tuning vary, but the notes indicated in Figure 291 are those scored by Haydn, and hence can always be counted on. They have a gentle, harplike tone, no louder than *mezzo-forte* (when overplucked they go sharp), and the lower ones may sustain for as long as six seconds. The equivalent of *sul ponticello* and *sul tasto* effects can be produced on these strings by plucking respectively near the nut or near the body of the instrument. In writing these "harp" tones, remember that the left hand must also finger the primary strings on the other side of the neck. While fingering the lowest string, it is possible to pluck only the highest sympathetic string; conversely, only the highest main string can be fingered when the lowest sympathetic string is to be plucked.

Left-hand stretches for the viola d'amore and baryton are roughly equivalent to those for viola and cello, respectively. The neck of the baryton is provided with (usually) seven inlaid or tied frets; the viola d'amore is unfretted. On both instruments, the ability to sustain multiple stops is the same as that of a viol.

MUSICAL EXAMPLES

VIOLA D'AMORE:

Vivaldi, Concerto in D minor for lute, viola d'amore and muted strings, P. 266
Hindemith, *Kammermusik* No. 6

BARYTON:

Haydn, Baryton Trio in D, Hob. XI, 97
Divertimento a 8 in A, Hob. X, 3

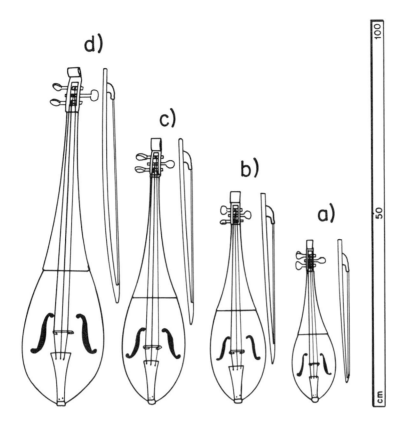

FIGURE 292. *Rebecs: (a) soprano; (b) alto; (c) tenor; (d) bass.*

THE REBEC

With its gut strings and fretless, raised fingerboard the rebec is one of the ancestors of the violin. These small, acoustically inefficient instruments have a much different tone, however: it is thin, choked, and nasal, almost as if it were electronically filtered.

The four discrete sizes and violin-like tunings of modern rebecs are modeled on a rather late stage of the instrument's development. Medieval rebecs were much more likely to have two strings than four, and were apparently tuned in all sorts of odd ways. Authentically, rebecs should not be held under the chin but in the hollow of the shoulder, on top of either shoulder, or horizontally across the chest. In medieval Spain they were held on the knee. The instrument is bowed overhand.

FIDDLES AND LIRAS

THE FIDDLE

The fiddle is the direct ancestor of the violin. It was and is so tremendously variable that it is difficult to say anything concrete about it, but two points are pretty much fixed: the instrument has five gut strings, and it sounds rather like a choked, weak violin or viola. Historically

name of instrument	abbreviations	approximate dates of original use	range (written & sounding)	tuning	availability
soprano rebec	sreb.	1000–1600	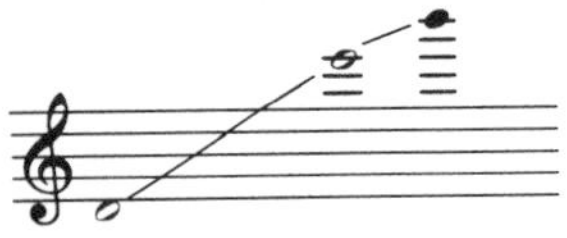 loudest: *f* ___ softest: *ppp* ___		very rare
alto rebec	areb. reb.	1000–1600	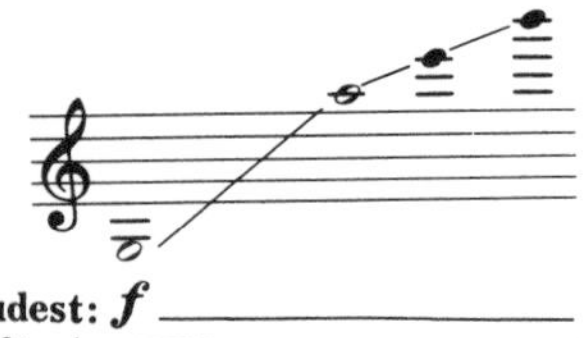 loudest: *f* ___ softest: *ppp* ___		rare
tenor rebec	treb.	1000–1600	 loudest: *f* ___ softest: *ppp* ___		very rare
bass rebec	breb.	1000–1600	 loudest: *f* ___ softest: *ppp* ___	 or a step lower	very rare

FIGURE 293. *Rebecs—vital statistics.*

it was made in sizes ranging from that of the violin to that of the guitar. Most modern examples are viola-sized, with the lowest string tuned to d^0 or c^0. Medieval fiddles frequently descended to G_0, though few modern ones are large enough for this. On the other hand, at least one modern maker builds a bass size descending to D_0, as well as a soprano going no lower than g^0. All sorts of tunings may legitimately be used, but the highest string should never be more than two octaves above the lowest. The fifth string was usually used as a drone and therefore may be tuned higher than the fourth.

Most modern fiddles follow a fifteenth-century pattern, with fingerboards long enough to allow ascent up to an eleventh above the pitch of the open string. They are also occasionally provided with seven tied frets (first used in the fourteenth century), which can of course be removed. Fiddles of truly medieval pattern have no frets, and the fingerboard allows ascent of only a sixth above the open string.

Correctly, the fiddle should be held in one of the manners listed above for the rebec, but many players insist on holding it on the knee, gamba-fashion, or under the chin, violin-fashion.

The fiddle is bowed overhand.

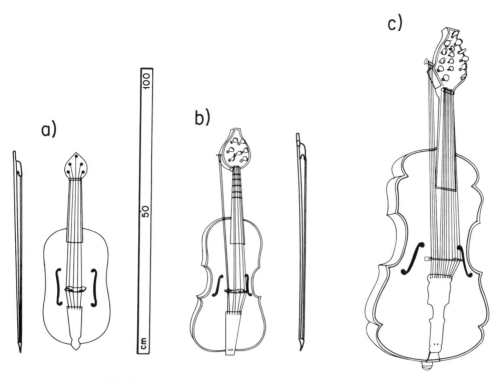

FIGURE 294. *Fiddle and liras: (a) fiddle; (b) lira da braccio; (c) lira da gamba.*

THE LIRAS

The lira da braccio is the (unfretted) Renaissance version of the medieval fiddle, from which it differs mainly in the addition of a sixth course as an off-board drone. The fifth and sixth courses are geminated at the octave. The full name "lira da braccio" is necessary because the term "lira," unadorned, has been and is used to refer not only to this instrument but to the rebec, lyre, lyra viol, and hurdy-gurdy.

The lira da braccio is about the size of a treble viol, but is held against or on top of the left shoulder and bowed violin-fashion. The lowest on-board course is stopped by the left thumb, which reaches around the back of the neck to a point opposite the index finger, as in folk-guitar technique—not around the front, as with a cello.

name of instrument	abbreviations	approximate dates of original use	range (written & sounding)	availability
fiddle	fid. fdl.	1000–1500	variable loudest: f softest: ppp	rare

FIGURE 295. *The fiddle—vital statistics.*

name of instrument	abbreviations	approximate dates of original use	range (written & sounding)	availability
lira da braccio	ldb.	1450–1625	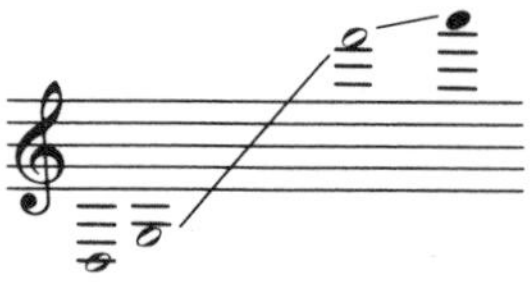 loudest: *f* ———— softest: *ppp* ————	very rare
lira da gamba	ldg. lne.	1560–1650	 loudest: *f* ———— softest: *ppp* ————	very rare

FIGURE 296. *Liras—vital statistics.*

Historically, the lira da braccio was primarily a solo instrument, providing improvised chordal accompaniment to a singer, but there is no reason why it cannot be used in ensemble music. The violin family first appeared around 1530 (as popular instruments) and by 1600 had effectively ousted the lira da braccio.

The **lira da gamba** or **lirone** is a bass-range lira designed to play chords easily. The bridge is so gently curved that chords of up to six notes can be fully sustained, and it is almost impossible to play on one string alone (except, of course, for the first and last). The instrument has nine to fourteen melody strings and two—sometimes more—off-board drones. The tuning is a staggered ascending cycle of fifths ending with $c\#^1$ or (late in the history of the instrument) $a\#^0$ (see Fig. 294). This pattern may descend in strict order all the way to the last off-board drone, or the lowest four or six strings may be tuned in octave pairs (D_0, d^0, G_0, g^0, etc.), grouped in staggered fourths (as in the example just cited) rather than fifths.

The lira da gamba is fretted, held, and bowed like a bass gamba. Historically, it functioned as a continuo instrument (e.g., in Francesca Caccini's *Il Liberazione di Ruggiero*), where the exact tuning pattern did not matter provided that chords of all sorts could be easily produced.

Both lira da braccio and lira da gamba make frequent use of the barre in producing chords.

THE HURDY-GURDIES

Hurdy-gurdies are keyboard instruments of a sort, but somehow they seem to fit best here, at the tail end of the list of instruments. The hurdy-gurdy is essentially a mechanized string instrument; this complete mechanization of both the left and right hands seems strangely out of place in the Middle Ages, and would be more fitting as a product of the gadget-happy eighteenth century.

name of instrument	tuning
lira da braccio	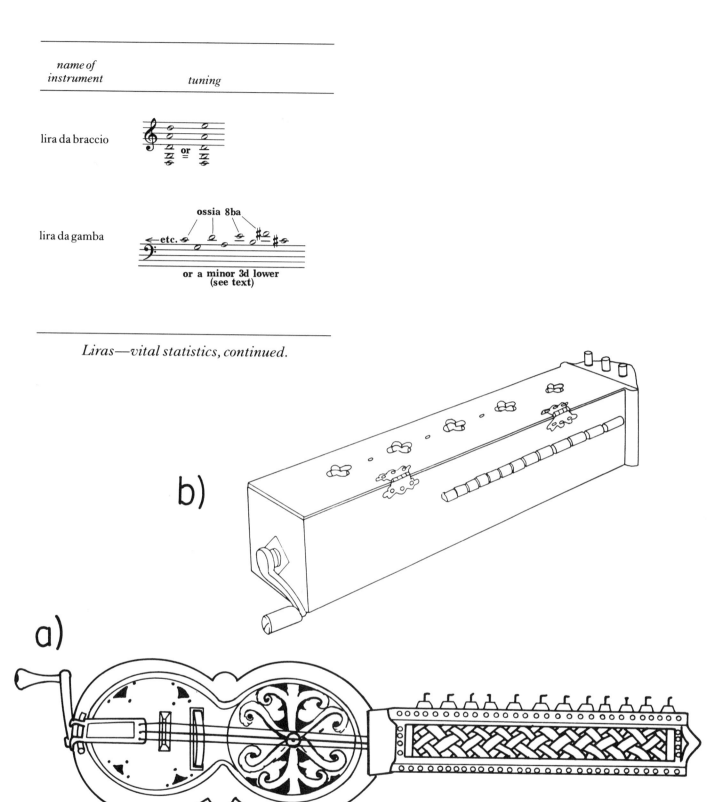
lira da gamba	

Liras—vital statistics, continued.

FIGURE 297. *Hurdy-gurdies: (a) organistrum; (b) symphonia.*

name of instrument	abbreviations	approximate dates of original use	range (written & sounding)	availability
organistrum	orgst.	1125–1300		very rare
symphonia	symph.	1250–1400		very rare

loudest: *f* _____
softest: *mp* _____

loudest: *f* _____
softest: *mp* _____

FIGURE 298. *Medieval hurdy-gurdies—vital statistics.*

The bow is replaced by a rosined wheel cranked by the right hand. The wheel is in constant contact with the strings, all of which sound simultaneously for as long as the wheel is turned. The natural expression of a hurdy-gurdy, then, is a continuous legato from beginning to end of whatever is being played; articulation is possible, however, albeit clumsy and slow. More rapid articulation can be achieved by giving the wheel a series of little extra pushes in the desired rhythm; this does not break the legato but accents the notes in question. The dynamic level is varied by turning the wheel at different speeds—the faster the louder.

As with the bagpipe, lyre, and harp, modern hurdy-gurdies reflect medieval reality very badly. Virtually all those now made are based—sometimes very carefully—on fifteenth- to nineteenth-century folk instruments. These have one or more unison or octave-tuned melody strings (**chanterelles**) with a range of two chromatic octaves upward from g^1, and numerous drone strings. In fairness it should be noted that such instruments are exactly what is needed for the spate of bucolic music with hurdy-gurdy and/or bagpipe parts cranked out (if the pun may be forgiven) by eighteenth-century composers.

The earliest type of hurdy-gurdy is the **organistrum**, a guitar- or cello-sized instrument with three chanterelles and no drones. The strings are stopped by a set of bridges on rotating keys manipulated by the player (Fig. 299a). This rather clumsy technique requires the use of both hands; the organistrum is therefore laid across the laps of two players, one of whom manipulates the keys while the other turns the wheel.*

The awkwardness of organistrum technique has been somewhat overemphasized by modern writers. While it is indeed a slow-moving instrument, it can attain fairly considerable speed whenever only one bridge need be turned to change a pitch. The following, for instance, is entirely idiomatic:

* Historically, many organistra were made with push-pull instead of rotary action. These could be played by a single person, but much of the following discussion would still hold. As far as I know, no organistra of this type are now made.

FIGURE 299. *Mechanism of (a) the organistrum; (b) the symphonia and later hurdy-gurdies.*

The important thing to remember is that in order to move from a given note to a lower note, all intervening bridges must be rotated out of the way. The following passage is impossible because the player would be required, before the final downward leap, to move six bridges while the c¹ was sounding, and a seventh to make the leap itself—this is just not possible with only two hands.*

But these *are* possible:

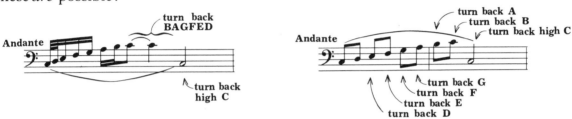

The three strings of the organistrum are tuned c⁰, g⁰, c¹, and each bridge stops all three; thus, the instrument constantly plays in parallel fifths and octaves. This effect is not intended as "instant harmony" but as an intensification of the main (lowest) note by reinforcing it with its second partial and the 3/2 privileged frequency; therefore, in reading from written music only the lowest of the three simultaneous pitches need be considered.

The organistrum seems to have been exclusively a church—or at least clerical—instrument; its use in medieval music should be limited to doubling chant, playing the tenors of melismatic organum, and playing slow-moving motet tenors.

The **symphonia**, on the other hand, seems to have been a strictly secular instrument. It differs from the organistrum in being smaller and higher-pitched and in having a much more efficient key action. In the symphonia the keys are placed on the bottom of the instrument and pushed up to stop the chanterelle(s), falling back of their own weight when released. This system, which permits extremely rapid playing, is used on all later types of hurdy-gurdy. Only one player, fingering the keys with the left hand and cranking the wheel with the right, is needed.

Classically, the symphonia had three strings—a chanterelle probably tuned to c¹, a⁰, or g⁰ and two drones tuned to the finalis of whatever was being played and/or its fifth. The drones make the instrument suitable only for monophonic music. Modern symphoniae, un-

* Presumably, though, the second player, whose left hand is free, could help with this—but the passage would still probably be unplayable.

der the retroactive influence of later types of hurdy-gurdy, tend to have two unison chante-relles tuned to g^1 (as given in Fig. 298). The box-shaped symphonia shown in Figure 297 is just one type; others are made in more or less the same shape as the organistrum.

Hurdy-gurdies of all types have a very thin, whining tone that is nonetheless quite ro-bust and powerful—at times, almost reminiscent of the noise of a power saw. Articulation noise is an important part of the timbre: the wheel makes a slight grunting or coughing sound as it starts and stops, and the tangents or bridges produce a distinct, organ-like "chiff" as they come in contact with the vibrating string. The pitches of both organistrum and symphonia can be adjusted slightly by varying the position of the bridge or the pressure on the key, respectively, and a vibrato can be made by this means.

APPENDIX I

Proposed Special Clefs

For Very Low and

Very High Notes

The practical ranges of most instruments have been gradually expanding for two centuries, and some are beginning to become notationally unmanageable. The indications "8va_____" and "8ba_____," traditional answers to the problem of excessive ledger lines, have never been satisfactory. The introduction of two special clefs—two octaves higher than the treble clef and two octaves lower than the bass clef, respectively—clarifies the notation of passages in extreme registers, making them easier to read and less cumbersome to write than they are with the traditional "8va" and "8ba" signs. Anyone wishing to adopt these "descant" and "contrabass" clefs in their scores must explain them, since very few players will have seen them before.

The following examples should make clear the usefulness of the new signs.

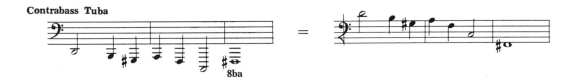

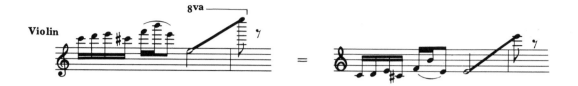

These clefs have the further advantage of enabling the notation of all parts in a concert-pitch score at actual pitch, eliminating octave transpositions entirely.

APPENDIX II

Student and Amateur Ranges

of Common Instruments

The ranges are given as written for the instruments, and are calculated at about high school senior or college freshman level. For transpositions, see the main text heading for each instrument.

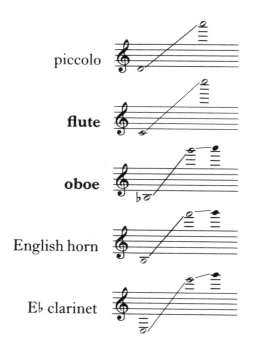

B♭ clarinet

alto clarinet

bass clarinet

contra-alto clarinet
contrabass clarinet

saxophone (all sizes)

bassoon

horn

trumpet in C

trumpet in B♭

trombone

flügelhorn

alto horn

baritone horn

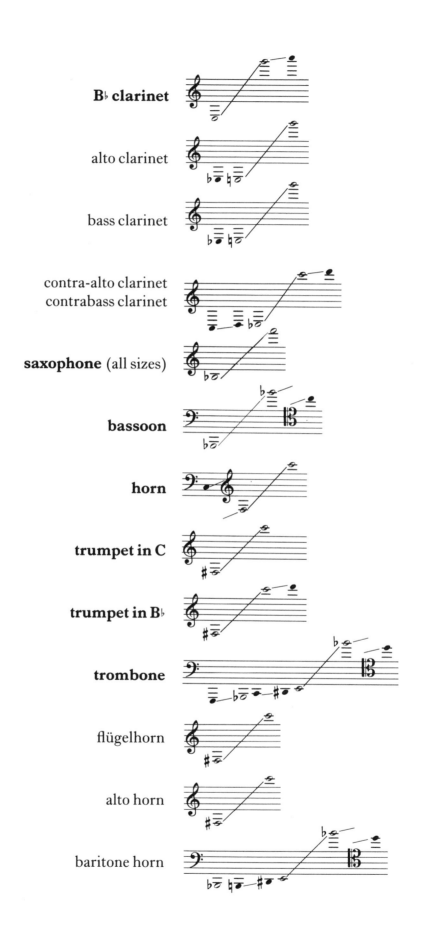

tuba (bass or contrabass)

timpani

chimes

xylophone

marimba

glockenspiel

vibraphone

celesta

piano
electric piano   } full normal range
organ

harp

guitar

violin

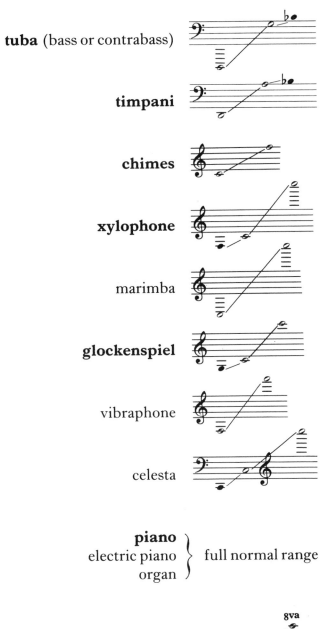

viola

cello

contrabass

soprano recorder

alto recorder
sopranino recorder

tenor recorder

bass recorder

harpsichord   8′, 4′

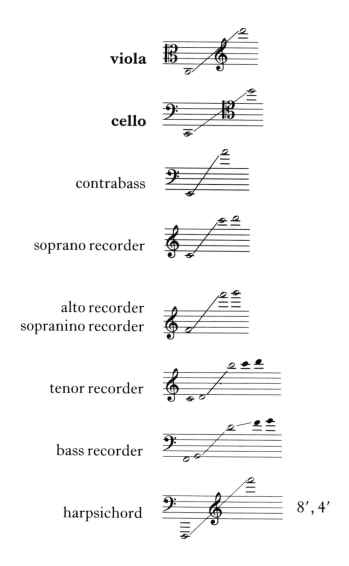

APPENDIX III

Foreign-Language Equivalents

of Terms Used in This Book

Items marked ≈ are only approximately equivalent to the English word.

PART ONE: MODERN INSTRUMENTS

ENGLISH	DEUTSCH	FRANÇAIS	ITALIANO	ESPAÑOL
Wind (instruments)	**Bläser**	**Vents**	**Fiati**	**Ventos**
bore	Bohrung	perce	tubatura canale	perforación
bell	Schallbecher Schalltrichter	pavillon	campana	campana
mouthpiece	Mundstück	embouchure	bocchino	embocadura
embouchure	Embouchure	embouchure	imboccatura	embocadura
fluttertongue	Flatterzunge	trémolo	frullato	tremolo dental frullato
double-tongue	Doppelzunge	double articulation	doppio colpo (di lingua)	doble articulación
cyclic breathing	Zirkulationsatmung			respiración continua
multiphonic	Mehrklang	multiphonique	multifonico	multifónico

ENGLISH	DEUTSCH	FRANÇAIS	ITALIANO	ESPAÑOL
Woodwind(s)	**Holz (-blasinstrument)**	**Bois**	**Legno (Legni)**	**Madera(s)**
reed	Rohrblatt	anche	ancia	lengüeta
key	Klappe	clef	chiave	llave
hard (tone)	(schall)hart	dur	duro	duro
muffled (tone)	matt	sourd	sordo	mate
breathy (tone)	hauchig	≈murmuré	soffiato	≈susurrado
fingering	Fingersatz	doigté	diteggiatura	digitación
half-hole	Halbdeckung	demi-obturé	mezzo buco	semiobturado
Flute	**Flöte**	**Flûte**	**Flauto**	**Flauta**
piccolo	kleine Flöte	petite flûte	flauto piccolo ottavino	flautin piccolo
alto flute	Altflöte	flûte alto	flauto contralto	flauta contralto
bass flute	baßflöte	flûte basse	flauto basso	flauta baja
foot joint	Fußstück	patte	pezzo inferiore	pata
harmonic	Flageolett-Ton	flageolet	suono flautato	armónico
whistle tone	Whistle-Ton			whistle-tone
Oboe	**Oboe**	**Hautbois**	**Oboe**	**Óboe**
English horn	Englischhorn	cor anglais	corno inglese	corno inglés
heckelphone	Heckelphon	heckelphone	Heckelphon	heckelphon
oboe d'amore	Liebesoboe	hautbois d'amour	oboe d'amore	óboe de amor
liebesfuss	Liebesfuß	liebesfuss	liebesfuss	liebesfuss
staple	Hülse	corps	corpo	cuerpo
bocal	Stift	bocal	esse	bocal
Clarinet	**Klarinette**	**Clarinette**	**Clarinetto**	**Clarinete**
A♭ clarinet	As-Klarinette Sextklarinette	petite clarinette en la♭	clarinetto piccolo in la♭ sestino	requinto en la♭
E♭ clarinet	Es-Klarinette	petite clarinette en mi♭	clarinetto piccolo in mi♭	requinto (en mi♭)
alto clarinet	Altklarinette	clarinette alto	clarinetto contralto	clarinete (contr)alto
bass clarinet	Baßklarinette	clarinette basse	clarinetto basso	clarinete bajo
contra-alto clarinet	Kontra-Altklarinette	clarinette contre-alto	clarinetto contra-alto	clarinete contra-alto
contrabass clarinet	Kontrabaßklarinette	clarinette contrebasse	clarinetto contrabbasso	clarinete contrabajo
basset horn	Bassetthorn	cor de basset	corno di bassetto	corno di bassetto
lay (of mouthpiece)	Bahn	table	tavola	asiento

ENGLISH	DEUTSCH	FRANÇAIS	ITALIANO	ESPAÑOL
alto **Saxophone**	**Alt**saxophon	**Saxophone** alto	**Sassofono** contralto	**Saxofón** contralto
soprano saxophone	Sopransaxophon	saxophone soprano	sassofono soprano	saxofón soprano
tenor saxophone	Tenorsaxophon	saxophone ténor	sassofono tenore	saxofón tenor
baritone saxophone	Baritonsaxophon	saxophone baryton	sassofono baritono	saxofón barítono
bass saxophone	Baßsaxophon	saxophone basse	sassofono basso	saxofón bajo
Bassoon	**Fagott**	**Basson**	**Fagotto**	**Fagot**
Contrabassoon	Kontrafagott	contrebasson	contrafagotto	contrafagot
crook	S	bocal	esse	bocal
wing joint	Flügel(röhre)	petit corps	aletta	pieza superior
butt joint	Stiefel Bogen	culasse	sacco	culata
bass joint	Baßröhre	grand corps	grande corpo	cuerpo central
Brass (instruments)	**Blech- (instrumente)**	**Cuivres**	**Ottoni**	**Metales**
pedal tone	Pedalton	son pédale	suono-pedale	sonido fundamental
valve	Ventil	piston	pistone	pistón
tuning slide	Stimmbogen	corps de réchange	ritorto	corredera
lips	Lippen	lèvres	labbri	labios
mute	Dämpfer	sourdine	sordina	sordina
brassy tone (cuivré)	schmetternd	cuivré	suoni metallici	sonidos metálicos
half-valve	Halbventil			medio pistón
(French) **Horn**	**Horn**	**Cor**	**Corno**	**Trompa**
stopped	gestopft	bouché	chiuso	tapado
Trumpet	**Trompete**	**Trompette**	**Tromba**	**Trompeta**
piccolo trumpet	kleine Trompete	petite trompette	tromba piccola	trompeta pequeña trompeta piccolo
trumpet in D (E♭)	D (Es)-Trompete	trompette en ré (mi♭)	tromba in re (mi♭)	trompeta en re (mi♭)
tenor trumpet	Tenortrompete	trompette ténor	tromba tenore	trompeta tenor
bass trumpet	Baßtrompete	trompette basse	tromba bassa	trompeta baja
straight mute	gerader Dämpfer	sourdine droite	sordina diritta	sordina recta
harmon mute	Harmon-Dämpfer	sourdine harmon	sordina harmon	sordina harmon
cup mute	Cup-Dämpfer	sourdine cup	sordina cup	sordina cup
plunger mute	Plunger-Dämpfer	sourdine plunger	sordina plunger	sordina plunger
buzz mute	Mirliton-Dämpfer	sourdine mirliton	sordina mirliton	sordina mirlitón
bucket mute	Bucket-Dämpfer	sourdine bucket	sordina bucket	sordina bucket

ENGLISH	DEUTSCH	FRANÇAIS	ITALIANO	ESPAÑOL
solotone mute	Solotone-Dämpfer	sourdine solotone	sordina solotone	sordina solotone
practice mute	Übungsdämpfer	sourdine d'exercice	sordina di esercizio	sordina de ejercicio
Trombone	**Posaune**	**Trombone**	**Trombone**	**Trombón**
contrabass trombone	Kontrabaßposaune	trombone contrebasse	trombone contrabbasso	trombón contrabajo
slide	Zug	coulisse	pompa a tiro	vara
trigger	Wechsel	piston	pistone	piston
bass **Tuba**	**Baßtuba**	**Tuba** basse	**Tuba** bassa	**Tuba** baja
flügelhorn	Flügelhorn	bugle (à pistons)	flicorno	fliscorno
alto horn	Althorn	bugle alto	flicorno contralto	fliscorno contralto
baritone horn	Tenortuba	tuba ténor	tuba tenore	tuba tenor
contrabass tuba	Kontrabaßtuba	tuba contrebasse	tuba contrabbassa	tuba contrabajo
cornet	Piston Kornett	cornet (à pistons)	cornetta	corneta cornetín
Voice	**Stimme**	**Voix**	**Voce**	**Voz**
vowel	Vokal	voyelle	vocale	vocal
consonant	Konsonant	consonne	consonante	consonante
rounded	gerundeter	arrondi	chiuso	cerrada
unrounded	entrundeter	non arrondi	aperto	abierta
plosive	Verschlußlaut	plosive	plosivo	explosiva
fricative	Reibelaut	fricative	fricativo	fricativa
voiced	stimmhaft	voisé	sonoro	sonoro
unvoiced	stimmlos	non voisé	sordo	muda
bilabial	mit beiden Lippen	bilabiale	bilabiale	bilabial
labiodental	Lippenzahnlaut	labiodentale	labiodentale	labiodental
dental	Zahnlaut	dentale	dentale	dental
alveolar	Alveolarlaut	alvéolaire	alveolare	alveolar
retroflex	zurückgebogen	rétroflexe	retroflesso	retroflexo
palatal	Gaumenlaut	palatale	palatale	paladial
lateral	Seitenlaut	latérale	laterale	lateral
velar	Velarlaut	vélaire	velare	velar
uvular	Zäpfchenlaut	uvulaire	ugolare	uvular
pharyngeal	Kehllaut	pharyngéale	faringeo	faringeo
chest register	Brustregister	registre de poitrine	registro di petto	registro de pecho
head register	Kopfregister	registre de tête	registro di testa	registro de cabeza

ENGLISH	DEUTSCH	FRANÇAIS	ITALIANO	ESPAÑOL
falsetto	Falsett	fausset	falsetto	falsete
whistle register	Pfeiffregister	petit registre registre de sifflet	registro di campanello	registro de silbato
growl register	Strohbaß Schnarregister			
male (voice)	Männerstimme	masculin d'homme	maschile	maculino
female (voice)	Frauenstimme	féminin de femme	femminile	femenino
Soprano	**Sopran**	**Soprano**	**Soprano**	**Soprano**
Alto	**Alt**	**Alto**	**Alto**	**Alto**
Tenor	**Tenor**	**Ténor**	**Tenore**	**Tenor**
Baritone	**Bariton**	**Baryton**	**Baritono**	**Barítono**
Bass	**Baß**	**Basse**	**Basso**	**Bajo**
countertenor	Contratenor	contraténor	contratenore	contratenor
mouth	Mund	bouche	bocca	boca
tongue	Zunge	langue	lingua	lengua
diaphragm	Zwerchfell	diaphragme	diaframma	diafragma
whispered	flüsternd	chuchoté	bisbigliato	susurrado
spoken	gesprochen	parlé	parlato	hablado
sprechstimme	Sprechstimme	sprechstimme	canto-parlato	cantar hablando
megaphone	Megaphon	mégaphone porte-voix	megafono	megáfono
bullhorn	Lautsprecher	haut-parleur	altoparlante	altavoz
kazoo	Mirliton	mirliton	mirliton	mirlitón
(to) whistle	pfeifen	siffler	fischiare	silbar
Percussion	**Schlagzeug**	**Percussions** **Batterie**	**Percussione** **Batteria**	**Percusión**
traps	Jazz-Schlagzeug	batterie de jazz	batteria di jazz	bateria
roll	Wirbel	roulement	rullo	redoble
Mallet **Stick**	**Schlegel**	**Baguette** **Mailloche**	**Bacchetta**	**Palillo** **Baqueta**
hard	hart	dur	duro	duro
soft	weich	molle	morbido	blando
heavy	schwer	lourde	pesante	pesado
light	leicht	légère	leggiera	ligero
wound	umwickelt	couverte	involto	envuelto

ENGLISH	DEUTSCH	FRANÇAIS	ITALIANO	ESPAÑOL
unwound	nicht umwickelt	non couverte	non involto	no envuelto
felt	Filz	feutre	feltro	fieltro
rubber	Gummi	caoutchouc	gomma	goma
plastic	Kunststoff	plastique	plastica	plástico
metal	Metall	métal(lique)	metallo (metallica)	metál(ica)
wood	Holz	bois	legno	madera
hammer	Hammer	marteau	martello	martillo
knitting needles	Stricknadeln	aiguilles à tricoter	ferri da calza	agujas de tejar
switch	Rute	verge	verga	vergueta
wire brush	(Jazz)besen	brosse métallique balai métallique	spazzola metallica	escobilla metálica
superball stick	Superball-Schlegel	baguette "superball"	bachetta "superball"	palillo "superball'
fingers	Fingern	doigts	diti	dedos
fingernails	(Finger)nageln	ongles	unghie	uñas
thumb	Daumen	pouce	pollice	pulgar
Drum	**Trommel**	**Tambour**	**Tamburo**	**Tambor**
drumhead	Fell Membrane	peau membrane	pelle membrane	membrana
shell	Holzrand	caisse	cassa	caja
rim	Reifen	(re)bord	cerchio	borde
edge	Rand	près du rebord	margine	orilla
center	Mitte	centre	centro	centro
timpani	Pauken	timbales	timpani	timbales timpani
tomtoms	Tomtoms	tom-toms	tom-toms	tomtoms
timbales	Timbales	(timbales) créoles timbales cubaines	timbales	timbales (cubanos)

snares	Schnarrseiten	timbres	corde	cuerdas
				(with snares = con
				    timbre)
				(without snares = sin
				    timbre)

Snare drum	**kleine Trommel**	**Claisse claire**	**Tamburo militare**	**Caja militar**
field drum	Paradetrommel	≈tambour militaire	Tamburo militare	Caja militar
long drum	Landsknechts- trommel ≈Rührtrommel	≈caisse roulante	≈cassa rullante	≈redoblante
tenor drum	Tenortrommel ≈Rührtrommel	≈caisse roulante	≈cassa rullante	≈redoblante

ENGLISH	DEUTSCH	FRANÇAIS	ITALIANO	ESPAÑOL
bass drum	grosse Trommel	grosse caisse	gran cassa	bombo
Indian drum	indianische Trommel	tambour indien	tamburo indiano	tambor indio
frame drum	Rahmentrommel	tambour sur cadre	tamburello	tambor de marco
tambourine	Tamburin Schellentrommel	tambour de basque	tamburo basco	pandereta
rototoms	Tom-Tom-Spiel Rototoms	rototoms	rototoms	rototoms
bongos	Bongos	bongos	bongos bonghi	bongos
congas	Congas	congas	congas conghe	congas
dumbegs	Darabukken	darbukkas	darabukki	darbukas
boobams	Boo-Bams Bambustrommeln	boo-bams	boo-bams	boobams
string drum	Löwengebrüll Reibtrommel	tambour à corde	tamburo a corda	tambor de fricción
Idiophone	**Idiophon**	**Idiophone**	**Idiofono**	**Idiófono**
wood	Holz	bois	legno	madera
metal	Metall	métal	metallo	metál
glass	Glas	verre	vetro	vidrio
Rattle	**Rassel**	**≈Hochet**	**≈Sonaglio**	**Sonajero**
sistrum	Sistrum	sistre	sistro	sistro
jingles	Schellenrassel	cymbalettes	pandereta brasiliana	pandereta brasileña
Mexican bean	Mexican Bean	Mexican bean	Mexican bean	semilla de flamboyán
maraca	Maraca	maraca	maraca	maraca
cabasa	Cabaza	calebasse	cabasa	cabaza
agbe shekere	Agbe Schekere	agbé shékéré	agbe shekere	agbe shekere
sleighbells	Schellen	grelots	sonagli	cascabeleo
string rattle	Reihenrassel	string-rattle	sonaglio a corda	string-rattle
chains	Ketten	chaîne	catene	cadena
windchime	Pendelrassel Windglocken	wind-chime	wind-chime	mobil de viento
shell windchime	Muschelpendelrassel	shell-chime	shell-chime	mobil de caracol
vibraslap	Vibraslap	vibraslap	vibraslap	≈quijada
ratchet	Ratsche	crécelle	raganella	carraca
Rasp	**Raspel**	**Râpe**	**Raspa**	**Raspador**

ENGLISH	DEUTSCH	FRANÇAIS	ITALIANO	ESPAÑOL
güiro	Guiro	güiro	guiro	güiro
sandblocks	Sandblocks	papier de verre	carta vetrata	papel de lija
washboard	Waschbrett	washboard	tavola da lavare	washboard tabla de lavar
bell tree	Bell-tree	≈clochettes	bell-tree	bell-tree
castanets	Kastagnetten	castagnettes	castagnette	castañuelas
slapstick	Peitsche	fouet	frusta	zurriago
rods	Stäbe	tiges	≈stecche	varillas
triangle	Triangel	triangle	triangolo	triángulo
clock coil	Glockenspirale	cloche spirale d'horloge	spiro d'orologio	campana espiral de reloj
auto coil	Autospirale	spiral d'auto	spiral d'auto	espiral de auto
claves	Claves	claves	claves	claves
stones	Steinen	pierres	sassi	piedras
anvil	Amboß Metallblock	enclume	incudine	yunque
(softwood) planks	Bohlen	planches	assi	tableros
clap (hands)	klatschen	battre (les mains)	batter (le mani)	palmear
snap (fingers)	schnippen	faire claquer (les doigts)	schioccare	castañetear
stamp	stampfen	frapper (du pied)	pestare	patalear
slab (of wood, metal)	Platte	plaque	piastra	plancha
practice pad	Trommel- Übungsgerät	plaque d'exercice	piastra di esercizio	plancha de ejercicio
wood plate drum	Holzplattentrommel	tambour en plaque de bois	tamburo con piastra di legno	tambor con cara de madera
tin can	Blechdose	≈bidon	latta	lata
wastepaper basket	Papierkorb	corbeille à papier	cestino	cesto para papeles
garbage can	Mülleimer	poubelle	≈bidone (per spazzatura)	latón de basura
steel drum	Trinidad- Gongtrommel Blechtrommel Stahltrommel	steel-drum	tamburo di latta	steel-drum
water gourd	Wassertrommel	tambour d'eau	tamburo di acqua	jícara de agua
woodblock	Holzblock	bloc de bois bloc chinois	(blocco di) legno	bloque de madera
slit drum	Schlitztrommel Holztrommel	tambour de bois	tamburo di legno	tambor de madera

ENGLISH	DEUTSCH	FRANÇAIS	ITALIANO	ESPAÑOL
temple blocks	Tempelblocks	temple blocks	temple blocks	temple blocks
mokugyos	Mokugyos	mokugyos	mokugyos	mokugyos
Bells	**Glocken**	**Cloches**	**Campane**	**Campanas**
almglocken	Almglocken	almglocken	almglocken	almglocken
flower pots	Blumentöpfe	pots à fleurs	vasi da fiori	tiestos (de flores)
agogo bells	Agogo-Glocken	cloches agogo agogos	agogos	agógos
cencerros	Cencerros	cencerros	cencerros	cencerros
bottles	Flaschen	bouteilles	bottiglie	botellas
electric bell	electrische Klingel	sonnette électrique	campanello elettrico	campanilla eléctrica
Sansa	**Sansa** **Zanza**	**Sanza**	**Zanza**	**Zanza**
kalimba	Kalimba	kalimba	kalimba	kalimba
marimbula	Marimbula	marimbula	marimbula	marimbula
lujon	Lujon	lujon	lujon	lujon
musical saw	singende Säge	scie musical	sega	serrucho
flexatone	Flexaton	flexaton	flexaton	flexaton
cricket	Knackfrosch			
thundersheet	Donnerblech	plaque de tonnerre	lastra (del tuono)	hojalata de trueno
suspended **Cymbal**	**Becken** freihängend	**Cymbale** suspendue	**Piatto** sospeso	**Platillo** suspendido
dome	Kuppel	tête	campana	cuenco
edge	Rand	bord	bordo	borde
sizzle cymbal	Nietenbecken	cymbale sur tiges	piatto chiodato	cimbalo sobre palillos
Chinese cymbal	chinesische Becken	cymbale chinoise	piatto cinese	platillo chinesco
crash cymbals	Schlagbecken	cymbales de concert	piatti da concerto	platillos de concierto
finger cymbal	Fingerzimbeln	cymbales digitales	cimbalini	cimbalillos digitales
hi-hat	Hi-hat	hi-hat	hi-hat	hi-hat
gong	Gong	gong	gong	gong
tam-tam	Tam-Tam	tam-tam	tam-tam	tam-tam
bell plate	Plattenglocke	cloche plaque	campana a lastra	plancha de campana
crotales	Krotalen	crotales	crotali	cimbalos antiguos
chimes	Röhrenglocken	cloches tubes	campane tubolari	campanas tubolares
metal tubes	Metallröhren	tubes métalliques	tubi mettallici	tubos metálicos

ENGLISH	DEUTSCH	FRANÇAIS	ITALIANO	ESPAÑOL
brake drums	Brake-drums	brake-drums tambours de frein	brake-drums	brake-drums tambores de freno

Mallet instruments (no straightforward equivalents to this term)

ENGLISH	DEUTSCH	FRANÇAIS	ITALIANO	ESPAÑOL
xylophone	Xylophon	xylophone	xilofono	xilofón
marimba	Marimbaphon	marimba	marimba	marimba
bass marimba	Baßmarimbaphon	marimba basse	marimba bassa	marimba baja
glockenspiel	Glockenspiel	jeu de timbres glockenspiel	campanelli glockenspiel	juego de campanas juego de timbres glockenspiel
vibraphone	Vibraphon	vibraphone	vibrafono	vibrafón
pedal	Pedal	pédale	pedale	pedal
motor	Motor	moteur	motore	motor
bass metallophone	Baßmetallophon	métallophone basse	metallofono basso	metalofon bajo
lithophone	Lithophon	lithophone	litofono	litófono
wind machine	Windmaschine	machine à vent	eolifono	eolifón máquina de viento
(friction) birdcall	Grille	cri-cri grillon	grillo	grillo
water whistle	Nachtigallenpfeife	rossignol	usignolo	ruiseñor
signal whistle	Signalpfeife	sifflet d'appel	≈fischietto	≈silbato
referee's whistle	Trillerpfeife	sifflet à roulette	fischietto a pallina	silbato de árbitro
slide whistle	Lotosflöte	flûte à coulisse	flauto a tiro zufolo a pistone	flauta de émbolo
ocarina	Okarina	ocarina	ocarina	ocarina
siren	Sirene	sirène	sirena	sirena
mouth siren	Sirenenpfeife	sifflet sirène	fischio sirena	silbato sirena
Keyboard (instrument)	**Tasteninstrument**	**(Instrument à) Clavier**	**Strumento a tastiera**	**Instrumento de tecla**
key	Taste	touche	tasto	tecla
keyboard	Klaviatur Tastatur	clavier	tastiera	teclado
action	Mechanik	mécanique	meccanica	mecanismo acción
stop (knob)	Zug	registre	tirante	registro
rank	Pfeifenreihe (organ) Saitenreihe (harpsichord)	rang	fila	fila
register	Register	registre	registro	registro
right (hand)	Rechte	droite	destro	derecho

ENGLISH	DEUTSCH	FRANÇAIS	ITALIANO	ESPAÑOL
left (hand)	Linke	gauche	sinistro	izquierdo
tone cluster	Tonballung Cluster	groupe de notes cluster	gruppo di note cluster	racimo de notas cluster
keyboard glockenspiel	Klaviatur-glockenspiel	glockenspiel à clavier	glockenspiel a tastiera	glockenspiel de teclado
celesta	Celesta	célesta	celesta	celesta
toy piano	Kinderklavier	piano des enfants	pianoforte dei bambini	piano de niños
Piano	**Klavier**	**Piano**	**Pianoforte**	**Piano**
grand piano	Flügel	piano à queue	pianoforte a coda	piano de cola
upright piano	Pianino	piano droit	pianoforte verticale	piano vertical
damper pedal	Fortepedal	pédale forte	pedale di risonanza	pedal fuerte
soft pedal	Moderatorpedal Leise-Pedal	sourdine	pedale del piano	pedal celeste
sostenuto pedal	Sostenuto-Pedal Mittelpedal	pédale centrale	pedale centrale	pedal central
plucked	gezupft	pincé	pizzicato	punteado
lid	Deckel	couvercle	coperchio	tapa (del piano)
frame	Panzerplatte	cadre métallique	armatura (in ghisa)	marco metálico
(to) strike	schlagen	percuter	percuotere battere	percutir
prepared piano	präpariertes Klavier	piano préparé	pianoforte preparato	piano preparado
electric piano	elektrische Piano	piano électrique	pianoforte elettrico	piano eléctrico
clavinet	Klavinet	clavinette	clavinet	clavinet
Free reed	**Durchschlagzunge**	**Anche libre**	**Ancia libera**	**Lengüeta libre**
Harmonica	**Mundharmonika**	**Harmonica (à bouche)**	**Armonica a bocca**	**Armónica (de boca)**
blow	blasen	souffler	soffiare	soplar
draw	einatmen	inspirer	inspirare	inspirar
chromatic	chromatisch	chromatique	cromatica	cromática
diatonic	diatonisch	diatonique	diatonica	diatónica
melodica	Melodika	mélodica	melodica	melódica
Accordion	**Akkordeon**	**Accordéon**	**Fisarmonica**	**Acordeón**
bellows	(Blas)balg	soufflet	mantice	fuelle
button keyboard	Knopfgriff	clavier à boutons	tastiera a bottoni	teclado de botones
Stradella system	Stradellasystem	système Stradella	sistema Stradella	sistema Stradella
(chromatic) free-bass	chromatische	chromatique	cromatico	cromático

ENGLISH	DEUTSCH	FRANÇAIS	ITALIANO	ESPAÑOL
Organ	**Orgel**	**Orgue**	**Organo**	**Órgano**
pipe	Pfeife	tuyau	canna	tubo
flue pipe	Lippenpfeife	tuyau à bouche	canna ad anima canna labiale	tubo labiado
reed	Zunge	anche	ancia	lengüeta
diaphone	Diaphon	diaphone	diaphon	diaphon
console	Spieltisch	console	consolle	consola
blower	Windmotor Balgentreter	soufflerie	meccanica dell'aria tira-mantici	motor de alimentación
manual	Manual	manuel	manuale	manual
pedals	Pedal Pedalklaviatur	pédales pédalier	pedale pedallera	pedal pedalero
swell (organ)	Oberwerk	récit	organo recitativo	recitativo
great (organ)	Hauptwerk	grand orgue	grand'organo	gran órgano
choir (organ)	Positiv Unterwerk	positif	organo positivo	cadereta positivo
full organ	volles Werk	pleine orgue	organo pieno	
swell box	Schwellkasten	boîte expressive	cassa espressiva	caja expresiva
swell pedal	Schwelltritt	pédale de la boîte expressive	staffa crescendo	pedal del crescendo
crescendo pedal	Progressions- schweller	crescendo	crescendo generale staffa crescendo	pedal del crescendo
coupler	Koppel	accouplement tirasse	accoppiamento	acoplador
piston	≈Fußdrücker	piston	pistone pistoncino	pistón
foundations	Grundstimmen	fonds	fondi	fondos
flutes	Flötenwerk Flötenstimmen	flûtes	flauti	flautado
strings	streichende Stimmen Streicherchor	gambes	archi	gambas
mutations	Aliquoten Wechselregistern	aliquotes mutations simples	mutazioni semplici	alícuotas
mixture	≈Mixtur	mixture	mistura	mixtura
celeste	Celesta	célesta céleste	celesta	celesta
reeds	≈Schnarrwerk	anches	registri ad ancia	lengüeteria
imitative stop	Imitator	jeu imitatif	effetto imitativo	juego imitativo
percussions	Perkussions	percussions	percussiones	registros de percusión

ENGLISH	DEUTSCH	FRANÇAIS	ITALIANO	ESPAÑOL
tremulant	Tremulant	tremblant	tremolo	trémolo
toe	Zehe	orteil	punta	punta (del pie)
heel	Ferse	talon	tallone	talón
electric organ	elektrische Orgel	orgue électronique	organo elettrico	órgano eléctronico
melotron	Melotron	mélotron	melotron	mélotron
performance synthesizer	Performance-Synthesizer	≈synthétiseur portatif	≈sintetizzatore portativo	≈sintetizador portátil
ondes martenot	Ondes Martenot	ondes Martenot	ondes Martenot	ondas Martenot
(loud)speaker	Lautsprecher	haut-parleur	altoparlante	altavoz
String instruments	**Saiteninstrumente**	**Cordes**	**Cordas**	**Cuerdas**
string	Saite	corde	corda	cuerda
course (of strings)	Saitenchor	chœur ordre	coro	coro
soundboard	≈Resonanzboden	table d'harmonie	tavola armonica	tabla de armonia
bridge	Steg	chevalet	ponticello	puente
fingerboard	Griffbrett	touche	tastiera	batidor
nut	Obersattel	sillet de la touche	capotasto	ceja
tailpiece	Saitenhalter	cordier	cordiera	cordial
scordatura	Skordatur	scordatura	scordatura	scordatura
natural harmonic	natürliche Flageolett-Ton	son harmonique naturel	(suono) armonico naturale	armónico natural
artificial harmonic	künstliche Flageolett-Ton	son harmonique artificiel	(suono) armonico artificiale	armónico artificial
cimbalom	Cymbal	cymbalum	cimbalom	cimbalón
Harp	**Harfe**	**Harpe**	**Arpa**	**Arpa**
pedal	Pedal	pédale	pedale	pedal
fork	Gabel	fourchette	uncino forchetta	horquilla
tuning key	Stimmeisen	accordoir	chiave per accordare	templador
Plucked instruments	**Zupfinstrumente**	**Cordes pincés**	**Strumenti a pizzico**	**Instrumentos punteados**
fret	Bund	sillet frette ligature	tasto	traste
pick plectrum	Plektrum	plectre	plettro	plectro
Guitar	**Gitarre**	**Guitare**	**Chitarra**	**Guitarra**
barre	Quergriffe	barre	capotasto	cejuela

ENGLISH	DEUTSCH	FRANÇAIS	ITALIANO	ESPAÑOL
capo	Capotasto	barre	capotasto	cejuela
bottleneck	Bottleneck(-spiel)	bottleneck	bottleneck	bottleneck
tambour	Tambour	tambour	tambour	efecto de tambor
mandolin	Mandoline	mandoline	mandolino	mandolina
banjo	Banjo	banjo	banjo	banjo
electric guitar	electrische Gitarre	guitare électrique	chitarra elettrica	guitarra eléctrica
electric bass (guitar)	electrische Baßgitarre	guitare basse (électrique)	chitarra bassa (elettrica)	guitarra eléctrica baja
pickup	Tonabnehmer	pick-up	rivelatore	pick-up
treble	Höhe	aigu	acuto	agudo
bass	Tiefe	grave	grave	grave
feedback	Rückkopplung	feed-back	feedback	feed-back
Bowed instruments	**Streichinstrumente**	**Instruments à archet**	**Archi**	**Arcos**
violin	Geige Violine	violon	violino	violín
viola	Bratsche Viole	alto	viola	viola
cello	(Violon)cello	violoncelle	violoncello	(violon)chelo violoncelo cello
contrabass	Kontrabaß	contrebasse	contrabbasso violone	contrabajo
endpin	Stachel	pied	puntale	puntal
bow	Bogen	archet	arco	arco
frog	Frosch	hausse	tallone	talón
tip	Spitze	pointe	punta	punta
thumb	Daumen	pouce	pollice	pulgar
downbow	Abstrich	tiré	arcata in giù	in giù tiré
upbow	Aufstrich	poussé	arcata in su	arcada arriba
(bowing) on the string	gestrichen	à la corde	alla corda	en la cuerda
spiccato	≈abgestossen	≈staccato	spiccato	spiccato
saltando	Springbogen	sautillé	saltando	saltado saltillo
jeté	Springbogen	jeté	gettando	jeté
martellato	≈markiert	martelé	martellato	martellato
double stop	Doppelgriff	doubles cordes	doppia corda	doble cuerda

ENGLISH	DEUTSCH	FRANÇAIS	ITALIANO	ESPAÑOL
triple stop	Tripelgriff	triples cordes	tripla corda	triple cuerda
quadruple stop	Quadrupelgriff	quadruples cordes	quadrupla corda	cuádruple cuerda
bariolage	Bariolage	bariolage	bariolage	bariolage
mute	Dämpfer	sourdine	sordina	sordina
practice mute	Übungsdämpfer	sourdine d'exercice	sordina di esercizio	sordina de ejercicio
Electronics	**Elektronik**	**Appareils électro-acoustiques**	**Apparecchio elettronico**	**Equipo electrónico**
Synthesizer	**Synthesizer**	**Synthétiseur**	**Sintetizzatore**	**Sintetizador**
mixer	Mischpult	console de mélange	mescolatore	mezclador
oscillator (VCO)	Oszillator VCO	oscillateur	oscillatore	oscilador
sine wave	Sinusschwingung	onde sinusoïdale	onda sinusoidale	onda sinusoidal
triangle wave	Dreieckschwingung	onde triangulaire	onda triangolare	onda triangular
sawtooth wave	Sägezahn-schwingung	onde des dents de scie	onda a dente di sega	onda en dientes de sierra
square wave	Rechteck-schwingung	onde carré	onda quadra	onda cuadrada
white noise	weißes Rauschen	bruit blanc	suono bianco	ruido blanco
pink noise	rosa Rauschen	bruit rose	rumori rosa	ruido rosa(do)
amplifier (VCA)	Verstärker VCA	modulateur d'intensité	modulatore d'ampiezza	modulador de amplitud
(power) amplifier	Verstärker	amplificateur (de puissance)	amplificatore	amplificador
high-pass filter	Hochpaß	filtre passe-haut	filtro passa-alto	filtro de paso alto
low-pass filter	Tiefpaß	filtre passe-bas	filtro passa-basso	filtro de paso bajo
band-pass filter	Bandpaß	filtre passe-bande	filtro passa-banda	filtro pasabanda
band-reject filter	Bandsperre	filtre à réjection	filtro eliminatore di banda	filtro eliminador de banda
reverb	(Nach)hall	réverbération	riverberazione	reverberación
trigger	Trigger Impuls	impulsion trigger	trigger	impulso de disparo
linear controller	Bandmanual	ruban mobile	nastro di controllo	control lineal
envelope generator	Envelope Generator Hüllkurven-generator	générateur d'enveloppe	generatore di inviluppi	generador de envolventes
sequencer	Sequencer	séquenceur sequencer	sequencer	sequenciador
timing pulse generator	Impulsgenerator	générateur d'impulsion	generatore di impulsi	generador de pulsáciones

ENGLISH	DEUTSCH	FRANÇAIS	ITALIANO	ESPAÑOL
ring modulator	Ringmodulator	modulateur en anneau	modulatore ad anello	ringmodulator
frequency shifter	Frequency Shifter	frequency shifter	frequency shifter	frequency shifter
vocoder	Vocoder	vocoder	vocoder	vocoder
phase shifter phaser	Phase Shifter	phaser	sfasatore	(des)fasador
envelope follower	Envelope Follower	détecteur d'intensité	rivelatore di ampiezza	detector de amplitud
frequency follower	Frequenz-demodulator Frequency Follower	détecteur de fréquence	rivelatore di frequenze	detector de frecuencia
spatial locator	Panoramaregler	panoramique	controllo panoramico	panorámica
oscilloscope	Oszilloskop	oscilloscope	oscilloscopio	osciloscopio
frequency counter	Frequenzzähler	compteur de fréquence	contatore di frequenze	contador de frecuencia
Computer	**Computer**	**Ordinateur**	**Computer**	**Computadora**
analog	analoge	analogique	analogico	analógico
digital	digitale	digitale	digitale	digital
Tape recorder	**Magnetophon**	**Magnétophone**	**Magnetofono**	**Grabadóra**
tape deck	magnetophon	magnétophone	magnetofono	grabadóra
(recording) tape	Tonband	bande (magnétique)	nastro (magnetico)	cinta magnetofónica
half-track	Doppelspur Halbspur	double piste	doppia traccia	doble pista
quarter-track	Vierspurig	à quatre pistes	a quattro tracce	de cuatro pistas
sel-sync	Synchronisierung	sel-sync	sel-sync	sel-sync
tape echo	Magnethall	réinjection	riverberazione magnetofonico	reverberación automática
feedback	Rückkopplung	feed-back	feed-back	feed-back
(to) splice	kleben	coller	congiungere	empalmar
tape loop	Bandschleife	boucle	nastro senza fine	loop
amplified	verstärkt	amplifié	amplificato	amplificado
microphone	Mikrophon	microphone	mircofono	micrófono
contact mike	Körper-schallmikrophon	micro(phone) à contact	microfono a contatto	contact mike
magnetic pickup	(magnetische) Tonabnehmer	pick-up	rivelatore (magnetico)	pick-up
transducer	(elektroakustische) Wandler	transducteur	trasduttore	transductor

PART TWO: EARLY INSTRUMENTS
IN MODERN RECONSTRUCTIONS

ENGLISH	DEUTSCH	FRANÇAIS	ITALIANO	ESPAÑOL
alto **Recorder**	Alt**blockflöte**	**Flûte à bec** alto	**Flauto dolce** contralto	**Flauta dulce** contralto
garklein Floetlein	garklein Floetlein	garklein Floetlein	garklein Floetlein	garklein Floetlein
sopranino recorder	Sopraninblockflöte	flûte à bec sopranino	flauto dolce sopranino	flauta dulce sopranino
soprano recorder	Sopranblockflöte	flûte à bec soprano	flauto dolce soprano	flauta dulce soprano
tenor recorder	Tenorblockflöte	flûte à bec ténor	flauto dolce tenore	flauta dulce tenor
bass recorder	Baßblockflöte	flûte à bec basse	flauto dolce basso	flauta dulce bajo
great bass recorder	Grossbaßblockflöte	grande flûte à bec basse	grande flauto dolce basso	gran(de) flauta dulce bajo
contrabass recorder	Kontrabaßblockflöte	flûte à bec contrebasse	flauto dolce contrabbasso	flauta dulce contrabajo
gemshorn	Gemshorn	Gemshorn cor de chamois	corno di camoscio	corno de gamo
tabor pipe	Trommelpfeife	galoubet	flauto a tre fori	flauta con tres agujeros
Renaissance flute	Renaissanceflöte	flûte antique (de la Renaissance)	flauto antico (del Rinascimento)	flauta antígua (del renacimento)
soprano **Shawm**	Diskant**schalmei** Diskant**pommer**	**Chalemie**	**Piffaro** **Bombarda**	**Chirimía**
sopranino shawm	klein Diskantschalmei klein Diskantpommer	chalemie sopranino	piffaro sopranino bombarda sopranino	chirimía sopranino
alto shawm	Altpommer	*Bombarde* contralto	bombarda contralto	*Bombarda* contralto
nicolo shawm	Nicolo-Pommer	bombarde nicolo	bombarda nicolo	bombarda nicolo
tenor shawm	Tenorpommer	bombarde ténor	bombarda tenore	bombarda tenor
bass shawm	Baßpommer	bombarde basse	bombarda bassa	bombarda baja
great bass shawm	Grossbaßpommer	grande bombarde basse	bombardone grande bombarda bassa	gran(de) bombarda baja
pirouette	Pirouette Lippenscheibe	pirouette	pirouette	tudel
fontanelle	Schutzkapsel Fontanelle	fontanelle	manicotto	fontanelle
bassanello	Bassanello	bassanello	bassanello	bassanello
bagpipe	Dudelsack Sackpfeife	cornemuse	cornamusa	gaita
drone	Bordun	bourdon	bordone	bordón
Crumhorn	**Krummhorn**	**Cromorne**	**Cromorno** **Storto**	**Orlo**

ENGLISH	DEUTSCH	FRANÇAIS	ITALIANO	ESPAÑOL
cornamuse	Dolzaina Cornamuse	douçaine	dolzaina	dulzaina
douçaine	Douçaine	douçaine médiévale	douçaine	douçaine
kortholt	Kortholt	≈courtaud	kortholt	kortholt
rauschpfeife	Rauschpfeife	rauschpfeife	rauschpfeife	rauschpfeife
schryari	Schryari Schreierpfeife	schryari	schryari	schryari
Curtal	**Dulzian**	**Basson antique (de la Renaissance)**	**Fagotto antico (del Rinascimento)**	**Bajón**
Rackett	**Rankett**	**Cervelas**	**Rackett**	**Rackett Cervelas**
Baroque rackett	Barockrankett Wurstfagott	basson à raquette	rackett barocca	rackett barroco
sordune	Sordun	sordun	sordone	sordón
cornettino	kleiner Zink	cornet à bouquin soprano	cornettino	cornettino
Cornett	**Zink**	**Cornet à bouquin**	**Cornetto**	**Corneta**
straight cornett	gerader Zink	cornet droit	cornetto dritto	corneta recta
mute cornett	stiller Zink	cornet muet	cornetto muto	corneta muda
tenor cornett	Baßzink grosser Zink	cornet à bouquin ténor basse des cornets	cornone corno torto	corneta baja
serpent	Serpent	serpent	serpentone serpente	serpentón
bass horn	Baßhorn	cor basse	corno basso	trompa grave
ophicleide	Ophikleide	ophicléide	oficleide	ophicleide figle
Sackbutt	**Renaissance-posaune**	**Saqueboute**	**Trombone antico**	**Sacabuche**
slide trumpet	Zugtrompete	trompette à coulisse	tromba da tirarsi	trompeta de varas
Baroque mute	Barockdämpfer	sourdine baroque	sordina barocca	sordina barroca
nakers	Päuklein	nacaires	nacchere	nácaras
tabor	Tabor	tambourin	≈tamburo	≈tamboril
timbrel	Renaissance-schellentrommel	tambour de basque antique	tamburello antico	pandereta antígua
Renaissance triangle	Renaissancetriangel	triangle antique (de la Renaissance)	triangolo antico (del Rinascimento)	triángulo antíguo (del renacimiento)
Harpsichord	**Cembalo Kielflügel**	**Clavecin**	**Clavicembalo**	**Clavicémbalo Clave(cín) Arpsicórdio**
jack	Springer	sautereau	salterello	macillo

ENGLISH	DEUTSCH	FRANÇAIS	ITALIANO	ESPAÑOL
quill	Kiel	plectre	plettro	plectro
lute stop	Nasalzug	jeux nasal	registro di liuto	registro nasal
harp stop buff stop	Lautenzug	registre de luth	"pizzicato"	sordina
coupler	Koppel	accouplement	accoppiamento	acoplador
virginal	Virginal	virginal	virginale	virginal
clavicytherium	Claviziterium	clavicytherium	claviciterio	clavicitério
spinet	Spinett	épinette	spinetta	espineta
Clavichord	**Clavichord**	**Clavicorde**	**Clavicordo**	**Monocordio**
fretted	gebunden	lié	legato	con trastes
unfretted	bundfrei	non lié	libero	sin trastes
tangent	Tangente	tangente	tangente	tangente
Bebung	Bebung	Bebung	vibrato	Bebung
Portative organ	**Portativ**	orgue **Portatif**	**Organetto** (Organo) **portativo**	Órgano **portátil**
Positive organ	**Positiv**	orgue **Positif**	(Organo) **positivo**	Órgano **positivo**
Regal	**Regal(orgel)**	**Régale**	**Regallo**	**Realejo**
Psaltery	**Psalterium**	**Psaltérion**	**Salterio**	**Salterio**
medicinale	Metzkanon	medicinale	mezzo canone	medio caño
dulcimer	Hackbrett	tympanon	salterio tedesco	dulcema
rote	Chrotta	rote	crotta	rota
lyre	Lyra	lyre	lira	lira
Renaissance **Lute**	Renaissance **Laute**	**Luth**	**Liuto**	**Laúd**
Baroque lute	Barocklaute	luth baroque	liuto barocco	laúd barroco
theorboed lute	Theorbenlaute	luth théorbé	liuto attiorbato	laúd-tiorba
archlute	Erzlaute	archiluth	arciliuto	archilaúd
theorbo	Theorbe	théorbe	tiorba	tiorba
chitarrone	Chitarrone	chitarrone	chitarrone	chitarrone
chanterelle	Sangsaite	chanterelle	antino	tiple
diapason	Baßchor	bourdon	bordone	bordón
mandora	Mandora	mandore	mandola	mandora
long-necked lute	Langhalslaute	luth long	liuto con manico lungo	laúd largo
Cittern	**Cister**	**Cistre**	**Cetera**	**Cistro** **Cedra**

ENGLISH	DEUTSCH	FRANÇAIS	ITALIANO	ESPAÑOL
citole	Ci(s)tole Zitol	citole	cetula citole	cítola
gittern	Gittern	≈guiterne quitaire	chiterna	mandora medieval
bandora	Pandora	pandora	pandora	pandora
orpharion	Orpheoreon	orpharion	orpheoreon	orfeoreón
ceterone	Ceterone	ceterone	ceterone	ceterone
vihuela	Vihuela	vihuela	vihuela	vihuela (de mano)
bass **Viol**	(Baß)**Gambe**	(basse de) **Viole** **Viole** de gambe	**Viola da gamba** **Viola** bassa	baja de **Viola** **Viola da gamba**
pardessus de viole	Pardessus de viole	pardessus de viole	pardessus de viole	pardessus de viole
treble viol	Diskantgambe	dessus de viole	viola soprano	soprano de viola
alto viol	Altgambe	haute-contre de viole	viola alto	contralto de viola
tenor viol	Tenorgambe	ténor de viole taille de viole	viola tenore	tenor de viola
violone (da gamba)	Grossbaßgambe	grande basse de viole	violone da gamba	gran(de) bajo de viola
division viol	Division Viol	division viol	division viol	division viol
lyra viol	Viola bastarda	viola bastarda	viola bastarda	viola bastarda
viola d'amore	Viola d'amore	viole d'amour	viola d'amore	viola d'amore
sympathetic strings	Resonanzsaiten	cordes sympathiques	corde simpatiche	cuerdas aliquotas
baryton	Baryton	baryton	viola di bordone	barítono
rebec	Rebec	rebec	ribeca	rabel
Fiddle	**Fidel**	**Vielle (à archet)**	**Viella**	**Fídula**
lira da braccio	Lira da braccio	lira da braccio	lira da braccio	lira da braccio
lira da gamba	Lira da gamba	lira da gamba	lira da gamba	lira da gamba
Hurdy-Gurdy	**Drehleier**	**Vielle à roue**	**Ghironda**	**Viela de rueda**
organistrum	Organistrum	organistrum	organistrum	organistrum
symphonia	Symphonia	chifonie	sinfonia	cifonía

APPENDIX IV

Master List of Musical Examples

Anon. (Pleyel?):

Feldparthie "Chorale St. Antonii"—
serpent

Babbitt:

Philomel—tape

C. P. E. Bach:

Sonata No. 4 from *Achtzehn Probe-
Stücken in sechs Sonaten*—
clavichord

J. S. Bach:

Brandenburg Concerto No. 5—
harpsichord
Suite in E minor, for lute, BWV 996—
Baroque lute

Bartók:

Bluebeard's Castle—orchestra
Divertimento—string orchestra
The Miraculous Mandarin—trombone
Sonata for solo violin—violin
String Quartet No. 4—string quartet

Bedford:

Music for Albion Moonlight—melodica

Berg:

Wozzeck—accordion

Berio:

Alleluia II—piccolo trumpet
Circles—percussion
Gesti—alto recorder
Sequenza II—harp
Sequenza III—female voice
Sequenza V—trombone
Sequenza VII—oboe

Berlioz:

Les Troyens—alto horn

Boulez:

Le Marteau sans maître—alto flute,
percussion, guitar, viola
Eclat—cimbalom

Britten:

Nocturnal—guitar

E. BROWN:

String Quartet—string quartet

CAGE:

Amores—percussion
Double Music—percussion
Sonatas and Interludes—piano
String Quartet in Four Parts—string
  quartet
Suite for Toy Piano—toy piano

CHAVEZ:

Sinfonia de Antigona—heckelphone,
  trumpet, harp
Sinfonia India—E♭ clarinet,
  percussion
Symphony No. 5—string orchestra

CHIHARA:

Branches—bassoon
Logs—contrabass
Willow, Willow—bass flute

COPLAND:

Piano Concerto—soprano saxophone

CRUMB:

Ancient Voices of Children—child's
  voice, toy piano, harp, mandolin
Black Angels—string quartet
Lux Aeterna—bass flute
Madrigals—contrabass
Music for a Summer Evening—
  percussion, piano
Night of the Four Moons—alto flute,
  banjo

CURTIS-SMITH:

Unisonics—alto saxophone

DEL TREDICI:

Vintage Alice—accordion

DES PREZ/SPINACINO:

La Bernardina—Renaissance lute

DOWLAND:

Forlorn Hope Fancy—Renaissance lute
Galliard, from the *Braye bandora
MS*—bandora

FALLA:

Concerto for harpsichord, flute, oboe,
  clarinet, violin, and cello—
  harpsichord
Psyché—harp

FELDMAN:

Eleven Instruments—tenor trumpet
The Viola in My Life—viola

G. GABRIELI:

Sonata No. 18 (a 14), from *Canzoni e
  Sonate* (1615)—cornett, sackbutts

D. GAULTIER:

La Rhétorique des Dieux, Suite II in
  A—Baroque lute

O. GIBBONS:

Fantasias a 3, from *Musique for the
  greate dooble bass*—viols

GRAINGER:

A Lincolnshire Posy—woodwinds,
  brass

HANDEL:

Rinaldo—recorders

HARRISON:

Canticle No. 1—percussion
Double Music—percussion

F. J. HAYDN:

Baryton Trio in D, Hob. XI, 97—
  baryton
Cassation in C for lute, violin, and cello
  (arr. from quartet Hob. III, 6)—
  Baroque lute
Divertimento a 8 in A, Hob. X, 3—
  baryton

HEINRICH:

Manitou Mysteries—serpent

HENZE:

El Cimarrón—male voice, percussion,
  guitar
The Raft of the Medusa—alto clarinet

L. HILLER:

Electronic Sonata—tape
Malta—tuba

HINDEMITH:

Kammermusik No. 1—accordion
Kammermusik No. 5—viola
Kammermusik No. 6—viola d'amore
Kammermusik No. 7—organ
Kleine Kammermusik—bassoon
Sonata for alto horn and piano—alto
    horn
Sonata for English horn and piano—
    English horn
Sonata for four horns—horn
Sonata for heckelphone, viola, and
    piano—heckelphone
Symphonie Mathis der Maler—
    orchestra
Symphony in B♭ for concert band—
    alto saxophone, woodwinds, brass
Trio for recorders—recorders

HOLBORNE:

Galliard for cittern and bass, from The
    Cittharn Schoole (1597)—cittern

HOVHANESS:

Symphony No. 4—trombone

IVES:

Memories—whistling
Piano Sonata No. 2—piano

JANÁČEK:

Capriccio for piano (left hand) and
    chamber orchestra—baritone horn
Concertino for piano and chamber
    orchestra—E♭ clarinet
Glagolitic Mass—organ
Sinfonietta—bass trumpet, orchestra

JOHNSTON:

Casta*—live electronics

KAGEL:

Improvisation ajoutée—organ
Match für drei Spieler—percussion
Musik für Renaissanceinstrumente—
    shawms, crumhorns, cornett,
    sackbutts, regal, positive organ

KOECHLIN:

Les Bandar-Log—soprano saxophone,
    contrabassoon

LANSKY:

Six Fantasies on a Poem by Thomas
    Campion—Tape

W. LAWES:

The Royal Consort, Suite No. 2 in D
    minor—theorbo
Six-Part Consort Suite No. 1 in C
    minor—viols
Suite No. 2 in C for division viols and
    organ—viols
Suite No. 2 in G minor for three lyra
    viols—viols

LIGETI:

Atmosphères—orchestra
Aventures/Nouvelles aventures—
    voices
Continuum—harpsichord
Requiem—contrabass trombone

MADERNA:

Concerto for oboe, chamber ens., tape
    ad lib (1962)—oboe, English horn

MAHLER:

Symphony No. 4—horn

MARTIRANO:

Octet—contra-alto clarinet

MAXWELL DAVIES:

Eight Songs for a Mad King—male
    voice, percussion
Hymnos—B♭ clarinet
Missa super l'homme armé—flute,
    piccolo, B♭ clarinet
Revelation and Fall—female voice

MESSIAEN:

Chronochromie—percussion, keyboard glockenspiel, orchestra
Les Corps glorieux—organ
Et exspecto resurrectionem mortuorum—woodwinds, trumpet in D, bass tuba, contrabass tuba, brass
Oiseaux exotiques—piccolo, woodwinds
Quatuor pour la fin du temps—B♭ clarinet, violin, cello
Turangalîla-Symphonie—celesta, piano, ondes martenot

MILAN:

Fantasia XI, from *El Maestro* (1536)—vihuela

MILHAUD:

L'Homme et son désir—percussion

MONTEVERDI:

Orfeo—regal, positive organ, chitarrone
Vespers (1610)—cornett

MORLEY:

The First Book of Consort Lessons, No. 12: "Goe from my window"—Renaissance flute, Renaissance lute, cittern, bandora, viols

MUDARRA:

Pavana III, from *Tres libros de musica* (1546)—Renaissance guitar

NONO:

Polifonica-Monodia-Ritmica—bass clarinet, alto saxophone, horn

NORDHEIM:

Osaka-Music Dinosauros—accordion

PARTCH:

The Delusion of the Fury—voices

PENDERECKI:

Capriccio for violin and orchestra—contrabass clarinet, baritone saxophone
Pittsburgh Overture—contra-alto clarinet

POUSSEUR:

Madrigal II—bass gamba

PROKOFIEV:

Quintet for winds and strings, Op. 39—contrabass

RAMEAU:

Pièces de clavecin II (1724)—harpsichord
Pièces de clavecin en concert, concert II—bass gamba

RAVEL:

Bolero—soprano saxophone, tenor saxophone
Ma mère l'oye—contrabassoon
Tzigane—violin

REICH:

Four Organs—electric organ

REVUELTAS:

Sensemayá—bass tuba

T. RILEY:

A Rainbow in Curved Air—electric organ

ROLDÁN:

Ritmicas V, VI—percussion

RUGGLES:

Men and Angels (1922)—bass trumpet

D. SCARLATTI:

Sonatas, K. 420 and 421—harpsichord

SCHEIN:

"Hosianna dem Sohne David," from *Opella nova*—tenor and bass shawms
Padovana for crumhorns, from *Banchetto musicale*—crumhorns

SCHMELZER:

Sonata a 7 flauti—recorders
Sonata a 8 duobus choris, from *Sacro-profanus concentus musicus* (1662)—cornettino
Sonata "La Carolietta" (1669)—bass curtal, cornett, tenor sackbutt

SCHMITT:

Dionysiaques—bass saxophone

SCHOENBERG:

Cello Concerto (after Monn)—cello
Friede auf Erden—chorus
Gurrelieder—tenor trumpet
Herzgewächse—female voice
Pierrot lunaire—bass clarinet
Theme and Variations, Op. 43a—woodwinds, flügelhorn, baritone horn, brass
Variations for Orchestra, Op. 31—mandolin
Von Heute auf Morgen—bass saxophone

SCHÜTZ:

Domini est terra—curtals
Erbarm dich mein, o Herre Gott, SWV 447—viols
Symphoniae sacrae, Pt. I,
Nos. 7–8, "Anima mea liquefacta est" / "Adjuro vos, filiae Jerusalem"—Renaissance flute
No. 13, "Fili mi Absalon"—sackbutts
Nos. 16–17, "In lectulo per noctes" / "Invenierunt me custodes civitatis"—curtals
Symphoniae sacrae, Pt. III,
No. 3, "Wo der Herr nicht das Haus bauet"—cornettino

STOCKHAUSEN:

Hymnen—tape
Klavierstück IX—piano
Mantra—live electronics
Mikrophonie I—live electronics
Momente—electric organ
Refrain—celesta
Stimmung—voices
Zeitmäße—English horn

STRAVINSKY:

Agon—flute, trumpet, mandolin, orchestra
Dumbarton Oaks Concerto—flute
Ebony Concerto—alto saxophone, tenor saxophone, baritone saxophone, trumpet, brass
Elegy for J. F. K.—alto clarinet
L'Histoire du soldat—trombone
Mass—child's voice
Les Noces—chorus, piano
Octet for Winds—bassoon
Renard—male voice, cimbalom
Le Sacre du printemps—horn, trumpet in D, tenor trumpet, baritone horn, bass tuba, orchestra
Symphonies of Wind Instruments—woodwinds
Threni—flügelhorn

TELEMANN:

Sonata in C for recorder and continuo, from *Der getreue Musikmeister*—alto recorder

THOMSON:

The Plow That Broke the Plains—banjo

VARÈSE:

Density 21.5—flute
Déserts—bass tuba, contrabass tuba, piano
Ecuatorial—brass, organ, ondes martenot
Intégrales—contrabass trombone
Ionisation—percussion
Octandre—piccolo, oboe, horn, trumpet
Offrandes—harp

VIVALDI:

Concerto in D minor for lute, viola d'amore, and muted strings, P. 266—viola d'amore

WEBERN:

    Drei Lieder, Op. 18—guitar
    Five Pieces for Orchestra, Op. 10—
        celesta
    Quartet, Op. 22—tenor saxophone
    Six Pieces, Op. 6 (original version)—
        orchestra

WEILL:

    Die Dreigroschenoper—baritone
        saxophone, voices

WERNICK:

    Songs of Remembrance—soprano
        shawm

WOLFF:

    Electric Spring No. 2—recorders

XENAKIS:

    Akrata—contrabass clarinet,
        contrabassoon, woodwinds, brass
    Anaktoria—B♭ clarinet, bassoon, horn
    Dmaathen—oboe
    Eonta—trumpet, trombone
    Nomos alpha—cello
    Nuits—chorus
    Oresteia Suite—piccolo trumpet,
        child's voice
    Persephassa—percussion
    Syrmos—string orchestra

POPULAR MUSIC

THE BEATLES:

    "I Want You (She's So Heavy)"—
        electric guitar, electric bass guitar
    "Strawberry Fields Forever"—
        melotron

CROSBY, STILLS, NASH, AND
    YOUNG:

    "Teach Your Children"—pedal steel
        guitar

BOB DYLAN:

    "I Dreamed I Saw St. Augustine"—
        harmonica

THE GRATEFUL DEAD:

    "The Dire Wolf"—pedal steel guitar

HERBIE HANCOCK:

    "Steppin' in It"—electric piano,
        harmonica
    "The Traitor"—performance
        synthesizer

THE INCREDIBLE STRING BAND:

    "Astral Plane Theme"—folk guitar

JEFFERSON AIRPLANE:

    "Embryonic Journey"—12-string
        guitar
    "The House at Pooneil Corners"—
        electric guitar, electric bass guitar

KING CRIMSON:

    "Elephant Talk"—Chapman stick
    "Sartori in Tangier"—Chapman stick

LEO KOTTKE:

    "Easter and the Sargasso Sea"—
        12-string guitar

JONI MITCHELL:

    "Little Green"—folk guitar

PAUL SIMON:

    "Congratulations"—electric piano
    "Papa Hobo"—bass harmonica
    "Peace like a River"—folk guitar

STEVIE WONDER:

    "Keep on Running"—clavinet

NEIL YOUNG:

    "Cowgirl in the Sand"—electric guitar,
        electric bass guitar

Manufacturer or Other Source
of Instruments Figured

piccolo: Artley
flute: Artley
alto flute: Artley
bass flute: Artley
oboe: Linton
English horn: Mirafone
Heckelphone: Heckel
Ab clarinet: Leblanc
Eb clarinet: Selmer
Bb clarinet: Yamaha
alto clarinet: Artley
bass clarinet: Artley
contra-alto clarinet: Leblanc
contrabass clarinet: Leblanc
soprano saxophone: Yamaha
alto saxophone: Yamaha
tenor saxophone: Yamaha
baritone saxophone: Yamaha
bass saxophone: unidentified
bassoon: Fox
contrabassoon: Heckel
horn: unidentified

piccolo trumpet: Getzen
Eb trumpet: Getzen
Bb trumpet: Getzen
tenor trumpet: Getzen
bass trumpet: Getzen
trombone: King
contrabass trombone: Mirafone
flügelhorn: Getzen
alto horn: Yamaha
baritone horn: Yamaha
bass tuba: Meinl-Weston
contrabass tuba: Meinl-Weston
traps: Slingerland
timpani: Ludwig
small kettle drums: Early Music Studio,
    Carroll
tomtoms: Ludwig
timbales: Ludwig
snare drum: Ludwig
field drum: Ludwig
long drum: unidentified
small double-headed drum: Ludwig

tenor drum: Ludwig
bass drums: Ludwig
Indian drums: Drums Unlimited, Drums
    Unlimited, Carroll
tambourine: Ludwig
rototoms: Remo
bongos: Latin Percussion
congas: Slingerland
dumbegs: Early Music Studio, Carroll,
    University of California at Davis
boobams: M. Grabmann
string drums: hypothetical, unidentified
sistrum: unidentified
jingles: Ludwig
Mexican bean: George Hole
maraca: Ludwig
soft rattle: Latin Percussion
cabasa: Ludwig
shekere: Latin Percussion
sleighbells: Ludwig
wooden string rattle: hypothetical
string of jingle bells: author's collection
chains: unidentified
wood windchime: author's collection
glass windchime: Carroll
shell windchime: author's collection
metal windchime: Latin Percussion
Mark tree: Carroll
vibraslap: Latin Percussion
ratchet: Ludwig
güiro: Ludwig
sandblocks: unidentified
washboard: author's collection
bell tree: Carroll
castanets: Ludwig
metal castanets: Zildjian
slapsticks: unidentified
rods: hypothetical
triangles: Latin Percussion, Latin
    Percussion, Ludwig
clock coil: hypothetical
auto coil: James Stamos
claves: Ludwig
Tibetan prayer stones: hypothetical
anvils: Deagan, hypothetical
softwood planks: hypothetical

practice pad: Ludwig
wood plate drums: unidentified
ping pong pan: Carroll
cello pan: Carroll
bass pan: Carroll
water gourd: hypothetical
woodblock: Latin Percussion
piccolo woodblock: Latin Percussion
slit drums: unidentified, Blocks, M.
    Grabmann
temple blocks: Ludwig
mokugyo: Horniman Museum
bells: Capella Antiqua Munich, Asian
    Percussion Products
glass bells: Harry Partch
almglocken: Drums Unlimited
flower pots: Plant Parlour Botanicus
cencerros: Carroll
agogos: Latin Percussion
bottles: unidentified
electric bell: hypothetical
treble kalimba: African Musical
    Instruments
alto kalimba: African Musical Instruments
marimbulas: Emil Richards, M.
    Grabmann
lujon: Alan Hall
musical saws: hypothetical, Carroll
flexatone: Latin Percussion
thundersheet: Alan Hall
suspended cymbals: Zildjian
sizzle cymbal: Zildjian
Chinese cymbal: Asian Percussion
    Products
crash cymbals: Zildjian
finger cymbals: Elton
hi-hat: Zildjian (Slingerland stand)
gongs: Paiste
tam-tams: Paiste
bell plates: Studio 200
crotales: Zildjian
chimes: Deagan
tubes: unidentified
brake drum: unidentified
xylophone: Musser
marimba: Musser

bass marimba: Deagan
glockenspiel: Musser
vibraphone: Deagan
lithophone: Robert Erickson
wind machine: Alan Hall
squeak: hypothetical
friction bird call: Duncraft
crow: Acme
razzer: hypothetical
water whistle: Ludwig
signal whistle: Acme
referee's whistle: Acme
slide whistle: American Plating and
    Manufacturing
ocarina: author's collection
siren: Carroll
mouth siren: Acme
keyboard glockenspiel: Mustel
celesta: Mustel
toy piano: Jaymar
piano: Steinway
electric piano: Yamaha
clavinet: Hohner
harmonica: Hohner
bass harmonica: Hohner
double bass harmonica: Hohner
melodica: Hohner
melodica bass: Hohner
accordion: Giulietti
organ: Wicks
electric organ: Kawai
melotron: Dallas
performance synthesizer: Roland
ondes martenot: Lutherie Electronique
cimbalom: unidentified
harp: Elysian
mandolin: Madeira
classical guitar: Madeira
folk guitar: Madeira
12-string guitar: Madeira
5-string banjo: Madeira
electric guitar: Guild
electric bass guitar: Guild
pedal steel guitar: Fender
Chapman stick: Stick Enterprises
violin: Scherl and Roth

viola: Scherl and Roth
cello: Scherl and Roth
contrabass: Andreas Postacchini
garklein recorder: Hopf
sopranino recorder: Moeck
soprano recorder: Moeck
alto recorder, Baroque: Moeck
alto recorder, Renaissance: Moeck
alto recorder, medieval: Atelier for
    Historic Wind Instruments
tenor recorder: Moeck
bass recorder: Moeck
great bass recorder: Moeck
contrabass recorder: Moeck
gemshorns: Brian Carlick
tabor pipe: Brian Carlick
Renaissance flutes: Theatrum
    Instrumentorum
sopranino shawm: John Hanchet
soprano shawm: John Hanchet
alto shawm: John Hanchet
tenor shawm: John Hanchet
bass shawm: John Hanchet
great bass shawm: Staatliches Institut für
    Musikforschung, Berlin (ca. 1600)
crumhorns: Moeck
cornamuses: Moeck
kortholts: Moeck
rauschpfeifen: Körber
schryari: Rolf Westenberg
soprano curtal: Moeck
alto curtal: John Cousen
tenor curtal: Graham Lyndon Jones
bass curtal: Graham Lyndon Jones
great bass curtal: Graham Lyndon Jones
contrabass curtal: Rainer Weber
racketts: Moeck
Baroque rackett: Moeck
sordunes: Theatrum Instrumentorum
cornetts: Christopher Monk
serpent: unidentified
slide trumpet: Philip Bate
soprano sackbutt: Helmut Finke
alto sackbutt: Meinl and Lauber
tenor sackbutt: Meinl and Lauber
bass sackbutt: Meinl and Lauber

nakers: Paul Williamson
timbrel: Traditional Percussion Workshop
Renaissance triangle: modified after
  Mersenne
early castanets: after Mersenne
harpsichord: Hubbard and Dowd
clavichord: Zuckermann
portative organ: Noel Mander
positive organ: Early Music Shop
regal: B. E. Shull
pig's-head psaltery: Alan Crumpler
medicinale: hypothetical
dulcimer: Tim Hobrough
medieval harp: Alan Crumpler
Gothic harp: G. R. Higgs
Irish harp: Michael Saunders
medieval lyre: G. R. Higgs (bow:
  Northern Renaissance Instruments)
Renaissance lute: Ian Harwood and John
  Isaacs
Baroque lute: Christopher Challen
theorbo: Ian Harwood and John Isaacs
chitarrone: Magno Tieffenbrucker (1608)
citoles: Bernard Ellis, Fabrizio Reginato
cittern: Early Music Shop
bandora: Donald Gill

orpharion: Robert Hadaway
ceterone: Robert Hadaway
Renaissance guitar: Christopher Challen
vihuela: Harold E. Snyder
Baroque guitar: Michael Heale
pardessus de viole: Michael Heale
treble viol: Dolmetsch
alto viol: hypothetical
tenor viol: Dolmetsch
bass viol: Dolmetsch (bow: Dörfler)
violone da gamba: Wolfgang Nebel
viola d'amore: unidentified
baryton: Michael Heale (bow: Dörfler)
rebecs: Bernard Ellis (bows: Northern
  Renaissance Instruments)
fiddle: Bernard Ellis (bow: Northern
  Renaissance Instruments)
lira da braccio: Staatliches Institut für
  Musikforschung, Berlin (sixteenth
  century) (bow: Northern Renaissance
  Instruments)
lira da gamba: Wendelin Tieffenbrucker
  (late sixteenth century)
organistrum: hypothetical
symphonia: Bernard Ellis

Bibliography of Works Consulted

A great deal of useful information was derived from the examination of literally hundreds of printed catalogs and advertisements from instrument manufacturers and dealers all over the world. As this material is not only ephemeral but mostly undated and unascribed, it was not considered worthwhile to include it here.

Apel, Willi. *Harvard Dictionary of Music.* Cambridge, Massachusetts: Harvard University Press, 1969.
——— . *The Notation of Polyphonic Music, 900–1600.* Cambridge, Massachussetts: Medieval Academy of America, 1961.
Avgerinos, Gerassimus. *Handbuch der Schlag- und Effektinstrumente.* Frankfurt a.M.: Verlag der Musikinstrumente, 1967.
Bacon, Tony, ed. *Rock Hardware: The Instruments, Equipment and Technology of Rock.* New York: Harmony, 1981.
Baines, Anthony. *Brass Instruments, Their History and Development.* London: Faber and Faber, 1976.
——— . *Woodwind Instruments and Their History.* New York: W. W. Norton, 1962.
Baines, Francis. "The Consort Music of Orlando Gibbons." Pp. 540–543 in *Early Music* VI, 4 (1978).
Bartolozzi, Bruno. *New Sounds for Woodwind.* London: Oxford University Press, 1967.
Bate, Philip: *The Trumpet and Trombone.* New York: W. W. Norton, 1966.
Benade, Arthur H. *Fundamentals of Musical Acoustics.* London: Oxford University Press, 1976.

————. *Horns, Strings, and Harmony.* Garden City, New York: Anchor, 1960.

Betteridge, Harold T. *Cassell's German-English English-German Dictionary.* New York: Macmillan, 1978.

Blades, James, and Jeremy Montagu. *Early Percussion Instruments.* London: Oxford University Press, 1976.

Brand, Stewart, ed. *The Next Whole Earth Catalog*, second edition. New York: Random House, 1981.

Smith Brindle, Reginald. *Contemporary Percussion.* London: Oxford University Press, 1970.

Bröcker, Marianne. *Die Drehleier.* Düsseldorf: Gesellschaft zur Förderung der systematischen Musikwissenschaft, 1973.

Carse, Adam. *Musical Wind Instruments.* New York: Da Capo (reprint), 1965.

Chion, Michel, and Guy Reibel. *Les Musiques électroacoustiques.* Aix-en-Provence: Chaudoreille-Edisud, 1976.

Clason, W. E. *Elsevier's Dictionary of Cinema, Sound, and Music.* New York: Elsevier, 1966.

————. *Elsevier's Dictionary of Electronics and Waveguides.* New York: Elsevier, 1956.

Denti, Renzo. *Dizionario tecnico italiano-inglese/inglese-italiano.* Milan: Ulrico Hoepli, 1976.

Eimert, Herbert, and Hans Ulrich Humpert. *Das Lexicon der elektronischen Musik.* Regensburg: Gustav Bosse, 1973.

Erickson, Robert. "Instruments for Cardenitas." Pp. 26–29 in *SOURCE* III, 1 (1969).

Farrell, Susan Caust. *Directory of Contemporary American Musical Instrument Makers.* Columbia: University of Missouri Press, 1981.

Fitzpatrick, Horace. "The Gemshorn: A Reconstruction." Pp. 1–14 in *Proceedings of the Royal Musical Association* XCIX (1972–73).

Fitzpatrick, Horace. "The Medieval Recorder." Pp. 361–364 in *Early Music* III, 4 (1975).

Forsyth, Cecil. *Orchestration.* New York: Macmillan, 1935.

Fox, Stuart. "The Classical Guitar." Master's thesis, University of Southern California, 1971.

Girard, Denis, et al. *The New Cassell's French Dictionary.* New York: Funk and Wagnalls, 1962.

Gleason, Harold. *Method of Organ Playing.* Englewood Cliffs, New Jersey: Prentice-Hall, 1962.

Grayson, John, ed. *Sound Sculpture.* Vancouver: A.R.C., 1975.

Green, Robert A. "The *Pardessus de Viole* and Its Literature." Pp. 301–307 in *Early Music* X, 3 (July 1982).

Gregory, Robin. *The Horn.* New York: Praeger, 1969.

Hamel, Fred, and Martin Hürliman, eds. *Enciclopedia de la musica*, transl. Otto Mayer Serra. Barcelona: Grijalbo, 1970.

Heffner, Roe-Merill S. *General Phonetics.* Madison: University of Wisconsin Press, 1969.

Holland, James. *Percussion.* London: McDonald and Jane's, 1978.

Howe, Hubert S., Jr. *Electronic Music Synthesis.* New York: W. W. Norton, 1975.

Howell, Thomas. *The Avant-Garde Flute.* Berkeley: University of California Press, 1974.

Inglefield, Ruth K., and Lou Anne Neill. *Writing for the Pedal Harp.* Berkeley: University of California Press, 1984.

International Association of Music Libraries. *Terminorum musicae index septem linguis redactus*. Kassel and Basel: Bärenreiter, 1978.

Irwin, Stevens. *Dictionary of Pipe Organ Stops*. New York: G. Schirmer, 1965.

Kennan, Kent. *The Technique of Orchestration*. Englewood Cliffs, New Jersey: Prentice-Hall, 1970.

Koechlin, Charles. *Traité de l'orchestration*. Paris: M. Eschig, 1954–56.

Kotonsky, Włodzimierz. *Schlaginstrumente im modernen Orchester*. Mainz: B. Schott's Söhne, 1968.

Lagueruela, Frank J. *Diccionario de electronica ingles-español*. Miami: Editorial Omega, 1963.

Langwill, Lyndesay G. *The Bassoon and Contrabassoon*. New York: W. W. Norton, 1965.

Little, Elbert L., Jr., and Frank H. Wadsworth. *Common Trees of Puerto Rico and the Virgin Islands*. Washington, D.C.: U.S.D.A. Forest Service, 1964.

Marcuse, Sybil. *Musical Instruments, a Comprehensive Dictionary*. New York: W. W. Norton, 1975.

———. *A Survey of Musical Instruments*. New York: Harper and Row, 1975.

Martin, John. *The Complete Musician*. Willits, California: Oliver Press, 1975.

Mersenne, Marin. *Harmonie Universelle 1635: The Books on Instruments*, transl. Roger E. Chapman. The Hague: Martinus Nijhoff, 1957.

Miller, Richard. *English, French, German and Italian Techniques of Singing*. Metuchen, New Jersey: Scarecrow, 1977.

Munrow, David. *Instruments of the Middle Ages and Renaissance*. London: Oxford University Press, 1976.

Nicolet, Aurèle. *Pro Musica Nova für Flöte*. Cologne: Hans Gerig, n.d.

Peers, Edgar Allison, et al. *Cassell's Spanish Dictionary*. New York: Funk and Wagnalls, 1966.

Peinkofer, Karl, and Fritz Tannigel. *Handbook of Percussion Instruments*. London: Schott, 1976.

Piston, Walter. *Orchestration*. New York: W. W. Norton, 1955.

Praetorius, Michael. *Syntagma Musicum II 'De Organographia' 1619*, transl. Harold Blumenfeld. St. Louis, 1949.

Ramm, Andrea von. "Singing Early Music." Pp. 12–16 in *Early Music* IV, 1 (1976).

Read, Gardner. *Contemporary Instrumental Techniques*. New York: G. Schirmer, 1976.

Rebora, Piero, et al. *Cassell's Italian Dictionary*. New York: Funk and Wagnalls, 1967.

Richardson, Edward. *The Acoustics of Orchestral Instruments and of the Organ*. London: E. Arnold, 1929.

Ripin, Edwin M., ed. *Keyboard Instruments*. New York: Dover, 1977.

Rushmore, Robert. *The Singing Voice*. New York: Dodd, Mead, 1971.

Sachs, Curt. *The History of Musical Instruments*. New York: W. W. Norton, 1940.

———. *Real-Lexicon der Musikinstrumente*. Berlin: Julius Bard, 1913.

Sadie, Stanley, ed. *The New Grove Dictionary of Music and Musicians*. London: Macmillan, 1980.

Santasusana, Juan Pich. *Enciclopedia de la musica*. Barcelona: Gasso, 1964.

Schmeckel, Carl D. *The Piano Owner's Guide*. New York: Charles Scribner's Sons, 1974.

Seeger, Pete. *How to Play the 5-string Banjo*. New York: Oak, 1962.

———. *The Steel Drums of Kim Loy Wong*. New York: Oak, 1964.

Smith, W. J. *A Dictionary of Musical Terms in Four Languages*. London: Hutchinson, 1961.

Smith Brindle, Reginald. *Contemporary Percussion*. London: Oxford University Press, 1970.

Solmi, Angelo, et al., eds. *Enciclopedia della musica*. Milan: Rizzoli Ricordi, 1972.

Spencer, Robert. "Chitarrone, theorbo and archlute." Pp. 407–423 in *Early Music* IV, 4 (1976).

Spencer, William. *The Art of Bassoon Playing*. Evanston: Summy Birchard, 1958.

Tarjáni Tóth Ida and Falka József. *Cimbalom Iskola*, vol. I. Budapest: Zenemükiadó Vállalat, 1958.

Taylor, Charles. *The Phsyics of Musical Sounds*. New York: American Elsevier, 1965.

Thurban, T. W., and E. H. Wickham. *How to Play the Harmonica in 30 Minutes*. Valley Forge: Sam Fox, 1965.

Tintori, Giampiero. *Gli strumenti musicali*. Turin: Unione Tipogràfico, 1976.

Turetzky, Bertram. *The Contemporary Contrabass*. Berkeley: University of California Press, 1974.

———. "Notes on the Double Bass." Pp. 64–66 in *SOURCE* I, 1 (1967).

Tyler, James. "The Renaissance Guitar." Pp. 341–347 in *Early Music* III, 4 (1975).

Vannes, René. *Essai de terminologie musicale. . . .* Thann, France: "Alsatia," 1925.

Westphal, Frederic William. *Guide to Teaching Woodwinds*. Dubuque: W. C. Brown, 1974.

Willets, Carl. *The Register of Early Instruments*. London: Oxford University Press, 1975, 1976.

Wood, Alexander. *The Physics of Music*. London: Methuen and Co., 1947.

Wright, Laurence. "The Medieval Gittern and Citole: a Case of Mistaken Identity." Pp. 8–43 in *The Galpin Society Journal* XXX (1977).

Index

Where there is more than one entry under a given heading, the main or defining entry for the term is shown in **bold-face type**. An x following the page number indicates a reference to a Figure.

Waveforms, electronic, 372
  clipper, 377
  computer-generated, 379
Wawa mute, 83
Wawa pedal, 386
Weill, Kurt
  Dreigroschenoper, 345
Whip. *See* Slapstick
Whispa mute, 83
Whistle register (vocal), 106x,
  108–9
  notation, 110
Whistles, 250–52
  bird. *See* Whistles, water
  musical examples, 136, 139
  pea. *See* Whistles, referee's
  police. *See* Whistles, referee's;
    Whistles, signal
  referee's, 250–52
  signal, 250–52
  slide, 250x, **252**
  water, 250–52
Whistle tones (flute), 30
Whistling, 115–17
White-noise generator, 373
Wiggle bar, 340
Windchimes, 172, **179–82**
  acoustics, 121

made of triangles, 191
  musical examples, 137–39
Wind machine, 249–51
  musical example, 136
Wire brush, 132x, **133**
Wobble-board, 222
Wolff, Christian, 284
Wood (sordunes), 424–25
Woodblocks, 204–5
  musical examples, 136–39
  See also Softwood planks
Wood chimes. *See* Windchimes
Wood drums. *See* Mokugyos; Slit
    drums; Wood plate drums
Wooden fish. *See* Mokugyos
Wood plate drums, 197–99
Woodwinds, 8, **13–24**
  acoustics, **13–16**, 18
  articulation, 22–23
  bore, 14–16
  double-tonguing, 22
  doubling, 19–20
  early, **395–96**, 403, 425
  fingering, **16–19**, 389
  fluttertongue, 22–23
  humming into, 23
  keys, 16–17
  large groups, 62

multiphonics, 20–22
  page position, 1–2
  quarter-tones, 19
  reeds, **14**, **15x**, 16
  registers, **18**, 20
  slap-tongue, 23
  special timbres, 20–22
  synthesizer. *See* Lyricon
  transposing, 19

X
Xenakis, Iannis
  Akrata, 61
Xylophone, 238–44
  bowing, 244
  musical examples, 137–39
  as organ stop, 298
  sticks, 130x
  student range, 481
Xylorimba, 240–41
  musical example, 137

Z
Zappa, Frank
  Uncle Meat, 386
Zither family, **315**, 447

DESIGNER: *Wilsted & Taylor*

COMPOSITOR: *Wilsted & Taylor*

PRINTER: *Malloy Lithographing, Inc.*

BINDER: *John H. Dekker & Sons*

TEXT: *Imprint*

DISPLAY: *Caslon Open Face*